That Noble Dream

IDEAS IN CONTEXT

Edited by Richard Rorty, J. B. Schneewind, Quentin Skinner, and Wolf Lepenies

The books in this series will discuss the emergence of intellectual traditions and of related new disciplines. The procedures, aims, and vocabularies that were generated will be set in the context of the alternatives available within the contemporary frameworks of ideas and institutions. Through detailed studies of the evolution of such traditions, and their modification by different audiences, it is hoped that a new picture will form of the development of ideas in their concrete contexts. By this means, artificial distinctions among the history of philosophy, of the various sciences, of society and politics, and of literature may be seen to dissolve.

Titles published in the series:

Richard Rorty, J. B. Schneewind, and Quentin Skinner (eds.), *Philosophy in History*

J. G. A. Pocock, *Virtue, Commerce, and History*

M. M. Goldsmith, *Private Vices, Public Benefits*

Laurence Dickey, *Hegel: Religion, Economics, and the Politics of Spirit, 1770–1807*

Margo Todd, *Christian Humanism and the Puritan Social Order*

Lynn S. Joy, *Gassendi the Atomist: Advocate of History in an Age of Science*

Edmund Leites (ed.), *Conscience and Casuistry in Early Modern Europe*

Wolf Lepenies, *Between Literature and Science: The Rise of Sociology*

T. Ball, J. Farr, and R. Hanson (eds.), *Political Innovation and Conceptual Change*

This series is published with the support of the Exxon Education Foundation.

That Noble Dream

The "Objectivity Question" and the American Historical Profession

Peter Novick
University of Chicago

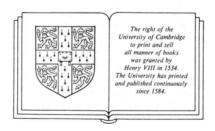

The right of the
University of Cambridge
to print and sell
all manner of books
was granted by
Henry VIII in 1534.
The University has printed
and published continuously
since 1584.

CAMBRIDGE UNIVERSITY PRESS

Cambridge

New York   New Rochelle   Melbourne   Sydney

Published by the Press Syndicate of the University of Cambridge
The Pitt Building, Trumpington Street, Cambridge CB2 1RP
32 East 57th Street, New York, NY 10022, USA
10 Stamford Road, Oakleigh, Melbourne 3166, Australia

© Cambridge University Press 1988

First published 1988

Printed in the United States of America

Library of Congress Cataloging-in-Publication Data
Novick, Peter.
That noble dream : the "objectivity question" and the American
historical profession / Peter Novick.
p.   cm.—(Ideas in context)
Includes index.
ISBN 0-521-34328-3.   ISBN 0-521-35745-4 (pbk.)
1. Historiography—United States.   2. Objectivity.   I. Title.
II. Series.
D13.5.U6N68 1988
907'.2073—dc 19   88–2606
                                                            CIP

British Library Cataloguing in Publication Data
Novick, Peter
That noble dream : the "objectivity
question" and the American historical
profession.—(Ideas in context).
1. American historiography
I. Title   II. Series
907'. 2073

ISBN 0 521 34328 3 (hard covers)
ISBN 0 521 35745 4 (paperback)

For V.J.Z.

We may look . . . with justifiable satisfaction on the impressive output of sound, creditable . . . works on American history. . . . dominated . . . by one clear-cut ideal—that presented to the world first in Germany and later accepted everywhere, the ideal of the effort for objective truth. . . . A year ago [Charles Beard] contended [that] the ideal of impartiality was an impossibility. . . . [A]t the end of fifty years of historical work the fundamental ideals that underlay it are positively rejected. A nonpartisan search for the truth . . . is declared to be impossible. . . . [A] growing number of writers discard impartiality on the ground that it is uninteresting, or contrary to social beliefs, or uninstructive, or inferior to a bold social philosophy. . . .

It may be that another fifty years will see the end of an era in historiography, the final extinction of a noble dream, and history, save as an instrument of entertainment, or of social control will not be permitted to exist. In that case, it will be time for the American Historical Association to disband, for the intellectual assumptions on which it is founded will have been taken away from beneath it. My hope is, none the less, that those of us who date from what may then seem an age of quaint beliefs and forgotten loyalties, may go down with our flags flying.

—Theodore Clarke Smith, 1934

Contents

Preface

In writing this book I have been stimulated and sustained by my friends in the Workshop in the History of the Human Sciences at the University of Chicago—Keith Baker, Arnold Davidson, Jan Goldstein, Bob Richards, and George Stocking: an exemplary intellectual community. Others who have read portions of the manuscript and contributed useful criticisms or suggestions include David Abraham, Susan Frank, Jim Grossman, Harry Harootunian, Don Levine, Don McCloskey, Bill McNeill, Joan Novick, Dorothy Ross, and Laurence Veysey, as well as anonymous referees. I could not begin to list the friends and colleagues, at the University of Chicago and elsewhere, who have supplied information, on whom I have tried out various ideas, or who have helped me in various ways, large and small; I thank them all.

Another sort of intellectual obligation is often acknowledged by bibliographical footnotes: "On this subject see. . . ." My indebtednesses of this kind are so numerous that had I listed them the notes would have crowded the text off the page, so except for a few instances where my treatment closely followed that of another writer, I have not done so. I trust this omission will not be considered ungenerous. The staffs of libraries and archives which I visited in the course of my research have been extremely helpful in furthering my work. My thanks to them, and to the staff of Cambridge University Press, in particular that paragon of an editor, Frank S. Smith, but also my production editor, Janis Bolster, and copy editor, Nancy Landau.

A few technical matters: I have been sparing with the use of initials for organizations and periodicals in both the text and the notes. The major exceptions are AHA and *AHR* for the American Historical Association and *American Historical Review*; MVHA and *MVHR* for the Mississippi

xi

Valley Historical Association and *Mississippi Valley Historical Review*; and after their names changed, OAH and *JAH* for the Organization of American Historians and *Journal of American History*. I have made archival citations as precise as I could, but in several cases collections were so disorganized (at least at the time when I used them) that no precise references could be given. Rather than further burden the footnotes with full information on the location of manuscript materials cited, I have used an abbreviated form, and included a list of the collections used in an appendix at the end. I have not repeatedly said "italics in the original" when quoting because all italics in quotations were in the originals. In one respect I have departed from standard scholarly practice: in quoting from letters I have corrected spelling and punctuation when the meaning was clear. In this context to truffle such quotations with "[*sic*]"s seemed to me mean-spirited.

Introduction

◁══════════════════════════════════════▷

Nailing jelly to the wall

At the very center of the professional historical venture is the idea and ideal of "objectivity." It was the rock on which the venture was constituted, its continuing raison d'être. It has been the quality which the profession has prized and praised above all others—whether in historians or in their works. It has been the key term in defining progress in historical scholarship: moving ever closer to the objective truth about the past. Anyone interested in what professional historians are up to—what they think they are doing, or ought to be doing, when they write history—might well begin by considering "the objectivity question."

In this book I explore the fortunes of the idea of objectivity among American professional historians over the last century. The book recounts how the idea was elaborated, modified, challenged, and defended; the ways in which the idea furthered (and some ways in which it retarded) professional historical scholarship; how other values and agendas of historians have sometimes complemented, and sometimes contradicted, the goal of pursuing objectivity. I do my best to sort out the influences which have moved successive generations of professional historians this way and that on the objectivity question over the past hundred years.

"Historical objectivity" is not a single idea, but rather a sprawling collection of assumptions, attitudes, aspirations, and antipathies. At best it is what the philosopher W. B. Gallie has called an "essentially contested concept," like "social justice" or "leading a Christian life," the exact meaning of which will always be in dispute.

The principal elements of the idea are well known and can be briefly recapitulated. The assumptions on which it rests include a commitment to the reality of the past, and to truth as correspondence to that reality; a sharp separation between knower and known, between fact and value,

1

and, above all, between history and fiction. Historical facts are seen as prior to and independent of interpretation: the value of an interpretation is judged by how well it accounts for the facts; if contradicted by the facts, it must be abandoned. Truth is one, not perspectival. Whatever patterns exist in history are "found," not "made." Though successive generations of historians might, as their perspectives shifted, attribute different significance to events in the past, the meaning of those events was unchanging.

The objective historian's role is that of a neutral, or disinterested, judge; it must never degenerate into that of advocate or, even worse, propagandist. The historian's conclusions are expected to display the standard judicial qualities of balance and evenhandedness. As with the judiciary, these qualities are guarded by the insulation of the historical profession from social pressure or political influence, and by the individual historian avoiding partisanship or bias—not having any investment in arriving at one conclusion rather than another. Objectivity is held to be at grave risk when history is written for utilitarian purposes. One corollary of all of this is that historians, as historians, must purge themselves of external loyalties: the historian's primary allegiance is to "the objective historical truth," and to professional colleagues who share a commitment to cooperative, cumulative efforts to advance toward that goal.

Although radically compressed, this is, I think, a fair summary of the original and continuing objectivist creed—an ideal to be pursued by individuals, policed by the collectivity. Some components of the concept have been reworked or reinterpreted over the last hundred years. There is nowadays, among even the firmest supporters of the idea of objectivity, a bit less confidence in the capacity of historians, no matter how rigorously trained, to completely purge themselves of all values; a resulting tendency to ground objectivity more in social mechanisms of criticism and evaluation, and less in the qualities of individuals. There is somewhat less talk, though still a good deal, of approaching the past "without preconceptions" and "letting the facts speak for themselves"; increased tolerance for hypotheses, and a greater emphasis on interpretations being tested by facts, instead of derived from them. Following from this there is a tendency to think of the collective voyage toward the truth as involving tacking, rather than sailing in a straight line toward that final destination. In recent discussions "contributions to knowledge" are somewhat more often seen as dialectical, rather than as permanent bricks added to an edifice. But despite these recent modifications, older usages remain powerful, and perhaps even dominant. The basic outlines and guidelines of the original program have remained remarkably enduring.

Ideas are frequently defined with reference to what they oppose. While in the late nineteenth century "objectivity" was usually contrasted with "subjectivity," in the last half-century "objectivism" has struggled against "relativism." The latter term refers not to a positive position but rather to a critical stance vis-à-vis various elements in the objectivist synthesis, and, in general, doubts about the coherence of the notion of objectivity as applied to history.[1]

One approach to the idea of historical objectivity which will not much intrude in my account, but one which has informed my inquiry, is to think of the idea as "myth." "Myth," of course, can be a fighting word, though perhaps a bit less these days than it used to be. Today academic Christians routinely speak of the myth of Christ's redemptive death; academic Marxists refer to the myth of the emancipatory mission of the proletariat; in neither case is there any implication that the myth in question is "false," or that the venture it sustains is dubious. My use of the term, in accordance with current practice, implies nothing about the truth or falsity of what is being discussed. Rather it is a device to illuminate the important functions which "historical objectivity" has served in sustaining the professional historical venture; and, since myths are by definition sacred, the tenacity, indeed, ferocity, with which it has been defended.

There are "founding myths": Mircea Eliade writes that myth is "the recital of a creation; it tells how something was accomplished, began to *be*. It . . . speaks only of *realities*, of what *really* happened, of what was fully manifested." The reality it describes is *sacred* reality: "a reality of a wholly different order from 'natural' (or 'profane') realities . . . saturated with being . . . equivalent to a *power*."[2]

A central problem for any new cognitive structure is to legitimize its epistemological foundation. This may involve a myth of an individual genius or hero whose personal qualities exemplify the way in which the new knowledge is acquired. Thus the cult of Newton, who "dared not to know," or of Freud, who heroically conquered anxiety in analyzing his own dreams. The epistemological claims of cultural anthropology rest heavily on the myth of Malinowksi's magical capacity to insert himself

[1] "Relativism" and "relativist" were usually labels applied by defenders of the idea of objectivity to their critics—not self-designations. The labels stuck, and have entered historians' language, so I have used them. "Objectivism" and "objectivist" are not terms which, until the last few years, were much used by historians, or even philosophers. For this reason, and because of my conservative resistance to neologisms, I have been reluctant to use them, but finally overcame my reluctance on grounds of urgent need. (It would be very difficult to write several hundred pages on the belief in the divinity of Christ, and on believers, without "Christianity" and "Christian.")

[2] *The Sacred and the Profane* (New York, 1959), 95.

within a culture so thoroughly that he could describe it "from the inside." As we shall see, the myth of Leopold von Ranke as value-free investigator, interested only in "the facts," played a not dissimilar role in American historiography. Without some such myth, cognitive structures lack grounding and authority. This is at least as important for the morale of practitioners as it is for the lay audience, which must be convinced of the superiority of what the new discipline has to offer: in the case of late-nineteenth-century professional historians, the superiority of their wares to the "partisan" and "tendentious" work of the gentleman-amateurs who had hitherto dominated American historiography.

But myths are not only concerned with origins; they function in the present. For Malinowski, myths were pragmatic charters of extant social institutions, closely corresponding to social and cultural arrangements. A myth is "not merely a story told, but a reality lived. . . . It expresses, enhances, and codifies belief; it safeguards and enforces morality; it vouches for the efficacy of ritual and enforces practical rules for the guidance of man." On this view, the myth of historical objectivity has served to safeguard and enforce norms of scholarly rectitude; it vouches for the efficiency of scholarly rituals: "purging oneself of preconceptions," procedures for the verification and criticism of sources, meticulous documentation.[3]

Emile Durkheim spoke of the indispensable integrative and stabilizing functions of myth for any social organization: to insure solidarity, to guard against lawlessness and chaos. The way in which norms of objectivity served to integrate and stabilize professional historical activity is a recurring theme of this work, and we will encounter repeated concern of scholars at the "anarchy" of competing truth-claims. In a very different spirit from Durkheim, Georges Sorel stressed the capacity of myths which looked toward the future to mobilize rather than stabilize. There is abundant testimony to the inspiration which historians derived from the conviction that they were participating in a collaborative effort which was progressing toward the ultimate and unitary objective historical truth; equally numerous are assertions by historians that without such faith they would see no point to scholarship, and would abandon it.

Claude Lévi-Strauss has maintained that "the purpose of myth is to provide a logical model capable of overcoming a (real) contradiction"—at least to mask or minimize the contradiction. For the founding fathers of the historical profession there was a contradiction between, on the one

[3]Bronislaw Malinowski, "Myth in Primitive Psychology" (1926), in his *Magic, Science and Religion and Other Essays* (Glencoe, Ill., 1948), 78–79.

hand, singular events in the past (there had been *one* American Civil War), and on the other hand, the existence of the most widely varying versions of those events. The *e pluribus unum* in the myth of historical objectivity promised to resolve the contradiction, through a unitary convergent history which would correspond to a unitary past.[4]

Students of primitive myths often tend to write of them as timeless and unchanging. But this is by no means always, or perhaps even typically, the case. Myths change, are questioned, or even abandoned, as the needs and purposes of actors change. Competing values intrude, which may demand modification in previously settled beliefs. For historians, periodic demands for the political mobilization of scholarship produced very serious strains in the myth of objectivity. Myths are at risk when that which they prophesy fails to materialize. Christian doctrine was strained by the indefinite postponement of the Second Coming; Marxism, by the failure of capitalism to collapse on schedule. In such cases some renew their dedication, others introduce doctrinal modifications, some abandon belief. Early professional historians were confident that they could move rapidly toward an agreed-upon objective historical truth; the repeated frustration of this hope produced the same range of responses as among Christians and Marxists, from neo-orthodoxy to apostasy. What was once functional in a myth may cease to be so in changed circumstances. In periods of ideological consensus, the conviction that "truth is one" has been reassuring; in more contentious times, a pluralist, perspectival orientation was more effective in maintaining professional civility between competing schools. Myths arise within the framework of surrounding cultural values, assumptions, and thoughtways; they flourish, more or less unaltered so long as these are stable. A sea change in the larger culture can threaten their viability. The most obvious instance in the last three hundred years of Western history has been the consequences of the growth of a scientific world view for religious myths. In the case of historiography, as particular axioms of "the scientific method" were called into question, ideas of objectivity rooted in older conceptions of science came to be seriously at risk.

Following the standard practice of historians treating any body of belief, "mythic" or otherwise, I put to the side questions of the truth or falsity of that which is being described. We live in an era of blurred genres and the collapse of many of the traditional boundaries between disciplinary approaches. But though the lines are fuzzy, there remain important differences between the approaches of the philosopher and the historian

[4]Lévi-Strauss, *Structural Anthropology* (New York, 1963), 229.

in dealing with the history of thought. Philosophers, as a result of both training and inclination, can rarely resist engaging in systematic critical evaluation of the thought they discuss. We historians, as a result of our training and inclination, are professionally sensitized to the historicity of intellectual life: the extent to which the emergence of ideas and their reception are decisively shaped by surrounding cultural assumptions, social setting, and other elements of their total historical context. We are thus reflexively loath to apply implicitly timeless criteria in judging what we describe and, historically, explain.

All of this is true, and needs to be said in making clear the nature of this undertaking. But it is more than a little disingenuous if it is taken to imply either that I have no views on the issues in debate, or that I believe I have succeeded in preventing those views from coloring my treatment. (Ridiculous notions.) Every reader wants to know "where an author is coming from," and insofar as I can do so briefly, I would like to respond to this perfectly appropriate curiosity. What I can't do is hope to satisfy those who exigently demand to know if I am "for" or "against" objectivity.

I don't think that the idea of historical objectivity is true or false, right or wrong: I find it not just essentially contested, but essentially confused. Many philosophical assumptions of the concept seem to me dubious; some of the key elements in the objectivist synthesis I consider psychologically and sociologically naive. As a practical matter, I think it promotes an unreal and misleading invidious distinction between, on the one hand, historical accounts "distorted" by ideological assumptions and purposes; on the other, history free of these taints. It seems to me that to say of a work of history that it is or isn't objective is to make an *empty* observation; to say something neither interesting nor useful. Another way of describing my stance is to say that, in general and on the whole, I have been persuaded by the arguments of the critics of the concept; unimpressed by the arguments of its defenders. Both sets of arguments are fully, and I hope fairly, set forth in the body of this work. No doubt many who read them will reach conclusions different from my own.

The immediately preceding remarks constitute a radically compressed summary of my philosophical position with respect to historical objectivity, offered not because it is of any inherent interest to anyone, and not as one I propose to defend with arguments, since this isn't that sort of book, but in the spirit of full disclosure. Insofar as philosophy aspires to monitor coherence, anyone who even briefly plays at philosophy may be said to be "against" the continued use of a concept he or she finds incoherent: in this case, for me, "historical objectivity." However, I am but a philosopher north-northwest; when the wind is southerly I know better than to declare myself for or against ideas solely on grounds of coherence. Consider the following:

> We hold these truths to be self-evident, that all men are created equal, that they are endowed by their Creator with certain unalienable Rights. . . . That to secure these rights, Governments are instituted among Men.

Rarely have so many ambiguous terms and dubious propositions been compressed into such a brief passage. By rigorous philosophical criteria the passage is nonsense. But far from being, in the well-worn phrase, "pernicious nonsense," it is *salutary nonsense*. Belief in these "self-evident truths" has for more than two hundred years provided one of the strongest bulwarks of liberty and equality in the United States. I don't know what it would mean if someone asked me whether I was for or against the ideas expressed in the passage, and I would have no idea how to respond.

Above all, the reason why I cannot take a position for or against objectivity is my historicism, which here means simply that my way of thinking about anything in the past is primarily shaped by my understanding of its role within a particular historical context, and in the stream of history. Sir Isaiah Berlin, following Hegel, has described the history of thought and culture as "a changing pattern of great liberating ideas which inevitably turn into suffocating straightjackets." As concerns the idea of objectivity, the characterization seems to me a bit exaggerated at both ends, but the general historicist point is clear enough. This is about as far as I think it appropriate to go in satisfying readers' curiosity as to "where I stand" on the objectivity question. An historian with a different position on the question would surely write a very different account. When one does, no doubt many of my astigmatisms will be corrected; it is likely that new ones will be introduced.[5]

"Nailing jelly to the wall" was a crusty political historian's characterization of the attempt to write intellectual history. Having attempted to deal historically with a concept as gelatinous as "historical objectivity," I am not inclined to quarrel with the description. I have said a bit concerning what I think about the jelly; a few words are in order about the wall, the nail, and the hammer I have chosen.

Practically all the work that has been done in the history of historical thought is biographical: studies of an outstanding individual historian, or at most of two or three outstanding individuals. Even works in historiography which are not explicitly biographical typically devote them-

[5]Berlin, *Concepts and Categories* (New York, 1979), 159.

selves to no more than a dozen major figures. If, when dealing with the outside world, historians have repudiated the "great man theory of history," there appears to be a residual great man theory of historiography.[6]

There's a good deal to be said for the biographical approach. Some historians are so interesting and influential that they certainly deserve extended treatment. Anyone who would seek to grasp the full richness and complexity of an individual's life and thought can do so in at most a handful of cases. But the sort of figures about whom biographies get written are exceptional, and it doesn't make much sense to ground generalizations about professional attitudes as a whole on the study of those who are most unrepresentative. Accordingly, I have spread my net much wider and have surveyed the writings, published and unpublished, of hundreds of members of the profession, scattered in dozens of collections across the country. My treatment retains an "elite bias" in that I have paid more attention to historians of some consequence or visibility. Even within this group, my survey has not been systematic, as rigorous quantifiers use the word. The English historian G. Kitson Clark has advised anyone venturing a generalization: "do not guess, try to count, and if you cannot count, admit that you are guessing." But this inquiry is not one that lends itself to counting. Thus my generalizations are, as Clark said of those offered by historians in these circumstances, "necessarily founded on guesses, guesses informed by much general reading and relevant knowledge, guesses shaped by much brooding on the matter in hand, but on guesses none the less."[7]

The price I pay for emphasizing breadth of coverage is that I am unable to offer rounded and nuanced treatments of the thought of the individuals whom I discuss. I have, of course, attempted to avoid misrepresenting their general postures, or overinterpreting their casual remarks or actions,

---

[6] The word "historiography" can be confusing. Running through the English language there is a distinction between "logys" and "graphys": "biology" (the science of life) and "biography" (the description of lives); "geology" (the science of the earth) and "geography" (the description of the earth); etc. The once respectable word "historiology" has dropped out of just about everybody's vocabulary, and "historiography" has had to do double duty for both "historical science" and descriptive accounts of historical writing. Strictly speaking, "the objectivity question" is an *historiological* issue, but all historians speak of it as "historiographical." Go fight city hall. Context will, I think, always make it clear in which of the two senses I am using the word.

[7] *The Making of Victorian England* (London, 1962), 14. In fact I tried to count and failed. Some time ago I spent the better part of two years coding the evaluative language used in thousands of historians' book reviews, punching IBM cards, and attempting to correlate the language employed with dozens of other variables having to do with historians' generation, field, status, etc. It was a total waste of time, producing nothing intelligible and permanently dampening my enthusiasm for introducing quantitative rigor into intellectual history.

but I am less likely to have succeeded in this attempt than a scholar who has made an intensive study of one or a few individuals. Scholarship, like all of life, is full of trade-offs. But what one loses in the ability to unpack the nuances and complexities of individuals' thought, in "doing them justice," one may gain in the validity of generalizations, and appreciation of the variety of contradictory currents within the profession, and their interaction.

If readers want to know where an author stands with respect to the subject at hand, colleagues are equally interested in getting a fix on the author's "school"—his or her methodological approach. In the history of science, and, by extension, the history of academic disciplines generally, there are "internalists" and "externalists." As the names suggest, those in the former camp concern themselves with what goes on inside the discipline, slighting or ignoring its relationship with the surrounding environment; the latter focus on one or another aspect of that external relationship. Cutting across this division, there are "cognitivists," who focus more or less exclusively on the substance of scientific or scholarly work and its rational development, and "noncognitivists," who stress psychological, sociological, political, or other factors in the development of disciplinary communities and their work.

My own deepest methodological commitment is to the "overdetermination" of all activity, including thought. Therefore, for me, explanation and understanding necessarily involve the exploration of the widest variety of overlapping influences, and this book straddles both the internalist versus externalist, and cognitivist versus noncognitivist divisions: explores them all, and does its best to integrate them. I discuss at length the development of intellectual arguments within the profession on the objectivity question; ways in which shifting external currents of thought shaped this discourse; aspects of the changing sociology and economics of the profession, and the psychology of historians; ways in which historians responded to various political and other demands from the larger society. This is the principal reason why the book is so long.

Such ecumenism might be thought to satisfy everyone (except those who like short books). But it won't. The oldest and still the most powerful tradition in intellectual history and the history of disciplines is both internalist and cognitivist—committed to the autonomy and rationality of either intellectual life in general, or of the work of a particular disciplinary community. Nowadays, those in this tradition feel under assault as a result of the growth in the number of externalists and noncognitivists, who are charged with "irrationalism" and "reductionism." Their interpretations, it is claimed, treat the substance of thought as "merely" or "nothing but" a reflection of social dynamics or external interests. Internalist cognitivists rarely consider what seems to me the self-evident truth that to treat thought as exclusively rational and autonomous is equally reductionist.

My multilayered approach should protect me against charges of reductionism. The question of whether my approach is "irrationalist" is more complex, and I am inclined to enter a plea of nolo contendere, or even "guilty with an explanation."

Most work in the history of disciplines deals with the development of substantive specialist knowledge: how chemists have changed their minds about chemistry, economists about economics. These processes—the development and refinement of theory, the discovery and interpretation of facts, carried out meticulously by trained investigators—are the essence of what we mean by "rationality." Recent work in the history, philosophy, and sociology of science has made us increasingly aware of the influence of external and social factors in theory choice, in deciding what is "a fact," and even in defining "rationality." Still, at least for our present purposes, I acknowledge that it is reasonable to expect that an inquiry into the development of substantive, specialist knowledge should direct itself primarily to the internal and the cognitive; only secondarily to the external and the "irrational."

The extent to which historians develop their substantive knowledge "rationally" is a tangled question, hinging largely on definitions of rationality, and also on whether by "knowledge" we mean relatively isolated factual propositions or broad interpretations. But—again, for present purposes—let us call it "rational." It certainly is true that with respect to particular issues, for example, the profitability of slavery, historians bring specialized knowledge and techniques to bear; that their conclusions are largely governed by historians' rules of evidence and inference which they have internalized, and which the historical community monitors; that whatever their backgrounds, whatever their desires, whatever they'd like to believe is true about the profitability of slavery, what they ultimately wind up concluding is powerfully constrained by all of these factors. For these reasons it would be appropriate to write of historians' changing views on the profitability of slavery as primarily the history of rational men and women bringing reason to bear on the question.

But the present work, unlike the vast majority of histories of history, is not concerned with the evolution of substantive historical interpretations. It concerns what historians have thought about the objectivity question—a subject about which they know less and care more. These differences are crucial with respect to the issue of "irrationalism."

On one level what is at stake in the objectivity question is a philosophical issue: a technical problem in epistemology. Very few historians have any philosophical training, or even inclination. (Not a crime; not even blameworthy; most philosophers are rotten historians.) Though all historians have had views on the objectivity question, these views have rarely been fully articulated; even more rarely have they been the fruit of systematic thought. The historical profession does not monitor the philosophical rigor of what historians have had to say on the question, and no historian suffers professionally as a result of demonstrated philosophical incompetence. All of which is to say that historians' reflections on objectivity, unlike their substantive historical work, have none of those positive attributes which privilege it as "rational" in the sense of discourse entitled to "professional courtesy."

But the objectivity question is far from being "merely" a philosophical question. It is an enormously charged emotional issue: one in which the stakes are very high, much higher than in any disputes over substantive interpretations. For many, what has been at issue is nothing less than the meaning of the venture to which they have devoted their lives, and thus, to a very considerable extent, the meaning of their own lives. "Objectivity" has been one of the central sacred terms of professional historians, like "health" for physicians, or "valor" for the profession of arms. A lawyer, whether prosecuting polluters or defending rapists, will have views on "justice" and how his or her work furthers it. A journalist, whether investigating municipal corruption or rewriting corporate handouts, will have views on "a free press in a free society" and his or her contribution to that role. It is quite possible that all four of those mentioned would have something interesting to say on the respective subjects. It is conceivable that some or all of these views might be the fruits of rational reflection, and study of the relevant theoretical literature. But I wouldn't start by assuming that was the case—with lawyers, with journalists, or with historians.

The horror of "irrationalism" in the history of disciplines confuses norms of scholarly discussion with procedures of scholarly analysis. Except with very good friends, it is considered tactless and discourteous to suggest that someone's views are a reflection of his or her background, prejudices, or psychic needs. We stick to the reasoned arguments advanced, even if privately we think those arguments are shallow rationalizations. The need to behave this way in scholarly discussion is obvious, as are the costs of violating the rule. But if, as historians of an ongoing discussion, we believe that the protagonists are in fact often disingenuous in their arguments, are following hidden agendas, and are expressing views shaped by "extra rational" factors, what kind of historians would we be if we suppressed this perception? (Of course, the perception might be wrong, but that is quite another issue.)

When historians discuss the most deeply rooted beliefs of "ordinary people"—workers, generals, priests, businessmen—we hardly ever assume that those beliefs are arrived at as a result of logical considerations. Out of understandable but misplaced tact and courtesy we apply a different standard when writing historically about historians—particularly, of course, living historians. Occasionally, when historians write of dead historians, they "sociologize" or "psychologize" their views, but here, too, there is a double standard at work: these noncognitivist explanations are almost always applied to the views of those with whom we disagree.

Neither of these double standards seems to me defensible. I have treated the views of historians—especially, but not exclusively, their views on highly charged issues—as being as likely to be "rational" or "irrational" as those of the rest of the human race; as certain to be overdetermined. And I do my best to extend such treatment evenhandedly: as much to the thought of those with whom I am in sympathy as to those whose views I dislike.

There is one final observation I want to make about the approach of this book—the genre to which it belongs, how it differs from previous work in historiography. Those of us interested in the development of academic communities and of organized knowledge often emphasize the distinction between "disciplinary histories," written by practitioners, and "histories of disciplines," produced by historians. The former, so we say, are characteristically distorted by "presentism": usually of the celebratory (how we got so wonderful) variety; occasionally denunciatory (settling scores with a dominant school of thought, or even the discipline as a whole). "Histories of disciplines," by (detached) outsider historians, are, in principle, free of these disfiguring characteristics. "A sociologist writing the history of sociology," Laurence Veysey observes, "remains, from the historian's point of view, an amateur, no different in principle from an untrained Mormon writing the history of Mormonism. Particularistic intellectual commitments inhibit balanced clarity of vision . . . in the academic world as in any other."[8]

In terms of this dichotomy, histories of history by historians are, in principle, an anomaly: neither fish nor fowl. But though works in historiography lack the more obviously ahistorical characteristics of "disci-

---

[8]"Reappraising the Chicago School of Sociology," *Reviews in American History* 6 (March 1978): 115.

plinary histories," in practice they mostly fall on that side of the line. If, as I suggested above, the great man theory of history survives, anachronistically, in historiography, so does the "Whig interpretation of history," which Herbert Butterfield described as "the tendency in many historians . . . to emphasise certain principles of progress in the past and to produce a story which is the ratification if not the glorification of the present."[9]

This is a characteristic not just of inferior work in historiography, but of the very best as well. I am thinking in particular of John Higham's *History: Professional Scholarship in America*, which has, since its publication in 1965, deservedly become the standard work in the field. It was written, he said, as an "affirmation of the historical vocation." Historians of bygone days were all treated with great respect and sympathy, though not uncritically. But he made it clear that in the case of the immediately preceding generation, their limitations— political naiveté, misguided attempts to make history directly "relevant," corrosive skepticism and relativism—had, after World War II, been "transcended"; that finally the American historical profession had "come of age." Higham, to his great credit, ruefully reflected several years later on the "consistently, indeed determinedly, cheerful" tone of his conclusions:

My summing up was an endorsement. History had renewed itself, finding directions that altered without abrogating earlier forms and achievements. Affluent, respected, and absorbed in studies of unchallenged worth, American historians could contemplate an enticing future continuous with their effective past.[10]

The point of mentioning this is not to establish that I am enlisted in the forces of light (histories of disciplines) as opposed to the forces of darkness (disciplinary histories). I would be well satisfied if colleagues found my work as enlightening and stimulating as I have found Higham's. But the celebratory tone of most of the disciplinary histories of history has created norms of discourse which may lead to a serious misreading of my own work. The expectations which have been established are so "accentuate the positive" that what I think of as my attempt at detachment may be read as hostility, on the grounds that the alternative to affirmation must be negativism. (The situation is not unlike that of textbook controversies, in which those raised on superpatriotic histories often think of more critical accounts as "anti-American.")

[9]*The Whig Interpretation of History* (1931; reprinted, New York, 1965), v.
[10]Preface to reprint of *History* (Baltimore, 1983), xii; "American Historiography in the 1960's" in his *Writing American History: Essays on Modern Scholarship* (Bloomington, Ind., 1970), 158; "Epilogue" to 1983 edition of *History*, 233.

My greater detachment, if that is what it is, may stem from the fact that I am, by background and training, an historian of Europe, writing about an American profession dominated by historians of the United States—a subject hitherto written about exclusively by specialists in American history. Carl Becker was also a Europeanist who wrote on American subjects. Reviewing Becker's *Declaration of Independence*, the Americanist Arthur Schlesinger, Sr. said—definitely not in praise—that the book was written "with so high a degree of detachment that one sometimes receives an impression of the author in the role of an entomologist studying a quivering specimen impaled with a pin." The comparison of myself with Becker is inexcusably immodest, but I think there may be something to the proposition that a certain distance or "marginality" has its advantages—and is often viewed with alarm by those more "central." Once again, there are trade-offs. When I wrote a book on a highly charged topic in the history of France (the purge of collaborators after World War II), several French reviewers commented on the advantages enjoyed by an outsider not caught up in internal polemics. What impressed *me* most forcefully when I wrote on France were all the things that as an outsider I felt I didn't adequately understand. In a similar fashion there may be advantages and disadvantages in my marginal relationship to American history.[11]

But my marginality is not just a matter of my Europeanist background. I have been a professional historian for over twenty years. I spend the majority of my waking hours reading, teaching, and writing history; I find it, most of the time, enjoyable and rewarding. But I am "unprofessional" in that I do not think that writing history is in any sense a sanctified vocation, or that it deserves to be spoken about reverently. The ways in which professional history is superior to the work of amateurs are not merely technical in the narrowest sense of the term, but its moral and political thrust have to do mainly, though not exclusively, with the context in which it develops. In the early decades of the twentieth century the most professionally accomplished work on Reconstruction—work hailed by the profession as the most objective, the most balanced, the most fair—was viciously racist; antiracist accounts were for the most part crude and amateurish. Nowadays generally the opposite is true; "progress," to be sure, from my point of view, but neither inevitable nor irreversible—nor, I think, attributable to history's becoming more professional. Despite my commitment (as a professional) to writing and teaching history, I am unable (as human being and citizen) to regard the

[11]Schlesinger review in *MVHR* 9 (1923): 334.

professional historical venture as unambiguously a blessing for mankind. This leads me to what those who see historical scholarship as a sanctified activity will call "negativity"; what seems to me a kind of "detachment."

And what is true of my attitude toward the profession as a whole and its work is also true of my attitude toward its members—an attitude which contrasts sharply with that of most historians, who generally write about their colleagues the way Arthur Schlesinger, Jr. writes about the Kennedys. In part what seems to some my negativity, or at least failure to be appropriately affirmative, is a function of my focus. Most histories of history concentrate on what professional historians do best, often superbly: write history. Although I constantly refer to historians' substantive work insofar as one or another aspect of it relates to my treatment of "the objectivity question," it is not my central concern, and I make no systematic attempt to evaluate it. And, inevitably, I spend a good deal of time talking about what historians do worst, or at least badly: reflecting on epistemology. This loads the dice against historians: something like a sportswriter reporting on their performances in the annual history department softball game.

But beyond this, my attitude toward the historians who appear in these pages is mixed. Going through the personal correspondence of historians, as anyone who has worked in private papers can testify, is a very intimate process. Often one develops sympathies or antipathies based on information which does not appear in one's text, because it is irrelevant to the issues under discussion. Some of those whom I have encountered in the course of my work display attributes I like very much. I think of Merle Curti's untiring efforts on behalf of Bert Loewenberg, whose Jewishness blocked his career; the gaiety and irreverence of the young Kenneth Stampp, Frank Freidel, and T. Harry Williams as they traded friendly insults with their mentor, William Hesseltine; the patience and tact of editors of the *American Historical Review* as they dealt with "difficult" authors. Other material I came across left a bad taste in my mouth. Based on my own values and preferences, "prejudices" if you like, I found a number of eminent figures to be insufferably pompous, arrogant, and self-satisfied. Others, particularly junior historians writing to their seniors, often struck me as sycophantic, self-absorbed, self-pitying "injustice collectors."

Some years ago I was fascinated by the findings of a sociologist who compared the workplace conduct of members of an advertising agency and of an academic department. The former, he said, behaved better on the whole. The sociologist's hypothesis was that those in advertising, nagged by guilt about their social product, felt obliged to expiate their sins by being nice to their colleagues. The academics, overwhelmed with the transcendent moral worth of their activity, believed that on that account they had a plenary indulgence to act badly. I was fascinated, but ultimately unpersuaded: too clever by half. Historians, and other academics, seem to me about the same as everyone else, displaying a normal distribution of the whole range of human strengths and frailties: extremes of dedication and cynicism, generosity and selfishness, kindness and cruelty.

"It is not that we are connoisseurs of chaos," writes Frank Kermode, "but that we are surrounded by it, and equipped for coexistence with it only by our fictive powers." The most universal of the "regulative fictions" which historians employ to make some order out of a chaotic past is "periodization," by which we cut the continuous thread of time into manageable lengths, and then do our best to present such divisions as natural rather than contrived. I have divided my account into four periods, corresponding to what seem to me to be the introduction of new sets of problems, turning points in historians' attitudes, or shifts in dominant sensibilities. But the reader is urged to be as aware as the author is of the artificiality of the periods, and the enormous difficulty in generalizing about historical thought at any time. Generations of historians do not replace one another on cue: at any given moment the historical profession includes individuals ranging from under thirty to over seventy, shaped by very different experiences—and, of course, responding very differently to the same experiences.[12]

The "plot" of this book is easily summarized. Part One, dealing with the years from the founding of the American historical profession in the 1880s down to the outbreak of the first world war, is concerned with the various reasons for the establishment of objectivity as the central norm of the profession. Part Two, treating the period of World War I and the interwar years, shows how a changed cultural, social, and political climate produced "historical relativism," which, though it never became the dominant view within the profession, did put believers in objectivity on the defensive. The theme of Part Three, covering the years of World War II and the cold war, is the attempt of the historical profession to establish a new, somewhat chastened, objectivist synthesis, trivializing the relativist critique by partially incorporating it. Part Four treats the years since the mid-1960s, and is a story, necessarily lacking an ending, of the many factors which caused the collapse of the postwar synthesis, leading to the present period of confusion, polarization, and uncertainty, in which the

---

[12]Kermode, *The Sense of an Ending: Studies in the Theory of Fiction* (New York, 1967), 64.

idea of historical objectivity has become more problematic than ever before.

Although the story can be easily summarized, it cannot be quickly or easily told: the weight of this volume is accounted for by my effort to detail what lies behind those innocent phrases in the previous paragraphs—"various reasons," "many factors." In casting my net as widely as I have, in exploring so many complex interactions, I have inevitably raised more questions than I have answered. This is as it should be in a work which attempts to open rather than close a subject: to stimulate others to inquire into areas on which I have touched lightly, and to reconsider and revise my conclusions. The book, though inevitably written from a point of view, presents no overarching thesis. If it is not a celebration, neither is it a jeremiad; it is not a call to arms, nor even a plea for reform. The book's aim is to provoke my fellow historians to greater self-consciousness about the nature of our work; to offer those outside the historical profession a greater understanding of what we're up to, together with some alternative ways of thinking about the products we present to them, and the claims we make on behalf of those products.

PART I

Objectivity enthroned

1

The European legacy: Ranke, Bacon, Flaubert

By 1884, the year of the founding of the American Historical Association, the United States had a favorable balance of trade: exports exceeded imports by over $100 million annually. The gap widened to over $500 million by the turn of the century, as more and more American cotton, wheat, machinery, and other products flowed abroad. But in these years, and for some time to come, the United States remained a net importer of ideas.

As American historians constructed their system of professional norms, and in particular the central norm of objectivity, they drew heavily on various European currents of thought. German historical scholarship was an unavoidable model—and had the advantage of borrowed prestige. Much the same was true of "scientific method," in an age when scienticity was the hallmark of the modern and the authoritative. They opted for an austere style which would clearly distinguish professional historical work from the florid effusions of the amateur historians whom the professionals sought to displace.

Based on their understanding of these currents—often, as we shall see, based on their misunderstanding of them—American historians laid the foundations of professional historiographical thought and sensibility in the United States.

I

"That Germany possessed the sole secret of scholarship," wrote Bliss Perry, "was no more doubted by us young fellows in the eighteen-eighties than it had been doubted by George Ticknor and Edward Everett when they sailed from Boston, bound for Göttingen, in 1814." During the course of the century, thousands of young Americans in search of advanced professional or academic training traveled to Göttingen, Heidelberg, Leipzig, Freibourg, Berlin, and the other German university centers. Graduate or professional training worthy of the name hardly existed in the United States until the century was well advanced. English universities were concerned with turning out gentlemen, not scholars— and until 1871 required degree candidates to sign the Thirty-nine Articles of the Anglican church. French universities offered no easily attainable advanced degree, and to contemplate study at the Sorbonne was to face perils of the flesh in the "vice dens" of the capital, while one's soul would have to brave the twin risks of "infidelism" and "popery." Also, study in Germany was inexpensive: in the late 1880s it was estimated that a year's study there, including transportation, cost a third less than a year spent at one of the leading American universities.[1]

In Germany, young American students of history found institutions of higher education whose structure and values were totally unlike anything they had known at home. The colleges they had attended in America were still primarily moral academies for the inculcation of "discipline"— mental, behavioral, religious. Student life was strangled in meticulously arrayed and rigidly enforced regulations; classroom work consisted, for the most part, of mechanical recitation; intellectual innovation was viewed as a threat to Protestant piety. In Germany they found the models that were to inspire a revolution in American higher education: the creation of new universities, like Johns Hopkins, Clark, and Chicago; the transformation of older ones, like Columbia, Harvard, Michigan, and Wisconsin. A "proper" university was a community of investigators, concerned with pursuing their researches while training the next generation of *Gelehrten*; rigorous scholarship, rather than religious or philosophical orthodoxy, was the criterion of academic excellence.

American students in Germany also found an intoxicating personal role model: the *Herr Professor*, who, unlike the shabby figure of fun they had known in the United States, was a personage of substantial wealth and even greater status. The average full professor in Prussia around the turn of the century earned twelve thousand marks—nine times as much as an elementary school teacher, who was himself far from the bottom of the economic ladder. The most successful university teachers might make more than forty thousand marks per year. Within the system of public ranks, a successful professor was close to the ministerial level. Those

[1]Perry, *And Gladly Teach: Reminiscences* (Boston, 1935), 88–89; Laurence R. Veysey, *The Emergence of the American University* (Chicago, 1965), 130.

most highly regarded were not infrequently personally ennobled. Even without that ultimate honor they were among the most respected figures in society, entitled to a deference that extended to the *Frau Professor* as well.[2]

In the *historische Vorseminarien* of their German mentors, graduate students encountered a dazzling array of refined and esoteric techniques for ferreting out and verifying the historical fact: paleography, numismatics, epigraphy, sphragistics, and many more. Technique was important, but even more important was rigor, assiduity in research, an infinite capacity for the most painstaking and arduous pursuit of the fact. Their ideal was the man who would "cross an ocean to verify a comma."

No merely professional motive could sustain such effort. Indeed, he who pursued knowledge, wrote one leading historian, was to be sharply distinguished from the "hackney professional"— he was rather a sanctified member of a "remnant" within society; his love of knowledge had to be "absolutely untainted by any sordid motives." The investigative mind, said G. Stanley Hall, required "whole-souled self-abandonment"; the researcher was a "knight of the Holy Spirit of truth." The ideal graduate student "must be gifted by nature with a certain amount of the celestial fire." The American historians who most fully embodied the German ideal of a holy "fanaticism for veracity" led driven existences. "Watching [Herbert Levi Osgood] at work," reported his son-in-law, Dixon Ryan Fox, "one could almost actually see the element of will pitilessly driving a poor body to the limit of its power. . . . He had dedicated himself to a service as unrelentingly as any monk." The Harvard medievalist Charles Gross, a colleague said, "worked with an absorbed intensity that was astounding, biting his nails all the while. . . . At Cambridge and in the British Museum he became so absorbed in his work that his meals were either entirely forgotten or taken at very irregular intervals, an element no doubt which contributed to his fatal illness."[3]

[2]Fritz K. Ringer, *The Decline of the German Mandarins: The German Academic Community, 1890–1933* (Cambridge, Mass., 1969), 37–38.
[3]Hermann Eduard Von Holst, "The Need of Universities in the United States," *Educational Review* 5 (1893): 117–19; Hall, "Address," in *A Record of the Commemoration, June Twenty-First to Twenty-Seventh, 1895, of the One Hundredth Anniversary of the Founding of Union College* (New York, 1897), 237; Hall, "The University Idea," *Pedagogical Seminary* 15 (1908): 104; W. G. Hale, "The Graduate School," *University Record* 1 (1896): 439; Fox, *Herbert Levi Osgood* (New York, 1924), 109–12; J. Sullivan, quoted in Veysey, *Emergence*, 152—the source of all quotations in this paragraph. Many American professional historians in this period were the children of clergymen; several— as well as others of nonclerical backgrounds—had themselves considered the ministry as a career before embracing scholarship; this may help to account for the religious zeal with which they threw themselves into their work.

The experience of the scholarly university, and visions of it being replicated in America; the dream of becoming, in Kansas and Kentucky, a figure as favored as the German professor; scholarship as a technical, specialized, and rigorous pursuit, to be followed as a sacred vocation: all these were brought back to the United States in more or less recognizable form, and all played an important role in shaping the sensibility of American professional historians. But when we move from the institutional, social, technical, and moral, to the explicitly philosophical and epistemological, a gap opens up between German reality and American perception—a gap which must be explored if we are to understand what became the distinctive American orthodoxy.

It is important here to look at the American reworking of what Edward A. Ross recalled as the "keynote" of his experience at the University of Berlin in the 1880s, "that majestic phrase, *wissenschaftliche Objektivität.*" How to translate *Wissenschaft*? On the denotative level, in German usage, any organized body of information is referred to as *eine Wissenschaft*, with the indefinite article; the collective activity of scholars in gathering and interpreting information is *die Wissenschaft*, with the definite article. *Die Wissenschaft* means "scholarship" or "learning," rarely "science"; *eine Wissenschaft* simply means a "discipline." "In English," as Fritz Ringer has remarked, "it is possible to argue about whether sociology or history is 'a science.' In German, history is *eine Wissenschaft* by definition, and to ask whether sociology is *eine Wissenschaft* is to wonder about its status as a distinct and clearly circumscribed discipline, not about its more or less 'scientific' methods." The connotations of the word were rooted in the idealist philosophical tradition within which it developed. *Wissenschaft* signified a dedicated, sanctified pursuit. It implied not just knowledge, but self-fulfillment; not practical knowledge, but knowledge of ultimate meanings. If *Wissenschaft* had vaguely idealist implications, there could be no doubt of the idealism implicit in the *Geisteswissenschaften*: idiomatically, "humanistic disciplines," but more literally and evocatively, "spiritual studies." History, together with philosophy, literature, and theology, was unequivocally *eine Geisteswissenschaft*. German historians reacted with outrage to the suggestion that *naturwissenschaftlich* approaches could be applied within their realm.[4]

[4]Ross, *Seventy Years of It* (New York, 1936), 38; Ringer, *Mandarins*, 102–3. It is a nice irony that the word *Geisteswissenschaften*, heavy with distinctively Germanic connotations, which those raised in the English empiricist tradition rarely appreciated, in fact was made popular in Germany by the translator of John Stuart Mill's *Logic*, in rendering Mill's phrase "moral sciences." Mill, unlike his German readers, thought the inductive methods of the natural sciences could be applied in this realm. (Hans-Georg Gadamer, *Truth and Method* [1960: English trans., New York, 1975], 5.)

Did late-nineteenth-century American historians, and especially that large portion of them who had studied in Germany, really think that *Wissenschaft* easily and naturally translated as "science"; that *wissenschaftlich* historical study meant the adoption of the (allegedly) purely empirical and neutral approach of the natural sciences? Such a suggestion beggars the imagination. Yet, as we shall see shortly, there is much to suggest that most historians believed something of the sort.

Translating *Wissenschaft*, difficult as it turned out to be in practice, ought, in principle, to have been possible. *Objektivität* was difficult in a different way. On the purely formal level it was exactly equivalent to the English "objectivity." Though "objectivity" had been an English word since the seventeenth century, it was employed with reference to the philosophy and psychology of consciousness and perception. In the sense with which we are concerned—representation of "the actual facts," un-colored by bias or preference—its appearance in English does not date from before the late nineteenth century, and entered into the language from Germany. George Bancroft, writing from Berlin in 1867, respond-ing to the observation that his history was "written from the democratic point of view," denied the charge, claiming that "if there is democracy in the history it is not subjective, but objective as they say here."[5]

As with any protean word, *Objektivität* was used in ways which, while overlapping, meant something slightly different to different intellectual communities, and to each individual within those communities. Even within an individual, the effort to derive a consistent usage depends on the arbitrary and unreal assumption of constant exquisite care in expres-sion. Typically, one received mixed messages. Hermann Eduard von Holst was a key figure in the transmission to America of the German ethos: at Freibourg he was the *Doktorvater* of Albert Bushnell Hart and James Harvey Robinson, subsequently the founders of dynasties at Har-vard and Columbia; immigrating to the United States, he was the first chairman of the History Department at the University of Chicago. Von Holst, with no apparent sense of inconsistency, could profess "the objec-tivity of the historian," of the "cool, unbiased student" aiming at the "stern historical truth," and yet praise Woodrow Wilson for being "no votary of that exaggerated, nay, impossible *objektivität*, which virtually amounts to a denial of his right to hold any political or moral opinion as to the events and men he is treating of. But he has no thesis to prove.

[5]M. A. DeWolfe Howe, *The Life and Letters of George Bancroft* (2 vols., New York, 1908), 2:183. Cf. Lord Bryce: "To complete the survey of the actualities of party politics by stating in a purely positive, or as the Germans say 'objective,' way what the Americans think about their system . . ." (*The American Commonwealth* [2 vols., London, 1894], 2:240.)

With unimpeachable honesty and undeviating singleness of purpose he
strives—as Ranke puts it—'simply to say how it was.'" The elusiveness
and ambiguity in Von Holst's usage was characteristic.[6]

The confusion in Americans' appreciation of what was meant by
wissenschaftliche Objektivität was most clearly demonstrated in their almost total misunderstanding of the man who to them embodied it more
completely than any historian who had ever lived: Leopold von Ranke.[7]

Ranke's name was constantly invoked as inspirational model by turn-
of-the-century American historians. William E. Dodd recalled that his
cohort of American students in Germany had, "with much objectivity
and little partisan or patriotic pleading . . . idolized" Ranke's "character
and work." "No purer or more exalted spirit than that of Leopold von
Ranke ever adorned the scholarship of any nation," wrote Herbert Levi
Osgood: "May his succession continue unbroken in his own country and
may men of his character be multiplied elsewhere, especially on this side
of the Atlantic, where the need of such is imperative. American scholars,
especially of the younger generation, owe a debt of gratitude to him
which cannot be easily repaid." Ranke was the first honorary member of
the American Historical Association. After his death in 1886 one of his
former students arranged for the purchase of Ranke's library, including
his portrait, study table, chairs, and pens, which were set up as a shrine at
Syracuse University.[8]

Justly regarded as the father of modern historical scholarship, Ranke's
greatest contribution was to apply to modern history those documentary
and philological methods which had been developed for the study of
antiquity. In assiduity and scrupulosity of research, in the critical treatment of a wide range of previously unused sources, in the volume of his
productivity, and in his development of the seminar for the training of
scholars, Ranke was unprecedented and unsurpassed. He was a supreme
representative of the romantic reaction against the universalistic, "materialistic," and "critical" philosophical thought of the Enlightenment—a
reaction which had stimulated the great flowering of historical studies in

---

[6]*The Constitutional and Political History of the United States* (8 vols., Chicago, 1876–92),
3:497; review of Wilson's *Division and Reunion* (1893), reprinted in Arthur H. Link, ed.,
The Papers of Woodrow Wilson (Princeton, 1966–), 8:222.
[7]The following discussion draws heavily on Georg G. Iggers's important article "The
Image of Ranke in American and German Historical Thought," *History and Theory* 2
(1962): 17–40.
[8]Dodd, quoted in Robert Dallek, *Democrat and Diplomat: The Life of William E. Dodd*
(New York, 1968), 19; Osgood, review of Ranke's *Zur Eigenen Lebensgeschichte*, *Political Science Quarterly* 6 (1891): 562; Charles W. Bennett, "The Ranke Library in America," AHA, *Papers* 3 (1889): 131–33.

the nineteenth century. For his friend Savigny, the founder of the German historical school of law, there was no antithesis between positive law and just law, between the actual and the ideal. Whatever the historical process had produced was to be not just accepted, but valued. So for Ranke, there were no rational or moral standards by which historical developments could be judged. Enlightenment "radicals" had criticized the past to awaken minds to the possibility of reform. Ranke, and German historicists generally, in reaction to the French Revolution, were wedded to the past, and accepted it as the basis of existing conditions. Ranke's abstention from moral judgment, rather than manifesting disinterested neutrality, was, in its context, a profoundly conservative political judgment. It is only a slight exaggeration to say that in his reaction to Enlightenment historiography he adopted a slogan from that epoch: "Everything is for the best in this best of all possible worlds." Nowhere was this more evident than in his celebration of the great nation-states. His "impartiality," real enough, compared with the nationalist partisanship of many of his contemporaries, was founded on pantheistic state-worship. All of the great powers were the objects of his veneration. They were "spiritual substances . . . thoughts of God."[9]

He was a thoroughgoing philosophical idealist, at one with Hegel in believing the world divinely ordered, differing with him only in his insistence on the extent to which that order was clearly manifested in existing reality. In repudiating an historiography based on a priori philosophy, he promoted an historiography grounded on the fundamental principle that the course of history revealed God's work. "The hand of God," "God's gift," "the judgment of God," are phrases which recur throughout his work. "God dwells, lives, and can be known in all of history," Ranke wrote. "Every deed attests to Him, every moment preaches His name, but most of all, it seems to me, the connectedness of history in the large. It [the connectedness] stands there like a holy hieroglyph. . . . May we, for our part, decipher this holy hieroglyph! Even so do we serve God. Even so are we priests. Even so are we teachers."[10]

[9] Leopold von Ranke, *The Theory and Practice of History*, ed. Georg Iggers and Konrad Von Moltke (Indianapolis, 1973), 119.

[10] Ranke, quoted in Theodore H. von Laue, *Leopold Ranke: The Formative Years* (Princeton, 1950), 29; Leonard Krieger, *Ranke: The Meaning of History* (Chicago, 1977), 361. Ranke's imagery could be erotic as well as religious. He referred to unexamined manuscripts as "so many princesses, possibly beautiful, all under a curse and needing to be saved"; a new Venetian archive was "a beautiful Italian, and I hope that together we shall produce a Romano-German prodigy"; a collection to which he had up to then unsuccessfully sought entry was "still absolutely a virgin . . . I long for the moment [when] I shall have access to her and make my declaration of love." (Krieger, *Ranke*, 105.)

The deciphering of the "hieroglyph" required "intuitive contemplation" (*Anschauung*) or "divination" (*Ahnung*).

No one could be more convinced than I that historical research requires the strictest method: criticism of the authors, the banning of all fables, the extraction of the pure facts. . . . But I am also convinced that this fact has a spiritual content. . . . The external appearance is not the final thing which we have to discover; there is still something which occurs within. . . . It is our task to recognize what really happened in the series of facts which German history comprises: their sum. After the labor of criticism, intuition is required.

Talent is an intimation [*Ahnung*], an immediate empathy with essence. I scent the track of the spirit. . . . The spirit from which things come, and the knower, will be one. In this theory of knowledge the most subjective is at the same time the most general truth.[11]

For Ranke the historian's greatest task was to penetrate to "essences." In his most quoted phrase he modestly forswore "judging the past"; his ambition was merely to show the past "wie es eigentlich gewesen." The phrase has habitually been translated "as it really was" or "as it actually was." In fact, as Georg Iggers has recently pointed out, in the nineteenth century, *eigentlich* had an ambiguity it no longer has: it also meant "essentially," and it was in this sense that Ranke characteristically used it. His wish, expressed in the preface to the *World History*, to "as it were extinguish myself," reflected a widespread romantic desire to open oneself to the flow of intuitive perception. (The young historian who in the 1970s proposed a "psychedelic" approach to history—altered states of consciousness as a means for historians to project themselves back into the past—was thus in some respects truer to the essence of Ranke's approach than empiricists who never lifted their eyes from the documents.)[12]

In Germany, Karl Lamprecht, from a positivist standpoint, attacked Ranke's continuation of the German idealist tradition, while Ranke's supporters, like Friedrich Meinecke, defended the tradition in defending Ranke. All German historians saw Ranke as the antithesis of a nonphilosophical empiricism, while American historians venerated him for being precisely what he was not.

To American historians their mythic hero was empirical science incarnate. Frederick Jackson Turner explained Ranke's orientation as a result of his having grown up in "an age of science." "That inductive study of

[11]Ranke, quoted in Leopold von Ranke, *The Secret of World History: Selected Writings on The Art and Science of History*, ed. Roger Wines (New York, 1981), 21; Krieger, *Ranke*, 11.
[12]Iggers, "Introduction" to Ranke, *Theory and Practice*, xix-xx; James B. Parsons, "The Psychedelic Approach," paper delivered at the 1971 meeting of the AHA.

phenomena which has worked a revolution in our knowledge of the external world was applied to history." For Dodd, "the fundamental principle of Ranke's method . . . was . . . no generalization, no interpretation and little exercise of native intuition—only the one question, 'what really happened.'" Ephraim Emerton of Harvard, describing Ranke as the founder of "the doctrine of true historical method," said that

If one must choose between a school of history whose main characteristic is *esprit*, and one which rests upon a faithful and honest effort to base its whole narration upon the greatest attainable number of recorded facts, we cannot long hesitate. . . . Training has taken the place of brilliancy and the whole civilized world is today reaping the benefit.

George B. Adams of Yale, hailing "our first leader" Ranke, said that his school had asked only

can methods of investigation which are strictly scientific be applied to the past action of the race, in such a way as to give our knowledge of what happened greater certainty? The school of Ranke has never endeavored to go beyond [this] question, but their answer to it has been a clear and, I believe, an indisputable affirmative.[13]

Because the alleged authority of Ranke was so often used to legitimate consensual American practice, it is worth considering the grounds of the misunderstanding.

Ranke had retired from his professorship before the great influx of American students in Germany, and no American had sustained firsthand contact with him. There is no reason to believe that Ranke's work, particularly his theoretical essays, was widely read. And there were programmatic statements by Ranke which, innocently taken out of context to illustrate the empiricist misconception, effectively furthered it: "Strict presentation of the facts, conditional and unattractive though they may be, is unquestionably the supreme law, for historical research is oriented by its very nature to the particular."[14]

[13]Turner, "The Significance of History," reprinted in *The Early Writings of Frederick Jackson Turner* (Madison, 1938), 51; Dodd, "Karl Lamprecht and His Work," 1908 draft manuscript in Dodd Papers, Box 6; Emerton, "The Practical Method in Higher Historical Instruction," in G. Stanley Hall, ed., *Methods of Teaching and Studying History* (Boston, 1886), 42; G. B. Adams, "History and the Philosophy of History," *AHR* 14 (1908–9): 236.

[14]Quoted in Krieger, *Ranke*, 5. As Krieger points out (p. 46), Ranke's "easy quotability . . . can yield a deceptively one-sided interpretation." There were two exceptions to the otherwise universal misreading: Earle Wilbur Dow, "Features of the New History: Apropos of Lamprecht's 'Deutsche Geschichte,'" *AHR* 3 (1897–98): 448; Carl Becker, "Some Aspects of the Influence of Social Problems and Ideas upon the Study and Writing of History," *American Journal of Sociology* 18 (1912–13): 657, 659.

Ranke's freedom from particularist nationalist partisanship had produced fierce opposition among more openly committed historians early in his career, and the "Prussian school" of German historians continued to denounce his universalism. To the extent that historians in the United States were aware of these conflicts, this was probably a factor in promoting his American reputation for neutral detachment. And by the 1880s and 1890s, the high point of the American pilgrimage to Germany, Ranke's name continued to be invoked there in support of an historiography whose tone had become considerably more secular.

Ranke's reputation as an unphilosophical empiricist underwrote an already existing American predisposition to disparage philosophical speculation about history; and this, in turn, served to perpetuate the reputation. "Philosophy of history," until well into the twentieth century, almost always meant grand speculative interpretive schemes rather than the analysis of historical epistemology. The repudiation of "philosophy of history" in this contemporary usage was inseparable from the establishment of the new historical scholarship, in the United States as in Europe. But American hostility to "speculative" philosophy of history quickly extended to any philosophical questioning of the self-evident dogmas of empiricism; indeed, to what one can hardly avoid terming "logophobia."

In the training of students, Ephraim Emerton wrote, a "brief excursion" into philosophy of history might be ventured, but it was a "dangerously speculative subject better reserved for later years in any deep way." George B. Adams, believing that "the first duty of the historian is to ascertain as nearly as possible and to record exactly what happened," thought it "not likely that historians of such training will be found to have concerned themselves with the problems of the science or of the philosophy of history to any greater extent than did other predecessors of earlier time. It remains true then that down to the present time professed historians have not dealt with these questions. They have left them to poets, philosophers and theologians." In his reply to Henry Adams's *Letter to American Teachers of History*, J. Franklin Jameson said that he was "precisely like old Scottish Janet, in my father's story: 'Dominie, that was a grand sermon ye gave us the Sawbath.' 'And did ye understond it, Janet?' 'Wad I hae the presoomption?!'" In a similar vein, Albert Bushnell Hart replied to the *Letter* by writing Adams: "What do speculations of any kind matter? The Harvard Baseball team will play Yale just the same, the President will build his freshman dormitories, the Panama Canal will be completed, Theodore Roosevelt will come out on top: why should anybody philosophize?"[15]

[15]Emerton, AHA *Annual Report*, 1893, 87; G. B. Adams, "History and the Philosophy of History," 236; Jameson to Ferdinand Schevill, 18 July 1919, in Elizabeth Donnan and

Despite the time that many American historians spent in Germany there was little understanding among them of the great gulf that separated the German and the Anglo-American cultural and philosophical contexts, and, of course, this was even truer of the majority of American professional historians who had not studied in Germany. Not until the initiative of James Harvey Robinson a few years before World War I was there any course in European intellectual history at an American university. Before the arrival in the 1930s of émigrés from the Third Reich there was little general understanding of German thought in the United States. Americans understood and enthusiastically adopted Ranke's critical use of sources and his seminar method; but they had no appreciation of the gulf which divided German and Anglo-American thoughtways, and as a result either distorted or disregarded what they couldn't comprehend.

The misinterpretation of Ranke can be considered part of a more general phenomenon. "One of the greatest misfortunes that can affect a writer of great intellectual seriousness and strong ethical passions," write Allan Janik and Stephen Toulmin, "is to have his ideas 'naturalized' by the English." Ranke's epistemology was "naturalized" into an English empiricist idiom. His "wie es eigentlich gewesen" was read as meaning that truth was accurate representation—the merest common sense in the English-speaking world, but a view not held in Germany since Kant. His desire to "empty himself" meant to Americans that he proposed turning himself into a Lockean "blank slate." German *Wissenschaft* became Anglo-American "science." It is to that conception of science that we now turn.[16]

II

Science ("objective science," the "scientific fact") was never more highly regarded in the United States, was never more of a cult, than in the late nineteenth and early twentieth centuries. Still for the most part intellectually accessible to the lay public, the triumphs and wonders of science were celebrated to an enthusiastic populace. There was no real substance

Leo F. Stock, eds., *An Historian's World: Selections from the Correspondence of John Franklin Jameson* (*Memoirs of the American Philosophical Society* 42 [1956]), 242–43; Hart, 2 May 1910 letter in Henry Adams Papers, Massachusetts Historical Society. I am grateful to my friend Mark Schwehn for making this document available to me.

[16] *Wittgenstein's Vienna* (New York, 1973), 19. Examples could be multiplied. Ernest Gellner observed that "in Cambridge, Michael Oakeshott developed a water-colour variant of Hegelianism designed mainly for the preservation of the amenities and privileges of rural England." ("Hegel's Last Secrets," *Encounter* 46 [April 1976]: 34.) In the United States, Sidney Hook turned Marx into a pragmatist. (*Toward the Understanding of Karl Marx* [New York, 1933].)

to the discussions about whether science should be valued for its utilitarian benefits, or "for its own sake": even the proponents of the latter view said only that one should not insist on immediately practical results. By the last decades of the nineteenth century there appeared to be abundant evidence of the technological payoff of "pure" science.

But, it was maintained, there was a moral and social payoff as well. The botanist John M. Coulter argued in 1900 for the social benefits that would come from the habit of "rigid self-elimination." "Emotional insanity" could result from not concentrating the mind on "objective material." While atomistic, individual truth claims acted like an "unruly mob," under the banner of objectivity they would march "in orderly array, battalion by battalion" toward a common goal. For the philosopher-scientist Karl Pearson, self-elimination would "lead to more efficient citizenship and so to increased social stability. Minds trained to scientific methods are less likely to be led by mere appeal to the passions or by blind emotional excitement to sanction acts which in the end may lead to social disaster." The astronomer and geologist Thomas C. Chamberlin saw "Fact and rigorous inductions from facts displace all preconceptions; all deductions from general principles, all favorite theories. The dearest doctrines, the most fascinating hypotheses, the most cherisht creations of the reason and of the imagination are put in subjection to determinate facts."[17]

Exactitude was at a premium in all walks of life. "The thing that was most notable about Aunt Fannie [Farmer]," recalled her nephew, the future historian Dexter Perkins, "was that she had a truly scholarly idea of her work. . . . She is described as 'the mother of level measurements,' perhaps an exaggerated phrase, but I believe that she was the first person to write all recipes with precision in mind, abandoning such vague terms as a 'heaping teaspoonful' or a 'scant cup.'" The Harvard economist Charles F. Dunbar held that the relation of an economic fact to its causes and consequences was "as certainly a question to be settled by appropriate scientific methods, as the perturbation of a satellite or a reaction observed by a chemist." Arthur O. Lovejoy led a movement within the American Philosophical Association to move philosophy toward the natural sciences, through adoption of an empirical methodology restricted to

---

[17]Coulter, *The Mission of Science in Education* (Ann Arbor, Mich., 1900), 13, 18–19, 27, quoted in David A. Hollinger, "The Struggle for the Banner of Science: Cultural Conflict and the Ideal of Objectivity, 1880–1920," paper delivered at the 1973 meeting of the AHA; Pearson, *The Grammar of Science* (1892; 3d ed., London, 1911), 9; Chamberlin, "The Ethical Nature of True Scientific Study," unpublished 1899 manuscript, quoted in Veysey, *Emergence*, 136–37.

"objective, verifiable and clearly communicable truths," so that philosophy would have "some hope of attaining the assured and steady march which should characterize a science." The Harvard athletic director said in 1888, "I aspire to be considered a scientific man," and spoke of the gymnasium as a laboratory.[18]

No group was more prone to scientific imagery, and the assumption of the mantle of science, than the historians. The historical seminar, said Herbert Baxter Adams, had "evolved from a nursery of dogma into a laboratory of scientific truth." The Johns Hopkins seminars were "laboratories where books are treated like mineralogical specimens, passed about from hand to hand, examined, and tested." He praised Albert Bushnell Hart, who had "traced the course of the late River and Harbor Bill as a biologist would study the life-history of a chick, or a tad-pole, or of yellow-fever germs." Ephraim Emerton of Harvard said that "what the laboratory is to physical science, the library must be to moral science. . . . Books must exist not so much to be read as to be studied, compared, digested, made to serve in the development of new truth by the method of practice with them." Another professor of history hoped to establish "a sort of working historical laboratory for students, that shall correspond to chemical and physical laboratories, and where the process of learning shall be much the same,—not memorizing a text-book, but, so to speak, manipulating literary, political, and historical apparatus."[19]

What are we to make of all this? What did it mean for a historian to be "scientific"? One thing it certainly did *not* mean for professional historians in this period was to be involved in a "nomothetic" (law-generating) rather than an "ideographic" (particular-describing) activity. There had been historians earlier in the century concerned with the development of laws of history (e.g., John William Draper); there had been historians across the Atlantic with similar aspirations (Henry Thomas Buckle was perhaps the best known); there were contemporary American amateur historians who sought such laws—Henry and Brooks Adams. But American professional historians of the turn of the century meant something

[18]Perkins, *Yield of the Years: An Autobiography* (Boston, 1969), 9; Robert L. Church, "The Economists Study Society: Sociology at Harvard, 1891–1902," in Paul Buck, ed., *Social Sciences at Harvard, 1860–1920: From Inculcation to the Open Mind* (Cambridge, Mass., 1965), 31; Daniel J. Wilson, "Professionalization and Organized Discussion in the American Philosophical Association, 1900–1922," *Journal of the History of Philosophy* 17 (1979): 55; the athletic director is quoted in Veysey, *Emergence*, 174.
[19]Adams, "Special Methods of Historical Study," in Hall, *Methods of Teaching*, 143; Adams, *The Study of History in American Colleges and Universities* (Washington, D.C., 1887), 175; Adams, "The American Historical Association," *The Independent*, June 2, 1887, 5; Emerton, "The Practical Method," 59–60; W. P. Atkinson, quoted in Holt, *Historical Scholarship*, 63.

quite different by "scientific history": they meant historical investigation
carried out according to "the scientific method."

"Ask a scientist what he conceives the scientific method to be," wrote
the Nobel laureate Sir Peter Medawar, "and he will adopt an expression
that is at once solemn and shifty-eyed: solemn, because he feels he ought
to declare an opinion; shifty-eyed, because he is wondering how to conceal the fact that he has no opinion to declare." Most scientists of the turn
of the century would no doubt have assumed the same expression,
though a few (like Sir Peter, a century later) were more forthcoming. And
there were—for better or worse—philosophers, and a philosophical tradition, to take over for them.[20]

Throughout the nineteenth century, and indeed, for many, well into
the twentieth, the definitive account of the scientific method had been
provided by Francis Bacon. A simplified and considerably vulgarized
version of his views carried the imprimatur of the Scottish commonsense
realists who provided official academic philosophy in the United States
and England. To the great majority of American philosophers and scientists Baconianism meant, in the first place, a rigidly empirical approach:
"observations" were sacred. One could not go wrong at this level. Error
could only come from mistaken or overly hasty inference from never-to-
be-doubted facts; the road to any needed correction was additional observations. Secondly, Baconianism meant the scrupulous avoidance of hypotheses, scorned by Bacon as "phantoms." It was unscientific to go
beyond what could be directly observed, to "anticipate nature." (Newton's "hypotheses non fingo" was the most often and most reverently
repeated scientific maxim of the period.) Finally, though this last point
was not as universally accepted, it meant the identification of all science
with taxonomy—the "nommer, classer, et décrire" of the French anatomist Georges Cuvier.

The Baconian view of science—and it bears repeating that it is the
dominant vulgarizations of Bacon's views with which we are concerned—was consistent with the blank-slate psychology of John Locke,
who in nineteenth-century America was almost as influential as an epistemologist as he was as a political philosopher. It received the slightly
qualified endorsement of John Stuart Mill, in his popular *System of Logic*:
following the "Canons of Induction," facts, appropriately arranged,
would reveal their inner connections. Mill's view of science was disputed
by William Whewell, who in his *Logic of the Inductive Sciences* argued
for the necessity of the mind imposing general ideas on the chaos of the

[20]*Induction and Intuition in Scientific Thought* (London, 1969), 11.

given facts. But in America even more decisively than in England, Mill's conception was by far the more widely accepted.

There were those in nineteenth-century America, coming out of a native or European transcendentalist tradition, who rejected Baconian inductivism and believed hypothesis indispensable in science, and in history as well. The Harvard philosopher Francis Bowen was one. "A naked record of facts," he wrote,

must . . . be untrustworthy; it will be not merely incomplete, but deceptive. It will give rise to undue impressions, and create false judgments. . . . It is impossible to write history without seeking, either avowedly or stealthily, or unawares, to verify some hypothesis, or establish some theory, which furnishes a reason and a guide for the selection and arrangement of materials. . . . The facts have no connection with each other, and the story has no unity, unless some doctrine lies at the bottom to which they are all, more or less related.

Another anti-Baconian was his colleague the great Swiss-born Harvard naturalist Louis Agassiz, who carried with him to this country German idealistic philosophy, and *Naturphilosophie* which he had learned directly from Schelling and Dollinger.[21]

The anti-Baconians' authority was fatally undermined by the great Darwin controversy of the 1860s and 1870s. Darwin himself was well aware that Baconian induction was a fiction, and privately expressed himself unequivocally on the subject. "About thirty years ago," he wrote in an 1861 letter, "there was much talk that geologists ought only to observe and not theorize; and I well remember someone saying that at this rate a man might as well go into a gravel-pit and count the pebbles and describe the colours. How odd it is that anyone should not see that all observation must be for or against some view if it is to be of any service!" In his public presentation of his findings, Darwin dissimulated to win acceptance. The very first paragraph of *On the Origin of Species* was calculated to deceive:

When on board H.M.S. "Beagle," as naturalist, I was much struck with certain facts in the distribution of the inhabitants of South America, and in the geological relations of the present to the past inhabitants of that continent. These facts seemed to me to throw some light on the origin of species—that mystery of mysteries, as it has been called by one of our greatest philosophers. On my return

[21]Bowen review of Richard Hildreth's *History of the United States of America*, *North American Review* 73 (1851): 412–13, cited in Donald E. Emerson, "Hildreth, Draper, and 'Scientific History,'" in Eric F. Goldman, ed., *Historiography and Urbanization: Essays in American History in Honor of W. Stull Holt* (Baltimore, 1941), 170.

home, it occurred to me, in 1837, that something might perhaps be made out on this question by patiently accumulating and reflecting on all sorts of facts which could possibly have any bearing on it. After five years work I allowed myself to speculate on the subject.

The deception was even more explicit in his *Autobiography*, where, describing his path to the theory of natural selection, he claimed to have "worked on true Baconian principles, and without any theory collected facts on a wholesale scale."[22]

The most prominent enemies of "Baconian induction" in America, such as Bowen and Agassiz, were opponents of Darwin on religious, a prioristic, grounds. His supporters were men like Asa Gray, inductivists who disliked theory and speculation. (The pattern was the same in England, where the Tory churchman Whewell, who had a much more sophisticated understanding of scientific method, opposed Darwin, while the liberal inductivists, Mill and Pearson, supported him.) As Darwinism triumphed, so did crude inductionism—the doctrine which Darwin, privately, mocked.

Another consequence of the Darwin debate—or rather of the attempt to moderate it, to allow those of various religious orientations to collaborate in the scientific venture—was the ideology of the rigid neutrality of science. Science, held Chauncey Wright and the evolutionary positivists, should be limited to factual description. Knowledge, Wright believed, becomes objective and scientific "when it ceases to be associated with our fears, our respects, our aspirations—our emotional nature; when it ceases to prompt questions as to what relates to our personal destiny, our ambitions, our moral worth." He distinguished between the "scientific mind," which limits itself "to the truth of things, whether good or bad, agreeable or disagreeable, admirable or despicable," and the "'philosophical habit of mind,' trained in the school of human life . . . viewing and interpreting nature according to its own dispositions." This, too, became part of the American historians' ideal of science.[23]

---

[22]Darwin to Henry Fawcett, 18 September 1861, in Francis Darwin, ed., *More Letters of Charles Darwin* (2 vols., London, 1903), 1:195; Darwin, *On the Origin of Species: A Facsimile of the First Edition* (Cambridge, Mass., 1964), 1; Francis Darwin, ed., *Life and Letters of Charles Darwin* (2 vols., London, 1887), 1:83. Darwin's strategy of dissimulation is established beyond any possible doubt by a letter he wrote to the young zoologist John Scott. "I would suggest to you the advantage at present of being very sparing in introducing theory in your papers (I formerly erred much in geology in that way): *let theory guide your observations* but till your reputation is well established be sparing in publishing theory. It makes persons doubt your observations." (Letter of 6 June 1863, *More Letters*, 2:323.)

[23]Wright, "The Philosophy of Herbert Spencer," in his *Philosophical Discussions* (New York, 1877), 49; "Evolution by Natural Selection," ibid., 196.

Finally, as American historians considered what it meant to be "scientists," they encountered the repeated suggestion that they were joining a finite venture, that science was approaching "completeness." When Max Planck chose science over classical philology or music in the 1870s, he did so against the advice of the professor of physics at the University of Munich, who warned him that there was nothing new to discover. Robert A. Millikan had the same experience at Columbia in the 1890s. Simon Newcomb, the dean of American astronomers, confessed in 1888 that "the work which really occupies the attention of the astronomer is less the discovery of new things than the elaboration of those already known." At the dedication of the Ryerson Laboratory at the University of Chicago in 1894, Albert A. Michelson thought it "probable that most of the great underlying principles have been firmly established." He quoted approvingly the remark of an eminent physicist, probably Lord Kelvin, that "the future truths of Physical Science are to be looked for in the sixth place of decimals."[24]

This, then, was the model of scientific method which, in principle, the historians embraced. Science must be rigidly factual and empirical, shunning hypothesis; the scientific venture was scrupulously neutral on larger questions of end and meaning; and, if systematically pursued, it might ultimately produce a comprehensive, "definitive" history. It was in the light of this conception of *wissenschaftliche Objektivität* that they regarded themselves as loyal followers of Ranke.

Other messages from across the Atlantic confirmed them in their course. The most widely used and influential manual of historical method was the English translation of Charles Victor Langlois and Charles Seignobos's *Introduction aux études historiques*. It taught that "Historical construction has . . . to be performed with an incoherent mass of minute facts, with detailed knowledge reduced as it were to a powder." At the 1900 Paris World Exposition, Henri Houssaye opened the first session of section one—general and diplomatic history—of the First International Congress of Historians by asserting,

If the nineteenth century began with Goethe, Lord Byron, Lamartine, and Victor Hugo, with imagination and poetry . . . it ended with Pasteur, Taine, and Mommsen, with science and history. . . . We want nothing more to do with the approximations of hypotheses, useless systems, theories as brilliant as they are decep-

[24]Walter Meissner, "Max Planck, the Man and His Work," *Science* 113 (1951): 75; *The Autobiography of Robert A. Millikan* (New York, 1950), 269–70; Newcomb, "The Place of Astronomy Among the Sciences," *Sidereal Messenger* 7 (1888): 69–70; Michelson, "Some of the Objects and Methods of Physical Science," *University of Chicago Quarterly Calendar* 3 (1894): 15. See Lawrence Badash, "The Completeness of Nineteenth-Century Science," *Isis* 63 (March 1972): 48–58.

tive, superfluous moralities. Facts, facts, facts—which carry within themselves their lesson and their philosophy. The truth, all the truth, nothing but the truth.[25]

In both their public and private utterances, turn-of-the-century American historians, both professionals and amateurs who had accepted the professional ethos, made clear that they had absorbed the lessons of inductive science. Albert Bushnell Hart, like most other readers of Darwin, accepted at face value Darwin's claim to have "worked on true Baconian principles" and, in his AHA presidential address, urged historians to follow his example.

What we need is a genuinely scientific school of history which shall remorselessly examine the sources and separate the wheat from the chaff; which shall critically balance evidence; which shall dispassionately and moderately set forth results. For such a process we have the fortunate analogy of the physical sciences; did not Darwin spend twenty years in accumulating data, and in selecting typical phenomena before he so much as ventured a generalization? History, too, has its inductive method, its relentless concentration of the grain in its narrow spout, till by its own weight it seeks the only outlet. In history, too, scattered and apparently unrelated data fall together in harmonious wholes.

Fred Morrow Fling wrote that "if sufficient evidence exists to enable the investigator to establish the facts and combine them into series, if he will gaze long and attentively at his series, if he will but press them for their larger significance and causal connection, he will seldom fail to get his reward."[26]

All would be well if one could rid oneself of preconceived ideas and so launder one's mind that it was capable of the immaculate perception called for by the Baconian model. Discussing the economist E. R. A. Seligman's "Economic Interpretation of History," Edward Cheyney objected to "beginning the examination of historical facts . . . with any theory of interpretation." Rather, "the simple but arduous task of the

[25]Langlois and Seignobos, *Introduction aux études historiques* (Paris, 1898; English trans., London, 1898), 214; *Annales Internationales d'Histoire, Congrès de Paris 1900, Première Section, Histoire Générale et Diplomatique* (Paris, 1901), 5–6. The English translation of Langlois and Seignobos's manual went through many editions and was the standard handbook down to World War II. Ernst Bernheim's 1893 *Lehrbuch der historischen Methode* was never translated into English, and was probably more cited than read.

[26]Hart, "Imagination in History," *AHR* 15 (1910): 232–33; Fling, *The Writing of History: An Introduction to Historical Method* (New Haven, 1920), 151. Even Brooks Adams, who unlike professional historians was avowedly seeking to develop a theoretical historiography, wrote of his *Law of Civilization and Decay* that "All theories . . . in the book . . . are the effect, and not the cause, of the way in which the facts unfold themselves. I have been passive." ([New York, 1896], v.)

historian was to collect facts, view them objectively, and arrange them as the facts themselves demanded." He thought that "many students had been led astray because they approached the past with predetermined principles of classification and organization." Historians had to eschew "philosophic considerations" because, as one explained,

such is the constitution of the human mind, or at any rate my own, that as I went through the mass of material I would have seized upon all the facts that made for my theory and marshalled them in its support while those that told against it I would have unconsciously and undoubtedly quite honestly neglected. . . . My aim therefore was to get rid so far as possible of all preconceived notions and theories.[27]

If the historian was conscientious, mastered *Quellenkritik* and the auxiliary sciences, avoided the "phantoms" of hypotheses, he could produce a body of reliable atomistic facts which "when justly arranged interpret themselves." The road to the ultimate history—the definitive, objective, re-creation of the historical past—was open. And the journey, while arduous, might not be that long. "Pas de documents, pas d'histoire" was a slogan made popular by Langlois and Seignobos: the beginnings of human history, for which there were no written records, could never be historically known. But there was a corollary: "Plus de documents, plus d'histoire":

The quantity of documents in existence, if not of known documents, is given; time, in spite of all the precautions which are taken nowadays is continually diminishing it; it will never increase. History has at its disposal a limited stock of documents; this very circumstance limits the possible progress of historical science. When all the documents are known, and have gone through the operations which fit them for use, the work of critical scholarship will be finished. In the case of some ancient periods, for which documents are rare, we can now see that in a generation or two it will be time to stop.

Arthur Schlesinger, arriving at Columbia to begin graduate study in 1910, "had formed the impression that nothing very important still remained to be discovered. My first-year seminar, with [William A.] Dunning on Reconstruction, did not dispel the idea. The topics he assigned involved little more than the threshing over of old straw." Schlesinger soon

[27]Cheyney, in "Proceedings," AHA, *Annual Report, 1901* 1:29; James Ford Rhodes to Charles Francis Adams, 19 March 1907, quoted in Robert Cruden, *James Ford Rhodes: The Man, the Historian, and his Work* (Cleveland, 1961), 226. By the time of his presidential address to the AHA many years later, Cheyney had greatly altered his views, and become one of the very few professional historians to urge that history concern itself with developing laws. See his "Law in History," *AHR* 29 (1924): 231–48.

changed his mind, and few believed that the task would be completed in the present generation. But the end could be imagined, "now," as one of the most prominent historians of the period announced, "that all information is within reach, and every problem has become capable of solution."[28]

III

The professional historians of the late nineteenth century, in pursuit of the authority of science, consistently distanced themselves from, and disparaged, "history as literature," "history as art." Paradoxically, novelists and painters, equally intoxicated with science, were moving rapidly in the same direction—indeed, in many respects anticipated them. The eminent French historian Henri Houssaye, in the 1900 paean to "facts, facts, facts" quoted above, noted the transformation of the novel during the last quarter century. "Today the novel is constructed with careful notes, direct observations, 'human documents'; invention, adventure, and romance are sacrificed to the study of the environment and the analysis of character; the novelist's approach is coming more and more to resemble the historian's."[29]

Flaubert's *Madame Bovary* (1857) and *Sentimental Education* (1869) introduced the objective, the omniscient, the impersonal, and the self-effacing narrator. For the literary realists, and their admirers, the direct appearance of the author was anathema. "The complex issues involved in this shift," writes Wayne Booth, "have been reduced to a convenient distinction between 'showing' which is artistic, and 'telling' which is inartistic." Flaubert insisted that *impassibilité*—flat affect—was the novelist's appropriate stance. His model was the scientist. Once we have spent enough time, he said, in "treating the human soul with the impartiality which physical scientists show in studying matter, we will have taken an immense step forward." Art had to achieve, "by a pitiless method, the precision of the physical sciences." Sainte-Beuve said of *Madame Bovary*, "Flaubert wields the pen as others wield the scalpel." He described the new style as the victory of the anatomist and physiologist in art. And Flaubert, of course, shared the Baconian conception of science:

[28]Albert J. Beveridge, *Abraham Lincoln* (New York, 1928), v; Langlois and Seignobos, *Introduction*, 316; Schlesinger Oral History Memoir, 1:39; Lord Acton, October 1896 report to the Syndics of the Cambridge University Press, in *The Cambridge Modern History: Its Origin, Authorship and Production* (Cambridge, 1907), 12.
[29]*Annales Internationales d'Histoire*, 7.

"That's what is so fine about the natural sciences," he wrote to his mistress, "they don't wish to prove anything."[30]

Flaubert thought that art had reached a scientific stage, and stressed the scientific, in particular the medical, nature of his observations, but saw science correcting and enriching art. Emile Zola went further. For him, art was the servant of science, and he considered himself a research worker. His rhetoric echoed many of the themes we have encountered among American scientists and historians:

Imagination has no longer place, plot matters little to the novelist, who bothers himself with neither development, mystery, nor denouement; I mean that he does not intervene to take away from or add to reality. . . . The work becomes a report, nothing more; it has but the merit of exact observation . . . of the logical connection of facts. . . . The novelist is but a recorder who is forbidden to judge and to conclude. The strict role of a savant is to expose the facts, to go to the end of analysis without venturing into synthesis; the facts are thus . . . and he stops there; for if he wishes to go beyond the phenomena he will enter into hypothesis; we shall have probabilities, not science.[31]

The same struggle against preconceived notions, in the service of empirical investigation of reality, occupied realist painters. As Constable sat down to paint from nature he tried to forget that he'd ever seen a picture; Courbet claimed not to know what he was painting. One of the most distinguished of present-day interpreters of the realist painters has summarized their program as "impartiality, impassivity, scrupulous objectivity, rejection of a priori metaphysical or epistemological prejudice, the confining of the artist to the accurate observation and notation of empirical phenomena, and the descriptions of how, and not why, things happen."[32]

With the Impressionists a scientific concentration on the discrete sense datum was carried further. Echoing Courbet, Claude Monet said in an interview: "Try to forget what objects you have before you. . . . Merely think, here is a little square of blue, here an oblong of pink, here a streak of yellow, and paint it just as it looks to you, the exact color and shape, until it gives your naive impression of the scene." Monet's longtime

[30]Booth, *The Rhetoric of Fiction* (2d ed., Chicago, 1983), 8; Flaubert, quoted in Marianne Bonwit, *Gustave Flaubert et le principe d'impassibilité* (Berkeley, 1950), 68; Sainte-Beuve, quoted in Arnold Hauser, *The Social History of Art* (4 vols., Vintage ed., New York, 1958), 4:75–76; Flaubert to Louise Colet, 27 March 1853, quoted in George J. Becker, ed., *Documents of Modern Literary Realism* (Princeton, 1963), 92.
[31]*The Experimental Novel* (New York, 1894), 123–25.
[32]Linda Nochlin, *Realism* (Harmondsworth, U.K., 1971), 43.

friend Georges Clemenceau described him as a laboratory technician: "He stands before a light, he takes that light, breaks it into its component parts, puts it together again. From the point of view of science nothing is more interesting."[33]

The scientifism of European literature and painting was echoed on the other side of the Atlantic, as part of a general shift in the taste of post-Civil War Americans toward the austere rather than the ornate, of a "professional distaste for a polite literature that was rotten ripe with idealizing sentiment and genteel affectation." Henry James became an apostle of European-style realism, and urged his friend William Dean Howells to "become the Zola of the U.S.A." He was preaching to the converted: Howells had already started to model himself after the hyper-empiricist image of Darwin, and became an indefatigable advocate of recording the facts of life, rather than poetic preconceptions. Realism had come to American literature, and, as Howells reported, seemed "to have come everywhere at once." By the turn of the century the genteel realism of Howells, who, in a famous phrase, thought "the smiling aspects of life are the more American," had given way to the naturalism of Stephen Crane, Frank Norris, and Theodore Dreiser. The rhetoric of the "objective, scientific posture" continued: Norris wrote that "no one could be a writer until he could regard life and people, and the world in general, from the objective point of view—until he could remain detached, outside, maintain the unswerving attitude of the observer." In painting, the shift from early-nineteenth-century romanticism to turn-of-the century realism was as manifest in America as in Europe, as can be seen in the work of Thomas Eakins, George Bellows, John Sloan, and William Glackens.[34]

During the last decades of the century the scientistic cult of the "objective facts" also took hold in American newspapers, hitherto unabashedly partisan. Reportage, for the first time, was to exclude opinion and literary flourishes. The *New York Times* began its climb to its leading position by basing itself on an "information" rather than a "story" model. "Facts, facts piled up to the point of dry certitude," recalled Ray Stannard Baker, "was what the American people really wanted." Whether or not it was what they wanted, it was what editors insisted their reporters produce.

[33]Both quoted in John Adkins Richardson, *Modern Art and Scientific Thought* (Urbana, Ill., 1971), 10–11, 22–23.
[34]Warner Berthoff, *The Ferment of Realism: American Literature, 1884–1919* (New York, 1965), 4; James, quoted in Kenneth S. Lynn, *William Dean Howells: An American Life* (New York, 1971), 244; Howells, quoted in Everett Carter, *Howells and the Age of Realism* (Philadelphia, 1954), 89; Norris, quoted in Malcolm Cowley, "A Natural History of American Naturalism," in Becker, *Documents*, 458.

H. L. Mencken recalled the "immense stress upon accuracy" during his journalistic apprenticeship. The *Baltimore Sun*, he recalled, "fostered a sober, matter-of-fact style in its men." Lincoln Steffens complained that on E. L. Godkin's *Evening Post*, "Reporters were to report the news as it happened, like machines, without prejudice, color, and without style; all alike. Humor or any sign of personality in our reports was caught, rebuked, and, in time, suppressed. As a writer I was permanently hurt by my years on the *Post*." The approved style at the *New York Tribune* was what one staff member called "The Grocer's Bill": "Facts; facts; nothing but facts. So many peas at so much a peck; so much molasses at so much a quart. . . . It was a rigid system, rigidly enforced."[35]

What was distinctive about the late-nineteenth-century sensibility in literature, painting, journalism, and history was not simply the cult of the fact. Romanticism, which had underwritten the development of historical scholarship in Germany in the earlier part of the century, had rhapsodized over the individual, idiosyncratic fact and insisted on its primacy over what were denounced as "abstract, universalistic systems." The change in the climate of taste was a change of tastes in climate. Whereas earlier in the century it was the warmth of the unique fact that was valued over the coldness of abstract systems, by the decades before 1900 it was the cold fact that was celebrated as instrument of liberation from the suffocating temperature and humidity of overarching systems. Whereas earlier the individual fact was fondled, celebrated, bejeweled, and dressed in layers of adjectives, by the 1880s and 1890s it was the plain and the unadorned fact which was à la mode. Thorstein Veblen and J. Franklin Jameson, both early members of the faculty at the University of Chicago, joined in declaring that the Gothic style with which they were surrounded was inappropriate to the austere modern sensibility. Veblen found the "disjointed grotesqueries of an eclectic and modified Gothic . . . consistently and unavoidably meretricious." It was outrageous to "hous[e] the quest of truth in an edifice of false pretences. . . . As an object lesson they conduce, in their measure, to inculcate in the students a spirit of disingenuousness." Jameson was explicit concerning the new stylistic imperative for historians—its origins, and its affiliations:

We dwell in an age of prose. The world cares less for eloquence than it did a generation ago. *Assez de lyre!* it says, as the shouting mob said to Lamartine. . . . The rise of professional or professorial history-writing coincided with the rise of realism in fiction. We may fairly maintain that both had the same cause, a discon-

---

[35]All quotations from Michael Schudson, *Discovering the News: A Social History of American Newspapers* (New York, 1978), 72, 77, 80.

tent with rhetorical and imaginative presentations of human life, bred in the minds of a generation to which Darwin and his fellows had taught the cogency and the pervasiveness of scientific laws. Since Darwin, it has been no more possible for the age to produce a crop of Macaulays and Michelets than it is possible for those who picture running horses to expel from their minds what they have learned from Mr. Muybridge's photographs of animal locomotion.[36]

"Le style c'est l'homme même," said Buffon in the eighteenth century; for twentieth century cultural anthropologists and art historians it is a window into the values of a society. "Style," writes Meyer Schapiro,

is, above all, a system of forms with a quality and a meaningful expression through which the personality of the artist and the broad outlook of a group are visible. It is also a vehicle of expression within the group, communicating and fixing certain values. . . . It is, besides, a common ground against which innovations and the individuality of particular works may be measured.

It was the transvaluation of "style" in this broad sense, in various areas of American culture, which accounts for much of the "scientific" professional historians' determination to distance themselves from their "literary," "gentleman amateur" predecessors of the early nineteenth century: George Bancroft, William Lothrop Motley, William H. Prescott, and Francis Parkman. What one was defining oneself against was as crucial for self-identification as any positive model.[37]

The issue certainly was not one of scholarship. Bancroft and Motley had both studied at Göttingen and Berlin, the former being perhaps the first American to win a German Ph.D. in history. All four had performed exhaustive labors with original sources, spending lavishly of their personal fortunes, and impressive royalties, on the purchase of manuscripts, trips to foreign archives, and the employment of copyists. Bancroft gathered documents from dozens of public and private collections throughout Europe, and had visited the archives of all thirteen of the original states. Motley wrote from the Saxon Royal Library that he was "working as hard as a wood sawyer," digging "raw material out of subterranean depths of black-letter folios in half a dozen different languages." The Harvard historian Roger B. Merriman praised the "scrupulous care and integrity" with which Prescott used his materials, "the pains that he took to find the exact truth." Scientific historians praised Parkman for "scrupulously and rigorously adhering to the truth of facts," and were uncertain whether, from the standpoint of scholarship, he should not be count-

---

[36]Veblen, *The Higher Learning in America* (New York, 1918; reprinted Stanford, 1954), 146–47; Jameson, *Historical Writing*, 137–38; Jameson, "The Influence of Universities Upon Historical Writing," University of Chicago *Record* 6 (1902): 297–98.
[37]Schapiro, "Style," in A. L. Kroeber, ed., *Anthropology Today* (Chicago, 1953), 287–88.

ed as one of them. It was not even a matter of the apparatus of scholarship: a third of Prescott's histories of Peru, Mexico, and Spain was given over to footnotes and bibliography, and the portion of their work devoted to this material by the others was only slightly less.[38]

But their scholarship appeared in a form and tone which rendered it unacceptable to those of the new sensibility, based as it was on a now discredited model of literary presentation. Bancroft, Prescott, Motley, and Parkman each, in at least one of their major works, employed the organization of the stage play, with a prologue, five acts, and an epilogue. Sir Walter Scott was, by a wide margin, the most popular and imitated author in the early-nineteenth-century United States, and the florid style of the "literary" historians gave clear evidence of his influence. In his old age, Parkman, attempting to bring his style in line with newer tastes, moved toward a more severe mode of discourse; Bancroft, with his wife's help, "slaughtered adjectives" in preparing his "Last Revision" in the 1880s. Critics noted the changes, but continued to find the older work "florid" and "turgid," unsuitable to a generation that "has grown accustomed to less use of literary as well as other stimulants," that "demands less color and more repose." The writings of the literary romantics failed to provide "the sober narration that an age of self-restraint demanded of its historians."[39]

But the difference between the older and newer sensibility was not simply one of forms of verbal expression; it involved the moral posture of the historian. The "gentleman amateurs" wrote not to keep the pot boiling, or out of professional obligation to colleagues, but because they had an urgent message to deliver to the general reading public. "If ten people in the world hate despotism a little more and love civil and religious liberty a little better in consequence of what I have written, I shall be satisfied," Motley wrote. They made no effort to achieve the authorial invisibility, the "rigid self-elimination" which had become normative by

[38]Motley, in G. W. Curtis, ed., *The Correspondence of John Lothrop Motley* (2 vols., New York, 1889), 1:145–46; Merriman article on Prescott in *Dictionary of American Biography*, 15 (New York, 1935), 199; Edward G. Bourne, "Francis Parkman," in his *Essays in Historical Criticism* (New York, 1901), 284; John Spencer Bassett, *The Middle Group of American Historians* (New York, 1917), ix; George H. Callcott, *History in the United States, 1800–1860: Its Practice and Purpose* (Baltimore, 1970), 126. The "romantic" historians were censured on one relatively trivial point of scholarship: Bancroft and Parkman—following the example of Jared Sparks, the early-nineteenth-century editor of George Washington's papers—rather freely "fixed up" the punctuation and spelling of documents they printed. Undoubtedly there is much to say for scrupulous editorial procedures, but it is dismaying to see the inquisitorial zeal with which the romantics were pursued on this point by historians whose greatest satisfaction in life seemed to come from inserting a "[*sic!*]" after every dropped comma.
[39]Bancroft, quoted in Russel B. Nye, *George Bancroft: Brahmin Rebel* (New York, 1944), 296; Jameson, *Historical Writing*, 106–7, 129; Bassett, *Middle Group*, 183–84, 202–3.

the late nineteenth century. One cranky commentator in the 1880s observed that Bancroft's *History of the United States* "should be entitled 'The Psychological Autobiography of George Bancroft, as Illustrated by Incidents and Characters in the Annals of the United States.' "[40]

They did not hesitate to "tell," in an era that preferred the writer to "show"; to make their political and moral judgments explicit. Of Bancroft's *History* it was said that "every page voted for Andrew Jackson." Motley wrote of Philip II that if he "possessed a single virtue it has eluded the conscientious research of the writer of these pages. If there are vices—as possibly there are—from which he was exempt, it is because it is not permitted to human nature to attain perfection even in evil." Prescott and Parkman regularly contrasted Protestant virtue and Catholic vice, Anglo-Saxon liberty with Latin absolutism. The combination of the "intrusive" authorial presence, the explicit moralizing, and overt partisanship, made their work unacceptable to the historical scientists. "The greatest price we have to pay for this ethical attitude toward history," wrote Edward Cheyney, "is the intense subjectivity it gives to it."

Everything comes to the reader as interpreted by the historian. Everything is seen through the medium of his personality. The facts of history when they are used to teach a moral lesson do not reach us in their entirety, nor grouped and generalized according to their internal relations, but selected and arranged according to the overmastering ideal in the mind of the historian. The reader is at the historian's mercy. . . . The conflicts of the past are perpetuated by the very chroniclers who recount their history. Thus history sells its birthright of truth for a mess of the pottage of partisanship.

The irascible Charles McLean Andrews termed Bancroft's work "nothing less than a crime against historical truth." The more serene Jameson, in his characteristic Olympian style, wrote of Motley that his "warm heart and enthusiastic, ardent temper . . . laid him open to dangers of partiality which, it must be confessed, he was far from wholly escaping." All of the new group of university-based historians agreed that as they came to constitute a "profession," they would put behind them the crimes and vices of amateur history.[41]

---

[40]Motley, quoted in Susan St. John Mildmay and Herbert St. John, eds., *John Lothrop Motley and His Family: Further Letters and Records* (London, 1910), 42; Edwin Percy Whipple, *American Literature and Other Papers* (Boston, 1887), 92.

[41]Motley, *History of the United Netherlands* (4 vols., New York, 1888–95), 3:534–35; Cheyney, "What Is History," 76; Andrews, quoted in A. S. Eisenstadt, *Charles McLean Andrews: A Study in American Historical Writing* (New York, 1956), 165; Jameson, *Historical Writing*, 119.

2

◁══▷

The professionalization
project

"Professionalism" has been a central term in recent historical discourse. Robert Wiebe interpreted professionalism as part of the "search for order" in late-nineteenth-century American society. Burton Bledstein saw a "culture of professionalism" as symbolic of the "vertical vision of life" central to the bourgeois world view—and described the new universities as the institutional embodiment of that vision. From a general concern with the phenomenon of professionalism, scholars quickly came to focus on academic disciplines. Developing a point made by John Higham in the early 1960s, Thomas Haskell devoted a volume to recounting how the emergence of professional social science served to resolve a crisis of authority in American intellectual life, while Mary O. Furner saw the tension between advocacy and objectivity producing "a crisis in the professionalization of American social science."[1]

What, in the case of historians, did "professionalization" mean? What was the relationship between the adoption by historians of the ideal of objectivity, and of the norms of professionalism?

I

The usual picture of the professionalization of history is one of a speedy and dramatic transformation, rapidly approaching the common list of

[1]Robert Wiebe, *The Search for Order: 1870–1920* (New York, 1967); Burton J. Bledstein, *The Culture of Professionalism: The Middle Class and the Development of Higher Education in America* (New York, 1976); John Higham et al., *History: The Development of Historical Studies in the United States* (Princeton, 1965), 8–9; Thomas L. Haskell, *The Emergence of Professional Social Science: The American Social Science Association and the Nineteenth-Century Crisis of Authority* (Urbana, Ill., 1977); Mary O. Furner, *Advocacy and Objectivity: A Crisis in the Professionalization of American Social Science, 1865–1905* (Lexington, Ky., 1975).

47

criteria of a profession: institutional apparatus (an association, a learned journal), standardized training in esoteric skills, leading to certification and controlled access to practice, heightened status, autonomy. Within a single generation graduate programs on the German model were established at several universities; the American Historical Association was formed, followed shortly by the *American Historical Review*; by 1900 the Ph.D. degree was a prerequisite for a professorial appointment at respectable colleges, and American universities had turned out more than two hundred doctorates in history. An often invoked symbol of the transformation was that only one out of the thirty-four contributors to Justin Winsor's *Narrative and Critical History of America*, which appeared in the late 1880s, had received professional historical training, and the great majority were not academics; whereas in the next multivolume general American history, the *American Nation* series, launched only fifteen years later, twenty-one of the twenty-four authors were university professors, and all but two had done graduate work in history.[2]

In fact, there was rather less here than meets the eye, and much of what passed for professionalization was superficial. The training which late-nineteenth-century American historians received, whether in Germany or in the United States, was usually not very impressive. J. Franklin Jameson, the first Ph.D. in history to emerge from Herbert Baxter Adams's famous seminar at Johns Hopkins, confided to his diary, his father, and friends that Adams was unscholarly, that seminar meetings were "tiresome," with "too much mutual admiration and not enough savage criticism"; "the staple of the meetings consists of outside 'attractions,' now a Confederate general to talk on a campaign, now an elderly party exhumed to 'reminisce' to us."[3]   American students in Germany generally received the doctorate within two years of their arrival, usually for a very brief dissertation based on printed sources—hardly more than what would later count as a seminar paper. Edward Channing's Harvard dissertation consisted of seventy-eight (badly) handwritten pages, completed within a year and a half of getting his B.A. While universities offering the Ph.D. thought of themselves as centers from which scholarly missionaries poured forth, often they were service stations for legitimation. In many cases a young man would impress his undergraduate teach-

---

[2]W. Stull Holt, *Historical Scholarship in the United States and Other Essays* (Seattle, 1967), 4–5.

[3]Elizabeth Donnan and Leo F. Stock, eds., *An Historian's World: Selections from the Correspondence of John Franklin Jameson* (Philadelphia, 1956), 19, 21–23. A few years later, Woodrow Wilson had a hardly more favorable response to instruction at Hopkins: he described Adams as "insincere and superficial." (Wilson to Ellen Louise Axson, 27 November 1883, in Arthur H. Link, ed., *The Papers of Woodrow Wilson* (Princeton, 1966–), 2:552.

ers, be kept on at the undergraduate institution for a year or two, then be sent away to a European or American university center for certification, and then, by prearrangement, be brought back home.[4]

If a "professional organization" meant an organization of professionals, the American Historical Association hardly qualified. According to one estimate, only about 25 percent of the members of the AHA in the period 1890–1910 were college teachers, compared to 80 percent of the members of the American Philological Association and Modern Language Association, 90 percent of the members of the American Philosophical Association. It was not until well into the interwar period that it became the rule for the presidency of the AHA to be bestowed on a college professor holding the Ph.D. Before 1907 the presidents were almost all amateurs; from 1912 through 1927 only one-third had the Ph.D.; from 1928 on, almost all were, by both training and occupation, professionals.[5]

In part the selection of amateurs as presidents of the association in the early days was a matter of legitimation, and accommodation with a still important constituency. But it was also true that much of the most distinguished historical work continued to be produced by those without Ph.D.'s or professorships. The most highly regarded multivolume works were written by men without formal training (J. B. McMaster's *History of the People of the United States*), without university affiliation (Ellis Oberholtzer's *History of the United States Since the Civil War*), or without either (James Schouler's *History of the United States Under the Con-*

[4]Davis D. Joyce, *Edward Channing and the Great Work* (The Hague, 1974), 11. Among the important historians who followed the circular rite of passage before World War I were Eugene C. Barker, John Spencer Bassett, Ephraim Emerton, Albert Bushnell Hart, Roger B. Merriman, Charles W. Ramsdell, Arthur M. Schlesinger, Charles S. Sydnor, Frederick Jackson Turner, and Claude H. Van Tyne.

[5]Figures on college teachers in professional associations from Laurence Veysey, "The Plural Organized Worlds of the Humanities," in Alexandra Oleson and John Voss, eds., *The Organization of Knowledge in Modern America, 1860–1920* (Baltimore, 1979), 71. All these figures are probably slightly low because of the estimating procedure employed. The transition to thoroughgoing "professionalism" in the AHA was very gradual, undramatic, and accomplished with relatively little bad feeling. Jameson has sometimes been represented as the symbol of "professional" opposition to Herbert Baxter Adams's catering to representatives of the older, "amateur," tradition. John Higham, for example, makes Jameson's election as AHA president in 1907 a turning point in the professionalization of the discipline (*History*, 20). There is some truth in this, yet Jameson himself, in a 17 November 1922 letter to Max Farrand, recalled that "the only two cases . . . in which I can remember to have taken a decided, and perhaps an initiative part in advocacy of a presidential nomination were those of the two *non*-academic ones, Goldwin Smith and Theodore Roosevelt." (Farrand Papers, 12:11.) Albert B. Hart is also named by Higham as a leader of "professorial" discontent with Adams (p. 16), but Hart, in a 2 January 1911 letter to Farrand, expressed the view that in choosing AHA officers a "distinct steer" toward "men non-academic and non-editorial" should be maintained. (Farrand Papers. 10:53.)

stitution, James Ford Rhodes's *History of the United States from the Compromise of 1850*). Many of the most important individual historical works of the period, universally acclaimed by the professional historical establishment, continued to be produced by independently wealthy amateurs: the medievalist H. O. Taylor, the historian of the Inquisition Henry C. Lea, the colonialist George Louis Beer. Undoubtedly, in the long run, a greater and greater portion of the more significant historical work was being done by professionals, but this was a slow process. Indeed, unlike the situation in other disciplines, nothing approaching a thoroughgoing monopoly by certified professionals was ever achieved.

The continued prominence of men like Schouler, Rhodes, and Lea serves as a reminder that for the historical community, professionalization did not serve as what Magali Sarfatti Larson has termed a "professional mobility project": an "attempt to translate one order of scarce social resources—special knowledge and skills—into another—social and economic rewards." One can clearly observe mobility projects at work when a previously existing occupation (e.g., dentistry) aspires to become a profession. But in the case of history the only full-time practitioners before the era of professionalization were the high-income, high-status "gentleman amateurs": the income and status of leading historians was higher before professionalization than it was afterward. For the professorate this period was the midpoint in a long slide in relative economic position. Before the Civil War the ratio of professorial income to that of unskilled urban workers was 9:1; at the turn of the century it was 4:1 or 5:1; by the 1950s and 1960s it was about 2:1. If the relevant comparison is to another profession, rather than laborers, turn-of-the-century academics seem to have averaged at least as large an income as physicians, while better-paid professors might earn four or five times the medical average. Of course, for an individual, entry into the profession might be a highly successful, and in this period very rapid, mobility project. In Germany, unlike the United States, the Ph.D. was not the final academic degree. After that came the *Habilitation*, earned on the basis of a substantial *Habilitationschrift*. Only then might one begin the slow climb up the academic ladder from *Privatdozent* (paid by student fees), through *Extraordinarius* (associate professor) to *Ordinarius* (full professor). In the expanding university system of late-nineteenth-century America, talented young men like Wilson or Turner might become full professors within a year or two of receiving the Ph.D.[6]

[6]Larson, *The Rise of Professionalism: A Sociological Analysis* (Berkeley, 1977), xvii; Colin B. Burke, *American Collegiate Populations* (New York, 1982), 233; Paul Starr, *The Social Transformation of American Medicine* (New York, 1982), 84–85.

II

It is true that many of the putative features of professionalism—esoteric skills, licensed monopoly, increased occupational status—were never attained by historians, and that others, such as relative autonomy from lay control, did not come for many years. But there were, in this period, many substantial changes in historical practice, usually considered part of the process of professionalization, which furthered the norm of objectivity, while the posture of objectivity simultaneously facilitated professionalization. The two were entangled in a complex symbiotic relationship which must be somewhat schematized in the interests of comprehensibility. Let us first consider the crucial role professionalization played in establishing historical knowledge as objective.

The adjective "objective," when applied to knowledge, has many meanings and implications. One of the most problematic, but at the same time one of the most highly valued of its connotations, is "authoritative." Objective knowledge is knowledge which commands assent, which is clearly distinguishable from "mere [i.e., subjective] opinion." Was there a severe crisis of intellectual authority in nineteenth-century America? Thomas Haskell, among others, argues that there was, and that the separation of objective truth from "charlatanism" and "quackery" was a central concern of Americans in the middle and late nineteenth century. Haskell has, in any case, demonstrated that at least some scholars and scientists experienced such a crisis, and sought its resolution in the creation of professional "communities of the competent" which were to

identify competence, cultivate it, and confer authority on those who possessed it in accordance with universalistic criteria—or, more realistically, criteria that were not in any obvious way personal, partisan, or particular. The criteria of judgment had to seem truly a product of consensus among the competent, beyond the power of any individual, clique, or party to control, and hence impersonal, objective, value-free—not mere opinion but "truth."[7]

[7]*Emergence*, 89. There were a few dissenters from this demand for closure—most notably William James. In 1894 and 1898 he testified against a bill in the Massachusetts legislature to license medical practitioners, arguing that since medical knowledge was highly imperfect and rapidly growing, it would be premature to exclude "non-professional" opinion and experience. His colleagues at Harvard Medical School were scandalized. He wrote to his friend John Jay Chapman: "Says I to myself, Shall civic virtue be confined entirely to Zola, J.J.C., and Col. Picquart? Never, says I, so in I goes." (Letter of 4 March 1898, cited in Ralph Barton Perry, *The Thought and Character of William James: Briefer Version* [Cambridge, Mass., 1948], 243–44.) James was a consistent opponent of the "search for order." He said to George Herbert Palmer: "Isn't it abominable that everybody is expected to spell in the same way? Let us get a dozen influential persons to agree each to spell after his own fashion and so break up this tyranny of the dictionary." (Quoted in Samuel Eliot Morison, *The Development of Harvard University Since the Inauguration of President Eliot, 1869–1929* [Cambridge, Mass., 1930], 6.)

"Truth" for Charles S. Peirce and many of his contemporaries was only to be identified by following the social process which produced it. Truth was "the opinion which is fated to be ultimately agreed to by all who investigate." It was in this spirit that Justin Winsor, at the founding convention of the AHA, observed that historians could "no longer afford to live isolated." They were obliged to "submit idiosyncrasies to the contact of their fellows, and . . . come from the convocation healthier and more circumspect." The foundation of an historical profession—a community of the historically competent—was, by this influential contemporary criterion, an indispensable prerequisite for the establishment, identification, and legitimation of objective historical truth.[8]

A related way in which professionalization served to consolidate the norm of objectivity was through its concentration on technique. The development and standardization of technique was, of course, the whole point of professional training; not, as J. Franklin Jameson wrote, "to evoke originality, to kindle the fires of genius . . . but to regularize, to criticize, to restrain vagaries, to set a standard of workmanship and compel men to conform to it." Standardized technique was the foundation of "transpersonal replicability"—one of the most important and perhaps the most coherent of all definitions of objectivity: it is objectively true that I am 5'11" tall because (and only because) all investigators agree that the technique of measuring height is to use a standardized yardstick, and anyone applying that yardstick to me will get the same result. By this criterion objectivity is a social phenomenon brought into existence by the establishment of methodological consensus. To the extent that it is professionalization which regularizes, promulgates, and enforces this consensus, objectivity cannot be said to exist before professionalization.[9]

A third way in which professionalization furthered objectivity was through a redefinition of the audience for historical work. Pre-professional work was directed outward, to the general reading public. Professional historical work was increasingly, though unlike other disciplines, never exclusively, directed to colleagues. To use a distinction advanced by Christopher Jencks and David Riesman, history became somewhat less of an "intellectual" and somewhat more of an "academic" enterprise.

An academic question is . . . one raised by some lacuna or ambiguity in the data or interpretations of a . . . discipline. It is a question asked by one's colleagues or on

[8]Peirce, "How to Make Our Ideas Clear," in Morris R. Cohen, ed., *Chance, Love and Logic* (London, 1923), 57; Winsor, in AHA, *Papers*, 1 (1884), 11.
[9]Jameson, "The Influence of Universities upon Historical Writing," University of Chicago *Record* 6 (1902): 299.

their behalf and answered primarily as a service to these colleagues. The term "intellectual" refers to an amateur role. Many people assume an intellectual role occasionally, and some do so almost constantly, but few make a living from it. Intellectual questions grow out of reflection on experience, are asked by all sorts and conditions of men, and are answered, insofar as they can be answered, in ways that make sense to such men. In an academic argument the participants are supposed to have professional detachment and to collaborate in the search for a generally acceptable answer. Moral and political questions that cannot be resolved by research and do not yield to cooperative investigation are almost by definition outside the academic orbit. The protagonists of an intellectual argument, on the other hand, are expected to be "interested parties." Heated debate is respectable for intellectuals, since the outcome of their argument is expected to have personal as well as professional consequences.

In "academicized" or "professionalized" history (in the present context the words can be used interchangeably) issues were much less charged than they were when history was part of general intellectual discourse. To the extent that this transformation was accomplished, the historian found it much easier to maintain the Flaubertian posture of *impassibilité*, the tone of cool detachment, which were the hallmarks of scientific objectivity.[10]

Historical professionalization, then, provided the underpinning of authority which the norm of objectivity sought. It offered, in standardized technique, the means of its operationalization, and it conduced toward an appropriate mode of discourse. But the relationship was reciprocal. Pre-professional historians and their lay readers might, for reasons of cultural taste, prefer that historical work be objective in one or more of the senses of that term. And I have attempted above to show that there were, in fact, strong currents running in that direction. But amateur historians and their readers need not have such a preference, and many did not. For the new profession of history, however, there were powerful reasons why the posture of objectivity was not just congenial, but vital.

III

The first service which the program of objectivity provided for the profession of history was the foundation of an acceptable reward system. Pre-professional historians had offered their wares in a classically free market: independent, unregulated producers received pecuniary or nonpecuniary rewards as a result of the consumer sovereignty of countless

[10]*The Academic Revolution* (New York, 1968), 242–43.

individuals of various tastes and preferences. Published evaluations (i.e., reviews) likewise were based on idiosyncratic criteria, and sophisticated readers, then as now, came to know the leanings and crotchets of reviewers—which ones experience had shown they should follow, and which to disregard. Though egos might be bruised or massaged, the material stakes were small. Few pre-professional historians made a living from history.[11]

Once historical work became institutionalized, and history became a full-time occupation rather than an avocation, anarchic criteria were no longer acceptable. Not the invisible hand of the market, but the visible and consensual judgment of the profession established the value of an historian and his work, and largely determined the course of his career. The profession was responsible for the award of fellowships, prizes, and honorific offices; the acceptance or rejection of submissions by journals; the evaluation of books in those journals; and, most crucially, though as yet far from autonomously, employment opportunities, promotion, and salaries. These were all, naturally, matters of the greatest concern to the new professionals, and the profession of history could hardly have functioned had these rewards not been distributed on the basis of what were perceived to be universalistic and objective criteria. Of course, in practice, these criteria were frequently honored in the breach; but that they were nonetheless honored, or at least appear to be honored, was indispensable. Thus, for example, the *American Historical Review*'s rule against a book's being reviewed by a teacher, student, or colleague of the author—a rule which was necessary, the editor explained to an associate, to avoid the possibility "that wicked persons might suspect us of partiality wholly foreign to our serene and lofty natures."[12]

A second problem of the profession was to make provision for those of mediocre talents. Few members of the late-nineteenth-century profession of history—or of any profession at any time—were distinguished by the

---

[11]This fact presumably accounts for a very different attitude toward what they called "borrowing" and what is nowadays designated "plagiarism." George Callcott writes: "The early nineteenth century historian . . . would not have understood why he should make a fetish of reworking material when what he wanted to say already had been better said by another. . . . There was little sense of competition among historians; it appeared entirely proper to borrow literally as well as factually. . . . Historians usually felt flattered rather than insulted when their words were used by another. The period is remarkable for the lack of scholarly rivalry, and writers who borrowed from each other remained on the warmest terms. One man, discussing his fellow historians, noted that he had 'availed myself of their labours with the same freedom which I would myself allow in like circumstances.'" (*History in the United States, 1800–1860: Its Practice and Purpose* [Baltimore, 1970], 136.)

[12]Jameson to A. C. McLaughlin, 31 August 1910, AHA Papers, Box 275.

power or penetration of their insight, or by their outstanding powers of literary expression. What was to become of them? Here, too, there is a marked contrast with the ethos of the survival of the fittest, and the banishment to other fields of endeavor of the unfit, which governed in the free markets of intellectual and cultural production. This was not a viable system in a growing profession hoping to recruit new members, and provide them with activity satisfying to both themselves and their colleagues. As Andrew Hacker has observed,

When individuals of average ability attempt to augment society's fund of information and understanding, they are soon led to recast hitherto prevailing conceptions of knowledge in such ways as to make its accumulation possible by persons of limited talents. . . . With so many careers at stake some variant of collective security comes into being, the chief article of agreement asserting that lack of surpassing ability need not exclude an individual from gaining a respectable reputation. The struggle for survival must by no means be a war of all against all. On the contrary, ententes can be drafted wherein all members are protected from unfair competition by pegging expectations of intellectual performance at a reasonable level. . . . Academic knowledge has ceased to be a broad-gauged pursuit of truth but . . . the accumulation of correct information and interpretations. The lifetime output of a modern scholar can therefore consist of quite reputable findings, not a single one of which is liable to attack on the ground that it is in error.[13]

J. Franklin Jameson, as founding and longtime editor of the *American Historical Review*, was the best placed person in the profession to evaluate the output of American historians. In the 1890s he described the period as one of "second-class work," in which professional historians would be most usefully employed in "laying up stores of well-sifted materials" which a subsequent generation would synthesize. As Richard Hofstadter noted, whereas the pre-professional historians, adumbrating moral visions with great literary skill, had produced works of art that were their own consummation, the new professionals, producing for the most part narrow and dull monographs, had to find their consummation in a collective enterprise that transcended their individual efforts.[14]

As we have seen, both natural scientists and historians in this period often voiced the expectation that their respective ventures might be finite.

[13]"Democracy, Mediocrity, and the Scholarly Calling," paper delivered at the 1968 meeting of the American Political Science Association, 4–5.
[14]Jameson, *The History of Historical Writing in America* (Boston, 1891), 132–33; Jameson, "The Influence of Universities," 300; Hofstadter, *The Progressive Historians: Turner, Beard, Parrington* (New York, 1968), 41.

Both groups employed the image of gradual additions to an edifice. Writing of the natural sciences, Karl Pearson said that

individual workers . . . were bringing their stones to one great building and piling them on and cementing them together without regard to any general plan or to their individual neighbour's work. . . . Yet this great structure, the proportions of which are beyond the ken of any individual man, possesses a symmetry and unity of its own, notwithstanding its haphazard mode of construction. . . . The smallest group of facts, if properly classified and logically dealt with, will form a stone which has its proper place in the great building of knowledge, wholly independent of the individual workman who has shaped it.

According to Edward P. Cheyney,

The scientific writer of history builds no Gothic cathedral, full of irregularities and suggestiveness, aspiring arches, niches filled with sacred or grotesque figures, and aisles dim with religious light,—that is work for the literary historian. But he builds a classic temple: simple, severe, symmetrical in its lines, surrounded by the clear, bright light of truth, pervaded by the spirit of moderation. Every historical fact is a stone hewn from the quarry of past records; it must be solid and square and even-hued—an ascertained fact. . . . His design already exists, the events have actually occurred, the past has really been—his task is to approach as near to the design as he possibly can.

Jameson wrote to Henry Adams: "I struggle on, making bricks without much idea of how the architects will use them, but believing that the best architect that ever was cannot get along without bricks, and therefore trying to make good ones."[15]

This conception of the historian's task—the patient manufacture of four-square factualist bricks to be fitted together in the ultimate objective history—had enormous professional advantages. It offered an almost tangible image of steady, cumulative progress. Although creating a grand synthesis might require an architectonic vision, almost anyone, properly trained, could mold a brick: worthwhile employment in making a contribution to the edifice was thus guaranteed to those of the most modest endowments. Because the method postulated that there could be only one appropriate brick for each niche, efficiency, a prime value of the age, would be assured by avoiding needless duplication of effort. Avoiding duplication of effort had two further functions. It made unlikely the confrontation of two irreconcilable versions of the same brick—a pros-

[15]Pearson, *The Grammar of Science* (1892; 3d. ed., London, 1911), 13; Cheyney, address delivered to Graduate School of University of Pennsylvania, 3 October 1907, reprinted as "What Is History?" in *The History Teacher's Magazine* 2 (December 1910): 79; Jameson letter of 31 October 1910, in Donnan and Stock, *An Historian's World*, 136.

pect which, if repeated with some frequency, could call the whole ideology of objectivity into question. And lessening the likelihood of confrontation would, of course, decrease the chance of controversy.

IV

This last point leads to a final dimension of the relationship between the programs of objectivity and professionalization in this period—a dimension filled with paradox as a result of strains within each of the two interacting ideas.

Perhaps the greatest appeal of objective knowledge was that it was incontrovertible and noncontroversial. At the same time an influential theory of objective knowledge held that controversy, the cut and thrust of debate and criticism, was indispensable to its production. This is, of course, not a logical contradiction. Indeed, it is a perfectly coherent and transparent dialectical process: icy-cold objectivity forged in the fires of disputation. But it suggests the possibility of a psychological contradiction: that those who prized what was objective precisely because it was noncontroversial might be at best ambivalent about participating in the processes of fierce controversy and sharp mutual criticism which, according to their theory, were necessary to generate it.

If there was a latent psychological contradiction in the idea of objectivity, there was a manifest behavioral contradiction in conflicting norms of professional behavior with respect to controversy and criticism. If the maxim of the free market is *caveat emptor*, the slogan of the profession is *credat emptor*: "the producer of these wares has been rigorously trained, and we vouch for both his competence and his ethics; the goods themselves have been subjected to the most rigorous testing and criticism; you may therefore take them on faith." In "free" professions like law and medicine, the emphasis is on the training and the ethical standards of practitioners, and the alleged willingness of the professional community to expel instantly those who fail to meet its high standards. (It is well known that in practice, except in the most outrageous instances, this almost never happens.) In academic or scientific professions the emphasis is rather more on the ferocious mutual criticism of findings within the disciplinary community. The scholar has been defined as "a man who has a quarrelsome interest in his neighbor's work."

But the norm of ruthlessness toward errant brethren, and no-holds-barred exposure of error, is in flat contradiction to equally important professional values: mutual respect and deference, preservation of the public fiction of the competence of all certified practitioners. One of the strongest of professional taboos is directed against criticizing a fellow professional in public, as evidenced by the frequent ostracizing of physicians who testify for the plaintiff in malpractice suits.

The nature of historical activity, of the early historical profession, and of contemporary norms of discourse, all worked to bring about the sacrifice of criticism to comity. Unlike more esoteric areas of scholarship, historical discussion was conducted in ordinary language, about comprehensible issues, and more or less in public. The *American Historical Review*, in its early years, was never directed exclusively to scholars; early meetings of the AHA were often more social than academic occasions, dominated by amateurs. The profession was so small that practically everyone knew everyone else, and was related to them by ties of friendship, patronage, or sycophancy. Nominated reviewers frequently declined to review books by friends when they had reason to suspect they would have to be critical. Fear by junior historians that they would damage their careers by criticizing their seniors was also common. The young Frederick Jackson Turner declined to publish a critique which he had delivered orally, lest he antagonize the sensitive and influential Hermann von Holst.[16]

But beyond these personal and prudential considerations, there was, in the genteel culture of the turn of the century, a widespread distaste for sharp controversy and criticism. It was, in fact, "unprofessional." The AHA program committee in 1901 hesitated to put "so controverted a field as the Reformation" on the agenda. A decade later Andrew C. McLaughlin demurred from discussing southern views of state sovereignty before the Civil War because "I do not like to use the Historical Association for the purpose of presenting this kind of controversial matter." Critical reviews in the *AHR* occasioned much pain, even among those not personally wounded. James Schouler expressed his "dislike of book reviews, etc., such as institute comparisons or make invidious remarks as between members of the Association." He preferred the rule of the Massachusetts Historical Society which forbade critical comments on the work of living members, and he deplored several instances in the *AHR* in which "opinions printed by the editors . . . are such as to produce rankling and ill feeling among our leading members, while on the other hand others have the good fortune to be praised and courted."

---

[16]Ray Allen Billington, *Frederick Jackson Turner: Historian, Scholar, Teacher* (New York, 1973), 149. In the early years of the *AHR*, reviews were sometimes anonymous. Jameson explained to a correspondent that among the reasons against signing one's name, "the one most often felt is the reluctance that arises from the consciousness that the writer has not praised the book as much as he would desire to do, so that if he signs it he feels a little uncomfortable when he meets the author at the next meeting of the American Historical Association." (Letter to Archibald Cary Coolidge, 16 July 1909, AHA Papers, Box 272.)

Albert Bushnell Hart of Harvard, agitated by what was in fact quite mild criticism in the *AHR* of books by some senior figures, complained that "every one of them has been corrected, told to stand with his heels on the line, not to squint, to put his shoulders back." "Not one of them," he said, "is a man who has need of reproof or admonition, or ought to be made the target for pop-guns." George Lincoln Burr of Cornell, then a member of the *AHR* editorial board, in general seconded Hart's views, believing that "scholars of proved worth and mature achievement in historical scholarship deserve from critics a certain deference of tone that others have not yet earned. There is to them, that is, an outstanding debt of gratitude." Even Jameson, who regularly decried the insufficiently critical tone of reviews, which he ascribed to excessive good nature in American culture, and amiability within the profession, thanked God "that we are not as the German *Gelehrten*, to many of whom it is a joy, sometimes the chief joy of life, to speak ill of each other."[17]

Professionalization, in some respects, brought a decline in rigorous criticism and fruitful controversy. In the 1860s and 1870s Henry B. Dawson's *Historical Magazine* had featured sharp and searching examination of the scholarship of Bancroft, Motley, and the elder Charles Francis Adams, among others. Dawson fulfilled his promise to his readers that he would always "fearlessly expose and condemn . . . what is known to be historically untrue . . . no matter by whom it may have been uttered." Criticism in the early *AHR* and other professional journals of the period was consistently more inhibited than Dawson's. In 1877 Henry Adams had proposed that Henry Cabot Lodge teach a course which would cover the same period as the one he offered. "His views being federalist and conservative," he wrote to President Eliot, "have as good a right to expression in the college as mine which tend to democracy and radicalism. The clash of opinions can hardly fail to stimulate inquiry among the students." In the era of professional territoriality no such suggestion was likely to be forthcoming.[18]

[17] C. H. Haskins to members of program committee, 15 March 1901, George Burton Adams Papers, 4:19; McLaughlin to Carl Russell Fish, 25 May 1910, Fish Papers, Box 1; Schouler to Herbert Baxter Adams, 1 December 1900, in W. Stull Holt, ed., "Historical Scholarship in the United States, 1876–1901: As Revealed in the Correspondence of Herbert B. Adams," *Johns Hopkins University Studies in Historical and Political Science* 61 (1938): 289–91; Hart to George Lincoln Burr, 26 October 1913, and Burr to Jameson, 17 November 1913, both in AHA Papers, Box 277; Jameson to Archibald Cary Coolidge, 16 July 1909, AHA Papers, Box 272.

[18] Dawson, quoted in David D. Van Tassel, *Recording America's Past: An Interpretation of the Development of Historical Studies in America, 1607–1884* (Chicago, 1960), 162; Adams, quoted in Seymour Martin Lipset, "Political Controversies at Harvard, 1636 to 1974," in Lipset and David Riesman, *Education and Politics at Harvard* (New York, 1975), 95.

Historians in this period might acknowledge those elements in the professional model which mandated sharp mutual criticism and controversy, as when Albert B. Hart described his colleagues as "more or less cannibals: they live by destroying each others' conclusions." In practice, the overwhelming majority—including, as we have seen, Hart himself— were repelled by these norms of academic professionalism, preferring those which stressed comity and gentility. Objectivity was valued not as the outcome of professional conflict, but as prophylactic against it.[19]

[19]Hart, "Imagination in History," *AHR* 15 (1910): 235.

3

◁══▷

Consensus and legitimation

No community can be satisfied that its discourse is objective—or even know what it would mean to be objective—without substantial agreement on values, goals, and perceptions of reality. All of the factors so far considered could not, in combination, have established objectivity as the accepted norm within the American historical community at the end of the nineteenth century were it not for one additional factor: the extraordinary degree of ideological homogeneity within that community.

If university administrators restricted their faculty members to the objective presentation of approved orthodoxy, this was not an onerous constraint on historians who showed no visible signs of serious heterodoxy. If scientific historians' involvement in producing historical work for schoolchildren was avowedly for purposes of legitimating the social and political order, this was untroubling to historians for whom that order was not at all problematic. By presenting an "impartial" account of the American Civil War and the American Revolution—in both instances, an account based on the "objective truth" of scientific racism—historians could simultaneously demonstrate their own detachment and render valuable public service by furthering the goal of reconciliation between North and South and between the United States and Great Britain.

The word "ideology" has been so loosely used and variously defined in recent years that I should, at the outset, make clear how I will be employing it. In orthodox Marxist usage the word refers to a viewpoint directly tied to the standpoint of a particular social class. This is not the sense in which I am using it. Rather I mean by the word simply an overarching, and at-least-tacitly-coherent outlook on the world. Ultimately, to be sure, every ideology implies—or is based upon—an ontology, an epistemology, an aesthetic, and so on. But if we limit ourselves to the explicitly social and political realms, ideology can be depicted, rather schematically, as consisting of three elements: (1) a picture of the way the world is; (2) a picture of the way the world ought to be; (3) a set of propositions about the relationship between the first and the second. (The third element has several dimensions: sheer distance, getting closer or getting farther apart, moving slowly or rapidly, evolving smoothly or requiring ruptures, etc.)

Social and political ideologies can be roughly categorized as "dominant," "accommodationist," and "oppositional." Dominant ideology, which in modern Western societies is rarely encountered in its pure form, sees the relationship between the way the world is, and the way the world ought to be, as one of identity, or near identity. Existing social and political arrangements are as good as man can make them. It is the ideology of celebration, complacency, and conservatism.[1]

"Accommodationist" ideology acknowledges problems and deficiencies. There is at least a moderate gap between the way things are and the way they ought to be. The various difficulties are, however, seen as unrelated: each requires its separate solution. Criticisms do not aggregate into a structural indictment. At least in the United States, the liberals, progressives, and reformers who are the spokesmen of an accommodationist ideology see the "is" as moving ever closer to the "ought"; they may be militant, but are not disaffected; often troubled, they remain at least moderately, and often immoderately, optimistic. Indeed, in their way, they may be as complacent as those in the first group: while the former take satisfaction from the contemplation of static perfection, the latter derive it from pride in the past record of closing the gap, and confidence in the future prospects of closing it further.

Finally there is "oppositional" ideology, whose hallmark is not so much the discrepancy between the way things are and the way they ought to be, though the discrepancy is typically seen as great, as the belief that the gap is unlikely to be easily or peacefully closed. Defects are not isolated but patterned and interrelated. The pessimistic, or "tragic," variety of oppositional ideology may see the gap as inexorably widening due to forces beyond our control. Conversely, the radical oppositionist rejects the possibility of substantially closing the gap without fundamental structural change: a decent society requires different foundations. It is the

---

[1]This taxonomy is taken from Ira Katznelson and Mark Kesselman, *The Politics of Power: A Critical Introduction to American Government* (New York, 1975), 356–59, in which they adapt to their (and my present) purposes a schema suggested by Frank Parkin in his *Class Inequality and Political Order* (New York, 1971), 82–83.

absence, or near absence, of oppositional ideology within the American political tradition, the relative triviality of the disputes between dominant and accommodationist camps, which the "consensus" historians were to emphasize after World War II. They argued that in comparison with Europe, where the bourgeois order was fundamentally rejected by ideologists of a wounded-but-not-yet-dead aristocratic arcadia and a struggling-to-be-born proletarian utopia, Americans, for most of the nation's history, have quibbled over how much or how little tinkering was needed. Whatever the analytic merits and limitations of a concentration on ideological consensus in understanding American history, it is clearly indispensable for understanding American historians around the turn of the century.

The consensus among historians in this period is in some ways surprising, for there was never another time in American history in which, overall, there was so little consensus. This was the era of the populist revolt and the free-silver campaign, of anarchist and trade-union violence; a time of unprecedented, unresolved social problems in cities which contained a larger body of unassimilated immigrants than ever before or since; a period which saw the rise of the Wobblies, and the Socialist Party seemingly on the verge of becoming, as in Europe, a serious contender for power. Amid all this turmoil, professional historians were, with the most partial and insignificant exceptions, serene and untroubled in their celebration of traditional pieties: an island of orthodoxy in a sea of heterodoxy. Before examining the specific elements which went into this remarkable consensus, let us look at some of the centripetal forces that generated and enforced it.

I

Whatever other attributes of a profession turn-of-the-century historians might claim, autonomy was not among them. The professionalization of history meant a change in the status of the historian from privileged, avocational, or entrepreneurial independence to that of salaried employee of a bureaucratic organization. Of course, members of other professions, too, are often employees, but a lawyer working for a salary in a large law firm, a doctor employed by a large hospital, is employed by a bureaucracy controlled by fellow professionals. It is fellow professionals who, even in these bureaucratic settings, control access to practice. The Ph.D. in history was never a formal license to practice history by writing it, for which you need no license. But neither was it a license to teach, for which you need students. In any meaningful sense, a usable and effective license to "practice" history—to teach history, and to have the facilities and time to write it—depended on getting a job in a college or university. By the second half of the twentieth century, hiring decisions were made by one's academic colleagues. While faculties rarely have formal appointment power, they characteristically take the initiative, and their recommendations are generally heeded; administrators and trustees almost never impose their own candidates on an unwilling faculty. This was far from the situation in the decades around 1900. College presidents, actively seconded by trustees, were the de facto, not just de jure, authority in personnel decisions: they conducted searches, did extensive interviewing, and closely monitored the utterances of professors, both before and after they were hired. There were exceptions, but their exceptional character is clear. Max Farrand, attempting to lure Carl Russell Fish to Yale in 1910, pointed out, as a singular feature of Yale's appointment procedure, that hiring was largely the prerogative of the faculty. Unlike the situation at other institutions, "when a man comes to Yale, he comes with the hearty approval and by the call of his colleagues. His appointment is welcomed, in no sense resented."[2]

"Philosophers," Brooks Adams once remarked to Justice Holmes, "were hired by the comfortable classes to prove everything is all right." It would be an exaggeration to say that Adams's observation defined the relationship between turn-of-the-century academics and the universities which employed them—but not that much of an exaggeration. "It is all very well to sympathize with the working man," William Rainey Harper, the first president of the University of Chicago remarked, "but we get our money from those on the other side, and we can't afford to offend them." Harper was careful to make sure that J. Franklin Jameson was acceptable to the university's patron, John D. Rockefeller, before appointing Jameson as Von Holst's successor. Nicholas Murray Butler told the Columbia Board of Trustees in 1910 that "Men who feel that their personal convictions require them to treat the mature opinion of the civilized world without respect or with contempt may well be given an opportunity to do so from private station and without the added influence and prestige of a university's name." When in 1915 the Board of Trustees of the University of Pennsylvania fired the economist Scott Nearing, an editorial in the *New York Times* expressed the opinion that

Men who through toil and ability have got together enough money to endow universities or professors' chairs do not generally have it in mind that their money should be spent for the dissemination of the dogmas of Socialism or in the

[2]Farrand to Fish, 8 February 1910, Fish Papers, 1:1910–11.

teaching of ingenuous youth how to live without work. Yet when Trustees conscientiously endeavor to carry out the purposes of the founder by taking proper measures to prevent misuse of the endowment, we always hear a loud howl about academic freedom. We see no reason why the upholders of academic freedom in this sense should not establish a university of their own. Let them provide the funds, erect the buildings, lay out the campus, and then make a requisition on the padded cells of Bedlam for their teaching staff. Nobody would interfere with the full freedom of professors; they could teach Socialism and shiftlessness until Doomsday without restraint.

Wealthy donors exerted not just generalized influence in defining the permissible limits of academic discourse through their membership on boards of trustees and via compliant administrators, but frequently sweetened the salary of a favored professor. Woodrow Wilson at Princeton and Frederick Jackson Turner at Harvard were among the beneficiaries of this sort of arrangement—one which, it goes without saying, was not extended to the even mildly heterodox.[3]

Criteria of religious orthodoxy were not uncommon: Bryn Mawr was something of a satellite of Johns Hopkins, and Wilson was backed for a job there by the influential Herbert Baxter Adams, but before he secured the position he had to satisfy the college president that he "believed that the hand of Providence was in all history; that the progress of Christianity was as great a factor as the development of philosophy and the sciences." The president agreed to recommend him to the trustees after he had become "assured that the moral and religious lessons of History will in thy hands be used to fortify a wide and comprehensive yet well defined faith in Christianity." Some years later, when Wilson moved on to Princeton, it was only after overcoming the concern of some who were worried that in his discussion of the origin of the state he had "minimise[d] the supernatural" and had left "the reader of [his] pages in a state of uncertainty as to . . . the place [he gave] to Divine Providence." The board of trustees "would not regard with favour such a conception of

[3]Holmes to Lewis Einstein, 1 June 1905, in James Bishop Peabody, ed., *The Holmes-Einstein Letters: Correspondence of Mr. Justice Holmes and Lewis Einstein, 1903–1935* (New York, 1964), 16; Harper quoted in Chester M. Destler, *Henry Demarest Lloyd and the Empire of Reform* (Philadelphia, 1963), 372; Harper to Rockefeller, 25 August 1900, reprinted in Clarence D. Karier, ed., *Shaping the American Educational State: 1900 to the Present* (New York, 1975), 43; Butler quoted in William Summerscales, *Affirmation and Dissent* (New York, 1970), 31; *Times* editorial quoted in Walter P. Metzger, "Academic Freedom in Delocalized Academic Institutions," in Metzger et al., *Dimensions of Academic Freedom* (Urbana, Ill., 1969), 13–14; Cornelius Cuyler Cuyler to Woodrow Wilson, 16 May 1898, and enclosure, in Arthur H. Link, ed., *The Papers of Woodrow Wilson* (Princeton, 1966–), 10:529–30; A. Lawrence Lowell to William Rand, Jr., 6 December 1911, Turner Papers, Box 16.

academic freedom or teaching as would leave in doubt the very direct
bearing of historical Christianity as a revealed religion upon the great
problems of civilization." Later still, when Wilson attempted to secure a
position for his fellow Hopkins alumnus Frederick Jackson Turner, the
latter's Unitarianism was too much for the Princeton trustees to swallow,
and Turner, for the time being, stayed at Madison. If state universities
were, in general, less inclined to impose religious tests, or be directly
answerable to wealthy trustees, they were hardly a secure haven. As
Arthur Schlesinger, Sr. said of a state university president a bit after the
period now under discussion, "He favors freedom of teaching in principle. . . . He would even protect a professor from outside criticism up to a
certain point. But if University appropriations are involved, then his
allegiance is to the appropriation."[4]

The prevailing standards of academic freedom, as all this suggests, were
narrowly defined and fitfully observed. Of particular importance for the
present inquiry was a marked contrast between American and German
conceptions of the relationship between objectivity and academic freedom. The German professor was expected to *profess*—to present, pas-
sionately and persuasively, with aggressive finality, deeply held convictions. There were a few who took a more cautious view: the pathologist
Rudolph Virchow, in the midst of the German Darwinian controversy,
warned that unproved hypotheses should not be presented as truth, and
that professors should "consult the *consensus gentium* before expressing
possibly dangerous beliefs." But the majority view among German academics was expressed by the biologist Ernst Haeckel, who in a famous
reply to Virchow maintained that in practice it was impossible to draw a
sharp line between knowledge and opinion, that science advances by the
clash of correct and incorrect views, and that requiring professors to
"stick to the facts" or defer to existing opinion would wind up subor-
dinating education to religious dogmatists.[5]

---

[4]Wilson to Ellen Louise Axson, 27 November 1884 and James E. Rhoads to Wilson, 1
December 1884, Link, 3:490, 502; Francis Landey Patton to Wilson, 18 February 1890,
Link, 6:527; Link, 12:290; Schlesinger to Upton Sinclair, 27 August 1922, Schlesinger
Oral History Memoir, 518–19.
[5]For Virchow and Haeckel, see Walter P. Metzger, "The Age of the University," in
Richard Hofstadter and Walter P. Metzger, *The Development of Academic Freedom in
the United States* (New York, 1955), 388. In practice the German universities' acceptance
of discourse which was not "objective" did not mean toleration of dissidents. "In Germany," Max Weber concluded in 1908, after his student Robert Michels was barred from
a teaching position, "the freedom of learning exists only within the limits of officially
accepted political and religious views." (Weber, quoted in Fritz Ringer, *The Decline of
the German Mandarins: The German Academic Community, 1890–1933* [Cambridge,
Mass., 1969], 143.)

The American conception of the permissible limits of academic discourse was quite different. Whereas in Germany, Friedrich Paulsen had defended the role of the professor as advocate on the grounds of the student's "complete freedom to accept or to reject," American educators thought of students as being in constant danger of mental seduction; what had earlier been fear of the student's exposure to heretical religious doctrine, became fear that students would succumb to "propaganda." The American insistence on professorial neutrality and objectivity was clearly expressed by President Charles W. Eliot of Harvard:

Philosophical subjects should never be taught with authority. . . . It is not the function of the teacher to settle philosophical and political controversies for the pupil, or even to recommend to him any one set of opinions as better than any other. Exposition, not imposition, of opinions is the professor's part. . . . The notion that education consists in the authoritative inculcation of what the teacher deems true may be logical and appropriate in a convent, but it is intolerable in universities.[6]

This was a view of the legitimate professorial function—and, by extension, of the limits of academic freedom—which was endorsed by teachers as well as administrators, liberals as well as conservatives. The professorial obligation to be "moderate" was stressed as the concomitant of academic freedom. The professor, John Dewey wrote in 1902, "needs tact as well as scholarship. . . . The manner of conveying the truth may cause an irritation . . . whenever the negative rather than the positive aspect is dwelt upon; wherever the discrepancy between the new truth and established institution is emphasized." The American Association of University Professors, in its inaugural manifesto in 1915, stressed the "relatively immature" minds of students: "In these circumstances it may reasonably be expected that the instructor will present scientific truth with discretion, that he will introduce the student to new conceptions gradually, with some consideration for the student's preconceptions and traditions, and with due regard to character-building." The AAUP accepted it as proper that

the university is . . . likely always to exercise a certain form of conservative influence. For by its nature it is committed to the principle that knowledge should precede action, to the caution (by no means synonymous with intellectual timidity) which is an essential part of the scientific method, to a sense of the complexity of social problems . . . to a reasonable regard for the teachings of experience.

[6]For Paulsen versus American conceptions, see Metzger, "Age of the University," 389, 402; Eliot, *Educational Reform* (New York, 1898), 7–8.

One of its most characteristic functions in a democratic society is to help make public opinion more self-critical and more circumspect, to check the more hasty and unconsidered impulses of popular feeling.[7]

Given this conception of the limits of the academically permissible, it was natural that dissidents could be removed for violating norms of scientific objectivity without raising legitimate questions of academic freedom. When the economist Edward Bemis was forced to resign from the University of Chicago for remarks that upset corporate contributors, J. Lawrence Laughlin, the chairman of the Department of Political Economy, explained that Bemis's removal was due to the "partisan unscientific methods" of his work, while President Harper described the dismissal as a consequence of Bemis having "confound[ed] personal pleading for scientific thought," of forgetting "that to serve the University we must employ scientific methods and do scientific work."[8]

II

Historians could scarcely have failed to be aware of the perils of dissent— that their views, if they deviated seriously from established orthodoxy, would fail the test of objectivity, and put their careers at risk. And it would seem reasonable to assume that this awareness had an inhibiting effect on heterodoxy. But it is only an assumption, for there is no direct evidence that early professional historians had any inclination to embrace heretical ideas. It would be puerile to explain ideological conformity on the basis of class and ethnic origin. Yet it is worth noting that there seem to have been no professional historians of recent immigrant background, none of working-class origin, and hardly any who were not Protestant. A handful, mostly at Ivy League institutions, sprang from what in America passed for an aristocracy; the overwhelming majority were from various strata of "the middle classes." Becoming a university professor, for most, meant some measure of upward mobility and entry into local, or, if they were particularly successful, national, elite status—presumably with the consequences for consciousness that such ascent generally produces. Their work, as Richard Hofstadter observed, "embodied the ideas of the possessing classes about industrial and financial issues, manifested the complacency of white Anglo-Saxon Protestants about social and ethnic

[7]Dewey, "Academic Freedom," *Educational Review* 23 (January 1902): 7–8; AAUP, "General Report of the Committee on Academic Freedom and Tenure" (1915), reprinted in Karier, 72–73, 71.
[8]Quoted in David Hogan and Clarence Karier, "Professionalizing the Role of 'Truth Seekers'," *Interchange*, 9:2 (1978–79): 47.

issues, and, on constitutional issues, underwrote the requirements of property and of national centralization as opposed to states' rights or regional self-assertion."⁹

Furthermore, with the development of new, autonomous, policy-oriented social science disciplines, there was a migration out of history on the part of those of more activist inclination. The tension between advocacy and objectivity existed among political scientists, sociologists, and economists—not historians. Some early historians, like Woodrow Wilson, knew from the beginning that their chief interest was in current affairs. In his first year as a graduate student at Hopkins he wrote of his discomfort at being surrounded by those whose "chief interest is in . . . the precise day of the month on which Cicero cut his eye-teeth." Many historians, like Wilson, retained their allegiance and affiliations to history, while also defining themselves as political scientists (John W. Burgess, William A. Dunning, Albert Bushnell Hart, Archibald Cary Coolidge, James T. Shotwell, Charles Beard). Others, like Edward S. Corwin,

---

⁹*The Progressive Historians: Turner, Beard, Parrington* (New York, 1968), 27. There is no substantial, "hard" data on the class background of early (or, for that matter, later) historians. There is a brief discussion, based in part on a modest quantitative survey, in John Higham, et al., *History: The Development of Historical Studies in the United States* (Princeton, 1965), 61–64. A recent local study suggests that "success in academia at the end of the century was tied more, rather than less, to social origins than it had been five decades earlier." (Alan Creutz, "Social Access to the Professions: Late Nineteenth-Century Academics at the University of Michigan as a Case Study," *Journal of Social History* 15 [1981]: 73–87.) Of four identifiably Jewish historians before World War I, two never sought regular academic appointments. Cyrus Adler held a position at the Smithsonian. The highly esteemed colonialist George Louis Beer was a wealthy German Jew who for several years after receiving his M.A. combined lecturing at Columbia with a business career, but he never enjoyed teaching, and after his retirement from business, pursued the life of a "gentleman scholar." Charles Gross, who held a Ph.D. from Göttingen, made a strong impression on Herbert Baxter Adams, who feared that "it will be very difficult for him to get a start as a regular instructor in an American College, on account of his Jewish connections. A University position must be created for him in some way, for he is really too brilliant and too well-trained for any subordinate kind of work." (Adams to Andrew D. White, 24 November 1883, in Holt, "Historical Scholarship," 69–70.) Adams's fears were, happily, unfounded, and Gross became a professor at Harvard, and twice chairman of its History Department. Archibald Cary Coolidge of Harvard at first found Frank Golder "a rather unusually insignificant looking little Jew whom we threw down hard the first time he tried his general examinations," but came to be "quite attached to him for he is a very good, kindly fellow." Golder held a variety of positions at minor universities before the war, and later wound up at Stanford. (Coolidge to Arthur Lyon Cross, 29 October 1924, Van Tyne Papers, Box 2.) Unlike the situation later on, there were so few Jews within the profession in this period that anti-Semitism was hardly an issue. Catholics were rare within the mainstream of the profession—they were mostly employed at their own colleges and universities—but were a significant enough presence for Jameson, in considering an article dealing with the Reformation, to worry that "we ought not to give needless offence to the Catholic part of our constituency." (Jameson to George Lincoln Burr, 8 September 1909, AHA Papers, Box 272.)

moved completely to political science or, like Albion W. Small, shifted to sociology. It was from policy-oriented social sciences, principally sociology and economics, that the protagonists in the notorious academic freedom cases of the era came: Bemis at Chicago, Nearing at Pennsylvania, Edward A. Ross at Stanford, Richard G. Ely at Wisconsin. History's principal contribution to society was not policy advice, or advocacy, but legitimation, which, when counterposed to objectivity, created a different set of problems.[10]

For the time being, however, these problems remained mostly latent, despite the deep involvement of early professional historians in that central arena of legitimation, the public school system. There were those among the historians, like Charles Kendall Adams, who thought that "from the college standpoint, it is a question whether history might not well be omitted in the lower schools. Poor teaching . . . gives indefinite ideas which are perhaps worse than none." But this was never a widespread view. Other considerations aside, there were urgent material reasons for professional historians to support the expansion of history in the schools. As Andrew C. McLaughlin, chairman of the AHA's Committee of Seven on history in the schools, wrote to a colleague,

We are at a critical time. A large committee of the Greek and Latin men . . . meet in New York this spring to push the claims of the classics and to urge, in all probability, six years of Latin and three years of Greek. . . . The Modern Language Association has a Committee of Twelve that is . . . discussing the whole subject of modern language teaching. How long are we to stand idle and see history neglected in the schools. . . . You must see that the graduate work in history in universities is dependent on a recognition by the schools of the fact that trained men are needed for teaching the subject. Where would German universities be if they were not engaged in preparing gymnasium teachers. The advancement of university work, therefore, depends upon the schools recognizing the high character of the work they are called upon to do, and upon their calling, therefore, for teachers that are thoroughly prepared for their task.[11]

Whether for reasons of professional aggrandizement, or from more disinterested motives, historians were committed to promoting history in the schools. But what sort of history should it be? How could they reconcile the seemingly contradictory demands of history for moral and patriotic indoctrination, and history as objective science? They were not

[10]Wilson to Ellen Louise Axson, 13 November 1884, Link, 3: 430.
[11]Charles K. Adams, quoted in "Minutes of the 1892 Madison Conference on History, Civil Government, and Political Economy," reprinted in Link, *Papers*, 8:63–64; McLaughlin to "My Dear Mr. Adams" (otherwise unidentified), 27 March 1897, McLaughlin Papers, Box 1.

unaware of the problem. At an 1892 conference on history teaching, Woodrow Wilson warned that "we must avoid introducing what is called scientific history in the schools, for it is a 'history of doubt,' criticism, examination of evidence. It tends to confuse young pupils. . . . What we need to study in schools is the united effort, the common thought, of bodies of men; of the men who make public opinion, that is of the uncritical and conservative rather than of the educated classes." Professor Lucy M. Salmon of Vassar, a member of the AHA's Committee of Seven, maintained that in the schools, as elsewhere, "the ultimate object of history, as of all sciences, is the search for truth, and . . . that search entails the responsibility of abiding by the results when found." Yet she was sure that in the discussion of national heroes one must avoid "the presentation to children of . . . blemishes the world has gladly forgiven and forgotten for the sake of a great work accomplished and a noble life lived."[12]

The contradiction, in this period, remained largely latent, and occasioned no discussion within the profession. Whatever their reluctance to introduce full-blown "historical science" into precollegiate instruction, professional historians were united in their determination to replace the exaggerated filiopietism of existing schoolbooks, and several leaders of the profession wrote texts for the schools. Four of the six best-selling school texts in the first decade of the twentieth century were by Channing, Hart, McLaughlin, and McMaster. The new texts, not surprisingly, were hardly models of austere, scholarly detachment, at least in part to placate school boards and patriotic groups who demanded celebratory accounts. They reflected the conventional pieties and prejudices of the era, they consistently dwelt on "the smiling aspects of life," discreditable incidents were generally swept under the rug. But such compromises of objectivity, if, indeed, they were perceived as compromises, seemed minor tactical retreats in the context of the sweeping victory the professionals were winning in ousting the older texts. Whatever their defects from a scholarly point of view, the new works were certainly more balanced and more critical than those they replaced. In the circumstances, the authors, and their colleagues, were not overly concerned with theoretical questions concerning objectivity which textbook treatments raised. They were replacing a "factitious" and "spurious" patriotism with one that was authentic and sound; a northern or southern "sectional

---

[12]Wilson quoted in "Minutes of the 1892 Madison Conference," in Link, *Papers*, 8:65; Salmon, *The Study of History in Schools: Report to the AHA by The Committee of Seven* (New York, 1899), 161; Salmon, "Some Principles in the Teaching of History," National Society for the Scientific Study of Education, *Yearbook* 1 (1902): 51.

patriotism" would give way to a broadly national patriotism; a chauvinistic patriotism "that would seek to present distorted ideas of the past with the idea of glorifying one country at the possible expense of truth" would give way to a broad and ecumenical, "an intelligent, tolerant patriotism." In the elaboration of that "intelligent, tolerant patriotism" they would express their most deeply held beliefs, serve the purposes of legitimation, and significantly elaborate the concept of objectivity.[13]

III

There is little disagreement about the general ideological posture of the early professional historians. John Higham has termed their stance "conservative evolutionist." American history was the story of "freedom realized and stabilized through the achievement of national solidarity." They favored institutional history, in part because it seemed more objective, but also because it represented unity, stability, and continuity. Inevitably their presentation of the past was, as Richard Hofstadter observed, "reshaped by current preoccupations with the problems of industrialism and the city, of agrarian or working-class revolts, of the immense waves of new immigrants that were sweeping into the country."

The mobs of the Revolutionary era could be depicted in such a way as to state a general point of view about law and order, Daniel Shays in such a way as to condemn contemporary agrarian radicalism; Jefferson could be used to condemn sentimental democracy and "radical" theorizing, Jackson to discredit spoilsmen, party machines, demagogues, and modern democracy.[14]

Ideological production of this kind was no doubt useful in its way, but it was a relatively marginal and ineffectual activity, and, if pushed too far, it might call their objectivity into question. There was, however, one most important realm in which historians could play a much more active and central ideological role while enhancing, rather than putting at risk, their reputation for objectivity. That was the great task of national reconciliation, healing the wounds of the Civil War and Reconstruction, repairing and deepening national unity, contributing to that shift in grammatical usage from the early nineteenth century, when one said, "The United States are . . ." to the twentieth-century version, "The United States is. . . ."

Pre-professional historical writing was overwhelmingly local and sec-

[13]*Report by the Committee of Seven,* 160–61, 74.
[14]Higham et al., *History,* 158–60; Hofstadter, *Progressive Historians,* 27.

tional, often in the most narrow and bigoted fashion. Sectional politicians, before the Civil War and after, called for schoolbooks "loyal to our own institutions," and the call was answered. Even those historians who painted on a national canvas often revealed a regional orientation. Bancroft, Motley, Parkman, and Prescott were all Harvard graduates, and New England dominance in historical writing extended well into the era of its professionalization. In 1903 Ulrich B. Phillips complained that "The history of the United States has been written by Boston and largely written wrong." In the AHA, and as editor of the *AHR*, J. Franklin Jameson waged unremitting warfare against the particularist antiquarianism of state and local historical societies, their "pettiness and sterility," and against locally focused historical work. The nationalization of historical perspective, the escape from parochialism, was a high-priority item on the professional historical agenda. Lord Acton, in his 1898 letter to the authors of articles in the *Cambridge Modern History* wrote:

Contributors will understand that we are established, not under the Meridian of Greenwich, but in Long. 30° W. [mid-Atlantic]; that our Waterloo must be one that satisfies French and English, Germans and Dutch alike; that nobody can tell, without examining the list of authors, where the Bishop of Oxford laid down the pen, and whether Fairbairn or Gasquet, Liebermann or Harrison took it up.

American historians had parallel aspirations for their collective labors.[15]

The word "impartiality" was often used as more or less a synonym for objectivity; and that word had more than a contingent etymological relationship with "loyalty to the part"—"particularism." If particularism and sectionalism could be eliminated from historical writing, impartiality and objectivity would be both furthered and demonstrated. A truly national historical profession would be created—and historians would simultaneously be contributing to the great task of reconciliation. John W. Burgess was explicit about the reconciliationist motives that led him to undertake

---

[15]Phillips to George J. Baldwin, 2 May 1903, cited in John David Smith, "Du Bois and Phillips—Symbolic Antagonists of the Progressive Era," *Centennial Review* 24 (1980): 94; Jameson to Herbert Baxter Adams, 21 February 1890, in Holt, "Historical Scholarship," 128; Acton letter reprinted in Fritz Stern, ed., *The Varieties of History: From Voltaire to the Present* (New York, 1956), 249. While undoubtedly sincere in his dislike of particularism, Jameson's animus was not evenhanded: "Western history is stupid," he wrote his father on 5 January 1889. (Elizabeth Donnan and Leo F. Stock, eds., *An Historian's World: Selections from the Correspondence of John Franklin Jameson* [*Memoirs of the American Philosophical Society* 42 (1956)], 46.) He was quite content with New England domination of the AHA and *AHR*: indeed he was its symbol; southern and western resentment of that domination was the principal motivating force behind a 1915 attempt by insurgents in the AHA to challenge his regime.

Objectivity enthroned

his work on the middle period. A publisher approached him with the
suggestion that

> the time had come for a more complete reconciliation of North and South in the
> juster appreciation of the views on both sides which led to the great struggle of
> 1861–65 and the reorganization of the Union through and after it, and . . . I
> undertook the work as a sacred duty to my country and carried it through with
> that feeling.[16]

The task of reconciliation was, of course, already under way. The year
of the founding of the AHA, 1884, was also the year which saw the
election of Grover Cleveland, the first Democrat to hold that office since
before the Civil War—elected against the warnings of those who thought
it might mean the resurgence of southern treason. Veterans of the Union
and Confederate armies began to hold joint "Blue and Gray" reunions. In
1892 the Populist presidential candidate was a former Union general from
Iowa; the vice-presidential candidate, a former Confederate general from
Virginia. But reconciliation was still a far from completed task. Many of
the founders of the AHA were veterans of the war, many more had at
least childhood recollections of the struggle, and, much more salient, of
course, in the South, of Reconstruction. At a minimum, deep vicarious
identification with one of the two sides was the rule until well into the
twentieth century.

In part the change in historiographical orientation toward the war and
Reconstruction was generational, and would have gone on whether or
not history had become professionalized. One can, to a very considerable
extent, discern a progressive decathecting of historical treatments, without regard to their authors' amateur or professional status, as one moves
from those with adult memories of the struggle (Schouler, Von Holst),
childhood memories (Rhodes, Hart), and no memories at all (Turner,
Dodd). But the deliberate negotiation of a mutually acceptable version of
the sectional conflict, of a consensual "usable past," was clearly a central
strategy of the new professionals. In effecting the reconciliation, they had
a powerful ally, whose contribution was indispensable: the pervasive
racism which—across regions, classes, and political persuasions—dominated the thought of the period.

Racism increased in the United States in the course of the nineteenth
century, particularly in educated circles, as it acquired the authority of
science. Social Darwinists were racists, of course, but so were Darwin's
opponents: Louis Agassiz wrote of the "natural impossibility" of racial
equality, since blacks were "in natural propensities and mental abilities

---

[16]*Reminiscences of an American Scholar* (New York, 1934), 289–90.

. . . indolent, playful, sensual, imitative, subservient, good-natured, versatile, unsteady in their purpose, devoted and affectionate." A physician who had undertaken a comparative study of black and white brains reported that "the one has a larger frontal region of the brain, the other a larger region behind; the one is subjective, the other objective."[17]

"Scientific" historians could hardly ignore the scientific consensus that blacks were genetically inferior. Albert Bushnell Hart was proud of his abolitionist heritage; he was the teacher and patron of W. E. B. Du Bois and of other black students at Harvard; there was no historian more energetic in promotion of black advance. At first he wavered, and was inclined to explain black deficiencies environmentally. Reviewing the literature which purported to demonstrate black inferiority, he conceded that "if provable, it is an argument that not only justifies slavery, but now justifies any degree of political and social dependence." Ultimately, he came down on the racist side:

The negroes as a people have less self-control, are less affected by ultimate advantages, are less controlled by family ties and standards of personal morality, than the average even of those poor white people, immigrants or natives, who have the poorest chance. . . . Race measured by race, the Negro is inferior, and his past history in Africa, and in America leads to the belief that he will remain inferior.[18]

Hart's conclusion was shared by other northern historians. James Ford Rhodes, citing Agassiz, said that "what the whole country has only learned through years of costly and bitter experience was known to this leader of scientific thought before we ventured on the policy of trying to make negroes intelligent by legislative acts." John W. Burgess wrote that "a black skin means membership in a race of men which has never of itself succeeded in subjecting passion to reason." For William A. Dunning, blacks "had no pride of race and no aspiration or ideals save to be like the whites." Ellis Paxson Oberholtzer quoted approvingly the southern observation that Yankees didn't understand the subject because they "had never seen a nigger except Fred Douglass." Blacks were "as credulous as children, which in intellect they in many ways resembled."[19]

[17]Agassiz to Samuel G. Howe, quoted in James Ford Rhodes, *History of the United States from the Compromise of 1850 to the Final Restoration of Home Rule in the South in 1877* (8 vols., New York, 1906), 6:37; Robert B. Bean, "The Negro Brain," *Century Magazine* n.s. 50 (1906): 784.

[18]Hart, quoted in James M. McPherson, *The Abolitionist Legacy: From Reconstruction to the NAACP* (Princeton, 1975), 337–38.

[19]Rhodes, *History*, 6:39; Burgess, *Reconstruction and the Constitution: 1866–1876* (New York, 1902), 133; Dunning, *Reconstruction, Political and Economic: 1865–1877* (New York, 1907), 211; Oberholtzer, *History of the United States Since the Civil War* (5 vols., New York, 1917–37), 1:73.

By the end of the century, American expansionism contributed its bit to the racist consensus. "Now that the United States has embarked in imperial enterprises," Burgess wrote in his history of Reconstruction,

the North is learning every day by valuable experiences that there are vast differences in political capacity between the races, and that it is the white man's mission, his duty and his right, to hold the reins of political power in his own hands for the civilization of the world and the welfare of mankind. . . . The Republican party, in its work of imposing the sovereignty of the United States upon eight millions of Asiatics, has changed its views in regard to the political relations of races and has at last virtually accepted the ideas of the South upon that subject.[20]

The near unanimous racism of northern historians—not, of course, peculiar to them—made possible a negotiated settlement of sectional differences in the interpretation of the Civil War and Reconstruction. By the 1880s and 1890s many southerners were, in varying degrees, willing to concede that secession had been unconstitutional, and that slavery, while its evils had been exaggerated by bigoted northerners, had been wrong, and had held back southern development. Increasingly, somewhat grudgingly, former Confederates expressed satisfaction with the outcome of the war. After all, as Senator John W. Daniel of Virginia, a former Confederate officer said, "The instinct of race integrity is the most glorious, as it is the predominant characteristic of the Anglo-Saxon race, and the sections have it in common." Insofar as the central contemporary issue was the continuation of white supremacy in the South, now accepted by all sections of northern opinion, the "lost cause" had perhaps not lost after all. Its supporters could afford to be gracious.[21]

Northern historians were more than willing to meet them halfway . . . and beyond. Most northern historians, especially of the older generation, were unbending on the constitutional issue. Von Holst's multivolume *Constitutional History of the United States* was one long legal barrage at the doctrine of states' rights. Burgess wrote that on constitutional questions, American history should be written from the northern point of view because it was, "in the main, the correct view. . . . Not one scintilla of justification for secession and rebellion must be expected." But as the century drew to a close—as a result of a racist downgrading of the Negro, the need for reconciliation of the sections, and the desire to strike a posture of impartiality, fairness, detachment, and objectivity—professional historians worked to revise previous northern views on several

[20]*Reconstruction and the Constitution*, viii-ix, 298.
[21]Daniel, quoted in Thomas J. Pressly, *Americans Interpret Their Civil War* (Princeton, 1954; 2d ed., New York, 1965), 153.

related questions. They became as harshly critical of the abolitionists as they were of "irresponsible agitators" in the contemporary world, they accepted a considerably softened picture of slavery, and they abandoned theories of the "slave power conspiracy." Above all, they joined wholeheartedly with southerners in denouncing the "criminal outrages" of Reconstruction, and this could lead to a reevaluation of moral judgments on other aspects of the conflict. Burgess acknowledged that "slavery was a great wrong, and secession was an error and a terrible blunder, but Reconstruction was a punishment so far in excess of the crime that it extinguished every phase of culpability upon the part of those whom it was sought to convict and convert." For his Columbia colleague William A. Dunning, Reconstruction was an unspeakable disaster, leading, among other atrocities, to "the hideous crime against white womanhood which now assumed new meaning in the annals of outrage." Its lesson was that slavery, while undesirable, had been a useful and natural modus vivendi between a superior and an inferior race.[22]

Through some give-and-take, a nationalist and racist historiographical consensus, which demonstrated historians' impartiality and objectivity, was achieved on the "middle period" of the nineteenth century. In fact, there was considerably more give on the northern side, more take on the southern. Carl Russell Fish, chairman of the AHA program committee in 1910, trying to persuade Andrew C. McLaughlin to deliver a paper, observed that "there is rather a disposition in the north at the present time to allow the southern view to go without any statement on the other side. This is a natural and commendable generosity, but it seems to me only fair that a sane conservative statement of the northern position should find some expression on the programme."[23]

There were several reasons for the imbalance. Of greatest importance, of course, was the consensual racism, which tilted matters toward the southern side. But there were other asymmetries. There were, so far as I have been able to determine, no northern historians employed in the South, while there were many southerners in the North: Woodrow Wilson, first at Bryn Mawr, then Wesleyan, then Princeton; Ulrich B. Phillips, who taught at Wisconsin, Michigan, and Yale; John W. Burgess, Benjamin B. Kendrick, and William P. Trent at Columbia; William E. Dodd at Chicago; Richard Heath Dabney at Indiana; John Spencer

---

[22]Burgess, *The Middle Period, 1817–1858* (New York, 1897), x-xi; Burgess, *Reconstruction and the Constitution*, 297; Dunning, *Reconstruction, Political and Economic*, 213–14; Dunning, *Essays on the Civil War and Reconstruction and Related Topics* (New York, 1931), 384.

[23]Fish to McLaughlin, 7 October 1910, Fish Papers, 1:1910–11.

Bassett at Smith; and the list could be extended. There were certainly no southern centers of pro-northern historiography to compare with Dunning's Reconstruction seminar at Columbia, which attracted scores of southern students, who under Dunning's direction turned out a stream of studies which lovingly detailed the iniquities of the period, state by state. Johns Hopkins, the first really "national" university, and the "birthplace of scientific history," perched just below the Mason-Dixon line, was a special case, which defies categorization. Its leading historian, Herbert Baxter Adams, was a northerner. But Adams, and the university, had many southern ties. Its location made it attractive to young southerners who could there imbibe scientific history without "crossing the line."[24]

There were sometimes, especially before the turn of the century, real or perceived constraints on southern historians in the North. Woodrow Wilson expressed his sympathy to his friend Dabney at Indiana in 1886: "In a word, you have gotten into a chair whose incumbent is expected to present, not the scientific truth with reference to our Constitutional history, whether that truth be on the side of Webster or of Calhoun in the great historical argument, but '*Yankee sentiments*'—sentiments agreeable to that eminent body of scholars, the Grand Army of the Republic." Constraints in the South were incomparably stronger, and lasted much longer—indeed, until well after World War II. Discussing "Some Difficulties of the History Teacher in the South," Dodd wrote:

Public opinion is so thoroughly fixed that many subjects which come every day into the mind of the historian may not with safety even so much as be discussed. . . . To suggest that the revolt from the union in 1860 was not justified, was not led by the most lofty minded of statesmen, is to invite not only criticism but an enforced resignation. . . . I have seen the very best books we have on American history ruled out of the South . . . for no board of education can live if it fail to heed the warning of the confederate veterans. . . . The confederate veteran works almost as great havoc in the field of history . . . as does the union veteran in the

---

[24]James W. Garner, in the Preface to his *Reconstruction in Mississippi* (New York, 1901), the first important monograph to emerge from Dunning's seminar, wrote that while passions had receded sufficiently for an unprejudiced study, the history of Reconstruction "ought to be written by a Southerner, for it is the Southerners who best understand the problems which the reconstructionists undertook to solve and the conditions under which the solution was worked out." This did not mean that it should be written "from the Southern 'point of view' or from any other 'point of view.'" The historian's job was "to *relate* and not to *judge*"; he "left the reader to form his own conclusions" (vii-viii). When Colonel J. Thomas Scharf of Baltimore donated his library to Hopkins in 1891 he wrote: "I have long noted with regret how imperfectly the history . . . of the Southern States has been written. . . . It is my hope that the Johns Hopkins University, founded by a Southern man in a Southern city, may see the way to do for the South what the Northern Universities have done for the North." (Quoted in Wendell H. Stephenson, "A Half Century of Southern Historical Scholarship," *Journal of Southern History* 11 [1945]: 6.)

neighborhood of the United States treasury. Time alone can work a cure in this respect.

John S. Bassett said in an 1897 speech that if an historian in the South departed from traditional views, "he has been denounced as a traitor and a mercenary defiler of his birthplace." (It was a prophetic observation: six years later Bassett's plea for racial conciliation, in the wake of a wave of lynchings, led to a furor which ultimately drove him to seek refuge in Northampton.)[25]

Albert B. Hart was, as his colleague Edward Channing said, "still unreconstructed." But he commissioned volumes by southern, or pro-southern, historians in the series he edited—especially for those volumes dealing with the crucial middle years of the nineteenth century. They generally resisted his quite mild editorial suggestions for the toning-down of their accounts. Woodrow Wilson wrote him, concerning a passage on Sherman's cruelty:

I have modified it a little; but really there is no more deliberately considered phrase in the book. I am painfully familiar with the details of that awful march, and I really think that the words I used concerning it ought to stand as a piece of sober history. . . . As for the treatment of prisoners in the southern prisons, that was doubtless heartless upon occasion; but the heartlessness was not part of a system, as Sherman's was.

When Hart penciled out Dunning's vituperative attack on Charles Sumner in his manuscript on Reconstruction for the *American Nation*

[25]Wilson to Dabney, 7 November 1886, Link, 5:384; Dodd, in *South Atlantic Quarterly* 2 (1904): 119–21; Bassett, quoted in Stephenson, "Half Century," 9. Bassett's most provocative assertion was to write that Booker T. Washington, although atypical of his race, was "all in all the greatest man, save General Lee, born in the South in a hundred years." Bassett closely averted dismissal from Trinity College (which later became Duke University) because Trinity's patron, Benjamin Duke, perhaps interpreting the attack on Bassett as part of a populist campaign against his influence, mobilized support for him. Ultimately, though his job was saved, he found the situation untenable and found employment in the North. (See the account in Metzger, "Age of the University," 445–50.) Although sometimes homesick for the South, and appalled by the Massachusetts winter, he was content at Smith. "I hope that I shall not be a failure," he wrote to William E. Dodd at the end of his first year, "the son of a confederate soldier, teaching the daughters of union soldiers the true story of the civil war and of reconstruction." (Bassett to Dodd, 28 April 1907, Dodd Papers, Box 5.) William P. Trent of Sewanee was another southern liberal—though certainly no egalitarian—who found it necessary to migrate to the North. As late as 1945, in an historiographical review, the leading southern historian Wendell H. Stephenson wrote that "Trent and other critical, liberal Southerners of the period exaggerated the evil influences of slavery. Dissatisfied with the uncritical writing of the past, they sought an objective approach to the study of southern history and literature. In their zeal for the new order, some of them went too far in repudiating institutions of the Old South and in condemning the philosophy of their ante-bellum ancestors." Trent, he reported sadly, had become "less objective." (Stephenson, "Half Century," 13–14.)

series, Dunning erased the suggested changes and sent the manuscript
back.[26]

In the extended negotiation of a consensus on slavery, the Civil War,
and Reconstruction, southerners managed to achieve a certain moral ascendancy. "Inflicting guilt," writes Phyllis Rose in her study of Victorian
marriage, "will always be a revenge of the less powerful, whether male or
female." And, indeed, there is something marital about the dynamics of
the reconciliation. Southerners saw themselves, and did their best to get
their northern colleagues to see them, as wounded victims of northern lies
and calumnies, which they were valiantly trying to correct. Any excesses
or exaggerations in the performance of that task were only attempts to
redress the balance. For northern historians to resist these efforts would
be "adding insult to injury," and would show a want of understanding
and sympathy. Reviewing a book by a young southern historian in the
AHR, U. B. Phillips criticized its old-fashioned partisan tone, but said it
was "one of the numerous protests from the thoughtful youth of the
South against the injustice done their people by the general American
historians." What better way for northern historians to show their fairness and impartiality than by bending over backward to appease the
southerners. In any case, the southerners cared so much more about the
points at issue that in the interests of professional comity it seemed wise
to let them have their way.[27]

IV

Although promoting Anglo-American reconciliation was by no means as
urgent an ideological task as that of helping to bring the American sections together, it, too, was part of the professional historians' agenda.
Like the revision of views on the Civil War, this program served several
functions, not the least of which was to promote and exemplify objectivity and impartiality. And, like reconciliation over sectional issues, the
new historiography of the colonial period and the American Revolution
was firmly rooted in contemporary racist doctrine.

In turn-of-the-century America it was not only blacks who were regarded as inferior. Not all whites were the natural rulers of society. If
blacks were, as one recent author has termed them, "outcasts from evolution," popular evolutionary thought, and those troubled by mass immi-

[26]Channing, quoted in Joyce, 28–29; Wilson to Hart, 20 December 1892, Link, *Papers*,
8:60; Dunning to Frederic Bancroft, 3 January 1908, cited in Philip R. Muller, "Looking
Back Without Anger: A Reappraisal of William A. Dunning," *JAH* 61 (1974): 333.
[27]Rose, *Parallel Lives: Five Victorian Marriages* (New York, 1983), 259; Phillips, review of
G. W. Dyer, *Democracy in the South Before the Civil War*, *AHR* 11 (1906): 715.

gration, distinguished between superior and inferior whites. The former were variously designated as "Teutons" or "Anglo-Saxons"; the latter were "Celts" (read "Irish"), "Latins" (the decadent French), and those from southern and eastern Europe. "They are beaten men from beaten races" said the amateur historian John Fiske, after he assumed the presidency of the Immigration Restriction League in 1894.[28]

"Anglo-Saxonism," the doctrine of the unique virtues and mission of that "race," had been circulating in the academic community since the 1870s. When Henry Adams was teaching at Harvard he taught himself Anglo-Saxon, and established, at his own expense, a special class of Ph.D. candidates to carry out research on Anglo-Saxon institutions. (Years later he ruefully observed: "Never did any man go blind on a career more virtuously than I did, when I threw myself so obediently into the arms of the Anglo-Saxons.") It was zealously promoted by Edward A. Freeman, Regius Professor of History at Oxford, during an American lecture tour in 1881–82. With the authority of scientific racialism, support for Anglo-Saxonism grew stronger as the century drew to a close. As an undergraduate at DePauw University in 1898, Charles Beard entitled his senior oration "The Story of a Race," and in it sung the glories of the "anglo Saxon race . . . the race of progress." The doctrine was not without its critics. William James, never one to be overly impressed with the pretensions of science, denounced it as "sniveling cant." Another minority voice was Mr. Dooley, who told Hennessy:

> The name iv Dooley has been th' proudest Anglo-Saxon name in th' County Roscommon f'r many years. . . . I tell ye, whin th' Clan an' th' Sons iv Sweden an' th' Banana Club an' th' Circle Francaize an' th' Pollacky Benivolent Society an' th' Rooshian Sons iv Dinnymite an' th' Benny Brith an' th' Coffee Clutch that Schwartzmeister r-runs . . . an' th' Holland Society an' th' Afro-Americans an' th' other Anglo-Saxons begin f'r to raise their Anglo-Saxon battlecry, it'll be all day with th' eight or nine people in th' wurruld that has th' misfortune iv not bein' brought up Anglo-Saxons.

But few historians dissented from Anglo-Saxonism, and most casually embraced it. Channing saw the nature of the "English race" as primarily responsible for America's political evolution.[29]

[28]Milton Berman, *John Fiske: The Evolution of a Popularizer* (Cambridge, Mass., 1961), 245.

[29]Adams to Henry Osborn Taylor, 4 May 1901, Worthington Chauncey Ford, ed., *Letters of Henry Adams, 1892–1918* (2 vols., Boston, 1938), 2:332; Beard essay quoted in Ellen Nore, *Charles A. Beard: An Intellectual Biography* (Carbondale, Ill., 1983), 10; James to Henry Rutgers Marshall, 8 February 1899, in Henry James, ed., *The Letters of William James* (2 vols., Boston, 1920), 2:88; Finley Peter Dunne, *Mr. Dooley: Now and Forever* (Stanford, 1954), 43–44; Channing, *A History of the United States* (6 vols., 1905–1925; reprinted, New York, 1925), 1:512.

Anglo-Saxonism provided support for American imperialism and for immigration restriction—causes congenial to many if not most professional historians. But for our purposes what is relevant about Anglo-Saxonism is its contribution to the revision of the history of the American Revolution. This contribution was both direct, stimulating historians to regret a quarrel with "race brothers," and indirect, insofar as it was a catalyst of the Anglo-American diplomatic rapprochement, which, in turn, led to revision of views on the Revolution for frankly pragmatic reasons.

The interpretation of the Revolution which began to emerge in the 1890s was the product of what has come to be referred to as the "Imperial school." Its leading figures were Charles McLean Andrews, Herbert Levi Osgood, and George Louis Beer. In their studies of the background of the Revolution—they rarely dealt with the Revolution itself—they disparaged American grievances, and often found the colonists ungrateful to Britain for the protection and fair treatment they had received. For most members of the Imperial school, the best vantage point from which to view the history of colonial America was that of the imperial administrators, with whom they sympathized and identified. (They were also considerably friendlier to the Loyalists—who around this time also began to receive sympathetic treatment in works by Moses Coit Tyler and Claude H. Van Tyne.) Some thought the Revolution avoidable, the result of misunderstanding and American selfishness. Others that it was the inevitable result of developments for which no one was to blame. All, in one way or another, regretted it.

The emergence of the Imperial school was, of course, overdetermined. Work in the British Imperial Archives could lead to an altered perspective. Identifying with the conservative and possessing classes of their own day, and with their values of order and stability, the members of the Imperial school naturally projected that identification back into the past. At the same time, their writings reflected their abhorrence of popular agitation and rebellion. After the Spanish-American War resulted in the United States acquiring an empire of its own, they sympathized with England's troubles in dealing with its colonies. The overwhelming majority of American professional historians in this period were of British descent, and in any case, they joined in the celebration of a shared cultural tradition.

The relationship between Anglo-Saxonism, a changed diplomatic climate, and the revision of views of the Revolution was made explicit by a number of historians. Albert Bushnell Hart, noting that a new, favorable attitude toward Great Britain had emerged in America at the time of the

Spanish-American War, urged that the American Revolution be taught as "a deep and broad Anglo-Saxon movement in which both sides had some rights and both had some wrongs." Moses Coit Tyler deplored the "race feud" that had separated America from England. George Louis Beer expressed the hope that in a new diplomatic climate, "the American Revolution will lose the great significance that is now attached to it, and will appear merely as the temporary separation of two kindred peoples." John Bach McMaster criticized contemporary textbooks in which "the schoolboy is taught to hate the only people on the face of the earth to whom we are bound by ties of race . . . the only people with whom it is possible for us to ever form a real and lasting alliance." The same argument was made by another historian when he offered a more favorable appraisal of Britain's role during the Civil War than had hitherto been common: "Today an undivided nation looks upon England not with the jealousies and suspicions of former days, but as a friendly power, and even as a possible ally in case of national danger."[30]

But besides representing an ideological service which historians could render to their conception of the national interest, and besides reflecting their own hopes, fears, and prejudices, the revised historiography of the Revolution was, as in the case of the negotiated consensus on the Civil War, a magnificent advertisement for impartiality and objectivity. The historical work of the Imperial school was a dramatic repudiation of the filiopietism of the older, "Whig" historians, a repudiation of their "twisting the lion's tail." It broke with the "factitious" and "spurious" patriotism of Bancroft's tradition, which had told a story of liberty against despotism, substituting an "intelligent, tolerant patriotism" which told of the sober evolution of institutions within a shared Anglo-Saxon community. (It is no accident that Andrews, a leader of the Imperial school, was the profession's harshest critic of Bancroft.) There was no significant protest from within the professional community against what today would be called the extreme "present-mindedness" of the new interpretation. It was the eminent amateur historian James Schouler who wrote Turner:

Just now we tend to a closer alliance of friendship with Great Britain, and it is in order to laugh at the earnest vehemence of our ancestors and the patriotic exag-

---

[30]Hart, "School Books and International Prejudices," *International Conciliation* 38 (January 1911): 12; Tyler, *The Literary History of the American Revolution, 1763–1783* (2 vols., New York, 1897), 1:ix; Beer, *British Colonial Policy, 1754–1765* (New York, 1907), 316; McMaster, "The Social Function of United States History," National Herbart Society for the Scientific Study of Teaching, *Yearbook* 4 (1898): 28; James Morton Callahan, *The Diplomatic History of the Southern Confederacy* (Baltimore, 1901), 274–75.

gerations of former school-history writers. But to go farther and argue that our
American independence was a sort of evolution, and that America had no just
grievance against England in 1775 . . . is a perversion of history. . . . Or to take our
own Civil War. I am said to write from a "Northern" standpoint; but one cannot
in truth picture both North and South . . . champions of human freedom and
champions of slavery, as equally right in their cause; though Americans on both
sides fought nobly and made patient sacrifice through conviction. In this day I
willingly let by-gones be by-gones and give the hand-grasp of fraternity for the
future; but the picture of our great four-years' struggle still preserves properly the
ideals and passions of the generation that fought it through.[31]

Professionals were neither more nor less present-minded or ideological
than their amateur predecessors. If their work was more systematically
racist than that of Bancroft, Motley, Parkman, and Prescott—and it
was—that is because they grew up in an intellectual climate in which
scientific racism was much more pervasive than it had been earlier in the
nineteenth century. Amateur historians in the era of professionalism were
influenced by the same intellectual currents as professionals. When the
first volumes of James Ford Rhodes's *History* appeared in the early
1890s, he was attacked by John W. Burgess and Woodrow Wilson for his
"abolitionist prejudices" which had resulted in an "antislavery pamphlet." By the time the last volume appeared, in 1906, Rhodes had totally
embraced the racist views of his critics. The work of the popular amateur
historian Sydney George Fischer on the Revolution was as Anglo-Saxo-
nist as that of any professional.[32]

For various reasons the work of professionals appeared to be less partisan. There was, for one thing, their stress on seemingly neutral institutional evolution. Also, they were addressing a more ideologically homog-
enous audience than the amateurs, who addressed the laity. There were
no poets within the professional community to point out to these historical M. Jourdains that they were speaking prose. Their austere stylistic
conventions, and the professional rejection of unabashed editorializing,
both adopted in the name of objectivity, meant that their ideological
assumptions and messages were less explicit than those of the amateurs.
Indeed, the assumptions at least were largely unconscious, and in consequence all the more powerful.

[31]Schouler to Turner, 25 May 1911, Turner Papers, Box 16.
[32]Wilson, "Anti-Slavery History and Biography," *Atlantic Monthly* 72 (1893): 272–74;
Burgess, review in *Political Science Quarterly* 8 (1893): 342–46; Fischer, *The True History
of the American Revolution* (Philadelphia, 1902). For the attribution of the (anonymous)
Atlantic review to Wilson, see Robert Cruden, *James Ford Rhodes: The Man, The Historian, and His Work* (Cleveland, 1961), 50; and for the evolution of Rhodes's views,
Cruden's chapter 8.

We have seen the ways in which professional historians' performance of ideological functions both reflected and reinforced their belief in objectivity. This was furthered by their social optimism. Their confident evolutionism gave an implicit moral meaning to history which made explicit moralizing superfluous. As Ranke's faith in history as the unfolding of God's grand design protected him from doubts about the objectivity of his labors, so the secular faith of the American professionals protected them. For them, as for Ranke, it guaranteed that their message, for all the austerity of its prose, was a profoundly moral one. There was no tension between disinterested scholarship on the one hand, and patriotic duty or moral engagement on the other: the former, through the self-evident ethical and political truths it revealed, satisfied the latter.

4

⊲══════════════════════════════════════⊳

A most genteel insurgency

Not all American professional historians before World War I accepted the orthodox scientific posture in toto. Especially among the elder statesmen of the profession there were those who retained elements of an earlier, pre-professional sensibility. Woodrow Wilson questioned the injunction to "Give us the facts, and nothing but the facts":

Without the colors your picture is not true. No inventory of items will even represent the truth: the fuller and more minute you make it, the more will the truth be obscured. . . . The investigator must display his materials, but the historian must convey his impressions. . . . The historian needs an imagination quite as much as he needs scholarship, and consummate literary art as much as candor and common honesty.

Edward Channing expressed a willingness to subordinate factual accuracy to a "truthful impression." He wrote that oftentimes the historian

must sacrifice absolute accuracy in detail and in perspective. If the impression produced upon his reader is truthful, it matters little whether all his dates are correct, all his names are properly spelled, or if all his facts are accurate. Indeed, his dates may every one of them be correct, his names may all be properly spelled, his facts may be absolutely accurate, and the impression left upon his reader be entirely false.

"It was all very well," wrote Albert B. Hart, "for Ranke to begin his lectures: 'I will simply tell you how it was.'" But, Hart asked, "did not his student really get 'how it was' as seen through the mind of Ranke?"[1]

[1]Wilson, "On the Writing of History," 1895 draft manuscript, in Arthur H. Link, ed., *The Papers of Woodrow Wilson* (Princeton, 1966–), 9:296, 304, 305; Channing, "The Present State of Historical Writing in America," *Proceedings of the American Antiquarian Society* 20 (1910): 430; Hart, "Imagination in History," *AHR* 15 (1910): 245.

More consequentially, in the years before World War I a number of new tendencies emerged within the historical profession. Some historians argued for the enlargement of the scope of history to include the social, economic, and intellectual as well as the political and constitutional. Connected with this development was a questioning of history's total separation from the social sciences. Some rather mild ideological heterodoxies emerged. A handful of historians suggested that the relationship of historical knowledge to contemporary problems be rethought. Though none of these movements for change directly challenged the prevailing norm of objectivity, in the long run many of the characteristics of the profession which provided indirect support for the idea were beginning to be subtly undermined. Perhaps in part because they sensed this, the traditionalists' reaction to the new developments ranged from nervous tolerance to barely controlled rage. Though these potential challenges to orthodoxy took several years to mature, any survey of the prewar scene which neglected them would be both deficient and distorted.

I

The first and most important development, of tremendous importance for historiography generally, but without obvious or immediate implications for epistemology, was a growing demand for the expansion of the scope of historical inquiry. The conservative evolutionism of the first generation of American professional historians had led them to stress the continuous growth of institutions—mostly, though not exclusively, political. In this they were faithfully following two major themes of nineteenth-century German historiography: a stress on continuity, against the threatening changes symbolized by the French and Industrial revolutions, and the hypostatization of the state. This tendency was most vividly exemplified in the "Teutonic-germ theory" which for several years dominated American historical thought.

Briefly summarized, the theory held that English and American democratic and liberal institutions had grown out of an institutional germ which developed in the forests of Germany in the remote past, and was transported to Britain by the Teutonic tribes in the fifth and sixth centuries. They maintained these institutions (and their racial purity) intact by exterminating the racially inferior Celtic Britons. This seed was responsible for the development of English institutions. When, in the seventeenth century, the descendants of the Teutons carried the seed to America, it grew with renewed vigor in the forests of New England, blossoming as the town meeting. "The science of biology," wrote Herbert Baxter Adams, the most zealous American promoter of the theory, "no longer favors the theory of spontaneous generation. Whenever organic life occurs there must have been some seed for that life. . . . It is just as improbable that free local institutions should spring up without a germ along American shores as that English wheat should have grown here without planting." Adams, for many years, set his seminar students to work tracing the course of Teutonic germs. By the 1880s, the Teutonic-origins doctrine was generally accepted within the historical profession.[2]

The hold of the "germ theory" on American historians proved short-lived, and by the early 1890s many were disenchanted. Edward Channing noted that "The argument that because a New England town and a German village were each surrounded by a defensive wall, the one is descended from the other, proves too much. A similar line of argument would prove the origin of New England towns to be the Massai enclosure of Central Africa." But the most important influence leading to the abandonment of the theory was Frederick Jackson Turner's alternative explanation of the expanding frontier and the availability of free land as the foundation of American democratic institutions. The stock of Turner's frontier thesis, first advanced in 1893, rose as Adams's fell.[3]

The substitution of the frontier thesis for the germ theory as the conceptual framework of American history had implications for the scope of history. Both approaches were consistent with an evolutionary model, but with a significant difference. Though Darwinism explained evolution as the result of interaction between the organism and the environment, biologists in this period attended almost exclusively to the former. Historians continued to be centrally concerned with institutions, but Turner's "environmentalism" implied a shift in emphasis from the institutions themselves to the social and economic matrix in which they developed, prefiguring a later shift in biologists' focus.

Even before he advanced the frontier thesis, Turner, in his teaching at

[2]Adams, "The Germanic Origin of New England Towns. With Notes on Cooperation in University Work," *Johns Hopkins University Studies*, 1st ser., 2 (1882), 1. The relentless pursuit of remote origins in the seminar irritated J. Franklin Jameson; he wrote his father: "Friday was spent at our tiresome history meeting, where a fellow read a paper on the origin of the military system of England, which he traced back *nearly* to when our ancestors chattered in the tree-tops. He couldn't *quite*, because, as I suggested to him, standing armies were impossible among those who held on to branches by their tails." (Letter of February 13, 1882, Elizabeth Donnan and Leo F. Stock, *An Historian's World: Selections from the Correspondence of John Franklin Jameson* [*Memoirs of the American Philosophical Society* 42 (1956)], 21.)

[3]Channing, remarks in communicating a paper on "The Genesis of the Massachusetts Town and the Origin of Town-Meeting Government," Massachusetts Historical Society, *Proceedings*, 2d ser., 7 (1892): 250.

Wisconsin, and in early essays, had been pushing the claims of social and economic history.

Behind institutions, behind constitutional forms, lie the vital forces that call these organs into life and shape them to meet changing conditions. . . . The institutional framework of the nation may be likened to the anatomy of the body politic; its physiology is the social and economic life molding this framework to new uses. Here it is that we find the field for widest study.

Although little substantive work illustrative of the new approach was produced, discontent with the narrowness of previous historical work became more and more general among younger historians. At the same time that Turner was pressing for attention to the social and economic, James Harvey Robinson at Columbia was introducing intellectual history as a respectable subject. William E. Dodd was an enthusiastic promoter of Karl Lamprecht's *Kulturgeschichte*. With Dodd's appointment at the University of Chicago in 1908, Turner's move to Harvard in 1910, and Robinson's creation of a community of "New Historians" at Columbia, which included Charles Beard, Lynn Thorndike, and James T. Shotwell, the program of expanding history's scope was firmly based at the center of the academic establishment.[4]

Few could object in principle to this expansion in history's scope, which by adding some new layers of brickwork to the political and constitutional edifice of historical knowledge might make it a bit more rambling, but still finite. The shift in focus nevertheless caused considerable unease. When William M. Sloane retired as chairman of Columbia's History Department in 1915 he wrote to university president Nicholas Murray Butler that Robinson and Shotwell had made a departure from traditional Columbia history which was

well enough perhaps in principle but in extent amounting almost to a secession and to the creation of a new department; to wit the establishment of elaborate courses in the history of thought and culture. In these courses they teach didactically and from a modernist point of view . . . everything except history, as their colleagues understand it. Neither is expert in any one of the subjects as discursively treated, and the departments of economics and sociology have been disturbed by the trespass.

Jameson, in a letter to Turner, discerned a threat to objectivity in extending historical inquiry beyond the political and constitutional. In social history, he wrote, "You do not have definitely limited bodies of materials, handed down by authority, like statutes or other manageable series,

---

[4]Turner, "Problems in American History" (1892), *The Early Writings of Frederick Jackson Turner* (Madison, 1938), 73.

but a vast blot of miscellaneous material from which the historian picks out what he wants, and so the effort to document must often be a process of selection, and if selection, always open to the suspicion of being a biassed selection, or one made to sustain a set of views." (The observation is a telling illustration of the early historians' confidence that the approved methods in the traditional areas could avoid questions of selection and bias.)[5]

An obvious corollary of the extension of historical scholarship into social and economic realms was a call for the establishment of a closer relationship between history and the newly established social sciences. Robinson rejected the widely accepted distinction between ideographic (individualizing) disciplines like history, and nomothetic (generalizing) disciplines like the social sciences. Turner, when he joined the *AHR* editorial board in 1910, advised Jameson that "in order to bring our work into more vital touch with current interests and needs . . . we should enter the overlapping fields more—the borderland between history in its older conception, and economics, politics, sociology, psychology, geography, etc."[6]

If the responses to general calls for the expansion of history's domain were, for the most part, temperate, the suggestion that history should ally itself with the social sciences provoked a fierce reaction from traditionalists. Responding to a paper at the 1903 AHA meeting by a sociologist, George Lincoln Burr invoked the ideographic-nomothetic distinction:

The theme of history has . . . been, not generalizations, but the lives and deeds of individuals—individual men, individual peoples, individual states, individual civilizations. Its method has been, not biologic, but biographic. Its prime aim, however obscured now and then by the prepossessions, theologic or sociologic, of the historian, has always been, in the simple phrase of Ranke, to learn and to tell *wie es eigentlich gewesen*.

In the same discussion, Ephraim Emerton could "not help thinking that under the seductive name of sociology we are here meeting once more the ghost of our ancient enemy, the philosophy of history."[7]

---

[5]Sloane to Butler and the Board of Trustees, 20 April 1915, quoted in Richard Hofstadter, "The Department of History," in R. Gordon Hoxie et al., *A History of the Faculty of Political Science, Columbia University* (New York, 1955), 235–36; Jameson to Turner, 25 November 1927, Jameson Papers, Box 132.
[6]Robinson, "The New Allies of History" (1910), reprinted in Robinson, *The New History* (New York, 1912), 73; Turner to Jameson, 23 January 1910, AHA Papers, Box 276.
[7]Paraphrase of Burr's remarks in discussion by Charles H. Haskins, "Report of the Proceedings of the Nineteenth Annual Meeting of the AHA," *Annual Report of the AHA for the Year 1903* (2 vols., Washington, 1904), 1:36; Emerton's remarks directly quoted, in Haskins, "Report."

This concern was echoed by George Burton Adams in his AHA presidential address, in which he wondered whether the invasion of the domain of history by the social sciences meant a "recrudescence of philosophy," and augured "passing from an age of investigation to an age of speculation." It was particularly disturbing that "this demand for a philosophy of history is not now made by poets, philosophers, or theologians," but by men who "invoke the name of science." For Adams the entire development was a "hostile movement," an "attack upon our position, systematic and concerted." "Certainly," he complained, "their attitude towards traditional history has not been that of dutiful children towards a parent," an image reiterated by William M. Sloane, for whom the social sciences displayed "the amusing independence . . . of children living on a handsome allowance from their parents." Political scientists, Sloane said, "announce a return to the method of induction in their study, but . . . they play fast and loose with the determination, statement, and meaning of the facts"; the work of contemporary economic historians was "as purely theoretic and deductive, and arid as was for long the most of their science"; the accounts of sociologists were "composed in the light of a predetermined theory." Adams feared "the controlling influence of the imagination in the new history in comparison with the stricter scientific faculties."[8]

Concern about the reintroduction of hateful "philosophy" into history was not restricted to traditionalists. Robinson confessed that some of social science's "more exuberant representatives . . . remind the historian disagreeably of the now nearly extinct tribe of philosophers of history, who flattered themselves that their penetrating intellects had been able to discover the wherefore of man's past without the trouble of learning much about it." But writing to Adams concerning the presidential address in which Adams had sounded the alarm, he warned against confusing the "boundless insolence and arrogance" of the older philosophy of history and "the far more reasonable pretensions of the modern social sciences." Robinson acknowledged that "the sociologist, anthropologist, and economist have doubtless often thought too fast and too recklessly, and this has engendered an excessive reserve in the historian, who has sometimes flattered himself on not thinking at all." In the long run, he thought, there was "more risk in thinking too little than too much."[9]

Turner, characteristically, was more cautious, and more representative of professional sensibilities in his fear that in borrowing concepts from

[8]G. B. Adams, "History and the Philosophy of History," *AHR* 14 (1909): 224, 228–30; Sloane, "The Substance and Vision of History," *AHR* 17 (1912): 235–37.
[9]Robinson, "New Allies," 99; Robinson to G. B. Adams, 19 October 1910, Adams Papers, 15:214; "New Allies," 100.

the social sciences, the historian would become the "prisoner" of "a priori" hypotheses, which he would be unable to evaluate "objectively." Accordingly, he was much more guarded in his endorsement of the social sciences, and much of his 1910 AHA presidential address was devoted to warning against dangers in their use.[10]

Early in his career Turner thought he had found a way of squaring the circle, by taking over from a geologist colleague a quixotic procedure which would avoid the problem of "parental affection for a favorite theory." The scientist or scholar had only to "bring up into view every rational explanation . . . develop every tenable hypothesis."

The investigator thus becomes the parent of a family of hypotheses: and by his parental relations to all, he is forbidden to fasten his affections unduly upon any one. In the nature of the case, the danger that springs from affection is counteracted. . . . The investigator at the outset puts himself in cordial sympathy and in parental relations . . . with every hypothesis. . . . Having thus neutralized the partialities of his emotional nature, he proceeds with a certain natural and enforced erectness of mental attitude to the investigation, knowing well that some of his intellectual children will die before maturity, yet feeling that several of them may survive. . . . If all rational hypotheses relating to a subject are worked coequally, thoroughness is the presumptive result.

Turner's own well-known failure to complete the synthetic work everyone expected of him is the best and most devastating judgment on this absurd and impossible program. But his enthusiastic embrace of it illustrates how historians' horror of the "preconceived notion" made them ambivalent toward new theoretical approaches which simultaneously promoted and threatened the goal of objectivity.[11]

II

The New Historians were "new" not just methodologically, but ideologically as well. Turner, Robinson, Beard, and here one must add the name of Carl Becker, were also "Progressive Historians."[12] The conservative

[10]"Social Forces in American History," reprinted in Turner, *The Frontier in American History* (New York, 1920), 311–34.

[11]Thomas C. Chamberlain, "The Method of Multiple Working Hypotheses" (1890), reprinted in *Science* 148 (1965): 754–59.

[12]"New Historians" is a designation generally given to the Columbia group around Robinson and Beard, and one which emphasizes methodology; "Progressive Historians" describes a descent from Turner and Beard, and emphasizes substantive interpretations of American history. The usage employed in the historiographical literature generally depends on the subject under discussion. Because Turner prefigured many New Historical themes, and Robinson, though a Europeanist, was the ultimate Progressive, all three of these men—plus Becker, the student of both Turner and Robinson, and an "associate member" of both groups—are here treated as both New and Progressive historians.

evolutionism of traditional historiography seemed to them inappropriate to the spirit of the age in which they lived. Commenting in 1914 on George Macaulay Trevelyan's assertion that it was a decline in the literary quality of historical writing which accounted for its decreasing popularity, Becker found the answer elsewhere:

In politics and morals the [French] Revolution unsettled all the old foundations . . . and men turned to the past with immense enthusiasm in order to rediscover there the principles of ordered social life. . . . But in our own day, when we are again, somewhat as men were in the eighteenth century, seeking a "new freedom," when we are less intent upon stability and more insistent upon "social justice," the past seems unable to furnish us what we want. The past seems to be on the side of vested interests. . . . The orthodox method of interpretation, surviving from an age when men feared revolution more than they do now, no longer ministers to the rising demand for social regeneration.[13]

Discontinuity, rather than continuity, struck these men as the most noteworthy feature of the recent past, and the political conclusions which they drew from that discontinuity led them to distance themselves a bit from the dominant conservative political outlook of the historical community. In this, as in other respects, they prefigured the partial and limited breakdown of the orthodox ideological consensus that became more marked in the interwar years.

The reputation of the eldest member of the group, Turner, was based on his noting an important symbol of discontinuity in the 1890 census report: the observation that it was no longer possible to map a frontier line on the American continent. Turner anticipated the New Historians who followed him in basing his work on the perception of discontinuity, and anticipated them also in drawing accommodationist, but not oppositional conclusions from the discontinuity. What would become of the democratic ethos with the disappearance of its foundation, the availability of free land? Turner's answer was progressive reform, but he was careful not to be publicly identified with the cause because "I am determined not to get so interested actively that I shall not be able to tell my story without prejudice or the reasonable apprehension of bias on my part by the class." His attempt to win a place in American historiography for the West, was, as Hofstadter termed it, a "most genteel insurgency . . . quieted at a relatively early point by its own success"; his historical writing, from beginning to end, was informed by his "deep and calm satisfaction with the American past."[14]

---

[13]Review of Trevelyan's *Clio, a Muse*, in *The Dial*, 56 (16 April 1914): 336.
[14]For Turner's reformism, see, e.g., "Social Forces," 319, 321; for his diffidence about active involvement, his letter to Edgar Eugene Robinson, 26 December 1911, printed in

In his consistent optimism and confidence in progress, his iconoclasm, and his hatred of what he perceived as a stultifying conservative orthodoxy, Robinson was perhaps a more representative Progressive Historian than Turner, who was reflexively cautious and establishmentarian. Robinson, too, was impressed by discontinuity in history, and, like Turner, placed it within the context of progressive advance. The principal task of the historian, and especially the intellectual historian, was to point out anachronisms in our thinking, to clear away inherited rubbish, to explain the circumstances that had given rise to inherited shibboleths. With a confidence that has been expressed from the Enlightenment to Freud, Robinson believed that to understand the origin of "error" was to exorcise it. "We are," he wrote, "in constant danger of viewing present problems with obsolete emotions and of attempting to settle them by obsolete reasoning. This is one of the chief reasons why we are never by any means perfectly adjusted to our environment."[15]

The key word in this passage is "adjusted"; the term "accommodationist" might have been coined with Robinson in mind. The trouble with conservatives was that they refused to see the "adjustments" and "accommodations" that had to be made to changing circumstances. Fervent in his denunciation of contemporary social evils and injustices, he never suggested that there might be anything fundamentally wrong with the social

---

Wilbur R. Jacobs, ed., *The Historical World of Frederick Jackson Turner. With Selections from His Correspondence* (New Haven, 1968), 136–37; Hofstadter, *The Progressive Historians: Turner, Beard, Parrington* (New York, 1968), 105. The frontier thesis, with its celebration of both American uniqueness and the ideology of individualism, was generally appealing to American historians, but especially to those not on the East Coast. It enabled them to do regionally and locally celebratory work under the aegis of this paradigm, and let them do professionally valued work with locally available archives, without the library resources of which the East Coast had almost a monopoly. Turner, among others, believed that the West represented distinct values. There were, he wrote to a fellow midwesterner, "characteristic Western ideals and social traits" resulting from "the experience of the frontier and of the democratic aspirations of the pioneer period" which were "in the position to arrest tendencies in the industrial life and society of the East, which if continued might result in the European type." (Turner to Becker, 21 January 1911, Turner Papers, Box 16.) There was also within the profession an undercurrent of "western" (i.e., midwestern) regional resentment of the East Coast historical establishment which survived until after World War II. Around 1910 Turner advised Clarence W. Alvord to moderate his assertions of the significance of the West for understanding British colonial policy lest he "offend the easterners without accomplishing any good result." "This most excellent advice was tinder to my essentially radical mind and so a few days later, I put my thought in the most emphatic manner possible and placed it at the opening of the book so that nobody could miss it" (Alvord to Becker, 23 April 1917, Becker Papers). At a time when the historical profession was dominated by the northeast, all four of the major New/Progressive Historians were from the Midwest. The common tie may have contributed to their sense of solidarity—and estrangement.
[15]*New History*, 251–52, 22.

order. Neither capitalists nor capitalism ever received any systematic criticism. The problem was to bring the system, and most particularly men's conceptions of the system, into line with current needs.

The apotheosis of Robinson's approach is in his essay "History for the Common Man": "What can be done for that very large class of boys and girls who must take up the burden of life prematurely and who must look forward to earning their livelihood by the work of their hands. . . . What . . . is it most necessary for them to know of the past in order to be as intelligent, efficient, and happy as possible in the life they must lead and the work they must do?" It was "of the greatest moment to society that this class should be recruited from those who have been taught to see the significance of their humble part in carrying on the world's work, to appreciate the possibilities of their position, and to view it in as hopeful a light as circumstances will permit." The New History held out an answer, by substituting for the old-fashioned history of battles and kings, history which would

explain our industrial life and make its import clear . . . explain the existence of the machine which the operative must tend . . . the very last link in a chain of marvelous discoveries reaching back hundreds of thousands of years . . . how the present division of labor, of which he seems to be the helpless victim, has come about . . . the rather hard terms on which things get made rapidly, cheaply, and in great quantities.

As the culmination of what seems an overly broad caricature of the creation of false and anodyne consciousness, "besides giving the artisan an idea of social progress and its possibilities, history will furnish him a background of incidental information which he can utilize in his daily surroundings, and which will arouse and foster his imagination by carrying him, in thought, far beyond the narrow confines of his factory."[16]

Carl Becker, the student of both Turner and Robinson, was, like his teachers, squarely in the Progressive camp. His first book, *The History of Political Parties in the Province of New York*, was a landmark in Progressive History, with its thesis that the issue of "who should rule at home" was as important as that of "home rule." After an early breakaway from the Republican upbringing which all four men shared, he was always a man of the moderate left, but his temperament was neither activist nor combative, and his political heterodoxies generally took the form of Voltairean shafts and ironic asides, not direct advocacy.

Very different was Charles Beard, the most activist, and the most

[16]Ibid., 132–33, 139–43.

heterodox, of the four major figures in the New/Progressive History. As Turner clung to the conservative edge of Progressivism, Beard was in the wing of the movement which shaded off into reformist socialism. As a graduate student in England he had, in collaboration with the Christian Socialist Walter Vrooman, and with the cooperation of English socialists and trade unionists, founded Ruskin Hall—a labor college which would "take men who have been merely condemning our institutions and . . . teach them how, instead, to transform them"; training students "to *raise* rather than *rise out of* the mass of their fellow workers." As a young instructor at Columbia he campaigned for the Socialist Morris Hillquit in New York's Lower East Side, and rang doorbells to raise money for the shirtwaist workers' organizing campaign.[17]

Like Becker and Robinson, Beard found Jaurès's *Histoire socialiste de la Révolution française,* "in spite of its ominous title and flaming red covers . . . a monumental contribution to the literature dealing with the Revolution." Like Robinson, Beard followed the economist E. R. A. Seligman, in his crude reduction of Marxism to economic determinism. Marx's theory, Robinson explained, "was misused by himself and his followers. . . . But in the sobered and chastened form in which most economists now accept the doctrine, it serves to explain far more of the phenomena of the past than any other single explanation ever offered." In his review of Jaurès, Beard explicitly endorsed Seligman's view that embracing Marx's philosophy of history need not lead one to endorse his socialism. It was Seligman's vulgar economic determinism which informed what was the greatest *succès de scandale* of the New Historians: Beard's *An Economic Interpretation of the Constitution of the United States,* published in 1913.[18]

No work produced by a professional historian before World War I ever stirred up such a storm. None of Beard's professional colleagues responded with quite the extravagance of the headline in the Marion, Ohio, *Star*: SCAVENGERS, HYENA-LIKE, DESECRATE THE GRAVES OF THE DEAD PATRIOTS WE REVERE.[19] Not quite, but almost. For Orin G. Libby the book gave aid and comfort to agitators, was "a partisan appeal to class prejudice" and "unmitigated rot." Edward

---

[17]Quoted in Ellen Nore, *Charles A. Beard: An Intellectual Biography* (Carbondale, Ill., 1983), 43.

[18]Beard, "A Socialist History of France," *Political Science Quarterly* 21 (1906): 120; Robinson, *New History,* 50–51.

[19]The news story which followed, based on reviews, said that Beard's book, "if correctly represented," was "libellous, vicious and damnable" and all patriotic citizens "should rise to condemn him and the purveyors of his filthy lies and rotten aspersions." (Nore, 63.)

S. Corwin saw it as "bent on demonstrating the truth of the socialistic theory of economic determinism and class struggle." The year after the book's publication, Andrew C. McLaughlin, in his AHA presidential address, without mentioning Beard by name, deplored materialistic interpretations of constitutional history, then pointedly skipped over the Constitution in a later section reviewing recent historiography.[20] Beard's exaggerations and provocativeness of expression made him particularly vulnerable. Thanking Max Farrand for a sympathetic review, he explained that he had been "more belligerent than was necessary and overemphasized a number of matters in order to get a hearing that might not have been accorded to a milder statement."[21]

In fact, as more than one commentator has pointed out, what was distinctive and provocative about Beard's treatment, and what produced the uproar, was not the assertion that the propertied classes had seen the Constitution as a bulwark against popular democracy. Many other scholars had held this view; but what his predecessors had approved as sane statesmanship aimed at controlling the irresponsible demos, Beard deplored—with what Justice Holmes called "a covert sneer." When, a few years later, Beard's student Arthur Schlesinger was about to publish his dissertation, he was advised by Beard not to mention his name in the preface: "It is the red rag to the historical bull."[22]

The Progressive Historians had lost faith in the conservative political pieties of their profession; the four men here discussed had lost their religious faith as well. The belief in secular progress was "almost the only vital conviction left to us." This belief—their confidence in the prospect of continuous amelioration "within the system"—kept their ideological heterodoxy from transgressing the limits of the accommodationist.[23]

[20]Libby review in *Mississippi Valley Historical Review* 1 (1914): 114; Corwin review in *History Teacher's Magazine* 5 (1914): 66; McLaughlin, "American History and American Democracy," *AHR* 20 (1915): 260, 265. William A. Dunning, in a 1917 summary of American historical writing during the previous thirty years, completely ignored his colleague's work ("A Generation of American Historiography," reprinted in his *Truth in History and Other Essays* [New York, 1937], 153–64).
[21]Beard to Farrand, 5 May 1913, Farrand Papers, 1:44.
[22]Holmes to Sir Frederick Pollock, 12 July 1916, in Mark DeWolfe Howe, ed., *Holmes-Pollock Letters: The Correspondence of Mr. Justice Holmes and Sir Frederick Pollock 1874–1932* (2 vols., Cambridge, Mass., 1942), 1:237; Beard to Schlesinger, 23 July 1917, Schlesinger Oral History Memoir, 2:322.
[23]Becker, "Some Aspects of the Influence of Social Problems and Ideas upon the Study and Writing of History," *American Journal of Sociology* 18 (1912–13): 663. The irreligiosity of the four, like their common midwestern origin, was mildly unusual, and perhaps also served to further set them apart from their colleagues.

III

The New Historians' commitment to progressive reform led naturally to
a stress in their programmatic statements on the present uses of history:
what would later be denominated, pejoratively, as "presentism." "The
value of our studies," the young Turner wrote to his teacher, "is not
merely historical. . . . If properly worked up they will be a basis for State
legislation—and that is the right kind of historical work." History, Turner said in an often quoted remark, should "hold the lamp for conservative
reform." Beard's *Economic Interpretation of the Constitution* was the
outstanding prewar example of presentist practice. Years later he said that
in writing it he "had in mind no thought of forwarding the interests of the
Progressive party or of its conservative opponents." In a narrow sense the
claim can be sustained: by 1913 he had rejected affiliation with the Progressives. But since his college days he had believed that the Constitution
had been "the bulwark of every great national sin—from slavery to monopoly." In a 1913 letter to Robert M. La Follette, Beard said that he
didn't agree that it was "a question of 'restoring' the government to the
people"; it was "a question of getting possession of it for them for the first
time." His book would show La Follette why he believed that "we did
not have a 'government of the people' to start with."[24]

Becker's presentism was explicit: "Historical thinking . . . is a social
instrument, helpful in getting the world's work more effectively done."
But of all the New Historians it was Robinson who was most insistent
that the study of the past was justified by the services it could render to
the present: "Our books are like very bad memories which insist upon
recalling facts that have no assignable relation to our needs, and this is the
reason why the practical value of history has so long been obscured. . . .
The present has hitherto been the willing victim of the past; the time has
now come when it should turn on the past and exploit it in the interests of
advance."[25]

Given the frequency with which historians are enjoined to "love the
past," it is not surprising that remarks such as this have led a number of
later commentators to charge Robinson with being "antihistorical." As
one historian recently remarked disapprovingly, "It seems fair to say that
he had a certain contempt for the past as such." "Loving the past" is, of
course, as much a value-laden attitude, which the historian holds in the

[24]Turner to William F. Allen, 31 December 1888, cited in Jacobs, *Historical World*, 124;
    Turner, "Social Forces," 323–24; Beard, preface to the 2d edition of *Economic Interpreta-
    tion of the Constitution* (New York, 1935), vi; Beard, quoted in Nore, *Beard*, 55.
[25]Becker, "Some Aspects," 642; Robinson, *New History*, 22, 24.

present, as is contempt for it. This truth is sometimes obscured by the historical profession's unreflective acceptance of the empathic imperative implicit in Ranke's historicist axiom that "each epoch is immediate to God." As we have seen, Ranke—and in this he was followed by the vast majority of European and American historians before 1914—limited his investigations to the history of states; it was these "thoughts of God" that were "immediate" to Him in each epoch. (Ranke differed from his contemporaries and immediate successors only in the ecumenism, the absence of narrow nationalism, with which he pursued this program.) So long as history was restricted to the political realm, it was a nationalist/patriotic imperative to "love the past" of one's institutions. The development of German historiography in the early and mid-nineteenth century is inseparable from nationalist frustration: since Germans could find neither unity nor glory in their country since the Middle Ages, they lovingly studied the glorious medieval German empire, and were—not innocently—heavily subsidized in the venture by the Prussian government. The English historical tradition was one of answering the question: How did our marvelous liberal and representative institutions develop? Even if one thought the later institutional forms a vast improvement over what had been, a loving regard for early and intermediate stages was appropriate.[26]

This orientation was shared by American institutional evolutionists— and by and large was as common among progressives as among conservatives. But when a linear progressivism was joined to an expansion of history into the social and intellectual realms, the situation was changed. It was easy enough—indeed, requisite—that one take a "loving" attitude toward landmarks in the development of liberty and constitutionalism, or toward moments in the expansion of national power. But the study of social and intellectual history involved immersion in a past made up of exploitative privilege, grinding rural poverty, and blind superstition (i.e., religion). How could one demand that the Progressive Historians, with their commitment to democracy, the fruits of modern industry, and the scientific outlook love *that* past? (Not surprisingly, Turner, with his recurrent regression to the celebration of a pastoral arcadia, was considerably more "past-minded" than the others here discussed.)

In any event, the "presentism" of the New Historians was, though distinctive and important, less heterodox in the eyes of their contempo-

[26]David Gross, "The 'New History': A Note of Reappraisal," *History and Theory* 13 (1974): 57. The situation in France was the exception that tests the rule. There, where institutional evolution was radically discontinuous and controversial, those who loved the institutions of the Republic hated those of the Ancien Régime, and vice versa.

raries than in the judgment of later commentators. Virtually all turn-of-
the-century historians believed in the manifest contemporary utility of
what they were doing. When they used the phrase "the past for its own
sake," as they occasionally did, they were, like Saint Augustine on marriage, speaking "by way of permission, not of commandment." They
were saying that historical study *need* not be immediately useful, not that
it *was* not. Historians like William M. Sloane, who detested the New
Historians, saw the historical discipline as "concerned not with the past
as a whole but only with so much of it as accounts for the present."

What is still alive and is still read . . . will be found to contain all [these] elements.
. . . It either rescues noble deeds from oblivion for the emulation of posterity; or,
it explains the present by just so much of the past as is needed; or it connects
causes and results in human conduct so as to establish law; or more likely still it
does all three in varied proportions.

"The past for its own sake" was not a significant element in prewar
professional ideology. The style and the thrust of the New Historians'
presentism was new: not "philosophy teaching by example," which,
despite disclaimers, many "scientific" historians believed in; not the celebration of national heroes or legitimation through continuity; but practical reform. The content of the rebels' presentism was new; their insistence that history should be useful in the present was not.[27]

IV

How much of a challenge did these unorthodox tendencies pose to norms
of historical objectivity? The entry of new approaches into history's domain had a threatening potential—especially the environmentalist intellectual history of Robinson and Becker, which could call into question all
norms, including the historians' own. The proposed alliance of history
with the social sciences was, as has been suggested, Janus-faced, working
toward both the reinforcement and the transvaluation of objectivity; but
at a minimum it undermined older, "no preconception" ideas of how
objectivity was to be achieved. The New Historians' ideological heterodoxy was, before the war, sufficiently moderate, and limited by social
optimism, to pose no major threat to the support for objectivity which
consensus offered; when optimism cracked, so did the consensus. The
new style of presentism, with its overt rather than covert principles of
selection, and open acknowledgment of didactic purposes, opened the

[27]Sloane, "Substance and Vision," 247–48.

door to a much more thoroughgoing critique of the posture of objectivity.

One can describe, in the abstract, a descent of attitudes concerning objectivity: that it is easily attainable, that it is attainable with difficulty, that it is unattainable but approachable, and that, at least in most common usages, it is an incoherent ideal. Despite some inductivist rhetoric which suggested that there was an algorithm for attaining objectivity, there were few who held the first position. To hold that objectivity was easily attainable would devalue professionalism—the rigorous training which made it possible for scientific historians to achieve that which the amateurs could not. Though one theme in the ideology of professionalism asserted that historical scholarship, like any other program of systematic inquiry, was necessarily social and collective, obstacles to objectivity were seen as primarily personal. The historian had to undertake the arduous task of purging his consciousness of every vestige of parti pris or bias; had to sufficiently polish his perceptual apparatus, or prose style, so that it accurately reflected reality. There was a belief, congenial to this morally strenuous age, that the obstacles to objectivity could be overcome by an effort of will.

Naturally historians differed in their estimation of their own success in this effort, and the differences were doubtless due less to any formal epistemological doctrines than to aspects of their character ("grandiosity," "negative capability"). William A. Dunning, who believed that he had attained a "purely impersonal and objective attitude" was startled and dismayed when his student Charles Merriam suggested that by "observing carefully his analyses and measuring emphasis and omission" it would be possible to infer his political preferences from his writings. Charles M. Andrews, writing in the evening of his life, denied that his writings had any relationship to his background: "It all depends on the conditions, not of one's ancestry or environment, but of one's temperament and freedom from bias."

This natural tendency has undoubtedly been cultivated by other circumstances— by my training at the Johns Hopkins University . . . and my desire to follow the leadership of the men in my profession for whom I had the greatest respect and admiration. I have never tried to analyze the exact state of my own mind and do not care to do so now. . . . I have had no philosophy of life and have never developed any system according to which I ought to shape my life.

Others, more modestly, acknowledged that no one, including themselves, could totally escape the influence of background and experience— but often suggested, particularly with respect to regional partisanship, that their background was balanced in such a way that influences canceled each other out. John W. Burgess made a point of the fact that he had been a Tennessee Unionist. Woodrow Wilson wrote a northern colleague that

Though born in the South and bred in its sympathies, I am not of Southern-born parents. My father was born in Ohio, my mother in England. Ever since I have had independent judgments of my own I have been a Federalist (!) It is this mixture of elements in me—full identification with the South, non-Southern blood, and Federalist principles—that makes me hope that a detachment of my affectionate, reminiscent sympathies from my historical judgments is not beyond hoping for.

Very occasionally an historian would report that despite his best efforts, he felt his consciousness to be shaped by insurmountable external circumstances.[28]

While a good deal of the building-block rhetoric—working toward the final completion of the edifice of objective historical truth—suggests that at least collectively, objectivity was attainable, it is probably a mistake to draw too sharp a line between those who thought it attainable and those who thought it merely "approachable." (Among other reasons, to do so would be to attribute to these historians a concern with precision of formulation on these questions which they did not have.) Objectivity, if conceived as only approachable was not a less worthy goal; indeed, it might be more worthy. In the early nineteenth century Schleirmacher had said that any worthwhile program for man should be impossible of achievement—only an unachievable goal could bring out man's powers to the full, so that we could know what they were. Statements about the attainment of total objectivity were not unlike statements about the "perfectibility of man"—although sometimes formulated in ways which suggested great naiveté, more often than not they were assertions about the possibility of moving ever closer to that goal. We cannot engage the dead in dialogue, though by preceding their words with our questions we sometimes pretend that we can. My strong suspicion is that, if pressed,

[28]Merriam, "William Archibald Dunning," in Howard W. Odum, ed., *American Masters of Social Science* (New York, 1927), 137; Andrews, quoted in Irving N. Fisher, "The Charles McLean Andrews Collection," *Yale University Library Gazette*, July 1967, 39–40; Burgess, *Reminiscences of an American Scholar* (New York, 1934), 289–90; Wilson to Albert B. Hart, 3 June 1889, Link, *Papers*, 6:243. In a similar vein Dodd wrote Jameson that he had been "reared in an old Whig county of North Carolina. . . . My mother . . . many a time told me that slavery had been a great wrong." (7 January 1918 letter, Dodd Papers, Box 9.) For an (atypical) acknowledgment by an historian that his attitudes had been firmly shaped by external factors, see Andrew C. McLaughlin, "American History and American Democracy," 258–59.

few turn-of-the-century historians would have said that objectivity was more than "approachable"—but they *would* have said that.

The final and greatest step in the descent, the disavowal of objectivity as an ideal, was not taken by any professional historian, "New" or "Old," before the war, with the exception of Becker. There are, to be sure, statements by others of the New Historians which, taken out of context, or read too literally, without allowance for excess or mindlessness of expression, seem to suggest that objectivity was a chimera—that it was not even a coherent goal.

"Each age," Turner wrote in 1891, "writes the history of the past anew with reference to the conditions uppermost in its own time." But this (by no means trivial) observation was, in context, hardly more than a suggestion that contemporary concerns might usefully direct our attention to hitherto neglected aspects of the past.[29] In his 1910 AHA presidential address there appeared a passage which some have seen as "anticipating" relativism:

> Those who insist that history is simply the effort to tell the thing exactly as it was, to state the facts, are confronted with the difficulty that the fact which they would represent is not planted on the solid ground of fixed conditions; it is in the midst and is itself a part of the changing currents, the complex and interacting influences of the time, deriving its significance as a fact from its relations to the deeper-seated movements of the age, movements so gradual that often only the passing years can reveal the truth about the fact and its right to a place on the historian's page.

But what appears to be—and perhaps to a very limited extent is—a questioning of the very foundation of empiricism, "the fact," was, in context, primarily an historicist criticism directed at the pretensions of social science, which offered its propositions as timeless truths, and a protest against historians being reduced to the role of data gatherers for social scientists. Immediately following this frequently cited passage he said:

> The economic historian is in danger of making his analysis and his statement of a law on the basis of present conditions and then passing to history for justificatory appendixes to his conclusions. . . . The historian . . . may doubt . . . whether the past should serve merely as the "illustration" by which to confirm the law

[29]*Early Writings*, 52. This reading is reinforced by Turner's repeating the observation, almost verbatim, in his "Social Forces in American History" (1910), and then glossing it as follows: "Each age finds it necessary to reconsider at least some portion of the past, from points of view furnished by new conditions which reveal the influence and significance of forces not adequately known by the historians of the previous generation." (*Frontier*, 323.)

deduced from common experience by *a priori* reasoning tested by statistics. In fact the pathway of history is strewn with the wrecks of "known and acknowledged truths" of economic law, due not only to defective analysis and imperfect statistics, but also to the lack of critical historical methods, of insufficient historical-mindedness on the part of the economist, to failure to give due attention to the relativity and transiency of the conditions from which his laws were deduced.

Though his language sometimes resembled that later employed by relativists, Turner was no relativist.[30]

Beard, who, with Becker, was the most influential interwar relativist, came to question the posture of objectivity only after 1918. Echoing Turner, he wrote in 1908 that "written history . . . from generation to generation . . . takes on new form and content, as the interests and intellectual preoccupations of mankind change"; his former students at Columbia recalled his emphasis on "the fickle and mutable nature of truth"; but the prewar Beard still believed in what he would later deride as the "noble dream" of objectivity.[31]

Like Beard's, Robinson's decisive break with the idea of historical objectivity only came after the war, but unlike Beard's, his epistemological dissidence began in the early years of the century. E. P. Cheyney recalled the Robinson who came to the University of Pennsylvania in the 1890s, after receiving his Ph.D. at Fribourg under Von Holst, as "fundamentally a well-trained, solid historical student with all the rigorous conceptions of historical research and statement that even the most pharisaical of the profession can lay claim to." It was Robinson's reputation as a close student of original source material that led Burgess, on Dunning's suggestion, to bring him to Columbia in 1895. One former student recalled that "when I first knew him back about 1903, he was not visibly disturbed by the forces of modernism." Another, who took his course in 1904–5, wrote that "he was as sympathetic with the scientific method championed by Ranke as he was unsympathetic with the political content of Ranke's historical writing." Robinson's student James T. Shotwell recalled that "historical scholarship controlled with relentless precision his reconstruction of the past. Textual criticism was the foundation of everything."[32]

[30]*Frontier*, 332–33.
[31]"Politics," in *Columbia University Lectures on Science, Philosophy and Art, 1907–1908* (New York, 1908), 8; Nore, *Beard*, 155–56.
[32]Cheyney to Harry Elmer Barnes, 3 March 1926, quoted in Barnes, "James Harvey Robinson," in Howard W. Odum, ed., *American Masters of Social Science* (New York, 1927), 334; ibid., 348 (no attribution, but probably Preserved Smith); Hayes, manuscript autobiography, in Hayes Papers, Box 8, 2:25; Shotwell to Barnes, 15 April 1926, quoted in Barnes, "Robinson," 349.

It is difficult to know precisely what turned the epistemologically orthodox Robinson of his Pennsylvania and early Columbia days into the moderate skeptic he had become by 1910. Was it the experience of teaching his famous intellectual history course in an increasingly environmentalist fashion? Did his daily lunches at Columbia with John Dewey revive the early influence of William James, the only teacher whose permanent influence he acknowledged, and lead him to embrace a "pragmatic theory of truth"? Or was it the experience of collaborating on a present-oriented textbook with his younger activist colleague Beard? In the absence of direct evidence, we can only speculate.

In any event, by the eve of World War I, Robinson had made a point of stressing the "relativity" of historical knowledge, but with a significant qualification which applies to the views of the other New/Progressive historians as well. History, he wrote, "should not be regarded as a stationary subject which can only progress by refining its methods and accumulating, criticizing, and assimilating new material." Historical truth was "relative," but "this relativity is conditioned by our constant increase in knowledge. . . . With our ever increasing knowledge . . . our opinions must necessarily change. To what may be called the innate relativity of things . . . we have added a dynamic relativity which is the result of rapidly advancing scientific knowledge, which necessarily renders all our conclusions provisional." Small wonder that a contemporary reviewer of *The New History* termed it a "timely . . . restatement of the scientific position."[33]

Prewar confidence in progress generally, and progress in scientific knowledge in particular, was a powerful limitation on the critique of historical objectivity. It blurred the line between those who thought objectivity approachable, though unattainable, and those who came close to questioning it as an ideal. Before the war, optimism was the great solvent of doubt in the epistemological as in the ideological realm. History, Robinson said, "is bound to alter its ideals and aims with the general progress of society and of the social sciences": who could doubt that as successive stages in the development of mankind became more rational and democratic, successive historical truths would become more accurate?[34]

That one man could we may infer from the fact that one man did. Carl Becker's 1910 essay "Detachment and the Writing of History" shows clearly that by that date all the elements of his later critique of the posture

[33]*New History*, 25, 130; Clarence W. Alvord's review, *Nation* 94 (1912): 457.
[34]*New History*, 25.

of objectivity were firmly in place. Whereas Turner's questioning of "the fact" was, as we have seen, more apparent than real, and directed against theorists rather than empiricists, Becker questioned the very notion of "cold facts" and "hard facts"; the fact, he wrote, was "almost impossible to distinguish from 'theory,' to which it is commonly supposed to be so completely antithetical." Going further than Beard would a generation later, he denied that the traditional distinction between (scientific) analysis and (interpretive) synthesis could be maintained. He doubted that interpretations would ultimately converge on the basis of scientific consensus: short-term convergence occurred "because there is, in every age, a certain response in the world of thought to dominant social forces." No historical synthesis could be "true" except "relatively to the age which fashioned it."[35]

Perhaps the most distinctive feature of Becker's prewar relativism was that, unlike Robinson's, it was self-referential. Robinson, as one commentator has observed, "might be called an 'environmental-relativist' when destructively criticizing ideas which he disliked, and a 'progressive-absolutist' when praising ideas of which he approved." Becker's skepticism extended to the progressive pieties to which he himself gave allegiance. In his review of *The New History*, with whose program he was in sympathy, he pointed out "a fundamental difficulty": Robinson could provide no fixed "standard of value" with which to answer the question "What, after all, is progress?"[36]

But Becker's radically skeptical writings appear to have had no discernible impact on historians before the war. (They generally appeared in nonprofessional journals.) When his writings were not misunderstood, they were greeted with a slightly nervous benevolence. Charles H. Haskins of Harvard, who had been one of Becker's undergraduate teachers at Wisconsin, wrote his former student that his criticisms of "Detachment and the Writing of History" were directed to "matters of omission rather than commission. . . . I realize . . . that your immediate business was rather to puncture certain prevalent misconceptions than to discuss how much practical truth might be left in them." Becker was known to most members of the profession as the author of Progressive monographs on the colonial period, and, above all, for his incisive and witty essay "Kansas," the highlight of the Festschrift presented to Turner in 1910.

[35]*Atlantic Monthly* 106 (1910): 524–36, reprinted in Phil L. Snyder, ed., *Detachment and the Writing of History: Essays and Letters of Carl L. Becker* (Ithaca, N.Y., 1958), 10, 15, 23, 28.
[36]Robert Allen Skotheim, *American Intellectual Histories and Historians* (Princeton, 1966), 80; Becker review of *The New History* in *The Dial* 53 (1 July 1912): 21.

Claude H. Van Tyne of the University of Michigan wrote Turner that he had found Becker's previous work "thorough, scholarly, patiently but heavily executed. Now, however, appears his essay, in your memorial volume, which is a brilliant, interpretative bit of work, written with real literary charm, and withal sound and convincing. It has revolutionized my opinion of his intellectual possibilities." The grace and optimism of "Kansas," unlike the corrosive skepticism of "Detachment," was a message to which the historical profession in 1910 could respond. Becker, unlike his contemporaries, did not need the catalyst of war, or a concomitant abandonment of social optimism, to turn him into a thoroughgoing relativist. Those forces, and others which will be discussed in succeeding chapters, had to unfold before he would win attentive listeners—and allies.[37]

The New Historians, with their varying degrees of dissent from orthodox epistemology, remained a minority within the historical community. But they were hardly marginal to the profession. By the beginning of the war, both Robinson and Becker were on the *AHR* editorial board. And, in the political jargon of a later day, they "had momentum." They were certainly attractive to many in the new generation of graduate students, who, before too many years had passed, would become leaders of the profession. To those of the students prepared to be challenged and stimulated, to look at history afresh, the representatives of the New History at Columbia were much more interesting than those who were purveying the Old.

Arthur Schlesinger, who was a graduate student on Morningside Heights just before the war, recalled that Dunning and Osgood "confined themselves to wholly traditional subject matter": Dunning's lectures "hardly did more . . . than repeat what he had already said in print" while Osgood "was a dry-as-dust lecturer who seldom lifted his head from his handwritten manuscript." But James Harvey Robinson's course on European intellectual history (dubbed by students "The Downfall of Christianity") was "the most provocative of any I took at Columbia and the source of endless argument among the students." Beard's "engaging personality invested everything he said with breathless interest. . . . These men, moreover, were more than just bookish people. They had been, or were still involved, in civic activities or governmental affairs, and in an undefinable way this, too, lent greater authority to their teaching."[38]

[37]Haskins to Becker, 18 October 1910, Becker Papers; Van Tyne to Turner, 16 February 1911, Turner Papers, Box 16.
[38]Schlesinger Oral History Memoir, 1:36–39.

Writing to William E. Dodd in 1913, James T. Shotwell expressed his confidence that "it will not be long before we shall be able to ignore to some extent the pious old gentlemen who attempt to hold down orthodoxy in history. All we have to do is to turn out our material and the world is ours."[39]

[39]Shotwell to Dodd, 23 January 1913, Dodd Papers, Box 10.

PART II

Objectivity besieged

5

Historians on the home front

In both European and American historiography there has been a tendency, over the last generation, to question the earlier view of World War I as a great watershed in intellectual history, and to point out that many important postwar currents had not only their roots but their first flowering in the decades before 1914. No doubt this is true, particularly for the study of the literary and artistic avant-garde, and for work on the cutting edge of philosophy and science as well. Even in the case of historians, a case could be made, as suggested in Chapter 4, for locating a turning point around 1910, rather than in 1914–18. However, concerning the "objectivity question," the dissident currents which emerged within the historical profession in the years just before the war were limited and hesitant. There was no change in the orientation of even a substantial minority before the interwar years. And, for a number of reasons, the war seems to me a more appropriate point to begin the discussion of that change—a change usually discussed with reference to the explicit "relativist" theses of Carl Becker and Charles Beard, but which, as we shall see, was a considerably more widespread, albeit minority, phenomenon.

The war posed a fundamental and sweeping challenge to the profession's posture of disinterested objectivity; to its pride in the distinction between the tendentious, superpatriotic, and propagandistic historical writing of benighted amateurs, and the austere detachment and evenhandedness of the professional. Many historians lost the optimism and faith in progress which, as we have seen, had grounded their faith in objectivity. And the war itself became the subject of interminable historical controversy, undermining faith that professional historical scholarship would converge on a consensual objective truth. Whereas before the war, American historians were largely isolated from modernist currents in philosophical, scientific, and social thought, after it, these currents became a significant factor in the rethinking of historiographical issues.

I

Between the summer of 1914 and the spring of 1917, American historians were no more successful than their compatriots in heeding President Wilson's injunction to be "impartial in thought as well as in action." Of the two opposing pulls on historians—attachment to Germany, where so many had studied, and the Anglophilia which the profession had in recent years done so much to promote—the latter was by far the more powerful.

There were, to be sure, a few for whom the German academic tie was decisive—"a powerful bond of connection between the two countries," said John W. Burgess, who had not only studied in Germany but had also been the first Roosevelt Professor at the University of Berlin in 1906. Long before the war he had become disturbed by the American tilt toward England.

If Great Britain is our motherland, Germany . . . is the motherland of our motherland; and when the Americans consent to dwell under the same diplomatic roof with the mother who has chastised them, they are not going to allow the grandmother, who has always taken their part, to be left out in the cold. . . . Britons will do well to . . . lay aside their imagined grievances against the Germans, their natural friends, and cease coquetting with the Romanic peoples, who, if ethnical, social and moral opposition breed enmity, may be called their natural enemies.[1]

After the outbreak of the war, Burgess struggled mightily to reverse the pro-Allied tide in the United States. To the dismay of other historians he argued, in books published in 1915 and 1916, that Germany had been the innocent victim of Entente imperialism and aggression.[2]

[1]"Germany, Great Britain and the United States," *Political Science Quarterly* 19 (1904), 9–10, 14. Burgess argued that German grandparents and American grandchildren shared racial traits absent in the intervening generation. During the Norman Conquest the Teutonic characteristics of the native English had become infected with French blood, which altered their character. When Englishmen came to America, however, the hardships of the wilderness scraped off the "Norman-French" taint, and brought "the German element in the English character again to the front." (*Germany and the United States* [New York, 1909], 8.)
[2]*The European War of 1914: Its Causes, Purposes, and Probable Results* (Chicago, 1915); *America's Relation to the Great War* (Chicago, 1916). Albert Bushnell Hart denounced him privately as a "doddering old idiot"; "an example of the American perverted by too close contact with Germany and German ideas." (Hart to Frank Taussig, 6 April 1915;

The German government, from the outset of the war, tried to use the academic connection to promote sympathy for their cause. The philosopher Rudolf Eucken and the biologist Ernst Haeckel announced the formation of a German University League. American professors would surely, on the basis of their graduate student experience, "know what German culture means to the world"; they expressed confidence that American scholars would accept the German interpretation of the war.[3]

If this was indeed their expectation, they were to be disappointed. The great American pilgrimages to Germany had been dwindling to a trickle in recent years, as the quality of the best American graduate training came to surpass that customarily offered in Germany. Nor had historians' German experience necessarily led to sympathy for the Hohenzollern regime. Many students' enthusiasm for *Wissenschaft* had been balanced by repugnance for *Militarismus*. And by the early years of the twentieth century the increasingly strident nationalism of German historical scholarship had offended many of its former admirers.

With the exception of a handful of older men like Burgess, Germany was to reap no political profit from the academic connection. Within three weeks of the outbreak of the war, William E. Dodd wrote his wife that he was "almost ashamed that I have my doctorate from such a people . . . the enemy of mankind in this war."[4] Nor did ethnic connection offer much more. The 1915 AHA program committee, arranging a panel on war issues, thought to achieve balance by including an historian of German extraction, William E. Lingelbach of Pennsylvania; he turned out to be more anti-German than any of the other participants.[5]

As might be expected, a number of fervently Anglophile historians

---

Hart to F. E. Chadwick, 18 October 1915: both cited in Carol S. Gruber, *Mars and Minerva: World War I and the Uses of the Higher Learning in America* [Baton Rouge, La., 1975], 49.) After the American declaration of war both books were withdrawn from circulation.

[3]Gruber, *Mars and Minerva*, 20.

[4]Letter to Mattie Dodd, 25 August 1914, Dodd Papers, Box 11. However, during the first two years of the war, Dodd kept up correspondence with his revered teacher, Erich Marcks.

[5]Cephas D. Allin to George M. Jones, 15 January 1916, cited in Gruber, *Mars and Minerva*, 47. One partial exception to this rule was Ferdinand Schevill of the University of Chicago, who before American entry into the conflict published the moderately pro-German *The Making of Modern Germany* (Chicago, 1916). He took, he acknowledged in the preface (vi), "a sympathetic approach," but one he hoped did "not preclude that patient search and philosophic objectivity which should be the historian's staff and scrip upon his pilgrimages. Moved by the desire to understand in order to explain, I have put to myself the question which, according to Ranke, should light the way for every worker in the field of history: *Wie ist es eigentlich gewesen?*" Schevill's pro-Germanism made his subsequent life at Chicago acutely unpleasant, and by the 1930s his position on "objectivity" was very different.

were strong interventionists. Indeed, George Louis Beer, together with George B. Adams of Yale, Dana C. Munro of Princeton, and James T. Shotwell of Columbia formed a semisecret organization to more effectively promote the allied cause by arranging propaganda which would "seem to originate in the West" rather than, as was the case, in the more interventionist East. At the same time, some historians, like Edward P. Cheyney of the University of Pennsylvania, a Quaker, opposed American intervention to the last. Albert B. Hart embodied the professional aspirations of many historians, if not their behavior, in laboring, until the eve of America's entry into the War, to separate his pro-Allied sentiments from his scholarly writing. In *The War in Europe: Its Causes and Results*, and in a series of other works, he attempted to balance rights and wrongs in the two camps, and endorsed the Wilsonian slogan of "peace without victory." The great majority of historians, like most other Americans, stayed aloof from the controversies surrounding the war. The only concerted action involving substantial numbers of historians was a 1916 petition urging representations to the German government for the release from internment of the Belgian historians Paul Fredericq and Henri Pirenne—offering them, if need be, temporary positions in the United States.[6]

On one issue American historians had been united since the summer of 1914: they were appalled at the prostitution of academic standards, and particularly historical scholarship, in all of the belligerent powers. The first dramatic example of the cooperation of scholars in wartime propaganda was "To the Civilized World," a 1914 manifesto signed by virtually every leading German scholar and scientist—Albert Einstein was the sole important exception—endorsing the most outrageously false German official assertions on the origin and conduct of the war. This "pitifully feeble" manifesto, said James Harvey Robinson, was "the sign and seal of the success of German *Kultur* in making all her subjects accept the Kaiser and his decisions in exactly the same unquestioning and dutiful spirit in which the Jesuit accepts the organization of the Roman apostolic church

---

[6]Gruber, *Mars and Minerva*, 83–85; Hart, *The War in Europe* (New York, 1914). Hart's pre-intervention evenhandedness resulted in his name appearing on a list of pro-Germans in the intercepted diary of a German spy. By the time this came to light, at the close of the war, Hart had become a superpatriotic propagandist; he apologized to a subcommittee of the Senate Judiciary Committee for the excessive fairness of the 1914 book. William M. Sloane of Columbia and Preserved Smith (later of Cornell, but at the time without an academic position) were other historians who, in 1914–17, criticized one-sided treatments of the war. In later years Smith recalled that his criticisms had "brought me no little odium and petty persecution during the war, but I am glad to be able to cite them now as my only contribution to the Kriegsschuldfrage." (7 June 1926 letter to Harry Elmer Barnes, Barnes Papers, Box 14.)

and the decrees of its head." Arthur O. Lovejoy pointedly drew the lesson of the manifesto for American scholars.

We have learned much from German scholars about historical "objectivity" and the niceties of historical criticism; what we receive when we look for an application of these principles to contemporary events, is a clumsy compilation of fictions, irrelevancies, and vulgar appeals to what are apparently conceived to be American prejudices. . . . The incident has in it too much of instruction and warning for Americans of the same profession, to be allowed to pass without notice. . . . It seems . . . to show that the professional class, in the country where it has played the greatest part, has signally failed, at the most critical moment in German history, to perform its proper function—the function of detached criticism, of cool consideration, of insisting that facts, and all the relevant facts be known and faced.[7]

A 1914 editorial in the *Mississippi Valley Historical Review* noted that

The war in Europe has brought the test to critical scholarship throughout the world, and, on the whole, scholarship has not withstood the strain. . . . The situation respecting historical scholarship calls for warning and rebuke. The daily papers abound in statements from scholars . . . in which the rumor is argued upon as though it were established, and in which the demonstrably untrue is certified to without attempt at truth. Scholars are of course human. . . . But when, from any side, they forget the difference between the scientific truths, established in the laboratory, and political convictions born in heat and tumult, they reveal the weakness of their scholarship and bring disgrace upon the world of letters. If there is today any place in which the world needs cold, hard truth, and refusal to be swayed from the proven fact, it is on the platform of the historian and in the columns of the critical journal.

In the following year another editorial reminded the American historian that the behavior of belligerent historians underlined the imperative that he "strip himself of all preconceptions and prejudices" so that "the exemplification of the past may safely be entrusted to him by the adherents of any and every creed, race, and political persuasion." In 1916 Andrew C. McLaughlin of the University of Chicago wrote of the urgent need to maintain objectivity and detachment amid the nationalistic excesses of wartime. In 1915 and 1916 the members of the American Historical Association heard presidential addresses which pointed to the wartime behavior of European historians and implored American historians to

[7]English translation of the 1914 German manifesto in Ralph Haswell Lutz, ed., *Fall of the German Empire, 1914–1918* (2 vols., Stanford, 1932), 1:74–78; Robinson, "War and Thinking," *New Republic* 1 (19 December 1914): 18; Lovejoy letter to the editor, *Nation* 99 (24 September 1914): 376.

guard their objectivity. "Woe unto us! professional historians, professional historical students, professional teachers of history," said H. Morse Stephens, "if we cannot see, written in blood, in the dying civilization of Europe, the dreadful result of exaggerated nationalism as set forth in the patriotic histories. . . . May we not hope that this will be but a passing phase of historical writing, since its awful sequel is so plainly exhibited before us." The lesson was clearly drawn, repeatedly invoked. And then the war came to America.[8]

II

For our purposes what is significant about the conduct of American historians in 1917–18 is not their wholesale abandonment of prewar norms of objectivity—a subject beloved of debunkers in the 1920s and later, who gleefully recalled the tendentious pseudoscholarship produced by the leaders of the profession during the war. For the present inquiry what matters is not the fact of propagandistic excesses, but the deep ambivalence experienced by many of the historians involved in them, their heightened awareness of strains in the concept of objectivity, and the long-run consequences of the experience for historians' reconsideration of their role and posture.

With the American declaration of war on Germany, doubts about the righteousness of the Allied cause all but disappeared within the profession. Virtually all shared the patriotic enthusiasm which, overnight, became de rigeur. Like Albert B. Hart, the University of Chicago Egyptologist James H. Breasted had held out against anti-Germanism before American entry into the war; like Hart, he attempted to keep up his old German academic associations and friendships. After April 1917, together with Hart, he became a propagandist for the National Security League, the most extreme and vitriolic of the wartime patriotic organizations. Breasted presented his son with the German dictionary he had used as a student, re-bound and retitled *Dictionary of the Enemy's Language.*[9]

Established historians were too old for active service, though some future historical luminaries saw combat. Some, like Ulrich B. Phillips, were commissioned in military intelligence. Others, disturbed at their

[8]Editorials in *MVHR* 1 (1914): 481, and 2 (1915): 303–4; McLaughlin, "Teaching War and Peace in American History," *The History Teacher's Magazine* 7 (1916), 259–64; Stephens, "Nationality and History," *AHR* 21 (1916): 236. Cf. George L. Burr, "The Freedom of History," *AHR* 22 (1917): 253–71.
[9]Charles Breasted, *Pioneer to the Past: The Story of James Henry Breasted* (New York, 1945), 227, 235.

inability to enter military service, sought the most satisfying form of direct involvement: Conyers Read worked with the Red Cross in France, Carl Russell Fish spent the summer working in a munitions factory, "the result of an effort to do something quite tangible . . . I believe that manual labor is now the prime necessity, and also that there are plenty of people who are willing to save the country by thinking and writing." Throughout the profession there was a desire to find the "moral equivalent of combat" in serving the national cause. But there were other considerations as well which account for the zeal with which historians sought to offer their skills to the crusade. [10]

In 1914 American historians had often blamed their European colleagues for promoting the nationalism which had led to war. With the entry of the United States into the conflict, the locus of guilt shifted: American historians' task was "repentance" and "expiation" for having insufficiently promoted American patriotism; for having left American youth morally unprepared for their military duties. [11] Germany had "used her schools for an ignoble purpose . . . we must not be behind her in the use of that weapon for . . . a very noble purpose." Participation of historians, as historians, in the war effort would demonstrate the usefulness of history. Everyone, wrote J. Franklin Jameson, was aware of the scientist's contribution to mobilization, but they were inclined to think of the historian as "occupied only with the dates and details of remote transactions having no relation to the fateful exigencies of the present day." Participation in the war effort would, wrote Frederick Jackson Turner to a colleague, enable historians to "feel better justified in following the scholars' calling," and, at the same time, "give greater zest to our research work." The war offered the historical profession "an opportunity for the greatest usefulness and for a corresponding increase in public estimation"; however "if it does not rise to this national emergency

[10]Fish to Charles H. Haskins, 7 June 1918, Fish Papers, Box 4. The University of Minnesota historian William Stearns Davis wrote Guy Stanton Ford that he was seeking employment as a carpenter in a shipyard since he felt that "This is one of the times when . . . the pen is NOT mightier than the sword." (Letter of 4 June 1917, quoted in Gruber, 114.)

[11]Arthur M. Schlesinger, "Mobilizing Ohio's Historical Resources: A Phase of Ohio's War Activities," *Ohio History Teachers' Journal* 11 (1918): 342. Historians had failed in this task because they were "for the most part ultraconservatives by temperament." They had, in his own state, failed to generate a "distinctive Ohio idea," a "distinctive Ohio tradition." As a result there was "lacking that stimulus that should incite an Ohioan to excel, not only because of the usual rewards of life but because he is an heir to and an upholder of the Ohio Idea. . . . The present situation of the world offers us the best opportunity we have ever had to do what we have hitherto left undone, namely, to formulate an Ohio idea and to insure its perpetuation for all time to come."

the sound teaching of history will receive a set-back from which it will not recover in this generation."[12]

Historians' wartime service took a variety of forms. A number of Europeanists did research on postwar problems for Colonel Edward House's "Inquiry." Others found their language skills mobilized for ferreting out signs of disloyalty in the foreign-language press. But historians' principal activity was the provision of serviceable propaganda; producing, in the phrase of the time, "a sound and wholesome public opinion." There was particular concern that "unwholesome" history might interfere with the war effort. Turner wrote to Max Farrand, in the first weeks of the war that

it will be possible for shallow historical argumentation and for sinister manipulators of public opinion to cloud the essential historical facts and conditions. . . . England's attitude, for example, in the period of the Revolution and of the Civil War can be made to serve as irritating and poisonous material by evilly disposed minds, to a degree unwarranted by all the facts, considered in the modern historical temper. . . . [M]en who have made a study of history . . . will feel a sense of treason to their cause if they are silent while pacifists set forth the meaning of American history.[13]

From the beginning, the enthusiastic desire to use history to promote patriotism and the Allied cause coexisted with uncertainty about how that could be accomplished without compromising the ideals of detachment, impartiality, objectivity. Some, to be sure, dealt with the problem by denying that any problem existed. Professor Samuel B. Harding of Indiana University, who as an official of the Committee on Public Information was responsible for promoting some of the most tendentious historical work, wrote that "not once have we consciously allowed our desire to win this war to do violence to our sense of historical truth." We would, he said, "gladly die for our country."

[12]Claude H. Van Tyne to F. B. Pearson, 31 August 1918, Van Tyne Papers, Box 2; Jameson, "Historical Scholars in War-Time," *AHR* 22 (1917): 831; Turner to Bernadotte Schmitt, 11 May 1917, Schmitt Papers, Box 2; Circular letter by Carl Russell Fish, 3 May 1917, Fish Papers, Box 4. After historians had been mobilized, Samuel B. Harding noted with satisfaction: "Before the war bookkeeping, typewriting, and various other vocational subjects were crowding subjects like History and English out of the curriculum. We shall have less cause to fear the eclipse of these subjects after the war. A knowledge of history, especially modern history, is now seen to be highly important even for the man of affairs. . . . The history teacher may look forward, therefore, with a certain degree of equanimity to the prospect which confronts him in the new era." ("What the Committee on Public Information and the National Board for Historical Service are Doing," *Association of History Teachers of the Middle States and Maryland: Proceedings* 16 [1918]: 16.)
[13]Andrew C. McLaughlin, "Historians and the War," *The Dial* 62 (1917): 428; Turner letter of 5 May 1917, in Wilbur R. Jacobs, *The Historical World of Frederick Jackson Turner with Selections from His Correspondence* (New Haven, 1968), 144–46.

The true scholar is one who would gladly die for Truth as he sees it. So, in the teaching of history, we must be on our guard to preserve the truth; not to do what Germany has done—not to falsify and distort truth in order to gain an advantage. The cause of the United States in this war, we believe, is a just and holy cause. . . . If I felt that the only way we could justify this war to our people was by falsification of the truth, I certainly could not work for it with the enthusiasm with which we all are endeavoring to work at the present time.

In the same vein, Harding's superior, Guy Stanton Ford, claimed that in the performance of his duties he had "been able to maintain the same standards that I have set for myself . . . as a member of the history department of the University of Minnesota."[14]

Some were less sanguine. "Perhaps few of us," wrote Andrew C. McLaughlin, "are able entirely to disentangle our scientific historical fibres from our swelling patriotic muscles, but most of us can try." McLaughlin wrote those words within weeks of American entry into the war; by late 1918 Albert Heckel, dean of Lafayette College, was skeptical of the result of the attempted disentanglement. Teachers, he said, "would have to be more than humanly endowed with the scientific spirit to avoid taking sides." The teacher "may be pardoned the feeling, though danger-ous, that at times there are possibly greater things in the world for him to accomplish than an absolutely cold recital of facts, and a pedantic slavish-ness to the so-called scientific spirit." "Of course," he added, "the histo-rian cannot sacrifice truth—even to patriotism." Claude H. Van Tyne of the University of Michigan went further in his impatience with the con-tinuation, in wartime, of the traditional scholarly posture. He did not, he wrote Jameson, like to see the *American Historical Review* "under the guise of intellectual neutrality, give its space to those cold-blooded intel-lectuals who assume a lofty superiority to the aroused moral indignation of the world. Only those who have cultivated mentality at the expense of moral fibre can at this stage take that attitude which they cynically call judicial."[15]

[14]Harding, 15; Ford, quoted in Gruber, *Mars and Minerva*, 141.
[15]McLaughlin, "Historians," 428; Heckel, "The War Aims Course in the Colleges," *Asso-ciation of History Teachers of the Middle States and Maryland: Proceedings* 16 (1918): 40–41; Van Tyne to Jameson, 26 April 1918, Van Tyne Papers, Box 2. In a similar vein, Frank Maloy Anderson of Dartmouth, praising a pseudoscholarly work by Charles D. Hazen on *Alsace-Lorraine Under German Rule*, spoke scornfully of unnamed scholars "for whom the Alpha and Omega of scholarship is restrained expression, a certain judicial pose." (*The History Teacher's Magazine* 9 [1918]: 326.) John Spencer Bassett of Smith thought some "concession to purposeful history" might be allowed since the "white-light-of-truth school" had so effectively routed "the filo-pietistics and the moralists" that the profession was "in no danger of going back to the old errors." ("The History Teacher and the League of Nations," *Association of History Teachers of the Middle States and Mary-land: Proceedings* 17 [1919]: 13.)

Few went as far as Van Tyne in his avowed renunciation of traditional scholarly norms. At the other extreme, there were a handful of historians who resisted participation in propagandistic activity, though in no case known to me on grounds of purely scholarly fastidiousness. Arthur L. Cross asked Edward P. Cheyney to contribute to a war-oriented series of "Timely Suggestions for Secondary School History." Cheyney wrote in reply that while he had opposed American entry into the war, he had "expected that when the die had been actually cast my doubts and disbeliefs would fall away and I would cheerfully turn in and do anything I could for our national success against our enemies."

But it has not turned out that way. Deeply and independently as I have thought upon the subject I have become more and more convinced that our going into the war was wrong, unnecessary, injurious to American freedom and world democracy and calculated to prolong the war—to the injury of the whole world. . . . But, you may say, what has all this to do with an outline of English History in the Tudor period? Why just that such an outline, drawn up in the [way?] that even you with your scholarly standards and fair minded habits would approve would be interpreted as a defense of the war, an indictment of other ideals than ours, . . . a seizing of the opportunity to impress on juvenile minds the superiority of our things; while what we and the world need just now in my judgment is recognition that other peoples' systems may also be good, that our own industrial and social system is grossly unfair and deficient. . . . Therefore when I think of putting before young people a plan of teaching English history in the 16th century, so as to show that the English and Dutch were right, the Spaniards and the Irish wrong, that the institutions then being developed were in themselves superior to those of other nations, with a constant suggestion of the righteousness of the present war and a deepening of the chasm between us and other nations—I simply cannot do it. Find somebody else—be a good fellow—and let me off.[16]

William S. Ferguson, chairman of the Harvard History Department reported a lack of enthusiasm among his colleagues for historical propaganda directed to the public. "The strongest dissentients are in this part indubitably the Irish. Now you know the situation here well enough to be aware that Harvard men are not particularly well pleased to do missionary work among them." If Ferguson and his Harvard colleagues were unhappy about addressing Irish audiences, the ancient historian William L. Westermann and some of his Wisconsin associates were displeased with the prominent role played by the New Historians on the National Board for Historical Service, the principal professional vehicle for propaganda activity. Carl Russell Fish reported that many of his colleagues

---

[16]Letter of 2 August 1917, Cross Papers, Box 2. Cheyney's relations with his professional colleagues were troubled throughout the war, though they smoothed out afterward.

were "afraid that the 'Robinson-Columbia' school of history has run us off our feet"; Westermann feared the Board's efforts would play into the "hands of the pseudo-historians of the ultra modern tendency." In consequence some members of the Wisconsin department participated only minimally and reluctantly.[17]

If few historians abstained from propagandistic work—and Cheyney appears to be the only one who did so on moral grounds—a certain nervousness, tentativeness, and ambivalence surrounded all aspects of the venture. In consequence, hypocrisy was a dominant motif: not a quality to be entirely despised, being, as La Rochefoucauld observed, "the tribute that vice pays to virtue." A prime example is the relationship between the AHA and the National Board for Historical Service, a volunteer organization set up in the first weeks of American participation in the war. Formed at the initiative of Jameson, managing editor of the *American Historical Review*, it was given office space by the *AHR* in the Carnegie Institution building; Waldo Leland, secretary of the AHA, also served as secretary of the NBHS; the principal outlet for NBHS materials was *The History Teacher's Magazine*, whose financing came from the AHA, and whose masthead after June 1918 carried the words "Edited in Cooperation with the National Board for Historical Service and under the Supervision of a Committee of the American Historical Association." But, it was repeatedly made clear, the AHA as such had nothing to do with the Board and its propagandistic work.[18]

So far as the *AHR* itself was concerned, Jameson thought the best course to follow was neither

that followed by the *English Historical Review*, which practically ignores the war, or that of the *Revue Historique*, which occupies many pages with war-matter, excellent of its kind, which, however, is more adapted to fortifying and encouraging its portion of the French public, than to stand the severest tests of impartial history. If we were in such an exigency as the French, it might be right to do this, but as it is, I think we should strive to avoid the printing of anything which twenty years from now will be subject to discount or looked upon by us with regret.

The *Review* should seek ways in which it "could be useful to the national cause . . . without at all stepping outside the proper province of such a

[17]Ferguson to Waldo Leland, 24 May 1917, quoted in Gruber, *Mars and Minerva*, 126; Fish to Charles H. Hull, 31 May 1917, quoted in Gruber, ibid., 127; Westermann to R.V.D. Magoffin, 10 July 1917, quoted in Harold Josephson, "History for Victory: The National Board for Historical Service," *Mid-America* 52 (1970): 217.

[18]See Josephson, "History for Victory," 207–9; Waldo G. Leland, "The National Board for Historical Service," *Annual Report of the AHA for the Year 1919* 1:163.

periodical." The judicious selection of topics—and treatments—was one
such way. He solicited, for example, an article on German rule in
Schleswig-Holstein which "would enable us all to judge how we should
like to be under German rule, which after all may be said to be the
essential point in our present national thinking."[19]

Properly chosen topics, properly treated, could "be of help to the
American public in right thinking respecting the war and the present
exigencies" on questions such as censorship. A letter from Jameson to
James G. Randall illustrates the disingenuousness and self-deception
which the historian's dilemma produced.

> Our newspapers are of course all banded together in a common endeavor, based
> upon a common pecuniary interest, to resist to the utmost any attempts to dictate
> to them as to what they shall print. . . . Things which are to be said upon the other
> side of the question are in danger of having no hearing at all. . . . The reasons for
> secrecy . . . can hardly find voice elsewhere than through such journals as this,
> which have no need to pay regard to newspaper opinion. . . . I should be very glad
> . . . if I could print in this journal an article showing what actually was the
> experience of our government with respect to newspaper disclosures during the
> civil war.

> This is not to say that I desire an article of propaganda or of one-sided argument.
> But the whole body of doctrine respecting the desirability of freedom of speech is
> so utterly familiar and the arguments on the other side are so much less constantly
> in people's minds, that I should have no hesitation in printing an article which,
> while consisting simply of historical facts, should nevertheless, by the facts thus
> massed, have a tendency to make people think as to what the proper limitations of
> newspaper freedom really are. With this in view, I should like to get an article
> which . . . should not dwell on the controversies aroused by efforts to restrain,
> not dwell mainly on the processes of restraint, but should on the other hand
> enlarge . . . upon the instances of disclosure (unwitting disclosure, almost en-
> tirely, no doubt) of military information which proved useful to the enemy—and
> similar aspects of the general theme.[20]

The activity which engaged the broadest range of historical talent was
the series "Timely Suggestions for Secondary School History," in which
scholars from a wide variety of fields cooperated to "show to what extent
if at all, the teaching of history in American schools should be made to
bear upon the present international situation of the United States . . . to
show teachers how far a selection of significant facts is warranted by true

[19]Jameson to Carl Becker, 2 May 1917, Becker Papers; Jameson to Laurence M. Larson, 4
May 1918, AHA Papers, Box 292.
[20]Letter of 17 July 1917, AHA Papers, Box 290.

historical method." This program was qualified by the warning that "There is one sacrifice no historian must make. He must not distort or pervert the facts of history to suit the present struggle." The most common theme of the contributions was continuous with the prewar tendency described in Chapter 3, the Anglo-American connection. Arthur Lyon Cross wrote on "Suggested Points for Emphasis in the Tudor Period" in a fashion which suggests that Cheyney had well appreciated the nature of the assignment he turned down:

At first sight the period of Tudor absolutism would seem to be a hopelessly empty place for the student of English origins of American free institutions to search. . . . However, the growth of free governments is a long process, compounded of many diverse, and at least on the surface, incongruous elements. . . . Tudor absolutism was peculiar . . . in that it served the needs of the rising agricultural and commercial classes. It might be argued that this is also true of the Hohenzollern, but the result has been different.

Andrew C. McLaughlin suggested that we "forget crazy old George III [who, as a number of other historians pointed out, was really a German] and . . . the rest of his tribe, and remember the men of the middle century, the creators of modern British liberalism—Cobden, Bright and Gladstone." One ancient historian reported that, in studying the distant forebears of our Italian allies, he found "qualities . . . duplicated in seventeenth century Salem"; one was "inevitably reminded of the eighteenth century struggle of the American colonies." For another, Roman history was "rich in parallels with present conditions":

The Germans are again invading northern France and Italy. . . . The invaders are murdering non-combatants or carrying them away into slavery; they are wantonly destroying monuments, priceless in their historical associations, irreplaceable in their beauty. . . . We have seen a race preeminent for its technical skill, reverting in its ideas of international morality to its ancestors of the wild German forests, to men like those described by Caesar, who measured their national glory by the extent of wasted country that surrounded their territory.

For still another, "The treachery to which Hannibal resorted in ambushing the Roman forces at Lake Trasimene has a modern parallel in von Hindenburg's butchery of the Russians in the swamps of Tannenberg." The medievalist James Westfall Thompson advised that

the present German Empire and the present program of German imperialism is the lineal descendant of the medieval empire both morally and politically. . . . Germany always has been, and still is, imperialistic and not national, in its political theory, its psychology, its past history and its present policy. It is not so far a cry as it seems from the hopes, aspirations, ambitions, policies, purposes, psychology of medieval Germany to the Germany of today. . . . Perhaps we may see in all this the persistence of a racial trait across the centuries.

The Americanist could also do his bit. In teaching the Civil War, said Carl Russell Fish, "it does not seem to pass the functions of the teacher of history to-day to call attention to the present enslavement of ten times as many individuals by Germany as were ever held in the South. Nor to call attention to Lincoln's reiterated insistence that the Civil War must end in victory, not compromise."[21]

Under the direction of Guy Stanton Ford, historians reached an even wider audience through their authorship of pamphlets—often, indeed, substantial volumes, though cheaply bound—for the Committee on Public Information. Though truffled with the apparatus of scholarship, they tended to be considerably less restrained than the material offered to schoolteachers. One genre was the documentary collection: two volumes on "German War Practices," edited by Dana C. Munro of Princeton; *Conquest and Kultur: Aims of the Germans in Their Own Words*, edited by Wallace Notestein of Minnesota. The chef d'oeuvre was the massive *War Cyclopedia*, which enlisted more historical talent than any other single venture. The entry on "Atrocities," written by Charles Beard, was typical of the volume in its uncritical retailing, and scholarly certification, of the most unrestrained propaganda: "The first months of the war witnessed the inauguration by Germany of a policy of terror in the invaded districts of Belgium and France, evidently premeditated. . . . Villages and towns were burned, wounded soldiers massacred, non-combatants shot or maimed, women outraged, and children tortured by the soldiery."[22]

The next-to-last pamphlet issued by the CPI, *The German-Bolshevik Conspiracy*, was subsequently its most embarrassing, because it was a pseudoscholarly certification of manifestly forged documents, which the American government had used to prove that Lenin and Trotsky were German agents. When the American press, following the lead of Euro-

---

[21]"To Those Who Remain at Home," *History Teacher's Magazine* 8 (1917): 212–13; Cross, "Suggested Points for Emphasis in the Tudor Period, 1485–1603," ibid., 8 (1917): 291–92; McLaughlin, "The Great War: From Spectator to Participant," ibid., 8 (1917): 187; William Stearns Davis, "The Study of the Roman Republic To-Day," ibid., 9 (1918): 14–15; William D. Gray, "The Great War and Roman History," ibid., 9 (1918): 138–39; John R. Knipfing, "The World War and the Teaching of Ancient History," *Ohio History Teacher's Journal* 30 (March 1918): 303; Thompson, "The Deeper Roots of Pan-Germanism," *Historical Outlook* 9 (1918): 360; Fish, "Internal Problems During the Civil War," *History Teacher's Magazine* 9 (1918): 199–200.
[22]Frederick L. Paxson et al., eds., *War Cyclopedia: A Handbook for Ready Reference on the Great War* (Washington, D.C., 1918), 22. For Beard's authorship of the entry, see George T. Blakey, *Historians on the Homefront* (Lexington, Ky., 1970), 51.

pean anti-Bolsheviks who had never swallowed the documents, raised questions about their authenticity, historians were once again mobilized. The CPI assigned Samuel N. Harper of the University of Chicago, and Jameson (who, not knowing Russian, couldn't read most of them) to examine the documents. Jameson described the task to a colleague as "a good seminary exercise, and . . . relatively not a difficult one." Their conclusions, while qualified on some matters of detail, certified the principal documents as genuine. *The Nation* labeled it a "sham investigation" deserving a "stern rebuke from every American historical scholar who values the good name of his profession."[23]

Of course, no such rebuke was forthcoming for the "grand old man" of the profession. But many historians viewed with alarm the activity of such zealots as Van Tyne, who, violating norms of professional solidarity, continually attacked colleagues for being lukewarm in their anti-Germanism.[24] And they were certainly not without private reservations about the activity with which they were involved. Charles H. Haskins complained that some of the CPI pamphlets reminded him of the "inspired narratives which Germany got out earlier in the war." Carl Becker suggested moderating propagandistic crudities—but with his typical diffidence dismissed his suggestions in advance as "perhaps mere hobbies of mine . . . not relevant to the purposes of the *Cyclopedia.*" Ferguson and Westermann implicitly criticized their colleagues by stressing, in their contributions to "Timely Suggestions," how limited was the power of historical analogy. Others, particularly those not yet well established, voiced concern over the effect of propaganda work on their scholarly reputation. One wrote of his "deep-seated aversion to the idea of being any man's hired hack writer or being placed in a position which would injure in any degree my reputation as being . . . all that a historical

[23]Jameson to Arthur I. Andrews, 24 January 1919, in Elizabeth Donnan and Leo F. Stock, eds., *An Historian's World: Selections from the Correspondence of John Franklin Jameson* (Philadelphia, 1956), 229; *Nation* 107 (23 November 1918): 616–17. There has been some controversy as to whether conscious dishonesty or self-deception was the principal factor at work in Harper and Jameson's certification. George F. Kennan takes the former view ("The Sisson Documents," *Journal of Modern History* 28 [1956]: 130–54); Gruber (*Mars and Minerva*, 151-57) argues—in my opinion more convincingly—for the second interpretation.

[24]Van Tyne publicly characterized the CPI's *Two Thousand Questions and Answers About the War* as "a masterpiece of pro-German propaganda." (*Nation* 107 [21 September 1918]: 312–13; Wallace K. Notestein to Arthur Lyon Cross, 27 September 1918, Cross Papers, Box 2; Blakey, *Homefront*, 89–97.) He embroiled himself in a long controversy with Frank Aydelotte, supervisor of the "War Issues Courses" for the War Department, over a text which he maintained "treats all matters from the point of view of the interests of Germany." (Van Tyne to Aydelotte, 11 November 1918, Van Tyne Papers.) Others associated with the National Security League were equally zealous—and burdensome to their colleagues.

student and writer ought to be." Wallace Notestein, after he edited *Conquest and Kultur*, wrote to George B. Adams of his hope that Adams would

find it a careful and fair piece of work. I have often wondered what you would think of this kind of work—propaganda work—whether a scholar should do it or not. . . . I hope the text and notes are accurate and painstaking and fair. I have tried hard to make them so. There are a few things I do not like but in them I had to yield to others. I would have kept my name out but Mr. Ford said otherwise—and Mr. Jameson advised me to put it in. If you and Professor [George Lincoln] Burr should feel the work unbecoming a student of theirs, I should regret having done it.[25]

Certainly the experience was rich in lessons about what a weak reed "professionalism" was in checking excesses. In fulfilling their propaganda tasks the wartime historians were almost always scrupulous about maintaining the formal norms of scholarship. Ford, for example, rejected work which had an unscholarly tone—which "sank to the level of vituperation and calling of names." Notestein, when editing *Conquest and Kultur*, followed all the scholarly rules of source criticism, accurate translation, and careful annotation, omitting documents of dubious provenance. But viewing the venture in the large, the participants could not escape the realization that one could quite easily be flagrantly propagandistic without violating norms of scholarship narrowly conceived. A project which failed to make the requisite point could be abandoned or modified. Ford suggested a pamphlet comparing German and American army field regulations in parallel columns, to show their fundamental difference in permitted norms of conduct. However, when the results were in he had second thoughts. "The more I look over our own field regulations with the citations from Moltke and other German writers and their utter confusion of necessity and right, the more doubtful I am about the effectiveness of the subject." The militarist and expansionist German pronouncements which Notestein amassed in *Conquest and Kultur* were individually accurate and collectively not an outrageously tendentious selection; in the absence of a parallel collection from the Allied camp they drove home the point that these characteristics were uniquely German.

[25]Haskins to Waldo G. Leland, 27 June 1917, quoted in Josephson, "History for Victory," 213; Becker to Ford, 13 May 1918, quoted in Gruber, *Mars and Minerva*, 149; Ferguson, "The Crisis of Hellenism," *History Teacher's Magazine* 8 (1917): 290–91; Westermann, "The Roman Empire and the Great War," ibid., 9 (1918): 86–87; D. D. Wallace to Van Tyne, 23 June 1918, Van Tyne Papers, Box 1; Notestein to Adams, 27 November 1917, Adams Papers, 18:265. Adams's response was reassuring. (Undated draft response, ibid., 18:265.)

The *War Cyclopedia* had entries on the Herrero insurrection, but not the Boer War; Karl Liebknecht, but not Bertrand Russell.[26] How did historians, in retrospect, evaluate the wartime experience? What lessons did they draw concerning the theory and practice of historical objectivity?

Those who had led the propagandist effort never gave any signs of second thoughts. Jameson, reviewing his wartime stewardship of the *AHR*, was well satisfied with the balance he had struck. Shotwell, looking back on his work with the NBHS, found it worthwhile, though perhaps not of great importance. Ford, in his later "Reminiscences," recalled that he had left the CPI "with the feeling that I would never regret or renege on anything that I did then. I never have." (The American Historical Association either approved, forgot, or forgave Ford's wartime role when it made him, on the eve of America's entry into World War II, executive secretary of the association and managing editor of the *Review*.)[27]

But the wartime experience was upsetting to many. Even while the war was on, Frank Maloy Anderson of Dartmouth thought historians' behavior cast doubt on the norms of scientific objectivity. Historians had been "claiming for history more than should be expected of it." William C. Binkley saw this as a widespread phenomenon: "doctoral candidates whose studies had been interrupted by the war returned to their history seminars to resume their apprenticeship in the application of the scientific method under the direction of men who, in many instances, were less sure of its finality than they had been a few years earlier." The economic historian Herbert Heaton reported the rumor that "those of our craft who wrote pontifically . . . during the war spent most of their subsequent vacations, sabbatical leaves and savings going round second-hand book shops, furtively buying and burning all the copies they could find of their war-time utterances."[28]

Some regarded the experience as an aberration, albeit a deeply disturbing one. J. W. Thompson said that he alternated between "indignation"

[26]Ford to Max Farrand, 2 March 1918; Notestein to Ford, 21 September 1917 (both quoted in Gruber, *Mars and Minerva*, 145, 147–48); Ford to James W. Garner, 7 June 1917, quoted in Gruber, ibid., 147. See also Blakey, *Homefront*, 46.

[27]Jameson to Paul Mijouef, 27 May 1922, in Donnan and Stock, *An Historian's World*, 273; Shotwell, "Reminiscences," Columbia Oral History Collection, 70; Ford, "Reminiscences," ibid., 2:419.

[28]Anderson, "The World War and the Historians," *History Teacher's Magazine* 7 (1916): 327–29; Binkley, "Two World Wars and American Historical Scholarship," *Mississippi Valley Historical Review* 33 (1946): 10; Heaton, "The War Historian's Dilemma," *Current History* 1 (1941): 1–2.

and "depression" when he contemplated the misrepresentation and corruption of history of which historians in every country had been guilty.[29]
James Harvey Robinson, who during the war had revised a textbook
twice, when the first revision was still adjudged insufficiently anti-German, thought that the wartime experience demonstrated that historians,
for all their erudition, were no wiser than anyone else. They had "applauded the old battle cries . . . blew trumpets and grasped halberds . . .
gulped down propaganda which in a later mood they realized was nau-
seous."[30] Frederic L. Paxson, editor of the *War Cyclopedia*, thought the
profession would have done well to heed Cheyney's warnings, and
ruefully characterized the work he and his colleagues had done as "mere
historical engineering." For Merle Curti, torn between pacifism and instrumentalism, the wartime experience of historians had at least had the
merit of breaking down "the traditional gulf between the thinker and the
actor, between idea and practice." William T. Hutchinson, who had been
in the trenches while the pamphlets were flying at home, reviewed his
colleagues' wartime behavior in detail, and reached a conclusion comfort-
ing to historians' consciences, but hardly consistent with the orthodox
view of the historian's detachment and autonomy: criticizing the historian for "yielding to the very strong pressures upon him" would be
unwarranted, "in view of the well-known axiom that a scholar inevitably,
and hence blamelessly, will mirror on his pages the temper of the times in
which he writes."[31]

III

Historians' evaluation of their wartime behavior was, of course, closely
connected with their retrospective evaluation of the conflict. America had
fought the war under liberal auspices and with liberal rhetoric. Indeed,
wartime enthusiasm had inspired idealism and resuscitated a somewhat
flagging Progressivism. Conyers Read wrote a colleague in 1918 that
"This great war and our own splendid part in it somehow has made me
less materialistic in my historical thinking than I used to be. I hope I don't

[29]Letters to J. Franklin Jameson, 15 January 1920, 21 January 1920, AHA Papers, Box 299.
The ancient historian Joseph Ward Swain thought most historians "smile sadly as we recall
many of the things said in 1917." ("What Is History?" *Journal of Philosophy* 20 [1923]:
347.)
[30]"The Newer Ways of Historians," *AHR* 35 (1930): 252. Theodore Roosevelt pronounced
Robinson's first revision of *Medieval and Modern Times* "an outrageous piece of German
propaganda . . . utterly unfit for use in American schools," and recommended an investigation by the National Security League. (See Blakey, *Homefront*, 82–83.)
[31]Paxson, "The Great Demobilization," *AHR* 44 (1939): 237; Curti, "The American Scholar in Three Wars," *Journal of the History of Ideas* 3 (1942): 257; Hutchinson, "The
American Historian in Wartime," *MVHR* 29 (1942): 183.

spring too far the other way but just now all about me I see so many men, high and low, rich and poor, sacrificing . . . for more spiritual things that I can't help reading a larger amount of this fine sentiment into the facts of the past." For prewar Progressives, the war, to justify its cost, had to have an aim greater than the defeat of Germany. Responding to a CPI request for suggestions for a Fourth of July appeal to foreign-born workingmen, Carl Becker warned that a "contrast between the horrors of German autocracy and the shining virtues of American and Allied democracy" would fall on deaf ears. Although the United States had "a certain political democracy, in industrial and economic organization we have never been so little democratic"—and this was well known to workers, "touched by the ideals of socialism," who encountered American institutions "precisely where they are least democratic, in big cities . . . and in connection with great corporations."

You talk to him of our ideals of liberty and he thinks of the shameless exploitation of labor and the corruption in government and of the ridiculous gulf between wealth and poverty. . . . The last thing the average foreign working man, either in Europe or in this country, wants is to establish American institutions as he knows them—the Capitalist and Bourgeois regime is precisely what he wants to destroy. To reach the foreign born laborer, therefore, it is necessary to make him feel that this war is not a Capitalistic war; that it is the culmination of a generation of Imperialistic reaction, a reaction which is not confined to Germany although there it has been most pronounced; and that we are in the war, not only to save France but to save our own soul, not only to safeguard democracy from German militarism, but against our own backslidings. The war will not touch this class of men much unless they are convinced that the war is to result in the real democratization of our industrial as well as of our political life.

In a similar vein, Charles Beard argued that "the world of democracy" for which European workers were willing to die "is not the world of Milner, Cecil, Maxse, and Balfour. . . . The kingdom of heaven for Kerensky and Liebknecht is not described in Lochner v. New York." The propagandist, it has been said, is his own first victim. Did Becker, Beard, and others inflate their expectations of the fruits of the war to match the wartime rhetoric they produced? In any event, with the Treaty of Versailles, followed by the "return to normalcy" of Republican administrations in the 1920s, and the rapid reconsideration by historians of the origins and nature of the war, disillusionment was deep and widespread.[32]

---

[32]Read to William E. Dodd, 23 July 1918, Dodd Papers, Box 13; Becker to Samuel B. Harding, 23 May 1918, quoted in Gruber, *Mars and Minerva*, 93–94; Beard, "The Perils of Diplomacy," *New Republic* 11 (1917): 137.

Disillusionment was particularly acute for historians, since it was "their" man in the White House, one of Herbert Baxter Adams's first Ph.D.'s, who had betrayed their hopes. William E. Dodd, almost alone in remaining loyal to his old friend and colleague, had to defend him against a barrage of bitter attacks from the historical fraternity. Carl Becker confessed to Dodd that he had "always been susceptible to the impression of the futility of life, and always easily persuaded to regard history as no more than the meaningless resolution of blind forces which struggling men . . . do not understand and cannot control."

The war and the peace . . . have only immensely deepened this pessimism. . . . [The war] was as a whole the most futile and aimless, the most desolating and repulsive exhibition of human power and cruelty without compensating advantage that has ever been on earth. This is the result of some thousands of years of what men like to speak of as "political, economic, intellectual, and moral Progress" . . .

The men recently convened in your city of Chicago were mostly good and honest men enough. Senator Harding is a good and honest man enough—born on a farm, member of the Baptist Church (against which no one can say a word, you least of all), upright citizen, never said or did anything ignoble. They are all honorable men, with clear consciences, loving their country and their fellow men, and firm in the belief that they are working for the welfare of all, including themselves. Yet the whole business there strikes me, in view of the state of the world at large and of America in particular, as so unreal, so false, as all compact of bunk and fustian and petty intrigue that one can only turn away in disgust or cynicism. . . .

What really irritates me, I will confess to you, is that I could have been naive enough to suppose, during the war, that Wilson could ever accomplish those ideal objects which are so well formulated in his state papers. A man of any intelligence, who has been studying history for 25 years, and to some purpose if I am to believe your high opinion of him, should have known that in this war, as in all wars, men would profess to be fighting for justice and liberty, but in the end would demand the spoils of victory if they won. It was futile from the beginning to suppose that a new international order could be founded on the old national order.

My present intention is to vote, if I vote at all, for Debs.[33]

---

[33]Becker to Dodd, 17 June 1920, Dodd Papers, Box 15. Replying to Becker, Dodd reported that at the University of Chicago, faculty hatred of Wilson was so strong and widespread that at the faculty club the management "took his picture down from a conspicuous place in the main room and put it behind the door upstairs." (Letter of 15 July 1920, Becker Papers.)

Becker's response, though perhaps not the depth of his despair, was echoed by other Progressive Historians like Beard and Robinson. In their prewar textbook *The Development of Modern Europe* the two had, in the spirit of those times, seen "the enormous number of men that would speedily be called into action . . . the disastrous effects of international conflict on industry and trade . . . the strong protest of workingmen and socialists against warfare" all combining to make war in Europe increasingly unlikely. Not long after Versailles, Beard, with gloomy prescience, was referring to the recent conflict as "The First World War." Robinson, in 1924, found it "almost as hard to reconstruct the bland assumptions of 1904 as those of the time of St. Louis or Augustus."

Our old moorings are lost and we are tossed about on the waves of illimitable doubt. . . . Twenty years ago . . . the unification of Germany and Italy and the Franco-Prussian war represented a natural *terminus ad quem*, as the Scholastics would have put it. The tale seemed to be nicely rounded out and the historian could lay down his pen . . . with a sense of provisional finality. . . . The Triple Alliance was a rumor in 1904 and the secret counter-understanding between France and Russia too well hidden to be reckoned with. Who could foresee that these and similar dark hints forecast a thoroughgoing revision of the whole perspective of modern history? History does not seem to stop any more. All the historian can do nowadays is to leave off, with a full conviction that he may have played up merely specious occurrences and have overlooked vital ones. . . . It is as difficult to tell where to start as where to stop. . . . I have come to think that no such thing as objective history is possible.[34]

Disillusionment and disorientation were, of course, not universal. When they were experienced, it was by no means always in equally profound or permanent ways. Robinson's conclusion was certainly not the only one which could be drawn. Not all historians were devastated by the Versailles Treaty; not all thought the war had made a shambles of previous conceptions of the meaning of the past; not all were repelled by "normalcy." Someone, after all, elected Harding, and there is no reason to believe that historians were underrepresented among his supporters. Indeed, on the basis of standard ethnic, class, and other predictors of electoral behavior, they were more likely to have been overrepresented.

But the war experience, and its fallout, touched all in one way or another—and many profoundly. Those of the older generation often experienced acute distress in attempting to assimilate the experience. Clarence W. Alvord, editor of the *Mississippi Valley Historical Review*

[34]*Development of Modern Europe* (2 vols., Boston, 1907–8), 2:368–69; Robinson, "After Twenty Years," *Survey* 53 (1924): 18–19.

described himself as an "historian of the old school" who had "conformed to the canons of my science . . . walked along the straight and narrow road of approved scholarship . . . learned to babble the words of von Ranke . . . prided [himself] on telling the story *wie es eigentlich gewesen*." In retrospect he saw how his generation's faith in objectivity ("few of us know its meaning") had been grounded in their sense of a determinate, progressive world. Now "all the spawn of hell roamed at will over the world and made of it a shambles. . . . The pretty edifice of . . . history which had been designed and built by my contemporaries was rent asunder. . . . The meaning we historians had read into events was false, cruelly false." The "science of history, as practiced by me and my fellows, appears to be mere 'bunk.'" He could not bring himself, in his sixtieth year, to abandon his prewar determinist faith, but neither could he resist the suspicion that the younger generation was correct: the historian's traditional program was "a mirage."[35]

Raymond J. Sontag, whose college years were interrupted by military service in the war, saw a clear break between "those whose minds were formed before 1914, and those, whatever their age, who began to think only in the years after 1918." He looked with admiration, but across a great chasm, at his elders, who were "confident that they understood the forces which shaped the past and that they could describe the past objectively and correctly." It was a confidence not easily shared by his own generation, "formed by a time of troubles."[36]

[35]"Musings of an Inebriated Historian," *American Mercury* 5 (1925): 434, 436, 441; "Historical Science and the War Guilt," ibid., 11 (1927): 324, 326.
[36]Review of James L. Cate et al., *Some 20th Century Historians: Essays on Eminent Europeans*, and Bernadotte E. Schmitt, *The Fashion and Future of History: Historical Studies and Addresses*, AHR 67 (1961): 90–91.

6

◁══▷

A changed climate

As cultural historians multiply, cultural epochs get cut finer and finer: where we once had the Age of the Baroque and the *Siècle des Lumières*, we now have characterizations of the culture of decades: "iconoclasm" for the 1920s; "radicalism" for the 1930s. But there was no shortage of superstition in the Age of Reason; plenty of traditionalism and complacency in the decades of iconoclasm and radicalism. It is almost always a minority who reflect and embody these "defining" currents. And this is particularly true when looking at the relationship of the professorate to the Zeitgeist. If, in hostile caricature, the archetypical intellectual goes whoring after every new current in thought and culture, no matter how shabby and evanescent, the archetypical academic ignores every new current, no matter how profound and substantial. (To succumb to such siren songs is to be "trendy," to cast doubt on one's "soundness.") In any event, we are concerned here with a heterodox minority of the historical profession—with the way in which they responded to aspects of interwar culture.

"Historical relativists" never presented either an overall philosophy or a positive program for historiography. Rather they offered a series of criticisms of the traditional posture of objectivity, and some suggestions as to how historians might proceed in the face of what they saw as the collapse of the profession's founding myth. In considering the intellectual origins of the relativist critique, I would suggest, as have many others before me in other arenas, Claude Lévi-Strauss's metaphor of *bricolage*. The term describes the work of the *bricoleur*, a jack-of-all-trades who collects odds and ends which might come in handy one day, and puts to his own improvisational use, heterogeneous materials originally meant for other purposes. Interwar culture was overflowing with "relativistic," "pragmatic," and iconoclastic ideas which historians took up in developing their critique of the received epistemology.

In the history of the avant-garde—literary, artistic, scientific, philosophical—the collapse of the stable norms of the nineteenth century is clearly a prewar phenomenon. A recent book on the revolution in thinking about time and space dates the change from around 1880; some years ago H. Stuart Hughes wrote that the refiguring of European social thought began about 1890; Morton White and Henry May, with an American focus, concentrated on the years around 1910–12. But the penetration of new currents into general intellectual and cultural discourse, and certainly into the discourse of historians, is just as clearly a postwar phenomenon. Apart from isolated and vagrant hints, there are no signs of awareness of new cultural currents among professional historians before the interwar years.[1]

After the Armistice the floodgates opened. New canons of representation in literature and art, new conceptions of mathematics, logic, and empirical science, and new currents in academic disciplines combined to render problematic nineteenth-century certainties in every realm of thought and culture. Nowhere was this more true than in literature and art. Nothing seems inherently closer to the historians' postwar problems of understanding and representation than modernism, with its sense of crisis, its self-skepticism, its violation of expected continuities, its unfolding and collapsing of time and space, its multiperspectivalism. But despite the countless parallels and logical connections between changes in artistic/literary and in historical consciousness, there is little evidence that American professional historians were in the slightest degree influenced by the modernist revolution. Because modernism in literature and the arts did not, so far as one can tell, concern interwar historians, it will not concern us here. It was quite otherwise with that activity which had been the foundation of the historian's self-image: the natural sciences.

I

Science had offered prewar historians not just a method—well or ill understood—but above all a vision of a comprehensible world: a model of certitude, of unambiguous truth; knowledge that was definite, and

[1] Stephen Kern, *The Culture of Time and Space, 1880–1918* (Cambridge, Mass., 1983); Hughes, *Consciousness and Society: The Reconstruction of European Social Thought, 1890–1930* (New York, 1958); White, *Social Thought in America: The Revolt Against Formalism* (New York, 1949); May, *The End of American Innocence* (New York, 1959).

independent of the values or intentions of the investigator. None of these characteristics were to survive the first third of the century. The very mathematical and logical foundations of empirical science seemed to be at risk in the interwar years. The development of non-Euclidian geometry had taken place gradually during the course of the nineteenth century and was little noted outside the mathematical community. The argument that geometries were wholly formal systems, with no necessary connection with any empirical reality, would not have had the impact it did, had not Einstein, in the "General Theory of Relativity" (1913), demonstrated that Euclidian geometry did not completely describe the physical universe. In discussing gravitation and the deflection of light rays, he had successfully applied Georg Riemann's geometry. At least one non-Euclidian system was not only internally consistent, but accurately described aspects of the physical universe. The eminent French mathematician Henri Poincaré, in the first volume of the *American Science and Education* series, advised that "One geometry cannot be more true than another, it can only be more convenient." "Euclidian" could now be used as a term of disparagement ("old-fashioned," "outdated"). For Charles Beard, arguing that the concept of balance in the American governmental system was inadequate to current demands, it was a "Euclidian theory."[2]

From non-Euclidian geometry it was a short step to non-Aristotelian, multivalued logics. The Harvard philosopher C. I. Lewis developed a five-valued logical system which he situated in a pragmatic framework. "There are no 'laws of logic' which can be attributed to the universe or to human reason in the traditional fashion." Logical systems and "laws" are constructed by men to serve their purposes. "Truth" and "falsity" cannot be the sole criteria in their employment, since the very terms are context-dependent. "The logical truths which are expressed by the laws of one system will not, in general, be expressible in terms of others." Before one could begin to reason, one had to choose between systems, and "in the nature of the case, the grounds of choice can only be pragmatic." The alleged implications of the new thoughtways in mathematics were quickly picked up by scholars in a variety of other fields, including history. "Logic," Carl Becker wrote in *The Heavenly City of the Eighteenth-*

---

[2]Poincaré, *The Foundations of Science* (New York, 1929), 65; Beard and John D. Lewis, "Representative Government in Evolution," *American Political Science Review* 26 (1932): 236. While several years later mathematicians concluded that only two non-Euclidian geometries were possible, and that only Riemann's had practical application, between the wars one could envision the possibility of an ever growing number of new systems.

Century Philosophers, "was formerly visualized as something outside us, something existing independently which, if we were willing, could take us by the hand and lead us into the paths of truth."

We now suspect that it is something the mind has created to conceal its timidity and keep up its courage, a hocus-pocus designed to give formal validity to conclusions we are willing to accept if everybody else in our set will too. . . . Logics have a way of multiplying in response to the changes in point of view. First there was one logic, then there were two, then there were several; so that now . . . the state of logic is "that of Israel under the Judges, every man doeth that which is right in his own eyes."[3]

Though new and disturbing developments in mathematics and logic were relevant to the collapse of received views in the interwar years, the revolution in physics was much more salient and dramatic. That revolution had, of course, begun in the first years of the new century, well before the war. But for laymen, including historians, pervasive awareness of the significance of the new physics dated from November 1919, when, in a report issued jointly by the Royal Astronomical Society and the Royal Society of London, it was announced that photographs of a solar eclipse had decisively verified Einstein's General Theory of Relativity. Within a month of the report, the *New York Times* published six editorials on theories of relativity. In the years that followed, the popular press was filled with endless discussions of the allegedly far-reaching implications of relativity; popularizing works on relativity by leading scientists and philosophers—Sir James Jeans, Arthur Eddington, Bertrand Russell—were repeatedly on best-seller lists.[4]

[3]C. I. Lewis, "Alternate Systems of Logic," *Monist* 42 (1932): 483, 500, 507; Becker, *Heavenly City* (New Haven, 1932), 25–26; for extensions to other fields, see Edward A. Purcell, Jr., *The Crisis of Democratic Theory: Scientific Naturalism and the Problem of Value* (Lexington, Ky., 1973), 62–73. The thrust of Purcell's argument is very different from mine. His point is the growth of an ethically relativist empiricism among social scientists, and the collapse of a rationalism counterposed to empiricism. He discusses neither the problematicizing of empiricism occasioned by the new physics, nor cognitive relativism, and excludes historians from his field of inquiry. So, though our trains are going in opposite directions, they are on different tracks, and there is no necessary crash.
[4]Paradoxically, Einstein's "relativity" theory—which provided the popular designation for all of the new physics, as well as new historical currents—was somewhat misnamed. Einstein himself, in private correspondence, referred to his *Invarententheorie*; as the eminent physicist Arnold Sommerfeld wrote, "Not the *relativizing* of the perceptions of length and duration are the chief points for him, but the independence of natural laws, particularly those of electrodynamics and optics, of the standpoint of the observer." (Gerald Holton, "Introduction: Einstein and the Shaping of Our Imagination," in Holton and Yehuda Elkana, eds., *Albert Einstein: Historical and Cultural Perspectives; The Centennial Symposium in Jerusalem* [Princeton, 1982], xv; Sommerfeld quoted in Lewis S. Feuer, *Einstein and the Generations of Science* [New York, 1974], 59.)

The traditional understanding of historical objectivity had based itself
on a conception of science as highly organized common sense, continuous with everyday experience. Defending historians' traditional posture
in the 1920s, the medievalist Carl Stephenson saw no reason why there
could not be "unquestioned facts of history . . . so long as there are
unquestioned facts of ordinary experience, and unquestioned facts of
science." The natural sciences, he went on, "consider only such phenomena as the normal observer can perceive in the physical world, and have
nothing to do with states of mind." In a similar vein, a fellow medievalist,
C. H. McIlwain of Harvard spoke of "the applied commonsense which
we call scientific method." It was precisely this conception of science, and
of "fact," which relativity seemed to challenge. Whereas hitherto science
had explained the common experiences of mankind, relativity explained
experiences which mankind did not have. Everyone experiences "absolute simultaneity" (at the moment of perception). In the rare instances
when this sense is violated, as in perceiving thunder some time after
lightning, we account for the elapsed time in ways which restore our
sense of simultaneity. But according to relativity theory, absolute simultaneity was not a characteristic of the whole universe; contrary to common experience there was no "now" shared by all natural events.[5]

Attempts to explain the physicists' new interpretations in language
comprehensible to the layman led to important misunderstandings.
Working within a tradition whose rhetoric was based on common human
experience, and human observational standpoints, popularizers made
analogies between relativity theory and the commonplace that "the aspect
of things" changed with the position of the observer, thus putting a
misleading emphasis on human perspective. In general, there was a conflation of "relativity" and "subjectivity." One early popularizer characterized the relativity theorists as revolutionary because they "substitute
mathematical symbols as the basis of science and deny that any concrete
experience underlies these symbols, thus replacing an objective by a subjective universe." Another writer, discussing art and relativity, saw Einstein's work as justifying the rejection of all absolute aesthetic standards
and legitimizing purely personal expression. Most misleading of all, since
Einstein's argument concerning the relativity of time had nothing whatsoever to do with consciousness, was the assertion, endlessly repeated in
various forms, that relativity was "just like" the common subjective experience that while awaiting one's beloved every minute seems like an hour;

[5]Stephenson, "Facts in History," *Historical Outlook* 19 (1928): 314; McIlwain, "Bias in
Historical Writing," *History* 43 (1926): 195.

when with her, every hour seems like a minute. It was explications of this sort which led Robert L. Schuyler, managing editor of the *American Historical Review* to protest "the indignity that astronomy has heaped upon us" by, as he (mis)understood it, "adopting the metaphysics of subjective idealism, which makes the very existence of the cosmos dependent upon consciousness."[6]

Other attempts at popular interpretation were disorienting when not misleading. The conception of a "space-time continuum," in which time was described as literally a "fourth dimension," contributed to confusion. Whereas in three-dimensional space, rotation can only occur around an axis line, one mathematical property of four-dimensional space is that rotation can occur around an axis plane. Efforts on the part of laymen to "visualize" such notions in the mind's eye, further opened the gap between traditional "common experience" and the latest scientific word on the nature of the physical world. The cult of incomprehensibility surrounding Einstein's theory, epitomized by his own joking remark that there were only twelve people in the world who understood it, opened the gap farther still. To cap the disorientation occasioned by Einstein's work, a public which wanted to know whether his theories were "true," found that scientists often resisted this formulation, in much the same way as did the mathematicians: the theories, rather, were "useful" or "successful": an unsatisfying answer to those who had grown up believing that the crucial question was always "truth" in the sense of "correspondence to what's out there."

While the layman was still attempting to assimilate the implications of Einstein's work, there quickly followed other scientific developments, also widely publicized and discussed, which further worked to overthrow older notions of scientific certainty. One was Niels Bohr's principle of "complementarity," which asserted that, depending on the kind of observation employed, electrons were either "like waves" or "like particles." Werner Heisenberg's "indeterminacy" followed from Bohr's complementarity. Describing its impact—in words which, not accidentally, prefigure the language of historical relativists—the physicist P. W. Bridgman said that the physicist "has learned that the object of knowledge is not to be separated from the instrument of knowledge. We can no longer think of the object of knowledge as constituting a reality which is revealed to us

---

[6]Alfred J. Lotka, "A New Conception of the Universe," *Harper's Magazine* 140 (1920): 477; L. T. More, "The Theory of Relativity," *Nation* 44 (1912): 370; Thomas Jewell Cravens, "Art and Relativity," *Dial* 70 (1921): 535–39; Edwin E. Slosson, "That Elusive Fourth Dimension," *Independent* 100 (1919): 298; Schuyler, "Some Historical Idols," *Political Science Quarterly* 47 (1932): 3.

by the instrument of knowledge, but the two together, object and instrument, constitute a whole so intimately knit that it is meaningless to talk of object and instrument separately." For interwar physicists, the fundamental elements of nature did not obey laws of causality as traditionally understood, and were not "out there" in the old sense. They could be known only as they were, in effect, "created" by the investigator. The old Cartesian dualism, which had been the foundation of Western science for centuries, was called into question.[7]

The extrapolation of principles of relativity and quantum mechanics into the cultural and social realms was often bizarre and laughable, but these ventures could hardly be dismissed as the work of cranks and scientific illiterates when conducted by such distinguished scientists as Jeans and Eddington. Bohr himself wrote popular articles extending quantum mechanics to the social sciences. Einstein termed the mass enthusiasm for relativity "psychopathological," and repeatedly disparaged the alleged philosophical implications of his work: "I believe that the present fashion of applying the axioms of physical science to human life is not only a mistake but has something reprehensible to it."[8]

Whatever the divergent views of physicists and philosophers about the legitimacy of extending the new ontology and the new epistemology outside its terrain of origin, such extension was widely practiced. And it is difficult to quarrel with the later observation of Lionel Trilling that the "exclusion of most of us from the mode of thought which is habitually said to be the characteristic achievement of the modern age is bound to be experienced as a wound given to our intellectual self-esteem. About this humiliation we all agree to be silent, but can we doubt that it has its consequences, that it introduced into the life of mind a significant element of dubiety and alienation?"[9]

Wedded as it was to the conception of "history as science," the historical community could hardly avoid noting that precisely those elements of science which had sustained them were crumbling under their feet, and many testified to the impact of the new scientific doctrines on their historiographical thought. There was widespread acknowledgment that the old, brute empiricism could no longer claim the mantle of science.

[7]Bridgman, quoted in Arthur March and Ira Freeman, *The New World of Physics* (New York, 1963), 161. See also Charles C. Lemert, "Sociological Theory and the Relativistic Paradigm," *Sociological Inquiry* 44 (1974): 93–104.
[8]Remarks quoted in Holton, "Introduction," xii; and Loren Graham, "The Reception of Einstein's Ideas: Two Examples From Contrasting Political Cultures," in Holton and Elkana, *Einstein*, 107.
[9]*Mind in the Modern World: The 1972 Jefferson Lecture in the Humanities* (New York, 1972), 13–14.

"Seeing," said the Americanist Roy F. Nichols, "is no longer believing." The European economic historian Charles W. Cole thought the physicists had led historians to a salutary reevaluation of the primacy of "facts." No longer, he said, would theories "cringe and cower like handmaidens before the queenly 'facts.'" Beard repeatedly alluded to a "crisis in empirical method" produced by the new scientific developments. Robert L. Schuyler, citing the work of Planck, Schrödinger, and Heisenberg, saw a crisis for traditional conceptions of science and scholarship with the abandonment of the goal of ever increasing accuracy.[10]

For some it was the scientists' abandonment of a determinate universe governed by strict causality that was most troublesome. For C. W. Alvord, a "deterministic" view was fundamental to a "science of history." "Introduce a broken link in the succession of causes, and there is nothing left except a point of view." Schuyler pointed out that while earlier historical determinism had a theological basis,

> Such support as the modern historical determinism has had came mainly from the scientific doctrine of causation. This support has of late been greatly weakened. . . . Acceptance of this doctrine has ceased to be a badge of the scientist. . . . Because determinism is losing its hold as a physical concept would not, in itself, be conclusive reason for discarding it in the realm of human history. The fact is, however, that it has been accepted, at least in modern times, in the realm of human history . . . mainly because it was accepted in the domain of the physical sciences. It may be that for philosophical or religious reasons we shall continue to believe in determinism—in natural phenomena, in human affairs, or in both—but this belief can no longer claim the prestige of science in its support.

For Beard, the collapse of older notions of causation produced an intellectual crisis which endured for the rest of his life.[11]

One of the most widely drawn lessons from the new view of science was the primacy of conceptual schemes, or what came to be most commonly designated "frames of reference." This was often joined to a recognition of the frankly pragmatic grounds for selection of a scheme or frame. Crane Brinton summed up the consequences for historians of the new approach.

> The historian can free himself from some of the unnecessary difficulties raised by Ranke's formula, *as it really happened*. That formula is in many ways still useful.

[10]Nichols, "History Teaching in this Intellectual Crisis," *Historical Outlook* 24 (1933): 359; Cole, "The Relativity of History," *Political Science Quarterly* 48 (1933): 170; Beard, "Fact, Opinion and Social Values," *Yale Review* n.s. 22 (1933): 596; Schuyler, "Indeterminism in Physics and History," *The Social Studies* 27 (1936): 511.
[11]Alvord, "Historical Science and the War Guilt," *American Mercury* 11 (1927): 326; Schuyler, "Indeterminism," 513.

. . . But the famous formula contained certain metaphysical overtones we are well rid of. As interpreted by many of the older historians it implied that a historian could somehow get at a reality that lay altogether outside his thinking—that "what really happened" was in itself a fact awaiting discovery. We can now admit that the past in this sense is forever lost to us; that the historian must relate his facts to a pattern, a conceptual scheme of which he can require only that it prove useful; that like the physicist's conceptual scheme for the electron, it proves a convenient way of accounting for known facts and for leading to the discovery of hitherto unknown facts. The historian can get rid of the incubus of absolutism implied in "as it really happened" and accept all the advantages of a frankly relativistic position.

Others were struck by the inevitably philosophical and value-laden foundation of conceptualizations, even in the "neutral" natural sciences. Becker quoted approvingly Alfred North Whitehead's observation that "No science can be more secure than the metaphysics which tacitly it presupposes." Merle Curti, whose conclusions from reading in science and philosophy of science were reinforced by a year he spent at Cal Tech, came to believe that "the scientific hypothesis is itself apt to have social and moral implications, apt to be affected by both subjective and objective factors, and functional in part to time and place and interest or value." "The natural scientists," as he saw it, "have given up many of the positions which historians adopted and which, I suspect, they have clung to."[12]

The historians just mentioned were among those who attempted to integrate the lessons of the new physics into their historical consciousness. Probably most historians retained an unshaken faith in scientific empiricism as applied to history. Although this was not a period in which relations between history and the social sciences were particularly close, some historians may have been sustained in their continued allegiance to the old ideal by the example of the newer social sciences, which were, in the 1920s and 1930s, becoming more and more committed to objectivity, empiricism, and inductivism. The sociologist Luther L. Bernard, shortly after the war, wrote that it was necessary for the scientific sociologist to "abandon the old subjective terminology" and replace it with "a description of the objective act—both overtly and neurally—thus following the newer behavior psychologists into the realm of biophysics and biochemistry." As the historians had done a generation before, social scientists invoked the crudest and most oversimplified versions of Bacon and Mill to justify a hyperempiricist approach. Stuart Rice's 1931 *Methods in*

[12]Brinton, "The 'New History' and 'Past Everything'," *American Scholar* 8 (1939): 153; Becker, review of Whitehead's *Adventures of Ideas*, *AHR* 37 (1933): 88; Curti to Becker, 4 March 1936 and 29 January 1940, Becker Papers.

Social Science: A Casebook, opened with a lengthy tribute to Auguste
Comte for having put aside "metaphysics" to focus on "observed
realities."[13]

But if this was the aspiration of the great majority of social scientists, it
was not necessarily how their product was perceived by historians. Ralph
H. Gabriel, reviewing Rice's *Case Book*, saw, in "the assumptions, concepts, and techniques of the investigators in the different social disciplines
. . . a picture of the momentary ideology of the twentieth century."
When, a few years later, Gabriel reviewed the final volumes of the *Encyclopedia of the Social Sciences*, it was not clear to him that even the
aspiration had survived. He noted the acknowledgment by the *Encyclopedia*'s editor, the economist E. R. A. Seligman, that his own discipline
would "perhaps ever continue to be the battle ground for rationalizations
for group and class interests"; the confession of another contributor that
"scientific detachment" was impossible; the observation by still another
of "increasing manifestations of disappointment with science." Gabriel
thought it possible that one day the *Encyclopedia* would be looked upon
as "the valedictory of an epoch."[14]

Many historians, locked into the old "history as art" versus "history as
science" dichotomy, opted for art. It is often very hard to get a clear idea
of what they meant by this. For some, reacting against the perceived
aridities of late-nineteenth-century scientific history it meant a nostalgia
for the style and manner of Macaulay and Bancroft. (It was much less
important for later generations of professional historians to distinguish
themselves from their "literary" forebears than it had been for the founding fathers of the profession; indeed, there may have been something like
the third-generation phenomenon which Marcus Hansen noted in the
case of European immigrants—a desire to recapture old-country values
and identities.) For some, retreating in confusion from history modeled
on a science whose meaning had become problematical, "history as art"
could mean a desire for a history more "representational" than contemporary science. No doubt many, for whom science still had the old objectivist connotations, meant to signal a relativistic orientation by describing
history as art; but a number of those most prominent in the "history as
art" camp, like Allan Nevins and Samuel Eliot Morison, were also fierce

---

[13]Bernard, "The Objective Viewpoint in Sociology," *American Journal of Sociology* 25
(1919): 298; McQuilkin DeGrange, "The Method of Auguste Comte: Subordination of
Imagination to Observation in the Social Sciences," in Stuart A. Rice, ed., *Methods in
Social Science: A Casebook* (Chicago, 1931), 19–58.
[14]Review of *Case Book*, *AHR* 36 (1931): 786–87; review of *Encyclopedia*, *AHR* 41 (1935):
113–16.

defenders of objectivity against the relativist heresy. As Hayden White once observed, the twentieth-century debate between "history as art" and "history as science" anachronistically counterposed early-nineteenth-century notions of art and late-nineteenth-century notions of science. A number of historians followed Carl Russell Fish in making a questionable distinction between "recovering history . . . which is a scientific process" and "presentation . . . which is an artistic process."[15]

II

There is no doubt that the prevailing wind from the social sciences was empiricist—and, in its general tendency, objectivist. In terms of cultural values and ideological significance, scientific empiricism was bivalent in this period. Before World War I, empiricism had been presented as a doctrine of liberation from "metaphysical" absolutes, often religious. After World War II—in a society based on naturalistic foundations, where the most obvious alternative to empiricism was not conservative traditionalism but Marxism—empiricism was primarily a doctrine of cultural and ideological legitimation. Between the wars, depending on individual or group orientations, empiricism might be perceived as a doctrine either of liberation or of legitimation.

Despite the scientific empiricist thrust of interwar social science, there were in the interwar years at least two important academic developments with substantial affinities to historical relativism. Both illustrate important and relevant themes in the prevailing academic "climate of opinion"—itself a phrase (Whitehead's) of the period.

One was the development of cultural anthropology, which had counted for little in the American academic world before the war, and which, between the wars, was dominated by the doctrine of "cultural relativism." In a weak form, cultural relativism had always been present in ethnography, as a methodological injunction that one be sufficiently empathic to understand societies "in their own terms." This was a common heritage of anthropology and history, where "historicism" was reflected in Ranke's dictum that "every era is immediate to God." It is no accident that Herder is celebrated as a precursor of both anthropological and historical consciousness.

But when combined with a deeply held belief in progress and absolutist moral principles, this weak form of relativism was often little more than a

---

[15]Fish to Arthur M. Schlesinger, 6 December 1922, Fish Papers, Box 6; White, "The Burden of History," *History and Theory* 5 (1966): 126. (White in fact referred to anachronistic ideas of social science, but the general point remains.)

tool, slipped on and off like a stethoscope. Prewar taxonomies of cultures were generally hierarchical; cultures were moments in an evolution from savagery, through barbarism, to civilization. When, with the war, the only certain mode of progress seemed to be the increased efficiency with which millions could be scientifically slaughtered, and with the decline in absolutes, cultural relativism flowered not just as methodological imperative, but as a moral and intellectual posture. Not merely tolerance and understanding toward alien folkways, but a certain detached skepticism toward the norms of one's own society became common among leading anthropologists. This was true in the case of Franz Boas, whose religion and leftist politics made him something of an outsider not only in his native Germany but in America as well. For Ruth Benedict, and others of his students and followers, various reasons, including culturally disapproved sexual orientation, led to a sense of estrangement from the norms of the society around them which provided an emotional foundation for their relativism.

Cultural relativism led directly to ethical relativism, since a nonjudgmental attitude toward strange customs was its central core. It did not, logically, entail any form of cognitive relativism, and, indeed, a distinguishing hallmark of interwar social science was its combination of ethical relativism and objectivist empiricism. But from the outset cultural relativism had a potential for undermining absolutism in the cognitive as well as the ethical realm. From his earliest writings Boas stressed how different historically conditioned cultural systems imposed different patterns of meaning on experience, determined categories of thought, and shaped perceptions of the external world. This was a theme repeated in the work of Ruth Benedict and Margaret Mead, both influenced by gestalt or "configuration" psychology, first becoming known in the United States in the early 1920s, with its emphasis on a holistic view of perception.

Full acknowledgment of the cognitive relativism implicit in cultural relativism emerged only fitfully in the interwar years—in part as a result of the strength of scientism, in part as a result of contemporary ethnographers' emphasis on patterns of behavior, rather than structures of meaning and symbol. One form in which it did emerge was in the anthropological linguistics of Edward Sapir and Benjamin Lee Whorf, both of whom did their most important work in the interwar years. What later came to be termed the "Sapir-Whorf hypothesis" held that different linguistic systems played a substantial role in shaping distinctive conceptual schemes and world views, in imposing different systems of order on the "kaleidoscopic flux of impressions," and in determining what was perceived as fact. The implications of this view were sketched by Sapir in a 1924 popular article.

To pass from one language to another is psychologically parallel to passing from one geometrical system of reference to another. The environing world which is referred to is the same for either language . . . in either frame of reference. But the formal method of approach to the expressed item of experience . . . is so different that the resulting feeling of orientation can be the same neither in the two languages nor in the two frames of reference. . . .

The natural or, at any rate, the naive thing is to assume that when we wish to communicate a certain idea or impression, we make something like a rough and rapid inventory of the objective elements and relations involved in it, that such an inventory or analysis is quite inevitable. . . . We assume, naively enough, that this is about the only analysis that can properly be made. And yet, if we look into the way that other languages take to express [a] very simple kind of impression, we soon realize how much may be added to, subtracted from, or rearranged in our own form of expression without materially altering our report of the physical fact. . . .

It would be possible to go on indefinitely with . . . examples of incommensurable analyses of experience in different languages. The upshot of it all would be to make very real to us a kind of relativity that is generally hidden from us by our naive acceptance of fixed habits of speech as guides to an objective understanding of the nature of experience. This is the relativity of concepts or, as it might be called, the relativity of forms of thought. It is not so difficult to grasp as the physical relativity of Einstein. . . . It is the appreciation of the relativity of the form of thought which results from linguistic study that is perhaps the most liberalizing thing about it. What fetters the mind and benumbs the spirit is ever the dogged acceptance of absolutes.

But even putting the controversial Sapir-Whorf hypothesis to one side, the main thrust of cultural relativism in the interwar years furthered that disintegration of certainty and absolutes in every realm, of which historical relativism was both symbol and result.[16]

Another significant interwar current which, in a different way, paralleled and furthered historical relativism, was the Legal Realist attack on received views of the nature of the law and of judicial behavior. If the

[16]Sapir, "The Grammarian and His Language," *American Mercury* 1 (1924): 151, 154–55. Like historical relativism, cultural relativism had an instrumentalist, Progressive side which sought to make scholarship useful in the cause of social amelioration. One strand in cultural relativism—as in "historicism"—was a non-judgmentalism which, in a certain mode, was consistent with a purely spectatorial posture. It argued against anachronistic Europocentric standards in judging non-Western peoples, just as historicism argued against presentist standards in evaluating the past. In practice Boas used cultural relativism as a weapon in his lifelong campaign against racism, Mead to criticize a competitive social order; Benedict thought that through cultural relativism we could "train ourselves to pass judgment on the dominant traits of our own civilization." (*Patterns of Culture* [1934; Mentor edition, New York, 1960], 216.)

model of the scientist, and the approving adjective "scientific," were important in the self-image and discourse of historians, the model of the judge, and the adjective "judicious," were hardly less central. Related terms, like "impartial," "fair," "just," and "evenhanded," were among the most common in the historian's evaluative lexicon. Legal Realism challenged precisely those traditional defining attributes of the "judicial" posture which historians believed they should adopt.

Just as the prehistory of cultural relativism goes back to the work of Boas in the 1880s, so the origins of Legal Realism date back to Oliver Wendell Holmes, Jr.'s book *The Common Law*, published in the same decade. On the first page of that work he had said that the the development of the law, rather than being the result of logical deduction from settled principles, was the result of "the felt necessities of the time, the prevalent moral and political theories, intuitions of public policy, avowed or unconscious, even the prejudices which judges share with their fellow men." Holmes's writings had inspired, in the early twentieth century, a school of "sociological jurisprudence," of which the leader was Dean Roscoe Pound of the Harvard Law School. But though dissenting from what remained the conventional wisdom, the views of the conservative Pound on jurisprudence were considerably less radical than those of the skeptical, iconoclastic, and relativistic Holmes. It was only in the interwar years that the Legal Realists picked up Holmes's ideas and applied them systematically, and without watering them down. Karl Llewellyn, a leader of the movement, acknowledged in one of its early programmatic statements that "Holmes' mind had traveled most of the road two generations back."[17]

The orthodox view held that "the rules of law are founded upon principles of right and justice that never change." A judge would survey precedents and statutes to discover the applicable principle; "he then declares the rule of law which governs." The Realists attacked this view on a number of fronts. They denied, following Holmes, that clear principles led ineluctably to just adjudication. "No case can be settled by general propositions," wrote Holmes. "I will admit any general proposition you like and decide the case either way." For the Realists, The Law, with its majestic capitalization, was not a determinate entity but a happening: it was nothing more than "what judges do." Insofar as "the facts" determined a verdict, they were filtered through the prejudice, misunderstand-

---

[17]*The Common Law* (Boston, 1881), 1; Llewellyn, "A Realistic Jurisprudence—The Next Step," *Columbia Law Review* 30 (1930): 454. Pound and the Legal Realists quarreled over who held legitimate title to the mantle of Holmes.

ing, ignorance, and outright falsification of those who presented them, and through the bias and fallibility of the juries who evaluated them.[18]

Rather than serenely and impartially deciding cases on the basis of precedent, the Realists said, judges decided—necessarily decided, given the range of choice they had—on the basis of what they thought was socially desirable according to their personal and class beliefs. They argued that the "real" foundations of judicial decisions were not only unacknowledged but often unconscious. This theme was pressed farthest by the psychoanalytically oriented Jerome Frank, for whom the principal key to the mysteries of judicial decision making was awareness of the "multitudinous," "complicated," and "hidden" factors, which are "distinctively individual, unconscious, un-get-at-able," "concealed, publicly unscrutinized, uncommunicated . . . secret, unconscious, private, idiosyncratic." (At its most extreme, this approach led to what was caricatured as the "breakfast school" of interpretation: all might depend on whether the judge's toast had been burnt that morning.) Felix Cohen stressed the element of rationalization: "principles enunciated by courts as grounds for decisions represent nothing more objective than a resolution to use sanctified words wherever specified results are dictated by undisclosed determinants." The idea of law, and not only law, as mystifying rationalization, and the debunking of its pretensions to objectivity, was the theme of Daniel J. Boorstin's first work. "This book," he wrote in the preface to *The Mysterious Science of the Law*, "attempts to indicate how the ostensibly impartial processes of reason are employed by the student of society to support whatever social values he accepts."[19]

The Legal Realists were well aware that they were opening themselves to charges of "subjectivism," and "relativism." Karl Llewellyn acknowledged that following the Realist approach, "we desert entirely the solid sphere of objective observation, of possible agreement among all normal, trained observers, and enter the airy sphere of individual ideals and subjectivity." Max Radin saw very clearly the troubling implications of the Realist position, but insisted that those who held that position were simply . . . being realistic. "That this is pure subjectivism and therefore an

[18]Charles W. Bacon and Franklin S. Morse, *The Reasonableness of The Law: The Adaptability of Legal Sanctions to the Needs of Society* (New York, 1924), iii, 145; Holmes to Harold Laski, 19 February 1920, in Mark DeWolfe Howe, ed., *Holmes-Laski Letters: The Correspondence of Mr. Justice Holmes and Harold J. Laski* (2 vols., Cambridge, Mass., 1953), 1:243.

[19]Frank, "Moral Responsibility in Legal Criticism," *New York University Law Review* 26 (1951): 573; Cohen, *Ethical Systems and Legal Ideals: An Essay on the Foundations of Legal Criticism* (Ithaca, N.Y., 1933), 237; Boorstin, *Mysterious Science* (Cambridge, Mass., 1941), vii.

unfortunate situation is," he said, "beside the point." Walter Wheeler
Cook of the Johns Hopkins Law School said that human knowledge had
"reached the era of relativity . . . a point of view, which, whatever may
happen to specific doctrines, seems destined to remain as a permanent
achievement in human thought."[20]

For Holmes, that archetypical skeptical relativist, "logical method and
form flatter that longing for certainty and for repose which is in every
human mind . . . certainty generally is an illusion, and repose is not the
destiny of man." This theme was echoed by Realists like Jerome Frank,
and his Yale Law School colleague Thurman Arnold, who both thought
the search for certainty was motivated by psychological insecurity. Frank
went beyond most of his fellow Realists in designating the quest for
certainty as, literally, childish. The "legal absolutist mind" was an outcome of childhood patterns which led to a search for an authority figure
to substitute for the "Father-as-Infallible Judge." He speculated that the
subject matter of the law "is one which evokes, almost irresistibly, regres-
sive emotions." The solution was to grow up—accept change and doubt
as healthy. He ended *Law and the Modern Mind* with a tribute to the
maturity of Justice Holmes, "The Completely Adult Jurist."[21]

From one point of view, Legal Realism is part of Morton White's
"Revolt Against Formalism," or Edward Purcell's "Scientific Naturalism." In this sense it is reasonable to treat the Legal Realists as empiricists, aiming at a more objective science of law than that offered by the
"deductivists." Yet from another perspective, focusing on a different axis
of thought, the work of the Realists challenged a scientific empiricist view
of the legal process. The Realists, following Holmes, had defined the
essence of the law as predictions about judicial behavior. While this conceptualization was not part of the discourse of the older tradition, and
they no doubt would have found it insufficiently respectful, their practice
was perfectly assimilable to this model. Knowledge of the preexisting
principles of law, and the facts of the case, together with the rules of
logic, should, in principle, make judicial decision perfectly predictable.
This traditional procedure is, in effect, the mirror image of the positivist
conception of science. Like that conception it assumes that attachment to
theory and appreciation of the fact situation are "disinterested," and that
one is validated, or invalidated, by the other. In the sciences one tests

[20]Llewellyn, "Legal Tradition and Social Science Method," in Brookings Institution, *Essays
on Research in the Social Sciences* (Washington, D.C., 1931), 100; Radin, "Statutory
Interpretation," *Harvard Law Review* 43 (1930): 881; Cook, "Scientific Method and the
Law," *American Bar Association Journal* 14 (1927): 304–5.
[21]Holmes, quoted in Max Lerner, ed., *The Mind and Faith of Justice Holmes* (New York,
1943), 80; Frank, "Moral Responsibility," 19, 98.

theory by laying it alongside the (privileged) empirical facts. If the theory fails to match the facts, so much the worse for the theory: it is abandoned. In the law, a litigant's case is laid alongside the (privileged) settled principles of jurisprudence. (In constitutional cases, the law, in the famous phrase, is "laid alongside the [privileged] constitution.") If the former fails to square with the latter, so much the worse for the former: "case dismissed," "the law is unconstitutional." There is a predictive algorithm.

The Realists challenged two crucial assumptions of this conception: first, in their denial that one could easily or regularly tell what was or was not an acceptable fit between fact and theory; second, in their denial that judicial rationality and disinterestedness could be assumed. If either of these challenges were admitted, scientific predictability disappeared. To be sure, it was claimed by the Realists that because of its fallacious assumptions, the old tradition made bad predictions, and that a model which acknowledged and explored irrationality, and sought to probe its origins and nature to reduce its mysteriousness, could in principle make better ones. Jerome Frank, in language which paralleled that of historical relativists when dealing with similar questions, argued that the old myth did not make judicial action more predictable: "It serves only to make it seem more predictable than it can be—and, indeed, less predictable than it could be if it were not conducted in the intellectual semi-darkness created by that myth." But Realists' stress on judges' social background, prejudice, and psychodynamics gave the process a much less determinate air than it had in the older model. In practice they might achieve a higher level of predictability; in principle they disclaimed the degree of certainty claimed by the older school. If it was science, it was science very attuned to the age of Bohr and Heisenberg.[22]

Legal Realism had its scientistic side, but it deserves a place among the iconoclastic, diffusely relativist, and, to its enemies, "irrationalist" currents of the 1920s and 1930s. As one of its historians has written,

Without straining too hard, one can discern parallels to the thought of Frank and his fellow Realists in twentieth-century art and science. Stravinsky, Picasso, Joyce, Einstein, and Freud each radically challenged the effort to structure objective reality into a single determinate rationalizable order. Moving beyond this, each inaugurated a search for a new kind of order consistent with their attack upon the simpler conception of rationality held by their predecessors.[23]

---

[22]Frank, quoted in Wilfred E. Rumble, Jr., "Legal Realism, Sociological Jurisprudence and Mr. Justice Holmes," *Journal of the History of Ideas* 26 (1965): 565.
[23]Bruce A. Ackerman, "*Law and the Modern Mind* by Jerome Frank," *Daedalus* 103 (1973) ["Twentieth-Century Classics Revisited"]: 125–26.

Given historians' penchant for assuming a "judicial" posture, the Realists' "sociology of jurisprudential knowledge" suggested the possibility of a parallel "sociology of historical knowledge." If judges' findings—despite their claims to be operating on the basis of reason and logic—were likely to be heavily influenced, if not determined, by "intuitions . . . avowed or unconscious," what reason was there to believe that the same was not true of historians' conclusions? If it was not only common, but inevitable and proper, that judicial opinions were influenced by judges' "consideration of what is expedient for the community," might this not be true for historians as well?

These paired questions suggest the existence of two separable strands in Legal Realism which were paralleled in historical relativism. One was represented by the aloof Holmes: deeply skeptical about the role of reason in human affairs, and with an ironic detachment toward projects for social betterment. His much celebrated defense of free speech was rooted in his belief that words alone rarely threatened the social fabric, and that radical speech was so wrongheaded that it was especially unlikely to be influential. The other strand was symbolized by the activist reformism of Thurman Arnold, determined that scholarship descend from Mount Olympus and throw itself into the struggle for reform. These two strands, and the tension between them, can be differentiated within historical relativism—in Becker at his most elitist and cynical, Beard at his most energetically populist.

III

The adjective most often attached to the interwar historical relativists is "pragmatic": the leading scholarly treatment of interwar historical relativism is entitled *The Pragmatic Revolt in American History*. The philosophical school associated with Peirce, James, and Dewey was, of course, established before the war: James died in 1910, Peirce in 1914; by the year of the Versailles Treaty, Dewey was sixty—though he remained active and productive until his death at age ninety-two in the early 1950s. In a 1909 commentary on pragmatism, Bertrand Russell pronounced it "singularly well adapted to the predominant intellectual temper of our time." To the temper of philosophers, perhaps, but not to that of most American historians. "As to Pragmatism," Jameson wrote to his friend Francis Christie in 1910, "nothing doing in this office. I am not going to throw myself into it unreservedly or make it the foundation of my existence until I can remember from one day to the next what it is." A not unreasonable position at a time when Arthur O. Lovejoy was distinguishing "The Thirteen Pragmatisms." Though James Harvey Robinson had been

William James's admiring student, Charles Beard a close friend of John
Dewey at Columbia, and Carl Becker included a reference to pragmatism
in his 1910 "Detachment and the Writing of History," there is little
reason to believe that pragmatism had any substantial connection with
historical thought until the interwar years.[24]

Even then, the relationship was far from straightforward: it was neither
one of historians "embracing" the pragmatist philosophers' views on history, nor of being heavily and systematically "influenced" by them.
Throughout the vast corpus of their writings the leading pragmatists—
Peirce, James, Dewey—paid practically no attention to historical issues,
and, when they did address them, did so very ambiguously. A handful of
historians mention having been influenced by pragmatism. Roy F. Nichols, for example, recalled that his graduate education and early teaching
at Columbia in the early 1920s had the result of "fitting my thinking into
a frame of pragmatism." Beard occasionally cited James, called pragmatism the only philosophy in harmony with American life and culture, and
regretted that the pragmatists had never worked out a theory of history.
Becker was not ungenerous in acknowledging intellectual debts—he regularly, for example, paid tribute to Whitehead. But he very rarely mentioned pragmatism, and said almost nothing about James. In a contribution to a symposium on "Books That Changed Our Mind," Becker wrote
that "John Dewey's books I find hard to understand, but his ideas,
coming to me through other writers, have confirmed a native tendency to
pragmatic theory."[25]

[24]Cushing Strout, *The Pragmatic Revolt in American History: Carl Becker and Charles
Beard* (New Haven, 1958); Russell, "Pragmatism," *Edinburgh Review* 209 (April 1909),
reprinted in his *Philosophical Essays* (rev. ed., London, 1966), 79; Jameson, letter of 2
February 1910, AHA Papers, Box 274; Lovejoy, in *Journal of Philosophy* 5 (1908): 5–13,
29–39. Robinson's privately expressed assertion of James's influence on him left few
discernable traces in his prewar work. Beard's friendship with Dewey seems to have been
based on a shared interest in various reform projects. The notes in Becker's papers on
James's 1909 *A Pluralistic Universe* are undated; his reference to pragmatism in "Detachment" was very casual. (Phil L. Snyder, ed., *Detachment and the Writing of History:
Essays and Letters of Carl L. Becker* [Ithaca, N.Y., 1958], 7.)
[25]The most extended—albeit quite brief—treatment of history by a pragmatic philosopher
is chapter 12 of Dewey's *Logic: The Theory of Inquiry* (New York, 1938). Burleigh
Taylor Wilkins is struck by its "almost point-by-point similarity to Becker's presentism."
(*Carl Becker: A Biographical Study in American Intellectual History* [Cambridge, Mass.,
1961], 174.) But on other issues in the chapter Dewey's views diverge substantially from
Becker's, and the date of the work—long after the major statements of historical relativism, and when in fact it was on the brink of dissolution—raises the question of the
direction of the lines of descent. For Nichols, see *A Historian's Progress* (New York,
1968), 49; for Beard, "The Economic Basis of Politics," *New Republic* 32 (1922): 128–29,
and "The Development of Social Thought and Institutions: Individualism and Capitalism," in E. R. A. Seligman and Alvin Johnson, eds., *Encyclopedia of the Social Sciences*,
vol. 1 (New York, 1930), 147; (with Mary R. Beard), *The American Spirit* (New York,
1942), 670; for Becker, *New Republic* 97 (1938): 135.

Yet in a larger sense Cushing Strout was quite right to call interwar historical relativism a "pragmatic revolt." There were in pragmatism values, insights, and approaches—above all, a tone, a style, a posture, a sensibility—which were clearly paralleled in the relativists' work.

First of all, there was the attitude of the pragmatists toward science. In the late nineteenth century the principal opponents of scientistic claims had been disturbed by the cultural implications of its critical spirit—the way in which it undermined older dogmas and certainties. These were critics from outside science: from philosophy, religion, to a lesser extent, from literature; they saw themselves as a rearguard, defending a prescientific culture. The pragmatists, too, were concerned with the cultural implications of science, but theirs was a critique from the inside. Both Peirce and James were practicing scientists; Dewey always operated within a scientific frame of reference. Though the pragmatists were relentless critics of the vulgarization of Baconian induction which was still widely considered the proper scientific (and historical) method, their criticism went further. They rejected the dominant view of the world as, in David Hollinger's words, "a hard object gradually being discovered by means of the suppression of human subjectivity." Science, like any other human activity, was rooted in human interests, and reflected those interests. As James observed the proliferation of scientific theories in the late nineteenth century he was led to abandon the view of science as offering an exact copy of "a definite code of non-human realities," and to adopt "the notion that even the truest formula may be a human device." Scientific developments in the early twentieth century gave interwar thinkers added reason to feel that James had it right when he stressed the contingent, mutable, and probabilistic nature of "truth."[26]

"Truth" for James and Dewey was man-made, social, and perspectival; not a "stagnant property" but something that "*happens* to an idea. It *becomes* true, is *made* true by events. Its verity *is* in fact an event, a process." A true idea was one which "will carry us prosperously from any one part of our experience to any other part, linking things satisfactorily, working securely, simplifying, saving labor." Truth—or rather, "truths," for they were plural—were ever changing, and what was true for one purpose was not true for another. The proponents of the "pragmatic conception of truth" sought to supplement, rather than supplant, the notion of truth as "correspondence to" or "agreement with" reality, which none of them denied was relevant, but which, because of ambigu-

---

[26]Hollinger, "William James and the Culture of Inquiry," *Michigan Quarterly Review* 20 (1981): 267; James, *The Meaning of Truth* (1909; Cambridge, Mass., 1975), 40.

ity in key terms, they thought inadequate. As with relativity, the metaphors employed in attempts to explain complex notions spread confusion
and misunderstanding. This was certainly the case with what Kenneth
Burke called the "disastrous felicity" of James's phrase "cash value" to
explain the worth of ideas. There was, of course, no warrant at all in the
writings of the pragmatists for the notion that if Johnny's story that the
dog ate his homework "worked" in allowing him to escape being kept
after school, it was therefore "true." The proposition that "truths" are
multiple and perspectival never had the corollary that there was no such
thing as error or mendacity.[27]

One of the defining characteristics of the pragmatic tradition, one that
made it attractive to some and anathema to others, was its break with the
quest for certitude; its acceptance of the contingent nature of knowledge.
"Objective evidence and certitude are doubtless very fine ideals to play
with," wrote James, "but where on this moonlit and dream-visited planet
are they found?" Scientific or scholarly caution seemed to James an over-
rated virtue.

Believe truth! Shun error!—these . . . are two materially different laws; and by
choosing between them we may end by coloring differently our whole intellectual
life. . . . Believe nothing [Clifford] tells us, keep your mind in suspense forever,
rather than by closing it on insufficient evidence incur the awful risk of believing
lies. . . . For my own part, I have also a horror of being duped; but I can believe
that worse things than being duped may happen to a man in this world. . . . Our
errors are surely not such awfully solemn things. In a world where we are so
certain to incur them in spite of all our caution, a certain lightness of heart seems
healthier than this excessive nervousness on their behalf.[28]

The principal themes and the temper of pragmatism connected at almost every point with the spirit of historical relativism: not least in its
common enemies, like Arthur O. Lovejoy and Morris Cohen. Pragmatism's crusade against the worship of facts, its skepticism about claims of
objectivity, its consistent reluctance to accept a hard-and-fast fact-value
distinction, its emphasis on change and flux, on the human and social
elements in knowledge, and the stress on the practical consequences of
knowledge—all these were at the center of the relativist sensibility. Pragmatism's "democratic" antiprofessionalism—the insistence that all men,
inevitably, were philosophers, was very close to "Everyman His Own

---

[27]James, *Pragmatism*, 97; James, quoted in David A. Hollinger, "The Problem of Pragmatism in American History," *JAH* 67 (1980): 97.
[28]James, "The Will to Believe" (1896), in John J. McDermott, ed., *The Writings of William
James* (New York, 1967), 725, 727.

Historian"; the "Will to Believe" not that far from history as an "Act of Faith."[29]

IV

Other influences on historical relativism—or other elements of sunshine, wind, rain, and fog that made up the climate of opinion in which it flourished—can be treated more summarily, for two reasons. The more decisive of the two is the absence of evidence, or even good reason to believe, that they influenced more than a handful of historians. But it is also true that many other relevant tendencies overlapped with, or were in part secondary reflections of, elements already mentioned. This is even true, to a limited extent, in the case of Benedetto Croce, who had been an active participant in debates over the new physics, supporting Poincaré's view that scientific facts were no more than concepts in the mind of the observer, and who had been touched by the wave of enthusiasm for American pragmatism in Italy at the turn of the century.[30]

Croce's influence on American historians is difficult to assess. Croce's work, according to Roy Nichols, was a topic of frequent debate among young historians at Columbia in the 1920s—but who knows what they made of it? Croce's elusive mode of expression must have been a barrier to understanding, and his neo-Hegelianism was surely less comprehensible to interwar Americans than it would have been a half century earlier. Both Becker and Beard acknowledged intellectual debts to Croce, but the relationship of their thought to that of the Italian philosopher is very ambiguous.[31]

Becker, in the 1938 symposium "Books That Changed Our Minds" said that Croce's writings "helped to shape my ideas about history, which I set forth in the address, 'Everyman His Own Historian.'" This is an acknowledgment best read narrowly: Croce contributed to the particular

[29]Without pressing the point, it seems to me that just as, in the Legal Realist movement, Holmes and Arnold reflected divergent aspects of the tradition which roughly corresponded to differences between Becker and Beard, so in the case of pragmatism, Becker seems more in the spirit of James, Beard more in the spirit of Dewey. Beard's association with Dewey in various social reform activities has already been mentioned. They also collaborated in the movement for "progressive" educational reform. My suggestion of parallelism is not helped by Becker's relative silence concerning James, who, a priori, would seem to have been a congenial vicarious companion. One possible explanation—made, as Becker used to say, *sans peur et sans recherche*—is that the determinedly secular Becker was put off by James's "softness" toward religious impulses.

[30]See his *Logic as the Science of the Pure Concept* (1909; English trans., London, 1917). By noting overlap I imply no reductionism: the most important roots of Croce's thought were clearly Hegelian.

[31]Nichols, *Historian's Progress*, 49–51.

formulation of those of Becker's ideas about history which he expressed in "Everyman." Becker's basic positions were well established before the war; he did not read Croce until the early 1920s, when, in a joint review, he compared Croce's detached idealism with James Harvey Robinson's social commitment, to the latter's advantage. In 1936 he wrote that the group of which Croce was spokesman "remain confident that the Idea will see us through; but the world is in no mood to heed, even if it could understand, this survival of nineteenth century idealism."[32]

Beard, too, thought that Croce's works deserved a place among those that had "changed our mind." "Confidentially," AHA executive secretary Conyers Read wrote to Becker in 1933, Beard was "a bit hipped on Croce." Beard tried, unsuccessfully, to bring Croce to the United States to speak at the 1933 AHA annual meeting, and arranged that a letter from Croce be printed in the *AHR* following the text of his own presidential address. But Croce's extreme idealism was even less congenial to Beard than to Becker, and, even more than Becker, he cited Croce very selectively—not to say opportunistically.[33]

Becker and Beard could admire Croce's anti-Fascist stance, and the fact that during World War I he had held out against nationalist hysteria. They joined with him in rejecting Marxism—with which Croce, unlike the two Americans, had flirted. But their sense of the inevitably political nature of historiography meant that they could not share the grounds of Croce's rejection of Marxism—that it was too bound up with the passions of "politicians and revolutionists." There was much in Croce they could unreservedly applaud without accepting his underlying metaphysics, for example, the assertion that "every true history is contemporary history"—distinguishable from "dead chronicle" as it took on relevance for the historian's own time. Also congenial were Croce's

---

[32]*New Republic* 98 (1938): 135; ibid., 30 (1922): 174–76; *Progress and Power* (Stanford, 1936), 5. Chester McArthur Destler has argued that Becker was not just influenced by Croce, but plagiarized him from 1910 onward and then deviously concealed the crime. ("The Crocean Origin of Becker's Historical Relativism," *History and Theory* 9 [1970]: 334–42.) The absurdity of Destler's argument was effectively demonstrated by Hayden V. White, in "Croce and Becker: A Note on the Evidence of Influence," ibid., 19 (1971): 222–27. A comparison of Becker's 1922 review of Croce's *History: Its Theory and Practice* and his 1931 "Everyman" makes clear that Croce's suggestion that history be considered an extension of memory stimulated Becker to the formulations in his presidential address. In the review Becker first tried out the exact analogies—for example, taking out a memorandum book and reading "pay Smith's coal-bill today"—that he made famous nine years later.

[33]Malcolm Cowley and Bernard Smith, eds., *Books That Changed Our Minds* (New York, 1938), 19; Letter of 12 May 1933, AHA Papers, Box 456; *AHR* 39 (1934): 229–30. For the ambivalences in Beard's response to Croce, see his review of Croce's *History of Europe in the Nineteenth Century, Journal of Modern History* 6 (1934): 84–85; and Ellen Nore, *Charles A. Beard: An Intellectual Biography* (Carbondale, Ill., 1983), 158–62.

insistence that determining the facts and judging or interpreting them were inseparable, and his attempt to sever the ruptured link between history and philosophy. Most important of all, perhaps, was their shared common enemy, and their admiration for his devastating and sarcastic attacks on the objectivism of the "dead chroniclers." If Croce was, as H. Stuart Hughes has suggested, "more successful in defining what history was not than in stating exactly what it was," the same was true of Becker and Beard.[34]

There is some evidence for the impact, at least on Becker and Beard, of other relativist currents in philosophy, many of them arguably of pragmatist cast. Becker seems to have been alone among interwar historians in thinking there was something to be gained from reading Nietzsche, whose thought, recent commentators have maintained, parallels that of James in important respects. Becker quoted, with evident delight, Nietzsche's portrayal of "the objective man,"

accustomed to prostration before everything that wants to be known, with such desires only as knowing or "reflecting" imply. . . . Whatever "personality" he still possesses seems to him . . . disturbing; so much has he come to regard himself as the passage and reflection of outside forms and events. . . . Should one wish love or hatred from him . . . he will do what he can. But one must not be surprised if it should not be much. . . . He is an instrument . . . but nothing in himself—*presque rien!*

Both Becker and Beard greeted with enthusiasm the 1924 English translation of Hans Vaihinger's *Die Philosophie des Als Ob*, termed by Philip Wiener "a pragmatic masterpiece." And their thought has been linked with that of Wilhelm Dilthey, whom one commentator called "the German William James."[35]

---

[34]Croce, *Historical Materialism and the Economics of Karl Marx* (1899; English trans., London, 1914), 50; Hughes, *Consciousness and Society*, 212.

[35]Becker, "Detachment," 8–9. For the connection between Nietzsche and James, see Arthur Danto, *Nietzsche as Philosopher* (New York, 1965), chap. 3; Richard Rorty, "Nineteenth-Century Idealism and Twentieth-Century Textualism," in his *Consequences of Pragmatism* (Minneapolis, 1982), 150–56. Both Becker and Beard put *The Philosophy of As If* in the "changed our minds" category. Wiener's characterization is in his article "Pragmatism," in Wiener, ed., *Dictionary of the History of Ideas* (4 vols., New York, 1973), 3:566. The connection between the American relativists and Dilthey is made in Maurice Mandelbaum, *The Problem of Historical Knowledge: An Answer to Relativism* (New York, 1938), chap. 1. For at least Beard's acquaintance with Dilthey, see Nore, *Beard*, 164. The characterization of Dilthey—who knew and admired James—is by Albert Salomon, "German Sociology," in Georges Gurvitch and Wilbert E. Moore, eds., *Twentieth Century Sociology* (New York, 1945), 591. H. Stuart Hughes wrote that "Like his contemporary Henry Adams, Wilhelm Dilthey was so old-fashioned that by the end of his life he had become a modern." (*Consciousness and Society*, 192.)

The United States was not the only country in which the war was a catalyst for the undermining of older historical consciousness. The "Crisis of Historicism" in Germany, like the questioning of norms of objectivity in the United States, followed a similar temporal pattern. Manageable prewar doubts reached crisis proportions only in the interwar years. But both before, and especially after, the war, the German crisis was considerably more profound, with much broader cultural ramifications. Both were crises of relativism, but whereas in the United States it was problems of cognitive relativism which were central to historians, in Germany the cognitive dimension was subordinate to a much more deeply felt crisis of ethical relativism—calling into question the objectivity of traditional religious and political values.

The strength of the Idealist tradition in German historiography had depended on belief in an orderly and progressive world. Whereas American notions of objectivity were tied to the concept of a "value-free" historiography, the German historicist tradition had found "objective values" in history. Though before the war Dilthey, Ernst Troeltsch, Heinrich Rickert, and others had begun to concern themselves with the viability of traditional notions of the objectivity of values and knowledge, these doubts were no more than troublesome and did not have substantial resonance within the historical profession. The war, infinitely more cataclysmic in its impact on thought in Germany than in the United States, shattered faith in "the victory of reason." In 1916, in the middle of the war, Troeltsch could no longer evade the conclusion that historical study, rather than providing understanding, had fatally undermined "all stable norms and ideals of human nature," and its own scholarly method as well. Theodore Lessing described history as pure myth building: not science (*Wissenschaft*) but will (*Willenschaft*). His *Geschichte als Sinngebung des Sinnlosen* caused a storm of controversy in the postwar years, which also saw a revived interest in the more skeptical of Dilthey's prewar writings. By 1932 Karl Heussi's *Die Krisis des Historismus* described, with some exaggeration, a total breakdown of faith within the historical profession in the possibility of an objective study of history.[36]

Among American historians only Charles Beard seems to have interested himself in the German controversies. Throughout the 1930s Beard never ceased urging his colleagues to read Dilthey, Troeltsch, Rickert, Georg Simmel, Kurt Riezler, and especially Heussi. Beard's immersion in

---

[36]Troeltsch, quoted in Georg G. Iggers, "The Dissolution of German Historism," in Richard Herr and Harold T. Parker, eds., *Ideas in History: Essays in Honor of Louis Gottschalk* (Durham, N.C., 1965), 304.

German thought was purposive. Setting out on a trip to Europe in 1927, he wrote William E. Dodd that "We have too much noise in this country and too little quiet thinking. I am guilty, but shall try to make reparations." In Germany he established relations with a number of leading German historians, most notably Riezler. On his journey, and in his subsequent reading, Beard had the guidance of his son-in-law, the German historian and expressionist poet Alfred Vagts. The extent and nature of the impact of German thought on Beard is difficult to evaluate, and a matter of controversy. It seems most likely that he used it, as he used Croce, very selectively, and primarily to confirm and deepen preexisting dispositions. It is not at all hard to evaluate the success of his efforts to direct his colleagues' attention to the German crisis. They were a total failure.[37]

None of the works which Beard urged his colleagues to read had been translated into English, which, in the United States, is almost always fatal for the prospect of substantial or widespread intellectual influence. While the problems which the literature of the German crisis addressed paralleled the concerns of American historians, the idealist/historicist tradition confronted by the Germans framed their problems very differently. By the time that Beard was promoting German historiographical writings, the triumph of Hitler, and the relative warmth with which Nazism was greeted by most German historians, made Germany a somewhat less attractive place for Americans to go for guidance. The trickle of émigré German historians (almost all Jewish, part Jewish, or married to Jews) were much too busy scrambling to find positions to serve as expositors of the "Crisis of Historicism" to their new compatriots. With the sole exception of Beard the German crisis had no discernable influence on American historians.[38]

[37]Beard to Dodd, 30 July 1927, Dodd Papers, Box 27. In speculating as to why Beard ("in many ways a very big man") had "in recent years gone haywire on history," Robert L. Schuyler wrote a colleague that he "sometimes wonder[ed] whether his German son-in-law Alfred Vagts (a very nice fellow, by the way) has not had a good deal to do with Beard's recent addiction to German historical metaphysics." (Letter to Charles W. Ramsdell, 17 April 1941, AHA Papers, Box 339.)
[38]Perhaps one should add—though the extent of the influence is highly problematic—the name of Merle Curti. In 1925, while a graduate student at Harvard, Curti wrote to Frederick Jackson Turner of his summer in Berlin, where he had met a group of younger German historians. "Like many of the German psychologists, these people feel that the older reliance on scientific method has failed to give satisfying results. . . . They insist that we should learn from the psychologist that objectivity and impartiality in making historical judgments is impossible. Therefore we must define our 'standpoint' if we would be honest intellectually, and treat history as a point of view. . . . I felt that there was a degree of truth in some of the things they said. I emphasized the need of the discipline history had been subjected to, and asked why the scientific method need be abandoned. Surely, from a long distance point of view, it is much too young for one to distrust its potentialities." (Letter of 26 September 1925, Turner Papers, Box 34A.)

In fact, there was one work often considered an outgrowth of the "Crisis"—written by a sociologist who became an émigré from Nazism, and translated into English in 1936—which did have some impact on Americans. Karl Mannheim's *Ideology and Utopia* introduced the fledgling "sociology of knowledge" to the United States. By 1938 Maurice Mandelbaum said that Mannheim was "among the most influential of the recent upholders of historical relativism" whom Mandelbaum was attempting to refute. Mannheim certainly attracted the attention of historians. Beard praised, quoted, and paraphrased him often, as did the now largely forgotten but then respected Columbia historian Vladimir Simhkovitch. Becker, though he identified key weaknesses in Mannheim's argument, thought it held much that was "penetrating and suggestive." New currents are most likely to have the greatest impact on those whose minds are still being formed, as in the case of Roy Nichols's encounter with Croce in the early twenties. Richard Hofstadter was a graduate student in the late thirties; Mannheim, he reported, "provided the link I had been seeking between ideas and social situations."[39]

Mannheim's discussion of "ideologies" and "utopias" (in later terminology, "dominant" [legitimating] ideologies" and "oppositional" ones), had its origin in Marxism. It emphasized and analyzed the relationship between social location or interest and what was accepted as truth. All of this was dangerous relativist doctrine to traditional defenders of objectivity in the United States, like Mandelbaum. But Mannheim, together with others, was attempting to *escape* relativism. He offered three doors through which one could move toward at least a greater degree of objectivity. In the first place, the very awareness of the problem was part of the solution. Beard, who was impressed with this argument, wrote that though the historian could never completely escape social influences, "he can acquire at least partial emancipation from their tyranny by becoming aware of them." Becker was skeptical: "Having relentlessly pressed all our heads down below the surface of the flowing social process, [Mannheim] first assures us that we can never get out, and then tells us that we can after all escape drowning by frankly recognizing that we are under water."[40]

Mannheim's second door, which he labeled "relationism" as opposed

[39]Mandelbaum, *Problem of Historical Knowledge*, 67. Beard, *The Nature of the Social Sciences in Relation to Objectives of Instruction* (New York, 1934), 19–20; Beard, *The Discussion of Human Affairs* (New York, 1936), 110–13, 116–18; Becker, review of *Ideology and Utopia, New Republic* 89 (1937): 388; Simhkovitch, "Approaches to History [in several installments]," *Political Science Quarterly* 44 (1929): 481–97; 45 (1930): 481–526; 47 (1932): 410–39; 48 (1933): 23–61; 49 (1934): 44–83; Hofstadter, "History and the Social Sciences," in Fritz Stern, ed., *The Varieties of History* (New York, 1956), 362.
[40]Beard, *Nature of the Social Sciences*, 19–20; Becker, review of *Ideology and Utopia*, 388.

to the relativism he wished to avoid, was the assertion that, though all knowledge was perspectival, the multiplication of perspectives, and their attempted reconciliation, could move one closer to objectivity. A "dynamic" political science, Mannheim had said, "accepts no theoretical construction as absolutely valid in itself, but reconciles the original standpoints . . . and tries to understand the whole of the views derived from the various perspectives through the whole of the process." Becker found this "not too clear."

If it means only that the political scientist should endeavor to understand the "whole of the process" with as little bias and as much intelligence as may be, nothing could be better—or more elementary. But if it means, as it seems to, that this enlarged "view of the whole" is not itself conditioned by the social situation in precisely the same way that the "original standpoints" are, then it denies the assumptions upon which all of Professor Mannheim's work is based.[41]

Mannheim's third door was the idea of a relatively socially detached, "free-floating intelligentsia," not subject to the processes of social influence at work on lesser breeds. Leszek Kolakowski is one among many who has suggested that it is a trompe l'oeil rather than a genuine egress:

To put the point bluntly, in Mannheim's opinion every social group which shares particular interests produces its own peculiar, and distorting, cognitive perspective—every group except one: the group to which Mannheim himself belonged. I do not say this maliciously, but only to point to a circumstance which Mannheim neglected. It is obvious that intellectuals have much better chances than members of other social groups of avoiding the influence upon their thinking of extra-cognitive situations, in the sense, namely that they are much more likely to subject themselves to the rules of correct thinking in their cognitive activity. But it is equally obvious that intellectuals are also the people who define what is, and what is not, correct thinking. Such definition is an essential part of their social function. One may therefore suspect that the privilege is a merely apparent one, like the old privilege of the Prince of Wales with respect to men's fashions. The Prince of Wales was always a model of fashionable dress, because men's fashions were largely defined by the way the Prince of Wales dressed. A critic might therefore say that the intellectuals' epistemological privilege is nothing more than the privilege of imposing universally obligatory norms of thought and, as such, offers no evidence for the extra-situational validity of these norms.[42]

Ideology and Utopia is interesting not so much because of its influence on historians in the 1930s (though that was real), nor as still another

---

[41]Becker, ibid.
[42]"The Epistemological Significance of the Aetiology of Knowledge: A Gloss on Mannheim," *TriQuarterly* 22 (1971): 229–30.

A changed climate 161

example of the ubiquity of relativist currents in the period (though it is
that too), but because it illustrates so clearly the variety and ambivalence
of responses to the arrival on the scene of a perspectival view of
knowledge.

Further examples could be offered of currents within the academic
world which contributed to the relativist climate of opinion in the interwar years. In both economics and political science there were attempts—
often quixotic, when not just silly—to assimilate non-Euclidianism and
relativity theory. Though Walter Lippmann never held an academic position, his writings on politics, beginning with *Public Opinion* in 1922, had a
substantial influence on interwar political science's stress on the irrational, and on the fictive nature of abstractions. Semanticists and literary critics—Alfred Korzybski, I. A. Richards, C. K. Ogden, Kenneth Burke—
discussed symbol systems, ambiguities of meaning, and "arbitrary" linguistic conventions in ways that made repeated reference to relativity
in physics, and had clear relativistic implications in the social realm.
(Work in this tradition reached a more than academic audience in Stuart
Chase's *Tyranny of Words* and Thurman Arnold's *Folklore of Capitalism*.)
Reinhold Niebuhr was not, in the interwar period, the cultural hero he
became after 1945, but he was a figure of some consequence in more than
scholarly theological circles. He wrote a friend that he stood "in the
William James tradition"; like James he stressed the inevitably partial,
perspectival, and relativistic nature of the truth available to mankind. The
University of Chicago philosopher T. V. Smith, a great admirer of
Holmes (and of Becker) argued that skepticism and relativism were the
most stable foundations of democracy.[43]

Skepticism about objectivity, and an implicitly or explicitly relativist
orientation, were not restricted to the academic world and the arts. It was
manifest in the highly visible realm of journalism. The austere posture of
factualist objectivity discussed in the previous chapter gave way, in the
interwar years to an emphasis on "point of view." In the *New York Times*

[43]For economics, see Purcell, *Crisis of Democratic Theory*, 64–65. For political science, William Bennett Munro's 1927 presidential address to the American Political Science Association, "Physics and Politics—An Old Analogy Revised," *American Political Science Review* 22 (1928): 1–11, and ibid., chap. 6. Merle Curti briefly discusses the work of Korzybski et al. as part of the relativist tradition in *The Growth of American Thought* (New York, 1943), 728–29. For Niebuhr on his pragmatism, letter quoted in June Bingham, *Courage to Change: An Introduction to the Life and Thought of Reinhold Niebuhr* (New York, 1961), 224; for his relativism, "The Tower of Babel" (1937) in his *Beyond Tragedy: Essays on the Christian Interpretation of History* (New York, 1965), 44–45. For Smith, see his *Beyond Conscience* (New York, 1934) and *Creative Skeptics: In Defense of the Liberal Temper* (New York, 1934); see also Michael Kammen, ed. *What Is the Good of History: Selected Letters of Carl L. Becker, 1900–1945* (Ithaca, N.Y., 1973), 349–51.

by-lines had been rare in the early twenties; they were common by the
late thirties. In 1925, when the Associated Press distributed a story with a
by-line it was explained away as a special case; within a few years they
were a matter of course. The political columnist, who provided what "the
facts" alone could not, emerged in the twenties: David Lawrence, Mark
Sullivan, Heywood Broun, and, in 1931, Walter Lippmann. The title of a
popular journalism textbook was changed, in its 1938 revision, from
Reporting for Beginners to *Interpretative Reporting*. The change, the
author explained, reflected "changing social conditions" which were
causing changes in journalism. "The trend is unmistakably in the direction of combining the function of interpreter with that of reporter after
about a half century during which journalistic ethics called for a strict
differentiation between narrator and commenter." Nowhere was the new
attitude more manifest than in that enduring contribution of the twenties
to American journalism, *Time*. "Show me a man who thinks he's objective," said its proprietor, Henry Luce, "and I'll show you a man who's
deceiving himself."[44]

Journalistic objectivity as an ideal was not without defenders, but the
nature of the defense illustrated the extent to which the concept had
become problematic. Walter Lippmann argued that "as our minds become more deeply aware of their own subjectivism, we find a zest in
objective method that is not otherwise there"; and he continued to promote it as an heroic ideal. But his writings suggested that it might be an
impossible, or at least an unrealistic, ideal. With Charles Merz of the
New York *World* he wrote a critique of the *New York Times*'s coverage
of the Russian Revolution. After documenting the pervasive anti-Bolshe-

[44]Curtis MacDougall, *Interpretative Reporting* (New York, 1938), v; Luce, quoted in W.
A. Swanberg, *Luce and His Empire* (New York, 1972), 142–43. *Time*'s cynicism about
the manipulation of fact for "interpretive" purposes is too well known to require documentation. The attitude received pseudoscholarly theorization in the writings of the pioneer public relations men. If the founding myth of the historical profession was the idea
of objectivity, the founding myth of the public relations profession was that objectivity
was a chimera. Ivy Lee quoted Walter Lippmann on the impossibility of presenting "the
whole of the facts," then went on to cast suspicion on the very notion of the fact. "The
effort to state an absolute fact is simply an attempt to achieve what is humanly impossible;
all I can do is to give you my interpretation of the facts." Disinterestedness, he argued,
was impossible: "All of us are apt to try to think that what serves our own interests is also
in the general interest. We are very prone to look at everything through glasses colored by
our own interests and prejudices." (*Publicity* [New York, 1925], 21, 38.) Whereas Lee
stressed that opinion was necessarily self-interested, the other great public relations pioneer, Freud's nephew, Edward L. Bernays, stressed the irrationality of all opinion,
which could be neither true nor trustworthy. (*Crystallizing Public Opinion* [New York,
1923].) My discussion of journalism—here, as in Chapter 2—is largely drawn from
Michael Schudson, *Discovering the News: A Social History of American Newspapers* (New
York, 1978), 135–58.

vik bias of the *Times*, they concluded: "The news as a whole is dominated by the hopes of the men who composed the news organization. . . . In the large, the news about Russia is a case of seeing not what was, but what men wished to see. . . . The chief censor and the chief propagandist were hope and fear in the minds of reporters and editors." Leo C. Rosten interviewed Washington correspondents for a doctoral dissertation in 1935–36, and found that by a two-to-one margin they endorsed the proposition that "it is almost impossible to be objective" and that they were "psychologically driven to slant [their] stories."[45]

The issue of objectivity came before the Supreme Court in 1937 when Morris Ernst appeared as a friend of the court in *Associated Press v. National Labor Relations Board*. The NLRB had ruled that the AP had fired a reporter for his loyalty to the Newspaper Guild, while the press association claimed that he was dismissed for writing biased, pro-labor stories. Ernst observed: "The Constitution does not guarantee objectivity of the press, nor is objectivity obtainable in a subjective world . . . the question . . . really raised is not whether news shall be unprejudiced but rather whose prejudices shall color the news." The Supreme Court upheld the NLRB position. Michael Schudson, concluding the section of his history of American newspapers dealing with the interwar period, observed that objectivity came to be enunciated as a journalistic ideal "precisely when the impossibility of overcoming subjectivity in presenting the news was widely accepted" and "precisely *because* subjectivity had come to be regarded as inevitable."[46]

V

In the preceding pages I have tried to indicate some of the heterogeneous materials on which the historical relativists could draw in practicing their *bricolage*. With some additions and subtractions, and changes in relative

[45]Lippmann, *Public Opinion* (New York, 1922), 256; Lippmann, *American Inquisitors* (New York, 1928), 46; Lippmann and Mertz, "A Test of the News," supplement to *The New Republic* 23 (4 August 1920): 3; Rosten, *The Washington Correspondents* (New York, 1937), 351.

[46]Ernst, quoted in Herbert Harris, *American Labor* (New Haven, 1938), 185; Schudson, *Discovering the News*, 157–58. From 1937 on, over the opposition of some of its members (Lippmann resigned in protest), the Guild began to endorse political resolutions. Publishers, whose principal objection to the Guild was that it was a militant union, used the fact that Guild stands to raise the issue of objectivity in support of their denial of recognition to the union. "We do not deny that causes require champions, and that progress springs from the genius of advocates. Equally important to society, however, are those who report the controversial scene. It is the newspaperman's job to do that, not as a partisan but as an objective observer." (*Editor and Publisher* 70 [3 July 1937]: 3.)

weight, dissidents in other disciplines drew on a similar stockpile in conducting their own *bricolages*. The precise forms which epistemological dissidence took varied from discipline to discipline, as did the reaction against dissidence. But just as there were elements in common among academic dissidents, so there were common elements in the conservative academic response, which enlisted men who had not previously thought of themselves as conservatives. The very *bricolé* quality of the dissidence, which its opponents, much more often than its proponents, characterized as "relativist," made it seem particularly pervasive and insidious. It was "at one with the recent novel, drama, music, painting, and sculpture in attaching greater value to novel impressions and vehement expression than to coherency and order." It was a nihilistic campaign against fundamental axioms of a stable and comprehensible world, against the quest for certain and absolute truth, against the very notion of rationality. The rebellion was "anti-intellectual," and "irrationalist." On its success or failure hung the future of Western civilization.[47]

The language of assault by revolutionary forces was employed by scholars of the period who felt themselves besieged. Arthur O. Lovejoy, as we saw in Chapter 1, wished to see philosophy "attain the assured and steady march which should characterize a science" through adopting a method restricted to "objective, verifiable and clearly communicable truths." He had, before the war, criticized the pragmatic theory of truth because it offered no certitude in the present, condemning the intellect to "subsist wholly by a system of deferred payments." By 1930, James, Dewey, Whitehead, Eddington, and Born were seen by him as soldiers in a far-reaching "revolt against dualism" which was "subjectivist," "relativist," and "anti-intellectual."[48]

If Lovejoy was, as a contemporary said, "the Edmund Burke of the epistemological revolution," Morris Cohen's rhetoric made him appear as

[47]Morris R. Cohen, "The Insurgence Against Reason, I," *Journal of Philosophy* 22 (1925): 113. The conflation of threats to order in cultural, political, and scientific realms was a recurring theme. One of the *New York Times* articles on relativity theory was entitled "Jazz in Scientific World" (16 November 1919, 8); it described non-Euclidian geometry as the consequence of "Bolshevism enter[ing] the world of science." Professor Charles Lane Poor of Columbia saw disturbing new scientific developments as fruits of a worldwide "mental as well as physical . . . state of unrest . . . the strikes, the socialist uprisings . . . futuristic movements in art . . . [the] easy way in which many cast aside the well tested theories of finance and government in favor of radical and untried experiments." (*Gravitation versus Relativity* [New York, 1922], v.)
[48]Lovejoy, "Thirteen Pragmatisms," 12; *The Revolt Against Dualism: An Inquiry Concerning the Existence of Ideas* (New York, 1930); see especially chapter 4 for his argument that the relativism of the revolt undermined objectivity. I have, of course, greatly simplified Lovejoy's position; for a full exposition, see Daniel J. Wilson, *Arthur O. Lovejoy and the Quest for Intelligibility* (Chapel Hill, N.C., 1980).

its Joseph de Maistre. Like Lovejoy, Cohen included Marx and Freud as part of what he termed "the insurgence against reason." He had "little doubt that this distrust of reasoning and intellect has its roots deep in the temper of our age. The art, literature, and politics of Europe and of our own country show an ever-growing contempt for ideas and forms." Croce and Nietzsche were included in a list of pernicious influences along with James, who, in the words of Cohen's biographer, was "representative of the ideas Cohen most wanted to destroy," his "lifelong exemplar of passionate, wrongheaded irrationalism." The "insurgence" could be found in all realms: "The romantic or 'Dionysiac' contempt for prudence and deliberative (so-called bourgeois) morality is simply a more intense, if not more crude, expression of the reaction against scientific or rigorous intellectual procedure." While it would, he admitted, be an exaggeration to attribute politicians' mendacity to "the systematic scorn heaped by modernistic philosophies on the old ideal of the pursuit of truth for its own sake 'in scorn of consequences,' " he believed that the "decline of respect for truth in public or national affairs is certainly not devoid of all significant connection with its decline in philosophy and art." He gave qualified endorsement to the view that "by removing the political and economic restraints which had kept the multitude from the realm of education, the Industrial Revolution and its political consequences let loose a horde of barbarians for the invasion of the fields of intellectual culture that had hitherto been restricted to those elaborately trained or specially gifted."[49]

Lovejoy and Cohen, as philosophers, were following their calling as traditionally defined in spinning out what they saw as the logical implications of "relativism," "irrationalism," "skepticism." The games philosophers play—surely no less worthy than those the rest of us play—have to do with syllogisms, axioms and corollaries, entailments. They do not, as philosophers, concern themselves with the ways in which ideas emerge from experience, with the affective meaning ideas have to men and women, with the uses they make of them in their personal and professional lives, with their role in the social world. Lovejoy, Cohen, and those who shared their response to new thoughtways, believed with every fiber of

---

[49]The sobriquet for Lovejoy is attributed to Arthur Murphy in Lewis S. Feuer, "Arthur O. Lovejoy," *American Scholar* 46 (1977): 358. Feuer's article is a moving evocation of Lovejoy's bewildered sense of having been rendered irrelevant. Cohen's quoted remarks from his "Insurgence," 113–14, 115–16. The characterization of Cohen's view of James is from David A. Hollinger, *Morris R. Cohen and the Scientific Ideal* (Cambridge, Mass., 1975), 53. As in the case of Lovejoy, such radical compression must inevitably involve distortion, if only by omission; see Hollinger's biography for a rounded treatment of his thought.

their being in the existence of objective, in-principle-knowable truth. That belief was for them the axiomatic foundation of the whole scholarly venture; it does not seem too extreme to say that for many of them it was the foundation of their existence. Those whom they denounced as relativists, irrationalists, and skeptics were involved not just in (corrigible) error, but (secular) sin; guilty of "treason to the life of the mind." The emotionality of the issue for the defenders of traditional epistemology perhaps accounts for the looseness with which these epithets were applied.

The principal argument of the historical relativists—and let me repeat, this was a term applied to them by their opponents, not a self-description—was that so far as they could see, historical interpretations always had been, and for various technical reasons always would be, "relative" to the historian's time, place, values, and purposes. They never maintained that historians had a choice in the matter. They differed in the equanimity with which they met what they saw as an inevitable reality. For many of their opponents, the greatest sin of the relativists was not so much that they were wrong about the situation they described, but that they weren't sufficiently unhappy about it.

"Irrationalism," like "relativism," was employed at least as often for purposes of denunciation as for description. Was "irrationalist" a characterization of the thought processes of those to whom the label was applied, or an expression of dismay at the insistence of the "irrationalists" that human thought does not in fact follow the rules and standards, timeless or contingent, of "rationality"? Was it, as so often seems to have been true with respect to relativism, a case of "kill the messenger"?

It is certainly true that Becker, Beard, Robinson, and others of the historical relativists came, particularly after World War I, to abandon earlier assumptions of human rationality, and surely this changed perception fed into their relativism. "Very few people think with their minds," Becker wrote to Dodd in 1920. "That is an unusual accomplishment, like . . . always telling the exact truth, or reading a foreign language. People commonly think with their emotions. I don't see history quite as much in terms of a conscious class struggle of conflicting economic interests, as you seem to do. People's minds are far too muddled to carry on any such struggle for more than a short time. . . . What historical research needs is a more subtle psychology." Robinson, before the war, had seen recent history as the triumphal march of scientific rationality; by 1921, in a chapter entitled "Our Savage Mind," he wrote of mankind as "lethargic, easily pledged to routine, timid, suspicious of innovation." Beard, in his later years, acknowledged that in his enduring commitment to the proposition that "economics explained the mostest," he might have erred in having "neglected the irrational." The word "irrationalist" is used so variously that it is often hard to know what it is meant to suggest, and whom it fits. Often it carries an implication of "intuitionism," as opposed to disciplined inquiry. Though this may be an appropriate observation in the case of some European theorists, I can think of no American "historical relativist" to whom it applies.[50]

"Skepticism," as a philosophical designation, is distinguished from "relativism" in that the former denies that true knowledge is possible, while the latter stresses the plurality of criteria of knowledge. In practice they are often conflated since they both, though on different grounds, deny the possibility of knowing absolute, objective, universal truth. Philosophers should keep them straight; historians' usage in the period was often a bit muddled, but there were no professional American historians, unguarded and casual remarks aside, who denied that at least singular factual statements about the past could be "true" for practical purposes. There was, however, considerable "skepticism" about the likelihood, or possibility, of creating a cumulative, convergent, "corresponding" picture of significant events and epochs in the past. It is the professional and experiential, as opposed to the philosophical and a priori, grounds of that "skepticism" to which we now turn.

[50]Becker to Dodd, undated, but from context, summer 1920, Dodd Papers, Box 16; Robinson, *The Mind in the Making* (New York, 1921), 81; Beard remark from Diary of Alfred Vagts, quoted in Higham, et al., *History*, 230.

7

Professionalism stalled

Prewar historians had been exhilarated at the speed with which they had professionalized the historical venture, and were confident that a bountiful harvest would result. Building on the foundation they had laid, the new profession would achieve greater and greater status and authority. It would, like the natural scientific disciplines which were its model, establish rigorous norms of mutual criticism based on universalistic standards. A professionalized, scientific, history would rapidly construct the cumulative and convergent edifice of historical truth which figured so frequently in their rhetoric. For older historians the less attractive features of professional scholarship, principally its narrow pedantry, were temporary, attributable to the newness of the venture. Jameson, who had acknowledged that the turn of the century was an era of "second class work," thought that the first world war would usher in "an age of generalization, of synthesis, of history more largely governed and informed by general ideas."

We have passed through what is apparently the greatest crisis in history, have undergone what is apparently the greatest calamity that has ever befallen the human race. . . . Now any study of the history of historical writing makes clear the fact, that each great crisis in human affairs has evoked in the next generation a striking access of interest in human history and a crop of great historians to meet the need.

The New Historians who had emerged in the immediate prewar years shared the faith of the founders, differing only in their conception of the scope of the historical venture. If anything, they were even more sanguine than the traditionalists, since their new approach had not yet had a chance to bear its expected fruits.[1]

For many, perhaps most, American historians, these prewar hopes were disappointed in the interwar years. Professional historians' status not only failed to rise, but in important respects it declined. They lost ground to educationists in the schools, and to amateurs with the general reading public. The scholarly work produced in the twenties and thirties did not live up to expectations, either quantitatively or qualitatively. The New History agenda remained largely unfulfilled. The bland tone of professional discourse was a continuing irritation to younger historians who wished to see more hard-hitting mutual criticism. Most decisively, historical writing failed to converge into a coherent, consensual structure. It moved, in fact, in the opposite direction, a process which will be discussed in the next chapter. In considering the period before the first world war, I attempted to show the reciprocal relationship between the process of professionalization and the goal of objectivity; how ideological convergence sustained that goal; and how the New Historians believed that they could achieve a wider and deeper objectivity. The checking or reversal of these tendencies, a widespread sense that the professional project had stalled, contributed—sometimes in specifiable ways, more diffusely in the creation of a general sense of malaise—to a questioning of the profession's founding assumptions.

I

Before 1914 the professionalization of history had served as a dramatically successful ladder of personal social and economic mobility for dozens of small-town boys of lower-middle-class backgrounds. In the rapidly expanding university world of prewar America, it was not unusual for a bright young man to become a full professor within a few years of receiving the doctorate, and to achieve national eminence before he was out of his thirties. Salaries, for the most successful, compared favorably with those of many other professionals. In the more difficult to measure area of status, the college professor was a figure of consequence in the local community; culturally, he commanded substantial respect.

Professorial prospects declined considerably after the war. The openings available to new holders of doctorates were, for the most part, no longer in leading universities but rather in small colleges and in state

[1]Jameson, *The American Historian's Raw Materials* (Ann Arbor, 1923), 41, 43.

universities of the second or third rank, many of which showed neither much growth nor much vitality in these years.[2] And once settled in the minor leagues, it was difficult to rise out of them. Fred Shannon, who had won the Pulitzer Prize for history in 1929, stayed at Kansas State Agricultural College for thirteen years, and this was by no means an exceptional case.[3] The purchasing power of average professorial salaries did not reach prewar levels until the early 1930s, when a slight improvement for those with jobs was balanced by the inability of newcomers to gain entry into the academic market. Even for those most favorably situated, who did not experience an absolute decline in living standards, the relative rewards of a professorial career failed to keep pace with those offered by other professions and by business. The sense of relative deprivation was furthered by the decline between 1890 and 1940 in the ratio between the average academic salary and that of an unskilled laborer from more than 5:1 to less than 2:1. There were widespread complaints that it was impossible to sustain the requisite amenities of middle-class life on a professorial income.[4]

Low salaries had consequences which went beyond the personal hard-

---

[2]Julius W. Pratt, who was chairman of the University of Buffalo History Department for twenty-two years, starting in the 1920s, reported that in all that time only one full-time history appointment was made (Selig Adler). (Interview with Pratt by Shonnie Finnegan, in Pratt Papers.) Bernadotte Schmitt wrote to his friend Stanley K. Hornbeck in 1923 that although his claims to promotion at Western Reserve were theoretically recognized, "there is a tradition of having only one full professor in a department, and my chief is good for another fifteen years!" Schmitt, then thirty-seven, sought Hornbeck's assistance in gaining entry into the Foreign Service, but was too old to be accepted. (Letter of 4 May 1923, and other correspondence, in Schmitt Papers, Box 2.) Schmitt, in the event, did not have to stay at Western Reserve; he moved to the University of Chicago in 1925.

[3]Shannon's wife wrote her husband's mentor, Arthur Schlesinger: "Does Fred have a chance to progress in research and in the teaching of history, or is the depression responsible for his failure to achieve that which means so much to him? . . . He was confident he would thrive in history as much as was possible for a person to do. It is a fight to try to prove his real worth, also humiliating to be still teaching in a school of this kind, when his aim has always been higher. In the last three years I have destroyed several letters which I had written to you (the only man Fred is devoted to) because it isn't customary and just is not done, so please don't ever let Fred know that I laid aside my pride to write like this. I love him so much, it would hurt me more to see him hurt by me, than to witness his growing discouragement day by day." (Mrs. Edna M. Shannon to Schlesinger, 10 May 1937, Schlesinger Papers, Box 12.)

[4]Clarence D. Long, "Professors' Salaries and the Inflation," *Bulletin of the American Association of University Professors* 38 (1952–53): 577–88; Colin B. Burke, *American Collegiate Populations: A Test of the Traditional View* (New York, 1982), 233. A typical complaint was that voiced by A. T. Volwiler to his former teacher Herman V. Ames in 1928. He was getting the top salary offered by Wittenberg College ($3,000), but felt that he was "not playing fair with my dear wife and boy. . . . I have not yet cleared up my [1922] Ph.D. debt, nor could I afford a small car for the family nor a radio, nor other modest comforts." (Letter of 21 September 1928, Ames Papers, Box 1.)

ships of professors. For one thing, they inhibited potential recruits from embarking on an academic career. William E. Dodd saw

the ambitious young folk enter business, for that leads to what modern society calls success, the handling of vast sums of money or evidences of money. The second class or even the third class of young folk enter upon the professions, perhaps the lesser lights upon the profession of teaching. . . . What we have then is to take in the main the poorest material and make of it the thinking element of the country. The problem of the doctorate then resolves itself into a task of teaching weak minds to use what talents there may be.[5]

Jameson, in 1923, described history graduate students as "a less able body than they were ten years ago," a phenomenon he attributed to declining material rewards, and he acknowledged that the training and professional habits of the historian "will often leave him dull." The latter observation was representative of spreading acceptance, within the academy, of the interwar stereotype of the "dryasdust" professor, a pedantic and ineffectual figure of fun. The decline of respect for academic pursuits ran parallel to a decline in the social background of those who joined the professorate. While no substantial systematic data has ever been compiled on the class origin of historians, one estimate suggests that whereas about a quarter of prewar professional historians came from relatively privileged families, this was only true of one-eighth of those trained in the thirties.[6]

The fact that professional historians were coming from lower social strata was not lost on contemporaries, and it distressed them. "The aesthetic sense," John Spencer Bassett, secretary of the AHA, wrote, "is not a thing that comes hit or miss."

One has it by inheritance or by long training in the things that stimulate taste and intellectual harmony. It is more apt to be found in persons who are born of and trained in families of long standing in the upper classes of society than in persons who have sprung from the class that is accustomed to the plainer ways and thinking of the world. The leading historians of the past, for the most part, belonged to this class. The men going into history to-day do not come from the

---

[5]Quoted in Marcus W. Jernegan, "Productivity of Doctors of Philosophy in History," *AHR* 33 (1927): 19. Dodd was here echoing the widely quoted remark of the literary critic Stuart Sherman: "The very best men do not enter upon graduate study at all; the next best drop out after a year's experiment, the mediocre men at the end of two years; the most unfit survive and become doctors of philosophy, who go forth and reproduce their 'kind.'" (Quoted in Logan Wilson, *The Academic Man: A Study in the Sociology of a Profession* [New York, 1942], 17.)
[6]Jameson to Henri Revardin, 24 May 1923, and Nathan G. Goodman, 27 February 1925, in Elizabeth Donnan and Leo F. Stock, eds., *An Historian's World: Selections from the Correspondence of John Franklin Jameson* (Philadelphia, 1956), 287–88, 306; John Higham et al., *History* (Princeton, 1965), 63.

same social class. An undergraduate body at one of our large universities will contain many students of striking personality, the inheritors of culture by family and class tradition. But of that class almost none go into the graduate schools in the arts. . . . They . . . come from another stratum of society.

It would be untrue and also unkind to say that these persons do not make good teachers of their subjects. As a class they are as satisfactory in imparting information and in doing the pedagogical tasks intrusted to them as any teachers we have ever had. . . . Some of them show, despite their early lack of taste, remarkable grasp of its quality. But the majority take a long time to acquire it, and some never manage to reach it. . . . Left alone they are apt to fall into the dull and dreary habits of amassing information without grace of form and without charm of expression.[7]

Concern with checking the declining social status of the historian almost certainly contributed to the widespread anti-Semitism within the profession in the interwar years. Academic anti-Semitism in interwar America was much stronger in *geisteswissenschaftlich* disciplines like history (particularly American history) and English than it was in the sciences, or in the newer social sciences. Selig Perlman, a professor of economics at Wisconsin, is said to have regularly summoned Jewish graduate students in history to his office and warned them, in a deep Yiddish accent, that "History belongs to the Anglo-Saxons. You belong in economics or sociology." The academic patrons of Jewish graduate students often despaired of finding them jobs. Writing on behalf of J. H. Hexter, Crane Brinton said, "I'm afraid he is unemployable, but I'd like to make one last effort in his behalf."[8]

It is impossible to disentangle, from fragmentary evidence, the components of academic anti-Semitism. Concern with lowering the status of the profession merged into concern with who should be entrusted with the guardianship of the *Geist*, and with reservations about the allegedly aggressive intellectual and personal style of Jews: a concern that discourse and social life within the profession would become less genteel if it became less gentile. Letters of recommendation repeatedly tried to reassure prospective employers on this point: Oscar Handlin "has none of the

---

[7]"The Present State of History-Writing," in Jean Jules Jusserand, et al., *The Writing of History* (New York, 1926), 117–18.
[8]The Perlman story, which may be apocryphal, is reported in J. Anthony Lukas, "Historians' Conference: The Radical Need for Jobs," *New York Times Magazine*, 12 March 1972, 40; Brinton to R. L. Schuyler, 19 February 1938, AHA Papers, Box 329. It is noteworthy that the best-known Jewish historians in the interwar years were Europeanists: Leo Gershoy, Louis Gottschalk, J. Salwyn Schapiro, Lawrence Steefel.

offensive traits which some people associate with his race," and Bert J. Loewenberg "by temperament and spirit . . . measures up to the whitest Gentile I know" (Arthur Schlesinger); Daniel J. Boorstin "is a Jew, though not the kind to which one takes exception" and Richard Leopold was "of course a Jew, but since he is a Princeton graduate, you may be reasonably certain that he is not of the offensive type" (Roger B. Merriman); Solomon Katz was "quite un-Jewish, if one considers the undesirable side of the race" (Merrill Jensen); variations on the formula were endlessly repeated.[9]

The number of Jews within the profession who were discriminated against in this period was probably smaller than the number of those who, knowing what they were in for, stayed out of it. No matter what its roots—status anxiety, preservation of genteel norms, or unadorned prejudice—anti-Semitism within the profession between the wars represented another way in which fully professional scholarly norms, in this

---

[9]On Handlin, recommendation without addressee specified, dated 12 February 1935; on Loewenberg, 6 May 1930 letter to Carl Wittke; Schlesinger Papers, Boxes 10 and 6 respectively. On Boorstin, 12 January 1934 letter to Master of Balliol; on Leopold, 28 March 1939 letter to W. K. Jordan, Merriman Papers. On Katz, 21 May 1936 letter to William B. Hesseltine, Hesseltine Papers, M68–25/1. The exquisite ambiguity of the phrase which Schlesinger applied to Handlin—simultaneously embracing and distancing oneself from the stereotype—commended itself to Harvard historians, who repeatedly used it. Variations on the theme were widespread. Raymond Turner of Johns Hopkins said of a candidate that he would not recommend him "were it not that in my opinion he is, for those who may object to Jews, the least objectionable Jew engaged in teaching that I have ever seen" (15 February 1928 letter to C. H. Van Tyne, Van Tyne Papers, Box 2); Bernadotte Schmitt of the University of Chicago wrote to the same effect about Leo Gershoy (9 October 1926 letter to William E. Dodd, Dodd Papers, Box 25). Bruce Kuklick found similar locutions in letters of recommendation written by Harvard philosophers at around the same time. Kuklick's view is that those who employed such phrases, even if not themselves anti-Semitic, "participated in, and therefore in some measure reinforced, a vicious system of prejudice." (*The Rise of American Philosophy: Cambridge, Massachusetts, 1860–1930* [New Haven, 1977], 456–57.) This seems to me a bit overjudgmental. If those seeking to find jobs for Jewish students in an anti-Semitic environment took a high moral ground, it probably would have been at the expense of the students. But the whole question is shrouded in ambiguity. Before Schlesinger (who was himself half Jewish by ancestry) moved to Harvard, and learned its ritual phrases, he said of a candidate for an instructorship that he was "a little afraid of employing a Jew unless I know him personally." (Letter to Harry Elmer Barnes, 13 May 1921, Barnes Papers, Box 9.) Some gentile job applicants—for example, Wallace Notestein and Frederick L. Nussbaum—ran into difficulty because of their names, and prospective employers had to be prevented from leaping to the wrong conclusion. Charles W. Hull of Cornell reassured C. M. Andrews of Yale, where Notestein was under consideration, that "his family are all Presbyterians, very much so, except Wallace himself, who is a somewhat straying sheep." (Letter of 28 November 1927, Andrews Papers, Box 47.) On Nussbaum, see Edward P. Cheyney to Laura A. White, 24 April 1925, Cheyney Papers, Box 1.

case the norm of universalism, were far from having been achieved in those years.[10]

Whatever the contribution of low salaries to difficulties in recruitment, they also inhibited scholarly productivity. Although there are widely differing estimates of how many members of the professional historical community made regular and substantial contributions to scholarly literature, contemporaries frequently voiced their disappointment with the level of productivity.[11] Despite the development of a few fellowship pro-

---

[10]"Universalism" was equally absent in the relation of Catholics to the historical profession, though the circumstances were quite different than in the case of Jews. American Catholic historians—at least those born into that faith—inhabited a separate scholarly world. The handful of American-born Roman Catholics who had any prominence in the interwar historical profession were all converts: Carlton J. H. Hayes, Raymond J. Sontag, Parker T. Moon, Robert H. Lord, Gaillard Hunt. (There were a few European Catholic émigrés, like Oscar Halecki, who also entered the mainstream of the profession.) Bookish Catholic youngsters, as had been true of Protestants a few generations earlier, frequently wound up as clerics. The very substantial number of historian-priests (and nuns) who earned their Ph.D.'s at Catholic universities spent their academic careers in religious institutions, with usually only the most tenuous relationship with the rest of the profession. There was considerable antipathy to Catholics among many Protestant historians, who often believed, as one put it, that "a Catholic cannot teach history and be a true Catholic." (W. H. Mace to Harry Elmer Barnes, 5 March 1922, Barnes Papers, Box 10.) Catholics, understandably, were hypersensitive to possible signs of prejudice—which could produce amusing results. When a book by the Catholic scholar Peter Guilday received an unfavorable (anonymous) review in the *AHR*, the Jesuit historian John J. Wynne wrote a letter of protest concerning the "dishonest" review. He observed that, as Jameson might recall, "This is not the first time . . . that I have deemed it necessary to point out to you symptoms of bias in some of your contributors and reviewers." His postscript noted that he had enclosed a carbon of the letter for the reviewer, "which I trust you will send to him, not, however, with my compliments, as one who can write in such fashion deserves no respect." Jameson replied that he was "duly appreciative of the lofty tone of your concluding paragraph, and do not need to be reminded that this is not the first time that you have thus addressed me *de haut en bas*. As to sending to the reviewer the carbon of your letter, I would not think of it for a moment. Gentlemen do not like to be told that they are dishonest, and no gentleman will willingly accept the office of transmitting such accusations." Jameson did not tell Wynne that the reviewer was Austin Dowling, the Roman Catholic Archbishop of St. Paul, who had chosen anonymity to spare Guilday's feelings. (Wynne to Jameson, 8 February 1923, and Jameson to Wynne, 12 February 1923, both in AHA Papers, Box 299; Dowling to Jameson, 2 November 1922, ibid., Box 296.)

[11]Cf. Jernegan, "Productivity"; William B. Hesseltine and Louis Kaplan, "Doctors of Philosophy in History: A Statistical Study," *AHR* 47 (1942): 765–800; AHA Committee on the Planning of Research, *Historical Scholarship in America: Needs and Opportunities* (New York, 1932); Chester P. Higby, "The Present Status of Modern European History in the United States," *Journal of Modern History* 1 (1929): 3–8. As publishing costs soared, requirements that doctoral dissertations be published were progressively abandoned, or honored in the breach. One of the few bits of systematic data on publication of theses is a 1954 "Survey of Illinois History Ph.D.s" which shows that in 1906–20, eleven of twelve dissertations were published; from 1921–30, fourteen of twenty-eight, and from 1931–40, seventeen of fifty. (University of Illinois History Department Archives.)

grams, there was generally little support for research expense, which could be very substantial when it involved trips to distant archives. The publishers of academic works frequently demanded of authors subsidies for publication which could run to half or more of a typical annual salary. A fortunate choice of students or of relatives could make the difference between publication and nonpublication: Herbert Levi Osgood's *American Colonies in the Eighteenth Century* saw the light of day as the result of a gift of five thousand dollars from his former student Dwight Morrow; Lawrence Henry Gipson's *British Empire Before the American Revolution* appeared only because his brother owned a printing company in Idaho.[12]

The need to augment salaries led to summers being devoted to extra teaching rather than research, and to writing aimed at keeping the pot boiling. The ten or twenty dollars a professor could earn for reviewing a book in a popular magazine could be an important item in the household economy, not to mention the temptation of more rewarding pseudo-scholarly ventures. Charles W. Ramsdell excused himself to a friend for writing work for a popular audience on a subject of which he knew nothing, but confessed that he would "undertake to write a dissertation on Chinese history for $100.00."[13]

Also relevant in this regard is the very partial and uneven extent to which an ethos of scholarly productivity dominated American higher education in the interwar years. The understandable concentration of historians of education on the development of the cult of research at a handful of institutions like Johns Hopkins, Chicago, and Cornell can lead to the incorrect assumption that such an orientation had become general throughout the world of colleges and universities by the twenties and thirties. Although no institutions remained unaffected by the spirit of research, there were only a few where it was dominant, and many where its impact was minimal. Teaching loads were heavy, often fifteen or eighteen hours a week, and library resources in most places all but nonexistent. Ivy League institutions were often ambivalent about research: most had active doctoral programs, but many of the faculty modeled themselves after Oxford and Cambridge dons rather than productive

---

[12]Dixon Ryan Fox to Arthur M. Schlesinger, 14 September 1922, Schlesinger Papers, Box 1; Gipson, "Reflections," *Pennsylvania History* 36 (1969): 14–15. Cf. Oscar Oshburn Winther, "Strictly Personal," *Western Historical Quarterly* 1 (1970): 134, for his dependence on a wealthy patroness to get his first book published.

[13]Letter to Paul Leland Haworth, 8 June 1926, cited in Wendell Holmes Stephenson, "Charles W. Ramsdell: Historian of the Confederacy," *Journal of Southern History* 27 (1960): 523.

scholars on the German model. One dyspeptic commentator noted that "the professor of medieval history at Harvard University for three decades after Haskins was a tweedy-looking gentleman who in his whole career published two insignificant articles."[14]

As in the prewar years, the selection of new faculty, at all but the largest institutions was still generally a presidential prerogative, and the criteria of selection were often other than academic. Robert L. Schuyler, later managing editor of the *American Historical Review*, recalled that when the president of Carleton College interviewed him for a position, "the conversation turned mainly on my denominational affiliations and my wife's vocal capacity—the choir, it seems, needed a little new blood. The subject of history was studiously avoided." President Faunce of Brown University rejected the candidacy of Frederick Merk because, though he liked Merk personally, he was "a little lacking socially" and "would not fit into the life of Providence" as well as the previous Americanist had.[15] Teaching was almost always valued more highly than research, and often scholarly productivity ranked third behind "public service." This was true at the departmental as well as the administrative level: Wallace Notestein reported that his value to the University of Minnesota was judged by his chairman "less by the research I may do than by the activity I might display in the pedagogical circles of the Twin Cities." At this stage in the development of the "social relations of historical production," in collegiate cultures in which scholarly publication

[14]Norman Cantor, *The Meaning of the Middle Ages* (Boston, 1973), 22–23. Fred Shannon reported in 1926 that the annual library appropriation for history at Kansas State Agricultural College was $125, "although it is no uncommon thing to spend $500 for a blooded rooster." (Letter to Arthur Schlesinger, 1 November 1926, Schlesinger Papers, Box 3.)
[15]Schuyler to Randolph G. Adams, 12 March 1941, AHA Papers, Box 329; W. H. P. Faunce to Carl Russell Fish, 24 May 1920, Fish Papers, 6:1920. Questions of church affiliation were less important as the years passed, but arose repeatedly throughout the interwar period. The purpose of religious criteria—and what could satisfy them—varied considerably. Robert R. Palmer found that in the small colleges where he was trying to get a job in 1934, "a vague 'Protestant ancestry' which is all I can lay claim to is hardly enough to make a man 'safe.'" Merle Curti, negotiating with American University in 1937, was told that whereas his particular denominational affiliation was unimportant, it was the rule that all permanent faculty members belong to some Church "and show thereby their sympathy with Christian ideals." When Fred Shannon was being considered by the University of Illinois in 1939 the university, as a public institution, could not afford to be as open about religious tests, so the head of the Illinois History Department asked the university librarian to make a confidential inquiry of the Kansas State librarian. (Palmer to Carl Becker, 10 July 1934, Becker Papers; E. N. Anderson to Curti, 2 February 1937, Curti Papers, 2:14; Paul L. Windsor to Grace E. Derby, 5 April 1939, Records of University of Illinois, Liberal Arts and Sciences/History/Staff Appointments 1916–66, University of Illinois Archives, Box 2.)

often brought no career advancement, the payoff of scholarly work, even when based on calculation of long term return, was problematic.[16]

Much more troubling than the question of the quantity of scholarly historical work being turned out in the interwar years was its quality. Both contemporary and subsequent commentators voiced considerable disappointment at the narrow, factualist character of professional American historical scholarship in this period—the absence of major interpretive works. In an observation that was repeatedly echoed, Joseph Ward Swain complained that professional historical research had "given us more facts than we know what to do with."[17]

In ancient and medieval history the most important work of the major American figures like Charles Homer Haskins and James Henry Breasted dated from earlier years. There had been very little written in modern European history before 1914, so that the interwar work cannot be said to represent a decline, but apart from a good deal of writing on recent European diplomatic history, most of the scholarship in this broad field clustered in studies of the Reformation and the French Revolution. Work in the former area was often narrowly sectarian, and on the latter, the closest historians came to a conceptual issue was the debate over the relative characters of Danton and Robespierre. Surveying interwar work in modern European history a generation later, Leonard Krieger remarked on the absence of "originality in method or of brilliance in conception"; on the persistent gap between "reach and grasp." He noted that there were, in the period, repeated calls for "a large coherence, whether in the overt form of a conceptual unity or in the covert form of a social history that would provide a substantive unity"; what appeared was the "assemblage of material." "American writing of European history in this period," Krieger concluded, "was in many ways the typical product of the tyro."[18]

On the American side the pattern was much the same. A survey of professional historians conducted shortly after World War II solicited

[16]Wilson, *Academic Man*, 97–112; Jernegan, "Productivity," 5–6; Notestein to George Burton Adams, undated, Adams Papers, 3:18.

[17]"History and the Science of Society," in *Essays in Intellectual History Dedicated to James Harvey Robinson by His Former Seminar Students* (New York, 1929), 325.

[18]"European History in America," in John Higham et al., *History* (Princeton, 1965), 272, 281. For Krieger's detailed evaluation of interwar work, which in important respects is more positive than the quoted passage suggests, see pp. 268–87, passim. My remarks in the introduction on the Whiggish and celebratory character of Higham's essay in this volume apply to Krieger's contribution as well—as does my appreciation of the richness and subtlety of his analysis.

opinions on the best interwar historical work. Of those most often
named, a number were by nonhistorians (e.g., Pérry Miller, Vernon
Parrington, Van Wyck Brooks); many represented the belated publication of work substantially completed before the war (e.g., Turner's *Frontier in American History,* Jameson's *American Revolution Considered as
a Social Movement,* Channing's *History of the United States*); while five
of the top ten choices were massive, multivolume compendia, more often
cited than read (e.g., Andrews's *Colonial Period* in four volumes, Gipson's *British Empire Before the American Revolution* in seven volumes).
Even political history languished in the interwar years, as did economic.
There was little to show in intellectual history, save Becker's *Declaration
of Independence.* The more notable achievements—Parrington's *Main
Currents of American Thought* and Perry Miller's Puritan studies—came
from outside the discipline, and were little noted by historians.[19]

     For many, the greatest disappointment was that the New Historians'
agenda for a systematic social history hardly advanced beyond programmatic statements. Of these there was an endless stream, with the most
zealous and consistent promoters of a more "social scientific" history
being Arthur Schlesinger and Harry Elmer Barnes, who had both been
graduate students at the prewar Columbia of Robinson and Beard. Their
writings called repeatedly for the expansion of history's domain into such
fields as the history of cities, of immigration, of women, but with a few
exceptions the call went unanswered.[20]

     The chef d'oeuvre of interwar social history was the twelve-volume
History of American Life edited by Schlesinger and Dixon Ryan Fox. As
a model it was, as Richard Hofstadter later observed, "a still-birth," an
attempt to integrate a vast array of phenomena without any unifying
ideas. It represented the New History at its worst: shapeless and sprawling; "liberal" in its avoidance of issues of power (social history as "history
with the politics left out"); "progressive" in its emphasis on rapid social
change with no attention to long-range structural dynamics. Negative
evaluations of the venture were not just retrospective; they were repeatedly voiced at a meeting of the American Historical Association in 1936.
Beard, reviewing Schlesinger's own volume in the series, *The Rise of the*

---

[19]John Walton Caughey, "Historians' Choice: Results of a Poll on Recently Published
American History and Biography," *MVHR* 39 (1952): 289–302. Caughey conducted
separate polls for 1920–35 and 1936–50. I have here conflated the results of the first with
the 1936–41 selections in the second. In the list of preferred biographies, as with histories,
five of the first ten choices were multivolume works.
[20]Schlesinger's and Barnes's principal manifestos (each produced many others) were, respectively, *New Viewpoints in American History* (New York, 1922), and *The New History
and the Social Studies* (New York, 1925).

City, noted his former student's apparent belief that "interpretations are wrong, that none is possible, and that impressionistic eclecticism is the only resort of contemporary scholarship." Becker, whom the publisher had imposed on Schlesinger and Fox as a consulting editor, was thus constrained from commenting publicly, but in private correspondence with the two men he reiterated the same themes. He thought it "a mistake to write social history with politics omitted. . . . I never understood why politics is not social." He had never, he wrote Schlesinger, "made any secret of my lack of enthusiasm for the kind of thing these books attempt to do."

The attempt to survey and present all the so varied and (superficially at least) so unrelated activities of a whole people during a short period makes it difficult if not impossible to get any clarifying unity into the book—does sure enough land one in a "mire of stubborn fact." So much in the mire . . . that the most one can do is to shovel the mucky things, more or less according to their external appearances, into whatever rough and ready compartments or categories may be available. This may be called a synthesis: in a sense it is—in the sense that any literary presentation of factual material is a "putting together." But to my way of thinking *classification* describes it better.[21]

In the interwar period, and subsequently, "social scientific" history had an ambiguous relationship to received notions of objectivity and the relativist critique of that ideal. Some of the second-generation New Historians—Schlesinger, Dixon Ryan Fox, Harry Elmer Barnes—never questioned the idea of objectivity, which remained as unproblematic for them as it was for Turner. Schlesinger repeatedly emphasized that the New History involved no epistemological break with the values of scientific history. He replied to Beard's insistence on the inevitably evaluative nature of frames of reference by asserting that objectivity was "the only proper goal of the historian," that he wished only to describe and not to judge, that he did "not propose consciously to be concerned with whether the 'damned human race' is growing worse or better." Soliciting Barnes's participation in the *History of American Life* series, he said that the facts should "be allowed to speak for themselves." Barnes, in reply, assured Schlesinger that he would intrude no point of view. Fox spoke of

[21]Hofstadter, "History and Sociology in the United States," in Seymour Martin Lipset and Richard Hofstadter, eds., *Sociology and History: Methods* (New York, 1968), 8; comments at the AHA session on the Schlesinger-Fox series were published in William E. Lingelbach, ed., *Approaches to American Social History* (New York, 1937); Beard review, *AHR* 38 (1933): 780; Becker to Schlesinger, 14 February 1933, in Schlesinger Oral History Memoir, Appendix J: "An Account of the Editing of *A History of American Life* (1927–1948)," 1215–16.

the volumes he and Schlesinger edited as preliminary contributions toward a "final interpretation." None of these were casual utterances; they
were reiterated countless times in countless ways, and expressed their
deepest values and beliefs. For this group, as for the prewar New Historians, a social scientific historiography would be more objective.[22]

Other historians who, in the interwar years, participated in the preliminary rapprochement between history and the social sciences—Roy
Nichols, Thomas Cochran, Merle Curti—evolved in a relativist direction, with growing awareness that their conceptual schemes reflected
their values and intentions. But even members of the first group, like
Schlesinger, were compelled, in consequence of their theoretical commitment to explicit conceptualization, to disavow the older view of objectivity as attainable via the "blank slate." Schlesinger acknowledged that
this idea had to be abandoned, and that it would be desirable if historians'
assumptions and criteria of selection were "drag[ged] into the open." This
much, at least, of relativism was a necessary precondition for a social
scientific history. Historians attracted to the social sciences were to remain sharply divided over whether, as Beard and Becker maintained,
their "frames of reference" were at least tacitly evaluative.[23]

II

If academic anti-Semitism was a relatively minor breach of the scholarly
norm of universalism, continued regionalism within the profession, and
in American historical writing, was more serious, representing a defeat
for the aspirations of the founding fathers of the profession to create a
community which was truly national, and manifestly contradicting the
notion, central to the conception of objectivity, that "truth is one."
There were mutually entangled social and intellectual dimensions to regionalism. Insofar as they can be extricated, the former will be discussed
here, the latter in the chapter which follows.

The job market which new history Ph.D.'s entered was largely regional
in the interwar years. The overwhelming majority of state universities

---

[22]Schlesinger on the New History in his "History," in Wilson Gee, ed., *Research in the
Social Sciences: Its Fundamental Methods and Objectives* (New York, 1929), 217; reply to
Beard in letter of 20 July 1933, Schlesinger Oral History Memoir, 4:778–779; Schlesinger
to Barnes, 10 May 1923, Schlesinger Papers (Houghton); Barnes to Schlesinger, 25 May
1923, ibid.; Fox to Schlesinger, 6 February 1933, quoted in Schlesinger Oral History
Memoir, Appendix J, 1215.
[23]"History," 232–33.

which offered the doctorate both drew on a local constituency and supplied local markets, and while the leading institutions drew their students from various parts of the country, their graduates for the most part remained within the market area served by the school. One study of the interwar market for historians showed that well over half of Harvard Ph.D.'s, more than two-thirds of those from Columbia, and three-quarters of those from Yale stayed in the Northeast; three-quarters of Johns Hopkins graduates remained in the South; over 80 percent of those with doctorates from the University of Chicago (a center of southern studies) taught in the Midwest or the South. "In a 'buyers' market,'" the authors of the study concluded, "each chairman attempts to control the part of the market nearest him and where he can exert his greatest influence. Moreover, college presidents and deans usually insist that their teachers should be spiritually attuned to the region. They demand 'Southerners who understand Southern people,' men who 'understand the local situation' in the Middle West, or teachers who will not offend the delicate ears of New England students with the outlander's harsh accents."[24]

Southern and midwestern historians had long resented what they saw as control of the profession by a northeastern (and especially New England) elite, and an American historiography which concentrated on that area to the neglect of their own. Harvard was a particular object of resentment: as promoter of disproportionate historical attention to the New England settlers in general and Puritans in particular; for its perceived domination of the historical "establishment"; and as symbol of miscellaneous undesirable characteristics observed by a Wisconsin historian who was a visiting professor there in 1937:

Most people here are quite unaware of the rest of the country—except perhaps to resent it. The tone is naturally conservative; I've heard that Schlesinger is called a red in these parts: what a reputation for such a respectable gentleman. . . . There is a very large element of rich men's sons. . . . Hence if you're not a conservative generally you have to be an intellectual water boy for the rich. . . . The European[ist]s seem to be firmly in control, as they outnumber the American[ist]s three or four to one. Of course the Eastern upper class worship of things European and English accounts for much of this. As far as I can judge most of the men here are not engaged in any great enterprises. McIlwain, Ferguson, Merriman, and Haring seem to have done their bit and are coasting into port. Schlesinger, Brinton, Merk, Buck and Fay strike me as men who have made great exertions

---

[24]Hesseltine and Kaplan, 783–88; quotation from 784. The figures are based on the 1939 affiliation of those who received the Ph.D. in 1926–30.

from which they are resting. . . . Langer seems to be the most active. Morison is a terrific worker.[25]

Southern regional consciousness did not find institutional expression until 1934 with the establishment of the Southern Historical Association (and *Journal of Southern History*) in 1934, but it was no less strong for that; indeed, it could be said that it was so strong, so taken for granted, that it didn't need institutional expression. Midwesterners, and some southerners, were organized in the Mississippi Valley Historical Association from 1907; its *Review* began publication in 1914. The MVHA was founded to serve the professional interest and ambitions of American historians within that region and to celebrate its historic role. The association's perennial secretary-treasurer, Clara S. Paine, decreed that "officers and editors should not be elected who reside outside the confines of the valley"; at its first annual meeting one of the founders voiced the association's dedication to showing that "the planting of Boonesboro in Kentucky or of Marietta in Ohio is of equal importance to the landing of the Pilgrim fathers at Plymouth."[26]

The founding of the midwestern association, and its unwillingness to accept the status of a regional subsidiary of the AHA, was a defeat for the centralizing/nationalizing tendency of Jameson, who was alarmed when he discovered that this sectional association's *Review* proposed to review books not exclusively concerned with midwestern history. Not all Americanists in "the valley" affiliated with the MVHA: historians at more cosmopolitan institutions like the University of Chicago and the University of Michigan were underrepresented in its ranks; its moral center was divided between Madison, shrine of the Turnerian mystique, and Lincoln, the locus of the "Nebraska matriarchy" which administered the organization for almost a half century.[27]

[25]Curtis P. Nettels to William B. Hesseltine, 14 November 1937, Hesseltine Papers, M68–25/2. Resentment of Harvard was not restricted to Americanists or those outside the Northeast. When the AHA was being reorganized in 1940, Robert L. Schuyler of Columbia grumbled that "Harvard remains triumphant. A Committee of Five (four of Harvard provenience) reports to an Executive Committee of six (five, Harvard) nominating a Harvard man for two of the three most important non-honorary offices of the Association, the other being filled by a Harvard man. As an old New Yorker, I have to concede with mortification that Tammany Hall is an incompetent duffer." (Letter to Conyers Read, 1 June 1940, AHA Papers, Box 343.)

[26]Paine quoted in Ray Allen Billington, "From Association to Organization: The OAH in the Bad Old Days," *JAH* 65 (1978): 76; C. W. Alvord quoted in James L. Sellers, "Before We Were Members—The MVHA," *MVHR* 40 (1953): 10.

[27]Jameson to C. W. Alvord, 27 February 1914, AHA Papers. Jameson discouraged all independent ventures: when the Agricultural History Society was founded he wrote Andrew C. McLaughlin that "the organization should be somehow kept under the foster-

Despite a determination voiced in the 1920s by the editor of the *Review* that it would focus on "that comparatively small segment of the past which had its setting in the Mississippi Valley" and that its task was "the promotion of the historical interests of mid-America," the *Review*, and the association, gradually became national in scope. By 1940 the chairman of the MVHA program committee declared that "the association has long since outgrown its regional beginnings, and its very name has only an antiquarian significance." But it was to be another quarter century until, over the bitter and last-ditch resistance of regional loyalists, what had long since become a national organization of Americanists became the "Organization of American Historians," and its *Review* the *Journal of American History*; a testimonial to the endurance of particularist sentiment within the profession.[28]

By establishing an alternative center of professional allegiance for Americanists in the Midwest, and reducing their participation in the American Historical Association, the MVHA furthered one of the phenomena that had called it into being: control of the AHA by the "eastern establishment." That "establishment," led by Jameson, had decisively defeated an ineptly led grass roots revolt against its rule in 1915, and accepted some moderate reforms, but its domination continued unabated, as did resentment in the outback. That domination was symbolized by the Convivium Historicum which Jameson, from 1917 until his death twenty years later, convened every summer at a Connecticut resort hotel. He described the week-long assemblage as "a gathering of professors, chiefly New England professors, of history, who come together not for any formal exercises, but for sociability, talk, and the

ing wing of the AHA, perhaps as a section"; some years later when Chester P. Higby was trying to set up the *Journal of Modern History* Jameson did his best to discourage him. (Letter to McLaughlin, 13 February 1919; letter to Higby, 13 December 1926; in Donnan and Stock, *An Historian's World*, 231, 321–22.) William E. Dodd of Chicago never joined the MVHA; his colleague Andrew C. McLaughlin, after having been made president, let his membership lapse. The University of Chicago History Department did once enter an unsuccessful bid to have the *MVHR* based there, to find useful employment for its unproductive candidate for editor, Chauncey S. Boucher, who later became a dean. (John D. Hicks to Avery O. Craven, no date but summer 1936, Hicks Papers, Box 1.) The phrase "Nebraska matriarchy" refers to the administration of the association's affairs by the Paine family from 1907 to 1953. Clarence S. Paine, secretary of the Nebraska Historical Society, was the principal founder of the organization. When he died suddenly in 1916, his widow, Clara, became secretary-treasurer, the association's only permanent officer. She held this position until 1952, when she retired and passed it on to her son, Clarence II. His tenure in office was short: in 1953 he embezzled the association's funds, thus ending the "Nebraska matriarchy." (Details in Sellers Papers, Series 4, Box 5, Folder 1.)
[28] Milo M. Quaife and William B. Hesseltine, respectively, quoted in Richard W. Leopold, "The MVHA and the OAH," *OAH Newsletter* 11 (February 1983): 3, 4.

making of acquaintance." But it also offered an opportunity, as Jameson informed invitees on one occasion, for the executive secretary to "consult members considerably interested in the Association's affairs as to the making of plans for using the larger means which the Association is now acquiring." Dexter Perkins (Harvard '14) recalled that "there was not much to do but talk . . . and play croquet. It was very likely through this contact that, on the death of John Spencer Bassett in 1928, I was offered the job of secretary of the AHA."[29]

Resentment by those outside the Northeast at what they saw as that region's domination of the AHA's affairs was widespread. Bernadotte Schmitt of the University of Chicago, as far from an insurgent as could be imagined, told Dexter Perkins in 1936 that "the Association is drifting towards a situation comparable to that of 1915, when . . . there was a protest against the so-called oligarchy in control." He heard "from various quarters complaints that the Association is once more in the hands of a small coterie of Easterners." James C. Malin wrote to his friend and fellow midwesterner James L. Sellers of "the little group who constitute themselves into mutual admiration societies and promote themselves and their own students accordingly." When William E. Dodd was elected AHA president in 1931 he wrote his father that he was "the only southern man chosen to the place in thirty years." By 1940 discontent had risen to the point that an administrative reorganization was devised to take the key offices of AHA executive secretary and managing editor of the *AHR* out of the hands of their eastern incumbents, and consolidate them in those of Guy Stanton Ford, retiring president of the University of Minnesota.[30]

Regional loyalties among historians received psychological, if not logical, legitimation from the later work of Frederick Jackson Turner, dedicated to establishing "sectionalism" as the central theme in American history from the early nineteenth century onward. Turner's argument was not as influential within the profession as his earlier frontier thesis had been, but his authority and prestige were so great that the concept of section remained important throughout the interwar period. It was challenged by Beard, among others, on the grounds that it diverted attention from economic conflict, and other developments, such as urbanism, that

[29]Jameson's description of the Convivium and the plan for consultation are from his circular letter of 20 June 1928, Cross Papers, Box 3. For Perkins, see his *Yield of the Years* (Boston, 1969), 67.
[30]Letter of 25 November 1936, Schmitt Papers, Box 4; Letter of 7 January 1936, Sellers Papers, Box 1; Dodd to his father, 2 January 1931, Dodd Papers, Box 38.

were at least as important. But Beard's own conception of nineteenth-century struggles, stressing the conflict between agricultural and industrial forces, could be assimilated to a regional orientation, meshing with a southern and midwestern populist/agrarian sense of struggle against "eastern industry."

As an historical construct, regionalism, or "sectionalism" was value-neutral. The assertion of the centrality of sections and sectional rivalry in American history did not logically entail sectional loyalty on the part of historians, any more than the assertion of the centrality of class and class struggle by other historians entailed class loyalty on their part. But just as the prewar nationalist interpretation of American history as the struggle for unity had been both normative and descriptive, so the concept of section was, in practice, not a purely neutral instrument. Nationalism in American history was still powerful, but after the experience of the war the term had lost something of its glow. A good deal of work in European history, of which Americanists were certainly aware, was dedicated to disparaging it. Turnerian sectionalism, either joined to an economic interpretation, or, as Beard saw it, as a reactionary technique for avoiding such an interpretation, provided important intellectual support for regional consciousness within the historical community. By the end of the interwar period the evidence of that consciousness was manifold: the AHA program committee scheduled a session to consider the extent to which "the methods and techniques of objectivity [have] been affected by the regional background of the historian."[31]

III

De jure or de facto monopoly is the aspiration of every professionalizing group, and historians were no exception. In the late nineteenth century newly professionalized historians had expected that they would, in short order, be able to establish their hegemony over the production and consumption of history at every level—in the schools, in the colleges, in the literary marketplace. In the interwar period it became clear that only the second of these professional aspirations was to be realized: control of history in the schools slipped through their fingers, and professional historians failed to displace amateurs with the book-buying public.

From around the time of World War I professional historians' influence on the precollegiate curriculum began a long period of decline. In

[31]Howard K. Beale to John D. Hicks, 3 April 1940, Hicks Papers, Box 6.

the mid-1930s, Beard summed up the evolution in his characteristic incisive (and smart-alecky) style:

In the long ago, a committee of historians framed a program of history for the
public schools. Being historians by trade they thought history was a good thing
for the schools and, naturally, the more of it the better. So they put a lot of it into
the program for the grades, and grabbed nearly four full years in the high schools.
. . . In those simple and easy days, history was history—wars, diplomatic negotiations, presidential administrations, and such things . . . It was taught in the
universities. Simplify it, boil it down, and hand it to "educators" in desiccated
form. . . . Teachers were at first glad to have "something definite." There it was,
all laid out in books, chapters, and paragraphs, with questions and tables of dates
appended. Dozens of texts were written to fit the stereotype. They were adopted
by eager school boards and sold by the millions. To the intellectual interests of
historians as such were added the pecuniary interests of authors and the huge
vested interests of publishers. Hence, an academic enterprise became entangled
with economic enterprise, and a powerful interlocking directorate was enlisted on
the side of the history program. . . .
    But about the time of the World War unrest broke out. Some of it appeared
among the historians. . . . How did it happen that the historians who knew so
much history had so poorly prepared mankind for enduring more history in such
frightful form? Historians were not so sure of themselves after 1918. School
teachers . . . had other grounds for discontent. Pupils did not just take to prescribed history like ducks to water. . . . Moreover, school teachers did not live in
the ivory towers of universities where pay checks came regularly and no questions
were asked. They saw face to face the boys and girls who had to study history
and, what is more, to withstand . . . a bitter struggle for existence in the cold
world. So teachers began to ask: What relation do the Wars of the Roses . . . have
to the life these boys and girls will soon enter, most of them unsupported by
inheritances and trust funds? That was a perplexing question for professors high
up in the ivory towers. . . . In fact, they could not answer it at all. The more they
tried, the more school teachers suspected the worth and validity of the history
stereotype imposed on them by the adepts.[32]

    Beard's account is, on the whole, accurate enough, though it is less
than fair to historians, few of whom had a pecuniary interest in the
existing school curriculum, and somewhat idealizes the postures of
schoolteachers, who had their own agenda of professional aggrandizement. The latter were presiding over a phenomenal growth-industry.
Between 1890 and 1924 the number of high schools in the country increased from fewer than five thousand to almost twenty thousand (more
than one public high school was founded every day during those years).

[32]"The Social Studies Curriculum," *The Social Frontier* 2 (1935): 78–79.

The increase in enrollment was even more dramatic: in 1890 three out of every thousand Americans were high school students; by 1924 the proportion had increased tenfold. The growing educational establishment controlled not just the rapidly expanding high schools, but the "normal schools" which produced their teachers—sinking the hope of the university historians that they could dominate the preparation of history teachers in the schools as did their colleagues in France and Germany. With all this came a new assertive and self-confident "professional" spirit on the part of educators: a disinclination to accept historians' offerings passively, as they had in the 1890s. Other academic disciplines began to be heard from—demanding their piece of the action. The terms of trade between university historians and schools changed from a sellers' to a buyers' market.[33]

In the 1890s history's place in the schools had been justified by a potpourri of rationales: it produced "mental discipline," taught "historical-mindedness," socialized immigrants into the American tradition, inculcated "civic virtue." The particular justifications had been of little account. The central fact was that conservative, traditionalist, and deferential educators, as yet unsure of their own authority, accepted uncritically a curriculum devised by university historians which consisted

---

[33]Economists, seconded by bankers, thought it urgently important that the basic principles of economics be included in the curriculum: an official of the American Bankers' Association said there would be nothing to fear from radicalism if students learned the "unchangeable laws" underlying business and government. (Early pleas for the treatment of economics in the schools are contained in Simon Patten, "Economics in Elementary Schools," *Annals of the American Academy of Political and Social Science* 5 [1895]: 461–62, and Frederick R. Clow, "Economics As a School Study," *Economic Studies* 4 [1899]: 172–246. The intervention of the bankers is reported in "The Proposed Scholarships of the American Bankers' Association," *School and Society* 22 [1925]: 458.) A committee of the American Political Science Association belligerently challenged history's dominant position in the curriculum. History, it said, was "essentially a study of things accomplished and on record"; government was "essentially a study of things in the doing, institutions in the making, of things projected, of what ought to be done." It asked rhetorically whether the schools' purpose was "to promote the development of history or to develop the American boy and girl and fit them for their citizen-duties and responsibilities?" (The political scientists' claims are in "Report of the Committee of Five of the American Political Science Association on Instruction in American Government in Secondary Schools," *Proceedings of the American Political Science Association* 4 [1908]: 239–45.) The National Security League, formed in World War I (when its principle curricular intervention was to eliminate the teaching of the German language from the schools), lobbied in the early 1920s for teaching of the Constitution. By the summer of 1923 twenty-two states had enacted laws requiring continuous instruction in the glories of the founding document. Sociologists and anthropologists made no claims for disciplinary representation in school curricula, but the former, insofar as they concerned themselves with the schools, advocated a present-oriented rather than an historical emphasis.

of a steady diet of academic history: ancient, medieval, English, French, and American history filling up the high school years.

Now it was the educators who were calling the tune, and they were taking a new look at the rationale for history's dominant position. They embraced the "progressive" doctrine of education for "social efficiency." In a report issued in 1916 the National Education Association defined "the cultivation of good citizenship" as the "conscious and constant" purpose of the social studies in the schools; history had a role only insofar as it could be related to "the present life interests of the pupil, or can be used by him in his present processes of growth." It would accomplish little for high school students, wrote one educator, for them to "master a few dissociated, disconnected, and well-nigh useless historical facts about the Egyptians, Babylonians, or nomadic tribes of other lands. Live, dynamic, functional social training is what is needed, and not cold-storage historical facts." David Snedden insisted that vague claims for the utility of history were unacceptable; it should be "a handmaid to the study of the social environment of the child—an extension of his social study into fields which are inaccessible to direct observation." History should be "drawn upon when and where needs are indicated by a . . . plan of civic education in much the same way that navigation or bridge-building draws upon mathematics for materials needed at the moment."[34]

The programmatic justification for social studies programs which increasingly drove "straight" history from the schools came from educationists and those, like John Dewey, who were allied with them. But the new approach derived considerable support from those within the historical profession who were equally dissatisfied with traditional historiography, the New Historians. Educators seeking support for their vision of a curriculum which would be "relevant" and up-to-date cited Robinson's

---

[34]*The Social Studies in Secondary Education* (Washington, D.C., 1916), 9, 12, 44; Joseph Roemer, quoted in Rolla M. Tryon, *The Social Sciences as School Subjects* (New York, 1935), 210–11; Snedden, "History Study as an Instrument in the Social Education of Children," *Journal of Pedagogy* 19 (1907): 261–65; Snedden, "History Studies in Schools: For What Purposes?" *Teachers' College Record* 25 (1924): 7–9. Snedden was one of the most influential interwar educationists, and his presentism was even more than ordinarily shortsighted. To illustrate the futility of history for civic education he proposed that "we take from Truslow Adams' great 'Epic' two very large, and in their day poignantly significant, subordinate 'epics'—that of the subjugation of the Indian tribes by the white invaders, and that of the train of consequences attending the institution of slavery. Have the 'histories' of these two any possible contribution towards the more adequate preparation of our young citizens to solve the problems certain to come to them in their local and state governments from 1940 to 1980? Probably only romantics can think so. . . . In brief, it is a mistake to assume that the history studies are going to prove of more than incidental worth as sources of functional civic learnings." ("The Social Studies—For What?" *School and Society* 36 [1932]: 362.)

essays in *The New History* more than any other source. They had another
ally in Beard, who before World War I argued, in light of his "entirely
utilitarian view of history writing and instruction," for an emphasis on
recent history in the schools. "The history which does not emerge into
the living present," he wrote, "is sterile when viewed from the standpoint
of public need, however diverting it may be as a subject of interested
speculation on the part of private persons." Becker also thought a radical
reorganization of the history curriculum was necessary. "Considering
how little students actually get out of the study of history in schools," he
thought it might be better to "throw all of the high school instruction in
history, economics, government, etc., into one three year course" with
history's share about one third.[35]

Those professional historians, and they appear to have been the great
majority, who wished to defend "the integrity of history" were in an
unenviable strategic situation. Their previous dominant position in the
schools had been based on the historians' assertion that history, in not
very clearly specified ways, contributed to "civic education." As educators increasingly came to define this goal in terms of familiarity with
contemporary problems, and indoctrination in desirable social attitudes,
the traditional historians' stress on continuity, "historical-mindedness,"
and an austere factualism seemed less self-evidently satisfactory. If the
historians dug in their heels in defense of "history for history's sake" they
lost their major selling-point with those whom they had to convince.
Alternatively, the acceptance of the educationists' aggressively presentist
criteria for choosing the history to be taught meant, for many historians,
at best a pyrrhic victory for their subject.

In practice, the historical establishment veered back and forth ineffec-
tually. A 1907 AHA curriculum committee formed in response to complaints about overemphasis on ancient history in the schools made only
the most modest concessions to modernism, and met with a cool response
by schoolteachers. When an AHA committee on History and Education
for Citizenship, a few years later, proposed eliminating ancient history to
make space for contemporary studies, its report was rejected by the AHA
Council. An editorial in *The School Review* was dismayed by the decision, and predicted—correctly—that the AHA would not be able to
"blockade a movement which is . . . going forward in the schools."

---

[35]Beard, "A Plea for Greater Stress Upon the Modern Period," *Sixth Annual Convention of
the Association of History Teachers of the Middle States and Maryland* (1908): 13; Becker,
"History in the High School Curriculum," *Educational Administration and Supervision* 2
(1916): 377; Becker to Henry Johnson, 24 October 1922, Schlesinger Papers, Box 1.

If historians are going to continue to regard themselves as the guardians of the social studies in high schools, they will have to give up the hope of spending three-fourths or even one-half of the time of students in laying what they please to call the foundation. The American student must be taught something about the community which is all around him. Either this instruction in modern social conditions must be worked out apart from history or the historians must begin to act quickly.[36]

By the late 1920s the AHA attempted another rapprochement with the educationists by joining in the sponsorship of a lavishly funded Commission on the Social Studies—formally headed by the medievalist August C. Krey but in fact dominated by Charles Beard and the commission's research director, George S. Counts. While the commission made no specific curricular recommendations, the principal thrust of its final report was toward an activist and reformist program of social education— suitable for the "new age of collectivism" which the commission saw emerging as "the age of individualism and *laissez faire* drew to a close." The AHA never officially accepted or endorsed the commission's report, and doubtless many of its members were appalled by its leftist/activist orientation. But the association could hardly repudiate its Beardian conclusions, appearing as they did during Beard's term as president of the AHA. Historians, on the whole, ignored it.[37]

They may have done so in part because the Commission on the Social Studies explicitly raised an uncomfortable issue: the inevitability of "indoctrination." Counts, the commission's research director, had posed the question directly in his *Dare the Schools Build a New Social Order?* and the issue was a frequent topic of debate in the late 1930s. "Neutrality with respect to the great issues that agitate society," wrote Counts, "is practically tantamount to giving support to the forces of conservatism."[38]

"Indoctrination" was an uncomfortable issue for historians, many of whom recognized that history and the social studies in the schools were necessarily involved in the inculcation of values, but who shied away from the implications of that fact for the historian's posture.[39] James

[36]"Conservatism in History," *School Review* 28 (1920): 167.
[37]AHA, Commission on the Social Studies, *Conclusions and Recommendations* (New York, 1934), 16.
[38]*Dare the Schools Build a New Social Order?* (New York, 1932), 54.
[39]The proposition that the function of education was indoctrination and legitimation was a commonplace among "advanced thinkers" throughout the interwar years. In 1922 Robert Morss Lovett called education "the dominant superstition of our time": "Though the humble and obscure teacher, like the Lollard parson, may puzzle his brains about the why and how and purpose of his being here, his superiors, the bishops, the papal curia, know the reason. Education is the propaganda department of the State, and the existing social system." ("Education," in Harold E. Stearns, ed., *Civilization in the United States* [New York, 1922], 88–89.)

Sullivan, the official New York State historian, saw, on the one hand, illegitimate propaganda, which "looks to the undermining of the social body and those institutions to which it has grown accustomed," and, on the other hand, that which "we cannot denominate as propaganda: the teaching of such elements as have for their object the maintenance of the institutions of the society." Elmer Ellis of the University of Missouri sketched the professional and ideological background of the dilemma in which many found themselves on the issue of indoctrination:

There have been many to urge that we should indoctrinate for a new but indefinite social order; there have been more to insist that we should indoctrinate to retard the processes tending toward change; and finally there is the force of our own tradition which echoes that we should not indoctrinate at all. . . . The history which we were taught to revere paid lip service, at least, to Von Ranke's standards. . . . The impact of intellectual and economic change has destroyed this structure; objective history seems an already ancient cult without a single follower. . . .

It is inescapable that some general philosophy—legitimately called indoctrination—is behind our selection of facts, generalizations, and attitudes to be acquired in school. . . . Contrary to the accepted theory of a few years ago, the kind of social studies teaching that has been general in American schools has not only been broadly indoctrinating but has embodied an immense amount of very narrow, although unacknowledged, indoctrination. . . . The general framework of our dominant upper middle class has generally been indoctrinated, even to such fundamentally reprehensible ideas as the belief that money income measures the social value of individual effort. . . .

In place of the older type of social studies philosophy, the Commission recommended a frame of reference which was far less specific than the one in use in most schools. It took no great insight to see that the most emphatic objections to the report came from those accustomed to think in terms of this still more specific, but unacknowledged, frame of reference, which was believed to result in a different distribution of privileged positions within society. But of course the attack was upon the idea of having a frame of reference, or perhaps one should say more upon the fatal admission of having one.[40]

As if in expiation for associating themselves with the radical Commission for the Social Studies, professional historians' final venture in the area of precollegiate curriculum before World War II was to cooperate in the College Entrance Examination Board's Commission on History, whose report gave short shrift to "social studies," and whose sole concession to "modernity" was to endorse historical studies which included the

[40]Sullivan, "History Teaching as Propaganda in Dealing with After-War Problems—Its Use and Abuse," Association of History Teachers of the Middle States and Maryland, *Proceedings* 17 (1919): 26–27; Ellis, "The Dilemma of the Social Studies Teacher," *Social Education* 2 (1938): 79–81.

social and economic, as well as the traditional political fare. Conyers Read, who served on the College Board Commission while executive secretary of the AHA, expressed in a private letter the problems of those historians who wished to take a middle course between left and right, while defending history through an accommodation with the educationists:

> Unless we are alert to the necessity for constant readjustment we create a condition of maladjustment which is the inevitable forerunner of Revolution, whether that Revolution take the Russian or the Italian form. . . . I believe that the study of history has an important social function to perform of just this sort. If Karl Marx was wrong, Edmund Burke was also wrong. There is a way of orderly progress somewhere between the two and I believe that the study of history serves to strengthen the faith of those who are of that persuasion. I am as far as possible from believing that history should countenance propaganda of any sort, but unless we can show that it has some significance in terms of contemporary problems, it is going to have to yield its place in a curriculum of the social studies, and we are going to have to accept the substitution of economics, civics and sociology as more pertinent to the needs of a bewildered world.[41]

History was never, in fact, completely displaced by social studies—the result of the failure of educationists to produce a coherent program, the conservatism of school boards which distrusted the "progressive" air of the new approach, and of that greatest of all social forces—inertia. But there was a pessimistic, beleaguered tone to historians' discussions of history's place in the schools throughout the interwar years. Henry Johnson thought it likely that the educationists, "freed from all control by historical scholarship," would "reduce history to the casual place it occupied in the school curriculum 300 years ago." The AHA's secretary, John S. Bassett, pleaded with historians to "fight for history, since no one else will do it for us. . . . If we wait we are beaten." By 1935 Carlton J. H. Hayes thought they already had been. In the schools, he said, "it is now *de rigeur* to regard history not merely as a step-sister of the social sciences but as an ugly and fallen sister, one whose very name should be avoided in polite circles and when referred to at all should be mentioned apologetically and with blushes. No longer, in any part of the country, or in any kind of school, is there a history program." Hayes's picture was vastly overdrawn—more reflective of historians' despondency over the direction of change than of what was actually occurring. But after the twen-

---

[41]Letter to Paul Cram, 10 April 1937, copy in Schlesinger Papers, Box 12. (Cram was the spokesman for a group of Harvard instructors who thought the College Board History Commission had gone too far in its concessions to the social sciences.)

ties, history never recovered the position it had held in the nation's schools before World War I, and this was not the least of the dimensions of historians' professional frustration during the interwar decades.[42]

The failure of professional historians to win a lay audience was less disturbing than their increasing marginalization within the school system, but it was nevertheless galling; the more so since the interwar period was one which saw the emergence of a substantial popular market for historical writing. It was amateur historians who cashed in on that market. Often, like Frederick Lewis Allen, Claude G. Bowers, and Matthew Josephson, they were journalists, but the ranks of successful interwar amateur historians also included a former U.S. senator (Albert J. Beveridge), and a poet (Carl Sandburg), as well as independent scholars like James Truslow Adams and Van Wyck Brooks. Foreign authors also cashed in on the boom: no biographer was more popular than the German émigré Emil Ludwig; *The Story of Mankind* by the Dutch writer Hendrik Willem Van Loon was a longtime best seller; H. G. Wells's *Outline of History* sold more than a million and a half copies in the United States.[43] By way of contrast, restricting ourselves to just two of the acknowledged scholarly classics of the era, J. Franklin Jameson's *American Revolution Considered as a Social Movement* sold less than a thousand copies; it took seventeen years to sell fifteen hundred copies of John D. Hicks's *Populist Revolt*.[44]

Most professional historians expressed dismay at the work of their amateur competitors. Wood Gray of George Washington University wrote a colleague that until professional historians displaced amateurs "Clio is going to be just a gal-about-town on whom anybody with two bits worth of inclination in his pocket can lay claims." Charles M. Andrews complained in his AHA presidential address that laymen had yet to esteem historians as highly as other professional experts, and gave as much confidence to Hume, Gibbon, Prescott and Bancroft as to "the most advanced and best trained historians." A 1935 presidential address to the Mississippi Valley Historical Association regretfully reported that after fifty years of professional historical scholarship, despite victory in

---

[42]Johnson, *AHA Annual Report, 1921*, 74; Bassett, ibid., *1924*, 65; Hayes, "History and the Present," *Proceedings of the Middle States Association of History Teachers* 33 (1935): 23.
[43]Wells's sales figure from Higham, et al., *History*, 74. The line between professional and amateur was not always easy to draw: Van Loon had a Ph.D. in history from the University of Munich; Douglas S. Freeman, the popular biographer of Lee, had a Johns Hopkins doctorate, but worked all his life as a journalist, and wrote in his spare time.
[44]W. Stull Holt, "Who Reads the Best Histories?" *MVHR* 40 (1954), reprinted in his *Historical Scholarship in the United States and Other Essays* (Seattle, 1967), 70.

the occasional skirmish, "we have won no major engagement outside our own ranks."[45]

If amateur historians in general were held in low regard by professionals, the iconoclastic "debunking" historians, who enjoyed a vogue in the twenties and thirties, were regarded with horror and anger. William E. Dodd found the debunkers offensive because they were "flippant": "History is not flippant; it is tragic." Carl Russell Fish of the University of Wisconsin thought there were two possible ways to deal with the problem. One, which he thought impractical, was "the recognition of the historical profession as a definite discipline . . . such as the medical profession, and its recognition as such by the licensing of historians who can show proper training." His preferred solution was "a statutory declaration that the truth (not opinion) in history is a public property and misstatements of the truth liable to grand jury indictment and prosecution by the proper authority."[46]

There were attempts, sometimes quixotic, to bring scholarship to the masses. Louis Gottschalk, who was disturbed by historical inaccuracies in Hollywood films like *The Scarlet Pimpernel*, wrote the head of Metro-Goldwyn-Mayer Studios to suggest that "if the cinema art is going to draw its subjects so generously from history, it owes it to its patrons and its own higher ideals to achieve a greater accuracy. No picture of a historical nature ought to be offered to the public until a reputable historian has had a chance to criticize and revise it."[47]

A more substantial venture to bring historical scholarship, if not to the masses, at least to the middle classes, came within a whisker of enlisting the official support of the profession. During the 1930s the AHA had several times agreed in principle that it would be worthwhile to sponsor a popular historical magazine. In 1938 Allan Nevins—a journalist who had become a professor of history at Columbia—together with Conyers Read, the AHA's executive secretary, and a few others, presented the association with a detailed plan under which the AHA, in collaboration with the magazine publisher Condé Nast, would issue an expensive and lavishly illustrated periodical "cocktail table book," much like what later emerged as *American Heritage*. Read described it privately as "aimed at

[45]Letter to William B. Hesseltine, 17 January 1941, Hesseltine Papers, M68–25/4; Andrews, "These Forty Years," *AHR* 30 (1925): 226–27; Lester Burrell Shippee, "A Voice Crying?" *MVHR* 22 (1935): 13.
[46]Dodd to Albert B. Hart, 22 December 1926, Dodd Papers, Box 24; Fish to Congressman Brooks Fletcher, 9 March 1927, Fish Papers, Box 7.
[47]Letter to Samuel Marx, 18 April 1935, Gottschalk Papers, 1:6.

the rich" who were "more in need of historical-mindedness than the poor." Subscribers, whom the promoters enthusiastically estimated would soon number a hundred thousand, would become nonvoting associate members of the AHA. In return for conferring this status on subscribers, and for lending its name to the venture, the association would receive an estimated $150,000 annually.[48]

The proposal at first sailed through the AHA executive committee with only a single dissenting vote, but opposition grew, and it barely squeaked through a meeting of the executive council. Those hostile to the plan, led by Frederick Merk of Harvard, and Robert L. Schuyler, managing editor of the *AHR*, were concerned with what they saw as the slick and commercial nature of the venture. Merk feared that the proposal to raise a $300,000 fund to launch the project, among wealthy "historical-minded persons" who had previously contributed to the AHA, would "dry up for years to come the sources of benevolence to which we might later wish to turn for our own proper projects." Schuyler was concerned that the hundred thousand who were made associate members (to "gratify their vanity and . . . enable them to pose as intellectuals in their respective Main Streets") "would not permanently remain 'political mutes.'" And as *AHR* editor he feared that, with a well-paying alternative outlet for articles, "some of our more fiscally-minded brethren will be seduced from their old allegiance." At the December 1938 membership meeting of the association the plan was tabled by a vote of 69 to 62.[49]

Nevins was enraged by the rebuff and produced two responses, which existed in uneasy balance. The first was the organization of a new, by-invitation-only, Society of American Historians, which would join amateurs and professionals in sponsoring the popular magazine. He rapidly enlisted virtually all leading amateur historians (and several historical novelists) together with an impressive list of professionals, including over twenty past and future presidents of the AHA.

Then, in what looked to many like a Declaration of Independence for the new group, Nevins published an angry attack on the historical profession in the *Saturday Review of Literature*. Historical writers, he said, were divided into three groups: at one end, pedants ("dryasdust monographers"); at the other, popularizers, like George Bancroft ("careless or

---

[48]Read to President James Phinney Baxter III of Williams College (another partisan of the project), 14 September 1938, Buck Papers, I/3.

[49]Merk, "To the Members of the Council of the AHA," 12 December 1938, Buck Papers, I/3; Schuyler to Charles A. Beard, 14 February 1939, AHA Papers, Box 330; Schuyler to Wallace Notestein, 10 February 1939, ibid., Box 337.

even contemptuous of precision and thoroughness"); in the middle, "true historians" who "reconcile fact and art." It was the pedant, with his "morose jealousy of intellectual superiors" who was "far and away the more dangerous"; he who was "chiefly responsible for the present crippled gait of history in America."

His touch is death. . . . He has found means in our university system and our learned societies to fasten himself with an Old Man of the Sea grip upon history. . . . They teach ambitious spirits to look for petty monograph subjects, drill them in their own plodding, barren discipline of footnotes and bibliography, and kill the vital spark. They gain control of the research funds that might provide some leisure for really talented men. They try constantly to fasten an autocratic, intolerant grip upon societies founded with broad and generous aims, like the American Historical Association, and to reduce them to strictly academic and narrowly "learned" bodies. . . . The worst examples of how history should never be written can be discovered in past files of the *American Historical Review*. . . . The unescapable fact is that organization must be fought with some degree of organization. Some body should be created to unite the best of the university writers of history—those really interested in its presentation in attractive literary form—with the best of the outside writers.[50]

Schuyler, on behalf of the *AHR*, wrote an angry reply to Nevins's article, and rejected his invitation to join the new society: "that would be disloyal to the American Historical Association . . . and to the memory of all the fine spirits—Jameson, G. B. Adams, Dunning, Osgood and all the rest—who gave themselves with utter unselfishness and the highest idealism to the cause of that history which is close to my heart, though you call it 'pedantic.'" Schuyler urged others to do likewise as an act of solidarity—and a few did. Charles and Mary Beard, who had been listed as sponsors before the *Saturday Review* article appeared, telegraphed their resignation to Nevins. Wallace Notestein wrote Schuyler that the Yale historians were meeting so that they could act collectively. In the event, he and Michael Rostovtzeff refused to join the society because of Nevins's attack on the AHA. But their Yale colleagues Samuel Flagg Bemis, Ralph H. Gabriel, Stanley Pargellis, and Harry Rudin affiliated with the new group. Similarly at Harvard, Roger Merriman reported that most members of the History Department were opposed to the new venture, but Crane Brinton, Paul H. Buck, C. H. Haring, William L. Langer, Samuel Eliot Morison, and Arthur Schlesinger all signed on. Carl Becker somewhat apologetically explained his affiliation with Nevins's

[50]"What's the Matter with History," *Saturday Review of Literature* 19 (4 February 1939): 3–4, 16.

group by observing that "The way aristocrats lose revolutions is by refusing to take any part in them."[51]

The willingness of so many prominent professional historians to align themselves with the new organization by no means signaled their repudiation of the AHA and its "pedantry." But in the context of Nevins's attack, and in the face of pressure to close ranks against it, their action was hardly an overwhelming vote of confidence for the professional status quo.[52]

IV

In addition to those realms in which, as we have seen, the prewar program of historical professionalization was checked or reversed between the wars, there were other areas as well in which the norms of "scientific professionalism" were unfulfilled.

Full professional autonomy eluded historians, not only because of the limited autonomy which departments had vis-à-vis college and university administrations, but also as a result of continued dependence on private patrons. At the University of Michigan, the wealthy businessman William Clements, who endowed the university library, held a veto over the appointment of a faculty member in American history whose duties would include overseeing the library. At the University of Chicago, William T. Hutchinson's academic future depended on satisfying, in his commissioned biography of Cyrus McCormick, the claims of one branch of the McCormick family over another concerning credit for the invention of the reaper. (The salaries of many of the members of the University of Chicago History Department were provided—in whole or in part—by earmarked contributions from wealthy Chicagoans, whom William E. Dodd was continually courting.) The business historian Thomas Cochran had an "irritation of long standing" at the censorship under which he had continually worked.[53]

---

[51]Schuyler to Nevins, 10 February 1939, AHA Papers, Box 337; Charles Beard to Schuyler, 18 February 1939, ibid., Box 339; Notestein to Schuyler, 11 February 1939, ibid., Box 337; Rostovtzeff to Nevins, 12 February 1939, Notestein Papers, I/7; Merriman to Conyers Read, 27 February 1939, Merriman Papers; Becker to Notestein, 18 February 1939, Notestein Papers, I/1.

[52]John Higham, in his discussion of the incident (*History*, 80–82), interprets it very differently—seeing it as a decisive victory for the "old guard."

[53]For Clements's role at Michigan, see correspondence between Claude H. Van Tyne and Verner W. Crane during 1922–23 in Crane Papers, Box 1. Dodd arranged for Hutchinson to write the biography which would support Cyrus's claims—and, his descendants hoped, win him election to the Hall of Fame. (The question of who invented the reaper was not straightforward, since it was a matter of evaluating the relative significance of

The numerous historians who relied on textbook writing to supplement their incomes sullenly acquiesced in the demands of ethnic and patriotic groups for additions, omissions, and alterations, a practice which went back to the early days of the profession, and did not at all improve during the interwar years.[54] There was a surge of pressure on textbooks in the aftermath of World War I. In part this was a continuation of wartime superpatriotism, in part a reflection of the Red Scare. Another factor was reaction by Irish and German groups against the Anglophile version of the American Revolution promoted by historians during the war, this last often exploited by local demagogues like Mayor "Big Bill" Thompson of Chicago. A committee on textbooks appointed by the superintendent of schools of New York City insisted that "Truth is no defense to the charge of impropriety. 'The Aristidean sense of justice' which would spread upon the pages of a textbook the weaknesses of our heroes . . . may find a place and an audience somewhere. That place must not be the public school. . . . To preserve unsullied the name and fame of those who have battled that we might enjoy the blessings of liberty, is a solemn and sacred obligation." Andrew C. McLaughlin, writing to Claude H. Van Tyne, his collaborator on a popular text,

incremental improvements to the basic mechanism, contributed by various members of the family.) Although Hutchinson's compensation was not conditional on his coming to conclusions acceptable to the family, they reserved the right to withhold the book from publication if they were not satisfied with it—sufficient leverage in the case of an assistant professor, dependent on a record of publication to advance academically. At the same time, Dodd was working on the family to secure an endowed research professorship for himself, and their repeated half promises insured that he would keep Hutchinson on track. Only Hutchinson did well out of the arrangement: Cyrus failed of election to the Hall of Fame; the family finally decided that they had to tighten their belts as a result of the Depression, and there would be no chair for Dodd. (Material covering these arrangements—as well as other fund-raising activities carried out by Dodd, is scattered through his papers, especially Boxes 31–38, and in Hutchinson's manuscript diary in the Joseph Regenstein Library, University of Chicago.) For Cochran, see his 12 March 1941 letter to Ralph Hower, Cochran Papers, Box 4.

[54] In 1897 John Bach McMaster wrote the head of the Textbook Committee of the veterans of the Grand Army of the Republic that "the suggestions you were kind enough to make have all been used." The first edition of his text included a footnote which doubted the Norse discovery of America. A textbook salesman wrote back to headquarters that "The discovery of America by the Norsemen is believed in by our Norse population as they believe in their Bible. . . . In some counties in Minnesota, Wisconsin, and South Dakota . . . the omission of the name of Leif Erikson . . . will effectually shut the book out of all the schools." In later editions the reference was suitably altered. Edward Channing's correspondence reveals an equal willingness to make changes in his textbook to placate significant constituencies; he wrote his publisher, "I have this moment finished the first draft of the 'Book of Lies' otherwise known as Channing's 'Elements of United States History'." (Eric F. Goldman, *John Bach McMaster: American Historian* [Philadelphia, 1943], 86–87, 94; Davis D. Joyce, *Edward Channing and The Great Work* [The Hague, 1974], 174, 176.)

expressed his dismay at the pressure to "don't never mention the fact that no American never did no wrong. Weren't they the ancestors of Mr. Walsh, and Mr. Cohen, and Mr. Podofsky and Mr. Adrionapolis and Mr. and Mrs. Popeyeski?"[55]

Historians regularly "adjusted" their textbooks to meet criticisms from local, regional, religious, ethnic, or patriotic pressure groups. (Carl Becker, for example, after his text was attacked for pro-Communism, was led to substitute the phrase "so called 'scientific' socialism" for "Marxism" at several points in his *Modern History*, and to reduce the use of Marx's name to a minimum.) Variant editions of texts were issued for southern schools, Catholic schools, and other special constituencies. Minimal authorial duties were required of those with "salable" names: "Your name will give the book standing throughout the South," Eugene C. Barker wrote William E. Dodd, "there is the bold, sordid truth." Barker insisted to the publisher that Dodd was "as entitled to dividends on [his] name as [the publisher] was on his stock."[56]

As a rule, historians, with a resignation that often shaded off into cynicism, were convinced of the impossibility of resisting pressure to modify texts. Dodd thought that "if the history of the United States were written exactly as it happened the author would probably be landed in jail." Marcus W. Jernegan believed that "about all one can do is to 'get by' with as much as possible and be satisfied with that." An editorial in the *Mississippi Valley Historical Review* expressed little sympathy with the naive textbook writer who "seeks to picture the past as it really was, to tell the truth without regard to present-day sentiments or sensibilities: he can hardly escape incurring the characteristic pains of martyrdom."

The public which controls the schools will dictate, whenever it sees fit, the history that is taught in them. . . . Mr. Bryan, who in the course of his career subscribed to many errors, stated as clearly as language permits, the fundamental issue here involved. In the course of his famous crusade against the teaching of evolution in the schools, he observed that someone must evidently determine the way this subject was to be taught, and he followed this with the unescapable proposition that this authority must rest with the public for whom the schools exist. The historian, no less than the religious teacher, deals with the dearest concerns of those who support him in his work. It is the business of a leader to lead; but the

---

[55]"Report on History Textbooks used in the Public Schools of New York City," *Historical Outlook* 13 (1922): 253; McLaughlin to Van Tyne, 29 September 1921, Van Tyne Papers, Box 1.

[56]For Becker, see his correspondence with the Silver Burdett Company, 1941 and 1942, Becker Papers; see also Barker to Dodd, 22 November 1926, 10 January 1929, Dodd Papers, Boxes 25 and 31 respectively.

indispensable condition of leadership is the ability to win followers. The historian who does not care whether anyone reads his work may enjoy a substantial scholarly independence; he enjoys, also, complete uselessness in so far as his work is of any influence upon his fellows. The historian who would be read must win the good will and esteem of his readers. To do this he must consult their sensibilities and prejudices.[57]

More bothersome than continued reminders of limitations on professional autonomy, particularly to younger historians, was the quality of historical discourse—in exposition, disputation, and criticism. Though subject to continual challenge, the dominant mode of presentation remained doggedly factualist. Articles in the *American Historical Review* were devoted to "General Robert E. Lee's Horse Supply, 1862–1865"; "The Shield Signal at Marathon." A substantial portion of every issue was given over to a "Documents" section: "President Hayes's Notes of Four Cabinet Meetings"; "The Financial Plight of a Queen's Consort." Communications to the *AHR* were limited to "matters of fact, capable of determination one way or the other, for such discussion is likely to add to the reader's knowledge"; excluded were letters having to do with "matters of opinion," about which historians "might differ endlessly, with little profit to the reader."[58]

In discussing historical professionalism before the first world war, I noted the tension within the idea of scientific professionalism: between norms of the most ruthless mutual criticism and norms of comity and conflict-avoidance. Before 1914 a genteel cultural climate, and a cumulativist/empiricist view of the growth of knowledge, tipped the balance decisively toward conflict-avoidance. Between the wars, in a cultural climate which found controversy more congenial, and with an increasing number of historians abandoning the cumulativist/empiricist posture, there were

---

[57]Dodd to Barker, 28 October 1932, Dodd Papers, Box 39; Jernegan to Dodd, 1 July 1934, ibid., Box 44; *MVHR* 14 (1928): 575–77. In 1941, in the wake of a widely publicized campaign by the National Association of Manufacturers against "subversive doctrines" in history textbooks, the AHA issued a statement deploring the attacks, but wrapped itself so tightly in the American flag that its defense of the historian's freedom and autonomy was rather muffled: "Among [the AHA's] presidents have been two Presidents of the United States. Its membership embraces many veterans of the Spanish-American War and the First World War. In every section of the Union, members of the Association have attested their devotion to the commonweal, not only by conscientiously discharging their professional duties but also by participating in a wide variety of civic activities. It is not reasonable to suppose that men and women of this type would write and use textbooks calculated to undermine the loyalty of their students." ("Freedom of Textbooks," *Social Education* 5 [1941]: 487–88.)
[58]J. Franklin Jameson to Harry Elmer Barnes, 13 February 1926, Barnes Papers, Box 14.

growing complaints from historians about the bland and irenic nature of professional discourse—calls for more rigorous criticism, and the legitimation of controversy. But by no means all of those who accepted or even relished conflict had abandoned empiricism—they wanted to argue about "the facts." Such disputes were more likely than conceptual confrontations to be bitter, unpleasant, and productive of ill will, because they always at least implicitly carry a hint of sloppy or even fraudulent use of evidence. In consequence they stimulated a professional reflex to shun them in the interests of comity. All of this made for confusing alignments.

The frequently unsatisfactory nature of empiricist historical controversy in the interwar years is well-illustrated by the "Appraisal" of Walter Prescott Webb's *The Great Plains* conducted by the Social Science Research Council in 1939. Following previous conferences devoted to the work of a sociologist and an economist, Arthur Schlesinger, the AHA's representative on the SSRC, commissioned Fred A. Shannon of the University of Illinois to produce a critique of Webb's volume, which would serve as the basis for a conference. Shannon was a hyperempiricist, deeply skeptical of claims for the heuristic value of frames of reference not arrived at inductively. He produced a lengthy recital of errors and alleged errors, which was so devastating that Webb, in a state of shock, decided "not to accept it as an appraisal"; he had never asserted, he said, that his book was history—it was "a work of art." "I did not undertake to conform to professional standards," Webb wrote Schlesinger, "but to make a new synthesis that would give a better understanding to western life. . . . It happens that I like the book and my opinion of it is in no way dependent on the opinion of others. . . . It is its own defense, its sole defense. I shall never question it by defending it." Webb reluctantly agreed to attend the conference, but said that he would not foolishly charge the matadors, but rather, like Ferdinand, would "sit on his tail and sniff the fragrant flowers."[59]

In the circumstances the conference was something of a shambles. Shannon's 109-page critique did not lend itself to discussion—though the deliberations were enlivened by splenetic outbursts by Webb's defenders, which were later deleted from the transcript. It was a *dialogue des sourds* between factualists like Shannon and those, like the sociologist Louis Wirth, and the historian Roy F. Nichols, who thought the episode was a

[59]Webb to Schlesinger, 22 June 1939; Edwin Nourse to Schlesinger, 27 July 1939; Schlesinger Papers, Box 14.

case study in what Nichols called "the most stimulating controversy among historical scholars in my time": that concerning the relative role of fact and frame of reference, and the possibility of objectivity in history.[60]

In postconference evaluations, Thomas A. Bailey was disturbed by the "ill-will created in the fraternity"; Henry S. Commager thought it "left a lot of bad feeling and didn't advance the cause of history perceptibly"; Edward S. Kirkland couldn't see how such procedures could avoid "degenerating into a dogfight"; and John A. Krout reported a widespread feeling that "it was not in the tradition of . . . gentlemanly reviewing. . . . We just did not do that to professional historians' books." Schlesinger thought the response reflected badly on the profession: he complained that "We seem to be so obsessed by the genteel tradition that honest, forthright criticism arouses passionate emotions." There was some truth in this view, but Schlesinger's assessment took no account of the paradoxical consequences of "hard-hitting" criticism within a strictly empirical framework. Dumas Malone delivered a more nuanced verdict on the conference, one which pointed to continuing dilemmas for the profession:

I certainly don't want to say that scholars are too careful, or careful enough in the work they do. The mistakes that I myself have observed have been unbelievable. I do think, however, that the scholarly world is organized in a way to prevent errors of fact and hasty generalization in so far as these can be prevented. . . . What has most alarmed me among scholarly writers is something quite different, namely, their fear of the criticisms of their colleagues and their excessive timidity of mind. The standards that are now generally in effect make them fearful of factual error and discourage them from generalization. . . . What I have in mind is the comment of William James that men . . . can be so fearful of error that they fail to pursue truth. . . . We can never get along without the critical spirit, but we can emphasize it so much that creativeness may be stifled at its birth.[61]

The aspect of professional historical discourse which came in for the greatest criticism by younger historians was book reviewing, which David Potter later characterized as the "bland, incestuous back-scratching and mutual admiration which for so many years chloroformed the

---

[60]Social Science Research Council, *Critiques of Research in the Social Sciences, III: An Appraisal of Walter Prescott Webb's The Great Plains by Fred A. Shannon* (New York, 1940), 188–89, 190–91.

[61]Letters to Merle Curti from Bailey (17 January 1944), Commager (11 January 1944), Kirkland (24 January 1944), in Curti Papers, Box 37; Krout quoted in typescript minutes of SSRC "Conference on Trends in Research in American History," 8 November 1942, Gottschalk Papers, 13:9; Schlesinger to Curti, 7 January 1944, and Malone to Curti, 8 January 1944, both in Curti Papers, Box 37.

review sections of American historical journals." The norms of science made it imperative that there be the most ruthless mutual criticism of scholarly work; only in this way could the community move forward. In a book-oriented discipline like history, the primary vehicle for this was the book review. But given the complex nexus of professional relationships within which reviewers were entwined, and the heavy consequences of negative reviews—material for younger authors, moral for their seniors—it was the rare independent (or cantankerous) historian who ventured to be sharply critical.[62]

It was extremely common for nominated reviewers, when they thought they would be impelled to be critical, to turn down assignments on grounds of some, often quite remote, association with the author. To take at random a not untypical example, Henry E. Bourne declined to review a book by Louis Gottschalk for the *AHR* because he thought he would have to criticize it sharply; because he had just accepted Bernadotte Schmitt's invitation to join the editorial board of the new *Journal of Modern History*, and Gottschalk was Schmitt's assistant, "this might seem lacking in courtesy."[63]

Under that monument of rectitude, J. Franklin Jameson, who was managing editor of the *AHR* until 1928, it was "a fixed principle . . . that

[62]Potter, review of David H. Fischer, *Historians' Fallacies, Journal of Southern History* 37 (1971): 87. Exceptions to the rule could sometimes be explained by special circumstances, such as religious antagonism, as in one confrontation between Harvard and Manhattanville College of the Sacred Heart. Reviewing William T. Walsh's *Philip II* for the *AHR*, Roger B. Merriman employed very "unprofessional" language: "The standpoint from which it is written is violently Roman Catholic . . . and the author's ignorance and credulity are appalling"; he revealed his "preposterous incompetence"; "his prejudices and ignorance are so obvious that no one with the slightest smattering of historical knowledge or training will be in any danger of taking it seriously." Walsh replied in kind: his book annoyed Merriman because "it exposed the shabby and slipshod and bigoted methods by which he, and the whole anti-Catholic historical conspiracy to justify the wretched division of Christendom, have dealt with Catholic Spain and the Church; it explained the part played by Jewish spies and Jewish finance in the Protestant revolt, a part that they have passed over in silence." (Merriman review, *AHR* 44 [1939]: 342–44; Walsh's reply in 19 April 1939 "Letter to the Editor," AHA Papers, Box 342. In the version of the letter printed in the *AHR* [together with Merriman's response] the reference to Jews was deleted. [*AHR* 45 (1939): 265–67.])
[63]Bourne to Dana C. Munro, 23 April 1929, AHA Papers, Box 315. Similarly, Becker told Jameson that he had initially turned down an invitation to review a book by C. W. Alvord because he had thought, from what he'd heard of it, that he "entirely disagreed with his main thesis; and I did not want to review it for that reason—reviewing has already made me some cool friends." He had subsequently heard that the book was not as first reported, and "if it is one which I should not have to disagree with too radically" he would take on the assignment. "There are some reasons why it would be rather ungracious in me to review Alvord's book if I had to take an entirely unfavorable attitude towards it." (Letter of 5 December 1916, AHA Papers, Box 288.)

we cannot allow the selection of reviewers to be made by the authors of the books."[64] Under his successors the rule remained in force, but was often honored in the breach, in response to a steady stream of requests from authors to solicit, or bar, a particular reviewer. Overly critical reviews of senior figures might be defanged, with or without the reviewers' consent, in the *AHR*'s offices.[65] One source of repeated maneuvering was the convention that scholars whose help was acknowledged in a book's preface were ineligible to review it. "This acknowledgment of indebtedness business is becoming a great nuisance," complained Robert L. Schuyler, who edited the *AHR* in the late 1930s. "All that authors have to do to prevent competent critics from reviewing their books is to debar them all in advance by a public expression of indebtedness." And the game could be played in reverse: Jack Hexter, after confirming with Schuyler the rule against books being reviewed by those mentioned in prefaces, removed Wallace K. Notestein's name from the preface of his *Reign of King Pym* so that Notestein could review it for the *AHR*.[66]

In this discussion of "professionalism stalled" I have deliberately stressed those elements in interwar professional life which produced disenchantment with the professional project among historians. There was, to be sure, another side. The number of Ph.D.'s in history awarded grew at the geometric rate which, with temporary setbacks for the two world wars, remained steady from the 1890s to the 1970s. There was a gradual expansion in the size of departments, and in the number of historical journals, university presses, and fellowship programs. There were,

---

[64]Letter to E. M. Coulter, 7 April 1924, AHA Papers, Box 300. Those who solicited a reviewer were politely but firmly rebuffed. Jameson was not averse to suggesting that a reviewer be particularly charitable in special circumstances. He suggested leniency to C. H. Van Tyne in dealing with a book by an author who had suffered a mental breakdown. He asked N. W. Stephenson to soften a review of a book by a woman historian because Jameson had personally requested a review copy from the woman herself: "I hesitate to put myself in a position where a lady can think, even unjustly, that I have behaved shabbily toward her." (Letter to Van Tyne, 28 March 1914, Van Tyne Papers, Box 1; Letter to Stephenson, 28 August 1923, AHA Papers, Box 298.)

[65]Roger B. Merriman wrote Schuyler, "As between old friends, *how* could you give Crane Brinton's book and mine to that little squirt [Eugen] Rosenstock-Huessy?" "*Entre nous* and strictly *sub rosa*," Schuyler replied, "I endorse your opinion . . . 100%. . . . I edited his original review rather drastically, and he didn't like it." (Merriman to Schuyler, 31 July 1939; Schuyler to Merriman, 2 August 1939; AHA Papers, Box 342.) The published review (which Schuyler's editing reduced to virtual incoherence) is in *AHR* 44 (1939): 882–84; the manuscript original is in AHA Papers, Box 339.

[66]Schuyler to Henry Steele Commager, 2 April 1941, AHA Papers, Box 331; Hexter to Schuyler, no date, AHA Papers, Box 346. Schuyler had implied that he was not averse to sending the book to Notestein, but was meanwhile replaced as editor by Guy Stanton Ford, who assigned it to another (and, as it turned out, very favorable) reviewer.

throughout the period, hundreds of historians who unstintingly gave their time to the service of the profession.[67]

Experiences with the profession, and with the very idea of professionalism, were clearly mixed. C. Vann Woodward recalls that as a graduate student in the 1930s, poring over the standard professional texts, he repeatedly asked himself, "My God, is this what I have dedicated my life to?" Oscar Handlin, reflecting on the same period in his life, in the same years, remembers the almost religious feeling he had at joining a profession that was "internally cohesive and held together by adherence to common standards and convictions," with "a sense of unifying purpose that overrode differences in background, interpretations and points of view." There is no conceivable way of determining which of the two attitudes was more "representative."[68]

But there were surely sufficient grounds in these years for many historians to feel disenchanted with "the professional project"; to be nagged by the feeling that it had not turned out as the founders expected. Professionalism, as an ideology in its own right, has prospered in times of stability and self-confidence; is called into question in periods of crisis and uncertainty. Before the war, as we have seen, enthusiasm for the professionalization project played an important role in sustaining faith in objectivity: indeed, the two were so intimately linked that they furthered each other when both were in the ascendancy. Between the wars the connection endured, but the direction of movement was reversed: declining confidence in professionalism helped call its associated doctrine into question.

[67]John Higham errs, I believe, in inferring stagnation in "professional" growth from interwar AHA membership figures. (*History*, 27.) As noted above, perhaps as much as three-quarters of the membership of the AHA around the turn of the century was "nonprofessional," whereas by the eve of World War II the vast majority of its members were academic historians. In addition, for various reasons many professional historians affiliated with the MVHA, the Southern History Association, or other regional bodies, rather than the AHA, and were not, in consequence, less members of "the profession."

[68]Woodward quoted in John Herbert Roper, "C. Vann Woodward's Early Career—The Historian as Dissident Youth," *Georgia Historical Quarterly* 44 (1980): 18; Handlin, *Truth in History* (Cambridge, Mass., 1979), 4–5.

8

Divergence and dissent

From the standpoint of the historical profession's founding program of objectivity, the most troubling aspect of interwar historiography was its failure to converge—to move toward a single, integrated edifice of historical truth.

Before the war this had seemed a plausible goal. The profession was only beginning to accumulate reliable, documented monographs on various aspects of the American past, and matters were not that much farther advanced in other fields of history. Historical production was still at the stage of "primitive accumulation." It did not, at that point, seem palpably absurd for historians to devote themselves, as Jameson put it, to "making bricks without much idea of how the architects will use them." To alter the metaphor, when first beginning to assemble a thousand-piece jigsaw puzzle, no one is troubled by their inability to foresee where a particular piece will fit. The prewar concentration on the political and constitutional realms furthered optimism about a convergent, cumulative picture emerging—in American history, as the successive completion of studies of parallel processes in the different states, and of developments in successive periods, promised to eventuate in an overarching narrative synthesis; in European history, as studies of various countries fell into the Actonian paradigm of advancing liberty, democracy, and international comity. There was, overall, substantial agreement on the picture that would emerge when all the pieces had been fitted together, and it was possible to see ways in which monographic work carried out within the framework of that picture actually was falling into place.

By the early thirties, as professional historical scholarship in America approached its fiftieth anniversary, convergence seemed more distant than it had in the days of the founders. Bricks were accumulating which

206

didn't seem even potentially part of the same structure. It became increasingly clear that the profession included those with very different architectonic visions and commitments.

Before turning to a discussion of the general breakdown of ideological and interpretive consensus within the profession, it will be useful to examine in some detail the two best-known and most divisive interwar historical controversies: one having to do with the "war guilt question"; the other, or rather, others, having to do with the issues surrounding the American Civil War. The first involved Europeanists; the second, Americanists. The first was played out principally in the twenties, the second in the thirties. Both, as well as exemplifying the breakdown of consensus, illustrate other issues relevant to the question of historians' faith in the objectivity of their professional venture.

I

In the light of the disillusionment with the fruits of World War I that most historians shared with their fellow citizens, and of the bad conscience so many of them had about their propagandistic excesses, it was predictable that after the war there would be a reexamination of former assumptions about the origins of the conflict. But no one could have predicted that the controversy would be as acrimonious and as polarizing as it turned out to be. A more and more extreme "revisionism" with respect to war origins confronted an often intransigent "orthodoxy," and American historians increasingly chose up sides in the postbellum hostilities.

Many accounts of the war's origins in the immediate postwar period were content to repeat what Beard characterized as the "Sunday-school theory": "three pure and innocent boys—Russia, France and England—without military guile in their hearts, were suddenly assailed while on the way to Sunday school by two deep-dyed villains—Germany and Austria—who had long been plotting cruel deeds in the dark." In 1920 Carlton J. H. Hayes, while acknowledging that international anarchy was a remote cause of the war, held that its outbreak was solely due to the actions of Germany; Charles D. Hazen described the war as the consequence of the "sinister and Brutal challenge" of Germany to civilization; Roland G. Usher took the same line in his *Story of the Great War*.[1]

---

[1]Beard, "Heroes and Villains of the World War," *Current History* 24 (1926): 733; Hayes, *A Brief History of the Great War* (New York, 1920): 1–17; Hazen, *Modern Europe* (New York, 1920), 690; Usher, *The Story of the Great War* (New York, 1920).

But in the same year that these accounts were being published, the *American Historical Review* started to run the first of three articles by Sidney B. Fay, which marked the beginning of American revisionist scholarship on war origins. During the war, while teaching at Smith, Fay had become convinced that "we . . . were being fed a great deal of silly propaganda . . . and that some day documents would be published which would allow sober historians to arrive at a more just estimate." Working from newly published materials, Fay's *AHR* articles attacked the notion of a deliberate German drive to war. His work attracted the attention, and aroused the enthusiasm, of Harry Elmer Barnes, a Columbia New Historian, who in 1923 was to become Fay's colleague at Smith. With Barnes's entry into the discussion of war origins the controversy was to take a new shape.[2]

In the early twenties Barnes seemed slated for a brilliant academic career. William A. Dunning wrote a colleague that his "learning and his capacity for turning out masses of good stuff in incredibly short time is the most striking thing that has come to my attention among our students in thirty years." A full professor at the age of thirty, he was invited by Arthur Schlesinger and Dixon Ryan Fox to contribute the volume on the most recent period to the *History of American Life* series. During the war, Barnes had surpassed most of his fellow historians in his enthusiasm for the Allied cause. Guy Stanton Ford recalled that Barnes had been "one of the most violent sort of shoot-them-at-sunrise Chauvinists"; the material he submitted to the National Board for Historical Service was "quite too violent to be acceptable." Cheerfully admitting his previous gullibility, Barnes, with the zeal of the repentant sinner, found in the "revisionism" of Fay's articles the cause that was to consume the rest of his life.[3]

In a lengthy review of Hazen's text Barnes flayed its author (and, in passing, E. Raymond Turner of Johns Hopkins) for having continued into the postwar period the wartime prostitution of historical scholarship. He found it scandalous that a professional historian could be so lacking in objectivity as to continue to argue "the thesis of a deliberate German plot against the peace of the world in the summer of 1914"—a

[2]Sidney B. Fay to Selig Adler, 25 August 1948, Adler Papers, II-5; Fay's "New Light on the Origins of the World War" was published in three parts: *AHR* 25 (1920): 616–39; 26 (1920): 37–53; 26 (1921): 225–54.
[3]Dunning to G. H. Blakeslee, 19 March 1919, Barnes Papers, Box 8; Schlesinger to Barnes, 4 May 1923, ibid., Box 11; Ford to Bernadotte Schmitt, 7 December 1926, Schmitt Papers, Box 3.

thesis contradicted by Fay's work, as well as that of other scholars. In a characteristic peroration, he wrote that

when a reputable historian refuses absolutely to take cognizance of a vast mass of first-hand source material which has completely revolutionized our knowledge of what he himself regards as the greatest crisis and episode in human history, we clearly have a case of "criminal levity" which is beyond the scope or competence of the historical critic and must be referred to the psychiatrist with his proficiency in dealing with such mechanisms and complexes as the flight from reality, compensation, projection, defense-mechanisms, the Jehovah complex, and the fixed-idea.

The charge against Hazen was "his offence against objective historical scholarship." The question was

Shall we require historians to make a decent and respectable effort to tell the truth, so that we may rely upon them for indispensable material in the guidance of intelligent public thinking, or shall we have to admit that history is, in varying degrees, but disguised personal, partisan, religious or national prejudice and bias, and come to the conclusion that it is worse than "bunk"? If history is to be "mere literature," then we should dispense with professional historians and call in the novelists.[4]

The review, not surprisingly, outraged its targets, and delighted the friends of the revisionist cause. H. L. Mencken wrote Barnes that "Your neat and complete disembowelment of Hazen gave me great joy. He has been one of my favorite asses for years." *The Nation* took the unusual step of publishing an editorial praising a review in a rival journal. While endorsing Barnes's substantive conclusions, what particularly impressed them was that Barnes, "a sound delver into the truth of history without fear or favor," had "dared to handle delinquent members of his craft without gloves."

By doing so he has violated one of the most firmly established traditions of the historical set. If you are a historian the first canon is to say nothing unkind about any co-worker in your field lest thirty years later that become a stumbling block to your rising to the presidency of the American Historical Association. . . . We wish that there were a chance that his challenge to his craft to bring Professors Hazen and Turner "to judgment before the bar of professional historical opinion," might be taken up; in our judgment that would be the best thing that has

4"Seven Books of History against the Germans," *New Republic* 38 (19 March 1924), 2:10–15; reply to letter from Hazen, ibid., 38 (7 May 1924): 285; reply to letter from Turner, ibid., 38 (9 April 1924): 186.

ever happened to the teaching of history in America. If the American Historical Association were worth its salt it would set the wheels in motion without further delay.[5]

The surprisingly high level of popular attention the dispute attracted was a reflection of many factors: a reaction to historians' wartime propaganda, the general climate of disillusionment, and the close connection between the issue of "war guilt" and the continuing controversies over the reparations clause of the Versailles Treaty, and the related question of Allied war debts. Beyond that, in a larger sense, the scholarly debate on the origins of the war in Europe was something of a surrogate for a debate on American entry into the war, a subject which never engaged much attention from American professional historians in the interwar years, though there was a good deal of popular writing on the subject later on, in the thirties. Then, too, there was a certain prurient interest in the squabbling of professors, particularly when enlivened by Barnes's provocative style, and the responses it brought forth. More than any other interwar controversy, the *Kriegsschuldfrage* was a subject of heavy coverage in the middlebrow press.

Even before the dust had settled on the controversy occasioned by his *New Republic* review, Barnes was at work on a fuller treatment of the question, a long article "Assessing the Blame for the World War," which appeared in the May 1924 issue of *Current History*. The article was free of invective against other historians, fulsome in its acknowledgment of indebtedness to scholars in the field, and, on the whole, moderate and balanced in tone, though somewhat underplaying German militarism while stressing that of France and Russia. He concluded, not surprisingly, that the "scape-goat theory of complete, sole and unique guilt on the part of Germany or any other single State can no longer be supported. . . . Deeper than any national guilt is the responsibility of the wrong-headed and savage European system of nationalism, imperialism, secret diplomacy and militarism which sprang into full bloom from 1870–1914." Until this system was attacked, there could be no hope of permanent peace in Europe. On the question of individual national guilt, he thought that "the majority of competent students would assign the rela-

---

[5]Turner's and Hazen's letters of reply to Barnes's review (with Barnes's response) are in *New Republic* 38 (9 April 1924): 184–86, and 38 (7 May 1924): 284–86; Mencken to Barnes, 19 March 1924, cited in Warren I. Cohen, *The American Revisionists* (Chicago, 1966), 64; "Historians and the Truth," *Nation* 118 (21 May 1924): 576.

tive responsibility for the outbreak of hostilities in about this order: Austria, Russia, France, Germany, England."[6]

Barnes's article was printed together with an exasperated rebuttal by Albert Bushnell Hart, chairman of the magazine's Board of Associates. "Perhaps without so intending," Hart began disingenuously,

the author denies the honesty of the Allies and the reality of our appeal to justice and humanity. He makes the American people a set of fools. . . . The subject is too involved . . . to make any review of printed testimony a safe basis for changing an opinion which was forged by the fires of war. . . . If Barnes is right, Roosevelt was wrong, Wilson was wrong, Elihu Root was wrong. Ambassador Page was wrong, everybody was wrong.

Hart's rebuttal was, as Arthur Schlesinger wrote to Barnes, "the best argument that has been yet adduced in favor of your position."[7]

With enemies like this, Barnes did not need friends, but he had them. The June issue of *Current History* featured a symposium in which leading historians were invited to comment on Barnes's article. Lucy M. Salmon of Vassar endorsed his conclusions without reservation. Carl Becker, while he thought the very term "responsible for the war" misleading, said that he and Barnes "do not seriously disagree . . . on any material point." Others, not in the symposium, aligned themselves with Barnes either publicly or privately. William L. Langer had long been a steadfast ally: he had been "delighted" with the review of Hazen ("I . . . hope this roast will act as a healthy deterrent to others"); he had assisted Barnes with the *Current History* article; and in a letter to *The New Republic* he declared that he was "only too ready to take my stand by him and suffer the consequences." Beard wrote Barnes to express his approval of both the review and the article, though including a word of caution:

You delivered terrific blows at the old fiction and came out with flying colors. I am sorry that you were so savage with Hazen, but still his offence against decency was great. It is better to be too savage than a lily-livered creeper around the throne

---

[6]"Assessing the Blame for the World War: A Revised Judgment Based on All the Available Documents," *Current History* 20 (May 1924): 171, 194. "Revisionism" at this time carried a taint of treasonous pro-Germanism, illustrated by the fact that the article was preceded by an editorial note which informed readers that Barnes was "of a long line of American ancestry of original English and Dutch stock" and that Barnes "authorizes the statement that he has never had German or Austrian affiliations either in study or in any personal relationships, his attitude during the war having been strongly pro-English and pro-French."

[7]Hart, "A Dissent from the Conclusions of Professor Barnes," ibid., 195–96; Schlesinger to Barnes, 9 May 1924, quoted in Cohen, *American Revisionists*, 69.

of the great gods in the American Historical Association. Go to my boy, you have the brains and the drive and you will bust old follies all along the line; but subdue your wild steed a bit.[8]

Other historians were decidedly in the opposing camp. Charles Seymour of Yale rejected Barnes's exculpation of Germany; Frank Maloy Anderson of Dartmouth expressed his general agreement with Hart, and thought Barnes's article was "likely to exercise an unfortunate influence" on American public opinion; A. E. Morse of Princeton wrote that it was "difficult to see how anybody but a German would be satisfied or convinced by this account." More than academic issues were at stake, even for academics. Andrew C. McLaughlin of the University of Chicago was distressed to learn that someone in his own department had said that "Barnes is right." "I lost a boy in that war," he wrote to Dodd. "And I don't take any pleasure in having it announced that poor old Germany was the innocent victim and that he lost his life fighting on the wrong side."[9]

This first round of the controversy, opened by Fay in 1920, and continued with the savaging of the upholders of "orthodoxy" by Barnes, had produced clear signs of a polarization of scholarly opinion by 1924. Though not all participants fit into the two categories, there was a suggestive lineup of New Historians (Barnes, Schlesinger, Becker, Beard, and one can add the name of the consistently "revisionist" Preserved Smith) against a solid Ivy League phalanx (Hazen of Columbia, Hart of Harvard, Seymour of Yale, Morse of Princeton, Anderson of Dartmouth).[10] The next two rounds, fought between 1926 and 1930, were to see a bitter wrangle between Barnes and Bernadotte Schmitt, and a more temperate, though no less significant, controversy between Schmitt and Fay and their respective followers. These later rounds gave continued evidence of the absence of convergence in interpretations of World War I, but also raised important professional and intellectual issues about the nature of historical discourse and authority.

In both disposition and outlook, Schmitt was the exact opposite of

---

[8]Salmon and Becker in "Assessing the Blame for the World War: A Symposium," *Current History* 20 (June 1924): 458, 455–56; Langer to Barnes, 10 February and 10 May 1924, Barnes Papers, Boxes 11 and 12 respectively; Langer's published declaration in *New Republic* 38 (30 April 1924): 260; Beard to Barnes, 28 June 1924, Barnes Papers, Box 79.
[9]Seymour, Anderson, and Morse in "Assessing the Blame," 452–53, 459–60, 455; McLaughlin to Dodd, 7 July 1924, Dodd Papers, Box 24.
[10]Age may also have been a factor. Schlesinger wrote Barnes that "we of the younger generation must stand together, especially in the face of such a controversy as that in which you are now engaged with the Elder Statesmen." (Letter of 9 May 1924, Barnes Papers, Box 12.)

Barnes. Where Barnes was flamboyant and given to extreme overstatement, Schmitt was reserved and expressed himself in terms so highly
qualified that they were often capable of diverse readings. In addition,
Schmitt was a thoroughgoing Anglophile and Germanophobe, who never
doubted the righteousness of the Allied cause, or the responsibility of the
Central Powers for the conflict. At the outset, Barnes had misunderstood
Schmitt's position, and taken him for a fellow revisionist. The public
clearing-up of the confusion occasioned some mutual embarrassment,
and though there was a surface restoration of cordial relations, it probably rankled on both sides. By the time the *Current History* symposium
was published in June 1924, Schmitt had clearly emerged as Barnes's
leading scholarly opponent. Rejecting Barnes's rank order of responsibility, he placed the burden of guilt on the Central Powers: "Austria would
come first by all means. But why? Only because of the promise of German support. . . . Therefore I should put Germany second in the list.
Probably Russia would not have mobilized without assurances from
France; so they tie for third place. And England last of all."[11]

In a cordial letter to Schmitt at this time Barnes said he would admit,
"indeed I have publicly stated, that there is an abysmal gulf between your
scholarship and mine"; the only difference he saw in their positions was

---

[11]"Symposium," 462. Schmitt's views, which led Barnes to conclude that he was in the
revisionist camp, were contained in a talk at the December 1923 AHA meeting, subsequently published as "Triple Alliance and Triple Entente, 1902–1914" in the *AHR* 29
(April 1924): 449–73. Barnes, in an exchange with Turner in *The New Republic*, referred
to his own forthcoming article in *Current History* and observed that "the same general
position is to be found in the abler and more scholarly article by Professor Schmitt in the
April number of the American Historical Review." In the *Current History* article Barnes
acknowledged a critical reading by Schmitt and Langer which "added much to the general
interpretation and saved me from many slips in matters of detail." When Schmitt saw the
reference to "the same general position" in *The New Republic*, he sent a letter to the
magazine denying "that my position is substantially the same as his own," and wrote
Barnes that he was doing so. Barnes replied, citing a letter Schmitt had sent him when
returning Barnes's manuscript, in which Schmitt had said that "while I have criticized
some of your statements our positions are not so far divergent." Schmitt was mortified.
"You clearly have me in a hole," he told Barnes. In the light of his remark Barnes was
"certainly justified in claiming for our two articles 'the same general position.' I quite
forgot that I had made such a statement. . . . You are entitled to an *amende honorable*, and
I apologize gladly and sincerely; indeed I am writing to the *New Republic* to ask it, if not
too late, not to publish my letter." It was in fact too late, and Barnes replied to Schmitt in
The New Republic by citing Schmitt's original comment. Barnes concluded the exchange
with Schmitt by suggesting "that we shake hands epistolographically and call it a draw. I
may have the best of you in the New Republic, but you will worst me in the Current
History where I shall have no chance to reply. . . . I trust that this may be the end of all
unpleasantness between us." (Schmitt to Barnes, 9 May 1924; Barnes to Schmitt, 15 May
1924; Schmitt to Barnes, 18 May 1924; Barnes to Schmitt, 20 May 1924; all in Schmitt
Papers, Box 2.)

"the wholly arbitrary and interpretative matter of the serial grading of the guilt"; he hoped that he was "through with the Kriegsschuldfrage for good."[12] But, in the historical discourse of the twenties, the "serial grading of the guilt" was the contested issue, and Barnes was too much of a controversialist to stay away from it. Moreover, his position hardened in a more revisionist direction, while Schmitt was moving the other way. Neither man's list remained as it had been in 1924: Barnes moved Germany to the bottom, while Schmitt moved her to the top.

In 1924 and 1925 Barnes had in fact largely put the *Kriegsschuldfrage* behind him. In those two years he wrote four books, edited three others, and published numerous articles, all on questions unrelated to the war. But he continued to lecture on the subject, and when the editor of *The Christian Century* heard a speech by Barnes he invited him to contribute a series of articles. At the conclusion of the series, the magazine asked a number of leading historians to respond. For various reasons the invitations were refused. E. Raymond Turner declined because no "historian of established reputation will much care to compete with the sensationalist effusions of this writer"; Carl Becker because, though he differed with Barnes's conception of "responsibility," and with his belief that "by exposing the criminals the world can be enlightened and induced to take a radically different attitude towards wars," he was in "essential" agreement with Barnes "so far as the brute facts are concerned."[13] Alfred Knopf asked Barnes to expand the articles into a book, which appeared in 1926 as *The Genesis of the World War*. His overall conclusion on the "order of guilt" was that

the only direct and immediate responsibility for the World War falls upon France and Russia, with the guilt about equally distributed. Next in order—far below France and Russia—would come Austria, though she never desired a general European war. Finally, we should place Germany and England as tied for last place, both being opposed to war in the 1914 crisis. Probably the German public

---

[12]Barnes to Schmitt, 20 May 1924, Schmitt Papers, Box 2.
[13]Turner's remark was quoted in a letter from C. C. Morrison, editor of *The Christian Century*, to Barnes, 3 February 1926, cited in Cohen, *American Revisionists*, 79. Becker's reason for declining is in his 21 February 1926 letter to Barnes in Barnes Papers, Box 14. Becker went on to say: "I couldn't write in the vigorous, superlative, sledgehammer way you do, but that doesn't mean that I protest, or that I don't enjoy what you write. I do. It can't I think do any harm. On the contrary it is probably the only way to jar people loose and make them think a little. You have done more probably to keep this question alive and make the public, or some of them realize that there are two sides to the question than any one else. Fay's kind of writing is probably more judicious and watertight than yours; but Fay might write to the end of time and no one the wiser except a few university professors. So I say, more power to your arm—and perhaps it would have more power if it were a bit more supple and not quite so heavy."

was somewhat more favorable to military activities than the English people, but as we have amply explained above, the Kaiser made much more strenuous efforts to preserve the peace of Europe in 1914 than did Sir Edward Grey.[14]

The Genesis met a reception which was, given the polarization of opinion on the subject, predictable. It was praised in *The Nation* and *The New Republic*, and by historians like William Langer, Preserved Smith, and Ferdinand Schevill who were sympathetic to the revisionist cause. Schevill acknowledged that "dry-as-dust scholars will not fail to complain that the book lacks that air of frozen detachment which is their fetish except when under the illicit inspiration of other idols they grind out wisdom for Mr. Creel's bureau of information." But Barnes's thesis of French and Russian war guilt "must in all its essential features be held as proved."[15]

Some expressed qualified approval. Beard agreed with the disproof of the charge of German war guilt in the Versailles Treaty, but was bothered by "the attempt to whitewash the German Kaiser, the Crown Prince, the war party and super-patriots of the Fatherland." Antirevisionists attacked it roundly. Preston Slosson in the *American Historical Review* termed it "no judge's verdict but the brief of a rather emotional advocate." The sharpest attack was by Barnes's old adversary Bernadotte Schmitt, in *Foreign Affairs*. Barnes, he said, had not "blazed his own trail through the documents" and let them "speak for themselves"; instead he had "swallowed whole" unreliable accounts which bolstered his case. His book fell "far short of being that objective and scientific analysis of the great problem which is so urgently needed."[16]

Unlike some other New Historians, Barnes never wavered in his belief in objective historical truth, and the parallel belief that on the war guilt question he was its spokesman. And, of course, since his own view was objective, Schmitt's was not. In his article "Mr. Bernadotte Everly Schmitt and the Question of Responsibility for the Outbreak of the World War," Barnes addressed himself to the "Schmitt legend" of "icy detachment, absolute absence of any special favoritism or prejudices, complete fearlessness. . . . the abstract historical ideal, of which the

---

[14]*The Genesis of the World War: An Introduction to the Problem of War Guilt* (New York, 1926), 658–59.
[15]Review in *Nation* by Frederick Bausman (123 [1 September 1926]: 198) and in *New Republic* by G. Lowes Dickinson (47 [28 July 1926]: 284–85); Langer to Barnes, undated, Barnes Papers, Box 82; Smith to Barnes, 7 June 1926, ibid., Box 14; Schevill review in *Christian Century* 43 (17 June 1926): 778–80.
[16]Beard, "Heroes and Villains of the World War," *Current History* 24 (1926): 733; Slosson, *AHR* 32 (1927): 319; Schmitt, "July, 1914," *Foreign Affairs* 5 (1926): 143, 132, 147.

youthful Leopold von Ranke dreamed a century ago, suddenly become flesh and dwelling in our midst." Much of Barnes's article was devoted to Schmitt's "personal equation" in accounting for his lack of objectivity. During his time at Oxford he had succumbed to "the subtle, encompassing and penetrating charm which is English." Schmitt, who was of Swiss origin, lived "in daily dread of being mistaken for a member of the detestable Teutonic breed." The evidence for this, and for the proposition that Schmitt had made up his mind before examining the documents, was Schmitt's having inserted, in his *Who's Who* entry in 1921, the information that in "a lecture on 'Germany in the Reign of William II,' given in Cleveland in January, 1914, he predicted that Germany was preparing to begin a European war." Further, in what was unquestionably the most gratuitously offensive passage in the article, Barnes wrote that "one must not forget the astute academic strategy of Mr. Schmitt in remaining quite 'correct' and immaculate in his theories of war-guilt."

No person, once he had thought the matter over, would care to challenge the sound and approved doctrine of war-guilt held by the chiefs of his profession . . . if he desired to rise to any dizzy heights in the conventional departments of history in our most respectable universities and to bask in the favor and honorific emoluments of the American Historical Association. . . . Mr. Schmitt has, indeed, guessed right. In 1924, he was an associate professor in Western Reserve University; to-day he is a full professor of modern history in what is by many legitimately held to be the best department of history in the United States. We cannot say that he was translated to Chicago simply because of his pussy-footing on the war-guilt matter, but it is wholly safe to say that if he had come out four-square in the controversy of two years ago, in a manner like Professor Becker, [or] Professor Langer . . . he would still be fretfully languishing in the confines of the Cleveland institution.[17]

No scholarly exchange had ever so enlivened discourse within the American historical profession. One can only speculate concerning Schmitt's initial reaction upon receipt of the article. As Crane Brinton wrote, eulogizing him, Schmitt had "a sense for the decencies, for decorum, for *pietas* in the Roman sense toward the establishment; and he has the obverse of such feelings, a distrust for the noisy innovator and crusader, . . . for the disturber, for the radical." Schmitt circulated to 170 historians a dignified "brief statement to a few friends." He acknowledged that the *Who's Who* entry was "an exhibition of vanity on my part . . . I have long regretted it." He addressed himself to three other personal

[17]*The Progressive*, 1 December 1926, 86, 91, 87. Copies of the article were widely distributed, almost certainly at Barnes's initiative, within the historical profession.

charges in Barnes's article, and with respect to the indictment for academic careerism said that "Such a charge needs no comment."[18]

While a handful of hard-line revisionists like William L. Langer and Ferdinand Schevill expressed approval of Barnes's attack, they were in a distinct minority within the profession.[19] The great majority of historians who commented on the exchange expressed sympathy with Schmitt. J. Franklin Jameson voiced the outrage of many in a letter to the Chicago professor:

> Never in my rather long lifetime . . . has any American professor ever gone so far in insolence, or for that matter, in the exhibition of self-conceit and wounded vanity. All those around here who have read his disgraceful article have agreed with me that it ought to kill him, so far as any standing in our profession is concerned, and though perhaps it will not do that, because in our profession there are some who are not revolted by such outrages, still I do not think that you need to apprehend that anything Barnes has said, or may say in the future, will do any damage to you in the eyes of any member of the profession whose good opinion you would care to have. Every one of that sort knows a cad when he sees him.[20]

Other letters of support which Schmitt received questioned Barnes's mental stability. Wallace K. Notestein suggested that Barnes "has some 'complex' about academic position"; Thad W. Riker thought that "when a man of his years behaves in that way one wonders if he is not a paranoiac." Riker would seem to have been right. There is abundant evidence that Barnes repeatedly saw himself as the victim of persecution and conspiracies, and was so out of control that he was blind to the perfectly predictable way in which the attack injured him much more than it did Schmitt. His charge that Schmitt had adjusted his findings for purposes of

[18]Brinton, "The Historical Work of Bernadotte E. Schmitt," *American Oxonian* 48 (April 1961): 53; *Private and Confidential*; "'Mr. Bernadotte Everly Schmitt and the Question of Responsibility for the Outbreak of the World War' By Harry Elmer Barnes; Some Comments by Bernadotte Schmitt," two pages, mimeographed, in Schmitt Papers, Box 54. The figure of 170 is drawn from a checklist of those to whom it was sent in the Schmitt Papers. The other charges to which Schmitt addressed himself are too complex to detail here, but it should be said that, although one cannot be certain, Schmitt's version in each case seems much more plausible than Barnes's.

[19]Langer, reviewing a collection of Barnes's essays which included his attack on Schmitt, said that he had "reduced many of his opponents *ad absurdum* and the process is highly illuminating and instructive." Schevill, Schmitt's colleague at Chicago, wrote Barnes that "when you psycho-analyzed Schmitt, you did, in my opinion, a good piece of work and did not go beyond the limits of propriety because, though you employed highly personal matter, you made use of it in an impersonal way to the end of uncovering a situation and clarifying an attitude." (Langer review of Fay's *Origins of the World War* and Barnes's *In Quest of Truth and Justice*, *Nation* 127 [1928]: 623; Schevill to Barnes, 13 June 1928, Barnes Papers, Box 17.)

[20]Letter of 14 March 1927, Schmitt Papers, Box 3.

professional advancement may or may not have been a reflection of Barnes's own frustrated ambitions. In any case, it was inconsistent with Barnes's demonstration that Schmitt had been a Germanophobe for many years. Barnes had contrasted Schmitt, who moved up the academic ladder through opportunism, and Langer, whose career was blocked by his principled revisionism; the contrast lost a good deal of its force when, a few months after Barnes's article appeared, Langer received an offer from Harvard.[21]

Carl Becker and Preserved Smith, besides regarding Barnes's attack as "an exhibition of extremely bad manners," and "discourteous," addressed the epistemological issue raised by the attack. Both did so in a way problematically consistent with their "relativist" principles. "The validity of your conclusions regarding the origins of the war," Becker wrote Schmitt, "does not . . . depend on the question of whether you did or did not desire a professorship at Chicago, any more than the validity of Barnes' conclusions depend on the question of whether he likes or does not like to shock conventional people." Smith wrote Barnes to tell him that he was hurting himself, along with the revisionist cause by bringing in "irrelevant" considerations:

If we indulge in personalities it will not only create an unpleasant atmosphere, but will damage cool and scientific research. . . . I esteem the question of Schmitt's complexes and motives of very slight importance and irrelevant to the question of war guilt. Prove the truth of your assertions objectively without going into the problem of what warps Schmitt's judgment of the facts. I do not mind what you say about Gray and Poincaré, for they were important actors in the drama; but the truth or falsity of a historical thesis can be and should be settled by appeal to evidence alone. By dragging in your critic's private opinions you act as George

---

[21]Letters from Notestein, 14 January 1927, and Riker, 15 January 1927, in Schmitt Papers, Box 3. Barnes's correspondence constitutes a full clinical record of his abusiveness toward critics, cries of betrayal, and conviction that he was the victim of conspiracies. He wrote James T. Shotwell: "I have taken in silence some eighteen years of unprovoked double-crossing, treachery and sneaking backbiting on your part. . . . You probably think that I have been unaware of what you have been up to all these years. . . . If I had wished to sell my intellectual services I could probably be enjoying as enviable an income as you are . . . instead of having to work hard 365 days a year to make a sheer living. . . . As the leader of the group that Charley Beard calls 'the Boardinghouse Americans' [Shotwell was Canadian-born], you doubtless find it hard to conceive of anybody holding a pro-American point of view and being without guile." (Letter of 26 March 1940, Barnes Papers, Box 25.) He had alternative explanations of his column in the *New York World-Telegram* being dropped: "the British Intelligence Department turned on the heat via the Morgan banks"; "pressure of the Jewish Department Store Owners in New York City, who threatened Roy Howard with loss of all advertising if he kept me on any longer." (Barnes to Ted O. Thackrey, 26 May 1940, ibid., Box 25; Barnes to Sidney Rosenblum, 17 October 1954, ibid., Box 42.)

Berkeley did when he attacked Newton's theory of fluxions by alleging that Newton was an atheist, or at least a deist. If saying this much proves that my attitude toward history is no longer modern, I must confess that my arteries are hardening.[22]

Both deplored Barnes's "personal" attack on Schmitt's reputation for impartiality and disinterestedness, and his attempt to show Schmitt's deep Anglophilia and Germanophobia.

Clearly, in practice, Barnes's attack on Schmitt was offensive, wrong-headed, and ill-considered, but was it illegitimate in principle? Is the *argumentum ad hominem*, as Becker and Smith held, a "fallacy" when applied to historical work?[23]

In twentieth-century usage, an *ad hominem* argument is a device intended to divert attention from the critical examination of the substance of an argument, and to discredit that argument by dragging in irrelevant considerations having to do with the character or motives of its author. That this is a disreputable procedure is clear enough in cases where the argument itself is "followable": in which those being addressed have the opportunity of addressing themselves systematically and exclusively to "relevant" considerations. The impersonal ethos of science is based on the proposition that what science offers is "public knowledge," subject to critical examination by the scientific community. The "replicable experiment" is the prime example of this characteristic of science. Sir John Ziman, in an influential work, has argued that better than any other

---

[22]Becker to Schmitt, 14 January 1927, Schmitt Papers, Box 3; Smith to Barnes, 13 January 1927, Barnes Papers, Box 16.

[23]The origin of the phrase is obscure. *Ad hominem* arguments were not listed in classical or medieval taxonomies of fallacies. Its first use in English dates from Locke, and he neither meant by it what is commonly meant today, nor did he regard its employment as necessarily fallacious. He listed, among arguments "that men, in their reasonings with others, do ordinarily make use of to prevail on their assent, or at least so to awe them as to silence their opposition," one which he said was "already known under the name of *argumentum ad hominem*": "to press a man with consequences drawn from his own principles or concessions." (*An Essay Concerning Human Understanding* [1690; edited with an introduction by John Yolton, 2 vols., London, 1961], 2:278–79.) By a multistage process of transformation, a phrase which had originally been used to describe a rhetorical device to *convince an opponent*, by showing that certain conclusions followed from his or her principles (whether or not the one employing the device accepted those principles), came, by the nineteenth and twentieth centuries, to mean an attempt to *discredit an opponent in the eyes of third parties* by questioning the motives or character of that opponent. There is no satisfactory account known to me of precisely how the transformation was effected, but the fullest discussion of the question, with hints as to how it probably took place, is in C. L. Hamblin, *Fallacies* (London, 1970). Chaim Perelman and Lucie Olbrechts-Tyteca have coined the term *ad personam* to describe what in twentieth-century usage is called *ad hominem*, while preserving the original meaning of the older term. (*The New Rhetoric: A Treatise on Argumentation* [1958; English trans., Notre Dame, Ind., 1969], 111–12.)

criterion, the public nature of the knowledge which science offers is its principal distinguishing feature. The assimilation of historical knowledge to this model was, as we have seen earlier, a key move in the establishment of objective, scientific history. On this assumption, *ad hominem* arguments are surely an irrelevancy, and should be scornfully dismissed.[24]

But are the characteristic products of historians like this? The historian has seen, at first hand, a great mass of evidence, often unpublished, and difficult of access. The historian develops an interpretation of this evidence based on years of immersion in the material—together, of course, with the perceptual apparatus and assumptions he or she brings to it. Historians employ devices, the footnote being the most obvious example, to attain for their work something resembling "replicability," but the resemblance is not all that close.[25]

Most historical writing is, at best, "semipublic" in Ziman's sense. The historian is less like the author of a logical demonstration, though he or she is that in part; more like a witness to what has been found on a voyage of discovery. And arguments which are illegitimate when addressed to the author of a transparently followable syllogism are quite appropriate in the case of a witness. A standard logic textbook, contemporaneous with the Barnes-Schmitt controversy, advanced the commonplace position that "the individual motives of a writer are altogether irrelevant in determining the logical force of his argument, that is, whether certain premises are or are not sufficient to demonstrate a certain conclusion." But the authors go on to acknowledge that "certain motives weaken our competence and our readiness to observe certain facts or to state them fairly.

[24]Ziman, *Public Knowledge: An Essay Concerning the Social Dimension of Science* (Cambridge, 1968).
[25]The footnote has various functions, rhetorical and otherwise, but in this connection it proclaims: "This is where you can find the document which I have cited; if you are skeptical of its existence, or of my interpretation, look for yourself." But it only weakly assimilates historical scholarship to the scientific norm of replicability. If the material referred to is readily available (which is almost never the case with respect to archival citations), a singular assertion can be checked, even a handful of assertions. But when citations, several thousand from among the millions which might have been chosen, are illustrative of a synthetic interpretation arrived at through "deep immersion," even the demonstration that several citations are faulty is far from constituting a refutation of the thesis they underpin, just as their verification does little to sustain it. The contrast between history and science in this regard should not be overdrawn. Many scientific experiments (whose cost can run to millions of dollars) are replicable only with the greatest difficulty. In science, as in history, mere replication carries low payoff and is rarely undertaken. And in many cases scientific theories are (quite properly) maintained even in the case of "experimental falsification."

Hence the existence of such motives, if such existence can be proved in any given case, is relevant to determine the credibility of a witness."[26]

Relativists within the historical profession faced a continuing dilemma. They thought it axiomatic that every historical account, before it saw the light of day, inevitably passed through the filter of the preconceptions, interests, and intentions of the historian. A clear corollary was that the evaluation of the historical account demanded the closest examination of these preconceptions, interests, and intentions. But the imperatives of professional demeanor and comity, as exigent for relativists as for others, made such an examination intolerable—the more so, in this instance, as a result of the egregiously offensive content and tone of Barnes's assertions. It is a nice paradox that it was the antirelativist Barnes who, as a result of his fanatical faith in the objectivity of his conclusions, proposed a procedure which Becker's relativist principles legitimated, but which Becker's sense of professional decorum made him disparage.

In most lists of "fallacies," the mirror image of the *argumentum ad hominem* is the *argumentum ad verecundiam,* or "argument from authority."[27] Whereas the former says, "Distrust this proposition—it is offered by a bad (unreliable) person," the latter says, "Believe this proposition—it is offered by a good (reliable) person." If professional exigencies led historians to reject the *argumentum ad hominem,* the *argumentum ad verecundiam* elicited an overwhelmingly positive response, as well it might, since most of what historians (as well as other people) know, apart from a few things touching their personal lives, and a handful of phenomena they have investigated personally, they know because they rely on some authority. As we have seen earlier, the aim of establishing "authority," and "authoritative consensus," was central to the professionalization of history and other academic disciplines. Consensual, ex-

---

[26]Morris R. Cohen and Ernest Nagel, *An Introduction to Logic and Scientific Method* (New York, 1934), 180.

[27]Like *ad hominem,* this argument, whose root word means "shyness" or "modesty," was first explicated by Locke—who, as in the former case, did not clearly designate it as a fallacy. It consisted, he wrote, of alleging "the opinions of men whose parts, learning, eminency, power, or some other cause has gained a name and settled their reputation in the common esteem with some kind of authority. When men are established in any kind of dignity, it is thought a breach of modesty for others to derogate any way from it, and question the authority of men who are in possession of it. This is apt to be censured as carrying with it too much of pride, when a man does not readily yield to the determination of approved authors which is wont to be received with respect and submission by others; and it is looked upon as insolence for a man to set up and adhere to his own opinion against . . . that of some learned doctor or otherwise approved writer." (Locke, *Human Understanding,* 2:278–79.)

pert, professional authority would substitute a single, reliable, objective truth for the cacophony of competing truth claims. But what if authority ceased to be consensual?[28]

In the late nineteenth century the anomaly of clearly conflicting versions of the same historical event could be attributed to "preprofessional" habits of untrained and thus "unauthoritative" amateurs. When such anomalies appeared in the first decades of organized scholarship, a certain allowance could be made for the vestigial presence of old habits. But in the event, the problem rarely arose, because there were institutional and disciplinary mechanisms which made it unusual. The AHA's register of dissertation topics, and other less formal mechanisms for the avoidance of duplication, averted confrontations; warded off, that is to say, precisely that "transpersonal replicability" which was the touchstone of objectivity in the natural sciences. To a considerable extent the nature of the discipline, with its heavy emphasis on excavating new, verified, factual materials from the archives, a process often requiring several years, discouraged duplication. Such duplication was likely to be as unproductive for the individual's career as it was for the "efficient" deployment of the resources of the profession as a whole.

Implicitly discrepant pictures of the same phenomenon could usually be attributed to the fact that the two scholars' work, while overlapping in treatment, was directed to different aspects of the subject. When contradiction occurred between two works in successive generations, the differences could be attributed, sometimes even legitimately, to "newly discovered sources." The third round of the war guilt controversy in the United States saw one of the rare occurrences of stark, contemporaneous confrontation in historical scholarship.

Throughout the early and mid-twenties the scholarly community was frustrated by the absence of an "authoritative," "definitive" account of the causes of the war by an acknowledged specialist in European diplomatic history. When such a work appeared, there would be an end to vulgar polemics by flamboyant controversialists like Barnes; scholarly harmony could be restored around consensual truth. In 1928 Sidney B. Fay, universally acknowledged to be a sober and meticulous scholar, published his long-awaited *Origins of the World War*, a "moderate revi-

[28]In 1914, Beard, angry at what he thought was unfair criticism of his work by an anonymous reviewer in the *AHR*, wrote Jameson asking who had written it. Beard argued against anonymity on the ground that the validity of general evaluative remarks "rests upon the authority of the person who speaks." Jameson defended the right of a reviewer to remain anonymous if he wished, "letting his review rest upon the authority of this journal." (Beard to Jameson, 8 October 1914; Jameson to Beard, 10 October 1914; both in AHA Papers, Box 279.)

sionist" statement. It was enthusiastically received—in part because the desire for closure was so strong that scholars of very different views proclaimed themselves satisfied with Fay's work.

"Those who have fought in the last years in the cause of historical truth," wrote William L. Langer, "may rest their case . . . and those who have been on the fence can use this authoritative work as a stepping-stone into the revisionist camp." Barnes's review was entitled "The Revisionists Vindicated." Preston Slosson, a dedicated antirevisionist, refused to classify Fay with the revisionists because he had separated himself from "unwelcome allies of the 'extreme left'" and did not accept the thesis of a Franco-Russian conspiracy to wage war. Raymond Turner claimed that Fay assigned Germany a role second only to Austria in causing the war, an assertion which led Fay to protest in the *New York Times* about people who "get out of a book what they are looking for, rather than what is actually in it."[29]

As Fay's work had neared completion, Schmitt, following norms of priority and conflict-avoidance, had abandoned his own plans to produce a synthetic treatment of war origins. But antirevisionists like Archibald Cary Coolidge and James T. Shotwell convinced him that it was his duty to combat the pernicious influence of Fay's work. Two years after the publication of Fay's magnum opus, Schmitt's two-volume *The Coming of the War, 1914* appeared. It was respectfully received and, in what may have been more a political than a literary or scholarly judgment, received the Pulitzer Prize. But even friendly academic reviewers generally compared it unfavorably to Fay's work, a verdict Schmitt attributed to the pro-German "climate of opinion." Even more disturbing to Schmitt than his book's cool reception were the epistemological and professional implications of the disagreement between Fay and himself:

This has always troubled me. We had both taken advanced degrees at eminent universities. . . . We used the same documents and read the same biographies and memoirs in preparing our respective books—and came up with quite different interpretations. . . . Is there something wrong with our methods of historical

[29]Langer, review of Fay, *Nation* 127 (1928): 623; Barnes review in *Current History* 29 (1928): 443–48; Slosson review, *AHR* 34 (1929): 337; Turner review, *American Journal of Sociology* 34 (1929): 932; Fay letter to *New York Times*, 7 December 1928, 30. The only important dissent from the chorus of approbation was Schmitt's systematic critique, which was a magnificent catalogue of exquisitely polite formulae: "Professor Fay very curiously fails to mention . . ."; "It is apparently unknown to Professor Fay that . . ."; "one important fact not mentioned by Professor Fay . . ."; "Professor Fay has failed to notice . . ."; "Professor Fay does not make clear that . . ." (*Saturday Review of Literature*, 2 March 1929, 726.)

study and training when two scholars draw such conflicting conclusions from the same evidence?

Others were led to believe that there might be "something wrong" with the traditional assumption that "conflicting conclusions" were an anomaly, and that authoritative, objective consensus could be expected on important historical issues.[30]

II

The controversies over the origins of World War I had mainly concerned Europeanists, and were carried out largely in the twenties. The other set of controversies which we will examine—those concerning slavery, Reconstruction, and the origins of the Civil War—were the province of Americanists, and these disputes took place, for the most part, in the thirties. Whereas prewar historiography had been clearly converging on these issues, and, as we saw, this convergence had given prewar historians confidence in the objective fruits of their labors, interwar historical thought was equally clearly diverging—a development which, in this as in other realms, was seriously troublesome for the program of demonstrating the objectivity of professional historical scholarship.[31]

Controversies over these issues were, of course, related to the regionalism within the profession, discussed in Chapter 7. Yet although southern regional consciousness remained high, and sometimes assumed new and more strident forms, the mutually incompatible interpretive frameworks of interwar historians did not necessarily follow regional lines. Historians within both North and South differed sharply on issues which shaped the historiography of mid-nineteenth-century struggles: the Beardian em-

---

[30]Coolidge to Schmitt, 27 September 1926 and 3 November 1927; Shotwell to Schmitt, 18 January 1927—all in Schmitt Papers, Box 3; Schmitt, *The Fashion and Future of History* (Cleveland, 1960), 4–5. Fay accepted the difference with greater serenity: "Two travelers may approach a mountain from opposite sides. Each may describe very accurately and honestly what he sees, and yet the two pictures of the mountain—its outline, its wooded base and snow-capped peaks—may appear very different according to the point of view or the time of day at which each traveler makes his description. Mr. Schmitt seems to have looked at it from the west, from the Entente point of view, in the evening, when England and France appear in rosy colors and the deeds of Germany look dark. Some critics of the present reviewer believe that his approach was from the east in the morning, with a reversal of effects." (Review of *The Coming of the War, 1914, Journal of Modern History* 3 [1931]: 147.)

[31]To say that historical interpretations were diverging is not to say that a static measurement would show interwar historians farther apart than their prewar predecessors: indeed, such an absolute measure, if it were possible, might show the reverse. But whereas between 1884 and 1914 there was substantial movement toward consensus, between World War I and World War II—and particularly during the 1930s—there was increasing dissensus within the profession.

phasis on economic and class conflict, the "lessons" of World War I for the interpretation of the Civil War, and, above all, on race.

In Chapter 3, I showed how before 1914 growing agreement on racist premises was the foundation of a convergence of historical interpretations on issues surrounding the Civil War. After World War I, divergent attitudes on black inferiority led, directly or indirectly, to historiographical dissensus. For a variety of reasons a growing number of white historians—though still, throughout the period, a minority—began to question racist assumptions previously taken for granted. For some the teachings of the new, antiracist anthropology appear to have been crucial; others were repelled by lynchings and other fruits of twentieth-century southern racism; for still others, leftist political commitments seem to have been the decisive element; in most cases it is impossible to say for sure.

Historians of southern origin or residence were of course more likely to be racist than their colleagues who were born in the North or lived there, but these weren't the only factors. More general ideological considerations, or the question of generation, were often of equal importance. Northern-born historians whose intellectual formation had taken place during the era of scientific racism were firmly set in their attitudes. Milo M. Quaife, Iowa-born editor of the *Mississippi Valley Historical Review*, published an editorial in that journal in 1926 which expressed alarm that "men eminent in American life and scholarship" had lent their support for the Association for the Study of Negro Life and History, with its absurd doctrine of racial equality: "It is proper that the negro contribution to civilization (whatever it may consist in) should be accorded its due meed of recognition, but the practical consequence of inculcating the rising generation with the idea that all the races of mankind occupy one common level of mediocrity seems to us as appalling as the teaching itself is unhistorical." Northern historians who made their commitment to racial equality clear were generally younger, and frequently on the left: Socialists like Fred A. Shannon, Communists like James S. Allen, Herbert Aptheker, Philip S. Foner, Herbert Morais.[32]

---

[32]*MVHR* 12 (1926): 629. There is a casual, matter-of-fact racism in the writing of many interwar northern historians. Arthur M. Schlesinger, who served on the board of the Association for the Study of Negro Life and History for more than twenty years, believed it likely that high achievement among blacks was the result of an "infusion of white blood." (*Rise of the City*, 385–86.) Paul H. Buck, in the concluding paragraph of *The Road to Reunion: 1865–1900* (Boston, 1937) expressed satisfaction with the northern decision to accept white domination of blacks in the South: "The unchanging elements of the race problem had become apparent to most observers. . . . Once a people admits the fact that a major problem is basically insoluble they have taken the first step in learning how to live with it."

The combination of generational and ideological factors can be seen in the racial attitudes of southern-born historians resident in the north. Ulrich B. Phillips became more conservative, and more racist, with the passing years. In his early years at the University of Wisconsin he had been a passionate Progressive; he often attributed "Negro inferiority," albeit ambivalently, to environmental factors; his writings on race were directed in the main against reactionary southern extremists. In the course of the 1920s his target shifted to egalitarians, who had scarcely existed when he began his career, and he asserted that "the cardinal test of a Southerner and the central theme of Southern history [was] a common resolve indomitably maintained that it shall be and remain a white man's country."[33]

When William B. Hesseltine came up from Virginia to study at Ohio State in 1926, the thing he liked least, he wrote his mother, was "the damned Yankees all around on all sides."

> Another thing is the Negroes. I am beginning to get used to sitting in classes with them but have not gotten to the place where I welcome them. . . . One old negro is in my classes. . . . The other day he spoke to me. I was not thinking . . . and said unconsciously, "how do, uncle." He has not spoken to me since. I really didn't mean to offend the old fellow but he looks to me as tho he should be following a mule in Arkansas instead of following History in a university.

Within a few years Hesseltine, who had in the interim joined the Socialist Party, became one of the most savage critics of reactionary and racist southern historiography. The "real central theme of Southern history," he wrote, was "the maintenance of the planter class in control." Racism had been an effective instrument for preventing unity among the exploited, except briefly during the days of Populism; now, once again, "depression-born necessity [has] brought tenant farmers of both races to stand shoulder to shoulder against their oppressors."[34]

Southern historians who remained in the South demonstrated as much divergence as their transplanted brethren Phillips and Hesseltine, though as a result of massive pressure for conformity, the full extent of their dissidence did not always appear.[35] Most southern historians had ab-

---

[33]"The Central Theme of Southern History" (1928), in Phillips, *The Course of the South to Secession* (New York, 1939), 152.
[34]Hesseltine to his mother, 11 July 1926, Hesseltine Papers, M77–88; "Some New Aspects of the Pro-Slavery Argument," *Journal of Negro History* 21 (1936): 14.
[35]For the sake of symmetry something should be said about the fourth cell created by classifying historians according to region of birth and of residence. Unfortunately, it is difficult to make generalizations about this category, since there were (to the best of my knowledge) only two northern historians in the South in this period: Ella Lonn, who taught at Goucher throughout the interwar years, and Howard K. Beale, who was at the

sorbed traditional racial attitudes in their youth, and had them reinforced daily by their environment; their defense of these attitudes often became more strident as they began to come under attack. Frank L. Owsley, who became president of the Southern Historical Association in 1940, was one of the "Vanderbilt Agrarians" who composed the 1930 manifesto *I'll Take My Stand* in defense of traditional southern values and culture. In his contribution to the volume he wrote of "half-savage blacks . . . some of whom could still remember the taste of human flesh and the bulk of them hardly three generations removed from cannibalism." Both before and after the Civil War tranquil race relations in the South had been disturbed by northern troublemakers, who had bamboozled the "childish and naive" blacks into believing that the white man was his oppressor. He proposed to Robert Penn Warren that a secret organization be formed to bolster southern morale in combating the interlopers: members would be required to read *I'll Take My Stand*, Avery Craven's biography of Edmund Ruffin, and Allen Tate's life of Jefferson Davis, and to visit Confederate cemeteries. If that didn't work, if "smart lawyers" (read "Jewish lawyers") continued to come to the South to stir up blacks, he threatened a revival of the Ku Klux Klan.[36]

Owsley was not untypical of interwar southern historians; he was certainly closer to the norm than Francis B. Simkins who, like Owsley, served as President of the Southern Historical Association. In 1927 Simkins published an article in the *Journal of Negro History* mocking the pretensions to gallantry of the KKK in Reconstruction, and detailing its corruption, brutalities, and atrocities. In 1939, in the *Journal of Southern History*, he directed his colleagues' attention to the findings of modern anthropology, which contradicted their assumption of innate Negro inferiority, and led to "rejection of the gloomy generalization that the race, because of its inherent nature, is destined to play forever its present inferior role."[37]

University of North Carolina. Lonn appears to have completely assimilated southern racial attitudes. Beale was an outspoken egalitarian: he attacked segregation in his *Are American Teachers Free?* (New York, 1936), and the assumption of Negro inferiority, which had distorted historical scholarship, in "On Rewriting Reconstruction History," *AHR* 45 (1940): 807–27. The University of North Carolina was by far the most "enlightened" southern university in this period, but even there, Beale's views created difficulties for him and contributed to his departure.

[36] "The Irrepressible Conflict," in *I'll Take My Stand* (Nashville, 1930), 62; "Scottsboro, the Third Crusade: The Sequel to Abolition and Reconstruction," *American Review* 1 (1933): 265, 285; Letter to Warren of 12 January 1935, quoted in Edward S. Shapiro, "Frank L. Owsley and the Defense of Southern Identity," *Tennessee Historical Quarterly* 36 (1977): 84–85.

[37] "The Ku Klux Klan in South Carolina," *Journal of Negro History* 12 (1927): 606–47; "New Viewpoints of Southern Reconstruction," *Journal of Southern History* 5 (1939):

By the 1930s a new generation of southern historians was emerging with different experiences and assumptions. Owsley had been born in 1890 and completed most of his education before World War I; Simkins, born in 1897, had done his graduate work in the 1920s. Comer Vann Woodward was born in a tiny village in Arkansas in 1908; as a teenager he saw lynch mobs gather. While a student at Emory University in the late 1920s he decided that segregation was "nonsense," and he single-hand-edly "desegregated" a dance at one of the local black colleges, "to the total embarrassment of everybody concerned." He followed the Scottsboro case from Moscow, where he had gone in the summer of 1932. While Owsley was fulminating at the role of outside Communist agitators, Woodward joined, and briefly headed, the committee to defend Angelo Herndon, a black Communist organizer sentenced to death under an old statute against "insurrection." (After a time he left the committee in disgust with what he regarded as opportunistic and manipulative behavior by the Communists.)[38]

At the University of North Carolina in the mid-1930s an older but still very much alive tradition of southern scholarship encountered a newer one, still struggling to be born, as Woodward sat in the classroom of Joseph G. de Roulhac Hamilton. Woodward fumed as Hamilton held forth on blacks' innate inferiority, and the appropriateness of Jim Crow. He had come to North Carolina to work on Tom Watson, to furnish "evidence against the once prevalent . . . assumption that 'things have always been the same.'" His interest was in the Populists' early challenge to segregation. "If there had indeed been no exceptions, no breaks, and things had always been the same, there was little hope of change." The final fruit of Woodward's work at North Carolina was the publication of *Tom Watson: Agrarian Rebel* in 1938. That his revised dissertation was reviewed on the first page of the *New York Times Book Review* was a

---

58. Simkins was not, however, a consistent crusader for racial equality: in his presidential address to the Southern Historical Association some years later, he said that "The histo-rian of the South should accept the class and race distinctions of his region unless he wishes to deplore the region's existence. He should display a tolerant understanding of why in the South the Goddess of Justice has not always been blind, why there have been lynchings and Jim Crow laws." ("Tolerating the South's Past," *Journal of Southern Histo-ry* 21 [1955]: 7.)

38 Woodward's comments on desegregating the dance are quoted in Larry Van Dyne, "Vann Woodward: Penetrating the Romantic Haze," *Chronicle of Higher Education* 22 (8 May 1978): 13–14; other biographical material in this and the following paragraph from infor-mation supplied by Woodward in John Herbert Roper, "C. Vann Woodward's Early Career—The Historian as Dissident Youth," *Georgia Historical Quarterly* 44 (1980): 7–21.

fitting recognition of the emergence of a radically dissonant tendency in southern historiography.

The breakdown in historians' consensus on race was reflected directly in the historiography of slavery and of Reconstruction. An idyllic picture of the plantation had been presented in Ulrich B. Phillips's two influential works, *American Negro Slavery* (1918) and *Life and Labor in the Old South* (1929). Felicitously written, based on monumental research, and filled with important insights into the complexities of the slave-master relationship, his work was firmly grounded in his belief in Negro inferiority. The slaves were, he wrote, innately "submissive," "light-hearted," "amiable," "ingratiating," and "imitative." Phillips's books went beyond a "sympathetic treatment" of slavery—they all but recommended it.[39] No alternative overall synthetic treatment of slavery appeared during the interwar years, and many works dealing with the South written by authors out of sympathy with Phillips either skipped over slavery or treated it summarily. As a result, Phillips's version held the field. Samuel Eliot Morison and Henry Steele Commager, in a best-selling textbook of the period, wrote that

Sambo, whose wrongs moved the abolitionists to wrath and tears . . . suffered less than any other class in the South from its "peculiar institution." . . . The majority of slaves were . . . apparently happy. . . . There was much to be said for slavery as a transitional status between barbarism and civilization. The negro learned his master's language, and accepted in some degree his moral and religious standards. In return he contributed much besides his labor—music and humor for instance—to American civilization.[40]

But there were a number of historians, North and South, who were unwilling to accept Phillips's version. David Muzzey, congratulating Carl Becker for having, in a textbook, painted an unflattering portrait of slavery, said he was "sick of the pussy-footing of authors who know what a damnable cause the South fought for, and yet are so gentle with the

[39]*American Negro Slavery* (New York, 1918), 291–92; Phillips indeed came close to urging the revival of the substance, if not the letter, of slavery. Earlier, stressing the economies of scale, division of labor, and rationalization of production on the plantation, he had attributed the postbellum economic backwardness of the South to the breakup of the system. The "ignorance, indolence, and instability" of the black would "prevent him from managing his own labor in an efficient way. . . . It is a dead loss for a good manager to have no managing to do. It is also a dead loss for a laborer who needs management to have no management." ("The Economics of the Plantation," *South Atlantic Quarterly* 2 [1903]: 233–36.) His solution, advanced in 1925, was restoration of the plantation system with Negro wage labor on long-term contracts: "voluntary indenture," he called it. ("Plantations with Slave Labor and Free," *AHR* 30 [1925]: 750.)
[40]*The Growth of the American Republic* (New York, 1930), 415, 418.

sophistries of the Stephens and the Davises." William E. Dodd privately expressed disapproval of Phillips's "strong tendency to plead a cause." In 1931 Frederic Bancroft, an older northern historian whose father had been an abolitionist, published a volume on *Slave Trading in the Old South* which challenged Phillips on a number of central issues. Bancroft's book was greeted warmly by blacks and liberals. Monographic works contradicting Phillips's picture of slavery—some by blacks, others by Marxists—increasingly came to be taken seriously by those who rejected the Georgian's magnolia-scented portrait, but were unable, as yet, to offer up an alternative synthesis. The emerging generation of graduate students in particular were more and more hostile to the benign interpretation of the "peculiar institution." Richard Hofstadter thought it "a latter-day phase of the pro-slavery argument." But it was to be another few years before the discontent which younger historians in the 1930s felt with Phillips's version of slavery was to find voice in the writings of Hofstadter, Kenneth Stampp, and others of their generation.[41]

The received view of Reconstruction, even more than that of slavery, came under systematic assault during the interwar period, though, as with slavery, no comprehensive alternative synthesis emerged. The orthodox version of the episode was established by professional historians in the early twentieth century, principally through the work of William A. Dunning and his students, many of whom, like Walter Fleming, Charles W. Ramsdell, and J. G. de Roulhac Hamilton, were among the most influential of interwar southern historians. During the 1920s these men, and their students, produced a stream of monographic studies which sustained and extended Dunning's picture. This view became a staple of popular fiction (often assigned in history classes) such as Thomas Dixon's *The Clansman*, translated by D. W. Griffith into the epic *Birth of a Nation*. Before the war it was embodied in the work of the highly respected amateur historian James Ford Rhodes. During the interwar period it attained its popular apotheosis, reaching hundreds of thousands of readers, in Claude G. Bowers's 1929 *The Tragic Era*. Paradoxically, Bowers's interpretation, written for partisan purposes—to discredit the Republican Party in the South—closely paralleled that of early-twentieth-century northern historians who had accepted the southern version of Reconstruction for purposes of nonpartisan sectional reconciliation. In reviewing Bowers's book, professional historians occa-

[41]Muzzey to Becker, 16 October 1920, Becker Papers; Dodd to F. Stuart Chapin, 17 November 1925, Dodd Papers, Box 22; Hofstadter, "U. B. Phillips and the Plantation Legend," *Journal of Negro History* 29 (1944): 122.

sionally deplored his rhetorical excesses, and manifest political partisanship, but generally acknowledged that, as Arthur Schlesinger said in reviewing it, its conclusions were in accord with contemporary scholarship.[42]

The traditional view, from Dunning and Rhodes through Bowers, viewed Reconstruction as an unprecedented atrocity. Vindictive radicals imposed on the prostrate South a regime of humiliation, corruption, and exploitation by carpetbaggers, "scalawags," and impudent freedmen. A united white population struggled manfully to remove the yoke of oppression, a struggle symbolized by the activities of the gallant knights of the Ku Klux Klan. The North eventually realized the folly of the experiment—which had been dictated by venality, the search for partisan advantage, and crackpot theories of Negro equality—and after 1877, the South, though crippled by the experience, was permitted to direct its own affairs, and in particular its race relations, without destructive northern interference.

There had been critics of this view all along: Harvard-trained professional historians who had challenged its biases and distortions. But their criticisms could be safely disregarded because, being black, they were manifestly and visibly incapable of being impartial or objective on the subject. When Carter G. Woodson wrote a scathing review of *The Tragic Era* in the *Journal of Negro History*, William E. Dodd, who had praised Bowers's treatment, chided Woodson for having "slightly weakened your hold . . . no one has a right strictly to the title of historian if he cannot make it clear that he neither condemns nor endorses beyond the point of positive impartiality . . . your estimate of Bowers' book did lead me to think you had forgotten for a moment this fundamental dictum." In any event, with the exception of an article by W. E. B. Du Bois in the *American Historical Review* in 1910, almost all of the work of black professional historians—Du Bois himself, Woodson, and Alrutheus A.

---

[42]*New Republic* 110 (1929): 210–11. (Cf. Charles R. Lingley review, *AHR* 35 [1930]: 382–83; James C. Malin in *MVHR* 16 [1930]: 561–64.) Bowers, a strong Democratic Party loyalist, hoped that his work would help to undo the cracks in the "solid South" created by the 1928 presidential candidacy of the Catholic Al Smith. He wrote a Democratic Party official that the book "will be the most powerful single factor in bringing the South back into line. . . . It is the true story of . . . this period during which the Republican Party solidified its power by bayonets and corruption . . . the most tremendous indictment of that party ever penned in history. . . . If I do not have the appreciation of the Democratic Party for this work on which I near broke myself down by day and night labor for five years I have written my last line in an attempt to serve it." (Letter to Jouett Shouse, 26 August 1929, in David E. Kyvig, "History as Present Politics: Claude Bowers' *The Tragic Era*," *Indiana Magazine of History* 73 [1977]: 27–28.) The appreciation was forthcoming: Roosevelt appointed him ambassador to Spain.

Taylor—appeared in the *Journal of Negro History* or in privately printed monographs, and was generally disregarded.[43]

As with the historiography of slavery, the early thirties marked the emergence of a new school of Reconstruction historians sharply critical of the old. Discontent with the received view focused on both its racism and its class bias. Implicit in any synthetic interpretation is a normative vision—explicit or implicit. The historiography of the French Revolution is difficult to sort out without knowledge of the visions of "the good society" held by the historians who contributed to it: the stable, traditional, hierarchical society of the Ancien Régime (tragically destroyed); enlightened constitutional rule by moderate elites (abandoned when the revolution "went astray"); a radical, popular, and egalitarian democracy (snatched from the people by a panicky bourgeoisie). So in the case of Reconstruction, those for whom it had destroyed a honeysuckle-draped aristocratic arcadia based on a stable racial caste system were challenged by those whose vision was of racial equality, of poor whites escaping the domination of the planter class—or a merger of the two egalitarian visions in hopes for a black-white populist coalition.

In 1932 two southerners, Francis B. Simkins and Robert H. Woody, published a work on Reconstruction in South Carolina which did not gloss over the intimidation and brutalizing of Negroes, and argued that the received interpretation of Reconstruction had been more harmful to the state than Reconstruction itself. A few years later, Simkins wrote that rather than Reconstruction's having been a failure because it was excessively radical on racial issues, its failure was a consequence of accepting

---

[43]Woodson review of Bowers, *Journal of Negro History* 15 (1930): 117–19; Dodd to Woodson, 5 April 1930 and 15 April 1930, Dodd Papers, Box 34. Du Bois's "Reconstruction and Its Benefits" appeared in the *AHR* 15 (1910): 781–99. August Meier reports, on the basis of an interview with the black historian Benjamin Quarles, who was a graduate student at Wisconsin in the 1930s, that Carl Russell Fish and the other Wisconsin historians "assumed that blacks could not write 'objectively' about their own past and were reluctant to permit their occasional Negro graduate students to do dissertations in Negro history." Because of Hesseltine's interest in Frederick Douglass he made an exception in Quarles's case and permitted him to do his thesis on the black abolitionist. ("Benjamin Quarles and the Historiography of Black America," *Civil War History* 26 [1980]: 101–2.) With the exception of Max Yergan, who briefly taught Negro History at CCNY in the late 1930s as the result of pressure from Communist students at the college, it was unthinkable in the interwar period that a Negro be employed at a white institution. There were paradoxes worth savoring in the exclusion of blacks. John Hope Franklin reports that at Harvard, while his classmates received assistantships which entailed teaching duties, he was given a fellowship—"one that didn't require work and would avoid the problems the University seemed to think I might have if I had to grade white students' papers." (Franklin quoted in Jack Star, "Above All a Scholar," *Change* 9 [February 1977]: 29.)

the continuation of white domination and indeed allowing southern whites to "tighten the bonds of caste."[44]

For other historians coming to prominence in the 1930s it was the class bias in traditional Reconstruction historiography which was most offensive. As Simkins's views of Reconstruction were shaped by a vision of racial equality, William B. Hesseltine's were consistent with his socialist convictions. "The Reconstruction struggle in the South," he wrote in 1934, "was the struggle of the grasping gentry to exploit the lower classes of whites and Blacks."

I've lived too long in the South to have any delusions left as to the honesty, probity, or excellence of the white classes. I counted up in Rhodes and found that in one chapter on reconstruction he uses the expression "property and intelligence" fifteen times. Rhodes was a damned snob. Moreover, the bargain which Hayes made with the Southerners to withdraw the troops was a bargain of the conservative classes of the country to cooperate in the great task of suppressing the lesser ranks of economic men. There's been too damned much oozy morality spread over the period of reconstruction. The capitalists secured their grip on the nation under the cover of loud outcries about public honesty and morality in public office. The doctrine of honesty is just a bit of propaganda by which the property holder seeks to protect his holdings. Under cover of its preachments, he steals the more.[45]

Howard K. Beale's critique of scholarship on Reconstruction combined racial egalitarianism and an insistence on the centrality of class. In an article in the *American Historical Review* surveying interwar work in the field, he found that even many of the more enlightened southern historians "never quite got away from [the] instinctive assumption that their race must bar Negroes from social and economic equality." For most historians of Reconstruction, he wrote,

the offense of the Radical leaders [was] that they sought to serve the interests of *poor* men. . . . The Radical attempt to establish democracy was not a success. But the Conservative white solution has been little better, save for property owners. It has kept the Negro in his place by creating a caste system. It has kept millions of whites dependent and docile politically by keeping them dependent economically as mill workers and tenant farmers.

Significantly, when listing those historians who had made the most important contributions to the reinterpretation of Reconstruction, he

---

[44]Simkins and Woody, *South Carolina During Reconstruction* (Chapel Hill, N.C., 1932); Simkins, "New Viewpoints," 55–57.
[45]Letter to Frank W. Prescott, 14 January 1934, Hesseltine Papers, M66–132/4.

named, along with southern liberals like Woodward and Simkins, black historians and historians who wrote from a Marxist perspective: Du Bois, Horace Mann Bond, Roger Shugg, and James S. Allen. The admission of these voices into scholarly discourse on Reconstruction was symbolic of the collapse of consensus on this highly charged issue.[46]

If there was a collapse of consensus on the objective truth about the slave system before the Civil War, and the Reconstruction which followed it, the historiography on the causes and nature of the war itself became totally fragmented. One standard survey of the historiography of the causes of the Civil War contrasts the situation between 1900 and 1930, when "historians had generally been credited with objectivity" and "criticisms were usually in good spirit," with the acrimonious debate and "name-calling" after 1930.[47]

The older nationalist consensus on the origins of the Civil War had stressed constitutional issues, and, to a lesser extent, slavery. Neither were regarded as central by interwar historians. In line with what Morton White called the "revolt against formalism," concern with abstract questions of constitutionalism seemed old-fashioned. In a 1922 essay on "The State Rights Fetish," Arthur Schlesinger mocked the idea that this had been a decisive issue. Most New Historians were strongly inclined to downgrade the proposition that mere principles, constitutional or abolitionist, had the explanatory weight of tangible material interests. No influential interwar work on the Civil War presented either the constitutional question or the slavery issue as decisive. Without directly attacking the old conceptual scheme on which professional consensus had been reached, interwar historians simply abandoned it, in favor of new, and mutually irreconcilable, interpretations. The new views, while often colored by older sectional loyalties, generally cut across these: they were based on new intellectual currents, and rooted in experiences other than that of the "late unpleasantness between the states."[48]

[46]"On Rewriting Reconstruction History," *AHR* 45 (1940): 819, 827, 809.

[47]C. E. Cauthen, "The Coming of the Civil War," in Arthur S. Link and Rembert W. Patrick, eds., *Writing Southern History: Essays in Historiography in Honor of Fletcher M. Green* (Baton Rouge, 1965), 234.

[48]Schlesinger's essay appeared in his *New Viewpoints in American History*. Becker, in an undated letter to Schlesinger, criticized "Beard & people of his way of thinking"—in which category he clearly included Schlesinger—for being unduly scornful of professions of principle. "This comes from an inadequate psychology." (Michael Kammen, *"What Is the Good of History?" Selected Letters of Carl L. Becker, 1900–1945* [Ithaca, N.Y., 1973], 59.) The constitutional issue, though downgraded by both northern and southern professional historians, was very much alive for "unreconstructed" southerners like Ruth Lawton, president-general of the United Daughters of the Confederacy. "We are suffering now," she complained to Arthur H. Brook of the Yale University Press, "from the

The first important entrants into what became a free-for-all on the Civil War were Charles and Mary Beard, who in *The Rise of American Civilization* termed it "The Second American Revolution," a "social war" which rearranged "classes and . . . the accumulation and distribution of wealth." It was "a social cataclysm in which the capitalists, laborers, and farmers of the North and West drove from power in the national government the planting aristocracy of the South." The war marked the dividing line between the agricultural and industrial eras in American history. Its essence was the struggle of classes and economic systems; only by the "accidents of climate, soil, and geography" was it a sectional dispute. The war itself was inevitable; it was an "irrepressible conflict."[49]

The Beards' treatment of the Civil War defended neither side in the conflict. It could be used by partisans of either North or South to sustain their case. Their view of the war as a Second American Revolution was broadly consonant with the view that Marx and Engels had taken of the American Civil War. A Communist historian, Herbert Morais, in the introduction to a 1937 collection of Marx and Engels's writings on the war, described *The Rise of American Civilization* as being, despite "certain limitations inherent in the liberal bourgeois approach . . . probably the best description of the Civil War." For Marxists the Second American Revolution was historically "progressive" in its consequences; politically it was a necessary precondition to working-class development. Their commitment to the Negro cause made them hail it as an epochal step in Negro liberation. They identified wholeheartedly with the North.[50]

But the Beards' historical framework had never been Marxist. They had no strong identification with the working class, and they had never been much interested in the Negro cause. Their criticism of postbellum northern capitalism was so unrelieved in the chapters dealing with the late nineteenth century that, as one commentator noted, "the Southern planters very nearly became the heroes of the narrative," and the Beards "very nearly became the ally of John C. Calhoun." Their ambivalence about the fruits of the war did not make them Confederate sympathizers, but the

domination in history . . . by the middle West, and we see the influence of those who have no conception of the sovereignty of a State because they were not born nor educated in a State which was sovereign." (Letter of 13 June 1927, Ralph H. Gabriel Papers, Add. I, Box 2.)
[49]*The Rise of American Civilization* (2 vols., New York, 1927), 2:53–54.
[50]Karl Marx and Frederick Engels, *The Civil War in the United States* (New York, 1937), xviii. The Beards were criticized for insufficient stress on the contribution of the working class and Negroes to the Union cause. Morais, a 1934 Columbia history Ph.D., taught in the New York City college system and wrote under the name "Richard Enmale" (ENgels-MArx-LEnin).

thrust of any work is inevitably contextual, dependent on what it alters or revises. The nationalist interpretation, which provided the backdrop against which the Beards wrote, had stressed the wrongs of slavery and secession, and the long-run positive fruits of its defeat and the triumph of the northern cause. By their silence on the former issues, and ambivalence on the latter, they produced a work which southern historians could use to vindicate the Confederacy.[51]

The South in the interwar years saw a revival of regional consciousness which reversed the movement toward national integration before 1914. The Scottsboro and Herndon trials, as well as northern agitation about lynchings, led a number of southerners to close ranks on the race question. The agricultural depression of the 1920s, and problems connected with farm tenancy and fitful attempts at industrialization, produced a belief among many southerners that they were an exploited colony of the industrial North. The Scopes trial of 1925, which seemed to contrast enlightened science with benighted southern Bible-thumpers, led the authors of *I'll Take My Stand* to condemn science as an ally of industrialism.

By no means all of the renaissance of southern regional consciousness took a Beardian standpoint. Much of it simply revived older attitudes. But even members of the ultraconservative *I'll Take My Stand* group, like Frank Owsley, could take over the Beards' framework of a confrontation between industrial and agrarian society, and their bleak picture of industrial capitalism, and weave out of it a vindication of the South in the Civil War, and the agrarian society which it represented. On at least partially Beardian grounds, Owsley could explain the causes of the Civil War as the result of the "egocentric sectionalism" of the industrial plutocratic North. A similar line was taken by Charles W. Ramsdell of the University of Texas, one of the founders of the Southern Historical Association, and, like Owsley, one of its early presidents. Following the Beards, he argued that rather than solving national problems, the Civil War had created new ones, by removing the planter counterweight to industrialism. Benjamin B. Kendrick, whose generally Progressive outlook made him a more thoroughgoing Beardian than either Owsley or Ramsdell, was explicit about how the Civil War had enabled northern industrial interests to relegate the South to colonial status.[52]

If Beardians divided over allegiance to agrarian or industrial values,

[51]Thomas J. Pressly, *Americans Interpret Their Civil War* (Princeton, 1954), 242.
[52]Owsley, "The Fundamental Cause of the Civil War: Egocentric Sectionalism," *Journal of Southern History* 7 (1941): 3–18; Ramsdell, "The Changing Interpretations of the Civil War," ibid., 3 (1937): 3–27; Kendrick, "The Colonial Status of the South," ibid., 8 (1942): 3–22.

there was another polarization between those, whether of the Beardian or the older nationalist persuasion, who regarded the Civil War as unavoidable, and those for whom it was, preeminently, "the repressible conflict." The "revisionist" school of Civil War historiography argued that inept statecraft and irresponsible extremism had produced a "needless war." Avery O. Craven asserted that the conflict was "the work of politicians and pious cranks"; for James G. Randall it was the combination of "fanaticism" and "bogus leadership" of a "blundering generation." While sectional loyalties had a good deal to do with the reception this interpretation received, its origins were neither sectional nor ideological, but rather were rooted in interwar disillusionment with strident nationalism, bellicose patriotism, and the bloodshed they had so recently produced. The two most prominent exponents of the revisionist interpretation both had strong pacifist leanings, and shared in the general discouragement with the fruits of the world war. Craven was a lifelong Quaker, dedicated to understanding "why humans must settle differences by shooting at each other." "Those who force the settlement of human problems by war," he wrote, "can expect only an unsympathetic hearing from the future. Mere desire to do 'right' is no defense at the bar of history." "It is more than one can endure," Randall wrote in his diary during World War I, "to think of . . . young men becoming cannon fodder." In his essay on "The Blundering Generation," Randall said that instead of the word "war," the "realist" should use words like "organized murder" or "human slaughterhouse." In the era of *All Quiet On the Western Front* and the Nye munitions inquiry, the Civil War, for Randall, became "less a matter of yellow sashes and tassels, of swords and roses."

It becomes known for the ghastly scourge that it was, a scourge in which prison misery and preventable disease took heavier toll than bullets and in which desertion, corruption, and greed were as widespread as romantic gallantry. Guerrilla fights, criminality, and the underworld of vice were more prevalent than most readers would realize. The horror of the war in what it did to human bodies is not commonly revealed. In its mental attitudes the war emerges from restudy as a thing of twisted ideology. Indeed, the war mind is one of the most ghastly features of the struggle; minds that should have kept serene were swept into excesses of propaganda, intolerance, and hate.

For the Civil War revisionists the statesmen of 1860 could no more be excused from responsibility for the horrors they had unleashed than could those of 1914.[53]

---

[53]Craven, "Coming of the War Between the States: An Interpretation," *Journal of Southern History* 2 (1936): 305; Randall, "The Blundering Generation," *MVHR* 27 (1940): 15; Craven to Max Farrand, 13 October 1936, Farrand Papers; other remarks by Craven

On the Civil War, as with slavery and Reconstruction, what had previously been a convergent historiography became not just divergent, but
cacophonic. Most of the contestants in the controversies about these
issues were convinced of the scientific, detached, and objective quality of
their scholarship. This was certainly true of Phillips; of Beard, who collaborated on the *Rise of American Civilization* before his epistemological
crisis; undeniably true of the Marxists; and true also of the black historians who saw themselves as correcting the biases of whites. Occasionally
the language of detachment and objectivity was used cynically for rhetorical effect: Frank Owsley wrote to his friend Allen Tate, "The purpose of
my life is to undermine by 'careful' and 'detached,' 'well documented,'
'objective' writing, the entire Northern myth from 1820 to 1876."[54]

But the cumulative effect of historical dissonance on these questions
was, at a minimum, to raise questions about the objectivity of the collective venture. Allan Nevins saw that Phillips and Bancroft "were in possession of much the same body of facts regarding slavery; they were both
thoroughly honest, and determined to tell the uncolored truth as they
saw it; but one arrived at a friendly, the other at hostile conclusions upon
slavery as an institution." For him this illustrated the truth that "facts
cannot be selected without some personal conviction as to what is truth
. . . and this conviction is a bias." Awareness of the ubiquity of racism in
southern historiography led Hesseltine to the realization of how, in good
faith, and quite unconsciously, one could "use the methods of scientific
history to bolster up a prevailing concept and furnish a pseudo-historical
philosophy to a dominant group." The role of ideological and sectional
commitments in determining which variations were played on the Beardian theme became manifest. It was equally manifest how disillusionment
with World War I had led to the "revised" version of the origins of the
Civil War; indeed, the revisionists themselves avowed that this was true.
And it was also clear that the Civil War revisionists' central point was
normative: what nineteenth-century statesmen should have done, as contrasted with their actual behavior.[55]

quoted in John S. Rosenberg, "Toward a New Civil War Revisionism," *American Scholar*
38 (1969): 251; Ruth Painter Randall, *I Ruth: Autobiography of a Marriage* (Boston,
1968), 160; "Blundering Generation," 7; Randall, "The Civil War Restudied," *Journal of
Southern History* 6 (1940): 457.
[54]Quoted in M. E. Bradford, "Frank L. Owsley," in Clyde N. Wilson, ed., *Twentieth-
Century American Historians* (Detroit, 1983), 337.
[55]Nevins, *The Gateway to History* (Boston, 1938), 38–39; Hesseltine, "A Quarter Century
of the Association for the Study of Negro Life and History," *Journal of Negro History* 25
(1940): 444–45; for Randall's acknowledgment of the role of World War I in shaping Civil
War revisionism, see Rosenberg, "Civil War Revisionism," 251.

If before World War I the negotiated convergence of historical writing on these questions was the most dramatic demonstration of the plausibility of the profession's goal of closing in on the objective truth, the collapse of consensus in this realm between the wars was for many a powerful demonstration of how problematic that program was coming to seem.

III

Beyond particular controversies, there was a more general breakdown of agreement on the meaning of the past, and in particular the American past. Whereas before the war ideological consensus had worked to further the goal of a convergent corpus of historical writing, between the wars, ideological dissensus frustrated the achievement of that expected state. Before 1914 American historiography had reflected the values of conservatism, continuity, and comity. The interwar period saw a split between those who clung to the older orientation, and the growing number of reform-oriented scholars who stressed conflict and discontinuity; saw American history as the story of perpetual conflict between "the people" and "the interests."[56]

By the standards of the late 1960s, or of continental Europe, the ideological split within the American historical profession in the interwar years was not that great. But it was substantial compared to the prewar years. Perhaps more important, whereas before the war the tendency was, on the whole, in the direction of ideological consensus, and convergent historical interpretations, increasingly during the interwar years the direction of change was toward dissensus and divergent interpretations. Alongside this development, there was an increasing acknowledgment by historians that the writing and teaching of history, when not narrowly antiquarian, inevitably had political implications of one sort or another. As the domestic and international crises of the thirties made political neutrality or inaction seem less and less tolerable, there was a marked increase in the extent to which explicit and avowed political

---

[56]Divergent ideological commitments were most obviously reflected in substantive historical interpretations, but they had methodological consequences as well: much of the attack on the "new social history" reflected conservative distaste for the "liberal," "progressive" aura which surrounded it. The relationship between political conservatism and a critical attitude toward the new social history is made explicit in Wilbur C. Abbott, "New Methods of Writing History: A Criticism," *Current History* 31 (1929): 93–98; Eugene C. Barker, "The Changing View of the Function of History," *The Social Studies* 29 (1938): 149–54; Crane Brinton, "The New History: Twenty-Five Years After," *Journal of Social Philosophy* 1 (1936): 135–47.

purposes appeared in historians' books and classroom lectures. Both growing dissensus and increasing acceptance of the use of history for political purposes undermined the old view of an austere, detached community of scholars working together toward convergent, objective, historical truth.

There was no across-the-board confrontation between the Progressive Historians and their conservative antagonists between the wars. The Progressives seemed clearly in the ascendancy. After the war, what had been localized dissidence spread, as its original constituency, the graduate students of the second decade of the century, became the influential historians of the third and fourth decades. Within the intellectual community at large in these years, Beard was *the* American historian. In the 1938 *New Republic* symposium on "Books That Changed Our Minds," Beard was ranked second only to Veblen in influence, ahead of Dewey and Freud. A study of college textbooks in 1936 showed that his *Economic Interpretation of the Constitution* had become virtual orthodoxy. *The Rise of American Civilization*, the work of synthesis which Beard, with his wife Mary, published in 1927, received wide popular and professional acclaim, selling over 130,000 copies. In those years, wrote Richard Hofstadter, "all American history seemed to dance to Beard's tune."[57]

Some, to be sure, followed a different drummer. Carl Russell Fish denounced Beard to a correspondent as "a yellow historian, with strong socialistic proclivities." Frederic L. Paxson, reviewing *The Rise of American Civilization*, sarcastically observed that "To those who do not believe that the American experiment has been, on the whole, an exhibit in successful government, and to those who do not believe that the right to enjoy the fruits of industry is worth protecting, the picture here presented may be convincing." Ralph H. Gabriel deplored the book's emphasis on "sordid and unpleasant motives," and thought the work marred by its "persistent flavor of sarcasm and cynicism."[58]

But no alternative conceptualization of the sweep of American history emerged in the interwar years. While work in older traditions, reflecting values of continuity and tradition, continued to appear, it seemed to younger historians part of a vanished vision. At the 1934 meeting of the AHA, George M. Dutcher deplored the neglect of constitutional history,

---

[57]Malcolm Cowley and Bernard Smith, eds., *Books That Changed Our Minds* (New York, 1938); Maurice Blinkoff, *The Influence of Charles A. Beard Upon American Historiography* (Buffalo, 1936); Howard K. Beale, ed., *Charles A. Beard: An Appraisal* (Lexington, Ky., 1954), 311; Hofstadter, *The Progressive Historians* (New York, 1968), 299.
[58]Fish to John W. Stewart, 23 February 1927, Fish Papers, 7:1927; Paxson review in *MVHR* 14 (1928): 232; Gabriel review in *Yale Review* 17 (1928): 404–6.

"with its emphasis upon the permanent rather than the transitory aspects of government and politics." In colonial history, though the older Imperial school continued to be represented with the continued appearance of volumes by Lawrence Henry Gipson, the "conflict" interpretations of Schlesinger, Becker, Fox, and Nettels clearly held the field. With no tradition of conceptual or ideological debate within the profession, works reflecting different commitments went past each other.[59]

Progressive History was not, in fact, all that radical, no matter how offensive its tone to outraged conservatives. For all of its supporters' criticism of the abuses of capitalism, they were rarely systematically anti-capitalist—certainly Beard personally was not—and they were usually optimistic about the ultimate victory of "the people" over "the interests." Some more radical currents appeared in the historical profession in the twenties, as part of a polarizing influence exercised by the war and the revolutionary events in Europe which accompanied it, moving prewar conservatives to the right, prewar Progressives to the left.

John W. Burgess, a vocal Germanophile until America's entry into the war, wrote Franz Boas that "the Germany of Ebert and Barth and Schei-demann and Liebknecht is not the Germany I knew and respected, but it is the Germany which, in my day, was regarded as little less dangerous to our Western Civilization than the present Bolshevism of Russia." Burgess's horror of Bolshevism was shared by his Columbia colleague Parker T. Moon, while at Harvard Albert B. Hart wanted American troops to stay in Europe to repress the Red Menace, and Wilbur C. Abbott summed up his appreciation of revolutionary currents in *The New Barbarians*. Native American anti-Bolshevism among historians was reinforced by the arrival of émigrés from the new Russian regime like George Vernadsky and Michael Rostovtzeff, both of whom joined the Yale faculty in the twenties, and Michael Karpovitch, who went to Harvard at about the same time.[60]

For other historians in the twenties the wartime experience seemed to reinforce, deepen, or mobilize more radical sentiments. Edward P. Cheyney described himself as a socialist; Becker told a friend of his intention to vote for Debs in 1920; Schlesinger flirted with socialism; Dodd expressed his total agreement with the Socialist leader Norman Thomas, and thought the United States "fast becoming a great new

---

[59]Dutcher, quoted in Henry E. Bourne, "The Fiftieth Anniversary Meeting," *AHR* 40 (1935): 426.
[60]Burgess, undated letter, quoted in Carol S. Gruber, *Mars and Minerva* (Baton Rouge, 1975), 51–52; Moon to Walter Lippmann, 30 April 1919, Lippmann Papers, I/31/833; Hart, quoted in *New York Times*, 16 November 1918.

feudalism with business in the saddle." But theirs was, for the most part, a very diffident and ambivalent radicalism. Cheyney, Becker, and Schlesinger were not activists by temperament, and Dodd's political activities were mostly confined to the Democratic Party. Dissidence was risky, and inevitably constrained by prudence throughout the interwar period, and particularly in the twenties.[61]

Historians' ideological commitments became even less consensual in the depression decade. Accounts of ideological polarization in the United States in the 1930s are often overdrawn. Those who were led to reject capitalist democracy from the left or right were a small minority. But historians were, at a minimum, aware of living in an increasingly polarized world. If their hyperbolic statements cannot be taken at face value, neither are they without significance. Frank Owsley saw the United States on the brink of revolution, while William B. Hesseltine thought "the signs and the portents [were] on all sides" that fascism was coming. Beard wrote a younger historian that "capitalist henchmen will give intelligence no choice except communism." Marcus Jernegan doubted that the New Deal programs, of which he approved, could be implemented "without resort to physical violence." Merle Curti, at Smith, said he was "very blue and discouraged" at finding himself surrounded by "a whole crew of young people . . . that are reactionary and fascist," while John Hall Stewart at Western Reserve reported being isolated as a "non-Marxian." Harry R. Rudin at Yale and Crane Brinton at Harvard both saw the world, and particularly youth, making a choice between communism and fascism. The "Fabian 'liberalism' of 1890–1910," Brinton wrote, "signally fails to attract the brightest minds of the new generation." James

---

[61]Cheyney said in a 12 December 1932 letter to Harold Mager that he had been regularly voting for socialist candidates for some time. (Cheyney Papers, Box 1.) For Becker, see Chapter 5, above. Schlesinger's (brief and ambivalent) involvement with socialism is recounted in his Oral History Memoir, 2:305–6, 414–15. See Dodd to Thomas, 15 January 1930, and Dodd to "Mr. Loomis" [otherwise unidentified], 6 March 1926, Dodd Papers, Boxes 34 and 25. Carl Wittke had been discreet in his support of La Follette in 1924, but not discreet enough—and he was convinced that this cost him a job at the University of Iowa. While the university's president "could not get rid of those now on the staff he would be careful to make no additions to the faculty from among the ranks of the discontented." When the ancient historian Solomon Katz was interviewed by the president of the University of Washington, he was asked, "Are you a Red? We have some men here who devote half their time to working for old age pensions, and I don't want any more of them." At the University of Chicago, Dodd wrote a colleague that freedom of teaching depended on the trustees' ignorance of what went on in the classroom. "The more closely even so liberal a man as Harold Swift [chairman of the university's board of trustees] looks into University details, the more certain he is to cut down on social science appropriations. It can not be otherwise." (Wittke to Schlesinger, 4 April 1925, Schlesinger Papers, Box 2; William B. Hesseltine to John D. Hicks, 4 July 1936, Hicks Papers, Box 1; Dodd to J. Fred Rippy, 26 October 1925, Dodd Papers, Box 22.)

Harvey Robinson told friends that "much as the liberal spirit may appeal to us, the fact remains that it is inadequate to a world divided into acutely hostile groups of the right and left and that in consequence the only way out is in a Communism à la Americaine."[62]

Many historians, almost certainly the majority of younger historians, were either New Dealers or critics of Roosevelt from the left. On the right there were predictions of the catastrophic consequences of the New Deal. "We are all in a motor car being driven by a drunk chauffeur at sixty miles an hour," Wallace Notestein wrote to a friend, and the result would make "the last panic . . . seem a minor matter." For some, like Samuel Flagg Bemis, opposition to the New Deal combined with a preference for solutions that seem fairly characterized as fascist:

We must have national organization of industry . . . we must have a wider and more powerful national police to wipe out the sanctuary of conflicting state jurisdictions. . . . This nation today stands powerless and on the verge of collapse for want of strong national government. The forces of localism thanks to the influence of modern mechanics and science on society are strangling the forces of national righteousness. . . . What we need is a benevolent dictator. . . . If this sounds like treason to the old states right democrat, the time has come to declare it, to frankly face the facts and stand up straight as a nation before we crumble into a honeycomb of corruption, anarchy and general noisesomeness.

Just as some historians on the left (e.g., Leo Gershoy) expressed qualified admiration for Stalin's Russia, so there were historians (e.g., Carl Russell Fish, Shepard B. Clough) who were among those American intellectuals who looked with favor on Mussolini's regime. At Harvard in the thirties Crane Brinton was a core member of the "Pareto Circle," led by Lawrence J. Henderson, an outspoken admirer of Hitler and Mussolini as "empiricists." Members of the circle sought in Pareto's equilibrium model an answer to the Marxism by which they felt themselves besieged. Another dimension of right-wing thought was represented by the Catholic convert Carlton J. H. Hayes, for whom the disastrous state of the world in the 1930s was the consequence of "the rise of liberalism with its atomizing of society," of "a decline of traditional religion and an obscur-

[62]Owsley to William E. Dodd, 8 March 1932, Dodd Papers, Box 38; Hesseltine to Frank W. Prescott, 10 November 1935, Hesseltine Papers, M66–132/4; Beard to Merle Curti, 20 January 1934, Curti Papers, 4–13; Jernegan to Dodd, Dodd Papers, Box 44; Curti to Harry Elmer Barnes, 12 December 1934, Barnes Papers, Box 21; Stewart to Carl Becker, 15 January 1936, Becker Papers; Rudin to Wallace K. Notestein, 14 January 1937, Notestein Papers, I-7; Brinton, "The New History: Twenty-Five Years After," *Journal of Social Philosophy* 1 (1936): 145; Robinson's remarks are paraphrased by Hartley Grattan in an undated letter to Harry Elmer Barnes, Barnes Papers, Box 15.

ing of religious values," and, above all, of the "emergence of the masses, an upsurge of the multitude, from relative quiescence and respect for an elite of brains or wealth or both, to self-conscious and commanding importance."

It has been in progress a long time, certainly since the rise of radical religious sects in the sixteenth century, but it has gathered great momentum only since Jean Jacques Rousseau and his disciples romanticized the common man, since crowds of peasants and slum-dwellers found they could exert decisive influence on the French Revolution, and since English workmen discovered in trade unionism a potent means of alarming their employers. For 150 years now, the tide has been flowing ever fuller and stronger: here a wave of urban labor combinations . . . there a wave of agricultural unions . . . here a wave of political democracy and popular schooling and universal military service; there a wave of "popular fronts" and "soviets of workers, peasants and soldiers." The immemorial age of patricians has closed with Bismarck, Cavour, Nicholas II, perhaps Winston Churchill, and the age of plebeians is definitely ushered in by the porter's son Hitler, the blacksmith's son Mussolini, the cobbler's son Stalin, and who will it be in England?[63]

In a decade marked by the (final?) crisis of capitalism at home, the Five-Year Plans and the rise of Nazism abroad, an increasing number of historians found the traditional, approved historian's posture of aloof detachment intolerable. Curtis P. Nettels wrote to a colleague that

the study of history until recently was largely sustained by the idea of progress induced by a capitalist society in expansion. If that society is now in decline it becomes impossible to be neutral without admitting defeat—without admitting that your work has no purpose. Well, I suppose the whole thing hinges upon your view of the future of capitalism. I can not see the factors of revival and expansion; I don't like contraction and depression; hence the only alternative is to join with other forces that are working for something better.

[63]The observation by Notestein is from his 9 May 1937 letter to Paul Knaplund, Knaplund Papers, Series 7/16/20, Box 1. For Bemis on the New Deal, see his 24 February 1934 letter to William E. Dodd, Dodd Papers, Box 7; quoted passage from 1 April 1932 letter to Dodd, ibid., Box 38. For Gershoy, see his "Abdication Day" 1936 letter to Carl Becker, after a trip to the USSR, Becker Papers; for Fish, see unpublished manuscript in Fish Papers, Box 9 (undated, but from internal evidence written in 1931–33); for Clough, see John P. Diggins, *Mussolini and Fascism: The View from America* (Princeton, 1972), 260. For Brinton, see Barbara S. Heyl, "The Harvard 'Pareto Circle,'" *Journal of the History of the Behavioral Sciences* 4 (1968): 316–34; the characterization of Henderson is from Lewis S. Feuer, "Arthur O. Lovejoy," *American Scholar* 46 (1977): 360. The first two quotations from Hayes are from his "The Novelty of Totalitarianism in the History of Western Civilization," a 1939 lecture, in *Proceedings of the American Philosophical Society* 82 (1940): 95–96; the latter, from an unpublished address at the University of Pennsylvania Bicentennial, 18 September 1940. I am grateful to Professor Edward B. Segal for making the latter available to me.

"As I see it," he said, "the historians are gradually being driven from their positions of aloofness and detachment—and are openly or covertly, consciously or unconsciously taking sides on the issues of the day. I have made my choice."[64]

Relatively few historians sought "engagement" through organized political activity. William B. Hesseltine and Fred Shannon were, for a number of years, active members of the Socialist Party. The latter, to my knowledge the only interwar historian of any visibility who was of working-class origin, was proud that his socialism was "that of the factory and of the mill town and not that of the seminar." A number of others, Curti and Nettels, for example, considered themselves (small "s") socialists. Communist Party membership among historians seems to have been restricted to graduate students, or recent graduates. Frederick Merk is the only "mainstream" historian known to me who acknowledged having voted Communist, but no doubt there were others.[65]

The vehicle of political expression adopted by most *engagé* historians was that which lay most readily to hand: the teaching and writing of history. By the thirties, though few historians shared George Counts's illusion that the schools could "build a new social order," an increasing number acknowledged that history teaching inevitably served to either sustain or undermine existing arrangements, and that one could choose which goal one wished to promote.[66] The conservative Duke historian

[64]Letters to Merle Curti, 6 January 1936 and 24 November 1935, respectively, Curti Papers, 27:34.

[65]The quotation from Shannon is in his 16 October 1932 letter to Arthur Schlesinger, Schlesinger Papers, Box 9. For Curti, see his 25 June 1935 letter to Avery Craven, Curti Papers, 11–1; for Nettels, his 24 November 1935 letter to Curti, ibid., 27–34. A handful of history graduate students at Harvard in the late thirties (e.g., Daniel Boorstin, Richard Schlatter) were Communist Party members, but their association with the party was relatively fleeting, as was that of Richard Hofstadter at Columbia. Some Communist graduate students at Columbia (Herbert Aptheker, Philip S. Foner) remained with the party for many years; for others named at the time as Communists (Edward N. Saveth, M. I. Finley), the association with the Communist milieu, whatever its exact nature, was much briefer. Some of the Columbia Communist historians taught for a few years in the New York municipal colleges, but lost their jobs in the early forties as a result of the Rapp-Coudert investigations; apart from this contingent there were, so far as I can determine, no historians with academic appointments who were party members. Merk, in a 30 October 1944 letter to Paul W. Gates, wrote of being "tempted to vote communist again." (Gates Papers.)

[66]The choice was not unconstrained. Benjamin B. Kendrick, who taught at North Carolina College for Women, was impressed by Counts's arguments, but thought they raised a problem: "How can we 'educators' carry on a progressive propaganda in the schools and colleges when in the last analysis our jobs depend upon the very crowd of buccaneers and mossbacks against whom our propaganda is directed?" (Letter to Harry Elmer Barnes, 23 May 1932, Barnes Papers, Box 20.)

W. T. Laprade approvingly acknowledged that the function of history in the schools was "the inculcation of a species of patriotic religion."

Pupils learn reverence for certain saints and ikons which later facilitates the task of rulers who mobilize them in orderly array. . . . Nor need we condemn society for a disposition to perpetuate itself and a distrust of the ultra-critical or the revolutionary. It may not be prudent to tear down altars at which people bow until we know how to erect others in their stead. The Washington and Lincoln of the history books and the flag on the pole in the school yard are part of the ritual by which the country regiments its growing citizens and accustoms them to obedience. Whatever may be the case with a social scientist, an historian is ill qualified to erect other altars should he succeed in tearing these down.

Others were less happy with the legitimating function: Roy Nichols thought it scandalous that "children be brought up in a rapidly changing world to consider eighteenth century institutions as eternal."

Political history was bad enough but now we have a flood of economic history which . . . is dangerous, especially in this country. For in the United States it has taken the form of glorifying our economic prowess and picturing our ruthless and wasteful development of a great continent as one of the greatest achievements of man. So it is, but the acquisition of wealth for its own sake has been glorified to a degree which has been mightily effective, not in abolishing poverty, but in precipitating panics. The continual glorification of material gain to adolescents cannot fail and has not failed to weaken our spirit. In fact our government and our economic system have been so sanctified by historians that in some quarters it seems sinful to let children even suspect that either might be improved.[67]

Divergent ideological postures came to be more explicitly reflected in historical scholarship, and more openly referred to in scholarly discourse. On the left, Louis Gottschalk attempted to find proto-socialism in the rule of the Committee of Public Safety; Merle Curti wrote a friend of his intention to give "a socialistic if not a Marxian interpretation and evaluation" to his *Social Ideas of American Educators*; radicals in the South, like Vann Woodward and Howard Beale, were, as we have seen, explicit about the political agenda of their historical writing. On the right, Rostovtzeff's attempt to call into being an "ancient capitalism" tragically destroyed by "socialism" was recognized by contemporaries for the polemical exercise in projective nostalgia that it was. In the preface to *The Jacobins*, published at the beginning of the thirties, Crane Brinton said he had studied revolutions so that society could protect itself from them.

---

[67]Laprade, "The Function of the Historian," *Social Studies* 25 (1934): 74; Nichols, "History Teaching in This Intellectual Crisis," *Historical Outlook* 24 (1933): 361.

"Does not a knowledge of meteorology," he asked, "allow us to take steps to lessen damage from drouth and from storm?" (In *The Anatomy of Revolution*, published at the end of the decade, Brinton's metaphor for revolutions and their course became disease and fever.) By the late 1930s, Hayes's colleagues, frequently to their embarrassment, began to acknowledge the extent to which his work was suffused with antiliberal and antimodern ideology.[68]

As a coda to the ideological conflicts within the historical profession in the thirties there was the battle between interventionists and isolationists in 1940 and 1941. The most prominent isolationist among the historians was Charles Beard, and most of the other historians who followed him in oppposing Franklin D. Roosevelt's foreign policy were, at least in a loose sense, Beardians—Merle Curti, Merrill Jensen, William Hesseltine, Fred Shannon. Others, like Thomas Cochran, were drawn closer to Beard by their shared foreign policy attitudes.

But others who had been regarded as members of the Beard camp broke with him as war approached. James Sellers attempted to get the Mississippi Valley Historical Association to pass a resolution which would strengthen FDR's hand by urging the repeal of the requirement that treaties be voted by a two-thirds vote of the Senate, and, with John D. Hicks, attempted to tilt the 1941 program of the association in an interventionist direction. Frank Freidel, preparing for his oral examination at Wisconsin, was worried that Curtis Nettels, who had become a strong interventionist, would be one of the examiners and, outraged by Freidel's isolationism, would fail him. When the list of examiners came out, Freidel was "tremendously relieved . . . to find one name beautifully, gloriously missing. I am on the Lord's side, and the Lord protects the little sparrows, yea even the little isolationists." At the University of Washington, the young isolationist Merrill Jensen expressed concern at tension between himself and the senior Americanist, W. Stull Holt, a belligerent interventionist. At Harvard, Henry F. May felt "isolated and

---

[68]For Gottschalk, see, e.g., his review of F. J. C. Hearnshaw, ed., *The Social and Political Ideas of Some Representative Thinkers of the Revolutionary Era*, *AHR* 37 (1932): 320. For Curti, see his 27 March 1932 letter to Harry Elmer Barnes, Barnes Papers, Box 19. For contemporary comments on the ideological agenda of Rostovtzeff's work, see Tenney Frank, "Recent Work on the Economic History of Ancient Rome," *Journal of Economic and Business History* 1 (1928): 114; E. Raymond Turner, *The Great Cultural Traditions* (2 vols., New York, 1941), 2:935; Arnaldo Momigliano, "Rostovtzeff's Twofold History of the Hellenistic World," *Journal of Hellenic Studies* 63 (1943): 116. For Brinton, *The Jacobins: An Essay in the New History* (New York, 1930), 1. On historians' response to Hayes, see Carter Jefferson, "Carlton J. H. Hayes," in Hans A. Schmitt, ed., *Historians of Modern Europe* (Baton Rouge, 1971), 34–35.

helpless in the present wave of emotional interventionism." One younger historian perceived the split as generational. He reported that at the December 1940 meeting of the Pacific Coast branch of the AHA, one of his age-mates "even had the temerity to read a paper on war-mongering in John Adams' administration, which was filled with so many pointed barbs that we youngsters, lacking in all decency and true idealism, snickered and cheered, while the oldsters afterwards talked darkly of the Fifth Column in our profession."[69]

By 1941 interventionists were clearly in the ascendancy, within the professorate, as elsewhere, and John D. Hicks was ready to read out of the academy anyone so lacking in patriotism as to fail to rally around the Roosevelt foreign policy. Isolationists in the profession had their back to the wall. Roy F. Nichols and Merle Curti both saw war hysteria threatening scholarship as it had in 1917. At a small Illinois college, Frank Freidel didn't, he said, want to "put my head on the war chopping block. I prefer to work subtly on my students, who are remarkably quick to catch on to my insinuations." Kenneth Stampp, at the University of Arkansas, was required to teach a course on national defense problems. He worried about how he could manage it "without getting myself run out of town as a Fifth Columnist," but he was "darned if I'll turn the course into anything but a propaganda machine for the isolationists." The tone of Beard's jeremiads became more and more strident. And then Pearl Harbor put an end to the debate, though not, as we shall see in Chapter 10, to the fallout of the controversy for historians' later appraisal of Beard and all of his works, including the epistemological.[70]

American historiography in the thirties was not ideologically polarized in the European fashion, as in France, where royalist historians affiliated with the Action Française were arrayed against Marxist historians in or close to the Parti Communiste. No historian in the United States bitterly regretted the American Revolution; only a very few sought socialist transformation, or even wrote from an explicitly Marxist perspective. Historians' quarrels over American intervention, though sharp and divi-

[69]Sellers to Hicks, 8 March 1941, 18 March 1941, 16 April 1941, 30 April 1941, and Hicks to Sellers, 12 March 1941, Hicks Papers, Box 6; Freidel to Hesseltine, 6 November and 15 November 1941, Hesseltine Papers, M68–25/4; Jensen to Hesseltine, undated but summer 1941, ibid., M68–25/4; May to Harry Elmer Barnes, 1 December 1940, Barnes Papers, Box 26; Freidel to Hesseltine, 16 January 1941, Hesseltine Papers, M68–25/4.
[70]Hicks, 2 December 1941 letter to University of Wisconsin student newspaper, Hicks Papers, Box 6; Nichols, "The Historian's Dilemma," *Proceedings of the Middle States Association of History and Social Science Teachers* 38 (1940–41): 8; Curti, "The Responsibility of the Teacher in Times of Crises: Four Views," *Social Education* 5 (1941): 367; Freidel to Hesseltine, 2 November 1941, Hesseltine Papers, M68–25/4; Stampp to Hesseltine, 31 July 1941, ibid., M68–25/4.

sive, did not reflect a fundamental ideological cleavage, and coming as they did at the very end of the period, left no mark on interwar historical writing. But the overall development of American historical writing in the interwar years gave cold comfort to those who had pinned their hopes on a convergent, objective, historiography. And the passions of the period, as reflected in bitter controversy and the overt politicization of scholarship, suggested that the austere detachment which was the putative concomitant of objectivity was not likely to be found in times of troubles.[71]

[71]Not much Marxist historical work of any kind appeared during the 1930s (or, for that matter, in the succeeding three decades). Louis Hacker's *Triumph of American Capitalism* (New York, 1940) stands out, though technically Hacker was an economist, as does W. E. B. Du Bois's *Black Reconstruction* (New York, 1935). (As a black, teaching in a sociology department in a black college, Du Bois was even more marginal to the profession.) The only other Marxist work of any consequence by a professional historian was Roger Shugg's *Origins of Class Struggle in Louisiana* (University, La., 1939). I find incomprehensible Page Smith's assertion that during the decade Marxism "became for a few years the dominant school of historical interpretation." (*The Historian and History* [New York, 1964], 46.)

9

The battle joined

In the immediately preceding chapters I have traced the influences which, during the interwar years, produced a widespread questioning of the founding program of the American historical profession: the scientific and detached search for impartial, objective historical truth. In the largest sense the interwar criticism of the objectivist posture was a moment in a philosophical debate that went back to Aristotle and Protagoras. But the "why" and "how" of its development in these years were closely tied to the specific forms of the enduring factualist, inductivist orthodoxy against which the dissidents were revolting, and the contemporary influences which mobilized doubts and provided the rebels with ammunition.

The experience of the war, various intellectual currents, professional disappointment, and ideological controversy had the direct and immediate consequence of leading a number of historians to abandon objectivist orthodoxy. And during the decade of the twenties there were signs that a growing number of historians were assembling for themselves elements of what would come to be designated "historical relativism." James Harvey Robinson laid down as "law" that "what passes for history in any generation is what Voltaire called *une fable convenue*—only one of the many, many stories which could be told of man's doings." Allen Johnson of Yale, in a widely used manual of historical method, was sharply critical of the empiricist certitude in the works of Bernheim and Langlois and Seignobos. Selection of facts was necessarily a value-laden process, and we could only know history "as constructed in human consciousness under distinct limitations." There was "an inevitable relativity" in historiography. Conyers Read had become convinced that as soon as one went beyond the narrowest monograph "every generation will have to make its interpretations of the past for itself in accordance with its own pre-

250

possessions." An editorial in the *Mississippi Valley Historical Review* accepted Croce's dictum that "all history is contemporary history," and acknowledged that the historian "cannot step off his own shadow."[1]

Defenders of the orthodox posture decried the emerging sensibility, and argued for the continued validity of traditional norms. "Say what one may of historical philosophy," Frederick L. Paxson wrote, "history is a matter of facts"; the historian's business was to establish them, "desiccated as they may be." Carl Stephenson inveighed against various "skeptics" and "relativists" from Max Nordau to Allen Johnson: "In spite of everything we *will* have our history true. 'No fact, no history' has long been our slogan, and we cannot abandon it. . . . The arguments of the reputable historian . . . [are] the inevitable conclusions of any thinking man who cares to examine the evidence." C. H. McIlwain was distressed by what he saw as a growing "demand for bias," and urged, instead, ever greater "repression of our own views" and a "stricter adherence to actual fact." But in the 1920s these exchanges remained relatively marginal to historical discourse. A full-scale debate on the posture that was appropriate and possible for the historian did not come until the early thirties, when it focused on the much publicized major pronouncements of Carl Becker and Charles Beard, which synthesized much that had gone before, and opened up the issues to general discussion.[2]

It is impossible to speak with assurance about the relative size of the groups within the profession which responded in a friendly or hostile fashion to Becker's and Beard's theses. By no means all historians expressed themselves on the question; not all such expressions of opinion survive or were available to me. When historians expressed themselves on the issue, they often did so with less than complete frankness, out of politeness, opportunism, or other motives. Many were ambivalent. Arthur P. Scott of the University of Chicago confessed that "on Mondays, Wednesdays, and Fridays I sympathize with one school; on Tuesdays, Thursdays and Saturdays, with the other." What we can do is survey the range of these responses, and say what can be said about those features and implications of Beard's and Becker's writings about histo-

[1]Robinson, "Some of the Fruits of Historical Study," *Proceedings of the Association of History Teachers of the Middle States and Maryland* 23 (1925): 76; Johnson, *The Historian and Historical Evidence* (New York, 1926): 141; Johnson to William E. Dodd, 5 November 1927, Dodd Papers, Box 28; Read to Dodd, 21 January 1926, ibid., Box 25; *MVHR* 16 (1930): 600–602.
[2]Paxson (1926), quoted in Earl Pomeroy, "Frederick L. Paxson and His Approach to History," *MVHR* 39 (1953): 682; Stephenson, "Facts in History," *Historical Outlook* 19 (1928): 313–17; McIlwain, "Bias in Historical Writing," *History* 11 (1926): 197.

riography which called forth positive and negative reactions from their
colleagues.[3]

I

Most of the ideas men and women confront come in what might be called
"wrapped packages." They are not encountered in discrete, pristine form,
but appear with the authority (or anti-authority) of those who present
them, couched in attractive or off-putting language, and in association
with other ideas toward which we are well- or ill-disposed. Philosophers
are professionally concerned with the careful "unpacking" and disaggregation of complex ideas, reducing them to purely denotative expression, and considering them in isolation from their surroundings. It is not
thus with most of us in our daily lives (or even with philosophers when
off duty). It was not thus with interwar historians confronting the critique of objectivity.

No aspect of the wrapping of a set of ideas is more important than the
respect accorded those who present them. And there were no other historians in the early thirties whose reputation and influence equaled that of
Beard and Becker. Beard's immense authority within the interwar historical profession has been discussed in Chapter 8. He was accorded great
respect even by those who differed with him; his reputation extended far
beyond the limits of the profession. Becker, in this regard, ran Beard a
close second. His *Modern History* had an authority for Europeanists
analogous to that of Beard's *Rise of American Civilization* among Americanists. His historical works were enthusiastically received throughout
the profession, even among those whose orientation and sensibility were
very different from his own. Jameson called him "the most brilliant
historical writer that we have in this country." Many expressed good-
natured envy. Claude H. Van Tyne wrote Becker that he was himself "a
mere historian, capable of digging out the facts fairly well, and telling
them with some simple directness, but your remarkable gift of philosophical interpretation and charm of presentation is quite beyond me." "Your
soundness and your felicity are my despair," wrote Ulrich B. Phillips.
"How did you get that way?" Nonprofessionals added their tributes.
Carl Sandburg wrote while in general he found "the history writing tribe"
irretrievably "smug," Becker was one of the few with whom he felt "a
genuine fellowship." From the Yale Law School, Thurman Arnold, who

---

[3] "Schools of History" (lecture given before the Division of the Social Sciences, University
of Chicago, 6 April 1937), 13, in Gottschalk Papers, 11:8.

was not personally acquainted with Becker, wrote him of the "breathtaking experience" of sitting up until three A.M. reading his *Heavenly City of the Eighteenth-Century Philosophers*. "It may be that greater books have been written, but for the moment I do not know what they are." It would have been impossible to find two more influential critics of the doctrine of historical objectivity. And their major statements were delivered from the profession's most prestigious rostrum: Becker's 1931 "Everyman His Own Historian" and Beard's 1933 "Written History as an Act of Faith" were both presidential addresses to the American Historical Association.[4]

There were striking similarities between Becker and Beard. Born in the Midwest a few years apart, both studied with James Harvey Robinson at Columbia, and both were members of his circle of New Historians. Before the war each published a work of American history which became a landmark of Progressive historiography; during the war they shared in the production of atrocity propaganda; after the war they shared profound disillusionment with its fruits. Their political evolution ran parallel throughout their lives. Of Republican background, both were Progressives before the war, and gradually became, loosely speaking, social democrats. They were influenced by many of the same intellectual currents: Croce, the new physics, pragmatism. Both were almost reflexively irreverent toward traditional pieties. A particularly important common characteristic was that neither was a fully integrated professional. Both had, in Jencks and Riesman's terms, more of an "intellectual" than an "academic" orientation. "I have heard on good authority," Beard wrote to Becker, that you are no Historian; nothing except a Man of Letters. It makes me jealous. I wish God (or what is it) had made me a Man of Letters." Throughout their lives they were more concerned to grapple with questions they found personally and socially meaningful than with projects which followed the agendas of the discipline. (One consequence of this was that they directed most of their work to a lay audience.) Their surviving correspondence makes clear that they were united as well by mutual affection and esteem.[5]

---

[4]Jameson to Mrs. Grattan Doyle, 9 December 1935, in Elizabeth Donnan and Leo F. Stock, eds., *An Historian's World: Selections from the Correspondence of John Franklin Jameson* (Philadelphia, 1956), 359. Van Tyne to Becker, 11 November 1927; Phillips to Becker, 13 October 1925; Sandburg to Becker, 5 November 1937; Arnold to Becker, undated; all in Becker Papers. "Everyman" appeared in the *AHR* 37 (1932): 221–36; "Written History" in the *AHR* 39 (1934): 219–31. Both were reprinted in various places: my citations to Beard's address are to the *AHR*; those to "Everyman," to Becker's collection of essays issued under the same title (New York, 1935).

[5]Beard to Becker, undated, Becker Papers.

Their presidential addresses reflect a great many shared ideas. Indeed, when taken together with their other writings on historiography, there are hardly any themes developed by one of the men which is not echoed by the other. Overall, they were convinced that the goal of a comprehensive, definitive, objective reconstruction of the past was not just unattainable in practice, but a vacuous ideal in principle. They mocked the notion that "the facts spoke for themselves," and the old inductivist ideal of approaching the past "without preconceptions." "Hoping to find something without looking for it," wrote Becker, "expecting to obtain final answers to life's riddle by resolutely refusing to ask questions—it was surely the most romantic species of realism yet invented, the oddest attempt ever made to get something for nothing!" They were both convinced of the conservatism inherent in unadorned factualism. "The mere 'fact,'" Becker had written ten years before, "if you allow the wretched creature to open its mouth, will say only one thing: 'I am, therefore I am right.'" And they were equally convinced that, historically, the Rankean program of objectivity and abstention from judgment had been designed for conservative purposes. As Beard said in his address, "Ranke, a German conservative, writing after the storm and stress of the French Revolution, was weary of history written for, or permeated by, the purposes of revolutionary propaganda. . . . Written history that was cold, factual, and apparently undisturbed by the passions of the time served best the cause of those who did not want to be disturbed."[6]

The very process of deciding what was a fact, apart from traditional technical procedures of verification, the importance of which they did not question, depended on values. Even less were there any neutral criteria for selecting among the multitudes of facts, or interpreting them, for which one needed an "a priori," and at least tacitly evaluative, frame of reference. "Every student of history knows," said Beard, "that his colleagues have been influenced in their selection and ordering of materials by their biases, prejudices, beliefs, affections, general upbringing, and experience, particularly social and economic; and if he has a sense of propriety, to say nothing of humor, he applies the canon to himself, leaving no exceptions to the rule." Definitions of truth, they maintained, were always social. One generation's or society's truth was not another's. They agreed that increments in historical knowledge played a major role in changing interpretations. But, said Becker, it was an illusion shared by every age that "the present version is valid because the related facts are

---

[6]Becker, "Everyman," 250; Becker, review of John Spencer Bassett, *Our War with Germany*, in *The New Republic* 25 (1921): 382; Beard, "Written History," 221.

true, whereas former versions are invalid because based upon inaccurate or inadequate facts."[7]

Though they both deplored pedantry, neither man disparaged scholarship; indeed, they celebrated it. "One of the first duties of man is not to be duped," wrote Becker. "To establish the facts is always in order, and is indeed the first duty of the historian." Beard wrote that "the empirical or scientific method" was

the only method that can be employed in obtaining accurate knowledge of historical facts, personalities, situations, and movements. It alone can disclose conditions that made possible what happened. It has a value in itself—a value high in the hierarchy of values indispensable to the life of a democracy. The inquiring spirit of science, using the scientific method, is the chief safeguard against the tyranny of authority, bureaucracy, and brute power.

But the historian had a social as well as a scholarly obligation. No belief was more central to Becker and Beard than that history existed for man, not man for history. The historian's social responsibility was to provide an account of the past appropriate to society's current needs. The selection and organization of facts was an act of purposeful thought by the historian, controlled, in Beard's words, by a frame of reference composed of "things deemed necessary, things deemed possible, and things deemed desirable."[8]

If Beard and Becker had a great deal in common, there were significant differences in their characters and intellectual styles. Beard, from his earliest days, was an enthusiast, consumed with activist zeal. Throughout his life he threw himself into one cause after another, from his early efforts on behalf of workers' education and municipal reform to his last battles against American "globalism." Though no dogmatist, and no stranger to self-doubt or self-criticism, he gave a polemical edge to many of his works, which always aimed at winning converts to whatever point of view he was currently promoting. Whatever the relationship of his substantive historical interpretations to Marxism, his conception of the function of the intellectual was squarely in the tradition of the eleventh thesis on Feuerbach. Becker, in posture and sensibility, was at the opposite end of the spectrum. Shy, withdrawn, and frequently morose, he shrank from public involvement, and viewed the follies of mankind with a wry detachment that often shaded off into cynicism. It is a paradox which many commentators have noted that Becker, who mocked and

[7]"Written History," 220; "Everyman," 248.
[8]"Everyman," 249; "Written History," 226–27, 228.

disparaged the historian's posture of detachment, embodied it more completely than any of his contemporaries.

In part the differences between Becker's and Beard's addresses was a
matter of style in the narrower sense: Becker always had a lighter touch
than Beard. And some of their difference in tone may have been a reflection of the fact that whereas Beard was writing with the zeal of a recent
defector from objectivity, Becker was offering a more nuanced version of
themes he had been pondering for a generation. But their style differed on
a deeper level as well, and reflected, if not a difference in values, a difference in the relative weight they assigned to those values. Both men acknowledged a balance between fate and will in the writing of history. On
the one hand, the limitations imposed by the historian's milieu; on the
other, the deliberate choices of frame of reference, selection, and interpretation which the historian must make. But they diverged significantly
in which aspect they found the more important.

Becker, with his strong fatalist streak, though recognizing the role of
deliberate purpose, emphasized the external constraints on the historian:

We are of that ancient and honorable company of wise men of the tribe, of bards
and story-tellers and minstrels, of soothsayers and priests, to whom in successive
ages has been entrusted the keeping of the useful myths. . . . Mr. Everyman is
stronger than we are, and sooner or later we must adapt our knowledge to his
necessities. . . . We do not impose our version of the human story on Mr.
Everyman; in the end it is rather Mr. Everyman who imposes his version on us.
. . . We are surely under bond to be as honest and as intelligent as human frailty
permits; but the secret of our success in the long run is in conforming to the
temper of Mr. Everyman, which we seem to guide only because we are so sure,
eventually, to follow it.

Becker accepted the relativity of historical knowledge serenely. By 1931 it
was, for him, an old friend. He had learned to accept that the pasts which
men created were "in part . . . true, in part false; as a whole perhaps
neither true nor false, but only the most convenient form of error." "It
should," he thought, "be a relief to us to renounce omniscience, to recognize that every generation, our own included, will, must inevitably, understand the past and anticipate the future in the light of its own restricted
experience, must inevitably play on the dead whatever tricks it finds
necessary for its own peace of mind."[9]

Beard's encounter with the problem of historical knowledge had convinced him that his old objectivist faith could no longer be sustained. It

[9]"Everyman," 247, 252, 245, 253.

had to be discarded and "laid away in the museum of antiquities"; one had to admit that "one is more or less a guesser in this vale of tears." But what for Becker led to something very like resignation, was for Beard a challenge. In reflecting on the historian's social functions, Becker had stressed the inevitability of the historian's deferring to Mr. Everyman's perception of his needs. Beard focused on the act of faith by which the historian followed his own vision of what was requisite. *Sub specie aeternitatis* historical truth might be relative; in the here and now, this made choice all the more imperative. The historian who would make sense out of the past had first to choose whether to see it as chaos, as moving cyclically, or as progressing in some direction—and if the last, what that direction was.

> The historian . . . consciously or unconsciously performs an act of faith, as to order and movement, for certainty . . . is denied to him. . . . [I]n writing he acts and in acting he makes choices, large or small, timid or bold, with respect to some conception of the nature of things. . . . His faith is at bottom a conviction that something true can be known about the movement of history and his conviction is a subjective decision, not a purely objective discovery.

> The supreme issue before the historian now is the determination of his attitude to the disclosures of contemporary thought. He may deliberately evade them for reasons pertaining to personal, economic, and intellectual comfort. . . . Or he may proceed to examine his own frame of reference, clarify it, enlarge it . . . and give it consistency of structure by a deliberate conjecture respecting the nature or direction of the vast movements of ideas and interests called world history. This operation will cause discomfort to individual historians but all . . . are under obligation to perform it. . . . Does the world move and, if so, in what direction? If he believes that the world does not move, the historian must offer the pessimism of chaos to the inquiring spirit of mankind. If it does move, does it move backward toward some old arrangement . . . [o]r does it move forward to some other arrangement which can be only dimly divined—a capitalist dictatorship, a proletarian dictatorship, or a collectivist democracy? The last of these is my own guess, founded on a study of long trends and on a faith in the indomitable spirit of mankind.

> The historian may seek to escape these issues by silence or by a confession of avoidance or he may face them boldly, aware of the intellectual and moral perils inherent in any decision—in his act of faith.[10]

In their critique of the traditional posture of historical objectivity, Becker and Beard used strikingly parallel arguments. Those who re-

---

[10]"Written History," 226–29.

sponded, positively or negatively, to the critical part of their message
rarely made any distinction between the two men. Insofar as they sketched alternative postures for the historian, these pointed in quite different
directions. It would be much too crude to say that Beard sought in his
version of relativism a justification for an activist stance, while Becker
found in his a justification for abstention. Much too crude, but with more
than a grain of truth. In their responses to these dimensions of Becker's
and Beard's thought, professional historians could and did make distinctions, and often reacted very differently to the alternative implied
agendas.

II

No presidential addresses to the American Historical Association ever
occasioned as much discussion as Becker's "Everyman" and Beard's "Act
of Faith." "'Why that man is not merely a scholar and thinker; he's a
poet,'" Felix Frankfurter wrote to Becker after "Everyman" appeared.
"'And his last paragraph is as good as anything Proust has written.' Now
if that were just my judgment, you could take it as lightly as you usually
take lawyer's lore. But it's my wife's judgment, and she adores Proust
and distrusts pedants deeply." The University of Chicago philosopher
T. V. Smith wrote Becker that "it warms my heart to see a historian
debunk his subject without surrendering self- or even subject-respect."
The *New York Times* hailed Becker's speech in a long editorial.[11]

In response to praise from one enthusiastic historian, Becker said that
he thought there were "a good many people in the association (younger
people like yourself) whose ideas on this subject I did little more than
formulate." But expressions of agreement came from elder statesmen in
the profession as well. Ferdinand Schevill wrote, "I did not think I should
live to see the day when the president of the Am. Historical Association
would make so clear an analysis of this business of history and lay his
hammer to so many idols of the market-place. You positively have
thrown me into a mood of religious thanksgiving: Now can my spirit
depart in peace!" Preserved Smith told Becker that he had

disposed once for all of the *voranssetzungslose Geschichtswissenschaft* [presup-
positionless historical science] once lauded by the "objective historians." You
have killed the notion that facts have any meaning in themselves, apart from that
shed upon them by our own minds. They are dark objects, invisible and intracta-
ble until they shine and effloresce in the rays cast upon them by our ideas.

[11]Frankfurter to Becker, 4 February 1932, Becker Papers; Smith to Becker, 2 February
1932, ibid.; *New York Times*, 10 January 1932.

But the responses to Becker's address within the profession were far from uniformly positive. Schevill wrote Becker that at the University of Chicago, while the graduate students responded with "enthusiastic affirmation," most members of the History Department rejected his ideas. Two of his correspondents reported generally negative reactions among historians at Ohio State. The address "caused no end of confusion among the 'scientifically minded' in the department," reported one; "most of them disapprove of your notions," wrote the other.[12]

Beard's destruction of his incoming correspondence makes it difficult to report on private reactions to his address, but there is more than sufficient evidence from published sources to make it clear that it, like Becker's, elicited a strong response. His speech led Eric Goldman to hail him as "a pioneer in the attack on the ivory-tower complex among American historians." In an article in the *American Historical Review*, Theodore Clarke Smith attacked Beard for seducing historians away from the "noble dream" of the founders of the profession, the disinterested search for objective historical truth. Picking up on Smith's phrase, Beard promptly replied in "That Noble Dream," which satirized the ideal as vacuous. Edward Mead Earle of the Institute for Advanced Study thought Beard's reply "a breath of fresh air" in "a lousy world." In the other camp, C. H. McIlwain devoted much of his own presidential address to the AHA in 1936 to attacking the address Beard had given three years earlier. Robert L. Schuyler, managing editor of the *AHR* congratulated McIlwain for "speak[ing] out, emphatically and boldly, against the defeatists," and lauded the author of a book review for a sideswipe at those who "sneer at 'that noble dream.'" Allan Nevins singled out Beard as purveyor of a pernicious epistemology in his 1938 *The Gateway to History*. Beard counterattacked in a long review of Nevins's book. In the decade of the 1930s, all was far from quiet on the epistemological front.[13]

For all the sound and fury of historians' wrangles over Becker's and Beard's theses, these disputes had a curiously hollow center. Becker and Beard had advanced two sorts of propositions. The first, empirical, prop-

[12]Becker to W. Stull Holt, undated, but probably January 1932, in Michael Kammen, ed., *"What Is the Good of History?" Selected Letters of Carl L. Becker, 1900–1945* (Ithaca, N.Y., 1973), 155; Schevill to Becker, 9 February 1932, Becker Papers; Smith to Becker, 15 January 1932, ibid.; Schevill to Becker, 18 February 1932; Sidney Terr to Becker, 18 December 1932; Harold Landin to Becker, 5 April 1932; all in Becker Papers.
[13]Goldman, "Historians and the Ivory Tower," *Social Frontier* 2 (1936): 280; Smith, "The Writing of American History in America, from 1884 to 1934," *AHR* 40 (1935): 439–49; "Noble Dream," ibid., 41 (1935): 74–87; Earle to Harry Elmer Barnes, 6 December 1935, Barnes Papers, Box 22; McIlwain, "The Historian's Part in a Changing World," *AHR* 42 (1937): 207–24; Schuyler to McIlwain, 2 November 1936, AHA Papers, Box 337; Schuyler to A. B. White, 17 April 1941, ibid., Box 342; *Gateway* (Boston, 1938), 43–44; Beard review, "Another Battle of the Books," *Nation* 147 (1938): 300–302.

osition, buttressed with countless examples, was that all historians, including professional historians, right down to the present day, could be
shown to have been massively influenced in constructing their accounts
by their differing and changing ideological commitments. The second,
logical, proposition was that the problem of selection, and the valuations
implicitly embedded within frames of reference, made the ideological
nature of historical work inescapable. It was inherent in the venture, not a
consequence of personal weaknesses or inadequacies of individual historians. From these two propositions they derived their conclusions—supported, as they saw it, both inductively and deductively. The orthodox
view of the professional historical venture was misconceived, since its
terminus ad quem, a value-free and objective historiography, arrived at
by self-elimination, was chimerical. They went on, with, as we have seen,
different emphases, to suggest what they considered to be more realistic,
appropriate, and socially useful ways of thinking about the historian's
task.

What is striking about the debate over Becker's and Beard's critique of
objectivity, as conducted by historians during the 1930s, is that almost
none of the many historians who rejected their conclusions, who expressed dismay at the implications of those conclusions, or were appalled
by their alternative conceptualizations, ever challenged their arguments.
Those who endorsed Becker's and Beard's point of arrival often explicitly
registered their agreement with the road which had led them to it. Their
opponents rarely disputed either Becker's and Beard's evidence or their
logic, only its outcome. That task, insofar as it was undertaken at all
during the 1930s, was left to two philosophers, who, at the end of the
decade, took on the task of defending the foundations of historical
objectivity.

Arthur O. Lovejoy and Maurice Mandelbaum were to become the
favorite philosophers of objectivist historians from the late thirties onward. Lovejoy, as we have seen in Chapter 6, had long been an opponent
of the relativistic and pragmatic currents which flowed into the thought
of Becker and Beard. At the December 1938 meeting of the eastern division of the American Philosophical Association he delivered a paper entitled "Present Standpoints and Past History." It was not a frontal assault
on the relativist stance. After enumerating some of the main elements in
that position—the problems raised by selection, the necessity of a "present" problem which governs selection, the role of values in determining a
frame of reference—he acknowledged that they contained "much truth
. . . deserving of emphasis." He sought not so much to refute the arguments of those who argued for the relativity of historical knowledge as to

trivialize them. Granting that the historian's selection of data was determined by present concerns, he argued that these concerns need be no more specific than "interestingness," and the historian's claim of "importance" for his or her work "need not, and often does not, mean more than that other persons are also interested."

It does not appear to be a true psychological generalization that no question about the past is ever interesting to anybody unless the answer to it is conceived to be instrumental to the settlement of a present philosophic problem or the determination of a present program of action. The inquiry of the historian, to be sure, is always, in intent, instrumental to the present . . . satisfaction of having a verified probable answer to his *historical* question; and the knowledge of the answer, if attained, will presumably continue to afford some sort of satisfaction. But the answer need not, in any other sense, be assumed to be contributory to the solution of a problem which is *not* about the past.

Lovejoy was here offering an argument which, as we shall see, was one of those frequently employed after World War II to refute the instrumentalist presentism of interwar relativists. To the extent that Becker and Beard exaggerated historians' immediate social goals, and were insufficiently attentive to the range of their professional concerns, and the complex mediations through which their values and desires were transmitted, Lovejoy's criticisms were telling.[14]

Drawing his examples from his own field of intellectual history, but clearly with broader implications, Lovejoy reiterated the "historicist" position.

If any normative criterion for the intellectual historian's selection is to be set up, it is that the selection should be determined, not by what is important to him, but by what seemed important to other men; for it is precisely this that differentiates historical from any other type of relevance and significance. General histories of philosophy have sometimes been inadequate and misleading, as *histories*, through a disregard of this canon.

Lovejoy was at one with Becker's and Beard's critics within the historical community in his emphasis on the possible pernicious consequences of their arguments. (Relativists, of course, denied that the sort of anachronistic presentism which Lovejoy deplored followed from their doctrines; indeed, they argued, greater awareness of present presuppositions helped insure against it.) The historian, Lovejoy acknowledged, *might* draw his focus from present problems, but if one insisted that he do so,

Lovejoy saw "danger to the breadth, disinterestedness, and liberality of historical inquiries." Insofar as philosophers suggested that the historians' first business was something other than ascertaining the facts of the past, he said, they "tend to undermine his morals as a historian."[15]

Lovejoy's statement was to be much cited after World War II as a defense of historical objectivity. But appearing as it did at the end of the thirties, in a technical philosophical journal, it could hardly have had any impact on the thinking of historians in the interwar period. More attention was paid to Mandelbaum's revised doctoral dissertation, published in 1938 as *The Problem of Historical Knowledge: An Answer to Relativism*.

The book was primarily an answer to European "relativism," which was part of a very different tradition than that of the American historical relativists. Becker, describing the book to Beard, told him that Mandelbaum arrayed his targets "in the order of least importance. The first one introduced is Carl Becker, the second Charles Beard. His heavy guns are, naturally, reserved for the philosophers, Croce, Dilthey, and Mannheim—people who may be expected to know what they are talking about." In addition to the exposition of the views of those just named, Mandelbaum sought to analyze the weaknesses in the work of European "counterrelativists": Simmel, Rickert, Scheler, and Troeltsch. In a work of more than three hundred pages, scarcely a half dozen were devoted to Becker and Beard; and, as the two men maintained, in separate reviews, their views were seriously misrepresented.[16]

Mandelbaum had, for example, attributed to Beard the view that "the works of Ranke do not contain objective truth; whatever 'truth' they contain is limited by the psychological, sociological, and other conditions under which Ranke wrote." Mandelbaum, Beard replied, "does not cite any lines from my writings to prove this statement, and if I have ever printed anything like that, then I cannot write the English language."

Ranke's works do contain statements of objective truth, many truths. When Ranke says that some person was born on a certain day of a certain year he states a truth about an objective fact. I have never meant to say that whatever "truth" Ranke's works contain is "limited" by psychological, sociological, or other processes under which Ranke wrote. What I have tried to say . . . [is] that every historian's work—that is, his selection of facts, his emphasis, his omissions, his organization, and his methods of presentation—bears a relation to his own personality and the age and circumstances in which he lives. This is relativism as I understand it, and it is not the conception put forth by Mr. Mandelbaum . . . [who] has missed the whole point of the business.

15Ibid., 482, 484, 489.
16Becker to Beard, 27 December 1938, in Kammen, "*What Is the Good*," 265–66.

Becker also vigorously denied that he held the views attributed to him by Mandelbaum, for example, that he believed "that one cannot know *something* about an event because one cannot know *everything* about it. . . . No relativist (except Croce) supposes this."[17]

Much of the confusion stemmed from Mandelbaum's adopting the common antirelativist conflation of skepticism and relativism. Skepticism, as I have pointed out earlier, holds either that truth does not exist, or that it is inaccessible to mere mortals. Relativists were at one with skeptics in denying that there is a single, objective, absolute truth which is the same for everyone. But, unlike skeptics, relativists did not deny the existence or knowability of truth. Rather than saying that there was no criterion for what is true, they stressed the variety of criteria employed by different societies, epochs, and methodological assumptions. What they denied was the existence of a timeless and universally valid metacriterion for deciding between them. The distinction between skepticism and relativism, real and important to Becker, Beard, and those in their camp, seemed unreal and inconsequential to absolutists for whom "truth," to be worthy of the name, had to be singular and immutable.

Beyond his misrepresentation of Becker and Beard, and his critical exposition of the work of European theorists, Mandelbaum offered his own extended characterization of the process of historical construction, which seemed a caricature of the American empiricist misunderstanding of Ranke's views on fact and truth in history.

Every recognized historical account is a tissue of facts, and if the facts are objectively ascertainable by research, then they are not dependent upon the historian's activity. . . . The truth of a historical work consists in the truth of its statements. . . . The concrete structure and continuity to be found in every historical work is not the product of valuational judgments, but is implicit in the facts themselves.

In his published review Becker delicately said that as "a description of historical works as we know them" Mandelbaum's version seemed "inexact." Privately he described it to Beard as "quite confused . . . a clumsy work." Beard wrote back that "Despite my passionate effort to be objective about it, I am forced 'by the facts' to conclude that it is simply preposterous!"[18]

---

[17]Beard's review of Mandelbaum, *AHR* 44 (1939): 571–72; Becker's review, *Philosophical Review* 49 (1940): 361.

[18]*Problem of Historical Knowledge*, 200, 183, 270; Becker to Beard, 27 December 1938 (Kammen, "*What Is the Good*," 265–66); Beard to Becker, 31 December 1938, Becker Papers. To Robert L. Schuyler, Becker described the book as "a naive treatment enclosed in a lot of philosophic verbiage." (Undated letter, AHA Papers, Box 330.)

If other critics were more restrained in their comments, the reception of Mandelbaum's book, within both the historical and the philosophical communities, was generally cool, in marked contrast with the praise heaped on it after World War II. Shall we attribute this to relativist blindness to the cogency of its arguments before the war, or to antirelativists' desperate quest for an "answer to relativism" after the war? Those of different commitments will choose different explanations.[19]

III

If it is difficult to make firmly grounded generalizations about the distribution of attitudes within the historical profession on "the objectivity question," it is all but impossible to say anything with certainty about the basis on which these attitudes developed. One has no idea how many historians thought seriously about the question, or had anything that could be described as "a position" on it. My guess is that such people were a minority. Historians "reasonably," if not by the most desiccated standards, "rationally," concluded, on various grounds, that one or another posture toward objectivity "felt right," or had more congenial implications or consequences. No doubt the grounds of choice were usually mixed, but they can best be grasped by separating them, somewhat artificially, into the political, the professional, and the personal.

Neither objectivism nor relativism has any clear, permanent political valence. Both positions are defended from a variety of points on the political spectrum. Oliver Wendell Holmes, an archconservative on social questions, was a relativist to the marrow. And the left-wing Labourite Aneurin Bevan was just as much of a relativist. "This is my truth, now tell me yours," he would say. Like Becker and Beard, Bevan had been much impressed by Vaihinger's *Philosophy of "As If."* He described democratic socialism as "the child . . . of relativist philosophy."[20]

---

[19]Andreas Elviken, in the *Journal of Modern History*, found that Mandelbaum in his attempt to refute relativists had "warped the meaning of the theories advanced by them"; overall he "takes for granted points which most evidently need establishment." (11 [1939]: 568) In the *Journal of Philosophy* John Herman Randall thought that while "his criticisms are cogent against the idealistic relativisms, it is to be doubted whether they will seriously touch Americans like Carl Becker or Charles Beard, or furnish much guidance to the writers of history itself." (36 [1939]: 442.) George H. Sabine wrote to Becker: "He strikes me as a decent youngster who will probably grow as he gets further from [Wilbur Marshall] Urban's influence, which I judge to be warping." (Undated, handwritten comment by Sabine on bottom of Becker to Sabine, 5 February 1939, Becker Papers.) Cf. the interesting review by Lewis S. Feuer (in his Marxist days) in *Science & Society* 3 (1939): 417–19.

[20]Kenneth O. Morgan, review of reissue of Bevan's *In Place of Fear, Times Literary Supplement*, 24 December 1976, 1615; Michael Foot, *Aneurin Bevan: A Biography* (2 vols., New York, 1963–74), 2:370, 508.

Although in principle the political affinities of interwar objectivism and relativism were contingent, and might, in some counterfactualist's alternative political culture, have been the reverse of what they were, the affinities which historically they did have played no small role in determining alignments on epistemological issues. Broadly speaking, and with a few notable exceptions, in these years the criticism of objectivity came mostly from the moderate left; the defense of objectivity was undertaken largely by the right. Even before New Historians like Beard and Robinson had come to question objectivity as a norm, they had, from a left-of-center standpoint, been disputing the explicit and implicit claims of older, conservative historiography that it represented "the objective historical truth." As they came to question the ideal of objectivity itself, their attack on the ideological conservatism of traditional historiography merged with their criticism of its epistemological conservatism, and the two were seen as functionally related. We have seen this theme in the writings of Becker and Beard, and it can be found in the remarks of their followers as well. Eric Goldman wrote that "Ranke, the patron saint of the cult of objectivity, was quite content to keep things as they were, and, consequently, was interested in proving nothing except that he had nothing to prove." American historians, he thought, "would never have denied themselves the right to attack prevailing institutions and ideals had they not been convinced that by describing things as they were they were also describing things as they *ought to be*"; they would never have embraced the Rankean ideal "had they any fundamental quarrel with the contemporary America which the history they were describing had produced." Goldman found it natural that "the historians in the United States who have been the sharpest critics of the ideal of impartiality"—he mentioned Robinson, Beard, and Becker—"are those who are most sensitive to the inadequacies of contemporary society."[21]

Whereas historians of Goldman's persuasion could avow a relationship between their social values and their epistemological stance, historians on the right never to my knowledge explicitly asserted a functional or logical relationship between objectivity and conservatism. The relationship, however unavowed, was nevertheless real enough. If many Progressive Historians were led to doubts about the norm of historical objectivity by their perception of conservative bias in the work of self-styled objective historians of a previous generation, conservatives were undoubtedly moved to defend the norm in defending against Progressive assault the historical work carried out under the banner of objectivity.

In antirelativist manifestos the "collectivist" or "social revolutionary"

---

[21]"Historians and the Ivory Tower," 279–80.

thrust of relativism was often attacked. Thus, Theodore Clarke Smith charged Beard with holding that "the only valid history was that which traced the forward movement of society toward a collectivist democracy." Omitting, in his citation of it, the crucial indefinite article, he maintained that in writing *An Economic Interpretation of the Constitution* Beard, by virtue of adopting this approach, had "forgo[ne] all possibility of . . . impartiality in judgment." Eugene C. Barker, in defending "judicial detachment" and "the search for objective truth" against the relativists, charged them with advancing "half truth and clever suppression for a preconceived social end . . . to advance a social revolution." W. T. Laprade, in maintaining that belief in any "underlying factor" or "theory" is "excess baggage, impeding the work of the historian and hindering him in his search for an orderly arrangement of past events," clearly had certain kinds of theories in mind. It was, he said, a natural by-product of the study of history to make the historian conservative. "He has little faith that benefits will come from sudden change." Charles M. Andrews joined an insistence on the historian's being strictly nonjudgmental, and never viewing the history of the past from the present, to some lessons he had been able to draw from the disinterested study of history:

The people are not always the best governors. . . . It is perfectly legitimate to argue on historical grounds that order and not liberty is the purpose of government. So-called liberty has too often led to confusion, wearisome debate, inaction, and even licence. We have been overstressing the place of the people in history. . . . We have neglected the conservative aspects of history—the executive side of government, the rulers instead of the ruled, and those whose business it is to administer affairs in an orderly and efficient manner.[22]

Not all on the right defended the old objectivist faith. Crane Brinton combined profound conservatism with sharp criticism of traditional epistemology. If the relativism of many Americanists was a mechanism that served to distance them from capitalist ideology, or perhaps was a function of that distance, Brinton's sense of the transience of contemporary ideological assumptions was a mark of his disdain for the democratic and revolutionary currents he saw dominating Europe since the late eighteenth century. Author of a biography of Talleyrand, he repeatedly criticized his reform-oriented colleagues with the message of his hero, "Surtout, pas de zèle."

[22]Smith, "Writing of American History," 447–48; Barker, "The Changing View of the Function of History," *The Social Studies* 29 (1938): 151; Laprade, "The Function of the Historian," ibid., 25 (1934): 78–79; "Message From Dr. Charles M. Andrews," Middle States Association of History Teachers, *Proceedings* 31 (1933–34): 14–16.

If there were those on the right, like Brinton, who combined sympathy with the relativist critique of objectivity and distaste for the left-critical purposes to which it was put, there were those on the left who rejected relativism because of what they saw as its above-the-battle flavor, its absence of commitment. Not surprisingly, criticism of this kind was mostly directed at Becker, rather than Beard. Curtis Nettels thought that Becker's position was unacceptable to radicals because it led to "a wholly negative stand." Malcolm Cowley wrote Becker that in "Everyman" he had "class-angled [his] subject without seeming to realize that every man was a small capitalist and that history might appear differently to a fac-tory-worker or a farmer." But criticism for insufficient commitment could encompass Beard as well. The Marxist Louis Hacker, though he had "enlisted in a different army," saluted Becker and Beard for their "gallant service to our generation." "At bottom," he wrote, "their main hopes are my hopes, their ultimate goal, mine also." But their posture made them "shrink from the acceptance of a fighting philosophy that is prepared to battle for its faith."[23]

Brinton was far from the only historian on the right who joined in the critique of objectivity. Ralph H. Gabriel, for example, combined pessi-mistic political and social conservatism with a sort of "tragic relativism," noting that

"history" is that image of the past which filters through the mind of the historian, as light through a window. Sometimes the glass is dirty; too often it is dis-tressingly opaque. The long and sometimes unfortunate experience of mankind with history has taught the historian that the biases, prejudices, concepts, as-

---

[23]Nettels to Merle Curti, 6 January 1936, Curti Papers, 27–34; Cowley to Becker, 20 May 1935, Becker Papers; Hacker, joint review of Beard's *Discussion of Human Affairs* and Becker's *Progress and Power*, *New Republic* 86 (1936): 162. A few months earlier Hacker, in reviewing *Everyman*, in a not unfriendly fashion, had said that it was because Becker was an intellectual that "he shrinks from the consequences of the revolution." He thought it significant that in his substantive writings Becker had written almost exclusively about the preliminaries of revolution, which are "orderly and rational," rather than revolutions themselves, which are "violent, disorderly and cruel." "Carl Becker tries to brush away the necessity for a choice. But the extinction of all those things he holds dear must come if he and the middle-class intellectuals and professionals like himself do not align themselves with the living forces in society." (*New Republic* 85 [1936]: 260–61.) Invited by the editors to reply to the review, Becker declined in a fashion which perfectly illustrated the sensibility which exasperated his activist critics: "Since Mr. Hacker has done me the signal honor of selecting me as a 'case,' an objective item in social history well worth examina-tion, it would be out of place for me to reply. . . . How unsuitable . . . would I be as an object for methodical examination if, like the electron when exposed to light, I should be suddenly and uncertainly perturbed by the examination. My part, obviously, is to look natural when posed as an object interesting to science, to remain indifferent and un-deflected so long as there is any call for my services as a datum in sociology." (Ibid., 256.)

sumptions, hopes, and ambitions which have contributed to the opaqueness of the minds of his predecessors are a part of the past with which he must deal. If he be a conscientious craftsman, he explores his own mind to discover those distorting bubbles which play such pranks on light rays. But at the outset he is sadly aware that, although he may discover a few of the more obvious imperfections, his task is hopeless.

And there were many on the left—one thinks, for example, of the hyper-empiricist socialist Fred A. Shannon—who joined Hacker in his faith in the objectivity of history. But overall it remains generally true that in the interwar years relativism, not least because of the well-known social views of its two principal spokesmen, had a leftward spin, while the defenders of "the noble dream" of seeking objectivity were usually found on the right.[24]

Though the political undertones of epistemological postures played an important role in the reception accorded the relativist critique, considerations of its professional implications were of even greater importance. For many traditionalists in the profession, relativism partook of both "sacrilege" and "treason," to use the words employed by W. Stull Holt in hailing Becker's presidential address:

> You . . . took out their appendix—no, their backbone and other vital parts. You destroyed the most valued part of the work most of them had done, and only one who has read history could imagine they will go on doing the same thing in the same way, as they will. It was sacrilege against the deity, Scientific History, who has been enthroned for so long. It was treason against the profession. It was glorious. It was grand. But I marvel that you were not tied to a stake and pelted with heavy tomes full of actual, self-expressing facts.[25]

Objectivity, as I have suggested in the introduction, can be seen as the founding myth of the historical profession; the pursuit of the objective truth its sacred mission and raison d'être. Small wonder, then, that for many, especially, though not exclusively, those of the older generation, the theses of Becker and Beard were not just mistaken, but anathema. In this connection, it is worth noting a striking difference in tone between the critics of objectivity and its defenders. Becker (characteristically), Beard (uncharacteristically), and their supporters (for the most part) issued their challenge in moderate, good-humored accents, and, indeed, with a certain diffidence. The responses they received were often uttered in the voice of the Church denouncing and excommunicating heretics.

[24]Gabriel, review of Stuart A. Rice, ed., *Methods in Social Science: A Case Book, AHR* 36 (1931): 786.
[25]Letter of 13 January 1932, Becker Papers.

At the 1934 meeting of the American Historical Association, Theodore Clarke Smith celebrated the magnificent accomplishments of American historians during the first fifty years of the profession's existence. Throughout, their "intellectual assumption," their "clear-cut ideal," had been "that presented to the world first in Germany and later accepted everywhere, the ideal of the effort for objective truth." But now there were those who would challenge that intellectual assumption, "deliberately cast aside, for one reason or another, the whole ideal of impersonality and impartiality." His peroration conveys both the religious fervor and hint of despair among interwar defenders of the old faith.

It may be that another fifty years will see the end of an era in historiography, the final extinction of a noble dream, and history, save as an instrument of entertainment, or of social control will not be permitted to exist. In that case, it will be time for the American Historical Association to disband, for the intellectual assumptions on which it is founded will have been taken away from beneath it. My hope is, none the less, that those of us who date from what may then seem an age of quaint beliefs and forgotten loyalties, may go down with our flags flying.[26]

When Beard submitted his reply, "That Noble Dream," to the *AHR*, he accompanied it with a note to the managing editor in which he expressed his belief that "our good old Church (AHA) is broad enough to include true believers and heretics, Erasmus and even rambunctious Luther. I can get along with any kind of a heretic. It is the fellow who is sure that he has boxed the compass that bothers me, especially when he insists that I must believe in the compleat job of boxing. But I would not excommunicate him." Such latitudinarianism came easier to those whose world view was based on pluralism and doubt than it did to those dedicated to driving toward objective certitude.[27]

The religious metaphor can be extended by noting one respect in which the horror of relativism resembled the common horror of atheism. What confidence could one have that people would behave in an honest and upright fashion, even though they might outwardly appear worthy, if they were not constrained by fear of divine punishment. The question was all the more urgent when those concerned held a public trust. In the early American republic, when denominational tests for public office had disappeared, a belief in heaven and hell remained a requirement for offices which involved handling public funds. Surely, on the premise that only the threat of the fires of hell could restrain the constant temptation to undetectable peculation, a prudent requirement. So it must have seemed

[26]Smith, "Writing of American History," 445–46, 449.
[27]Beard to Henry E. Bourne, 22 July 1935, AHA Papers, Box 314.

to those raised in the traditional historical faith, in which the ever-present temptation to play fast and loose with the past in order to bring it into line with one's personal desires was held in check only by emptying oneself of presuppositions and attending only to facts which would speak for themselves. How could one trust the scholarship of historians, who *seemed* scrupulous, when they were not inhibited by an objectivist superego?

Excommunication from the profession was not a practical option for outraged defenders of "That Noble Dream," much as many seemed to have yearned to employ that instrument. One made do with denunciation. A common theme in antirelativist manifestos was "treason" to what Smith had called "forgotten loyalties." "Defeatist" was a commonly invoked term, used more than once by C. H. McIlwain in his 1936 blast at the relativists, and echoed by Allan Nevins two years later.[28] A related charge was of damaging the morale of historians. Dodd thought that Becker's address in its "total impression upon younger scholars" could "lead them to a certain feeling of futility."[29] Another count in the indictment for treason was Robinson's, Becker's, and Beard's consorting with the educationist enemy, through their cooperation in the replacement of straight history by social studies. And if it was treason against reason to suggest that historical interpretation rested, ultimately, on an act of faith, the notion of everyman his own historian was the ultimate treason against professionalism, received by many historians with the same dismay as those in other professions would greet the idea of everyman his own lawyer or everyman his own neurosurgeon.

But, as Holt's exulting in the term suggests, the idea of "treason against the profession" was not, by the 1930s, regarded by all historians as a capital offense. Professionalism, for reasons detailed in Chapter 7, was no longer as universally highly regarded in these years as it had been before the war. In 1914 all four of the leading New Historians had been firmly ensconced within the professional establishment. After the war this re-

---

[28]McIlwain, "Historian's Part," 209–10; Nevins, *Gateway*, 43. The charge was glossed by McIlwain, in the common conflation of relativism and skepticism, by his claiming that the relativists were maintaining that the historian could "know absolutely nothing," "never truly find out anything whatsoever."

[29]Dodd to Becker, 29 January 1932, Dodd Papers, Box 37. "Misunderstanding could hardly go farther than that," Becker wrote to W. Stull Holt. (Undated letter in Kammen, *"What Is the Good,"* 155.) His point, he said, was the indispensability of history. A sense of futility is necessarily personal. What many critics of Becker were in effect saying was "If *I* thought that my historical work was not 'moving toward objective truth,' which for me is indispensable to justify working at it, I would think history futile and would abandon it." A perfectly reasonable position, though not the only one possible.

mained true only of Turner, the oldest, and in every respect the most conservative, of the four. He followed a quite orthodox career, remaining an "historian's historian," distinguished only by his nonproductivity. The other three, all of whom broke decisively with the norm of objectivity, separated themselves from professionalism as well, though all became presidents of the American Historical Association, and used their presidential addresses to proclaim their epistemological heterodoxy. Robinson and Beard both left Columbia before 1920, never again to have a regular academic appointment. Much, in Robinson's case all, of their subsequent writings was directed to a lay rather than a professional audience. Becker, while remaining formally within the academy, never again wrote a scholarly monograph. Most of his writings were directed to the general intellectual community. From an internal immigration at Cornell he maintained an ironic detachment from professional norms.

For some younger historians who were disenchanted with many of the connotations of professionalism, the extent to which the relativist message was "unprofessional" was not one of its less attractive features. Becker and Beard repeatedly charged that the approved professional posture of icy impartiality was, albeit often unconsciously, dishonest. The only way to play fair with the reader was to make one's values and purposes explicit. Avery O. Craven developed this theme in commenting ironically on "historical soundness."

H. G. Wells . . . has become something of a "horrible example" to be held up to young historians. *He was not objective.* And that is an historical crime. . . . The great trouble with his history, to be perfectly honest, was that he wasn't skilled enough to hide the fact that he had a notion of what history teaches and what the future should be like, long before he acquired the facts for his history. It takes a more highly trained and more "scholarly" writer to do that. It takes more than two years of patient toil. No man can lay claim to scholarship who deduces his past from the values he holds *in* the present and *for* the future, if he does it in such blunt, honest fashion. Subtility is the essence of historical soundness.[30]

Others, for whom "professional" was unambiguously a badge of honor, sought to delegitimize the relativist message by questioning whether those who delivered it were bona fide professional historians. Homer C. Hockett, reviewing Becker's collected essays in 1935, suggested that their author should not, properly speaking, be considered an historian because his approach was "almost incompatible with usual historical procedure." His work "derived as much from the modern psy-

---

[30]"The Subjective and the Objective in History" (lecture given before the Division of the Social Sciences, University of Chicago, 20 April 1937), 6; Gottschalk Papers, 12:7

chologists as from Bernheim. Even in the studies which are most distinctively historical . . . he fails to show the conventional regard for events narrated in sequence." Reviewing the same work, Stanley Pargellis told those of Becker's readers who might be disturbed by his message that it was "worth remembering that he is not a 'professional' historian. . . . He never took seriously the scholar's paraphernalia of tools, or dug so intently among the dead facts that they came alive. . . . The best of the professional historians, who do their dissecting more deeply . . . do not end in Mr. Becker's disillusionment."[31]

No aspect of the relativist critique of the traditional norms of the profession was more central than its insistence on the historian's responsibility to descend from the ivory tower and contribute to social needs. This was an aspect of the New History inheritance which Robinson and Beard hammered home constantly, and if Becker had a considerably less activist orientation, his presidential address had been explicit about the historian's obligation to serve "everyman," and he consistently disparaged mere mandarin erudition. "No doubt the truth shall make you free," he wrote. "But free to do what? To sit and contemplate the truth?"[32]

This theme met an enthusiastic response from many, but it was very unprofessional. It ran counter to that central tenet of academic professionalism which regards scholarly work as self-justifying, an end in itself. The self-justifying nature of historical inquiry was to be a major theme in the objectivist counteroffensive against the relativist stress on knowledge that was useful to mankind in the here-and-now. Traditionalists, as we have seen, had attacked relativists by arguing that to turn history to utilitarian ends was, inevitably, to distort it. To this they added a positive alternative. Whereas Becker had taken it for granted that "if we are interested in, let us say, the fact of the Magna Carta, we are interested in it for our own sake and not for its sake," antirelativists elaborated the doctrine of "the past for its own sake."[33]

The phrase itself had been around for some time, expressing something of the aestheticism, celebration of technique, and the assertion of autonomy implicit in "art for art's sake," and "science for science's sake." The latter slogan had in fact hardly asserted more than that scientific investigation was worthwhile even if it had no immediate technological payoff. It was a plea for delayed gratification. No scientist doubted that in the long

---

[31]Hockett, *MVHR* 22 (1935): 332–33; Pargellis, *Yale Review* 25 (1935): 213–14.
[32]Review of William E. Barton, *The Life of Abraham Lincoln*, *New Republic* 44 (1925): 208.
[33]Becker, "What Are Historical Facts?" 328.

run, science was socially useful, and scientists delighted in presenting examples of pure research that later had the most utilitarian fruits.

Before the 1930s, on those rare occasions when American historians spoke of "the past for its own sake" they seem to have been mainly voicing the historicist caution against anachronistic backward projection of present categories, and arguing, like the scientists, for the value of work with no immediate, clearly specifiable, social utility. None doubted, all took for granted, that history was useful. The phrase acquired additional, different, and much stronger connotations when it became one of the principal slogans of the antirelativist counteroffensive.

The most vocal spokesman for "useless history" (his phrase) was Robert L. Schuyler, managing editor of the *American Historical Review*. From salutary warnings about the ways in which social purpose might distort the past, he moved to the assertion that any utilitarian purpose in historical study would always and inevitably produce distortion. The only valid history was history pursued "for its own sake." To ask "how we got this way" was to make a social engineer's, not an historian's, inquiry. The true historical spirit is moved by "disinterested curiosity about the past . . . in and for itself. . . . It seeks knowledge of the past as an end in itself, not as a means to some end. It is not perturbed by the utilitarian's contemptuous question, 'What's the use of such knowledge?' It is merely sorry for the questioner, because it looks upon knowledge as good in itself, as needing no ulterior justification, as its own reward." Not only was present social purpose dangerous to the historian, even knowledge of the present was dangerous. An historian of the medieval English parliament would be better off if he knew nothing whatsoever of eighteenth- and nineteenth-century developments. He would be "less likely to be led astray by modern developments."[34]

This was "the past for its own sake" with a vengeance. To the charge that professional historical scholarship had often descended into antiquarianism, the profession's most influential official responded with what can hardly be described as less than a celebration, indeed a mandating, of antiquarianism. It was a position considerably more extreme, and infinitely less tolerant, than any ever advanced by Becker or Beard.

Schuyler and others had been much impressed with Herbert Butterfield's *Whig Interpretation of History*, published in the same year in which Becker delivered "Everyman His Own Historian." Many of Schuyler's themes echoed those found in Butterfield's book: the reiter-

---

[34]Schuyler, "The Usefulness of Useless History," *Political Science Quarterly* 61 (1941): 27–28; "Can History Educate?" *Columbia University Quarterly* 27 (1935): 99; "Some Historical Idols," *Political Science Quarterly* 47 (1932): 16.

ated slogan of the "past for its own sake," concern with the present as the root cause of "all sins and sophistries in history," the suggestion that the historian who knew nothing of the present was better off, the privileging of the monographic, the hostility to theory, the injunction to the historian to "empty himself." Similar, too, was the political complexion of the prime villains. Butterfield's sparkling invective was systematically directed against liberal and progressive distortion. Schuyler, in an article discussing "Some Historical Idols," briefly noted in a single sentence that "apologists for the *status quo*" sometimes used history for their purposes; he then spent six pages on the pernicious consequences of "the idol of reform."[35]

While interwar historians' attitudes toward objectivity and the relativist critique had a good deal to do with their position on a right-left continuum, and with their attitudes toward professionalism, they were probably even more closely related to another set of issues which are difficult to label. Cognitive style? Sensibility? Personality type? All of these, and more; all interacting, and all inextricably mixed up with the political, the professional, the philosophical.

Psychologists speak of "tolerance for ambiguity" as a characteristic spread differentially through the population. On the one hand, those for whom a plurality of viewpoints and perspectives is perfectly acceptable, shading off into those who "flout reality in an extreme manner"; on the other hand, those for whom "things must appear as they are *known* to be," who, at the extremes, are "rigid, pedantic, compulsive." We are manifestly in the realm of phenomena it is difficult to describe neutrally. For Theodor Adorno and his associates, "intolerance for ambiguity" was associated with "the authoritarian personality." On the other hand, we have all encountered those who seem to belong in a nursing home for the terminally ambivalent.[36]

In a phrase whose meaning has been the subject of learned exegesis for over a century, Keats wrote of "Negative Capability": "when man is

---

[35]"Some Historical Idols," 8–13. Schuyler enthusiastically reviewed Butterfield's book in *The Historical Outlook* 23 (1932): 309–10. C. H. McIlwain's 1936 AHA presidential address, cited in note 13, also appears to have been strongly influenced by Butterfield.
[36]George S. Klein, "The Personal World Through Perception," in Robert R. Blake and Glenn V. Ramsey et al., *Perception: An Approach to Personality* (New York, 1951), 342–44. The concept of "tolerance for ambiguity" arose in a highly charged ideological context. The Nazi psychologist E. R. Jaensch had seen the characteristic as a pathological state, associated with decadent liberalism and relativism. (*Der Gegentypus* [Leipzig, 1938].) For the émigré psychologist Else Frenkel-Brunswick, who worked with Adorno, it was *intolerance* for ambiguity which was pathological. (See her "Intolerance of Ambiguity as an Emotional and Perceptual Personality Variable," *Journal of Personality* 18 [1949]: 108–43.)

capable of being in uncertainties, Mysteries, doubts, without any irritable reaching after fact & reason." He contrasted those possessing that characteristic with Coleridge, "incapable of remaining content with half knowledge," and with his friend Dilke: "a Man who cannot feel he has a personal identity unless he has made up his Mind about every thing. . . . Dilke will never come at a truth as long as he lives; because he is always trying at it." As Keats's biographer W. Jackson Bate has observed, with considerable relevance to the sense in which I am applying the term here,

The remark, "without any irritable reaching after fact and reason," is often cited as though the pejorative words are "fact and reason," and as though uncertainties were being preferred for their own sake. But the significant word, of course, is "irritable." We should also stress "capable"—"capable of being in uncertainties, Mysteries, doubts" without the "irritable" need to extend our identities and rationalize our "half-knowledge."[37]

Both Keats and the psychologists touch on aspects of a dimension no less real for being difficult to pin down. With all appropriate acknowledgment of exceptions and qualifications, it seems clear that cognitive style, sensibility, and personality played an important role in determining historians' attitudes toward objectivity and the relativist critique.[38]

In the interwar years, historians' responses to the relativists' theses are problematically separable from those historians' responses to the style of Becker and Beard—their irreverence, their suspicion of conventional pieties just because they were conventional pieties, their delight in puncturing the pretensions of the pompous, their mocking tone, which was frequently reflexive. Some found these characteristics appealing, others found them appalling. Before the war Andrew C. McLaughlin was uneasy about Becker's elevation to the *AHR* editorial board because of "a certain 'freshness' or smartness" in Becker's reviewing, which did not seem "the mark of solid and mature wisdom." It was not a characteristic which Becker, or Beard, ever lost. Nor, while they were undoubtedly sincere in acknowledging the indispensability of narrow, monographic

---

[37]*John Keats* (Cambridge, Mass., 1963), 249.
[38]In discussing these phenomena I am staying fairly close to the surface level of emotional and cognitive strategies, not probing their depths. If one accepts, as I do, the dialectical perspective of psychoanalysis, which suspects a yearning for the absolute in ambivalence, flight from pervasive doubts in dogmatism, one is immediately embroiled in an infinitely more complex pattern, if not infinite regress. It would be eminently worthwhile to explore these themes in the postures of historians. To do so here would take us too far afield, or, if done summarily, would be too facile by half. One can note in passing that Beard, for example, who frequently seemed to be hoping for certitude around the next corner, appeared less comfortable in the relativist posture than Becker; but I prefer to let it go at that.

work, did they altogether avoid a certain condescending tone when referring to it, a tone sometimes amplified in the remarks of their admirers.
Ferdinand Schevill wrote Becker that he thought historians had misunderstood "Everyman" when they concluded that Becker "refused to concede their minute graduate investigations any value."

> Of course you insisted that the value was small but you did not deny men the
> right to amuse their leisure, in the spirit of antiquarianism, with any odd junk that
> the past has spared and which happens still to be lying about. Since average
> human beings are justified in seeking honorable occupation of their free time, I
> for my part do not see why they should be forbidden the pleasure of collecting
> bric-a-brac and exhibiting it in the journals of history.

When glossed in this fashion, the relativist message was not likely to
commend itself to those whose greatest pride was in having added a small
brick to the edifice of knowledge.[39]

On the whole, though with important exceptions, the relativist critique
tended to be rejected by those whose reflexes were "establishmentarian,"
men like Jameson and Schuyler, while iconoclasts, the Cochrans and the
Woodwards, often found it attractive. (History teachers in the schools,
whose comparative status was enhanced by deflation of the superior authority of university historians, often seemed to be attracted to relativism
because it seemed to do precisely that.) If, other things being equal, the
iconoclastic flavor of relativism made it attractive to those who bridled at
the conventional wisdom, its tolerant perspectivism made it uncongenial
to iconoclasts like Fred Shannon, who were also ardent controversialists,
dedicated to proving an opponent wrong. Moderate revisionists on
World War I, like Sidney B. Fay, or on the Civil War, like Avery O.
Craven, might display a relativistic sensibility; the more zealous, like
Harry Elmer Barnes, were engaged in a holy crusade to replace error with
truth. The enthusiastic Civil War revisionist James G. Randall explained
that the activity he was engaged in had nothing to do with point of view.
"The scholarly revisionist overthrows only falsehood. Revisionism is not
a matter of promoting a theory. It is a matter of findings."[40]

Anguish and doubt are not the sine qua non of serious thought. To be
deeply troubled about the problem of historical knowledge, to be dissatisfied with conventional formulae, to wrestle with the issue—none of
these are any guarantee that the time and energy will have been well

[39]McLaughlin to J. Franklin Jameson, 9 December 1914, AHA Papers, Box 280; Schevill to
Becker, 9 February 1932, Becker Papers.
[40]"The Historian as Revisionist," *Indiana History Bulletin* 15 (1938): 99.

spent, or productive of wisdom. Clearly, one could embrace the relativist critique mindlessly. Equally clearly, one could, after deep and deliberate consideration, conclude that the pursuit of the old "noble dream" was a coherent and sensible program. All this said, it remains true that among the defenders of objectivity there was frequently an impatience with philosophical reflection which, continuous with prewar norms, verged on anti-intellectualism. In the preface to his *Gateway to History*, Allan Nevins informed readers that they would not be confronted with "that pseudo-philosophic jargon upon Historismus, frames of reference, patterns of culture, and cyclical phases of causation which I no more understand than do most of its users."[41] And there was, among some defenders of objectivity, like Arthur Schlesinger, a professional astigmatism, a magisterial aloofness from prevailing currents, that is awe-inspiring. During World War II, Perry Miller wrote him from Third Army headquarters about the "damned important job" of rewriting American history after the war: "When we think what a difference it made after the last war, how our view of the past had to be readjusted to what we thought was the utterly different frame of reference that that war had put us into, I am aghast to think, or rather to try to imagine, in what different lights we shall see everything from the colonies on down after we have found ourselves on the other side of this business." Schlesinger replied: "I don't understand your reference to the effect of the First World War on the rewriting of American history. I am not aware that it had any such effect. Maybe it will be different this time, but if so, we stay-at-homes have given the matter no thought except to wonder somewhat listlessly whether we won't have to take military history more seriously into account than in the past."[42]

The assault on objectivist epistemology, as elaborated by Becker, Beard, and their associates, opened up a long-overdue consideration of what historical scholarship could and should do; what it couldn't, and shouldn't try to do. Criticisms of previously unexamined assumptions entered the collective consciousness of the profession, and could never be permanently quieted. As a result of their work, future generations of historians found it immensely more difficult to proceed with the old serene confidence in the value of mindless cumulation of facts, though to be sure many persevered with the "business as usual" molding of bricks.

The relativist critique, though powerful, was seriously flawed. Neither

---

[41]*Gateway*, iii-iv.
[42]Miller to Schlesinger, 14 February 1945; Schlesinger to Miller, 14 March 1945, Schlesinger Papers.

Becker nor Beard was a systematic thinker, and their formulations were often loose and inconsistent—turgid and convoluted in Beard's case, allusive and aphoristic in Becker's. "Objectivity," in their discourse, was employed in ways so varied and mutually inconsistent that it is frequently impossible to pin down precisely what they meant. They operated on the basis of a fairly unsophisticated model of "ideological preconception," with scant attention to the complex mediations between interest and perception. Many weaknesses in their presentation were a consequence not of their exaggerating their case, but of their not pressing it far enough. Both Becker and Beard, particularly the latter, clung to a distinction between the allegedly direct and immediate observations of the natural scientist, and what the historian saw through a glass darkly, privileging the former.

Becker and Beard were well aware of the philosophers' alleged knock-down argument against relativism: that it is self-refuting, since relativism must necessarily be, by its proponents' own principles, itself a relative, rather than an absolute and timeless, truth. Indeed, they cheerfully accepted it, at least insofar as it stressed the historicity of historical relativism. Beard thought that one must ask: "To what spirit of the times, to the ideas and interests of what class, group, nation, race, or region does the conception of relativity correspond?" and accepted that the doctrine would "disappear in due course, beneath the ever-tossing waves of changing relativities." Becker concluded "Everyman" by telling his listeners that he was not offering his view of history as one that was "stable and must prevail."

Whatever validity it may claim, it is certain, on its own premises, to be supplanted; for its premises, imposed upon us by the climate of opinion in which we live and think, predispose us to regard all things, and all principles of things, as no more than "inconstant modes or fashions," as but the "concurrence, renewed from moment to moment, of forces parting sooner or later on their way."

Historiographical doctrines, he predicted, like substantive historical interpretations, would not remain stable "as mankind moves into the unknown future." They would, as we moved away from their point of origin, lose "some significance that once was noted in them, some quality of enchantment that once was theirs."[43]

Becker's confidence in the relativity of doctrines was to be confirmed by the next generation's rejection of his doctrine of relativism.

[43]"Written History," 225; "Everyman," 254–55.

PART III

Objectivity reconstructed

10

⊲══⊳

The defense of the West

The aftermath of World War I ushered in a period of negativity and doubt, the climate in which the relativist critique flourished. The coming of World War II saw American culture turn toward affirmation and the search for certainty. American mobilization, intellectual as well as material, became permanent in what most saw as one continuous struggle of the "Free World" against "totalitarianism"—first in its Nazi, then its Soviet embodiments. "Totalitarianism" as a theoretical and rhetorical construct had been employed occasionally and casually throughout the 1930s. For obvious reasons it succeeded in capturing the imagination of academics and publicists during the years of the Nazi-Soviet pact. For equally obvious reasons, use of the term dropped off during the wartime alliance between the United States and the Soviet Union. Then, for a generation after 1945, the construct served both as the principal theoretical underpinning of scholarly studies of Nazism and Communism in the United States, and as the foundation of American counterideology in the cold war.

As a predictive theory, "totalitarianism" ultimately proved of limited value, and was progressively abandoned by historians and political scientists from the 1960s onward. The concept pointed to real, important, and novel shared features of the Nazi and Soviet regimes. In practice, variants of the theory stressed elements from one or the other of the systems; efforts to analyze the behavior of one on the basis of propositions drawn from the other were generally unsatisfactory.

Politically, the theory of totalitarianism was used to assimilate the Soviet strategic posture in the late 1940s to that of Nazi Germany in the late 1930s, and to extend to the Soviet case the alleged systemic necessity of the Nazi regime to expand militarily or collapse. In postwar discus-

281

sions of foreign policy, it became a foundation stone of the "Munich analogy." Ideologically, it divided the world up into permanently antagonistic "free" and "totalitarian" segments, with the later addition of the "Third World." On the basis of the theory it was argued that the traditional taxonomy of regimes or movements along a left-right axis, based on attitudes toward private property, was obsolete. In the twentieth century, Arthur Schlesinger, Jr. said, the more relevant axis was that which placed libertarian and "gradualist" regimes at one end, authoritarian and "violent" regimes at the other. Moderate liberals and moderate conservatives had to join forces against the fundamentally similar totalitarians of the left and right. Most relevantly for our purposes, "totalitarianism" was a slogan which succeeded in justifying continuous mobilization of consciousness from the forties through the sixties: promoting currents of thought which furthered a militant posture and underwrote the belief in a dichotomized world; disparaging those currents, and their spokesmen, which did the opposite.[1]

I

Relativism, in its different embodiments, was a prime target of the campaign for ideological mobilization. The attack on moral relativism was part of an effort to rearm the West spiritually for the battle with the totalitarians. The attack on cognitive relativism aimed at making a clear distinction between the scholarship and science of the Free World and the debased practices of its enemies. Though politically complementary, and sometimes entangled in rhetorical practice, the two attacks were conceptually distinct, and, indeed, sometimes contradictory.

As Plato had charged the poets with corrupting the youth, a chorus of leading American intellectuals in the years before Pearl Harbor called for the repudiation of those modes of thought that had morally disarmed the United States for the coming struggle. Leading writers and intellectuals— Archibald MacLeish, Lewis Mumford, Van Wyck Brooks, Bernard De Voto, Waldo Frank—were joined by Protestant and Catholic theologians, freed by national intellectual mobilization from the marginal position they had occupied in a secular age. Agreement on the need for faith and commitment encouraged attacks on the "objectively pro-fascist" disseminators of skepticism, pragmatism, and relativism. Philosophers were urged to "surrender the shallow indifference about ultimate truth of the debased 'liberalism' of our recent past." Relativism, it was claimed, led to

---

[1]Schlesinger, *The Vital Center* (Boston, 1949), 145.

cynicism and nihilism. All traditional values had been "debunked." Just as, in the popular wisdom of the time, Marcel Proust was the real moral author of France's defeat, so "America was endangered . . . because debilitating relativism had spread widely and robbed people of their convictions and their will to fight."[2]

Historians, though clearly included in the indictment, were not singled out as the sole offenders. Litterateurs, like MacLeish and Brooks, directed most of their fire at their own tribe. Theologians attacked their old enemy, the unwillingness of a secular age to acknowledge absolutes which stood above society. Cultural relativism in anthropology was a prime target, since nothing could be more disarming in a global struggle of ideologies and social systems than to suggest that there was no universal, absolute standard by which belief systems and practices could be judged.

But historians came in for at least their fair share of the opprobrium heaped on moral relativism for weakening American fiber in its struggles with the totalitarians. Criticism came from both outside and inside the profession. Howard Mumford Jones, in 1938, was concerned that historians like Charles Beard had had "an unfortunate influence . . . from the point of view of keeping alive a necessary patriotic glow in the juvenile breast. . . . I wonder . . . what it is that American democrats are to believe in during the coming struggle?" Archibald MacLeish, whose article "The Irresponsibles" was the *locus classicus* of the attack on intellectuals' moral relativism, challenged Merle Curti to name for him the historians who had "faced the dreadful danger of our time . . . earnestly and indefatigably." The émigré Italian historian Gaetano Salvemini charged his American colleagues with a moral relativism which led to moral indifference. Roger B. Merriman of Harvard complained that students had told him, in the years before Pearl Harbor, that "the cynicism of some of their instructors had shaken the foundations of their faith."[3]

In all fields the most common response to the attack was retreat and repentance, and many of the attacks on moral relativism took the form of *mea culpa*s. An editorial in *The New Republic* announced that to the

---

[2]Arthur Murphy, "Ideals and Ideologies: 1917–1947," *Philosophical Review* 56 (1947): 386–87; Edward A. Purcell, Jr., *The Crisis of Democratic Theory: Scientific Naturalism and the Problem of Value* (Lexington, Ky., 1973), 221.
[3]Jones, "Patriotism—But How?" *Atlantic Monthly* 162 (1938): 589, 587; MacLeish to Curti, 12 December 1940, Curti Papers, 25–13; Salvemini, *Historian and Scientist: An Essay on the Nature of History and the Social Sciences* (Cambridge, Mass., 1939), 157; Merriman, "A Retrospect and a Prospect, or 'Lest We Forget'" (draft manuscript, undated, but from internal evidence probably 1945), Merriman Papers.

extent that it had published material of the type excoriated by MacLeish, "we hereby do penance for our sins."[4]

Anthropologists took a close look at the moral implications of cultural relativism and found it wanting. Elgin Williams, reviewing a 1946 reprint of Ruth Benedict's *Patterns of Culture*, observed that "the Gold Star Mother . . . is going to be reluctant about granting significance to Hitler's culture . . . and the remaining Jews of Europe . . . are going to be poor customers for gospels which hold that there are two sides to every question." But Benedict had already altered her perspective. In an unpublished manuscript dating from shortly after Pearl Harbor, she wrote that it was vital to "discover the ways and means of social cohesion. . . . This problem is *beyond relativity*." The task of anthropology, she said, was to discover "what it is that makes for well-being and a sense of freedom in tribes like the Blackfoot and for the conviction of doom in tribes like the Chukchee. We are fighting today a war which is to preserve freedom, and we need to know its proved strategy." She celebrated "civil libertarian" primitive cultures which, as in "the American dream," offered members "the opportunity to enter any profession according to a man's individual ability."[5]

Cultural relativists were on the defensive within anthropology during the postwar decades. When the American Anthropological Association in 1947 produced a draft Statement on Human Rights for the United Nations, its ultrarelativist author, Melville Herskovits, felt constrained to hedge on the question of accepting the integrity of cultural practices that denied human rights. (Of course, the very notion of a Universal Declaration of Human Rights was inconsistent with a thoroughgoing cultural relativism.) Some years later Herskovits backed off even farther from cultural relativism; he wondered how tolerant one should be of cultural practices which included Soviet slave-labor camps and the lynching of blacks in the American South. "What we face," he said, "is the gigantic task of devising ways of dealing with man's inhumanity to man. . . . These are questions not easy to answer."[6]

Symbolic of the postwar turn of American anthropologists away from

[4]"War and the New Generation," 103 (1 July 1940): 8.

[5]Williams, "Anthropology for the Common Man," *American Anthropologist* 49 (1947): 85; Benedict, "Ideologies in the Light of Comparative Data" (excerpt from an unpublished manuscript, ca. 1941–42); "Primitive Freedom," *Atlantic Monthly* 169 (1942); both reprinted in Margaret Mead, *An Anthropologist at Work: Writings of Ruth Benedict* (1959; reprinted, New York, 1973), quotations from 385, 391, 394.

[6]"Cultural Diversity and World Peace" (1956), in his *Cultural Relativism: Perspectives in Cultural Pluralism* (New York, 1973), 93, 94. The draft statement appears in *American Anthropologist* 49 (1947): 539–43; see correspondence, ibid., 50 (1948): 351–55.

relativism was the search for universals in cultural values. Ralph Linton discovered "a fundamental uniformity . . . behind the seemingly endless diversity of culture patterns." He was seconded by Robert Redfield, who asserted that though the contents of moral systems throughout the world were enormously divergent, values tended "to vary around basic similarities." This tendency received its fullest embodiment in the "Comparative Study of Values in Five Cultures Project" directed by Clyde Kluckhohn at the Laboratory of Social Relations at Harvard between 1949 and 1955, an attempt to discover "scientifically" nonrelativistic moral norms.[7]

By the mid-1960s, the article on cultural relativism in the *International Encyclopedia of the Social Sciences* treated it as anachronistic. While the empathy and temporary suspension of value judgments which it enjoined were still methodologically valuable in fieldwork, as a world view it had to be discarded. "Culture is not the measure of all things . . . there are more things in nature than are ever grasped through our human, cultural symbols." The "postulate of a metacultural reality renders scientific progress possible." Cultural relativism, said the author of the article, David Bidney, was characteristic of a naive, softheaded sensibility, out of date in the era of the global struggle with totalitarianism. It "assumed implicitly that there is a kind of pre-established harmony of cultures that makes it possible for all to coexist in a pluralistic cultural world. It has taken the shock of World War II, with its brutalities, to awaken this romantic cultural optimism of our modern Candides to the reality of cultural crises and the actual conflict of cultures."[8]

Historians joined the chorus of those repudiating moral relativism. Hans Kohn acknowledged that historians had "dull[ed] all sense of morality and of moral distinctions . . . and thereby destroyed the possibility of any effective resistance to fascism." Invoking a connection made by many others, he associated this amorality with "a complacent belief in economic and social factors as the prime motivation in man's life." Becker's former student Robert R. Palmer wrote to his old teacher just after the fall of France that he could "no longer rest content with the facile relativism" on which he had been raised. Reviewing the Beards' *Basic History of the United States* in 1944, Eric F. Goldman, who had been

---

[7]Linton, "Universal Ethical Principles: An Anthropological View," in Ruth Nanda Anshen, ed., *Moral Principles of Action: Man's Ethical Imperative* (New York, 1952), 646; Redfield, *The Primitive World and Its Transformation* (1953; rev. ed., Ithaca, N.Y., 1957), 159–69.
[8]Bidney, "Cultural Relativism," *International Encyclopedia of the Social Sciences* (New York, 1968), 3: 543–47.

Beard's protégé, noted that "war made psychologically uncomfortable the relativism that was becoming associated with an economic interpretation."

The great social danger of relativism is that, for good or for bad, men do not seem to be able to charge their actions with much emotion unless they believe that they are acting on *the* truth and *the* right. Before the war, liberal groups, especially groups of younger liberals, showed traces of the debilitating effects of relativism. War increased the psychological difficulty a thousandfold, for war admits of no relativism.[9]

Both Beard's and Becker's wartime writings took on a somewhat more affirmative tone. Beard, for example, took a less pragmatic and iconoclastic attitude toward the Constitution. But because this shift was connected to his concern with defending the Constitution against what he regarded as Roosevelt's abuse of constitutional authority for interventionist purposes, his altered perspective hardly placated critics of his "amoralism." Becker repudiated an extreme moral relativism which he had never really accepted: "that if morals varied with the customs of time and place, any custom that got itself established was moral, and one system of morality as good as another." But his acknowledgment that there were "Some Generalities That Still Glitter"—essentially, the values of liberal democracy—was too wrapped in his characteristic skeptical rhetoric to satisfy his critics. In his most "affirmative" work, *New Liberties For Old*, he referred to "convictions I entertain—prejudices, if you prefer—prejudgments as to the essential values of life." If the war made Becker less "detached," his conversion was to a more engaged, Beardian, "Act of Faith" relativism, not to the abandonment of his fundamental posture.[10]

The attack on moral relativism continued to be heard after World War II, and in a general way it helped establish the tone of affirmation which characterized postwar scholarship in the social sciences. But it was only in the case of anthropology, and, as we will see shortly, in jurisprudence, that the attack left an explicit, visible, permanent mark on the professional ideology of an academic discipline. Within the historical profession during the postwar decades there were occasional programmatic statements about the necessity of historians acknowledging "certain fundamental values as beyond dispute," and reiteration of historians' responsibility for "American spiritual unpreparedness for World War II." But on

---

[9]Kohn in symposium "On 'The Irresponsibles'," *Nation* 150 (1940): 680; Palmer to Becker, 30 June 1940, Becker Papers; Goldman, "A Historian at Seventy," *New Republic* 111 (1944): 696–97.
[10]*New Liberties For Old* (New Haven, 1941), 137, xvi.

the whole, after 1945, explicit attacks on moral relativism in scholarship came only from the conservative fringe of the academic world: from some Catholic scholars; from others, like Leo Strauss, in the natural law tradition; and from those offended by such examples of amoral social science as the Kinsey Reports on sexuality.[11]

The indictment of moral relativism had its short-term uses for purposes of mobilizing national morale, but it was a two-edged sword. MacLeish and his allies considered that the totalitarians "were stronger in arms because they were stronger in heart. It was their fanatical faith that gave them wings and fire. It was the singleness of their purpose that quickened the spearhead of their march." The attack on "debilitating moral relativism," which left the United States unprepared for global struggle, was uncomfortably reminiscent of Goebbels' crusade against decadent art and literature: "Kulturbolschewismus Is Here," Dwight Macdonald entitled his 1941 response to Van Wyck Brooks's strictures. The Soviet historian E. V. Tarle wrote of the failures of the recently purged Pokrovsky school of historians in terms which were virtually identical to those being used in the United States:

What went on, in essence, was the moral disarmament of the Russian people. If a nation consists only of drunkards, sluggards and idlers, of Oblomovs, is such a nation worth much? Is it possible that the "fair-skinned Aryans" are really right in committing their atrocities? Is General von Reichenau right in saying that there are no cultural values in Russia? Many who showed this tendency in their historical work did not think of these consequences and might have been horrified if they had seen them. But objectively their work was harmful.[12]

In indicting the moral relativism of American intellectuals MacLeish said that the scholar's sin was that he had adopted as words of praise "the laboratory words—objectivity, detachment, dispassion."

His pride is to be scientific, neuter, skeptical, detached—superior to final judgment or absolute belief. . . . To the scholar impartiality, objectivity, detachment were ideal qualities he taught himself laboriously and painfully to acquire. . . . Both writers and scholars freed themselves of the subjective passions, the emotional preconceptions which color conviction and judgment. . . . They emerged free, pure, and single into the antiseptic air of objectivity. And by that sublimation of the mind they prepared the mind's disaster.

[11]Quotations from the AHA presidential addresses of, respectively, Conyers Read ("The Social Responsibilities of the Historian," *AHR* 55 [1950]: 284) and Samuel Eliot Morison ("Faith of a Historian," *AHR* 56 [1951]: 267).
[12]MacLeish, *The American Cause* (New York, 1941), 12–13; Macdonald in *Partisan Review* 8 (1941): 442–51; Tarle, "Soviet Historical Research," *Science and Society* 7 (1943): 230–31.

For critics of moral relativism like MacLeish it was the "neuter" qualities of objectivity and detachment which had morally disarmed the West for the battle against totalitarianism. For critics of cognitive relativism, objectivity and detachment were the distinctive values of Western life and thought which distinguished the democracies from the totalitarian regimes. The two lines of criticism were conceptually quite distinct, not to say contradictory. One might, without too much exaggeration, designate them as the conservative and liberal attacks on relativism, the former stressing relativism's abandonment of moral absolutes and its critical/adversarial stance, the latter attacking relativism for its presentist willingness to employ scholarship for social ends and its abandonment of the posture of detached objectivity. The extent to which the two themes overlapped or coexisted peacefully was a sign of how conservative the liberal tradition became in times of national mobilization, of the strength of liberal values within American conservatism.[13]

There certainly were overlaps. Criticism of cultural relativism in anthropology, though primarily based on moral grounds, had a cognitive dimension as well. The attack on the relativism of the Legal Realists mixed moral and cognitive elements in a way it is difficult to disentangle. It was in response to the charge of moral relativism that Realists uttered their *mea culpas*. Karl Llewellyn, in 1940, acknowledged that the central problem for jurisprudence was ethical purpose in law, and pronounced himself "ready to do open penance for any part I may have played in giving occasion for the feeling that modern jurisprudes or any of them had ever lost sight of this."[14]

To the Realists' critics, their standpoint collapsed the distinction between judges in the Free World and those in the totalitarian states. Realism, it was said, was "prepar[ing] the intellectual ground for a tendency toward totalitarianism." Holmes's philosophy was "akin to Hitler's." For Ben Palmer, writing in the *American Bar Association Journal* in 1945, "the fact that Holmes was a polished gentleman who did not go about like a storm-trooper knocking people down and proclaiming the supremacy of the blonde beast should not blind us to his legal philosophy that might makes right, that law is the command of the dominant social group."[15]

As a movement, Legal Realism all but disappeared from American law

[13]MacLeish, "The Irresponsibles," *Nation* 150 (1940): 622–23.
[14]"On Reading and Using the Newer Jurisprudence," *Columbia Law Review* 40 (1940): 603.
[15]Edgar Bodenheimer, *Jurisprudence* (New York, 1940), 316; Francis Lucey, ·quoted in G. Edward White, "The Rise and Fall of Justice Holmes," *University of Chicago Law Review* 39 (1971): 66; Palmer, "Hobbes, Holmes, and Hitler," *American Bar Association Journal* 31 (1945): 569.

schools, though many of its critical insights continued to trouble legal scholarship. It was replaced for more than a generation by schools of legal thought which stressed the constraints of "the legal process," the necessity for "reasoned elaboration" in judicial opinions, and the search for "neutral principles of constitutional law": all strategies which put the maximum distance between current legal doctrine and the relativistic and sociological jurisprudential scholarship of the thirties.

As early as 1923 Bertrand Russell had made a connection between the pragmatic theory of truth and rigged trials in the Soviet Union. In a 1935 discussion of the ancestry of fascism he made it clear that doubts about the existence of objective truth figured prominently in that genealogy. Another allegedly relativistic current of the interwar years which was tarred with the totalitarian brush was Mannheim's sociology of knowledge. Robert K. Merton, in a 1938 essay, thought it "of considerable interest that totalitarian theorists have adopted the radical relativistic doctrines of *Wissenssoziologie* as a political expedient for discrediting 'liberal' or 'bourgeois' or 'non-Aryan' science. . . . Politically effective variations of the 'relationism' of Karl Mannheim . . . have been used for propagandistic purposes by such Nazi theorists as Walter Frank, Krieck, Rust, and Rosenberg."[16]

Within the historical profession the charge that cognitive relativism collapsed the distinction between Western scholarship and that of the totalitarians was made from the very beginning of relativism's vogue in the 1930s. Robert L. Schuyler, in 1932, cited history in the Soviet Union as an example of "present-mindedness run riot." In Theodore Clarke Smith's 1934 attack on Beard he expressed distress at "the ease with which a growing number of writers discard impartiality on the ground that it is uninteresting, or contrary to social beliefs, or uninstructive, or inferior to a bold social philosophy."

There are today countries where history, under the sway of precisely these ideals, has become so functional that it is systematically employed as a means for educating people to think as the ruling authorities wish them to do. We have Soviet history, and Fascist history, and we are to have National Socialist history as soon as it can be manufactured—in each case based on a definite philosophy as an act of faith.[17]

[16]Russell, "Can Man Be Rational?" (1923) and "The Ancestry of Fascism" (1935), reprinted in Russell, *The Will to Doubt* (New York, 1958), 11, 86–104; Merton, "Science and the Social Order," reprinted in Merton, *The Sociology of Science: Theoretical and Empirical Investigations* (Chicago, 1973), 260.
[17]Schuyler, "Some Historical Idols," *Political Science Quarterly* 47 (1932): 17; Smith, "The Writing of American History, 1884–1934," *AHR* 40 (1935): 449.

Claims that Becker and Beard's relativism legitimized Nazi and Soviet historical practice multiplied from the late 1930s onward. In 1938 Allan Nevins, in his *Gateway to History*, denounced relativism as "the doctrine to which historical writing has bowed under state pressure in Nazi Germany and Fascist Italy." Those asserting a relationship between relativism and Fascism often invoked the case of Croce. His relativism, according to one historian, had "in a sense . . . prepared the way for Fascism." Another historian, writing in the *American Historical Review* after the war, charged that "American relativists have neglected to indicate the intimate relation that the new Continental historiography has borne to the origins of Fascism. . . . The adoption of subjectivist-relativism as the basic historical theory contributed to the rise of Fascism and Nazism and their conquest of the universities."[18]

Throughout the postwar decades totalitarianism continued to be identified with relativism, and with disdain for "objective historical truth." George Orwell's *Nineteen Eighty-Four*, which more than any other work of the period established the popular conception of totalitarianism, was particularly important in furthering this association. Long before he wrote his classic novel, Orwell had been arguing that "The really frightening thing about totalitarianism is not that it commits 'atrocities' but that it attacks the concept of objective truth: it claims to control the past as well as the future." In *Nineteen Eighty-Four* the protagonist's occupation, under the ideal-typical totalitarianism of the future, was rewriting history, turning unwanted historical actors into "unpersons," stuffing truth down the "memory hole."[19]

Morton White thought relativism could be used to justify Soviet erasure of certain names from the history of the Russian revolution. "'Frame of reference' history," said Samuel Eliot Morison, "is of course the only kind that historians are allowed to write under a dictatorship," and he cited historical practice in *Nineteen Eighty-Four* as the logical consequence of relativist doctrines. Attacks on historical relativism as totalitarian often included personal attacks on Beard and Becker. Thomas A. Bailey charged Beard with having "prostituted" history to his own ends: "The Marxist-Leninist-Stalinist philosophy that the end justifies the means may be sound doctrine in Soviet Russia, but if we are to glorify it

[18]Nevins, *Gateway to History* (Boston, 1938), 43; R. V. Burks, "Benedetto Croce," in Bernadotte Schmitt, ed., *Some Historians of Modern Europe* (Chicago, 1942), 71; Chester McArthur Destler, "Some Observations on Contemporary Historical Theory," *AHR* 55 (1950): 525. Destler's charges against Croce are rebutted in a communication to the *AHR* by James Moceri (56 [1951]: 760–66.)
[19]*Tribune* column, 4 February 1944, reprinted in Sonia Orwell and Ian Angus, eds., *The Collected Essays, Journalism and Letters of George Orwell* (4 vols., London, 1968), 3:88.

in historical circles we might as well close up shop and try to earn an honest living." Repeating, years later, themes adumbrated in the late forties, J. H. Hexter saw an intimate connection between Becker's relativism and Nazi historical practice:

Many German professional historians were shortly to perform the service that Becker had prescribed. . . . The history they wrote was intended to do work in the world, to be living history that influences the course of history, to enlarge and enrich the specious present of the Nazi Everyman, to encourage him to embrace the thousand-year Reich. . . . How did such exponents of living history . . . suit Carl Becker? What did Becker make of the generous services that, following his prescription without being aware of it, so many professional historians in Germany rendered to Mr. Everyman, when he appeared in the guise of Herr Sturmer? He does not tell us directly; and he did not directly pass judgment on the historians in Nazi Germany, who along with the idea of blood and race gladly accepted from the Nazis the jobs of Jews and liberals who were displaced from university positions.[20]

The association of either Becker or Beard with totalitarianism was so outrageous that it is distasteful to say the charge had "greater justification" in one case than the other. Still, it is noteworthy that in the logic of those who connected totalitarianism with moral and cognitive relativism, Becker seems a more plausible target. He was much more of a moral skeptic than Beard. It was Becker, not Beard, who saw the historian as the relatively passive and acquiescent servant of society's demands. Yet in practice, attacks on Becker were infrequent and mild compared to those directed at Beard. For in Beard's case there was an aggravating circumstance: his opposition to Roosevelt's interventionist foreign policy, which, unlike most other pre–Pearl Harbor isolationists, he continued to express in historical works written during and after the war.

There is no need to concern ourselves here with the details of Beard's views on foreign policy. From the mid-1930s he had voiced concern that Roosevelt would seek escape from domestic economic difficulties through foreign adventure, and that involvement in war would spell the death of democratic institutions in the United States. In 1941, when most liberals were becoming at least reluctant interventionists, Beard testified against Lend Lease, seeing in it a prime symbol of unconstitutional executive aggrandizement. His isolationism produced increasing intellectual

[20]White, *Social Thought in America: The Revolt Against Formalism* (Boston, 1949), 232; Morison, "Faith of a Historian," 268; Bailey to Merle Curti, 17 March 1948, Bailey Papers, SC54/3–32; Hexter, "Carl Becker and Historical Relativism," in his *On Historians* (Cambridge, Mass., 1979), 38–39.

and personal isolation. "I wanted to speak out for peace," he told Matthew Josephson. "But I found that the wrong kind of people were in that camp, while those I like all seem to be on the other side." But Beard stuck to his (opposition to) guns throughout the war, and after the war as well. The principal theme of his two books on Roosevelt's foreign policy was the deception and dissimulation which FDR had employed in "lying" rather than "leading" the country into war.[21]

In the political climate of the forties Beard's stance made him a pariah. He was jeered at meetings of the American Historical Association and the American Political Science Association. Lewis Mumford, earlier a protégé of Beard's, said in a letter to the *Saturday Review of Literature* that Beard "has become a passive—no, active—abetter of tyranny, sadism, and human defilement." Allan Nevins threatened to resign from the National Institute of Arts and Letters when Beard, on the basis of his lifetime work, was made the recipient of an Institute medal. Perhaps the ultimate obloquy was when, after his death, he was, historiographically speaking, turned into an "unperson" à la Orwell. Oscar Handlin, the student of Beard's student Schlesinger, denied that Beard was an historian at all: "he had no students"; "His influence upon subsequent scholarship was slight."[22]

Beard's isolationism had no more logical connection with his relativism than Becker's ardent interventionism had with his. "It doth appear," Beard wrote to a friend, "that if you agree with me on Roosevelt, Hull, Stimson, and Co., you must also approve my views on virgin birth, marginal utility, infant damnation . . . total immersion, transubstantiation, and compensatory financing. Though an exigent old cuss, I make no such demands upon my friends." But Samuel Eliot Morison made a connection which others repeated. "It was not clear to everyone who heard Beard's [AHA presidential] address," Morison wrote, "exactly what he had in mind, but his later [anti-interventionist] works made it transparently clear. They have the same relation to 'Written History as an Act of Faith' as do Adolf Hitler's acts after 1933 to *Mein Kampf*."[23]

---

[21]Josephson, *Infidel in the Temple* (New York, 1967), 413–14.
[22]*Saturday Review* 27 (2 December 1944): 27; for Nevins's threat of resignation, Van Wyck Brooks to Mumford, 1 May 1948, in Robert E. Spiller, ed., *The Van Wyck Brooks-Lewis Mumford Letters* (New York, 1970), 333–34; Handlin, review of Richard Hofstadter, *The Progressive Historians, New York Times*, 17 November 1968, 7:28; Handlin, review of Lee Benson, *Turner and Beard, AHR* 67 (1961): 148.
[23]Beard to George Morgenstern, 12 April 1948, Morgenstern Papers, Box 2; Morison, *By Land and By Sea: Essays and Addresses* (New York, 1954), 328.

II

We have seen how, before World War I, inductivist conceptions of science helped to shape the consciousness of American historians, and, between the wars, the impact of physicists' conceptions of relativity and complementarity on historians' thinking. In the period now under discussion, images of science were not as directly reflected in historiographical thought as they were in these two cases. But in a larger sense, as an important element in the political and cultural climate of the postwar years, conceptions of science had a background influence, overwhelmingly anti-relativist and objectivist, which was of substantial importance. Whereas hitherto I have treated images of science in association with other academic and intellectual currents, in this instance I put it with foreign policy-related issues, for the framework within which science was conceived was often geopolitical. The science of the West was autonomous, empirical, and objective; that of the totalitarians was subordinated to the state, "ideological," and tendentious.

Scientists had long held to the principle that their work must be pursued "autonomously," without subordination to external control or direction. The "lessons of history," from Galileo's confrontation with the Holy Office to the Scopes trial in Tennessee, were that science could only function effectively when nonscientists kept their hands off it. This article of faith came to be challenged during the 1930s, when several leading British scientists, impressed with Soviet direction of scientific work to social ends, and the lavish funding accorded Soviet scientific ventures, began to make invidious comparisons between these practices and the anarchic, poverty-stricken state of British science. In a number of works, of which the best known was J. D. Bernal's *The Social Function of Science*, and in the foundation of a "Division for the Social and International Relations of Science" within the British Association for the Advancement of Science, arguments were advanced stressing the obligations of scientists to the social order, of the social order to science.

The "Social Relations of Science" movement, as it came to be called, was a product of the economic crisis of the 1930s, and of considerable sympathy for the Soviet Union among British scientists, many of whom joined, or worked closely with, the Communist Party. The reaction against that movement, symbolized by the formation of the Society for Freedom in Science in 1941, coincided with, and was part of, the redrawing of the intellectual map into "free" and "totalitarian" realms. Those in the Social Relations of Science movement had criticized the state of science in the capitalist West, denounced conditions in the Fascist regimes as considerably worse, and compared both unfavorably to those which obtained in the Soviet Union. On the contrary, said Michael Polanyi, one of the founders of the Society for Freedom in Science, "scientific thought is . . . nowhere oppressed so comprehensively as in the USSR, and this is due precisely to the fact that the thrust of violence is guided here by Marxism, which is a more intelligent and more complete philosophy of oppression than is either Italian or German Fascism."[24]

Either the subordination of science to ideology, or "mission-oriented" science, as in the totalitarian states, would mean the death of science. Only an autonomous, individualistic science, pursuing truth for its own sake, was faithful to the traditions of science, and would produce a bountiful harvest.

> Bernalism is the doctrine . . . that research workers should be organized in gangs and told what to discover. . . . If once Bernalists get power the fount of discovery will be dried up. If science is left free, incalculable benefits for human welfare, material and mental, will accrue as they have accrued in the past. . . . Geniuses have pursued knowledge for its own sake; and in doing so they have thrown off much that has been of tremendous significance for the practical affairs of mankind. . . . There is room for all in science. Let the gangsters work always in gangs and order one another about and improve whatever it may be that they tell one another to improve. . . . Let there be freedom, nevertheless, for those who lack the gang instinct but possess that insatiable curiosity sneered at by Bernalists as puerile, which is the source of all real advance in science.[25]

"Laissez-faire" opposition to the coordination and mobilization of science was being rendered anachronistic at the very moment it was being voiced. During World War II, and permanently thereafter, "gangster science"—highly organized, mission-oriented research—became the dominant mode of scientific organization. The old mystique of the autonomous, individualistic scientist increasingly became an arcadian fantasy, though it continued to be invoked as an ideal, used rhetorically to bargain for greater scientific influence on the direction of government spending, and advanced as an argument for the greater long-run payoff of pure research. But if opposition to planning in science declined, the distinction between free and totalitarian science became a major theme in cultural politics. The Society for Freedom in Science was transformed into a

---

[24]"The Rights and Duties of Science" (1939), reprinted in Polanyi, *The Contempt of Freedom: The Russian Experiment and After* (London, 1940), 21.
[25]John R. Baker (another founder of the SFS), "Counterblast to Bernalism," *New Statesman and Nation* N.S. 18 (29 July 1939): 174.

subcommittee of the CIA-financed Congress for Cultural Freedom, which in 1953 sponsored an elaborate international meeting on "Science and Freedom" with a star-studded list of participants. The Lysenko affair in the Soviet Union—in which ideological and bureaucratic control of genetics had consequences which were not just dysfunctional but murderous—became, for Western propagandists, the archetype of science under totalitarianism.

After the launching of the first Soviet space satellite in 1957, the proposition that "totalitarian science" was technically inferior to "free science" became harder to sustain. By the 1960s, for this reason among others, the invidious comparison of Western and Soviet science had ceased to be a dominant theme in cold war polemics. But for most of the 1940s and 1950s, it had great resonance and was used to establish the disinterested search for objective truth as the distinctive epistemological posture of the Free World.

This overall framework shaped, to varying degrees, the emerging subdisciplines of history, sociology, and philosophy of science. This was particularly clear with history of science. As of the early 1930s history of science was still largely the avocational pursuit of scientists, done in their spare time or in retirement. Whether in the hands of scientists, or the handful of historical scholars who pursued it, the field had taken for granted a purely internalist approach. Science was conceived as a self-contained activity, considered without reference to the surrounding material or cultural environment.

This consensual orthodoxy received a sharp challenge at the 1931 meeting of the International Congress of the History of Science and Technology, when, unexpectedly, a large Soviet delegation appeared, headed by the leading Bolshevik theoretician, Nicolai Bukharin. The *succès de scandale* of the 1931 congress was Boris Hessen's "Social and Economic Roots of Newton's 'Principia,'" a rather crude and reductionist materialist account which stressed the needs of developing English capitalism in explaining the emergence of Newton's mechanics. Hessen's paper, together with the other Soviet contributions, was widely circulated in an inexpensive edition immediately following the congress.[26]

Hessen's externalist and materialist approach was seen, by friends and foes alike, as the historiographical equivalent of the policy orientation of the scientists on the left. Where they were arguing that science should respond to social needs, Hessen maintained that it was historically the case that science had responded to those needs. The normative and the

[26]*Science at the Crossroads* (London, 1931).

descriptive became linked. Those on the scientific left turned to an externalist view of the scientific past; those hostile to proposals for the social control of science in the present denied that external factors had played any positive role in its past.

Internalism in the history of science became not just a method, but a fighting faith. At his speech to the opening session of the Congress for Cultural Freedom meeting on "Science and Freedom" in 1953, Polanyi listed the externalist approach as the first of the pernicious Marxist views of science which had to be combated. A considerable amount of academic energy was devoted to refuting what David Joravsky termed Hessen's "notorious" paper. "For several decades," writes Stephen Toulmin, "Hessen's paper served as an object lesson to scare younger scholars in the history of science away from social questions." To raise these questions was implicitly to question the austere and autonomous objectivity of the scientific venture. History of science in the United States remained deeply committed to internalism. As late as 1964, when Everett Mendelsohn began to publish papers on the social context of science, he felt "very much alone." The most highly regarded American work in the history of science during the postwar years described its progress as the advance of one field after another up to and across *The Edge of Objectivity.*[27]

Sociology of science was an even newer venture than history of science. Robert K. Merton, who began to publish on this subject in the late 1930s, was, for all practical purposes, the founder of the field. From the outset, his work was dominated by the "Free World versus totalitarianism" framework. In a 1938 paper, in which he first sketched his famous model of the fundamental norms of science, he repeatedly stressed the basic conflicts between totalitarianism and "the traditional assumptions of modern Western science." In the classic (1942) formulation of the Mertonian norms (universalism, commun[al]ism, disinterestedness, organized skepticism), he likewise emphasized their congeniality to a liberal-democratic society; their incompatibility with totalitarianism.[28]

---

[27]Polanyi, in *Science and Freedom: The Proceedings of a Conference Convened by the Congress for Cultural Freedom and Held in Hamburg on July 23rd-26th, 1953* (London, 1955), 36; Joravsky, *Soviet Marxism and Natural Science, 1917–1932* (New York, 1961), 185; Toulmin, "From Form to Function: Philosophy and History of Science in the 1950s and Now," *Daedalus* 106 (1977): 150; Mendelsohn quoted in Toulmin, 149; Charles Coulson Gillispie, *The Edge of Objectivity: An Essay in the History of Scientific Ideas* (Princeton, 1960).

[28]"Science and the Social Order," 260; "Science and Technology in a Democratic Order," *Journal of Legal and Political Sociology* 1 (1942), revised version in his *Social Theory and Social Structure* (Glencoe, Ill., 1949), 271. In the original versions of Merton's papers, though totalitarianism in general was invoked, and there were veiled allusions to the

The association between the values of disinterested, objective science and the liberal polity was continued in the work of sociologists of the Merton school such as Bernard Barber. He found a "relatively great congruence" between American liberal society and the environment which was ideal-typical for the advancement of science. The Nazi and Soviet cases demonstrated, negatively, "how necessary for modern science is the whole constellation of cultural values and social structural conditions that we have included in our 'ideal type.'" It was a view that had already become a commonplace in cold war culture. "Scholarly inquiry and the American tradition go hand in hand," said Harvard president James B. Conant. "Specifically, science and the assumptions behind our politics are compatible; in the Soviet Union, by contrast, the tradition of science is diametrically opposed to the official philosophy of the realm."[29]

One of the most striking aspects of sociology of science before the 1960s was its scrupulous, almost phobic, avoidance of any sociologically informed discussion of the content of science. Just as historians of science, who concentrated exclusively on the content of science, shunned the social dimension, sociologists of science avoided content. Sociology of science addressed itself to the ethical norms of the scientific venture, the internal social relations of science (productivity, reward systems, measures of influence), but, except for the repeated discrimination between Free World and totalitarian science, not to relations between science and society. In the conventional sociological wisdom of the day, external influence on science could only be malignant. One might grant that philosophy, theology, or ideology had from time to time intruded into the scientific realm, but the result was invariably a violation of scientific norms, and bad science. There could be a sociology of scientific error, but no sociology of scientific truth. To believe otherwise was to embrace the "radical relativism" Merton excoriated.

Most philosophers of science were less caught up in the epistemological politics of the cold war than were the historians and sociologists of science. Their objectivism stemmed from their positivistic commitment to a view of science as consisting entirely of claims about matters of fact. Scientific disputes were seen as essentially disputes about the facts, resolvable by appeals to evidence, according to rules of inference which the philosophers devoted themselves to explicating. Philosophical orthodoxy

USSR, the explicit negative examples were Nazi; when the 1942 paper was republished in 1949, specific reference to Soviet practices was added.
[29]Barber, *Science and the Social Order* (Glencoe, Ill., 1952), 110; Conant, "Scholarly Inquiry and the American Tradition," *Educational Record* 31 (1950): 282.

in this period radically disjoined the context of discovery, which defied logical analysis, from the formal context of justification. Any concern with the former led one into the swamps of "psychologism" or "sociologism"; the bottomless pit of "the genetic fallacy."

If, compared with the historians and sociologists, most philosophers of science in this period were relatively little influenced by contemporary political struggles, this was not at all true of the most important of them, Karl Popper. A powerful and original thinker, he was termed by one of his distinguished admirers, "incomparably the greatest philosopher of science that has ever been." That is as may be, but his was unquestionably the most influential voice in postwar discussions in the field. Whereas historians of science and sociologists of science turned to the project of distinguishing the science of the West from that of the totalitarians only in the 1930s, for Popper, a "life-long revulsion" toward Marxism, and dedication to exposing its unscientific character, dated from the Vienna of 1919, when he was sixteen years old. Certainly one cannot reduce Popper's philosophy to his struggle against Marxism, but that concern permeated all his work—and was highly relevant to the enthusiasm with which his writings were received in the West after 1945.[30]

Most readers outside the community of the philosophy of science first encountered Popper's epistemology imbedded in his widely read and discussed anti-Marxist volumes *The Poverty of Historicism* and *The Open Society and Its Enemies.* They represented what he called "my war effort." He explained in his autobiography that he was concerned that "freedom might become a central problem again, especially under the renewed influence of Marxism and the idea of large-scale 'planning'; and so these books were meant as a defence of freedom against totalitarian and authoritarian ideas, and as a warning against the dangers of historicist superstitions. . . . Both grew out of the theory of knowledge of [my 1934] *Logik der Forschung.*"[31]

---

[30]Sir Peter Medawar, quoted in W. W. Bartley, III, "A Popperian Harvest," in Paul Levinson, ed., *In Pursuit of Truth: Essays on the Philosophy of Karl Popper on the Occasion of His 80th Birthday* (Atlantic Highlands, N.J., 1982), 268; "Autobiography of Karl Popper," in Paul A. Schilpp, ed., *The Philosophy of Karl Popper* (2 vols., La Salle, Ill., 1974), 1:25.

[31]"Autobiography," 1:91. *Logik der Forschung*, Popper's major epistemological work, was translated into English as *The Logic of Scientific Discovery* (New York, 1959). *Poverty* first appeared in *Economica* 11 (1944) and 12 (1945), and was only published in book form in 1957; *The Open Society* was first published in London in 1945 in two volumes, and went through several editions. My citations to the former are from the third revised edition (New York, 1961); to the latter, from the fourth revised edition (2 vols., London, 1962). The historicism against which Popper inveighed was not the German *historismus* which writers in recent decades have translated as "historicism." "Historicism," in Popper's usage, was a neologism for any theory (ancient, medieval, or modern) which pur-

Popper's position on scientific epistemology was thoroughgoingly objectivist. He held unswervingly to a strong version (Tarski's) of the correspondence theory of truth; he never let slide an opportunity to denounce "subjectivist" interpretations of physics, "relativism" in any form, the "myth of the framework," or any attempt to "sociologize" knowledge. Though absolute certainty would always prove elusive, the closer and closer approximation of the objective truth about nature was to be found through the refinement of theory by "conjecture and refutation." Like the logical positivists of the Vienna Circle, with whom he was often confused, Popper was concerned to establish a demarcation criterion between "scientific" and "metaphysical" propositions. But whereas for the logical positivists, the verifiability of a proposition was the hallmark of its scientific status, for Popper the key was its "falsifiability." A theory was scientific only if, and to the extent that, one could specify the evidence which would falsify it; its truth was established insofar as it successfully resisted attempts at falsification.

Popper's principal technical concern in the half century following the publication of *Logik der Forschung* was the elaboration and refinement of his demarcation criterion, a venture few historians followed closely. A line of thought which attracted much more attention among historians, and the intelligentsia generally, was developed in *The Open Society and Its Enemies*. The "enemies" were "ideologies" which had had a "persistent and pernicious influence ⋮ . . from Heraclitus and Plato to Hegel and Marx." The assault on ideology was the obverse of the celebration of scientific modes of thought. Science and scholarship in the Free World could achieve objectivity, and mark themselves off from the totalitarians, by rigorously excluding the ideological.[32]

The denigration of ideology, one of the most characteristic features of American culture in the cold war era, was directly related to the celebration of objectivity as the hallmark of thought in the Free World. Indeed, the two terms defined each other. "The essential criteria of an ideology," wrote Talcott Parsons, "are deviations from scientific objectivity." For another commentator, thought related to "the *facts* of reality" was "like a pure stream, crystal-clear, transparent; ideological ideas [are] like a dirty river, muddied and polluted by the impurities that have flooded into it."[33]

ported to predict the future course of history; of any "lawlike" historical social science; more broadly, for any social outlook which aspired to more than "piecemeal social engineering."

[32]*Poverty*, viii.

[33]Parsons, "An Approach to the Sociology of Knowledge," *Transactions of the Fourth World Congress of Sociology* (Milan, 1959), 25; Werner Stark, *The Sociology of Knowledge* (London, 1958), 90–91.

The academic analysis of the malignancies of ideology fell more into the preserve of sociologists than that of historians. It was sociologists— Daniel Bell, Seymour Martin Lipset, and Edward Shils—who were most prominent in the proclamation, which was both descriptive and normative, of "The End of Ideology in the West." But historians were by no means in the rear guard. H. Stuart Hughes produced the first scholarly analysis of "the end of ideology," and his fellow historians participated actively in the disparagement of "ideological" thought. "Totalitarianism is ideology . . . ," wrote Jacques Barzun. "Democracy of the American brand is anti-ideology." "Isms," a colloquial equivalent for ideologies, had no place in academic discourse, according to Arthur Schlesinger, Jr. Words like "capitalism," he said, "belong to the vocabulary of demagoguery, not to the vocabulary of analysis." Echoing a theme which became dominant in American historiography during the 1950s, he explained that "the most vital" American thought had been "empirical." He made a sharp distinction between the ideals and the ideology of Jeffersonianism, and explained that "Fortunately, Jefferson himself preferred his ideals to his ideology. . . . The true Jefferson is not the ideological Jefferson."

The ideologist contends that the mysteries of history can be understood in terms of a clear-cut, absolute, social creed which explains the past and forecasts the future. . . . The history of the twentieth century is a record of the manifold ways in which humanity has been betrayed by ideology. . . .   Surely the basic conflict of our times, the world civil war of our own day, is precisely the conflict . . . between ideology and democracy.[34]

The disparagement of ideology and the concomitant celebration of American empiricism were among the forces which in the postwar years returned historiographical thought in the United States to older norms of objectivity. Though they had rarely used the word "ideology," the relativists' central argument was that historiography was inevitably ideological. The attack on ideology in scholarship and in society—on the sociology of knowledge, on "the myth of the framework"—struck at the basis of the relativist position. It helped to relegitimize that powerful factualist current in American historiography, that horror of preconceived notions, which the interwar relativists had challenged but never defeated.

The crusade against ideologies and ideological scholarship had other consequences for historiography. The principal function of the assault on

[34]Hughes, "The End of Political Ideology," *Measure* 2 (Spring 1951); Barzun, *God's Country and Mine* (Boston, 1954), 90–91; Schlesinger, "The One Against the Many," in Schlesinger and Morton White, eds., *Paths of American Thought* (Boston, 1963), 533–37.

ideologies was to spread an apolitical umbrella over an attack whose specific target was Marxism. Historians participated wholeheartedly in that attack. Marxism was uniformly equated with economic determinism of the crudest sort. Bemoaning the decline of biography, John A. Garraty laid some of the blame at Marx's doorstep: "If man was a mere pawn, helpless before the sweep of a relentlessly evolving universe, or a selfish animal motivated only by his material interests, he was scarcely worth careful study in all the loving detail required of biographers." Marx's insights, Page Smith explained, were "achieved at the price of uncritical devotion to an 'outside' ideology" which produced gross distortions. "Psychotics," he added, "have insights which are inaccessible to normal people." Probably the most visible effect of anti-ideological currents on historiography was the development of a school of interpretation for which the consistently unideological nature of American thought was the key to the nation's greatness: the "hallmark of a decent, free, and God-fearing society."[35]

In Mannheim's classic work he had distinguished between (legitimizing) "ideologies," which served the interests of the powers that be, and (delegitimizing) "utopias," which a later generation would term "oppositional ideologies." The denial that dominant thoughtways were ideological, that they were other than the plainest common sense, was, in Mannheim's view, the greatest strength of ideologies—the key move in the subordination of intellect to power. Postwar historians' insistence that their work was free of ideological taint provided a textbook illustration of the truth of Mannheim's assertion.

III

"Intellect has associated itself with power as perhaps never before in history," Lionel Trilling observed in 1952. With the exceptions of physics, it would be difficult to think of any academic discipline which, during World War II and the cold war, participated more wholeheartedly in that association than did history. The association took various forms, and although by no means all historians were directly involved, a great many were, and they came disproportionately from the elite of the profession. Some worked full-time for government agencies, others part-time or off

---

[35]Garraty, *The Nature of Biography* (New York, 1957), 109; Smith, *The Historian and History* (New York, 1964), 157; Daniel J. Boorstin, *The Genius of American Politics* (Chicago, 1953), 3–4. The "consensus" school of American historians, of which Boorstin was the most extreme representative, is discussed in Chapter 11.

and on; many more shaped their work in ways which contributed, directly or indirectly, to national mobilization.[36]

There is a sharp contrast between the mobilization of historians in 1917 and in 1941. In the former case the experience was extremely brief, well under two years. In the latter case, the involvement often extended for twenty or more years. Whereas in World War I the net effect of involvement with national mobilization was to raise questions about historical objectivity, in World War II and the cold war the consequence of involvement, although not without its ambivalences, on the whole sustained and reinforced the ideal.

In 1941–45 the war effort made little use of historians in a propagandistic capacity. The issues of the war appeared so straightforward, the support for the crusade against the Axis was so consensual, that the Allied cause needed no legitimation from historical propagandists. (In part reacting against inflated atrocity propaganda in World War I, Allied publicists in World War II systematically understated the horrors being committed by the Nazi regime.) The only activity the AHA undertook which was at all analogous to that of the World War I National Board for Historical Service was the preparation of pamphlets for servicemen: "Can War Marriages Be Made to Work?" "Shall I Buy a Farm?" and "Do You Want Your Wife to Work After the War?"

Some historians worked during the war, and thereafter, as official historians, most notably Samuel Eliot Morison, who rose to the rank of rear admiral as author of the multivolume *History of United States Naval Operations in World War II*. But by far the most significant wartime occupation for historians was intelligence analysis for the Office of Strategic Services. William Langer of Harvard, who headed the OSS research and analysis branch, scoured Ivy League history departments (and, in a pinch, those from below the salt) for scholars with useful expertise. After the war, OSS veterans were an elite cohort. Leonard Krieger, writing in the early 1960s, called them "the one identifiable cohesive group among the American historians of Europe today." Fritz Stern wrote that those like himself who missed this "almost legendary experience" regretted that there was "no 'moral equivalent' to the OSS in peacetime."[37]

Whether historians worked for the OSS, for the State Department, or for one or another branch of the military, their wartime labors, unlike

[36]Trilling, contribution to symposium "Our Country and Our Culture," *Partisan Review* 19 (1952): 319–20.
[37]Krieger, "European History in America," in John Higham et al., *History* (Princeton, 1965), 291; Stern, "Europe's Past and America's Experience," *New York Times Book Review*, 24 October 1965, 3.

those of the previous generation in World War I, involved neither pangs of professional conscience, nor retrospective regret. Whereas in World War I the most "useful" history was that which was most outrageously slanted, in World War II it was the historian's capacity for "detachment" and "objectivity," a willingness to voice unpleasant truths, that was most serviceable. (Thus Carl Becker's famed skeptical detachment was a positive contribution to the war effort, when, asked to advise the Pentagon, he cautioned against accepting grandiose Air Corps claims that their bombing would break German morale.) National service in an analytic, rather than a propagandistic capacity, underwrote, rather than undermined, the ideal of objectivity. One of the many meanings of objectivity, more properly, one of the strategies which gives it meaning, is what Alvin Gouldner has called "normative objectification." Thus the physician is not less objective because of his or her commitment to the patient and against the germ. Medical objectivity could be said to rest on the explicitness of this value commitment, which constrains the physician to observe and report things about the patient's condition that neither may want to know. From the early forties through the early sixties the normative objectification implicit in the consensual acceptance of the Free World vs. Totalitarianism framework was the guarantor of the objectivity of scholarly labors against the totalitarians.[38]

The OSS experience represented the first wholesale involvement of historians with the foreign policy establishment, but it was by no means the last. After V-J day most historians returned to civilian pursuits, where the OSS old school tie gave them a certain cachet. But many stayed on. H. Stuart Hughes, who had risen to the rank of lieutenant colonel in the OSS, moved over to the State Department, which, in addition to employing historians as analysts, for several years regularly enlisted prominent historians for a tour as cultural attachés. Other OSS veterans, like Sherman Kent of Yale, signed on with its successor, the Central Intelligence Agency. Some historians, like Kent, Raymond J. Sontag, James Billington, and Joseph Strayer, had long-standing connections with "the Agency." Some, like Langer and Robert F. Byrnes, were given leave from their universities to serve temporarily. Many more participated as consultants, or participants in the monthly conferences at Princeton, organized by Sontag, at which CIA estimates were reviewed. (There was, in fact, criticism within the CIA concerning what some considered the overrepresentation of historians within its ranks.)[39]

---

[38]Gouldner, "The Sociologist as Partisan," *American Sociologist* 3 (1968): 113–14.
[39]Sontag to Samuel Flagg Bemis, 14 May 1952, Bemis Papers, Box 35; "Report of the [Yale] History Department for 1956–57," Griswold Presidential Papers, Box 31; Bemis to K. C.

304   *Objectivity reconstructed*

Though the CIA made something of a fetish of keeping the identity of its analysts and consultants secret, to those involved, and to their colleagues, who, inevitably, usually knew of the association, their work seemed completely continuous with wartime OSS service, as indeed it was. It was likewise with other forms of historians' involvement with various components of the national security and foreign policy apparatus: Arthur Schlesinger, Jr.'s work with the Economic Cooperation Administration and Mutual Security Administration, Ernest May's service with the Joint Chiefs of Staff, Gordon Wright's tour of duty with the National War College. Older notions of an adversarial posture between intellect and power were abandoned as "immature." In 1967, twenty years after publishing his iconoclastic *American Political Tradition*, Richard Hofstadter, one of the few young historians not mobilized during World War II, apologized for the book's being written "from the personal perspective of a young man who has only a limited capacity for identifying with those who exercise power."⁴⁰

It was by no means the case that wartime or later government service inevitably led to an uncritical attitude toward American policy. Hughes, for example, shortly after leaving the State Department, was for a time a supporter of Henry Wallace's presidential campaign. But overall there can be little doubt that the experience of government service produced a substantial shift in historians' "capacity for identifying with those who exercise power": a step forward for empathy; a step backward for critical distance.⁴¹

Cole, 2 December 1953, Bemis Papers, Box 36; William H. Dunham, Jr. to A. Whitney Griswold, 1 November 1954, Griswold Presidential Papers, Box 31.
⁴⁰Preface to 1967 Hebrew edition of *The American Political Tradition*, reprinted in the American reedition (New York, 1973), xxv-xxvi. In the interim Hofstadter had argued repeatedly for the mutual benefits to be derived from the association of intellectuals with government. ("A Note on Intellect and Power," *American Scholar* 30 [1961]: 588–98; *Anti-intellectualism in American Life* [New York, 1963], 393–432.)
⁴¹The most extreme case of the permanently engaged postwar historian is that of Arthur Schlesinger, Jr., who capped his career of government service with his term on the White House staff, which was followed by his massive works on the Kennedy administration and on Robert F. Kennedy. With unconscious irony, Schlesinger wrote to Max Lerner: "I have been writing about the Kennedy administration precisely as I have written in the past about the Roosevelt and Jackson administrations." (Letter of 5 August 1965, Lerner Papers, 7–361Y.) In 1966, after the resignation of Eric Goldman, who succeeded Schlesinger as White House historian-in-residence, there was discussion within the Organization of American Historians of the importance of keeping an historian at the White House. According to Martin Ridge, managing editor of the *Journal of American History*, Goldman's resignation meant that "the profession stood to lose not only an eye and an ear in the White House, but also some status." Ridge urged a procedure by which the OAH would secure the right to nominate White House historians. (Ridge to Thomas Cochran, 12 December 1966, Cochran Papers, 6–21.)

Scholars could work to further American foreign policy through private scholarship as well as through public service. Not surprisingly, it was the community of diplomatic historians who contributed most wholeheartedly and directly to the support and defense of the American cause in the cold war. These scholars' principal contribution was providing a version of recent history which would justify current policy, linking America's struggles with the Axis and with the Soviet Union as successive stages in one continuous and unavoidable struggle of the Free World against expansionist totalitarians.

It is not always easy to distinguish between official and unofficial scholarship in this area, as historians moved in and out of government service. In the early 1950s William L. Langer and S. Everett Gleason produced a massive two-volume history of American entry into World War II, avowedly "calculated to offset any debunking of War aims and policies," and to chronicle "the tortured emergence of the United States of America as leader of the forces of light in a world struggle which even today has scarcely abated and is still undecided." The two men's labors were funded by the Rockefeller Foundation, and they worked under the sponsorship of the Council on Foreign Relations. They stressed in the preface to the first volume that "No one, in the State Department or elsewhere, has made the slightest effort to influence our views or to shade our conclusions. This book is in no sense an official or even a semi-official account." But they received privileged access to material denied other scholars, and while writing it, Langer was director of research of the CIA, and Gleason was deputy executive secretary of the National Security Council.[42]

During the late 1940s the primary political concern of diplomatic historians was to replace "naive optimism" about Soviet-American relations with a bleaker, more "realistic" perspective. Thomas A. Bailey, seeking

[42] Langer, *In and Out of the Ivory Tower* (New York, 1977), 209; Langer and Gleason, *The Challenge to Isolation, 1937–1940* (New York, 1952), xiv; *The Undeclared War, 1940–1941* (New York, 1953), xvi. A few years earlier, at the suggestion of Secretary of State Cordell Hull, Langer had written a defense of Roosevelt's controversial policy of wartime cooperation with the Vichy regime. Like the later volumes, it was written largely in his spare time while in government service, and on the basis of documents not available to other scholars. In this instance as well, Langer insisted that he was serving as "a dispassionate scholar, not as an apologist"; that no one in the government had "ever attempted to sway my conclusions or in any way to influence my work." (*Our Vichy Gamble* [New York, 1947], vii, ix.) For another view, see Louis Gottschalk, "Our Vichy Fumble," *Journal of Modern History* 20 (1948): 47–56. Special access to materials not otherwise available was frequently extended to those who were well connected and could be depended upon to use the data in question with discretion. (See Ernest May to Thomas A. Bailey, 2 April 1954, Bailey Papers, SC54/4–30; McGeorge Bundy to Herbert Feis, 8 March 1965, Feis Papers, Box 12.)

to persuade his publisher that there was a large potential market for his *America Faces Russia,* pointed out that the only other work in the field was inappropriate for the 1949 market since it was written "in an entirely different climate of opinion . . . when we were entertaining wishful thoughts about our wartime ally." "God forbid," Bailey concluded, "that the present cold war should develop into a shooting one, but if it does, I suspect that my book would be widely used in the armed services for indoctrination purposes."[43]

But by the 1950s the hesitations of the left were less troublesome for the foreign policy establishment than the belligerence of the right—the Taft-MacArthur wing of the Republican Party, and its bullyboy, Senator Joseph R. McCarthy. In 1954, at the height of the cold war, Raymond J. Sontag, who moved back and forth between the academy and the CIA, observed that there could be no domestic tranquillity until Americans reached substantial agreement on the foreign policy decisions of late 1944 and early 1945. "In those months the United States attained a peak of strength unparalleled in our history, and the decisions were made which were to place our country, and the Free World, in the mortal peril which continues to this day. The half-conscious groping of the American people for an explanation of this precipitous decline lies back of the darker side of American political life today." Sontag was willing to concede that Roosevelt and Truman had a somewhat "blurred" perception of Communism and Soviet policy at the end of World War II, but his principal concern was that historians establish the absurdity of charges of treason "so far at least as the leading characters are concerned."[44]

Textbooks in American diplomatic history were vehicles for exhortations on the necessity of an activist foreign policy. Julius Pratt's *History of United States Foreign Policy* concluded with the observation that the paramount question of the day was whether "the United States could successfully fill the role of leader in the struggle with Communist imperialism." Bailey ended his *Diplomatic History of the American People* by chastising some of his fellow citizens: "Not all Americans are bearing their new burdens cheerfully and responsibly. Not all of them are prepared to recognize that their very way of life is jeopardized by the Communist menace. Many are grumbling over defense expenditures, not realizing that to Moscow the most eloquent language is that of force. Many are blindly determined to have business as usual, profits as usual,

---

[43]Letter to Edward C. Aswell, vice-president of McGraw-Hill, 3 June 1949, Bailey Papers, SC54/4–2.
[44]"The Democracies and the Dictators Since 1933," *Proceedings of the American Philosophical Society* 98 (1954): 313, 315.

Cadillacs as usual." Other diplomatic historians went farther in their concern that the American people were not rising to the Communist challenge. In his presidential address to the AHA, Samuel Flagg Bemis said:

Have not our social studies been tending overmuch to self-study—to what is the matter with us rather than to perils and strengths that test our liberty? Too much self-study, too much self-criticism is weakening to a people as it is to an individual. There is such a thing as a national neurosis. A great people's culture . . . begins to decay when it commences to examine itself. . . . In self-study and self-indulgence we have been losing sight of our national purpose. . . . During the letdown of the last fifteen years we have been experiencing the world crisis from soft seats of comfort, debauched by mass media of sight and sound, pandering for selfish profit to the lowest level of our easy appetites, fed full of toys and gewgaws, our military preparedness held back by insidious strikes for less work and more pay, our manpower softened in will and body in a climate of amusement. Massive self-indulgence and massive responsibility do not go together. A great nation cannot work less and get more, with fun for all, in today's stern posture of power. How can our lazy social dalliance and crooning softness compete with the stern discipline and tyrannical compulsion of subject peoples that strengthen the aggressive sinews of our malignant antagonist?[45]

Whereas prewar historical treatments of turn-of-the-century imperialism had usually been highly critical, after 1945 the Spanish-American War, the taking of the Philippines, the Open Door, and the activities of Theodore Roosevelt received more sympathetic treatment, insofar as these demonstrated that American policymakers, though not yet the American people, were awakening to "the responsibilities of world power." Foster Rhea Dulles, a leading diplomatic historian, and cousin of the Secretary of State, reported sorrowfully that around 1900 the populace "developed . . . doubts and misgivings as to whether the nation had set out on the right course."

The American people became confused and uncertain. . . . They were still reluctant to accept the responsibilities and obligations inescapably inherent in the country's new position of strength and power. In spite of the appeals of Theodore Roosevelt, they remained highly dubious of his thesis that American politics had become world politics. . . . Only the dreadful experience of . . . two world wars was able to drive home the lessons that had not been learned in the opening years of the century. . . . Popular attitudes in the 1890s and early 1900s . . . have an

[45]Pratt, *A History of United States Foreign Policy* (New York, 1954), 780; Bailey, *A Diplomatic History of the American People* (rev. ed., New York, 1955), 852–53; Bemis, "American Foreign Policy and the Blessings of Liberty," *AHR* 67 (1962), 291–92, 304–5.

unexpected relevancy for a day in which the United States has assumed the obligations and made the commitments it so long refused.

Historians were unanimous in endorsing the broadest executive prerogatives in foreign policy, against foot-dragging legislators and a benighted populace. Bailey cheerfully acknowledged that "Franklin Roosevelt repeatedly deceived the American people during the period before Pearl Harbor," but explained that "because the masses are notoriously shortsighted and generally cannot see danger until it is at their throats, our statesmen are forced to deceive them into an awareness of their own longrun interests."[46]

Diplomatic historians believed their most urgent task to be combating the vestiges of isolationism, a phenomenon they frequently discussed as a form of psychopathology. In particular, historians dedicated themselves to holding the line against "revisionism," the carrier of the deadly isolationist virus. Revisionism with respect to World War I, wrote Dexter Perkins, had encouraged Germany and Japan to believe that they could "count on the indifference of the United States to the realization of their nefarious ambitions. A revisionist theory of World War II might well have the same result. It suggests that we can be secure if we abdicate our role as a world power; it suggests that we can and ought to watch the growth of a new totalitarianism without apprehension, without ever reacting emotionally against it. . . . Behind revisionism often lies the spectre of appeasement."[47]

The World War II revisionism, which Perkins feared might lead to a revival of isolationism and appeasement, never became a significant current in postwar historiography. The indefatigable Harry Elmer Barnes produced a stream of pamphlets denouncing the "historical blackout" by which professional academics conspired to hide the truth about Roosevelt's perfidy, and he served as recruiter and paymaster for wealthy patrons who covertly subsidized revisionist scholarship. The fruits of his brokerage were meager: a study of Henry Stimson by Richard Current which Barnes found insufficiently hostile; broken promises from historians like William B. Hesseltine, who accepted funds from Barnes to produce a muckraking study of Cordell Hull, but never delivered.[48]

---

[46]Dulles, *The Imperial Years* (New York, 1956), vii–ix; Bailey, *The Man in the Street* (New York, 1948), 11, 13. Commenting on this passage more than thirty years later, and with particular reference to the secret bombing of Cambodia, Bailey wrote in his memoirs that he did "not want to be thought to say that the people ought in all cases or even most cases to be deceived." (*The American Pageant Revisited* [Stanford, 1982], 167.)

[47]"American Wars and Critical Historians," *Yale Review* 40 (1951): 694–95.

[48]Barnes's principal angel was John W. Blodgett, Jr., a millionaire Oregon lumberman. Current's *Secretary Stimson: A Study in Statecraft* was dedicated to "J.W.B., Jr.," but

Barnes had always been, somewhat vaguely, a man of the left, but after the war his only support came from Roosevelt-haters on the extreme right. His crusade was hailed by William F. Buckley, Jr., who denounced "the intellectuals [who] have banded together to short-circuit any attempt by a truth-seeker to reveal the truth," but few outside of Buckley's Mc-Carthyite orbit expressed any interest in the movement. Whereas in the twenties Barnes's revisionism had attracted substantial support among academic historians, by the fifties he was a professional pariah. In part this was a result of his boisterous polemical style, which had not moderated since his earlier exchanges with Bernadotte Schmitt, but it was in equal measure a reflection of the tenacity with which post-World War II historians held to the axioms of what they called "internationalism"— what Barnes and a later generation termed "globalism." Revisionist history, Dexter Perkins maintained, unlike most orthodox history, was not "dictated by a pure and disinterested search for truth." Refereeing a revisionist manuscript for the *AHR*, Perkins wrote that "such history rests upon the assumption that our entry into the war was a mistake. . . . this proposition is—and must be—a highly subjective one." Neither Perkins nor any of his colleagues ever questioned the objectivity of the opposite assumption.[49]

Other forms of academic work which had no direct connection with government agencies were often oriented to the needs of national security. Particularly noteworthy were the proliferating area studies programs and institutes which sprang up after the war, and were largely devoted to training students for government service. In 1942 the sinologist John K. Fairbank, then with the OSS, wrote back to the Harvard

contains no acknowledgment of financial assistance. For correspondence between Current and Barnes concerning the grant from Blodgett, see Barnes Papers, Boxes 34, 37–41. Barnes initially kept Blodgett's identity secret from Hesseltine, and funneled the money through the Foundation for Foreign Affairs, headed by the right-wing publisher Henry Regnery. Hesseltine wrote Barnes on 26 August 1948: "Thank you for your assurances that the sponsor is a 100% American whose money is relatively untainted. I can readily believe that it's at least as untainted as a publisher's advance or a foundation's grant-in-aid! And, of course, you understand that I shall undertake this work with absolutely no preconceptions or prejudices and I shall let the chips fall where they may. If my investigations convince me that Cordell Hull was an honest man, a true patriot, and a statesman who contributed his bit towards leading us into a just and righteous war, I'll certainly say so. If I do, of course, I'll have to eat a lot of my own words for the past ten years. And, it follows naturally, if my researches convince me that he was a stuffed shirt, a fraud, a sycophant, and a highly-overrated politician and war-monger, I'll say that as vigorously as I can." (Barnes Papers, Box 34.) Barnes's subsequent efforts to get Hesseltine to return the moneys advanced to him were unavailing.
[49]Buckley, "The Colossal Flunk," *American Mercury* 74 (March 1952): 35–36; Perkins, "Was Roosevelt Wrong?" *Virginia Quarterly Review* 30 (1954): 372; Perkins to Boyd Shafer, 21 December 1955, AHA Papers, Box 495.

History Department urging the expansion of Asian studies after the war, on the grounds that "we must expect this country to assume responsibilities in Asia, particularly in the matter of supplying trained personnel for administrative purposes there." The Russian Research Center at Harvard and Columbia's Russian Institute were modeled after the OSS research and analysis branch, and OSS historians played a central role in setting them up. Such institutes and area studies programs, concentrating on portions of the globe deemed strategic, multiplied in the late forties and fifties, together with programs in "International Affairs," "Defense Studies," and the like.[50]

Private philanthropic organizations like the Rockefeller Foundation and Carnegie Corporation provided initial funding for most of these ventures until, as the academic cold war became institutionalized, a program of official government grants became established, mostly under one or another "national defense" rubric. By 1950 twenty-nine integrated area studies programs had been established in American universities, involving five hundred faculty members; by 1965 there were 153 such programs, with a total faculty of close to four thousand. In the cold war years one would have been hard-pressed to find scholars who would acknowledge publicly, or perhaps even to themselves, that there was anything less than objective about the "normatively objectified," mission-oriented scholarship of these programs.[51]

The influence of the Free World versus totalitarianism framework on Europeanists was not limited to those working in cold war–initiated institutes or area studies programs. In every field there was work which gave the appearance of having been carried out in serene isolation from contemporary currents, but the influence of the dominant framework was very widespread. Surveying postwar scholarship in modern European history, Leonard Krieger saw a "large-scale shift of attention to the history of the totalitarian 'enemy'" as one of the defining characteristics of the field. Russian history had barely existed as a field before the war; after 1945 it grew more rapidly than any other. Whereas before 1939 most historians of western continental Europe had specialized in France, after the war "the German problem" absorbed the attention of those who were to become the most influential Europeanists of their generation. Krieger, Carl Schorske, and Peter Gay launched their careers with works which explored why German liberalism and social democracy had not been up

[50]Fairbank to Frederick Merk, 23 June 1942, copy in Schlesinger Papers, Box 16.
[51]Robert A. McCaughey, *International Studies and Academic Enterprise: A Chapter in the Enclosure of American Learning* (New York, 1984), 129; Ford Foundation, *Context: The World* (New York, 1966), 3.

to the task of resisting Nazism, while Fritz Stern, George Mosse, and Gordon Craig wrote on movements which had prefigured or assisted the rise of the Third Reich. The main theme of most of these discussions was summed up by the awkward double negative in the title of Stern's collected essays: *The Failure of Illiberalism.*[52]

Before World War I, the dominant institutionalist-evolutionist orientation of American historians had led them to stress the English origin of American institutions, and made English history the centerpiece of European studies. Between the wars, most Americanists stressed the distinctiveness of American society, and were little inclined to emphasize links with Europe. It is difficult to locate any clear focus in the work of Europeanists in this period. After World War II, both Americanists and Europeanists joined in arguing that "the Atlantic community" was the appropriate framework for both American and Western European history. "To those who are interested in the survival of democracy," wrote Richard Hofstadter, "it is probably more important to see American democracy as a part of western European democracy than it is to stress its uniqueness." Allan Nevins saw a "nationalistic" view of United States history replaced by "the international view, treating America as part of a great historical civilization with the Atlantic its center, as the Mediterranean was the center of the ancient world." On the European side, Carlton J. H. Hayes, seeking to reverse continental drift, said that a historiography which treated "detached Eastern and Western Hemispheres" was "unrealistic, contrary to basic historical facts, and highly dangerous for our country at the present and in the future." Garrett Mattingly likewise stressed that American history was Western history: "moved by the same rhythms, stirred by the same impulses, inescapably involved in the same crises. Sharing the same past with the peoples of Western Europe, bound to them by a thousand daily ties, we go forward with them to a common destiny."[53]

Albert Soboul was no doubt being highly unfair when he designated work which posited an "Atlantic Revolution" in the eighteenth century as "NATO History." And it is certainly an exaggeration to say, as did Gilbert Allardyce, that "educators equated . . . the Western military alliance with Western civilization." Unfair, exaggerated, but with at least

[52]Krieger, in Higham et al., *History*, 293.
[53]Hofstadter, *The Progressive Historians* (New York, 1968), 135–36; Nevins, "New Lamps for Old in History," *North Carolina Historical Review* 31 (1954): 249; Hayes, "The American Frontier—Frontier of What?" *AHR* 51 (1946): 203; Mattingly, "A Sample Discipline—The Teaching of History," address delivered to Princeton University Bicentennial Conference, "The University and Its World Responsibilities," 20 February 1947, mimeographed copy in Gabriel Papers, Box 31.

a grain of truth, especially in the case of that great curricular innovation of the postwar years, the Western civilization course.[54]

In both its remote and immediate origins, "Western civ" was a war baby. The first such course was instituted at Columbia immediately after World War I, as a continuation of the "war issues" course offered during hostilities. It defined the traditions of the West as those for which the Allies had fought against the Hun. The course had few imitators between the wars, but after World War II it became the most widely taught history course on American campuses. Courses of this type were strongly urged by the influential report of Harvard's General Education Committee in 1945, whose principal concerns, according to a sympathetic commentator, were "'why we fight,' the principles of a free society, the need to provide a consistent image of the American experience, the definition of democracy in a world of totalitarianism, the efforts to fortify the heritage of Western civilization, and the need to provide a 'common learning' for all Americans as a foundation of national unity."[55]

There were features of the climate in which Western civilization courses were taught, and elements in the courses themselves, which made them important agencies of socialization into the values of cold war America. David Owen, professor of history at Harvard, describing one of the courses of this type offered at that institution, wrote of how it served to debunk "facile generalizations" like those of Marxism, and other "ideologies." George Mosse advanced a similar argument. Western civilization courses which stressed cultural themes would make students less vulnerable to Communist propaganda, and would, incidentally, bring Americans and their European allies closer together. The latter idea was also developed by Geoffrey Bruun, who thought that one could "obviate much current confusion" by changing the title of courses from "Western civilization" to "Atlantic civilization"; the ties of Western Europe to North America had always, he argued, been closer than its connection to Russia, and until recent decades there had been little Slavic immigration to the United States.[56]

The manifest definition of "the West" or "the Atlantic community" was cultural and historical. Its latent geopolitical dimension, the extent to which historians were involved in tracing the prehistory of the Free

---

[54]Allardyce, "The Rise and Fall of the Western Civilization Course," *AHR* 87 (1982): 717.
[55]Daniel Bell, *The Reforming of General Education: The Columbia College Experience in its National Setting* (New York, 1966), 39.
[56]Owen, "Harvard General Education in Social Science," *Journal of General Education* 5 (1950): 27; Mosse, "The Pragmatism of the Freshman History Course," *Social Studies* 48 (1957): 290–91; Bruun, "Western Civilization," in Erling M. Hunt et al., *High School Social Studies Perspectives* (Boston, 1962), 155–56.

World, was never far below the surface. The closer one moved to the present, the more exclusive the focus on the North Atlantic triangle. William H. McNeill was probably not far from the mark when he wrote that the fundamental ideas of Western civilization courses was that "Humanity has fumbled through the centuries towards truth and freedom as expressed in modern science and democracy, American style. . . . Meaningful history . . . is the record of the progress of reason and liberty; and the place where it happened was Greece, Rome, western Europe and latterly the United States." After the wars and "illiberal" revolutions of the twentieth century, the old Actonian paradigm of the history of Western civilization as the forward march of liberty received less explicit articulation. Indeed, as McNeill wrote, "the whole notion swiftly sank from consciousness."

Yet like an echoing nautilus shell, washed up on the beach after its living inhabitant has disappeared, the stately structure raised at the close of the nineteenth century to accommodate European history still stands. The roof may be leaky and the plumbing deplorable, but in the absence of any alternative housing for unmanageably ample data, the Victorian edifice continues to give shape to what school children as well as graduate students learn and what their teachers choose to emphasize amidst all the buzzing, blooming confusion of the accessible European past. . . . The basic shape . . . still maintains itself in the English-speaking world, more because it has been half forgotten and little examined than because it is any longer actively believed.[57]

In part, as McNeill argued, the structure endured mindlessly and *faute de mieux*, because no generally acceptable alternative conceptualization could be found. But whatever the limitations of the framework for directing research, or for organizing historical findings in a sophisticated fashion, it was admirably suited for the purpose of articulating the ideological stance of the West in the cold war, and socializing students to that stance. The axis of freedom, not that of attitudes toward the distribution of property, Schlesinger had argued in *The Vital Center*, was the salient dimension of politics in the twentieth century, and this theme was central in Western cold war rhetoric. Of the revolutionary triad—*liberté, égalité, fraternité*—the first was consistently privileged in defining the essence of Western civilization. It was the ground of invidious comparison on which the West was most comfortable. The latter two had, besides, acquired a suspicious taint from their centrality in Communist and fascist discourse. The reification of "the West," and the identification

[57]"History for Citizens," *AHA Newsletter* 14 (March 1976): 5; *The Shape of European History* (New York, 1974), 4, 11.

of its heritage with the struggle for freedom, was no small contribution to American ideological mobilization.

Not all Western civilization programs were founded with an eye to their relevance to foreign policy or "war issues." And whatever the origins of the course, curriculum committees propose; teachers in the classroom dispose. It is likely that with the passage of time few involved in the courses were conscious of their ideological roots. Indeed, they were undoubtedly frequently taught from idiosyncratic ideological perspectives, quite at odds with those of their founders.

The authors of the Harvard report, in proposing a course called "Western Thought and Institutions," noted that they had "considered the possibility of suggesting as a title for such a course 'The Evolution of Free Society,'" but that title, they explained, "carries with it implications of indoctrination which would be unacceptable to many." There is here not a trace of dissimulation or hypocrisy. The authors get the highest marks for making the problem open and explicit. It was one of many examples of the dilemmas involved in simultaneously mobilizing the West for world-wide ideological struggle, while parading disinterested objectivity as one of the West's distinctive values and institutions.[58]

IV

The term "cold war" makes for some awkward metaphors. On the one hand, relaxation of Soviet-American hostility is sometimes described as a thaw. But because the alternative to cold war is hot war, a thermometer is inadequate for measuring the intensity of the conflict. If one adopts the not unreasonable criterion of the degree to which general armed conflict between East and West seemed imminent, the late forties and early fifties would probably qualify as the height of the cold war. From the mid-1950s onward, though a cold war climate endured, various factors—above all the the fact that so many threatening crises had not, as anticipated, led to general conflagration—somewhat lessened the atmosphere of permanent high anxiety. But in the late forties and early fifties a sense of urgent crisis, and impending Armageddon, was widespread. When, in 1947, Louis Gottschalk of the University of Chicago was considering an offer from the University of Washington, he thought that "the question of relative locations and the atom bomb . . . a matter to enter into practical consideration." In 1950 Boyd Shafer, later to be executive secre-

---

[58]*General Education in a Free Society* (Cambridge, Mass., 1945), 213–14.

tary of the American Historical Association, "made the hardest decision I have ever had to make."

Because of the continuing international crisis I felt that I had to bring my family back to the States and this meant that temporarily I had to give up my research in France. . . . War and the Russians were too near. The first might come any minute and the Russians would sweep through in three days to two weeks. There would be no way out, especially for families with small children, and as one Fulbright official in Paris put it, "We'd be trapped like rats". . . . I came to believe that the Chinese intervention [in the Korean War] meant that the Russians were willing to have a world war now. . . . In quick succession I received three letters from valued friends indicating that they were of the same opinion, that the States were about to enter a general war, and advising us to come home. . . . And I looked at my kids and thought "I'd better get you home where you may not be safe but at least you'll be safer for a while."[59]

In circumstances of such urgent peril, it is not surprising that there were many voices in the historical community arguing for the mobilization of scholarship. "While the danger lasts," wrote Garrett Mattingly, "the safety of society must come ahead of individual preferences. . . . Any necessary inconvenience or expense, any necessary pruning of curricula . . . are all justified if the result is likely to be of use in this world emergency." George Mosse urged the much greater coordination and integration of history teaching "for citizenship" at all levels, arguing, with no perceptible irony, that "the effectiveness of such a course of study can be seen in the fact that National Socialist Germany had [such] a concerted plan. . . . This was history as political propaganda and it was enormously successful."[60]

But the characteristic posture of historians who had to deal with the tension between demands for mobilization of consciousness and for dispassionate objectivity was ambivalence, or more properly, what Orwell called "doublethink": "the power of holding two contradictory beliefs in one's mind simultaneously, and accepting both of them." Thus the militant cold warrior Samuel Eliot Morison maintained that "the historian who knows, or thinks he knows, an unmistakable lesson of the past, has the right and the duty to point it out," and he made clear the particular lesson he had in mind: Morison chastised interwar historians whose paci-

---

[59]W. Stull Holt to Samuel Flagg Bemis, 6 December 1947, Bemis Papers, 1946/47:H; Shafer to Guy Stanton Ford, 5 January 1950 (misdated—actually 1951), AHA Papers, Box 364.
[60]Mattingly, "A Sample Discipline," 6; Mosse, "Freshman History: Reality or Metaphysics?" *The Social Studies* 40 (1949): 102.

fism "rendered the generation of youth which came to maturity around
1940 spiritually unprepared for the war they had to fight. . . . Historians
. . . are the ones who should have pointed out that war does accomplish
something, that war is better than servitude." Depending on the phenomenon being discussed by the historian, Morison said, it should be treated
"with sympathetic warmth or appropriate indignation." Within a few
pages of these remarks he denounced the pernicious relativism which
would adapt the study of the past to present purposes. He declared his
unshakable commitment to the Rankean dictum which renounced the
high office of judging the past or instructing the present, in favor of
"simply explain[ing] the event exactly as it happened."[61]

Historians were prepared to respond to appeals to render patriotic
service in their writing so long as the contradiction between norms of
detachment and objectivity on the one hand, and of mobilization and
usefulness on the other, were not posed too sharply; so long as the
requirement for doublethink was not made too manifest. When calls for
the mobilization of historical consciousness made explicit the extent to
which they entailed the abandonment of scholarly norms, they were
angrily rejected.

In 1948 the Historical Society of Pennsylvania convened a meeting to
consider the question "Do We Need a 'New History' of American Political Democracy?" The conference opened with a call by Roy F. Nichols
for scholarly mobilization: "In this period of ideological struggle in
which a great contest for power seems imminent. . . . American democracy [is] facing hostile forces which are trying many weapons including the
potent one of propaganda. . . . Scholars . . . are hardly equipped . . . to
provide the counterpropaganda which will withstand these subtle and
surreptitious or openly brazen assaults." Generalities of this sort were
acceptable, but Pendleton Herring, then president-elect of the Social Science Research Council, went further. "We are," he said, "in the midst of
an ideological warfare with an inimical philosophy and system. . . .
Scholars themselves may be forced to choose sides." He had specific
recommendations about the direction historical writing ought to take—
recommendations whose weight was not diminished by the fact that they
came from the person assuming control of one of the principal sources of
outside funding available to historians. In its day, iconoclastic history had
been salutary in rousing Americans from complacency; today America
stood "at the opposite pole." American history had been "oriented too

[61]*Nineteen Eighty-Four* (New York, 1949), 215; Morison, "Faith of a Historian," 265, 267,
262.

much to the study of conflict and disagreement. Its true accomplishment is union and co-operation." He particularly commended to historians the idea that in rewriting American history they stress the contrast between Russian and American society.[62]

Beyond these particular suggestions, Herring spelled out what he saw as the necessary operational consequences of the cold war for the conceptualization of historical practice, making specific reference to propositions advanced by interwar relativists. "The touchstone for historical writing," he said, was "not accuracy nor objectivity, but relevance." Historians should abandon the illusion that they were making "timeless" contributions to knowledge. The historian's task was to "clear the contemporary minds for the tasks immediately ahead"; their function was fulfilled "if they perform this duty for their own generation." Herring rejected the view that "objectivity was an end in itself."

Men [are] seeking both direction and the reassurance of religious or ideological faith. They will not be content with cold treatises. . . . The distortion of history was a deliberate Nazi policy and continues as a propaganda device for the Soviets. The Muse has been routed from her ivory tower, and you may choose your metaphor in deciding whether, in Moscow, Clio has become a streetwalker or a bureaucrat. We can agree that in this country the Muse of History is a career woman; henceforth our task is to see that she does a good job. . . . I would insist that she cease to be a social butterfly.

He acknowledged that "a central value of our system is intellectual freedom and pursuit of truth." But America was entering a period which could not afford "the calm and detached spirit of traditional historiography"; he doubted whether "freedom can be promoted by scholarly detachment and truth equated with scientific objectivity."[63]

Herring's challenge was posed too provocatively to be acceptable to the assembled historians. One after another of the conferees arose to reject what they saw as his demand for a purely and avowedly instrumental standard of "relevance." The search for this kind of relevance, it was said, had led to countless distortions in past historical writing. Arthur Link was appalled by the suggestion that history be written "to serve certain

[62]Nichols, "Unfinished Business," *Pennsylvania Magazine of History and Biography* 72 (1948): 114–15, 110; Herring, "A Political Scientist Considers the Question," ibid., 124, 123, 127, 129. Guy Stanton Ford, managing editor of the *American Historical Review*, thought Herring's paper was sufficiently important to warrant publication in the association's official journal, but it had been already committed to the *Pennsylvania Magazine of History*. (Ford to Nichols, 17 February 1948; Nichols to Ford, 18 February 1948, AHA Papers, Box 354.)
[63]Ibid., 121–22, 126–27, 124.

interests or ideologies." The past, they insisted, using a phrase which perplexed Herring, should be studied "for the sake of the past." An attempt to "go all-out for relevance" was the greatest danger to historiography.[64]

The most explicit, extreme, and widely publicized call for historical mobilization in the cold war was presented the following year in Conyers Read's presidential address to the American Historical Association. "Words are weapons," said Read, "often the most dangerous type of weapons. . . . In the end, we assure ourselves, the truth will prevail. But what about in the meantime?"

> Total war, whether it be hot or cold, enlists everyone and calls upon everyone to assume his part. The historian is no freer from this obligation than the physicist. . . . We can never be altogether free agents, even with our tongue and our pen. The important thing is that we shall accept and endorse such controls as are essential for the preservation of our way of life. We shall . . . like the doctor, have to examine social pathology if only to diagnose the nature of the disease. But we must realize that not everything which takes place in the laboratory is appropriate for broadcasting at the street corners.[65]

At the Pennsylvania conference, Herring had expressed skepticism about whether historians, in the present crisis, could successfully "differentiat[e] between their functions as scholars and as citizens." The tension between the two roles, the strain experienced by historians with both a strong scholarly conscience and a deep sense of civic obligation, is exquisitely illustrated by the short-run and long-run response of Merle Curti to Read's address. His initial reaction was outrage. "He calls on us," Curti wrote a friend, "to abandon the critical attitude—the essence of scholarship—if research reveals 'pathological' weaknesses in the 'American way.' This is really dreadful from a president of the AHA." Curti unsuccessfully attempted to organize a collective public protest.[66]

A decade after Read's speech, Curti, with a grant from the Ford Foundation, was working on a study of American philanthropy abroad. Among the experts whose guidance he solicited was a political scientist who had written on Radio Free Europe. Curti was informed that it was well known to insiders that rather than depending on private donations,

[64]Synopsis of discussion of Herring's paper, ibid., 137–38; Link's remarks quoted ibid., 202.

[65]"Social Responsibilities of the Historian," 282–84.

[66]Herring, "A Political Scientist," 123; Curti to Louis Gottschalk, 15 February 1950, Gottschalk Papers, 3:8. Curti ultimately included a disapproving reference to Read's remark in his presidential address to the Mississippi Valley Historical Association in 1952. ("The Democratic Theme in American Historical Literature," *MVHR* 39 [1952]: 26.)

Radio Free Europe was the recipient of massive secret government funding. It was the perfect scenario: just the sort of thing, uncovered "in the laboratory," which Read, to Curti's horror, had suggested should be suppressed. When Curti's book appeared, he described Radio Free Europe as "supported by voluntary contributions."[67]

[67]Robert T. Holt to Curti, 6 June 1960, Curti Papers, 31–5; Curti, *American Philanthropy Abroad: A History* (New Brunswick, N.J., 1963), 538.

11

◁══▷

A convergent culture

As we saw in our consideration of the period before World War I, consensual values within the historical profession, and an overwhelmingly affirmative stance toward the American experience, resulted in a convergent, celebratory historiography, which in turn promoted confidence in the objectivity of the work produced. Between the wars this pattern was reversed: a breakdown in consensus, and an undercurrent of "negativism," contributed to a questioning of the norm of objectivity. After World War II the pattern was reversed once more, with an affirmative and consensual historiography again contributing to confidence in the old ideal. Looking back on Renaissance scholarship in the 1950s from the perspective of a quarter century, William J. Bouwsma noted the "abiding consensus among historians of any complex subject." He thought the "irenic mood . . . [the] amiable but slightly complacent consensus" was in part "a reflection of the general consensus of the Eisenhower years, when we were all beating our swords into ploughshares."[1]

The relativist critique had, as we have seen, been associated with an insurgent mood, a critical tone, and an adversarial posture. In the postwar decades all these were out of fashion. Orthodoxy, not heterodoxy, was à la mode. "Radical" interpretations were abandoned; dissidents were increasingly marginalized. Relativism had developed in contingent but intimate relationship with "progressive" interpretations of the American past, which stressed social conflict, the struggle of "the people" against "the interests." As this influential interpretive framework of the interwar years fell into disfavor after World War II, so did the epistemology with which it was associated. Furthermore, the perceived substantive errors of

[1]"The Renaissance and the Drama of Western History," *AHR* 84 (1979): 2.

Progressive Historians were held to be largely the result of their misguided presentism and relativism.

By the 1950s the historical profession was considerably more socially heterogeneous, and slightly more ideologically pluralist, than it had been a half century before. While the relativist critique was, when not totally rejected, contained and trivialized, there was nevertheless somewhat more modesty among midcentury historians about the extent to which their scholarship was value-free and objective. Still, as in the years before World War I, most of the "big truths" of history were so self-evident that, by a communitarian criterion of truth, to be within the consensus was, *ceteris paribus*, to be objective. With that recurrent conceit that is always guaranteed to produce a wry smile a generation later, postwar historians often assured themselves and others that whereas previous generations of historians had produced work deformed by contemporary preconceptions and preoccupations, their own historical writing was not thus disfigured by "presentism."

I

Circumstances of national mobilization are inherently inhospitable to dissent, and foreign involvement puts domestic insurgence on the back burner. George Orwell observed in 1939 that "a left-wing party which, within a capitalist society, becomes a war party, has already thrown up the sponge, because it is demanding a policy which can only be carried out by its opponents." The record of the American Communist Party during World War II, with its 200 percent Americanism, support of the "no strike pledge," and projection of an indefinite postwar era of class cooperation, fully bore out Orwell's remark. But the wartime alliance against fascism between the Western powers and the Soviet Union was, ideologically and rhetorically, a continuation of the Popular Front. The high point of Communist Party membership in the United States was not in the 1930s, but during the war. The liberal rhetoric with which the war was prosecuted made it seem not unpatriotic to criticize the administration from the left. Liberals and leftists attacked Roosevelt for foot-dragging in opening a "second front," and for what many thought was a too cozy relationship with the semifascist regimes of Marshal Pétain and Generalissimo Franco. The Massachusetts Historical Society expelled the French historian Bernard Faÿ, a devout Vichy supporter. At the 1944 meeting of the American Historical Association a group of Young Turks, including Richard Hofstadter and Kenneth Stampp, came close to preventing the election of Carlton J. H. Hayes as AHA president on the grounds of his antidemocratic sentiments and his friendly attitude toward the Franco regime in Spain, to which he had been Roosevelt's ambassador.[2]

The Indian summer of the Popular Front only gave way gradually to the new climate of the cold war. While many intellectuals had made a dramatic departure from the Communist Party at the time of the Hitler-Stalin pact, others stayed in the party or its periphery and only later drifted away, quietly, as East-West tension increased and repression deepened. When Truman succeeded to the presidency, many New Dealers became critics of the Democratic Party from the left. An ominous sign of the passing of the Roosevelt era was the election in 1946 of the 80th Congress, the most conservative in recent memory. Many who had expected an era of world peace following Hitler's defeat were dismayed by the breakdown of the wartime alliance with the USSR, and were critical of what they saw as the belligerent foreign policy posture of the United States. All of this was reflected in the enthusiasm of a number of left-liberals for the 1948 presidential campaign of Henry Wallace. Ray Billington, Curtis Nettels, and Paul Gates were among the prominent historians who took a leading role in the Progressive Party crusade. Some younger radicals, like Richard Current and Kenneth Stampp were "among the millions of rats who deserted the sinking Wallace ship before the election. Naturally enough, we finally decided to give our votes to Farrell Dobbs and the Socialist Workers."[3]

---

[2]Orwell, "Democracy in the British Army," in Sonia Orwell and Ian Angus, eds., *The Collected Essays, Journalism and Letters of George Orwell* (4 vols., London, 1968), 1:403. Others involved in the AHA rebellion—which sought to replace Hayes with Sidney B. Fay, who was next in the line of succession—included William O. Aydelotte, Richard Current, Dwight Dumond, Frank Freidel, Fred Shannon, and L. S. Stavrianos. The insurgents were outmaneuvered by the AHA "establishment." Wesley M. Gewehr of the University of Maryland, who was the group's spokesmen, had asked Julius W. Pratt, chairman of the AHA nominating committee, to let them know if Fay declined to accept their nomination, so that they could select another candidate. With the agreement of AHA executive secretary Guy S. Ford, Pratt, without telling Gewehr, declined to formally notify Fay. At the business meeting, Arthur Schlesinger read out a letter from Fay declining to serve, thus throwing the anti-Hayes ranks into confusion. Even so, they garnered 65 votes for Fay against 110 for Hayes, a result Ford found "startling and disturbing." (List of signers of Fay nominating petition in AHA Papers, Box 136; Gewehr to Pratt, 5 December 1944; Pratt Papers, Box 3; Pratt to Ford, 11 December 1944 and Ford to Pratt, 14 December 1944, ibid.; Ford to Pratt, 16 January 1945, AHA Papers, Box 136.)
[3]Stampp to William B. Hesseltine, 17 November 1948, Hesseltine Papers, M77–88. For Nettels's support of Wallace, see his 18 June 1948 letter to Arthur Schlesinger, Schlesinger Papers, Box 21; for Gates and Billington, Curti to Thomas Cochran, undated but early 1948, Cochran Papers, 6–4; cf. Gates to Charles J. Goldstein, 27 August 1948, Gates Papers. Curti, like many others, was at first inclined to support Wallace, but was alienated

But from 1948 onward, among historians as among other academics and intellectuals, there was an accelerating abandonment of dissidence, a rapid accommodation to the new postwar political culture. The Wallace campaign was a disillusioning experience for many, both in its failure to win more than a tithe of the ten million votes its backers had hoped for, and even more because of the perception that it was being cynically manipulated by the Communists. Paul Gates, who had been New York State treasurer of the Wallace campaign would not, by 1949, support the right of a Communist to speak on the Cornell campus. "The position of the American Communists is so utterly indefensible in terms of morality that I am not willing to make a fight for them on matters of civil liberties and freedom."[4]

Upon completing his *American Political Tradition* in early 1948, Richard Hofstadter described the book as being "slightly—tho not very much—to the left," and having a "disgruntled, critical, alienated tone." "I had the necessary courage to write it," he told Merle Curti, "but I am now beginning to wonder if I have the courage to see it through publication." A *Partisan Review* symposium in the early 1950s on "Our Country and Our Culture" found leading intellectuals eagerly renouncing "alienation" and "disgruntlement." Within a few years of writing *The American Political Tradition*, Hofstadter confessed to Curti that he had "grown a great deal more conservative in the past few years." "I do hope, at least," he added, "that my conservatism is libertarian in its bias." Where formerly he had amused his intimates with savage imitations of FDR ("our favorite non-hero," said his friend Alfred Kazin), by the mid-1950s he was celebrating the New Deal as the final triumph of rationality within a reform tradition whose previous manifestations he found "retrograde," "delusive," and "vicious." "Comity" and "civility" became, for him, the principal values. He came to define democracy in procedural rather than substantive terms.[5]

by what he perceived as his hewing to the Communist Party position. (Curti to Cochran, 7 April 1948, Cochran Papers, 6–4.) W. Stull Holt went a good deal farther; he wrote Samuel Flagg Bemis in early 1948 that he was "being convinced of your view of last year that Wallace is not a naive sentimentalist but a deliberate traitor." (Letter of 30 March 1948, Bemis Papers, 1948:H.)
[4]Gates to Margaret Beattie, 17 March 1949, Gates Papers. Of course, most liberal historians, like most liberals generally, never enlisted in the Wallace crusade. Early in 1948 the elder Schlesinger sought to persuade Dixon Wecter to insert a disparaging remark about Wallace in Wecter's book on the New Deal, then in galley proofs, but Wecter reported that he was unable to do so "without obviously dragging it in." (Wecter to Schlesinger, 24 January 1948, Schlesinger Papers [Houghton], 3–7.)
[5]Hofstadter to Curti, undated but early 1948, Curti Papers, 19–26; *Partisan Review* 19 (1952): 282–326, 420–50. 562–97; Hofstadter to Curti, undated but probably late 1953,

Hofstadter's conservatism indeed had a libertarian bias. In this it was reflective of a general redrawing of political frontiers among the American intelligentsia after 1945 along the lines suggested by Schlesinger in *The Vital Center*: the privileging of freedom over equality; the need for a coalition of centrists against those at either end of the spectrum. Cushing Strout suggested that the very categories "liberal" and "conservative" were anachronistic. He criticized those who so described themselves for "the tragic error of seeking allies in extremist advocates of similar-sounding goals rather than in opponents who shared a common respect for moderate means and non-utopian hopes." The contrast of the extremist and the moderate was a typical theme of the period, as was the disparagement of "utopian hopes."[6]

"Complexity"—and such attendant characteristics as "irony," "paradox," and "ambiguity"—became the most highly valued qualities in postwar intellectual life. They were continually counterposed to the "simplifications" and "schematizations" of previous thinkers, and contemporary leftists. Reinhold Niebuhr's variations on the theme of irony found echoes in the work of many of the period's leading historians. Hofstadter thought the "rediscovery of complexity in American history" was the greatest achievement of postwar historiography. There was a veritable cult of complexity, with its inevitable strong suggestion that any but the most piecemeal and modest tinkering with the social mechanism was ill-fated. Complementing the cult of complexity were diminished belief in social possibilities and human potential, and greater concentration on the limits of social action and "the sinfulness of man"— also Niebuhrian themes. The innocence and naiveté of earlier generations was compared invidiously with the postwar generation, which, in Daniel Bell's phrase, was "twice-born . . . find[ing] its wisdom in pessimism, evil, tragedy, and despair." H. Stuart Hughes thought that "all the more discerning historians of today . . . believe in . . . a mixture of 'piety' and 'irony' and a sense of tragedy in viewing the past." The study of history, said Alan Simpson of the University of Chicago, had a "chastening mis-

Curti Papers, 19–26; Kazin, *New York Jew* (New York, 1978), 22. In the 1960s Hofstadter noted that Frederick Jackson Turner spoke of democracy in terms of "sentiments and attitudes," and identified it with egalitarianism. "Most of us today are disposed to define democracy as a system of parliamentary government in which there is a universal or nearly universal base of suffrage, in which officeholding is not restricted to a limited class, in which criticism of the policies of the government is tolerated and takes an institutional form in an opposition party or parties, and in which there are adequate formal legal sanctions to protect such criticism." (*The Progressive Historians* [New York, 1968], 126.)
[6]Strout, "Liberalism, Conservatism and the Babel of Tongues," *Partisan Review* 25 (1958): 108–9.

sion"; it taught prudence; it was an antidote to "illusions about the perfectibility of human nature and the power of human reason to cure original sin"; its "supreme utility is to teach the limits of the possible."[7]

The deeply conservative implications of all of this are clear enough, and
were reflected in countless ways in postwar scholarship. Erstwhile radicals who did not share in the new movement of thought generally retreated in discouragement from political involvement. In 1951 Merle Curti
wrote Thomas Cochran of his dismay at growing reaction, repression,
and militarism in these "dark and wintry times." "I can't swim with the
current and being a notoriously poor swimmer I can't swim against it.
What one does under such circumstances I'm trying to find out. All my
work as an historian has denied the validity of the idea of any sort of
retreat or ivory tower. Now I'd like to find one but it's too late."[8]

Cochran, in this period, privately described himself as a socialist, but
one who in 1948 had felt unable to vote for Norman Thomas because of
Thomas's anti-Soviet foreign policy views. As of 1950 he remained convinced of the "essential soundness of most of historical materialism,"
though he was critical of "the failure of Marxian scholars to break away
from outworn conceptions and keep up-to-date." In response to Curti's
letter he wrote his old friend that, like him, he could "find no place for
[his] convictions in what is going on around us"; and, like Curti, with a
troubled conscience, he was "disinclined to try to swim against the overwhelming current." "I guess," he concluded, "what I've done is to build
an ivory tower called the Social Science Approach to History where I can
live wrapped up in social roles, and protected from reality by sanctions,
basic personalities and cultural themes."[9]

II

The disappearance of dissident currents in historiography, and the retreat
into quietude, was not always the result of unconstrained choice. The late
forties and fifties saw a wide-ranging effort to remove "reducators" from
American campuses—an effort which resulted in hundreds of dismissals
and a climate of caution and self-censorship which endured for several
years.

[7]Hofstadter, *Progressive Historians*, 442; Bell, "The Mood of Three Generations," in *The End of Ideology* (1960; rev. ed., New York, 1961), 300; Hughes, review of Herbert J. Muller, *The Uses of the Past*, AHR 58 (1952): 73; Simpson, "History in Education," *School Review* 66 (1957): 285–86.
[8]Letter of 3 March 1951, Cochran Papers, 6–4.
[9]Cochran to Curti, 10 October 1948, 9 March 1950, 10 March 1951; Curti Papers, 9–17.

There was a lively debate within academic circles in these years as to whether membership in the Communist Party was prima facie evidence of unfitness to hold an academic position. Both sides in the debate argued on objectivist grounds. Those who would automatically bar Communists did so on the grounds that, unlike other academics, they were incapable of impartiality or objectivity. They were enslaved in the straitjacket of party-line dogma in a way which, again, in implicit contrast to others, rendered them incapable of changing their minds. T. V. Smith wrote that for Communists, "there is no room for neutrality, no objectivity. . . . We cannot deal with Communists objectively, or objectively with any issue which concerns them; for they sneer at our whole notion of impartiality. He who is not for them is against them; and they are not for anything that we are for." This position was shared by a number of historians: Samuel Flagg Bemis, who had been a member of the American Association of University Professors for a quarter century, wrote asking that his name be stricken from its rolls when the AAUP refused to accept Communist Party membership as grounds for automatic dismissal of a professor. Arthur Bestor endorsed the view that any Communist professor should be fired because, unlike his open-minded colleagues, he was "no longer an intellectually free agent." And Richard Hofstadter did not feel that he could condemn the University of Washington for firing Communist professors: "I dislike these Stalinists so—and I wonder what they would do for us or to us if they had control of things."[10]

The alternative position was equally objectivist. Arthur Schlesinger, Jr. wrote to Sidney Hook, disagreeing with Hook's position that Communist Party membership should be grounds for dismissal, though acknowledging that "this is a close question, on which men of good will can easily disagree." Schlesinger pointed out that given "the number of people who have broken with the Communist party when asked to do something that went against the grain," the argument that Communists were uniquely resistant to changing their minds collapsed. In Schlesinger's view, and those of virtually all who opposed an automatic exclusionary rule, Communist professors should be fired only when it was established that their beliefs influenced their teaching—that they attempted to "indoctrinate" students. The civil libertarian position on Communist teachers was thus implicitly grounded on the view that the proper classroom posture was one of value-neutrality.[11]

[10]Smith, "Academic Expediency as Democratic Justice *in re* Communists," *American Scholar* 18 (1949): 343; Bemis to Ralph E. Himstead, 21 April 1953, Bemis Papers, Box 36; Bestor, *The Restoration of Learning* (New York, 1955), 418; Hofstadter to Merle Curti, Curti Papers, 19–26.
[11]Schlesinger, Jr. to Hook, 11 March 1953, copy in Schlesinger (Sr.) Papers, Box 24.

In the case of history, and, indeed, most other disciplines, debates about academic freedom for Communist Party members were truly "academic." By the late forties scarcely any professional historians were still closely associated with the party. Herbert Aptheker and Philip S. Foner are the only two known to me. Neither ever succeeded in securing a regular academic position during the cold war years. Aptheker, whose revised dissertation *American Negro Slave Revolts* attracted considerable attention when it was published in 1943, served as a party publicist and editor. Foner, who had lost his position in the City College of New York during a 1941 loyalty probe, thereafter taught at a variety of party-affiliated schools, while producing a stream of works in labor history, published by small leftist presses.

A number of alleged former Communists were called before congressional committees, either to perform ritual recantations or to be "exposed" and outfitted with the leper's bell if they refused to answer questions on the grounds of the Fifth Amendment. Neither position was entirely satisfactory to those who adopted it, and neither deserves the blanket opprobrium which, both at the time and in retrospect, opposite camps heaped on them. Motives were varied and mixed. Many cooperative witnesses had undergone conversion experiences to which they were anxious to attest. When they "named names" they rarely gave investigators information they did not already possess. If the posture involved a measure of self-abasement, this was a penalty which those involved often thought they deserved. Those who "took the Fifth" were often uncertain of the possible legal consequences of a candor many of them would have preferred; some were willing to talk freely about their own activities, but required the legal protection of the self-incrimination clause to avoid involving others in their testimony.[12]

Those who answered all the investigators' questions, and offered evidence of their current anti-Communist credentials, generally escaped at least outwardly unscathed. Among historians, Daniel J. Boorstin was the outstanding example of a cooperative witness. Called before the House Committee on Un-American Activities in 1953, he reported fully on his and his associates' activities during his brief membership in the party in

[12]The Rutgers historian Richard Schlatter had been a Communist at Harvard in the late thirties, leaving the party after the Hitler-Stalin pact. By the time he was called before the House Committee on Un-American Activities the committee already had all the names Schlatter was able to give them, but he nevertheless got in touch with all those individuals, and got their permission to name them again. Following its usual procedure, the committee first heard Schlatter in executive session, where he told them what he had done. The committee, which preferred either defiance or wholehearted cooperation in its public spectacles, did not ask Schlatter to testify publicly. (Ellen W. Schrecker, *No Ivory Tower: McCarthyism and the Universities* [New York, 1986], 196.)

1938–39. He agreed with his questioners that no Communist should be allowed to teach at an American university, and, after some prodding, that the committee had "not in any way impinged on my academic freedom." Asked to indicate the ways in which he had expressed his opposition to Communism, he said that although he was "not basically a political person," his opposition had taken two forms.

First, the form of an affirmative participation in religious activities, because I think religion is a bulwark against Communism. This has been expressed in my activities in the Hillel Foundation at the University of Chicago. . . . The second form of my opposition has been an attempt to discover and explain to students, in my teaching and in my writing, the unique virtues of American democracy. I have done this partly in my Jefferson book, which, by the way, was bitterly attacked in the *Daily Worker* as something defending the ruling classes in America, and in a forthcoming book called *The Genius of American Politics*.[13]

Uncooperative witnesses fared less well. The best-known case within the historical profession was that of the ancient historian Moses I. Finley, named as a Communist before a Senate subcommittee by his fellow historian Karl Wittfogel. Though willing to state to university authorities that he had not been a member of the Communist Party since the beginning of 1941, Finley, on Fifth and First Amendment grounds refused to discuss his affiliations with Senator McCarran's committee in his 1952 appearance. Overruling the recommendation of a faculty committee, the Rutgers University administration dismissed Finley. Rutgers president Lewis Webster Jones explained that universities were obliged to take account of their "responsibilities as key institutions in the defense of the free world. . . . They are at once the most characteristic expression and the principle guardians of the Western tradition of freedom. . . . They cannot confine themselves to techniques, and adopt an attitude of neutrality and withdrawal in the face of the central moral issues of our times." Finley emigrated to England, where his distinguished academic career was capped by a knighthood. (An attempt by the Cornell History Department to hire Finley in 1958 was vetoed by that University's administration.)[14]

Other historians figured on the list of those whose careers were

---

[13]Boorstin's testimony is most conveniently available in Eric Bentley, ed., *Thirty Years of Treason: Excerpts from Hearings before the House Committee on Un-American Activities, 1938–1968* (New York, 1971), 601–12.
[14]"Statement of President Lewis Webster Jones of Rutgers University on the Heimlich-Finley Cases, January 24, 1953," in Gates Papers, which also contain a documentary record of negotiations between the Cornell History Department and the university administration.

derailed by their failure to cooperate with government agencies, or because they were named as Communists before investigating committees. At Harvard, in 1954, Sigmund Diamond's appointment to a combined administrative and teaching position was canceled by Dean McGeorge Bundy because of Diamond's unwillingness to "name names" for the FBI. A few years later, Richard Reichard's appointment at George Washington University was canceled because he invoked the Fifth Amendment before the Un-American Activities Committee. Lee Benson was named as a former Communist before the same committee, and for many years despaired of getting a regular position on that account. And universities had long memories. "Whenever I am up for consideration in a state university," Edward N. Saveth wrote to a friend in 1967, "my involvement twenty-seven years ago in the Rapp-Coudert inquiry comes to the fore. College Presidents are most reluctant to take a chance."[15]

For the most part, historians sympathized with their colleagues who were the victims of government action, or of university administrations. During the loyalty oath controversy at the University of California both the American Historical Association and the Mississippi Valley Historical Association passed resolutions deploring the oath, and there were efforts on behalf of those historians—John Caughey, Ernst Kantorowicz, and Charles Mowat—who, on grounds of conscience, refused to sign and lost their jobs. Some, like Henry May, turned down jobs at California in protest against the oath. A number of those who signed it apologized to colleagues at other institutions for doing so. AHA executive secretary Boyd Shafer refused Val Lorwin's offer to withdraw from a program at the association's annual meeting when Lorwin was indicted for perjury in a loyalty investigation. The AHA's representatives to the International Congress of Historical Sciences, albeit somewhat nervously, stuck by their nomination of Owen Lattimore to give a paper at the congress when

---

[15]Diamond, "Veritas at Harvard," *New York Review of Books* 24 (28 April 1977): 13–17 (see also letters from McGeorge Bundy and others, issues of 26 May 1977, 9 June 1977, 14 July 1977); for Reichard, see "Academic Freedom and Tenure: The George Washington University," *AAUP Bulletin* 48 (1962): 240–47; Benson to Paul W. Gates, 7 January 1952 and 5 March 1955, Gates Papers; Saveth to Merle Curti, 12 February 1967, Curti Papers, 36–3. The question of whether to pass on information concerning an individual's problems with the security apparatus raised nice questions of conflicting loyalty. W. Stull Holt, who had been Diamond's undergraduate teacher, was asked to write a letter of recommendation for Diamond when he was being considered for a job at the University of Wisconsin. After having "debated a long time" he decided to mention the Harvard incident to Merle Curti. "To many or most academic people this stand is to his credit, and I personally think that former membership, especially when very young and in his circumstances, is irrelevant and not decisive. But if I withheld the information I would be making the decision for you and my obligation, as I see it, is to give you all the information I have which you might wish to have." (Letter of 12 December 1955, Curti Papers, 45–20.)

Lattimore was under fire in connection with the investigation of the Institute of Pacific Relations. And individuals resisted pressure to conform, or to be cautious, as when Oscar Handlin refused to delete specific criticisms of Senators McCarran and McCarthy from his contribution to a series of books sponsored by the Library of Congress.[16]

But it would be quite mistaken simply to portray a historical community responding to outside pressure for conformity and the repression of dissidence. Much of the most pervasive pressure came from within the community itself. Armin Rappaport's appointment at Berkeley in 1949 was held up until John D. Hicks, who was worried that Rappaport "might have some of the ultra left wing tendencies so common to the New York Jewish intelligentsia," could receive a guarantee that he was not an opponent of American foreign policy. At the same institution, in the following year, Raymond Sontag's fear that Joseph Levenson might be a Marxist had to be assuaged before he would assent to his appointment. John K. Fairbank conveyed his assurances that Levenson "tends to be eclectic in his thinking about politics. . . . His approach is an intellectual and aesthetic one and he is not especially concerned about politics." H. Stuart Hughes's appointment at Stanford was held up until he could be queried on his current political beliefs. Opposition had developed within the department, based on Hughes's brief involvement in the Wallace campaign in 1948. According to Stanford History Department chairman Thomas A. Bailey, several of his colleagues felt that "anyone that woolly witted had no business teaching on our faculty."[17]

[16]*MVHR* 38 (1951): 368–69; Carl Bridenbaugh to Guy Stanton Ford, 3 January 1951, AHA Papers, Box 361; Ford to Kantorowicz, 29 November 1950, ibid., Box 360; Bridenbaugh to Arthur Schlesinger, Sr., 28 February 1951, Schlesinger Papers, Box 23; John Higham to William B. Hesseltine, 15 April 1950, Hesseltine Papers, M68–25/2; Shafer to Merle Curti, undated but January 1954, Curti Papers, 1–19; Donald C. McKay to Waldo G. Leland (20 October 1954), Leland to Shafer (25 October 1954), Shafer to McKay (23 November and 17 December 1954), all in AHA Papers, Box 180; Verner W. Clapp, acting Librarian of Congress, to Thomas J. Wilson of Harvard University Press, 24 May 1954, copy in Gabriel Papers, Add. I, Box 5. In these years there were, additionally, various humiliations imposed by the loyalty mania which rankled historians. John K. Fairbank, accused of pro-Communism by Louis Budenz, felt obliged to circulate, in 1951, a long list of extracts from his writings to document his anti-Communism; Merle Curti, after including a somewhat gratuitous anti-Marxist statement in his AHA presidential address, at the last moment made it even stronger, "to be on the safe side." ("John K. Fairbank: Excerpts From Writings and Speeches, 1946–1950," Americans for Democratic Action Papers, Box 2–37–2; Curti to Catherine Seybold, 2 December 1954, AHA Papers, Box 366.)

[17]On Rappaport, Hicks to Bailey, 6 May and 17 May 1949, Bailey Papers, SC54/4–4; Hicks to George E. Mowry, 11 March 1949, Hicks Papers, Box 9. On Levenson, Woodbridge Burnham to Hicks, 3 January 1950, Hicks Papers, Box 4. (Quotation is Burnham's paraphrase of Fairbank's remarks.) On Hughes, Bailey to Stanford president Wallace Sterling, 20 March 1952; Bailey to Sturtevant Hobbs, 5 December 1951; Bailey Papers,

Political dissidence was a criterion in the evaluation of manuscripts as well as persons. In 1955 the young sociologist Norman Birnbaum submitted for consideration by the *American Historical Review* a critique of *The Social Sciences in Historical Study*, a report of the SSRC's Committee on Historiography. The manuscript was sent to Thomas Cochran for refereeing. Cochran responded with a detailed negative evaluation of Birnbaum's critique. In a rather obscure sentence, he said that his "chief fear is that historians lacking the background of present international cleavages in the social sciences would not realize the motivation of Birnbaum's essay." A handwritten note which Cochran attached to his referee's report removed the obscurity: "Dear Boyd: I am not putting this in my more formal letter as you should feel quite free to pass that around. I suspect that the motivation behind Birnbaum is that U.S. social science has left the party line. . . . The party line is to damn . . . empirically based social science. . . . I suspect that this essay is a labor both of duty and love, aimed to strike a blow for the cause." Birnbaum's critique—which, ironically, was much more Weberian than Marxian—was rejected by the *AHR*.[18]

Documented cases of the repression of dissidence in this period are, presumably, the tip of the iceberg. In the case of icebergs we know that the total mass is nine times what we see above water. What multiplier do we use in cases of repression? Nine? Ninety? More? Less? With respect to the consequences of repression one confronts the paradox that the measure of its effectiveness is the scarcity of overt instances. There was presumably a large "demonstration effect," but its extent is impossible to measure. A broadly based survey of the impact of the cold war climate on social scientists in the fifties found that almost half acknowledged that they had grown more cautious in their writings and speech out of fear of being labeled subversive. No doubt there were dissident or potentially

SC54/7–29 and SC54/5–11 respectively. Hughes's involvement with the Wallace campaign made difficulties for him at Harvard, both before and after the Stanford appointment. In 1948, when serving as associate director of the Russian Research Center, he was informed by his superior, Clyde Kluckhohn, that the Carnegie Corporation, which was supporting the center, found his presence an embarrassment, and that his continuation in office might endanger future grants. Hughes resigned the position. (Seymour Martin Lipset and David Riesman, *Education and Politics at Harvard* [New York, 1975], 184–85.) In 1956, when Harvard was considering both Hughes and Carl Schorske for a permanent appointment, David Owen thought that in the case of modern European historians Hughes's lack of "political sagacity" was a relevant consideration; but, Owen said, "Carl's record, if anything, has been worse than Stuart's." (Letter to Myron Gilmore, 29 January 1956, copy in Gottschalk Papers, 4:5.)

[18]Cochran to Boyd Shafer, 28 October 1955, AHA Papers, Box 368. I am grateful to Professor Birnbaum for making available to me a copy of the manuscript "History and the Social Sciences—A Sociologist's View."

dissident historians who "stayed in the closet," or subtly modified their manuscripts and teaching, or avoided research into perilous subjects. Lee Benson recalled twenty years later that his 1960 *Turner and Beard* was written from an "implicit Marxian standpoint," but when he wrote the book he did not have a tenured position, and was "afraid that I would never get one if I made my 'Marxian standpoint' explicit. During the 1950s, and for some time thereafter, I—for one—was intellectually terrified."[19]

But in most cases in which historians found it difficult to find employment for political reasons it was past dissidence, usually long since abandoned, which was the barrier. The occasional heterodox manuscript might be rejected by a journal or a publisher on political grounds. But in going through the editorial correspondence of the *American Historical Review* and *Mississippi Valley Historical Review* for the cold war years, what struck me most was the absence of such submissions. Like the apocryphal small-town Nazis who petitioned Berlin to send them a Jewish shopkeeper so they could boycott him, there may have been the will within the university and the profession to repress dissident historians and historiography, but there wasn't much dissidence to repress.

III

If one had to choose a single term to characterize the dominant tendency in postwar American historical writing, "counterprogressive" would seem the best choice, for no project was more central to historians from the late 1940s onward than the revision and refutation of the alleged deficiencies of the Progressive Historians who had preceded them. As is usual in such revisionist projects, the new school constructed something of a straw man to battle against. The hegemony which Turner, Beard, and the literary historian Vernon Louis Parrington had exercised over interwar historiography was exaggerated by the new generation, and their theses were often vulgarized so as to present a broader target.

The attack on the Progressive Historians featured variations on themes prominent in postwar intellectual life. The reformist optimism of Beard's generation was naive, and their activism skewed their perceptions. The approved postwar sensibility was "the tragic sense," and the approved posture, spectatorial. The previous generation had mistakenly thought

[19]Paul F. Lazarsfeld and Wagner Thielens, Jr., *The Academic Mind* (Glencoe, Ill., 1958); Benson, "Doing History as Moral Philosophy and Public Advocacy: A Practical Strategy to Lessen the Crisis in American History," paper delivered at the 1981 meeting of the OAH, note 21.

that the central theme of history had been struggles between haves and have-nots. Postwar historians saw the defense of freedom as the thread which wove American history together. Overall, the progressive emphasis on social conflict was rejected not just as overdrawn but as fundamentally wrongheaded; historians' focus shifted from the conflict of classes to a consensual culture.

"Consensus" became the key word in postwar attempts to produce a new interpretive framework for American history, focusing attention on what had united Americans rather than what had divided them. In the earliest general statement of the consensus orientation, Richard Hofstadter wrote in 1948 of his growing conviction of "the need for a reinterpretation of our political traditions which emphasizes the common climate of American opinion."

The existence of such a climate of opinion has been much obscured by the tendency to place political conflict in the foreground of history. . . . The fierceness of the political struggles has often been misleading; for the range of vision embraced by the primary contestants in the major parties has always been bounded by the horizons of property and enterprise. . . . The sanctity of private property, the right of the individual to dispose of and invest it, the value of opportunity, and the natural evolution of self-interest and self-assertion, within broad legal limits, into a beneficent social order have been staple tenets of the central faith in American political ideologies; these conceptions have been shared in large part by men as diverse as Jefferson, Jackson, Lincoln, Cleveland, Bryan, Wilson, and Hoover.

Hofstadter's attempt to identify and explicate the core ideology of Americans was carried farther by Louis Hartz, who in *The Liberal Tradition in America* produced the most elaborately worked-out argument for abiding American ideological consensus. Meanwhile, the third of the most influential consensus theorists, Daniel Boorstin, argued forcefully that rather than agreeing on an ideology, Americans were united by their rejection of the very notion of ideology, or indeed, of theorizing of any kind. "We do not need American philosophers," Boorstin explained, "because we already have an American philosophy, implicit in the American Way of Life. . . . Why should *we* make a five-year plan for ourselves when God seems to have had a thousand-year plan ready-made for us?"[20]

Counterprogressive or "consensus" history was not exclusively a re-

[20]Hofstadter, *The American Political Tradition* (1948; reprinted New York, 1973), xxxvi-xxxvii; Hartz, *The Liberal Tradition in America: An Interpretation of American Political Thought Since the Revolution* (New York, 1955); Boorstin, *The Genius of American Politics* (Chicago, 1953), 162, 179.

flection of postwar social values. In part it represented a natural swing of the scholarly pendulum. The Progressive Historians had, as Hofstadter said, "pushed polarized conflict as a principle of historical interpretation so far that one could go no further in that direction without risking self-caricature." Nor was the idea of consensus as a framework for analysis intrinsically or necessarily conservative. Hofstadter's initial statement of the consensus idea in *The American Political Tradition* had something of a Marxist cast, as did, somewhat more ambiguously, Hartz's *Liberal Tradition in America*. Hofstadter described "a democracy in cupidity rather than a democracy of fraternity." Hartz was acerbic about the Lockean straitjacket in which he found American thought constrained from the Revolution onward: "The psychic heritage of a nation 'born equal,'" he wrote, was "a colossal liberal absolutism, the death by atrophy of the philosophic impulse." Of the three principal consensus historians, only Boorstin from the outset unequivocally celebrated the consensus he described. When the first volume of Boorstin's *The Americans* appeared, Bernard Bailyn termed it an "apologia for his disillusioned conservatism."[21]

But if Boorstin's strident conservatism, boosterism, and unabashed patriotic celebration were not entirely typical of consensus history, neither was the "disgruntled, alienated, critical" tone of Hofstadter's early work. The consensus idea was an attempt to give some positive content and direction to the essentially negative and critical counterprogressive venture. To get some sense of the thrust of that venture, it will be useful to look briefly at three areas of postwar counterprogressive scholarship: the historiography of the late eighteenth century, of populism, and of business. In all three areas the relationships between postwar interpretive patterns and the contemporary political culture were fairly straightforward. All three became arenas in which charges and countercharges of "distorting presentism and relativism" were hurled, and opposing claims of disinterested objectivity contested.

No works were more central to the Progressive view of American

---

[21]Hofstadter, *Progressive Historians*, 439; *American Political Tradition*, xxxvi-xxxvii; Hartz, *Liberal Tradition*, 285; Bailyn, review in *The New Republic* 139 (15 December 1958): 18. *The American Political Tradition*, unlike Hofstadter's later work, was applauded by leftists and iconoclasts, and deplored by those concerned with its "delegitimating" implications. Morton Borden, in soliciting contributors for a volume on America's ten greatest presidents, explained that the project was stimulated by dissatisfaction with Hofstadter's book: "few undergraduates are sophisticated or well enough informed to read him without a measure of confusion and disillusionment. Everyone seems to have clay toe-nails, if not clay feet; everyone is a politician." (Letter to Norman Graebner, 13 June 1958, Graebner Papers.)

history as the enduring struggle between "the people" and "the interests" than two books by the foremost interwar relativists: Becker's *History of Political Parties in the Province of New York* and Beard's *An Economic Interpretation of the Constitution.* Becker's book, published in 1909, was the first and most influential characterization of the Revolution as class struggle: a conflict having as much to do with "who should rule at home" as it did with "home rule." Beard's celebrated book on the Constitution complemented Becker's on the background of the Revolution. It portrayed the events leading up to the Federal Convention of 1787 as the latest in a long series of struggles between rich and poor, farmers and merchants, debtors and creditors.

Both works came under sustained assault after the war, and critics repeatedly stressed the causal connection between Becker and Beard's skepticism about objectivity and their substantive mistakes. Robert E. Brown was perhaps the most important critic of the view, implicit or explicit in Progressive treatments of the eighteenth century, that there was a large, disenfranchised lower class in the colonies, and that class struggles were at the root of political conflicts in the colonies. Brown's first two books on the subject, dealing with Massachusetts and Virginia respectively, attacked Becker only indirectly, but he then made the relationship between Becker's epistemology and his interpretation of the Revolution the subject of a full-scale onslaught. Becker, he charged, had resorted to "deliberate falsification." He had "prostitute[d] scholarship" in the service of his preconceived leftist notions. Although no other counterprogressive historians matched Brown in his vituperation, which was generally deplored within the profession, the assertion that the Progressive Historians' view of the Revolution had been distorted by their presentism was commonly made.[22]

Brown was also the first to systematically challenge Beard on the Constitution, but he was soon followed by Forrest McDonald, who devoted two books to refuting Beard's economic interpretation. Both Brown and McDonald associated the shortcomings of Beard's account of the Constitutional Convention with his embrace of relativist doctrines. The first

[22]*Carl Becker on History and the American Revolution* (East Lansing, Mich., 1970), 39. Cf. his *Middle-Class Democracy and the Revolution in Massachusetts, 1691–1780* (Ithaca, N.Y., 1955) and (with B. Katherine Brown) *Virginia, 1705–1786: Democracy or Aristocracy?* (East Lansing, Mich., 1964). For Edmund Morgan on the "presentism" of progressive views of the Revolution, see Morgan, "The American Revolution: A Review of Changing Interpretations," in William H. Cartwright and Richard L. Watson, Jr., eds., *Interpreting and Teaching American History* [31st Yearbook of the National Council for the Social Studies] (Washington, D.C., 1961), 51; "The American Revolution: Revisions in Need of Revising," *William and Mary Quarterly* 14 (1957): 12.

chapter of Brown's *Charles Beard and the Constitution* discussed Beard's relativism as a necessary prolegomenon to the consideration of his substantive theses. McDonald, in the prefaces of *We the People* and *E Pluribus Unum*, did the same. In the latter work he attributed to Becker and Beard the view that accurate knowledge of the past was not only unattainable, but "not worth seeking."[23]

By the early 1960s it was generally accepted within the historical profession that Becker and Beard's Progressive version of the Revolution and the framing of the Constitution had been decisively refuted. American historians came to see the Revolution as a conservative and traditionalist response to recent provocations by England—indeed, hardly a revolution at all, and certainly not a social revolution of any kind. The framers of the Constitution, rather than having self-interested economic motives, were led by concern for political unity, national economic development, and diplomatic security. The counterprogressive picture of late-eighteenth-century American society and politics was characteristically advanced as the only view consonant with "the facts." Both Brown and McDonald asserted that their conclusions were those to which absolutely any fair-minded student of the evidence would ineluctably be led.[24]

Some scholars remained committed to older interpretations, or at a minimum were skeptical about assertions that the new version of early American history represented the antiseptic truth, uncontaminated by presentism. Max Savelle thought Edmund Morgan's version of *The Birth of the Republic*, written "in the flush times of mid-twentieth-century capitalism and of chaste and dedicated patriot-businessmen, has taken on the hue of Eisenhower prosperity." Responding to charges that the new interpretations of the American Revolution had "contemporary political overtones" or reflected "the conservative mood of the 1950s," Jack P. Greene wrote that while the Progressive Historians had responded to the spirit of the times, this was not true of present-day scholars.

There is no question that social determinants do affect the work of historians, but not necessarily in a way to make them all equally distorted reflections of that elusive, though theoretically attainable goal, objective historical truth. It can be

---

[23]Brown, *Charles Beard and the Constitution: A Critical Analysis of "An Economic Interpretation of the Constitution"* (Princeton, 1956), 9–13; McDonald, *We the People: The Economic Origins of the Constitution* (Chicago, 1958), vii–viii; *E Pluribus Unum: The Formation of the American Republic, 1776–1790* (Boston, 1965), xi–xii.

[24]Brown, *Reinterpretation of the Formation of the American Constitution* (Boston, 1963), 62–63; McDonald, *E Pluribus Unum*, xiii–xv.

argued, in fact, that environmental conditions in the post-World War II years have made possible an increasing detachment among historians of the Revolution. The absence of serious internal economic problems and the general levelling of society has enabled them to avoid that central preoccupation with economic questions that led many scholars of the progressive school to wrench Revolutionary events out of context.

This was, as Merrill Jensen observed, a "rather remarkable" assumption, but one not untypical of the self-confident historians of the postwar decades.[25]

No interpretive tendency of the 1950s was more typical of the general movement of intellectual opinion, or reverberated more widely throughout the culture, than the sharp downward turn in the historical reputation of the Populists. As postwar academics and intellectuals put greater and greater distance between themselves and traditions of dissidence and insurgency, the favorable view of the Populists associated with Progressive historical scholarship was an obvious candidate for historiographical revision. Rather than a democratic movement against exploitation, whose program prefigured subsequent reforms, the Populists came to be portrayed as a backward-looking band of nativist book burners obsessed with imaginary grievances.

Whereas the rise of counterprogressive tendencies in the historiography of the late eighteenth century remained a purely professional matter, of which most nonhistorians were hardly aware, the assault on Populism spread throughout the social sciences and the intellectual world at large. Richard Hofstadter was the principal historian involved in the attack on the Populists, but he was by no means alone and was joined by leading figures from other disciplines. The immediate context of the reevaluation of the Populists was the early 1950s phenomenon of McCarthyism, which a number of analysts quickly connected with agrarian radicalism, La Follette Progressivism, and, in particular, Populism. In this view McCarthy's crusade, like that of the Populists, was a democratic and anti-intellectual revolt of dispossessed groups against educated elites. Historians increasingly identified with elites, and disdained "vulgar levellers." Lawrence W. Levine recounts that as a graduate student working with

[25]Savelle, review of *The Birth of the Republic, William and Mary Quarterly* 14 (1957): 618; Greene, "The Flight From Determinism: A Review of Recent Literature on the Coming of the American Revolution," *South Atlantic Quarterly* 61 (1962): 258; Jensen, "Historians and the Nature of the American Revolution," in Ray Allen Billington, ed., *The Reinterpretation of Early American History* (San Marino, Calif., 1966), 121.

Hofstadter at Columbia he found William Jennings Bryan's "militant egalitarianism" to be among those of Bryan's characteristics which would "make even the most sympathetic historian shudder." Cushing Strout perceived "a populist current in both fascism and Communism."[26]

The approach which Hofstadter took to the Populists was the first important example of what became a common feature of cold war historical scholarship, the social-psychologizing of dissidence and insurgency. Taking up themes which received wide currency in *The Authoritarian Personality*, and the literature which grew up around that much discussed work, Europeanists discussed the irrational drives and longings which led people to embrace Nazism or Communism, while Americanists explored the unconscious forces which produced Populists, Progressives, and abolitionists. If those who wrote in this vein never went quite to the point of identifying protest per se with pathology, and acceptance of the status quo with mental health, they often came close to it.

The most controversial of Hofstadter's assertions about the Populists, certainly the one which attracted the greatest amount of attention, was the charge that anti-Semitism was central to their world view; indeed, that the Populists had "activated most of what we have of modern popular anti-Semitism in the United States." Privately, Hofstadter acknowledged that he had exaggerated Populist anti-Semitism, and that his treatment would "mislead anyone who had never heard of Populism from any other source," but he thought his overstatement justified in order to redress the balance, since previous historians had omitted any mention of Populist anti-Semitism.[27]

Hofstadter's strategy was consistent with his long-held view that "if a new or heterodox idea is worth anything at all it is worth a forceful overstatement," a position he contrasted with that of historians who "approach their work as though they were engaged in the final death grapple with error." But tacking toward a balanced view is a strategy which can easily go astray if one misjudges the direction of the wind. In the climate of the 1950s Hofstadter's exaggerations concerning Populist anti-Semitism, and in general his stress on the movement's "dark side," were not countering the conventional wisdom. Rather, his exaggerations were further exaggerated by other members of his generation with a less-well-developed sense of nuance, or whose move in a conservative direction was less ambiguous than Hofstadter's. The reevaluation of Populism

[26]Levine, "The Historian and the Culture Gap," in L. P. Curtis, Jr., ed., *The Historian's Workshop* (New York, 1970), 313; Strout, "Liberalism," 107–8.
[27]*The Age of Reform: From Bryan to F.D.R.* (New York, 1955), 80; Hofstadter to Merle Curti, 17 January 1956, Curti Papers, 19–26.

became a central symbol of the jaundiced view which postwar historians took of radicalism in its various embodiments.[28]

Hofstadter's interpretation of Populism, or variants of it, appeared in the work of Daniel Bell, Nathan Glazer, Oscar Handlin, Seymour Martin Lipset, Talcott Parsons, David Riesman, and Edward Shils, among others. Although their views remained dominant for a time, they did not go unchallenged. John D. Hicks and C. Vann Woodward defended their earlier, positive evaluation of the movement, and they were joined in criticizing the Hofstadter school by Howard K. Beale, William B. Hesseltine, John Higham, Walter T. K. Nugent, Norman Pollack, Theodore Saloutos, David Shannon, and William A. Williams. With minor exceptions (Parsons in the one camp, Pollack in the other), those critical of the Populists were Jews and from the Northeast; those defending them were gentiles, and from the South or Midwest. This feature of the controversy was well known to the participants and many contemporary observers, but was usually mentioned only obliquely, if at all. It tacitly raised issues of perspectivism and universalism which, for the moment, the profession preferred not to discuss openly.[29]

In the early 1960s Carl Bridenbaugh outraged a good many historians with his AHA presidential address. In what was universally taken to be a reference to Jews, who were for the first time becoming a significant presence in the profession, Bridenbaugh deplored the fact that whereas once American historians had shared a common culture, and rural upbringing, the background of the present generation would "make it impossible for them to communicate to and reconstruct the past for future generations." They suffered from an "environmental deficiency": being "urban-bred" they lacked the "understanding . . . vouchsafed to historians who were raised in the countryside or in the small town." They were "products of lower middle-class or foreign origins, and their emotions not infrequently get in the way of historical reconstructions. They find themselves in a very real sense outsiders on our past and feel themselves shut out. This is certainly not their fault, but it is true."[30]

---

[28]*Progressive Historians*, 119–20; Hofstadter, "The Historian's Risk," *Encounter* 12 (February 1959): 56–57.

[29]Hofstadter, the son of an Eastern European Jewish immigrant father and a Lutheran mother, was thus only half Jewish by inheritance—and as a child served as an Episcopalian altar boy. But, as he told an interviewer, he "spent a lot of years acquiring a Jewish identity, which is more cultural than religious . . . anyone who is part Jewish can only be a Jew." (Richard Kostelanetz, *Master Minds* [New York, 1969], 168.) The second half of Hofstadter's observation, as the case of Arthur Schlesinger, Sr. suggests, is extremely doubtful.

[30]"The Great Mutation," *AHR* 68 (1963): 322–23, 328.

Most of those who commented on Bridenbaugh's address had no hesi-
tancy in terming it anti-Semitic. They inferred, probably correctly, that
he was distressed and resentful at the entry of Jews into the profession.
No such inference seems justified in the case of those defenders of the
Populists who, directly or indirectly, publicly or privately, commented
on the background and ethnicity of the Populists' critics, sometimes
employing language which superficially resembled Bridenbaugh's. They
were simply seeking to account for what they considered to be an astigmatic perception.

Woodward, in an article critical of the "Hofstadter school," listed the
viewpoints found among the anti-Populists. They included, he said, "the
New Conservative, the New Liberal, the liberal-progressive, the Jewish,
the Anglophile, and the urban, with some overlapping," and he noted the
northeastern origin of the assault. Hicks believed that Hofstadter understood urban America well enough, but thought "his background . . .
quite inadequate for any reasonable understanding of Populism." Beale
wrote a colleague that Hofstadter had a "sophisticated New Yorker's lack
of understanding of the rest of the country." Hesseltine pronounced *The
Age of Reform* "not, technically speaking, a work of history . . . [but] an
asphalt-oriented piece of professorial punditry."[31]

Besides noting what they regarded as the critics' inadequate understanding of the rural context of Populism, the Populists' defenders
charged Hofstadter and his associates with "cavalierly disregard[ing] the
past and writ[ing] solely from the present" (Norman Pollack), and with
"a transformation of History into Ideology" (William A. Williams).
Many expressed irritation at Hofstadter's implicit denial that insurgents
had real grievances, and at what they regarded as his intoxication with
social psychological propositions about "status anxiety." "This is not
science," David Shannon wrote to Merle Curti. It was "what an intelligent person can do sitting in an arm chair." None, so far as I can tell,
ever advanced what seems to me the most compelling reason why a group

---

[31]Woodward, "The Populist Heritage and the Intellectual," *American Scholar* 28 (1959);
reprinted in Woodward, *The Burden of Southern History* (rev. ed., Baton Rouge, 1968),
145–46; Hicks to Theodore Saloutos, 25 January 1957, Hicks Papers, Box 4; Beale to
Merle Curti, 11 January 1956, Curti Papers, 45–21; Hesseltine review of *Age of Reform*,
Wisconsin Magazine of History 39 (1956): 280. When Hicks wrote to congratulate Woodward on his article, he observed that if he himself had written the piece he could not have
maintained Woodward's "good humor and lack of heat." Woodward replied that he had
"hesitated a long time to do it, because so many of our critics were long-time friends and
historians with whom I have much in common in the way of tastes and sympathies. Had
this not been the case, I doubtless would have been somewhat harsher in my strictures."
(Hicks to Woodward, 17 December 1959, Hicks Papers, Box 3; Woodward to Hicks, 4
January 1960, ibid., Box 9.)

of the background of Hofstadter, Bell, Lipset, and their friends should have taken such a uniformly and exaggeratedly bleak view of the Populists: they were all only one generation removed from the Eastern European *shtetl*, where insurgent gentile peasants spelled pogrom.[32]

The efforts of the new historians of Populism in turning the Progressive view of the American past on its head were complemented by "business history revisionism." Whereas the former downgraded erstwhile heroes, the latter refurbished the reputation of those who had hitherto been villains, the "robber barons."

Few professional historians had interested themselves in the history of business before World War II. As an academic specialty it had been (and to a considerable extent remained) within the jurisdiction of business schools. Most of the influential works which took a jaundiced view of business leaders had been the work of amateurs: Gustavus Myers and Ida Tarbell earlier in the century; Frederick Lewis Allen, Lewis Corey, and Matthew Josephson between the wars. Though the characterization of late-nineteenth-century entrepreneurs as "robber barons" did not originate with professional historians, an unsympathetic view of businessmen was common in professional historical work within the Progressive tradition. A typical characterization was one by Arthur Schlesinger, Jr. in what was perhaps the last important work of that school—*The Age of Jackson*, published in 1945. The business community, "moved typically by personal and class, rarely by public considerations . . . has invariably brought national affairs to a state of crisis and exasperated the rest of society into dissatisfaction bordering on revolt."[33]

Four years later, in his anti-Communist manifesto *The Vital Center*, Schlesinger was denouncing the "sentimentality" of progressives who deplored the work of the robber barons while enjoying its fruits. He asked rhetorically, whether the progressive would "reduce our industrial capacity to the point where it was when the 'robber barons' came on the

---

[32]Pollack, "Fear of Man, Populism, Authoritarianism, and the Historian," *Agricultural History* 39 (1965): 61; Williams, "The Age of Re-Forming History," *Nation* 182 (1956): 552; Shannon letter of 15 December 1965, Curti Papers, 36–15. There is an alternative explanation of Jewish responses to Populism. Daniel Bell recalled for an interviewer discussions about anti-Semitism he had with Richard Hofstadter in the early 1940s. "What arose in our conversations has, I think, shaped a lot of subsequent work. I mean a fear of mass action, a fear of passions let loose. A lot of this goes back in many ways to a particularly Jewish fear. In traditional Jewish life, going back particularly to the Assyrian and Babylonian episodes, the first creativity, there's a fear of what happens when man is let loose. When man doesn't have halacha, the law, he becomes chia, an animal." (23 February 1978 interview with Nathan Liebowitz, in Liebowitz's *Daniel Bell and the Agony of Modern Liberalism* [Westport, Conn., 1985], 70.)
[33](Boston, 1945), 521.

scene. Or has he some other formula for industrialization in a single generation?" Ironically, this was precisely the argument the pro-Soviet writers against whom Schlesinger was writing made with respect to critics of Stalinist industrialization. Reviewing Victor Kravchenko's *I Chose Freedom*, Frederick L. Schumann wrote:

Soviet collectivization and industrialization during the 1930's were agonizing ordeals. . . . The result, however, was victory in building the foundation of Soviet power and the expectation of a life of ultimate abundance and freedom for the Soviet peoples. The result is brushed aside in these pages, as in all the literature of this type. Yet had the victory not been won . . . the fascist powers would have beaten Russia and defeated the United Nations. . . . His preference, like that of Trotsky, Barmine, et al., is that the USSR should have gone under rather than have survived through the use of brutal measures to remake man and society and prepare against the day of attack.[34]

The argument that whatever the moral delinquencies of the robber barons, these were far outweighed by their decisive contribution to American military prowess, was frequently invoked by Allan Nevins. Without their efforts, he wrote, America would have lost the first and second world wars, and would, in the 1950s, be "cowering before the knout held by the Kremlin." In a 1951 speech which *Fortune* hoped might "mark a turning point in the reputation of businessmen and in the attitude of American youth toward business careers," Nevins denounced the "feminine idealism" characteristic of previous historians. They had been "apologetic about our . . . materialism . . . mentioned deprecatingly our worship of size and deplored our boastfulness about steel tonnage . . . spoke scornfully of the robber barons." The new perspective offered by America's emergence to world-power status would allow the so-called robber barons to "stand forth in their true proportions as builders of an indispensable might."[35]

[34]*The Vital Center* (Boston, 1949), 44; Schumann review, *New Republic* 114 (6 May 1946): 668.

[35]Nevins, "Should American History be Rewritten?" *Saturday Review of Literature* 38 (6 February 1954), reprinted in A. S. Eisenstadt, ed., *The Craft of American History* (2 vols., New York, 1966), 1:184; 1951 speech at Stanford Institute of American History, reported in *New York Times*, 6 August 1951; *Fortune* editorial, 44 (September 1951): 83. Nevins's Stanford speech was also hailed in editorials in the *New York Times* (7 August 1951) and New York *Daily News* (12 August 1951). Felix Edgar Wormser, who was heading the fund drive for Columbia's engineering school, wrote Nevins to tell him how much the Stanford speech aided his efforts. "One of the difficulties I have had is to meet the charge that Columbia is riddled with socialists, and even communists. . . . I think your viewpoint as expressed at Palo Alto goes a long way in dissipating this exaggerated and prejudiced viewpoint, for which I want to express to you my deep thanks." (Letter of 7 August 1951, Nevins Papers, Box 83.)

Though Nevins was the best-known voice raised on behalf of what came to be called "business history revisionism," his was by no means the most extreme. Nevins, and other revisionists like Edward Kirkland, had drawn the line at rehabilitating the rapacious speculator Jay Gould, a task undertaken by Louis Hacker in his study of the Gilded Age, or at celebrating the career of the notorious promoter Samuel Insull, which Forrest McDonald did in a 1962 biography. For some historians, like Stanley Pargellis of the Newberry Library, or Henrietta Larsen of the Harvard Business School, business history revisionism was a tool to combat pernicious New Deal antibusiness doctrines which historians had been deceived into embracing. At the other end of the spectrum there were those, like the erstwhile socialist Thomas Cochran, who wanted to leave the field of business history because of uneasiness with the way in which the neutral social scientism he espoused tended to conflate "understanding, explaining, and approving," turning him into an apologist for a system he disliked.[36]

Both business history revisionists and those who held out against them argued from a variety of epistemological standpoints. Allan Nevins had earlier indicated his fierce opposition to historical relativism in general, and Beard's version of it in particular. But in justifying the "new look" in business history, he argued on explicitly relativistic grounds. Foremost among the reasons for historical reinterpretation—more important than the development of new approaches or the discovery of new materials— was "the need of every generation for a reinterpretation to suit its own preconceptions, ideas, and outlook. Every era has its own climate of opinion. It thinks it knows more than the preceding era. . . . Every era, too, is affected by cataclysmic events which shift its point of view. . . . We now possess what Beard would have called a new frame of reference."[37]

[36]Cochran to Merle Curti, 9 March 1950, Curti Papers, 9–17.
[37]"Should American History be Rewritten?" 177–78. Nevins's "relativism" did not extend to permissiveness toward alternative "preconceptions, ideas, and outlook." When Chester M. Destler sought permission to consult Rockefeller papers under Nevins's control, he granted Destler access "With the single restriction that you show me your paper when finished, and if I regard the treatment of this material as unfair, make such modifications as I request. This may seem like a stiff condition! But I presume you have considerable trust in me as a historian, and in my general sense of fairness. I shan't in the least desire to control your conclusions or to affect your general treatment; only to see that Mr. Rockefeller's conversations, which have a peculiar character, shall not be used in a way that will needlessly and improperly damage his reputation." (Nevins to Destler, quoted in Destler to Paul W. Gates, 10 February 1944, Gates Papers.) After strong protests by Destler, Nevins relaxed his requirements. (Copy of Destler to Nevins, 10 February 1944, and Destler to Gates, 23 March 1944, ibid.)

If Nevins acknowledged that the new perspective on business was socially determined, Thomas Cochran, who publicly took a posture of austere scientism, privately suggested the influence on his own thought of much more subjective factors. He speculated to Kenneth Burke about the origin of the differences between himself and his old friend Matthew Josephson concerning robber barons.

The more I think it over the more my argument with Matty seems to rest on a difference in personality that leads to a different rhetoric. Matty deplores the man of power because he inwardly admires and/or envies him. Hence he likes to pick out the chief malefactors and give them the works. I don't think that ambivalence toward power is one of my neuroses—at least not directly. I have rather a passion for order, stemming I suppose from some insecurity feeling. Instead of joining the church I wish to be secure by living in an understandable world. Consequently I hunt for averages, types, patterns, etc., and this does not involve giving any individual much praise or condemnation. It also implies a persuasive rather than an admonitory or exhortatory rhetoric. Is this the standard rationalization for science?[38]

For other business revisionists a correct or "corrected" standpoint was not the result of changed perspective, values, or psychology, but was to be explained on purely factualist grounds—it was a question of available documentation. Stanley Pargellis was appalled at the hostile portrayal of business in the prewar work of Arthur Schlesinger, Sr., Henry Steele Commager, and Merle Curti, but insisted that all three were unsurpassed in "devotion to the standards of an exacting profession" and "allegiance to canons of accuracy and of faithfulness to the record."

What then is the answer? Why are well-trained and honest historians so grossly one-sided in their judgment? The answer is a ridiculously simple one. These men have told their story as they have because that is the only story which the documents available to them let them tell. The papers of hundreds of Farmers' granges are open to the historian; . . . the arguments of the muckrakers are spread in scores of articles and books; the files of congressional investigating committees are heavy with information. . . . But he cannot get into the records of a great corporation.

Pargellis was confident that as he and others succeeded in their efforts to persuade corporations to open their records to prudent, responsible, and objective scholars, "twisted and malformed" interpretations of business history would give way to "sounder evaluation."[39]

---

[38]Cochran to Burke, 1 July 1951, Cochran Papers, Box 1.
[39]Pargellis, *The Judgment of History on American Business* (Princeton, 1943), 17–18, 24. Cf. Edward Kirkland, whose enthusiasm for business history revisionism was tempered

The few who rejected business history revisionism were likewise divided between those of objectivist and relativist turn of mind. Sigmund Diamond, attacking Allan Nevins's biography of John D. Rockefeller, repeatedly hammered home the point that the discreditable features of Rockefeller's activity, features minimized or suppressed by Nevins, were not "a matter of interpretation," but of "fact." Gabriel Kolko, while a graduate student at Harvard, argued that the premises of business revisionism were the mirror image of Marxism in their deterministic, historicist, moral relativism: an "absolution of injustice and cruelty." While the amateur historian Matthew Josephson could hardly look with pleasure on the change in the Zeitgeist which was bringing his school of interpretation into disfavor, and while he thought the pace of change a bit rapid and "Orwellian," he took some comfort from reflecting on the teachings of Croce and Beard, which he endorsed and cited in an exchange with Nevins. He agreed with Nevins that "every era has its own climate of opinion," and acknowledged that the climate of 1933 when he wrote *The Robber Barons* was now a thing of the past.

Today is a different day, and the prevailing trade winds in this country drive us toward mental conformity. Our university scholars are but made of flesh. Even the Justices of the Supreme Court, it has been long said, "follow the election returns" in handing down their opinions. Should historians lag far behind in judging the shift of political power to conservative hands?[40]

If there was, as John Higham maintained at the time, a veritable "cult" of consensus in American historiography in the 1950s, and if counterprogressive themes were overwhelmingly dominant, they never, as we have seen, went completely unchallenged. The University of Wisconsin, not inappropriately, as the institution principally identified with Turner, was something of a Progressive redoubt, holding out against postwar tendencies. It was two Wisconsin products, Merrill Jensen and Turner's grandson Jackson Turner Main, who were the principal defenders of the Progressive view of the Constitution. John D. Hicks, who had spent his most active years at Wisconsin, and Theodore Saloutos, who had taken his degree there with Hicks, were leaders in the defense of the Populists against Hofstadter's criticisms. Higham, another Wisconsin Ph.D., repeatedly, albeit ambivalently, criticized the excesses of the consensus

by concern about how far the "frame-of-reference-boys" would carry it. ("The Robber Barons Revisited," *AHR* 66 [1960]: 73.)

[40]Diamond, "John D. Rockefeller and the Historians," in Sidney Morgenbesser et al., eds., *Philosophy, Science, and Method* (New York, 1969), 602–13; Kolko, "The Premises of Business Revisionism," *Business History Review* 33 (1959): 342; Josephson, "Should American History be Rewritten," in Eisenstadt, ed., *Craft of American History*, 187.

school, while Merle Curti, Wisconsin's most distinguished Americanist, defended the Progressive tradition in his presidential addresses to the Mississippi Valley Historical Association and the American Historical Association in 1952 and 1954. There was, within the Wisconsin community, a general sense of estrangement from prevailing currents. Richard Kirkendall, one of Curti's students, wrote him from Wesleyan in 1955:

> Your observation about Hofstadter's relationship to neo-conservatism is certainly true. If my sample of eastern intellectuals is an accurate one, I would say that among the younger generation liberalism is all but dead. Brockunier reminds me of my Wisconsin friends, but the people who are just emerging from Harvard . . . and elsewhere in the neighborhood tend to sneer at liberalism. . . . One of my friends . . . derided me the other evening as a "Son of the Middle Border." These people share many liberal values, but liberalism to them connotes first of all naiveté—tender mindedness—a failure to recognize the "sinfulness" of men.[41]

Above all, Wisconsin was dedicated to the defense of Beard's reputation, and, with some qualifications, of his teachings. Fred Harvey Harrington was, after the war, the only major diplomatic historian who taught from a "Beardian" perspective. Curti for some time hoped to write Beard's biography, but ultimately was forced to abandon the project because Beard's destruction of his papers left inadequate sources. Howard K. Beale, frustrated by defections on the part of many who had once voiced enthusiasm for the venture, finally brought a Beard Festschrift to completion in the mid-1950s. Warren Susman reported back to Paul Gates, his undergraduate teacher at Cornell, that

> there are three parts of the god-head here at Wisconsin—the Father, the Son, and the Holy Ghost—Beard, Parrington, and Turner. We have gotten to the point where we can admit some failings in Turner—but Beard looms as even a larger task. Even Bill Hesseltine who thinks nothing of damning Turner and even laughing a little at Parrington allows nothing of this when it comes to CAB. With Merle the mention of Beard or of John Dewey evokes a kind of sign of the cross. (In reality Curti is more sensible about the last Beard book and even Beale will admit that certain things shouldn't have been stated in the way they were, but. . . .)

Lee Benson was convinced he lost whatever chance he had for a position at Wisconsin when, at an AHA annual meeting, Beale overheard a con-

---

[41]Letter of 17 December 1955, Curti Papers, 22–17. The reference is to Samuel Brockunier (Ph.D., Harvard, 1937), a member of the Wesleyan History Department.

versation in which Benson had criticized Beard. Later the same day Curti remarked to Benson that he had been informed that Benson had "hopped on the currently fashionable anti-Beard bandwagon."[42]

But apart from occasional cannonades out of the besieged outpost in Madison, Beard's writings, and those of Becker, had few defenders in the 1950s; as few as the overall Progressive interpretation which they embodied and symbolized. Other historical theses with which the two men were closely associated met no better fate. Becker's interpretation of the Enlightenment was savagely attacked by Peter Gay, and came to be abandoned by all but a handful of his most devoted students. Beard's analysis of twentieth-century American foreign policy had even fewer defenders. In these instances, as with the repudiation of their work on the Revolution and the Constitution, it was frequently asserted, in either extenuation or exacerbation, that Becker's and Beard's relativism had helped to lead them astray.

It is difficult to say how important a role the scholarly rejection of Becker's and Beard's substantive work was to the declining influence of their epistemological doctrines. But surely just as the high reputation of their scholarship in the interwar years contributed to their influence as historiologists, the decline of that reputation must, to some indeterminate extent, have served to detract from the acceptability of their conception of the historian's task. Becker's works continued to be prized for their brilliance of style and flashes of insight, even when their principal theses were abandoned. And there was a substantial corps of still admiring students to keep his memory green through the postwar decades. Another reason for Becker's greater acceptability was his characteristic tone of gentle irony, which was fashionable in the fifties, unlike Beard's abrasive sarcasm, which was very much démodé. The efforts of Beard's Wisconsin defenders were unavailing. By the 1960s his reputation was, Hofstadter wrote, "an imposing ruin in the landscape of American historiography."

What was once the grandest house in the province is now a ravaged survival. . . . True, its lofty central portion, constructed in the days when the economic interpretation of history was flourishing, remains in a state of partial repair, and one suspects that several of the rooms, with a little ingenious improvisation, might still be habitable; but it has become shabby and suggests none of its former solidity and elegance. . . . The west wing, dedicated to continental isolationism, looks like a late and relatively hasty addition; a jerry-built affair, now a tattered

---

[42]Susman to Gates, 14 January 1950; Benson to Gates, 7 January 1952; both in Gates Papers.

shambles. . . . The east wing, inspired by historical relativism and showing a little sadly the traces of a wholly derivative design, is entirely neglected.[43]

IV

Consensus among American historians in the postwar decades was even more striking in that realm which had always been marked by the greatest amount of dissension: the long mid-nineteenth-century crisis over questions having to do, in one way or another, with race. Whereas in the establishment of the American historical profession before World War I, historiographical agreement on these issues was grounded on the objective truth of scientific racism, consensus among historians after World War II was based on the objective truth of scientific antiracism. World War II itself, in principle, if not in practice, an antiracist crusade, is sometimes said to have influenced historiography in this direction, and perhaps to a limited extent it did. But a more important factor was the coming to maturity and professional influence of a generation of historians whose antiracist consciousness was formed in the 1930s. Older historians, North and South, continued to write in the old way, but their work was increasingly disparaged—or disregarded. Having played out their role as targets for the new generation, they were rapidly swept into the dustbin of historiography. The transition was accomplished as Max Planck said it customarily was in the physical sciences: "a new scientific truth does not triumph by convincing its opponents and making them see the light, but rather because its opponents eventually die, and a new generation grows up that is familiar with it."[44]

Richard Hofstadter, during World War II, attacked the racism which lay at the foundation of U. B. Phillips's "Plantation Legend." After the war, in *The American Political Tradition*, the abolitionist Wendell Phillips was the only one of the book's protagonists of whom Hofstadter wrote warmly and approvingly. Northern-born historians began to find employment in the South, and brought with them a jaundiced view of local folkways. T. Harry Williams, who commenced a long tenure at Louisiana State University during the war, wrote back to his mentor William B. Hesseltine of the situation that developed when he was asked to give a talk at a local Negro college on southern history.

---

[43]*Progressive Historians*, 344. I have transposed the order of Hofstadter's description of the east and west wings.
[44]*Scientific Autobiography and Other Papers* (New York, 1949), 33–34.

Remembering my alien ancestry, I decided to get an O.K. from the president. After I told him the facts he said: "The Board will raise hell if you speak to niggers. Niggers are trying to get in to L.S.U. The Board wouldn't like it if you spoke to niggers and then came back and spoke to our children. . . ." I asked with sarcasm that wasn't appreciated, I mean he didn't get it, "Is it all right if I go out and look at the buildings?" That was all right. But think, I went out and looked at nigger buildings and then came back and looked at our white buildings. Damn you, don't use this in an article.

Kenneth Stampp, like Williams a student of Hesseltine's, wrote his teacher just after the war to let off steam about the older generation of Civil War historians.

James G. Randall is a damned Negro-hating, abolitionist-baiting, doughface. . . . I'm sick of the Randalls, Cravens and other doughfaces who crucify the abolitionists for attacking slavery. If I had lived in the 1850's, I would have been a rabid abolitionist. When the secession crisis came I would have followed the abolitionist line: let 'em secede and good riddance. . . . But once the war came, I would have tried to get something out of it. I would have howled for abolition, and for the confiscation and distribution of large estates among negroes and poor whites, as the Radicals (some of them) did. I would have been a Radical because there was nothing better to be. I couldn't have been a conservative Lincoln Republican and rubbed noses with the Blairs and Sewards; and I couldn't have been a Negro-hating copperhead. My only criticism of the Radicals is that they weren't radical enough, at least so far as the southern problem was concerned.[45]

The decade of the 1950s saw an ever increasing commitment of historians to racial equality—and greater zeal in its pursuit. Inevitably, like everything else in this period, racial questions were caught up in the cold war. There was an ultimately successful effort in the Mississippi Valley Historical Association to cease holding meetings in cities where only segregated accommodations were available. Howard K. Beale, the most

[45]Williams to Hesseltine, 19 April 1945, Hesseltine Papers, M66–132/5; Stampp to Hesseltine, 6 March 1946, ibid., M68–25/3. Williams shared Stampp's dismay that racist scholarship was not labeled as such. He wrote Hesseltine that "it's a crying shame the way the profession has reviewed [E. Merton] Coulter's godawful book on Reconstruction. Isn't someone going to have the courage to say it's based on race prejudice and distortion of the sources?" (Undated [probably 1948] letter, Hesseltine Papers, M68–25/3.) John Hope Franklin wrote a scathing review of Coulter's *The South During Reconstruction* for the *Journal of Negro History* and mailed five hundred reprints to historians all over the country. "The reaction was tremendous," Franklin recalled many years later. "I got a stack of letters two inches thick from the historians telling me that they were touched, that they hadn't looked at the book the way I had." (Jack Star, "Above All, A Scholar," *Change* 9 [February 1977]: 30.)

militant and impatient of those involved in the struggle, made it clear in a letter to Thomas Clark of the University of Kentucky that desegregating the MVHA was an anti-Communist duty:

I wonder if Mr. [Dwight] Dumond and his friends, who I am sure are devoted to America, have ever thought of the tremendous service they are doing to communism in her fight against America and democracy to put into communist hands to use with the millions of people that our government is trying to win away from Russian influence, the record of a scholarly organization that is threatened with disruption in democratic America because a group . . . insists upon maintaining distinctions of class and color[;] think what a service we will do world communism in its fight against our country if we support the belief that a man, however great a scholar, however loyal an American, and however true a gentleman, must not be allowed to sleep in the same building with other scholars and gentlemen, or to mingle with them socially at scholarly meetings because of his color.[46]

A number of historians worked on the NAACP brief in the epochal case of *Brown v. Board of Education*. By 1956, when the strife-ridden Brooklyn College History Department wanted to find a nominee for department chairman whom the president of the college couldn't turn down, they hit on the name of John Hope Franklin. By the late 1950s, as the civil rights movement gathered steam, an increasing number of young historians found in that struggle an outlet for social energies and idealism bottled up in the previous period of political quiescence. In the early 1960s some younger historians (Howard Zinn, Staughton Lynd) began teaching at southern black colleges. By-then-middle-aged historians like Walter Johnson, Hofstadter, and Woodward were marching with Martin Luther King from Selma to Montgomery.[47]

Historical controversies on race-related issues were considerably more

---

[46]Letter of 2 February 1954, copy in Shannon Papers, Box 2. Anti-Communism could work the other way as well. Protests by Negro students and others at the City College of New York were ultimately successful in ending the use of Samuel E. Morison and Henry Steele Commager's *Growth of the American Republic* in classes because of its racist characterizations of Negroes. But the initial reaction of the CCNY History Department was to defend the text—whose racism was privately acknowledged—because Communists were active in the campaign against it. (La Wanda Cox to Merle Curti, 6 October 1950, Curti Papers, 10–16.) Defending his characterization of slavery, Morison wrote a correspondent that "the Negroes were the most successful slave race; that is, as slaves, in modern history; much more satisfactory, as slaves, I mean, than the Greeks, the American Indians or any Oriental population. There must be some essential docility in their character that made it so." (Letter to Harvey Wish, 8 October 1952, Wish Papers.) Interestingly, in light of a later shift in terminological fashion, one of the criticisms of the Morison and Commager text was that it sometimes employed the term "blacks" instead of "Negroes." (*Time* 57 [26 February 1951]: 48–49.)

[47]Jesse D. Clarkson of the Brooklyn Department explained their strategy to Franklin when sounding him out about the possibility of coming to Brooklyn. Reported, on the basis of

decorous and limited in scope than they had been in previous years, or were to be again, later on, in the late sixties and seventies. Historical writing on these issues had often been characterized by highly emotive, and moralistic, language, generally regarded as an index of the sharpness of the differences which divided the contestants. But as the profession moved toward consensus on substantive issues of interpretation, the question of the appropriate tone for discussing the issues remained. Indeed, the question of rhetoric often became central, as substantive issues became resolved, or narrowed in scope. As consensus on issues of racial justice became not just broader but deeper and more passionate, agreement on "the facts" ceased to be associated with the detached posture and neutral descriptive tone the traditional norms of objectivity had mandated. Historians repeatedly had to address the relationship of moral commitment and moralistic language to historical scholarship.

The new antiracist consensus was most clearly manifest in the historiography of slavery and of Reconstruction. In both areas insofar as there were ideological differences between scholars they were fairly narrow, between moderate conservatives, who in glossing the Supreme Court's famous phrase on the pace of integration stressed the word "deliberate," and moderate liberals, who stressed the word "speed." The main thrust of postwar historical writing in both realms was to turn earlier evaluations on their head. Slavery was brutal and repressive rather than benign. Reconstruction was a "tragic era" not because of excesses in its treatment of whites, but because it stopped so far short of effective emancipation of the Negro.

In a 1952 survey of the scholarly literature on slavery, Kenneth Stampp noted that while members of the "scientific" and "subjectivist-presentist-relativist" schools were still debating whether historians were entitled to pass moral judgments, and whether they could succeed in transcending their own backgrounds, it was undeniable that "so far as Negro slavery is concerned we are still waiting for the first scientific and completely objec-

conversation with Franklin, by Horace S. Merrill to William B. Hesseltine, 8 January 1956, Hesseltine Papers, M66–132/8. One interesting index of the growth of antiracism was the change in the historiographical fortunes of the abolitionists, who had, during the preceding decades, generally been treated as troublemaking extremists. During the 1960s the abolitionists' stock simultaneously went up, as that of "moderates" on racial issues went down; and got lower, as standards for what counted as thoroughgoingly egalitarian racial attitudes got higher. In the early 1960s Martin Duberman, putting together an anthology of new essays on the movement, found it impossible to find any younger scholars who took the traditional view of abolitionists as "meddlesome fanatics." Those historians, North and South, whose work made clear their commitment to the cause of racial equality were frequently called "neo-abolitionists"—a not unfriendly characterization, and one which many so-designated embraced.

tive study of the institution which is based upon no assumptions whose validity cannot be thoroughly proved." Stampp acknowledged that the very act of disapproving slavery was a "subjective bias," but to assert innate Negro inferiority went beyond this. Such an assertion demonstrated inexcusable "ignorance of, or disregard for, the overwhelming evidence to the contrary," particularly that embodied in Gunnar Myrdal's *An American Dilemma*. And he set forth the essential precondition of a "scientific and completely objective study": "No historian of the institution can be taken seriously any longer unless he begins with the knowledge that there is no valid evidence that the Negro race is innately inferior to the white, and that there is growing evidence that both races have approximately the same potentialities." Stampp's 1956 *The Peculiar Institution* exemplified this outlook. In its most quoted sentence he made explicit his assumption that "the slaves were merely ordinary human beings, that innately Negroes *are*, after all, only white men with black skins, nothing more, nothing less."[48]

At the end of the 1950s Stanley Elkins published his *Slavery*, and initiated a long discussion on the slave personality. Elkins provoked many historians with his suggestion that just as Nazi concentration camps had "infantilized" their inmates, slavery had produced "Sambo." The stereotype of the grinning, shuffling, feckless, childish slave was not, said Elkins, a racist fiction, but the consequence of incarceration in the "closed system" of North American slavery. In his focus on the brutalities of the system, Elkins clearly aligned himself with Stampp rather than Phillips. But his acceptance of "Sambo" as psychic reality, rather than a form of "puttin' on ole massa," had implications for the twentieth century which were, for obvious reasons, not altogether congenial to most liberal integrationists.

Elkins had a certain ironic detachment from what he saw as Stampp's uncritical acceptance of liberal pieties. In Elkins's view these gave *The Peculiar Institution* an unacceptable moralistic tone, and an undeserved reputation for objectivity.

With the "proved assumptions" of the social sciences at his disposal . . . Stampp prepared to banish Phillips into full retirement and to produce the "objective study." In short, "objectivity" and the discrediting of Phillips were assumed to be not only fully compatible but inseparable. . . . To challenge Phillips' assumption of racial inferiority, Stampp made use of the extensive Myrdal material, whose scientific legitimacy had been unimpeachably established. But he did so without

[48]"The Historian and Southern Negro Slavery," *AHR* 57 (1952): 613, 619–20; *The Peculiar Institution: Slavery in the Ante-Bellum South* (New York, 1956), vii.

making much distinction between what was clearly "scientific" in it and what was earnestly and animatedly normative. Since the Myrdal studies themselves crackled with moral electricity, Stampp, by adopting their attitude (his own pages similarly crackle), was returning to a long-familiar moral position through the back door. . . . Numerous "scientific" possibilities . . . were ignored in *The Peculiar Institution*. Whatever submissiveness, cheerfulness, and childishness could be observed among the ante-bellum plantation Negroes was automatically discredited; these features could not be accepted as typical and normal—not for a white man, and therefore not for anyone: "Negroes *are*, after all, only white men with black skins, nothing more, nothing less." . . . Professor Stampp, like his abolitionist forbears, is still as much concerned as they to prove slavery an abomination and to prove master and slave equal before their Maker.[49]

C. Vann Woodward became the dominant figure in studies of the South in Reconstruction and thereafter. As Stampp's revised portrayal of the antebellum Negro had promoted a more hopeful view of the prospects for integration from one side, Woodward's writings on postbellum whites did so from the other. In a series of works of which the most influential was *The Strange Career of Jim Crow*, Woodward endeavored, as he had done earlier in his *Tom Watson*, to "indicate that things have not always been the same in the South"; to show that "the belief that [southern racial policies] are immutable and unchangeable is not supported by history." In *Jim Crow*, whose first chapter was significantly entitled "Forgotten Alternatives," Woodward attempted to show that the elaborate legal structure of segregation, which most southerners believed was timeless, had not been instituted until some time after the end of Reconstruction. He cited evidence of peaceful mingling of whites and blacks in saloons, restaurants, and trains. If in the late nineteenth century, why not in the mid-twentieth century?[50]

Many journals assigned the book to black reviewers, but black or white, all agreed in treating the book as a contribution to contemporary discussions of desegregation. Rayford W. Logan in the *American Historical Review* thought it showed that recent cracks in the Jim Crow wall were "understandable in part because of the relative recency of many of the segregation laws" and that "additional breakdowns of the barriers may be easier for the same reason." In the *Mississippi Valley Historical*

---

[49]*Slavery: A Problem in American Institutional and Intellectual Life* (Chicago, 1959), 22–23. It is noteworthy that Elkins omitted the key word "innately" in his quotation from Stampp, since David Potter did exactly the same thing when reviewing *The Peculiar Institution*, and subsequently apologized for having done so. (For the original review, *Yale Review* 46 [1956]: 261; for the apology, see I. A. Newby, ed., *The Civil War and Reconstruction, 1850–1877* [New York, 1971], 106–7.)
[50](New York, 1955), 47.

Review a white historian teaching at the University of Tennessee thought the book would "help materially in easing the adjustments of thinking and viewpoint made necessary by recent decisions of the Supreme Court." E. Franklin Frazier in the *Saturday Review of Literature* believed that Woodward had shown that "the race problem was *made* and that men can *unmake* it, as they are attempting today," while in the *Journal of Southern History* a black historian was pleased that the book was reaching the reading public "at the precise period when it can make a very significant contribution to the embattled forces of law and order, of sanity and reason."[51]

Woodward himself had reservations about the uses to which the book was put, distressed that there were those who took him to be saying that Jim Crow was "superficially rooted and easily eradicated." David Potter, surveying Woodward's work and career some years later, agreed that the arguments of *The Strange Career of Jim Crow* had often been vulgarized by its readers, but thought that Woodward himself was not without responsibility for misunderstandings. And he pointed to the source of an ambivalence which pervaded Woodward's work.

When an historian has a strong ideological commitment, a tension may be set up between his devotion to the commitment and his devotion to realism for its own sake. . . . His historical realism was pitted against his liberal urge to find constructive meanings in the past for the affairs of the present. His realism never lost hold, but his liberal urge constantly impelled him to emphasize viewpoints which his realism constantly impelled him to qualify and dilute. . . . The urgency of Woodward's desire to find answers in the past which would aid in the quest for solution of the problems of the present . . . distorted his image of the past, at least for a time and to a limited degree.

For Potter, Woodward's work raised but did not answer the question: "Can history retain its integrity as a rigorous and disciplined form of scholarly inquiry even while partaking of public and functional uses in our encounter with current issues?"[52]

By the 1950s the question of the origins of the Civil War was neither as much discussed nor as controversial as it had been in previous decades.

---

[51]Logan, *AHR* 61 (1955): 212; Stanley J. Folmsbee, *MVHR* 42 (1955): 579; Frazier, *Saturday Review* 38 (11 June 1955): 13; Rufus E. Clement, *Journal of Southern History* 21 (1955): 557.

[52]Woodward, "What Happened to the Civil Rights Movement?" (1967), in *The Burden of Southern History* (rev. ed., Baton Rouge, 1968), 183; Potter, "C. Vann Woodward," in Marcus Cunliffe and Robin Winks, eds., *Pastmasters: Some Essays on American Historians* (New York, 1969), 397–98, 401–2, 406–7.

But it was this subject which most clearly counterposed the rival claims of moral commitment and detached objectivity in historical writing.[53]

Writing in 1946, Bernard De Voto explained Civil War revisionism, the view that the conflict was avoidable, by the fact that revisionists like Avery O. Craven and James G. Randall "happened to be young and impressionable at a time when an intellectual fashion was developing the (erroneous) thesis that the United States could and should have stayed out of the First World War and the (false) theorem that we were betrayed into it by propaganda." It was the unwillingness of revisionists to acknowledge the great moral issue of the Civil War that outraged De Voto.

As for considering even theoretically that the problem of slavery may have involved moral questions, God forbid. History will not put itself in the position of saying that any thesis may have been wrong, any cause evil, or any group of men heretical. A thesis may have been insufficient and a cause may have been defeated but, even at the end of the [Second] World War, history will not deal with moral values, though of course the Republican radicals were, well, culpable.

A few years later Oscar Handlin struck a similar note in chastising Allan Nevins for failing to recognize that there was "surely a difference between being a fanatic for freedom and being a fanatic for slavery."[54]

The Dutch historian Pieter Geyl, writing in *The New England Quarterly*, thought that the Beards, though not themselves Civil War revisionists, had laid the groundwork for that "amoral" viewpoint by their "despiritualization" of the episode; had directed their focus away from the moral issue—the fact that behind the abolitionists stood "the silent condemnation of the free North, of Europe, of the world." In considering Lincoln's struggle to preserve the Union from the perspective of the early years of the cold war, Geyl was "almost tempted to believe that it

---

[53]David Donald suggested that one important reason for the neglect of the Civil War by consensus historians was that "so appalling an aberration is inexplicable, easiest to pass over in silence." ("American Historians and the Causes of the Civil War," *South Atlantic Quarterly* 59 [1960]: 354.) Daniel Boorstin confessed that the Civil War was an anomaly and an embarrassment for his interpretation, but undaunted sought to show how "the circumstances of the struggle circumscribed the Civil War debate and prevented it from becoming a free-for-all among political theorists [and] was even to reinforce our sense of the continuity of our history." (*Genius*, 99–100.) This led Richard Hofstadter to respond with a vision of a cartoon: "a Reb and a Yank meet in 1865 to survey the physical and moral devastation of the war. 'Well,' says one to the other consolingly, 'at least we escaped the ultimate folly of producing political theorists.'" (*Progressive Historians*, 462.) Probably the most important factor in the decline in Civil War studies was boredom with a subject which seemed, at least for the time being, to have been exhausted.

[54]De Voto, "The Easy Chair," *Harper's* 192 (1946): 124, 126; Handlin, review of *The Emergence of Lincoln, Nation* 147 (1950): 513.

was inspired by a prophetic vision of our own times." If the South had successfully seceded, "the world role played by the United States today, and the role which no doubt it will be called upon to play in the future, would be impossible."[55]

It was Arthur Schlesinger, Jr. who provided the most comprehensive statement of the necessity of considering the Civil War from the perspective of morality, and of twentieth-century diplomacy. In language which made manifest his debt to Reinhold Niebuhr, Schlesinger expressed his belief that

the vogue of revisionism is connected with the modern tendency to seek in optimistic sentimentalism an escape from the severe demands of moral decision; . . . it is the offspring of our modern sentimentality which at once evades the essential moral problems in the name of a superficial objectivity and asserts their unimportance in the name of an invincible progress. . . . We have here a touching afterglow of the admirable nineteenth-century faith in the full rationality and perfectibility of man; the faith that the errors of the world would all in time be "outmoded."

When Schlesinger reviewed Nevins's *Ordeal of the Union* in 1947 he saw it as taking a middle-of-the-road position on the question of revisionism, but he was bothered by what he took to be the book's implications.

The issue here posed—what policy would have averted war—goes down to the question we formulate today in terms of appeasement or resistance. A future historian might say, much in Mr. Nevins' language, that the primary task of statesmanship in the 1930's was to furnish a workable adjustment between the USA and Germany, while offering strong inducements to the German people to abandon the police state, and equal persuasion to the Americans to help the Nazis rather than to scold them. In essence, this is Mr. Wallace's current thesis about the Russians. Comparisons with the issues of the Civil War may be extreme: yet one must face the hard fact that closed and authoritarian social systems tend to create a compulsive intransigence in their own ruling groups—and that these groups may respond much more to a firmness which wakens them to some sense of actuality than to a forbearance which is never great enough and always to be discounted.

Two years later Schlesinger's position had hardened. By 1949 his tolerance for any hint that the Civil War was not inevitable had declined, and he now characterized Nevins's discussion of Civil War inevitability as showing "entire acceptance of revisionism." Whereas earlier he had sug-

[55]"The American Civil War and the Problem of Inevitability," *New England Quarterly* 24 (1951); reprinted in his *Debates with Historians* (Cleveland, 1958), 244–45, 261–62.

gested that the lesson of the coming of the Civil War was that an American policy of firmness with the Soviets might produce moderation of their conduct, now he went to the brink of saying that the lesson to be drawn was the inevitability of armed conflict. Then, as in 1949, one was in the presence of "moral differences far too profound to be solved by compromise." Small wonder that John Higham privately characterized Schlesinger's article on the causes of the Civil War as "an obvious exercise in historical rearmament for World War III."[56]

The presence of "moralism" in accounts of the Civil War was disturbing to two quite different groups of historians, each of which, though on completely different grounds, expressed a strong preference for a more austere and objective approach. For a number of pro-southern historians "moralism" in accounts of the Civil War was offensive because it was *northern* moralism. They somewhat disingenuously appealed to professional standards of impartiality. Nevins's work, unacceptable to Schlesinger because of its amoral "superficial objectivity," was the target of southern attacks for its moralistic departures from objectivity. Avery O. Craven called Nevins's work "shallow and biased," deficient in precisely the qualities of "objectivity and balance" which were most necessary in dealing with "a period when passions were aroused." Fletcher M. Green thought Nevins was "blinded by his sense of moral values." Robert H. Woody observed that "It may all be very well to take one's stand with freedom as against slavery; it is worth suggesting, however, that it makes difficult an impartial account."[57]

If for southerners the "moralistic" character of professional discourse

---

[56]"The Causes of the Civil War: A Note on Historical Sentimentalism," *Partisan Review* 16 (1949): 976, 979; review of *Ordeal of the Union, Saturday Review of Literature* 30 (18 October 1947): 9–10; "Causes of the Civil War," 977; Higham to Merle Curti, 9 January 1950, Curti Papers, 19–19. It was by no means gratuitous, or a sign of an unusually "presentist" frame of mind, for Schlesinger to draw contemporary lessons from Nevins's book, since Nevins himself had done so in the preface to *The Ordeal of the Union*: "Twice in a century and a half terrible calamities came; twice a failure of statesmanship if not of national character cost the country far more than it could afford to pay. The Civil War and the Second World War should have been avoidable. Because the people and leaders of the United States did not act with determination and sagacity in solving the problems of slavery, sectional irritation, and a right adjustment of races, part of the country was half ruined for generations, and all of it set back by decades. The subsequent failure to consolidate the victory won in the First World War—the refusal to help set up a system of collective security and to play a manly, farsighted part in the world community—imperilled the very existence of the republic. Only colossal effort and the sacrifice of a vast part of the national wealth saved it. Such errors can in time be largely retrieved. But they cannot be forgotten or forgiven, and their lessons should be driven home." (viii.)
[57]Review of *The Emergence of Lincoln* by Craven, *Yale Review* 40 (1951): 723; Green, review of *The Ordeal of the Union, MVHR* 35 (1948): 128; Woody, review of *The Ordeal of the Union, South Atlantic Quarterly* 47 (1948): 389.

on the Civil War was unsatisfactory because of its particular tilt, for others, northerners with no interest in defending the Confederacy, such an approach was unsatisfactory because it implicitly renounced the goal of moving toward consensus on the objective explanation of the Civil War. Historians of the Civil War who wanted to expel moralism and produce a convergent, value-neutral explanation of the conflict, sometimes invoked the authority of objectivist philosophers—Morris Cohen, Ernest Nagel, Karl Popper—and characteristically urged that quantification or more rigorous concepts borrowed from the social sciences would aid in the search for closure. Edwin Rozwenc of Amherst, editor of an anthology on the causes of the Civil War, considered various strategies for escaping the "chaos of historical discourse which is completely subjective and partisan." He thought the most fruitful approach, in "the day of the electronic computing machine and of the lavish research grant" was the mounting of "a comprehensive attack, with abundant tables and measurements, upon the causal variables in the explanation of the American Civil War." Lee Benson, in a series of papers, explored social scientific strategies through which differences over the causes of the Civil War could be "objectively resolved," eliminating unscientific explanations and assigning precise weights to causal variables.[58]

But in epistemological posture, as in substantive interpretation, this was a period of compromise and conciliation. Synthesis rather than polarization was the order of the day. Those historians who prized detachment and who sought certitude and closure were willing to grant that their attainment was problematic. Elkins, who wanted to replace moralistic treatments of slavery with a social scientific approach, acknowledged that even for the most disinterested of scholars, "how a person thinks about Negro slavery historically makes a great deal of difference here and now; it tends to locate him morally in relation to a whole range of very immediate political, social, and philosophical issues." Rozwenc admitted that

---

[58]Rozwenc, "The Present Crisis in the Historical Explanation of the Causes of the American Civil War," in his *The Causes of the American Civil War* (Lexington, Mass., 1961), 228–30; Benson, "Causation and the American Civil War," *History and Theory* 1 (1961), reprinted in his *Toward the Scientific Study of History* (Philadelphia, 1972), 96–97; Benson and Thomas J. Pressly, "Can Differences in Interpretations of the American Civil War Be Resolved Objectively?" paper delivered at the 1956 meeting of the AHA, 73. The same desire to escape moralism in historiography via a social scientific approach was found among historians in adjacent fields. Elkins had complained that down through the 1950s "the rhythm of 'right' and 'wrong' which characterized ante-bellum discourse on the subject of slavery has retained much of its original simplicity and vigor." David Donald found Reconstruction historiography trapped into trying to deal with "questions involving value judgments. . . . To such questions . . . there can be no final answers." (Elkins, *Slavery*, 1; Donald, *The Politics of Reconstruction, 1863–1867* [Baton Rouge, 1965], xiii.)

despite the utmost rigor of approach, "historical explanations will always tend to be tenuous and speculative." Benson, though indefatigable in his efforts to find ways to resolve differences objectively, and measure variables precisely, conceded that it was an open question whether this could in fact be accomplished.[59]

Views that were in any respect relativist were expressed with even greater circumspection. Vann Woodward was always very conflicted about the "presentism" of his work. He alternated between denying it, qualifying it, and apologizing for it. In three separate surveys of the literature on the causes of the Civil War, Howard K. Beale, Kenneth Stampp, and David Potter found no prospect of ultimate agreement, and all agreed on the "relativistic" proposition that differences in historians' background and philosophy, and changes in the climate of opinion, would continue to cause historians' interpretations to diverge. But none of the three saw in this any grounds for discouragement. Beale, despite finding that every recent interpretation had already been offered in the nineteenth century, saw "the constant striving toward never-fully-obtainable objectivity or fairmindedness [bringing] us closer than we were to a clear and true picture of the causes of the Civil War." Stampp, too, found that "twentieth-century historians often merely go back to interpretations advanced by partisans while the war was still in progress," but remained confident that "we have gradually enlarged our knowledge and deepened our understanding." And Potter thought that despite the persistence of disagreement, there was "objective progress" insofar as increased factual mastery "narrows the alternatives between which controversy continues to rage."[60]

The dramatic swings in the historical treatments of slavery, the Civil War, and Reconstruction during the course of the twentieth century produced a great many historiographical surveys, which sought to explicate and explain the evolution of interpretations over the years. In conducting such surveys, one could, on the one hand, stress the "plus ça change, plus c'est la même chose" dimension of scholarship—the extent to which changes in interpretation appeared cyclical, dependent on

[59]Elkins, *Slavery*, 1; Rozwenc, "Present Crisis," 230; Benson, "Causation," 97.
[60]For Woodward, see the successive editions of his *Strange Career of Jim Crow* and "The Strange Career of a Historical Controversy" in his *American Counterpoint: Slavery and Racism in the North-South Dialogue* (Boston, 1971), 234–60. Beale, "What Historians Have Said About the Causes of the Civil War," in Social Science Research Council, *Theory and Practice in Historical Study: A Report of the Committee on Historiography* (New York, 1946), 91; Stampp, *The Causes of the Civil War* (Englewood Cliffs, N.J., 1959), v–vi; Potter, "The Literature on the Background of the Civil War," in *The South and the Sectional Conflict* (Baton Rouge, 1968), 146–47.

changes in the idiosyncracies of historians and shifts in the climate of opinion. On the other hand, one could focus on growing sophistication of approach, increments in reliable information, the demolition of misconceptions. One approach was professionally discouraging, the other encouraging.

The growing professional self-confidence of these years, to which we will turn in Chapter 12, inclined historians to optimism. Shortly after his discharge from the army in 1945, Thomas J. Pressly began writing *Americans Interpret Their Civil War,* the most comprehensive survey of middle-period historiography published in these years. Looking back at it from the early sixties, in the introduction to a paperback edition, Pressly noted that his views had evolved. During the course of the 1950s he had come to believe that historians' disagreements were more likely to be based on factual differences than on the ideological differences he had earlier emphasized. The book he had written as a young man maintained that historians' experiences and presuppositions were often more influential than evidence in shaping their interpretations. He had concluded that, paradoxically, rather than the passage of time providing perspective, it seemed to increase emotional commitment to partisan viewpoints. He had stressed the ways in which the climate of opinion influenced trained scholars as much as it did laymen. Overall, the book had not "provide[d] much warmth for the ego of the historian"—particularly in its suggestion that contemporaries "have interpreted the crises of their age with as much understanding as has been mustered by trained historians of later generations."

Were he to rewrite the book, he reflected in 1962, it would strike a much more professionally affirmative note. He would balance what he had previously written with the "satisfying conviction" he had come to that " 'progress' in historical scholarship can be demonstrated."

This type of self-examination by historians, this type of historiography, can impart to the historian a proud sense of "guild expertise"—pride in the guild of historians whose members have been trained in techniques of historical research unknown to "laymen," pride in the guild whose members have collected a mass of information concerning past events, whose members have a perspective, due to the passage of time, which enables them to view the past with greater detachment and clarity than did participants in the past events.[61]

[61](1954; paperback, New York, 1965), 11–13, 335, 358.

12

An autonomous profession

In previous chapters we have seen how partially and incompletely historians had succeeded in meeting all the criteria of an academic profession, criteria drawn from models of the free professions and from scientific disciplines. Insofar as the concept "profession" remains an ideal type, it will by definition forever be imperfectly realized, but the postwar years saw dramatic progress in fulfilling the old program of professionalizing historical studies. Whereas in the interwar years historians had only indifferent success in achieving such key elements of academic professionalism as autonomy from lay control, heightened status, universalistic criteria of evaluation, and a dominant research ethos, the postwar years saw substantial advances in all these areas, producing a sense of self-confidence and self-satisfaction which clearly distinguishes this period from those which preceded and which followed. The doubts and discouragements which had characterized the interwar years, and which, as we have seen, had consequences for attitudes toward objectivity, gave way to an increasing sense that American professional historical scholarship was a vital, growing, and prospering venture.

John Higham, whose 1965 survey of the historical profession reflected contemporary mainstream opinion, wrote that "the depressing sense of a loss of status, which was so widespread in the first quarter of the twentieth century, has been dramatically reversed since World War II."

Instead of looking backward to the esteem attached to "character" and "culture" among the genteel classes of the late nineteenth century, college professors have become conscious of their rising importance as a relatively autonomous group on the national scene. The jibes that cultural critics of the 1920's leveled at the ineffectuality of academic men have all but vanished; and the stock figure of the absentminded professor is gone from our folk humor. . . . Certainly the university has never before played so large a part in American intellectual activity as it does today. . . . The professor has emerged . . . not only as the visible possessor of intellectual authority but also as the gatekeeper at the citadel of all of the elites. . . . In place of the reputation once derived from association with a social class, the professor has acquired a new, occupational prestige from his entrenchment in a mighty institution.[1]

Reconciling themselves to a loss of control over precollegiate history education, and less concerned than formerly with the lay audience, an increasingly professionalized discipline gloried in its autonomy from the norms of social science and from the epistemological conundrums of philosophers. Though assertions about objectivity were characteristically more qualified and nuanced than they had once been, there was a deep and widespread conviction that the profession was moving steadily in the direction of establishing objective historical truth.

I

Renewed professional self-confidence was in part a matter of sheer growth. Membership in the American Historical Association was not much higher in 1940 than it had been before World War I. It increased by more than 60 percent between 1940 and 1950, at the same rate in the decade of the fifties, and in the sixties grew by over 90 percent to a total of eighteen thousand. The overall size of the professorate increased fivefold between 1940 and 1970. During the 1930s about 150 history doctorates were awarded annually; after a wartime slump this grew to about 350 annually in the mid-1950s, 600 by the mid-1960s, and more than 1,000 by the end of that decade. Many of the new entrants to the historical profession found jobs in new and smaller institutions, but departments in major institutions also expanded substantially, growing to dimensions undreamed of in previous generations. Departments that once had no more than a handful of historians on permanent appointments came to count their tenured members in the dozens.

Rapid growth brought some unanticipated consequences. One was the feudalization of a number of major departments, as fields of specialization attained quasi-autonomous status, with a consequent narrowing of breadth among both faculty and graduate students. The multiplication of journals and societies for specialists in a variety of fields furthered the same development. Another unanticipated consequence was growing

[1]Higham et al., *History* (Princeton, 1965), 65–66.

"elitism" within the AHA. Whereas once the association could not fill its offices and major committees without reaching down to smaller colleges and institutions of the second rank, after the war those who held these positions increasingly came from a handful of major universities. The material rewards of the profession did not always keep up with growth in size. It was not until the 1950s that salaries (in constant dollars) caught up with prewar levels. After the swelling of student populations by veterans in the late 1940s there was a severe slump in the job market. But for the thousands who found jobs, morale was high. Low enrollments were clearly a temporary phenomenon, and academics knew that before long the baby-boom generation would arrive on campuses, bringing with them an academic sellers' market. Even when the current job market was bleakest, there was full awareness that better times were on the horizon. In the mid-1950s, 55 percent of undergraduate history majors with A averages planned to go on to graduate school. It was only after 1957 that Sputnik made investment in higher education a cold war imperative, but for some years previously there had been a steady increase in the availability of fellowship assistance for graduate students, particularly for research abroad.[2]

Even before the job market turned around, "professional autonomy" advanced steadily, as it became increasingly rare for administrators to make appointments without the agreement of departments. In the early 1940s most of the Berkeley History Department did not know that Raymond J. Sontag was even being considered for a position until he wrote to accept an offer, and John D. Hicks's appointment was arranged by the department head without its members being consulted. Within a few years such procedures would become unthinkable. The "department head," who was an agent of the central administration, gave way to the "chairman," who was, at most, *primus inter pares.*[3]

Democratization of hiring meant that outrageously inappropriate appointments became rarer, but so, too, did adventurous ones, as the need to satisfy a consensus often favored the bland and uncontroversial. Few historians, however, regretted the gradual disappearance of the wealthy patron who could specify the holder of a chair, or the replacement of an

---

[2]Confident predictions of a turnaround in the job market included J. F. Wellemeyer, "Survey of United States Historians, 1952, and a Forecast," *AHR* 61 (1956): 339, and Dexter Perkins, "We Shall Gladly Teach," *AHR* 62 (1957): 292. For history majors' career plans, see Dexter Perkins and John L. Snell, *The Education of Historians in the United States* (New York, 1962), 38. Thirty years earlier, in a roughly comparable survey, only 20 percent had such plans. (See Higham et al., *History,* 67.)
[3]Hicks to Robert Reynolds, 1 July 1943, Hicks Papers, Box 6.

"ad hominem" system of research support by one in which a system based on peer review dispensed foundation grants. The increasing availability of faculty fellowships was both cause and effect of a reorientation of the academic ethos toward scholarship. Compared with other disciplines, history remained relatively teaching-oriented, but there was an increased emphasis on research as compared with the interwar years— particularly at once somnolent Ivy League schools. As an interesting example of the shift, one can compare the remarks of John D. Hicks and Jack H. Hexter with respect to the relative importance of teaching and publication. Reflecting on the very small sales of his interwar *Populist Revolt* (1,500 copies in seventeen years), Hicks found solace in the thought that in a teaching career of thirty-five years, averaging one hundred students a year, a professor of history would have "left his mark on the minds of about 3,500 students in his time, and usually a much deeper mark than the mark most reference works ever make on anybody." Hexter, in the 1960s, wrote:

I have been a classroom teacher since 1936. In that time, on a fair estimate I have taught about 5000 students face-to-face. In the past three years I edited one book, contributed a large section to another, and wrote a third. All are for the use of college students. The combined sales of the three are already more than 100,000 copies and the end is not yet in sight. Therefore, in the past three years I taught 2000 per cent more students by publishing than I have taught face-to-face in thirty-three; and I will be teaching many more.[4]

Academic hiring became more meritocratic, and more universalistic. Even at Harvard, which continued to draw its tenured faculty overwhelmingly from its own students, there was some embarrassment at the institution's reputation for inbreeding, and Oscar Handlin urged the permanent appointment of an outsider over a homegrown product on the grounds that it "would do us a lot of good in the country (i.e., in the profession outside New England)." Handlin himself was a symbol of the most significant universalization of hiring criteria: the entry, for the first time, of a substantial number of Jews into the profession.[5]

[4]Hicks, "What's Right with the History Profession," *Pacific Historical Review* 25 (1956): 124–25; Hexter, "Publish or Perish—A Defense," *Public Interest* 17 (1969): 71. Though historians were increasingly research-oriented, they lagged behind other fields. Differences in modes of presentation make cross-disciplinary comparisons of productivity impossible, but when a survey of prospective graduate students in all academic fields asked respondents to rank their relative interest in teaching and research, future historians led all other fields in leaning toward teaching. (James A. Davis, *Great Aspirations* [Chicago, 1964], 224.)
[5]Handlin to David Owen, 4 November 1954, copy in Gabriel Papers, Add. I, Box VI.

After World War II anti-Semitism in the historical profession, as in society at large, was an embarrassing legacy to be exorcised. The selection of Louis Gottschalk as president of the American Historical Association at the extraordinarily young age, for an AHA president, of fifty-two was in part an expiation of past sins. In these years, relatively few Jews undertook graduate work in history, compared with other disciplines. Of a large sample of the B.A. class of 1961, only 7 percent of those planning graduate work in history were Jews, fewer than in any other disciplines save geology, biology, botany, and zoology. By the end of that decade Jews constituted 9 percent of academic historians, but 22 percent of the membership of history departments at highly rated universities. Of works in American history deemed outstanding in polls of historians, none published before 1950 was by a Jewish historian; of those published in the 1950s three out of ten were by Jews; in the 1960s, four out of ten. Jews also figured prominently in modern European, especially German, history in these years, with a particularly noteworthy role being played by those who had emigrated in the 1930s as children.[6]

Anti-Semitism by no means completely disappeared, and indeed for some the entry of Jews into positions of prominence was an added provocation. J. Fred Rippy of the University of Chicago History Department complained in the early 1950s that

Alfred Knopf does all he can to promote the Jews. . . . The Harris Foundation here is now largely Hebrew controlled. The Guggenheim Foundation favors the Jews in its awards. *Saturday Review of Literature* is now in the hands of Jews. . . . Jewish influence has been responsible for the choice of Louis Gottschalk as a member of UNESCO's committee to write a world history. . . . Enrollments have declined . . . the main cause . . . probably is the distaste for such an overwhelming number of Jewish refugees on the faculties.

But these attitudes became rarer, better hidden when they survived, and in consequence less influential, in part because they could be costly.

---

[6]Both Thomas Cochran and Merle Curti favored Gottschalk's selection as AHA president because it would establish the precedent of honoring a Jew. (Cochran to Curti, 15 July 1951, Curti Papers, 9–17; Curti to Cochran, undated, Cochran Papers, Box 1.) Figures on Jews in the historical profession are from Davis, *Great Aspirations*, 168, and Stephen Steinberg, *The Academic Melting Pot: Catholics and Jews in American Higher Education* (New York, 1974), 122. The surveys of outstanding works in American history are by John Walton Caughey, "Historians' Choice: Results of a Poll on Recently Published American History and Biography," *MVHR* 39 (1952): 289–302; John Edward Johnson, "Historians' Histories, 1950–1959" (Ball State University Ed.D. dissertation, 1972); Cornelius Eringaard, "Historians' Histories, 1960–1969" (Ball State University Ed.D. dissertation, 1972).

366 *Objectivity reconstructed*

When David Donald recommended six young Americanists to the University of Wisconsin in 1957, five of the six were Jews. By that point, the price of anti-Semitism was mediocrity.[7]

Recruitment to the profession also became more universalistic with respect to the class background of history graduate students. Precise information on this question does not exist, but there was a widespread impression, almost certainly correct, that young historians were increasingly being drawn from somewhat lower social strata. The chairman of Yale's History Department, for one, found the social origins of postwar graduate students distressingly low, as compared with those in the English Department at that institution.

Apparently the subject of English still draws to a degree from the cultivated, professional, and well-to-do classes, hence more young men and women from able backgrounds. By contrast, the subject of history seems to appeal on the whole to a lower social stratum. . . . Far too few of our history candidates are sons of professional men; far too many list their parent's occupation as janitor, watchman, salesman, grocer, pocketbook cutter, bookkeeper, railroad clerk, pharmacist, clothing cutter, cable tester, mechanic, general clerk, butter-and-egg jobber, and the like. One may be glad to see the sons of the lower occupations working upward. . . . It may be flattering to be regarded as an elevator. But even the strongest elevator will break down if asked to lift too much weight.[8]

In one important respect, universalism declined. The percentage of women in the profession fell precipitously after the war. From around

[7]Rippy to Harry Elmer Barnes, 7 September 1952 and 21 January 1954 (Barnes Papers, Boxes 39 and 42 respectively). Fred Harvey Harrington, memorandum of telephone conversation with David Donald, 4 March 1957, copy in Hesseltine Papers, M77–88. There was discrimination against Catholics, but its extent is very difficult to measure. Whereas Jews were substantially overrepresented at elite institutions (22 percent versus 9 percent in the profession at large), the situation with respect to Catholics was reversed (10 percent versus 21 percent in the profession at large). (Steinberg, 121.) But these figures can be misleading because a very high proportion of Catholic historians were part of a separate labor market: graduates of Catholic universities who spent their entire careers at Catholic institutions. One young Catholic historian in the 1950s wrote his (Protestant) graduate school mentor asking him to recommend a Protestant denomination for him to adopt so that he could evade discrimination: "In these past few years I have learned what 'Catholic' on an application blank can mean—teachers' agencies have made it plain enough. . . . Now my problem is what 'church affiliation' can I select which will be respectable in the majority of college employment circles? I don't give a bang if it's Mohammedan—it won't affect my beliefs—and certainly won't offend the God and Christ I believe in. . . . I am really shopping around for a Church. The way I figure it my God deserves the best—that includes a decent living too." The *Doktorvater* in question provided the requisite information, and in his next letter of recommendation, remarked— casually, in passing—"I think he is an Episcopalian."
[8]"Report of the History Department for 1956–57," 15 July 1957 (George W. Pierson to President A. Whitney Griswold), Griswold Presidential Papers, Box 31.

1910 to the late 1940s women accounted for about 20 percent of new doctorates in history. This dropped to 10 percent in the decade of the 1950s, and increased to only 12 percent in the 1960s. Until 1949 women constituted about 20 percent of the profession; this declined steadily to 12 percent by 1965, where it remained for several years. As in the case of Jews earlier on, it is hard to say how much of the underrepresentation of women was due to actual discrimination, how much to anticipated discrimination, and how much to internalized notions of appropriate occupational roles. Daniel J. Boorstin of the University of Chicago was undoubtedly voicing a widespread attitude when he told the AHA Committee on Graduate Education in 1959 that he had not "had a single really keen woman student" and in consequence was "not in favor of encouraging women students any more than they have been encouraged in the past." Since it is a sociological truism that nothing contributes more to the status of a vocation than the extent to which it is seen as a male calling, the change in the gender composition of the profession probably contributed to the enhanced occupational prestige of historians which Higham noted.[9]

Another dimension of universalism was the gradual decline of regional loyalties, a greater "nationalization" of historical consciousness. Assertive regionalism could not survive the ridicule and silent contempt of more cosmopolitan historians. Throughout the 1950s there were repeated skirmishes over the transformation of the Mississippi Valley Historical Association into a truly national organization of Americanists. Those favoring changing the name of the association, and its *Review*, were also those who urged that the MVHA meet only at unsegregated facilities and who battled for democratization of the association against the old guard. Though victory on all fronts was long in coming, the ultimate outcome was never in doubt from the mid-1950s onward. The general nationaliza-

---

[9]Percentages are my calculations based on figures in Douglas L. Adkins, *The Great American Degree Machine: An Economic Analysis of the Human Resource Output of Higher Education* (New York, 1975), 350–53, 514–15. Boorstin, quoted in AHA committee interviews, 12 May 1959, in Barzun Papers, Box 16. "Membership in the profession" is here defined as holding a doctorate in history. There is no reliable serial data on changes in the representation of women historians on the teaching staffs of institutions of higher education. It seems overwhelmingly likely that, as in other disciplines, it declined substantially after World War II. In the interwar years women were found disproportionately on the faculties of teachers' colleges and women's colleges, including many nuns at Catholic women's colleges. Virtually all of the women who held office in the AHA before the war were at women's colleges; hardly any women held positions at major research universities. With the postwar expansion of higher education the relative share of the market occupied by these institutions declined sharply. Also, many women's colleges after the war were for various reasons more disposed to hire male faculty.

tion of consciousness among American historians led to a widespread substitution of disciplinary for institutional loyalties, a shift greatly furthered by the enormous increase in horizontal mobility among senior historians in the 1960s.

Success in more closely approaching many goals of the professionalization project improved historians' morale. John Higham was undoubtedly correct when he saw this as contributing importantly to what he termed "emancipation from skeptical and derivative theories of history" which had flourished in the years of professional disillusionment. Paradoxically, failure to meet one of the earlier goals, across-the-board monopoly, also worked in an antirelativist direction.[10]

The postwar years saw the final collapse of the profession's original goal of having exclusive license to "prescribe" history for schoolchildren and the lay audience. In the interwar years historians had, as we have seen, veered back and forth between different strategies in seeking to recapture influence over precollegiate education. In the period now under discussion the profession, somewhat reluctantly and grumpily, reconciled itself to complete loss of control over history in the schools. In the 1930s the AHA had overall editorial and financial responsibility for the National Council for the Social Studies' magazines for high school teachers, and historians frequently contributed to their pages. After the war the relationship attenuated and then lapsed. Chester M. Destler, the AHA's representative on the board of *Social Education* in the late 1940s, reported that whereas in the thirties it was "accepted as sound doctrine that the . . . direction and leadership of instruction in history on all levels was an important obligation of our Association . . . this vital function, on non-college and university levels, has in the past few years been virtually surrendered." In 1947 the *Mississippi Valley Historical Review* discontinued its "Teachers' Section." James L. Sellers, in his 1953 presidential address to the MVHA, noted that the association's efforts on behalf of history in the schools had all but ceased.[11]

On two occasions during these years, "counterrevolutionary" movements arose to regain the place history had lost to social studies in the schools. In both instances the professional historical establishment declined to enter the lists, and tacitly accepted that authority over history in the schools had been ceded to the educationists. In the early 1940s *New York Times* publisher Arthur Hays Sulzberger, at the urging of Allan Nevins, commissioned a Pulitzer Prize-winning series of articles on stu-

---

[10]Higham et al., *History*, 132.
[11]Destler in AHA, *Annual Report, 1949* (Washington, 1950), 1:45; James L. Sellers, "Before We Were Members—The MVHA," *MVHR* 40 (1953): 21.

dents' ignorance of American history, based on a narrowly and doggedly factualist examination given to seven thousand students. The results, not surprisingly, showed substantial historical misinformation or lack of information, though the *Times* and those who endorsed its conclusions made rather too much of such academic commonplaces as a freshman writing of Lincoln's "emaciating" the slaves, and of those who confused Andrew and Stonewall Jackson. Both Nevins and the *Times* argued that American history was woefully neglected in high schools and colleges, and attacked its displacement by social studies. They joined in urging states to adopt legislation mandating compulsory instruction in American history at all levels.[12]

Most historians opposed the crusade. Some, like William B. Hesseltine, disliked the narrow factualist approach to history it seemed to recommend. He mocked the "Committee to Defeat America by Memorizing the Presidents." Others, like AHA executive secretary Guy Stanton Ford, the medievalist Joseph Strayer, and the Americanist Max Savelle, criticized the nationalism implicit in giving priority to American over European history. Merle Curti saw in the crusade an attack on the social studies movement, which he thought would "in the long run . . . justify itself." But his principal concern, shared by many others, was that "a legitimate demand for a wider and better understanding of American history [would] play into the hands of isolationists and reactionary chauvinists." John D. Hicks wrote a friend that he was "unconditionally opposed to making U.S. History a required subject."

The opposition to the Social Studies program out here [California] comes from people who are utterly uninterested in either content or method. All they want is indoctrination: (1) against the U.S. ever again abandoning Washington's doctrine of isolation, (2) that Great Britain is the chief enemy of the human race, and (3) that the American system of free enterprise, *as they interpret it,* is sacrosanct, and must never be criticized. The Hearst newspapers and a few misguided patriots out here are back of this program. . . . I don't want to join the bunch that is now determined to beat down anyone who teaches anything not included in the 6th grade textbooks once studied by W. R. Hearst.[13]

[12]For Nevins's original manifesto, which launched the campaign, see his "American History for Americans," *New York Times Magazine,* 3 May 1942. The principal *Times* articles (with many follow-ups and much subsequent correspondence) were by Benjamin Fine in the issues of 21 June 1942, 4 and 5 April 1943.
[13]Hesseltine to John D. Hicks, 10 May 1943, Hicks Papers, Box 6; Ford, "Your Business," *AHR* 49 (1943): 114; Strayer, "Compulsory Study of American History—An Appraisal," *Public Opinion Quarterly* 6 (1942): 537–48; Savelle in "Stanford Conference," 18; Curti to Arthur M. Schlesinger, 16 April 1943, Schlesinger Papers, Box 17; Hicks to Paul Knaplund, 23 April 1943, Knaplund Papers, Series 7/16/20, Box 1.

In the light of all of this, the historical establishment took steps to distance itself from the agitation begun by Nevins and the *Times*. In an effort to "gain the initiative, and forestall any unconsidered action" Ford arranged for yet another official study in the schools, this one jointly sponsored by the AHA, the MVHA, and the National Council for the Social Studies. The report, issued in 1944, studiously avoided any mention of the *Times* controversy which had prompted it, a fact noted caustically by several reviewers. Conservative historians like John D. Barnhart of the University of Indiana complained that it "seemed to be afraid to step on the toes of the educationalists." In its conclusions the report came out strongly against the danger of legislative enactments requiring American history in the schools, and voiced the opinion that "American history is now taught with sufficient frequency."[14]

In the early 1950s another campaign was launched to oust the social studies usurper and restore "straight" history in the schools, this time explicitly calling for the reassertion of professional historians' authority over school history. The prime mover of this effort was the University of Illinois historian Arthur E. Bestor, Jr., who, employing vintage cold war rhetoric, explained why the time for "appeasement" of the educational establishment was over.

Across the educational world today stretches the iron curtain that the professional educators have fashioned. Behind it, in slave-labor camps, are the classroom teachers, whose only hope of rescue is from without. On the hither side lives the free world of science and learning, menaced but not yet conquered. . . . The subversion of American intellectual life is possible because the first twelve years of formal schooling . . . have fallen under the policy-making control of educators who have no real place in—who do not respect, and who are not respected by— the world of science, of scholarship, and of the learned professions. The fifth column that engineered this betrayal was composed of professors of education.[15]

The *Times* controversy had erupted at a time when "progressivism," including "progressive education," was still respectable among many academics and intellectuals. By the 1950s counterprogressivism extended to the conviction that John Dewey had had a pernicious influence on American education, and that to combat "populist" anti-intellectualism, one had to return to a more traditional curriculum, and restore the authority

---

[14]Ford to members of the [AHA] executive committee, 14 November 1942, Buck Papers, I/4; Barnhart, "Report of the Committee on American History," *Indiana Magazine of History* 40 (1944): 71; *American History in Schools and Colleges* [Report of the Committee on American History in Schools and Colleges of the AHA, MVHA, NCSS, Edgar B. Wesley, Director] (New York, 1944), 118.
[15]"Aimlessness in Education," *Scientific Monthly* 75 (August 1952): 114.

of academic elites. Bestor presented a paper on "Anti-Intellectualism in the Schools" at the 1952 meeting of the AHA. In it he attacked

the arrogance of those secondary-school educators who believe that they own the schools and can mold them as they please without regard to the rest of the scientific, intellectual and professional life of the nation. . . . The learned world must speak with a voice unmistakably its own, and must not allow its words to be smothered or twisted or censored by others. . . . Scholars have not done this effectively in the past, and the views of the professional educators have prevailed largely by default.

In the months before the AHA meeting, Bestor circulated to his professional colleagues draft resolutions for presentation to the association's business meeting, which declared total war on the "educationists" and called for the creation of a "Permanent Scientific and Scholarly Commission on Secondary Education," to be made up exclusively of scholars and scientists, which would displace the anti-intellectual educationists in overseeing the nation's school system.[16]

Several dozen historians joined in endorsing Bestor's resolution, but more prudent heads prevailed. Bestor was persuaded to withdraw the resolution in favor of a bland expression of the AHA Council's judgment that "the problem presented by resolutions is a serious one, meriting close and thoughtful study before any action by the Association." The Committee on Teaching of History in the Schools which was established concluded that "it wanted to approach the problem from the positive rather than the negative point of view. . . . It is absolutely necessary to obtain the willing cooperation of administrators and teachers and this cannot be done through a negative approach." The committee's recommendations eventuated in the establishment of the AHA's "Service Center for Teachers." The center prepared book lists for schools, and sponsored a series of pamphlets summarizing recent historical interpretations, probably having a wider readership among graduate students preparing for oral examinations than among schoolteachers.[17]

By the late 1950s the historical profession had acknowledged that its expertise did not carry with it authority over the schools. The relationship of historians to history in the schools was defined by the phrase the

[16]"Anti-Intellectualism in the Schools," *New Republic* 128 (19 January 1953): 11–13 (an abridged version of the AHA address); "Proposals for a Permanent Scientific and Scholarly Commission on Secondary Education," reprinted in Bestor's *Educational Wastelands: The Retreat from Learning in Our Public Schools* (Urbana, Ill., 1953), 197–206.
[17]The AHA Council resolution (together with a list of sponsors of Bestor's original resolution) is in *Wastelands*, 205–6, 200–202. Draft report of Committee on Teaching of History in the Schools (6 December 1954) is in AHA Papers, Box 183.

British used to describe the proper role of scientists: historians would be "on tap but not on top." The post-Sputnik concern over the quality of American education furthered science, mathematics, and to a lesser extent the social sciences in the schools, often at the further expense of history. In the early 1960s Oscar Handlin thought it would be no loss if history ceased being taught in high schools altogether. By the latter part of that decade Charles G. Sellers, one of the few historians who continued to interest himself in precollegiate education, asked rhetorically, "Is History on the Way Out of the Schools and Do Historians Care?" The answers seemed to be, respectively, "yes" and "no."[18]

No dramatic controversies marked historians' abandonment of the aspiration to achieve a dominant position in providing history for the general reading public. There was merely a continuing decline, accompanied by occasional, and increasingly ritualistic, headshaking. Whereas before the war, the indefatigable Allan Nevins had been able to enlist a sizable portion of the historical profession for his project of a popular magazine of history, when it eventually appeared, as *American Heritage*, in the 1950s, hardly any major professional historians' work appeared in its bland, slick pages. (The venture was a runaway commercial success, attaining 300,000 subscribers within a few years of its launching.) Occasionally a work of serious scholarship, like Garrett Mattingly's *The Armada*, might achieve popular success, but for the most part best-seller-dom in history was reserved for amateurs like Walter Lord, Cornelius Ryan, William L. Shirer, John Toland, and Barbara Tuchman, whom most professional historians, justly or unjustly, regarded as the equivalent of chiropractors and naturopaths.

The continued decline in the popular market for professional historians' wares was the occasion of disappointment, but not of dismay. After the paperback revolution in the 1950s, works of serious scholarship could reach many more captive student readers than the most popular work of nonfiction in the free market, although, at paperback royalty rates, not with proportionate material rewards. In any case, improved economic circumstances turned historians away from potboiling popular writing. Foundation grants to visit London or Rome were in every way more rewarding than fees for lectures to women's clubs or book reviews for newspapers.

The erosion of historians' popular audience as well as of their relationship with the schools, produced a certain inward turn in the profession. Earlier the ethos of the historical profession, like other professions, had

[18]Handlin, "Live Students and Dead Education: Why the High School Must Be Revived," *Atlantic Monthly* 208 (September 1961): 32; Charles G. Sellers in *Social Education* 33 (1969): 509–16.

emphasized "service." (Crudely—perhaps too crudely—put, professions offer society a service ideal in return for licensed monopoly.) For reasons largely though not entirely beyond its control, the historical profession's two principal external clienteles decided they could get along without its services. The abandonment of aspirations to monopoly, and, *pari passu*, of the "service ideal," represented a defeat in terms of meeting the general norms of professionalism, but in fact it moved history closer to postwar norms of academic professionalism. For in terms of those norms, history's external clienteles, and concern with meeting their demands, had set history somewhat apart from other disciplines. Christopher Jencks and David Riesman, discussing the postwar university, noted that graduate schools of arts and sciences "occupy a position somewhat comparable to that of theology in the medieval university."

Other professional schools justify themselves (and their budgets) in terms of external problems and needs. The graduate academic departments are for the most part autotelic. They resent even being asked whether they produce significant benefits to society beyond the edification of their own members, and mark down the questioner as an anti-intellectual. To suggest that the advancement of a particular academic discipline is not synonymous with the advancement of the human condition is regarded as myopic.[19]

Historical work was increasingly, and less apologetically, directed to a "strictly academic" audience. Typical of a more academicized postwar sensibility was Bernard Bailyn's explanation of the criteria professional historians employ in selecting a topic:

Historians decide to study and write about something because they observe that in the present state of the historical literature there is a *need* for such work, a need in the sense that a proper utilization of known resources has not been made. . . . A second group of topics seems to be defined . . . by observations concerning the state of historical knowledge itself. These are topics that are suggested by what appear to be *gaps* in our knowledge. . . . A third group of topics is defined by the observation of (1) anomalies in the existing data, or (2) discrepancies between data and existing explanations.

Criteria of this sort were, of course, by no means new, but they tended to become more universal, crowding out older, competing aims, such as wrestling with a moral problem, the expression of a sensibility, or attempting to reorient public opinion.[20]

The inward turn of the historical profession meant the placing of a

---

[19]*The Academic Revolution* (New York, 1968), 250.
[20]"The Problem of the Working Historian: A Comment," in Sidney Hook, ed., *Philosophy and History: A Symposium* (New York, 1963), 95–96.

higher valuation on the exploration of technical questions of purely professional interest. In considering the audience for their works, historians felt freer to say, as Thomas Cochran did in a letter to a friend, "the public be damned." The historian no longer suffered under the burden of making those compromises with impartiality, detachment, and objectivity which had proven all but inevitable when writing for a lay public, and especially for the schools. To write solely for one's fellow historians could be a kind of liberation, allowing a less contaminated pursuit of the old ideal. At the same time, the proliferation of subcommunities of historians, pursuing parallel researches within a shared body of assumptions, also made the objectivity of individuals' efforts seem less problematic. All of this dovetailed nicely with the attack on "instrumentalism" which was part of the repudiation of the pragmatic currents of the interwar years. In the dominant postwar view, the best history, for some the only reputable history, was history written "for its own sake."[21]

As we have seen in our consideration of the critical reaction to Becker and Beard by their contemporaries, the proposition that the past should be studied for its own sake was a recurring theme in antirelativist discourse in the 1930s. That position had not hitherto been professional orthodoxy. In the early 1950s, Herman Ausubel published a study of AHA presidential addresses from the founding of the association down to 1945. He noted with dismay that

The scholar who believes that historical study should serve above all to explain the present and its problems . . . will find much to applaud in the presidential addresses. . . . The gildsman who believes that the past should be studied above all for the sake of the past and only incidentally for the sake of the present . . . will find much less and sometimes even nothing to applaud in the messages.[22]

After 1945 the ethos of "the past for its own sake" flourished and, as with the prototype, "art for art's sake," reflected a celebration of technical proficiency and virtuosity, a more detached and spectatorial posture, and a certain deliberate turning away from a sordid or threatening present toward more permanent values. "Life is so horrible," Flaubert had complained, "that one can only bear it by avoiding it. And that can be done by living in the world of art." A student of Merle Curti's recalls a "splendid" and "glorious" incident during the Cuban missile crisis, when he and his fellows were all convinced that they would die horribly in an imminent inevitable war. Curti expressed sympathy for their concern, but

---

[21]Cochran to Richard Hofstadter, 13 April 1948, Cochran Papers, Box 1.
[22]*Historians and Their Craft: A Study of the Presidential Addresses of the American Historical Association, 1884–1945* (New York, 1950), 13.

insisted on no deviation from the day's assigned seminar topic: "There is also merit in keeping the light of scholarship burning as long as possible."[23]

Like Herbert Butterfield, whose *Whig Interpretation of History* was a staple of postwar reading lists, American historians moved from salutary warnings against historical anachronism to insistence that historians totally disengage themselves from twentieth-century assumptions and concerns. This argument was carried farthest by Jack Hexter in his much praised 1954 article on "The Historian and His Day." With his characteristic panache Hexter presented what many believed to be a knockdown refutation of the "relativist" implications of the proposition that the "passions, prejudices, assumptions, prepossessions, events, crises and tensions" of the historian's own day inevitably permeate what he or she writes about the past. Hexter's argument was based on recounting his own "day," which was lived, as a professional historian's should be, immersed in the texts of his period, and for the most part isolated from contemporary currents.

I have never read the Social Security Act, but I have read the Elizabethan Poor Law in all its successive versions. . . . I have never read the work of a single existentialist but I have read Calvin's *Institutes of the Christian Religion* from cover to cover. . . . Instead of the passions, prejudices, assumptions and prepossessions, the events, crises and tensions of the present dominating my view of the past, *it is the other way about.* The passions, prejudices, assumptions and prepossessions, the events, crises and tensions of early modern Europe to a very considerable extent lend precision to my rather haphazard notions about the present. I make sense of present-day welfare-state policy by thinking of it in connection with the "commonwealth" policies of Elizabeth.[24]

Though Hexter's claim to live his affective life in another time and place was extreme, it found echoes in the postwar world. Roy F. Nichols had earlier criticized his colleagues for being too aloof from the world around them. History, he had said, was "too often the refuge for pedestrian minds and careful technicians who like to escape in the past." After the war Nichols reversed himself: he urged the historian to practice "historical yoga . . . a new asceticism . . . a metaphysics that transcends most of his own immediate experience . . . an emotional discipline based upon

[23]Flaubert letter of 1851, quoted in Arnold Hauser, *The Social History of Art* (Vintage ed., New York, 1958), 4:80; David W. Levy, "Merle Curti's Place in American Scholarship: A Consideration of the Controversy," *Journal of Thought* 6 (1971): 15.
[24]Originally published in *Political Science Quarterly* 70 (1954); reprinted in his *Reappraisals in History* (Evanston, Ill., 1961), 6–9.

the absence of both hope and fear." Even that most *engagé* of historians, Arthur Schlesinger, Jr., insisted (with a straight face?) that he had "always been among those who believe that history should be studied for its own sake."[25]

But the proposition that a true professional historian was disengaged from the actions and passions of the day was not always unambivalently accepted. As I have indicated earlier, there was a contradiction between the imperative to do one's part in the Manichean struggles of the midcentury while at the same time embodying values of disinterested objectivity. One interesting attempt at a symbolic reconciliation of the contradiction was the creation of a minor cult surrounding Marc Bloch, the eminent French medievalist executed by the Germans for his Resistance activity. His life and death, combining serene scholarly detachment in a field far removed from current struggles with heroic moral commitment in the great issues of the day, was a dramatic and reassuring example which suggested that detachment and commitment could coexist without either threatening the other.[26]

There were shifts in mood with respect to "the past for its own sake" as one moved from the late forties to the early sixties. In the first postwar years, under the impact of Hiroshima, William B. Willcox of the University of Michigan wondered about the historian's social responsibility at a time when "the coming generation will be faced with the choice of creating a new world or exterminating itself." "If there ever was an historian's ivory tower," he wrote his mentor, Wallace K. Notestein, "it's been vaporized by now." By the early sixties there were signs of restlessness with what some saw as the excessively antiseptic character which an overreaction to the perceived partisan excesses of a previous generation had brought to historiography. John Higham, though endorsing the common view that a person "not involved so immediately and urgently in

---

[25]Nichols, "Confusions in Historical Thinking," *Journal of Social Philosophy* 7 (1942): 340; Nichols, "Why So Much Pessimism?" in Marshall W. Fishwick, ed., *American Studies in Transition* (Philadelphia, 1964), 322; Schlesinger, "The Historian and History," *Foreign Affairs* 41 (1963); reprinted in A. S. Eisenstadt, ed., *The Craft of American History* (2 vols., New York, 1966), 1:107–8.

[26]The reconciling function the canonization of Bloch performed was furthered by some other considerations. He was, of course, a superb historian, and one of the founders of the *Annales* school, destined to be a major force in Western historiography in the postwar decades. His principal (posthumously published) excursion into historical theory, *The Historian's Craft* (New York, 1953), while containing much good sense, never addressed issues of objectivity and relativism. His politics were neither offensively chauvinist nor embarrassingly leftist. He was a Jew who had risen higher professionally than had any Jew in the United States before World War II. For the growing number of Jews in the historical profession he was thus an inspiration, while for gentiles the cult of Bloch was something of a talisman against the profession's reputation for anti-Semitism.

the struggles of his own times . . . may be able more easily to project himself into the past on something like its own terms," thought the pendulum had swung too far. The austere posture of detachment, reinforced by a university system which "rewards its employees with prestige and security for predictable quantities of passionless research" was, he thought, resulting in scholarship which "dehumanizes history . . . encourages fatalism . . . gives us nothing to admire." But Higham carefully avoided any concern with a socially relevant scholarship, asking instead for historiography that was morally relevant. The historian-as-moral-critic would judge his or her subject "for its intrinsic value as a gesture of the human spirit"—historiography as moral connoisseurship.[27]

II

No factor contributed more to postwar historians' heightened morale and professional self-confidence than the quantity and quality of the historical scholarship being produced. AHA executive secretary Boyd Shafer remarked proudly in 1956 that "The profession of history is thriving, the professors are vigorous. Historians are producing articles and books at an amazing rate." Vastly enlarged output naturally produced work of differential quality. Surveying the previous two decades of American historical writing from the perspective of 1967, Jack Hexter found two propositions to be simultaneously true, observing correctly that they were by no means mutually exclusive:

1. Never in the past has the writing of history been so fatuous as it is today; never has it yielded so enormous and suffocating a mass of stultifying trivia, the product of small minds engaged in the congenial occupation of writing badly about insignificant matters to which they have given little or no thought and for which they feel small concern.
2. Never in the past have historians written history so competently, vigorously, and thoughtfully as they do today, penetrating into domains hitherto neglected or in an obscurantist way shunned, bringing effectively to bear on the record of the past disciplines wholly inaccessible to their predecessors, treating the problems they confront with both a catholicity and a rigour and sophistication of method hitherto without precedent among practitioners of the historical craft.[28]

[27]Willcox to Notestein, 29 May 1947, Notestein Papers, I-9; Higham, "Beyond Consensus: The Historian as Moral Critic," *AHR* 67 (1962): 615, 609, 620–21.
[28]"Report of the Executive Secretary and Managing Editor for 1956," AHA, *Annual Report, 1956* (Washington, D.C., 1957), 1:8; Hexter, "Some American Observations," *Journal of Contemporary History* 2 (1967): 5–6.

When historians attempted to explain the first half of Hexter's observation, they often focused on the quality of graduate students. Probably no generalization about such a heterogeneous group is meaningful. Major institutions varied greatly in selectivity. The University of Chicago and the University of Pennsylvania accepted 90 percent of those who applied; Fritz Stern complained to an AHA committee that Columbia had "large numbers of inferior students"; other universities, like Princeton, accepted only a small percentage of applicants. In most respects history graduate students seemed to resemble those in other disciplines, but in two particulars they displayed notable characteristics. In a survey of the college class of 1961, those going on to graduate study in history were almost at the bottom of a list of several dozen disciplines in the extent to which they saw in their academic work an "opportunity to be original and creative." Only those going into geology, microbiology, and economics listed this ambition less often. And when asked to rate themselves on a scale running from "very conventional" to "very unconventional," prospective graduate students in history were almost the most "conventional," surpassed only by chemists, biochemists, and microbiologists.[29]

But most historians regarded the second half of Hexter's comment as the more noteworthy, and more relevant. The work of many of the leading postwar Americanists has been discussed in Chapter 11. European history in the United States after the war was enormously enriched and energized by the influx of refugees: historians like Hans Baron, Felix Gilbert, Hajo Holborn, Ernst Kantorowicz, and Hans Rosenberg; scholars from other disciplines like the philosophers Ernst Cassirer and Paul O. Kristeller, the classicist Werner Jaeger, the political scientists Hans Morgenthau and Franz Neumann. One would have been hard-pressed to find, in the interwar years, American Europeanists whose command of their respective fields equaled that of Gordon Craig in German history, Gordon Wright in French history, David Landes in economic history, Carl Schorske in intellectual history. By the early 1960s Leonard Krieger was pleased to report, in his survey of "European History in America," that "American historians . . . are now equal members of the Western historical community . . . represent[ing] an autonomous national dimension within the expanded historical universe."[30]

Americanists and Europeanists joined in making invidious com-

[29]Information on admissions standards from "Interviews with Historians by John L. Snell on Behalf of Committee on Graduate Education in History of AHA, 1958–60," and other notes in Barzun Papers, Box 16. Survey data on prospective graduate students from Davis, *Great Aspirations*, 175, 179.
[30]In Higham et al., *History*, 289.

parisons between the postwar and the prewar scene, and in heralding the dawn of a new historiographical era. Richard Hofstadter found that "the old idea that the historian has done his job if he gathers together a lot of related facts and puts them on a chronological framework in creditable prose is now largely dead among the younger generation of historians. No doubt a certain amount of historical work of this kind will continue to be done, but this is not what the able younger historians aspire to." John Higham said that "anyone who looks back at the frequently stiff and pedestrian articles in the leading historical journals during the Twenties and Thirties may feel reassured about the general level of contemporary work: it is more deft, often more perceptive, and usually more substantial." Like his Americanist colleagues, H. Stuart Hughes contrasted the postwar situation with the years before World War II, when the younger generation of historians had been radically dissatisfied with the discipline, "an intellectually invertebrate affair [with] no clear concepts and no recognized canon of interpretation." Hughes joined with others in connecting the "renewal" of history with the overcoming of relativist discouragement.

Armed on the one hand against intellectual naiveté and on the other against the corrosion of skepticism and self-doubt, contemporary historians are finding the courage to build structures of explanation which are both more inclusive and more logically consistent than has been conventionally true of the historian's craft. One of the most exhilarating aspects of directing advanced students in today's intellectual atmosphere is the shared sense of being on the verge of great discoveries. . . . I think it is quite possible that the study of history today is entering a period of rapid change and advance such as characterized the science of physics in the first three decades of the twentieth century.[31]

From the standpoint of professional academic historians perhaps the most disturbing aspect of the interwar relativist critique had been its sometimes explicit, and always implicit, skepticism about "progress" in historiography. Since the beginning of the twentieth century professional historians had been divided about the extent to which their discipline should be modeled on the natural sciences, but it was nevertheless professional orthodoxy that, as in the sciences, historical scholarship was cumulative; later interpretations were, other things being equal, presumed to

---

[31]Hofstadter, "History and Sociology in the United States," in Seymour Martin Lipset and Hofstadter, eds., *Sociology and History: Methods* (New York, 1968), 14–15; Higham et al., *History*, 59; Hughes, "The Historian and the Social Scientist," *AHR* 66 (1960): 20–21; Hughes, "What the Historian Thinks He Knows" (ca. 1961), in his *History as Art and as Science* (New York, 1964), 20–21.

be better than earlier ones, in terms of the stated or unstated criterion of
"moving closer to the truth." All of this the relativists had called into
question, with their emphasis on the functional adaptation of historiography to changing social needs, and its dependence on culturally determined "frames of reference." While the relativists had acknowledged that
the store of reliable factual data was growing, that previous errors and
misconceptions were continually being abandoned, and that fruitful new
approaches were being developed, their general posture had cast doubt on
the professionally satisfying assumption of cumulative disciplinary
progress.

As we have seen, the interwar relativists' skepticism about the principle
of progress in historiography gained plausibility from the widespread
contemporary perception that in practice historical writing did not seem
to be making much progress. After World War II agreement within the
profession that historical scholarship was advancing rapidly made the
relativists' skepticism about historiographical progress seem a timebound product of a temporary period of discouragement, and probably
contributed as much as any other single factor to relativism's eclipse.

The two realms of postwar historical scholarship which attracted the
most attention were intellectual history and "social scientific" history.
Each, in different ways, reflected contemporary attitudes on "the objectivity question."

Among intellectual historians there was a marked turn away from the
"pragmatic," "functional," or "environmental" study of ideas, a turn
which in many ways paralleled the repudiation of externalism in history
of science. At the very beginning of this period Arthur O. Lovejoy, a
thoroughgoing internalist, founded *The Journal of the History of Ideas*,
which became the principal journal in the field, attracting a large number
of historians to its editorial board, and featuring contributions from most
major intellectual historians in the years after the war. For many historians the exquisite dissection of ideas into their unitary components practiced by the Lovejoy school was rather too much of a good thing. But
their principal fire was directed against the previous generation of Progressive intellectual historians.

Perhaps the most highly regarded American intellectual historian in the
postwar years was Perry Miller, long a dedicated opponent of those who
studied thought from a functional or environmental perspective. He had
prefaced his prewar *Orthodoxy in Massachusetts* with the sarcastic observation that by ignoring economic and social context he laid himself open
to the charge of "being so very naive as to believe that the way men think
has some influence upon their actions, of not remembering that these

ways of thinking have been officially decided by modern psychologists to be generally just so many rationalizations constructed by the subconscious to disguise the pursuit of more tangible ends." After the war he attacked Beard and Merle Curti as dullards with no appreciation of "the life of the mind."

A generation ago historians began to reach into literature and into what they called "intellectual history"; the pioneers of the movement . . . assumed that they became historians of the mind by producing catalogues of names, titles, and isms, though they showed little or no aptitude for, or understanding of, the nature of thought itself. A younger group is now emerging, adequately trained in the methods of scholarship but capable of working within the structure . . . of ideas. They write from a depth and with a fluency unknown to Beard and Curti because they understand what ideas mean; they understand because they have taken the life of ideas into their own consciousness.[32]

Others, less irascible, or more diplomatic, than Miller, avoided his insulting language, but they made it clear that they welcomed the disaggregation of "social and intellectual history" so that the latter might "autonomously" devote itself to the life of the mind. The rise of a separate field of social history was welcome, said one leading student of American thought, because it "relieves the intellectual historian from overextended commitments." The desired autonomy of intellectual from social history was furthered by the development of the American Studies movement, which attempted, through the analysis of unifying myths and symbols, to define a national mind. With its talk of capturing "the spirit of an age" and penetrating to the central idea of an era, the American Studies program had a certain general affinity to the romantic, idealist agenda of Ranke, as well as some very particular connections to the cold war. John Higham expressed his preference for the phrase "spirit of an age" over "climate of opinion" for that which the intellectual historian sought to depict. The latter phrase, Higham thought, had unfortunate "relativistic" connotations. "I like the term 'spirit,'" he wrote, "because it implies a kind of energy, whereas 'climate' suggests merely a vaporous condition."[33]

---

[32]Miller, *Orthodoxy in Massachusetts, 1630-1650* (1933; 2d. ed., Boston, 1959), xi; Miller, review of Hofstadter's *American Political Tradition*, *Nation* 167 (1948): 440.

[33]Higham, "American Intellectual History: A Critical Appraisal," *American Quarterly* 13 (1961): 231, 221. Announcing the establishment of a program in American Studies at Yale, President Charles Seymour saw it as producing "solidified faith in the American philosophy and devotion to its maintenance." Rejecting the "negative path" of "insulating students from the study of Communist theory and practice," he recommended American Studies as a way in which "the Communist threat [could] nonetheless be met vigorously

Not all intellectual historians pursued myths and symbols, but almost all repudiated the "environmentalism" and "instrumentalism" associated with Parrington, Beard, and Curti. Reiterating the theme of the autonomy of intellectual history, members of the older school were charged with "not car[ing] greatly about intellectual history as such. . . . valu[ing] it more as an instrument for interpreting the multifarious doings of men . . . than as a subject with its own intelligibility and importance." The now ascendant school made its case on moral as well as professional grounds. Robert A. Skotheim noted with satisfaction that postwar intellectual historians placed primary emphasis on "the power of thought and the responsibility of the individual for his beliefs," and Higham was pleased that "the decline of a pragmatic approach to thought made for a greater interest in first principles, in values that have some ultimate claim and not a merely instrumental role."[34]

If the assertion of the autonomy of intellectual history was closely linked to repudiation of the relativistic environmentalism of the 1930s, it also reflected a desire to repudiate that mode of objectivism associated with the entry of a social scientific sensibility into history. For Higham, intellectual history was a characteristically humanistic pursuit in its tendency to "celebrate the finer products of mind, and . . . bring to a focus all of the characteristic consequences of an internal approach: a sensitivity to qualitative distinctions, an exaltation of creative thought, an appreciation of subjective criteria for judging it." He contrasted this with the "blunter" approach of the social scientist,

objectify[ing] ideas and values into forms of behavior. . . . Subjective categories appropriate to value judgments are rejected for principles derived from observations of how men behave. . . . Respect for the molding force of social controls replaces the humanistic emphasis on creative thinkers. . . . His stress on quantity, objectivity, and behavior will lead to external analysis.

"At some point in his thinking or research," Higham concluded, leaving no doubt about his own choice, "each scholar must choose."[35]

Not all historians in these years felt the necessity for choice as urgently

and in a positive sense." ("Seymour Cites Program to Combat Red Threat," *New Haven Register*, 22 February 1949.) But the movement was far from ideologically homogeneous, and some of its leading figures (Bruce Kuklick, Leo Marx) were sharp critics of American cold war policies.

[34] Skotheim, "The Writing of American Histories of Ideas: Two Traditions in the XXth Century," *Journal of the History of Ideas* 25 (1964): 278; Higham, "Critical Appraisal," 225, 232.

[35] "Intellectual History and Its Neighbors," *Journal of the History of Ideas* 15 (1954): 344–47.

as Higham did. History saw no across-the-board *Methodenstreit*, unlike adjacent disciplines, in which, in Hexter's words, "the wars of method are fought to the finish."

There every night becomes a night of the long knives, every day is St. Bartholomew's Day; the massacres initiated in the academic capitals spread outward and are recapitulated on a smaller scale, but sometimes with bloodier savagery, in the provinces, and the major holocausts are staged at the meetings of the professional associations where the halls and corridors are littered with slaughtered reputations of old and young alike, and made horrid by the screams of the maimed and the moribund.

Those historians who thought of themselves as social scientists were surely a minority of the profession in these years, but the presence of that increasingly visible minority produced something of a disciplinary identity crisis.[36]

If one had to name the single most important intellectual influence from the social sciences it would surely be Max Weber, whose work entered the mainstream of American academic discourse only after World War II. Weber's model of society was attractive as an alternative to Marxism. A somewhat oversimplified version of his doctrine of "value freedom" in scholarship, and the substitution of "neutral" for evocative language, was widely endorsed by social scientifically oriented historians. But the postwar social science with which some historians sought to affiliate had moved beyond the classic figures like Weber, Durkheim, and their contemporaries. Postwar sociology and political science, not to mention economics, were in their most hyperempiricist period, heavily committed to mathematical model building, and speaking a language of arcane symbols. H. Stuart Hughes, who had regarded himself as one of those historians most open to the social sciences, ruefully reported being told by social science colleagues that he was "two generations out of date."[37]

A handful of aggressive promoters of social scientific history, most prominently Lee Benson, the *enfant terrible* of the movement, made far-reaching claims for the fruits historians could reap from the codification of systematic procedures drawn from the social sciences. At the University of Iowa, and a few other centers, the application of quantitative techniques to the study of politics produced a certain missionary enthusiasm. But for the most part those promoting a social scientific approach to

---

[36]Hexter, "Some American Observations," 18–19.
[37]"The Historian and the Social Scientist," *AHR* 66 (1960): 34–35.

history, aware of the fierce resistance they faced in the profession, were careful to moderate their claims.

Their modesty was to no avail. Those opposing the introduction of the concepts and methods of the social sciences were much more zealous and strident than those promoting them. It would seem hard to quarrel with the reasonableness of G. Kitson Clark's admonition, that when you are generalizing about a group or a class, "Do not guess, try to count, and if you cannot count, admit that you are guessing." But Carl Bridenbaugh inveighed against those who would "worship at the shrine of that Bitch-goddess QUANTIFICATION," and Arthur Schlesinger, Jr. insisted that "Almost all important questions are important precisely because they are *not* susceptible to quantitative answers." At least for the time being, the opposition held the line. Surveying the putative impact of the social sciences on history from the perspective of the late sixties, C. Vann Woodward believed that "far from being revolutionized by new techniques, transformed beyond recognition, or swallowed up by the social sciences, much the greater part of history as written in the United States has remained obstinately, almost imperviously traditional. It could be read by historians of the past three generations with scarcely a tremor of surprise over methods and techniques."[38]

The grounds on which historians either favored or opposed a social scientific orientation for the discipline varied widely. Some of the social science enthusiasts were excited by conceptual schemes borrowed from other disciplines, or by the striking results which could follow the application of even the most elementary counting procedures to problems previously not treated in this way. There were historians in the social science camp who saw an alliance with sociology or political science as a strategy for checking history's relative decline vis-à-vis those disciplines. But the same phenomenon of perceived relative disadvantage in attracting students, in rate of professional growth, and in funding of research, was seen by others as a mortal challenge, mandating intransigent resistance. There were social scientists who believed, and were so ill advised as to give voice publicly to the belief, that historians would be most usefully employed in supplying them with reliable data. Historians reacted predictably. Roy F. Nichols admonished historians to "stop living by other people's wits . . . frantically seeking to adopt other people's jargon . . . humbly seeking to be recognized as faithful and reasonably satisfactory

[38]Clark, *The Making of Victorian England* (London, 1962), 14; Bridenbaugh, "The Great Mutation," *AHR* 68 (1963): 326; Schlesinger, "The Humanist Looks at Empirical Social Research," *American Sociological Review* 27 (1962): 770; Woodward, "History and the Third Culture," *Journal of Contemporary History* 3 (April 1968): 24–25.

handmaids worthy of Thursday afternoons and alternate Sundays on which to do what they really wish." (Concern about history being reduced to the role of "handmaid" to the social sciences was a recurring theme in the writing of those anxious that history be regarded as one of the humanities—or, more, generally, that its autonomy be preserved.)[39]

A number of historians voiced skepticism about claims made for social science findings: Robert R. Palmer wrote a Social Science Research Council Committee on Historiography that he found the maxims of La Rochefoucauld "as valid, useful and illuminating as any [generalizations] we are likely to get in social science, and about as much or as little capable of empirical verification by scientific method." Probably most important of all was a general defensiveness and fear of the new and strange. Richard Hofstadter thought that "at a very primitive level" many historians heard suggestions that their activity might be enriched by the social sciences as a reproach for "shoddy work or intellectual superficiality." For the many historians who had always thought of themselves as humanists, with all the richly evocative connotations of that term, the suggestion that history should not just use social science but be a social science violated their deepest sense of their identity.[40]

Issues having to do with objectivity cut across the line between those who favored and those who opposed the incorporation of social science into history or of history into the social sciences. One theme in the movement to introduce social science concepts and methods into historiography stressed greater exactitude, the use of nonevaluative language, and achieving results independent of the wishes or preferences of the investigator. Lee Benson thought *the* problem of historiography was "to work out a methodology which prevents . . . bias from coloring historical research." Edward N. Saveth wrote that resistance to the social sciences had been based on their association with reform and relativism. Now that those currents had subsided, a social scientific history could come into its own. But others, like Thomas Cochran and William O. Aydelotte, directed their principal fire at what they regarded as the naive, blank-slate objectivism of traditional historiography, and acknowledged that their proposed procedures had relativistic implications, that standards of proof were ultimately subjective, and that the conceptual schemes of the social sciences were at least implicitly value-laden. "It is too bad," Cochran wrote to Hofstadter, "that his [Beard's] stage of relativism ended just as

---

[39]Nichols, "Postwar Reorientation of Historical Thinking," *AHR* 54 (1948): 84.
[40]Palmer to Louis Gottschalk, 16 June 1958, copy in Cochran Papers, 6–17; Hofstadter, "History and Sociology," 11.

social scientists were giving us an interpretive framework congenial to it."[41]

The variety of epistemological positions from which a social scientific approach to history was defended meant that its proponents were under fire from those occupying different positions on the objectivity question. When Thomas Cochran delivered a plea for the use of hypotheses from the social sciences in history, Edward Kirkland saw historians being assaulted once again by the pernicious cliché of the "frame of reference" which had disoriented scholars between the wars. "I cannot forget," Kirkland said, "that one of the most impish protagonists of this theory, Charles A. Beard, was a social scientist, and I think it is a very common social-science theory." He contrasted distortions produced by "frames of reference" with "actuality." Whatever the grip of frames of reference on "the natural man," the historian, Kirkland said, "is not a 'natural man' he is a trained man, and the trained man will get nearer the fortress of certainty and actuality. He may even occupy a part of that fortress." The ancient historian Chester G. Starr was sure he could detect "hidden values" behind the "pleasant air of certitude" with which social scientific propositions were advanced. The Social Science Research Council's 1954 bulletin on *The Social Sciences in Historical Study* was anathema to John Higham because of what he felt was its positivist flavor. But for Lee Benson the document was absurd because of its authors' failure to realize that "simply by definition scientific methods are incompatible with subjective relativism which requires the individual's frame of reference to control his research and interpretation."[42]

From time to time the hoary squabble over whether history was an art or a science was trotted out, and one could always find a few—Lee Benson for the "scientists," Arthur Schlesinger, Jr. for the "artists"—to strike a provocative posture to enliven dull gatherings. But in the era of consensus and comity, most historians were happy to collapse the dis-

---

[41]Benson to Paul W. Gates, 5 January 1954, Gates Papers; Saveth, "The Conceptualization of American History," in Saveth, ed., *American History and the Social Sciences* (New York, 1964), 8; Cochran, "History and the Social Sciences," *Relazioni del X Congresso Internazionale di Scienze Storiche* (Florence, 1956), reprinted in Eisenstadt, ed., *Craft of American History*, 2:104; Aydelotte, "Notes on the Problem of Generalization," in Louis Gottschalk, ed., *Generalization in the Writing of History* (Report of the SSRC Committee on Historical Analysis) (Chicago, 1963), 158; Cochran to Hofstadter, 11 November 1968, Cochran Papers, Box 5.

[42]Kirkland in discussion of Cochran, "A Decade of American Histories," *Pennsylvania Magazine of History* 73 (1949): 173; Starr, "Reflections upon the Problem of Generalization," in Gottschalk, ed., *Generalization*, 12; Higham, review of *The Social Sciences in Historical Study*, *Pacific Historical Review* 24 (1956): 75–76; Benson to Paul W. Gates, 5 March 1955, Gates Papers.

tinction. John Higham had earlier called upon historians to "choose." His private view was that "history is fundamentally a story and an art." He thought the profession was composed of "a minority of social science enthusiasts, a majority of positivistic isolationists who resent the enthusiasts' clamor for largely old fogey reasons, and a small number who have thought about the matter and who align themselves in principle with the humanities." But by the mid-1960s his public posture was irenic: the distinction "misleads and stultifies." He was joined in this conciliatory stance by his Europeanist colleague H. Stuart Hughes who, though aligning himself on the other side of the divide, thought the historian "at least as much an artist as he is a social scientist," and called for "the imaginative fusion of these attributes."[43]

III

There is no better symbol of the transition from the historiographical sensibility of the 1930s to that of the 1950s than the reception accorded Bulletin 54 of the Social Science Research Council: *Theory and Practice in Historical Study: A Report of the Committee on Historiography*. Produced under the inspiration of Charles Beard, and the formal direction of Merle Curti, Bulletin 54 was conceived in the early 1940s, published in the mid-1940s, and the subject of continuing discussion throughout the late 1940s. The bulletin was made up of a number of loosely related essays, mostly of a markedly, albeit sometimes somewhat ambivalently, relativist cast. It became, for many in the postwar generation, the classic demonstration of the inadequacies and contradictions of that position.

The confusions in the document reflected its conflicting purposes. Among its aims was to promote an alliance between history and the social sciences; to combat "defeatism" based on the view that history had "little or no general social significance, little or no objective validity, little or no diagnostic or prognostic value"; and to serve as the vehicle for the expression of Beard's version of relativism. Above all, by circulating throughout the profession a list of "Propositions in Historiography" (drafted by Beard with the advice of the committee), and modifying them on the basis of the comments received, it aimed at establishing what a later generation would learn to call a "paradigm" for historical study, and what Beard himself, using Charles Peirce's phrase, called "a consensus of compe-

[43]Higham to Merle Curti, 8 July 1956, Curti Papers, 19–20; Higham, "The Schism in American Scholarship," *AHR* 72 (1966), reprinted in his *Writing American History* (Bloomington, Ind., 1970), 7; Hughes, *History as Art and as Science* (New York, 1964), 107.

tence." The preface to the draft propositions made explicit the committee's belief in the urgency of attaining consensus, in terms which uneasily combined a relativist and an objectivist sensibility:

Every science . . . rests upon a number of propositions accepted by persons competent in such science as valid in themselves and for application. . . . When accepted by competence as valid, such propositions form features of any program for the training of workers in the science and offer guidance and suggestions for new advances in the science. Advances in science, thus resting upon accepted propositions, are made by devising hypotheses or fictions for further appraisal, exploration, testing, correction, and generalization. . . . Any alleged science which can present no propositions on which workers in the science can agree upon is not a science; it is chaos with a pretentious name.[44]

The propositions were a peculiar mix. Some were banal, for example, an injunction to avoid saying that "history repeats itself." Some reflected the collective ideology of the committee, for example, a stern (and transparently anti-Catholic) ban on the historian's accepting "supernatural absolutes." A few represented particular hobbyhorses of Beard's: a pedantically reiterated distinction between history-as-actuality, history-as-record, and written history; injunctions to minimize or eliminate entirely any reference to "cause." There was a deference to the social sciences so far-reaching that it was later eliminated: "Since the historian is often not equipped to test the verisimilitude of [social science] statements the rule should be to accept well established principles on the basis of confidence in the methods of the other sciences involved." Their "methods, procedures, and findings" should receive "full faith and credence."

The principal thrust of the draft propositions was clearly relativist. It defined all but the narrowest monographs as "a selection of so-called facts made by some man or woman . . . under the influence of some scheme of reference, interest, or emphasis." Such an historical work was to be un-

---

[44]Aim of combating "defeatism" in minutes of August 1943 Conference on American Historical Thought and the Social Sciences, Curti Papers, 37–24; Beard's phrase in his "Grounds for a Reconsideration of Historiography," in SSRC, *Theory and Practice in Historical Study: A Report of the Committee on Historiography* (New York, 1946); [draft] "Propositions in Historiography," Curti Papers, 38–4. The published bulletin, in addition to Beard's essay, and the "propositions," contained an historical survey of "Controlling Assumptions in the Practice of American Historians" by the philosopher John Herman Randall, Jr. and the young historian George Haines IV; a survey of "What Historians Have Said About the Causes of the Civil War" by Howard K. Beale; philosopher Sidney Hook's glossary of terms commonly used (or misused) by historians; and a bibliography on historiography and philosophy of history by Ronald Thompson. Besides Beard and Curti the members of the Committee on Historiography were Shepard B. Clough, Thomas C. Cochran, Louis Gottschalk, Jeanette P. Nichols, Richard H. Shryock, and Alfred Vagts.

derstood "not only by an analysis of its structure and documentation but also by a study of the life and circumstances of the author." "What is called an 'understanding' of history or of historical events is often, if not always, the feeling of satisfaction which comes over us when a new impression or treatment . . . falls easily into one or another of the categories already accepted and established in our minds." But these propositions were sometimes qualified in ways which seemed to contradict and undercut them. The historian was enjoined to "confine himself to the making of verifiable statements about history-as-actuality." The hope was held out that through such clarification as was being advanced in the propositions, historians could "emancipate themselves from bondage to the subconscious, the routine, and the surreptitious and [be free] to seek the utmost impartiality or objectivity possible to the human mind."

Only about half of those asked to comment on the propositions did so, but those who did made a mockery of the committee's hope of arriving at a "consensus of the competent." Many of those replying found the phrasing of the propositions so confusing that they weren't quite sure what they thought about them, and had to go by instinct. John D. Hicks wrote Curti: "In so far as I understand these 'propositions' . . . I think I agree with them," while John Hermann Randall said: "I should quarrel violently, I presume, with Proposition XVI, if I knew what it meant." A number of respondents endorsed all of the propositions, but the general response was so highly critical that Curti felt it necessary to bowdlerize the précis of comments he circulated to the committee. "We have some very delicate problems facing us," he wrote Louis Gottschalk.

We mustn't stick our necks out merely to have the heads cut off, and that is what will happen unless we put a lot of time and thought into the revision of the propositions. And yet I must try to avoid hurting Mr. Beard's feelings. . . . The document you will presently receive does not contain the harshest criticisms—I feared they would so discourage Mr. Beard he would throw up the whole business.[45]

Some of those who declined to comment on the propositions did so on the reasonable grounds that the very venture of trying to establish epistemological consensus by plebiscite was absurd. This view was shared by a number who, out of courtesy, or personal friendship with members of the committee, did respond. One historian, after making specific criticisms, characterized the attempt to attain consensus on the propositions

[45]Hicks to Curti, 5 October 1944, and Randall to Curti, 25 November 1944, Curti Papers, 38:1; Curti to Gottschalk, 14 October 1944, Gottschalk Papers, 14:1.

as "oddly ecclesiastical." A number of respondents, including several who agreed with the general thrust of the propositions, thought them too negative. William T. Hutchinson could imagine a social scientist reading the propositions and saying:

Here once again the poor historian puts ashes on his head, confesses his sins to the world, and admits there is very little of value about the past which he can know with certainty. And yet, in spite of his self-acknowledged failure to be of much use, he apparently intends to insist upon his right to go on instructing the youth of the land and drawing his salary from society.

Fred Shannon thought the wording of the propositions "puts a weapon in the hands of those who are addicted to the notion that 'history is bunk.' . . . Why don't you people abandon this washing of dirty linen in public and at least protect the historian."[46]

A few historians found the propositions overly timid in their avowal of the relativity of historical knowledge. Henry Nash Smith thought the ambivalent lip service the propositions paid to "objectivity" and "impartiality" was ill-advised.

It seems to me that with the adoption of these terms you import back into the discussion a way of thinking which you were trying to get rid of. I recognize that there may be a strategic value in trying to capture these highly honorific terms from your opponents by redefining them; but it might be worth while to consider the value of a frontal attack, rejecting the terms altogether on the theory that they designate an inconceivable state of affairs.

But a larger number either objected to the propositions' relativism per se, or thought their formulations too extreme. James C. Malin said that he could

make no compromise with the school of thought that has . . . for the past generation deliberately sought to shake confidence in [history's] validity. . . . Scrap the present draft and start over. Certainly there must be available to the committee some vigorous young mind that has escaped the blight of frustration philosophy, one capable of a clean break with the ideology of the twenties and the thirties. That was a period of pathological aberration in the cultural development of the world.

Edward Kirkland saw the central propositions as reflecting the pernicious influence of recent psychology, "with its emphasis upon . . . sublimation,

[46]"Oddly ecclesiastical" was R. R. Palmer's phrase, undated comments on propositions in Curti Papers, 38–4; Hutchinson to Curti, 20 September 1944 and Shannon to Curti, 29 September 1944, ibid., 38–5.

rationalization, and the like." "I trust," he concluded, "that historiography will not demand of its practitioners a preliminary psychoanalysis. Perhaps it is sufficient to insist that historiographers be introverts and to warn extroverts that they need not apply for admission to the profession." For Robert R. Palmer the propositions "reflect a philosophy in which I was brought up, but which it seems to me we should try to get away from, not to sink into further." Eric Goldman wrote Curti that "The line between a recognition of the limitations of the historical method and an unsophisticated relativism is a thin one. Failure to emphasize it tends to create an anaemic intellectualism, sheepishly avoiding the emotional charge that is necessary to make history a powerful adjunct of public affairs."[47]

For several years after the bulletin's publication in 1946 it was the subject of dozens of reviews, articles, and extended discussions at professional meetings. There was as little consensus in the evaluation of the bulletin as a whole, and its other constituent parts, as there had been in the prepublication comments on its "propositions." Crane Brinton thought that an essay by John Herman Randall, Jr. and George Haines IV which reviewed historiographical thought from a relativist standpoint "should gain acceptance from all but the most devout believers in history *wie es eigentlich gewesen.* His Harvard colleague Oscar Handlin characterized the essay as "unsatisfactory . . . [filled with] shallow discussion and . . . flimsy generalizations . . . fail[ing] to lend conviction to the general thesis." Handlin expanded his criticism of the Randall-Haines essay in a memorandum on Bulletin 54 which he wrote for the SSRC. One of his arguments is an interesting illustration of how the growing emphasis on consensus and continuity in American history mitigated against one major relativist theme. Handlin quoted Randall and Haines's observation that "In 1944 the United States is not what it was in 1927. Hence the historian, facing the problem of selecting those facts in the American past that seem 'basic' for 1944 will not be able to make just the same selection that he made in 1927." "The whole statement," said Handlin, "is misleading."

While the United States is not now what it was in 1927 in some respects, in the more important respects it is now what it was then. . . . The focal point of history's concerns is continuity, and continuity implies that elements of sameness

[47]Smith to Curti, 19 September 1944, Curti Papers, 38–5; Malin to Curti, 26 September 1944, ibid.; Kirkland's undated comments, ibid.; Palmer's undated comments, ibid., 38–4; Goldman, quoted in Curti's 20 October 1944 précis of comments for committee members, Gottschalk Papers, 14:1.

persist. Although historians must call attention to the mutations, they must emphasize the elements of continuity. And to grant that continuity within change exists leads necessarily to the conclusion that the elements of continuity are the essentials, of mutation, the incidentals. Can we not then expect the historian, whether of 1927 or of 1944 to select the facts that bear upon the essential rather than upon the incidentals? The historian may seek to escape the problem by surrender, by concession that all is incidental. But he has a more worthy task. Working on the hypothesis that there is continuity to the human past, his primary mission is to define the nature of that continuity and of the media through which it operates.[48]

Few historians gave high marks to the bulletin as a whole. Even sympathetic commentators, like W. Stull Holt, said that the propositions revealed "a lack of systematic thinking, a confusion in thought, a frequent internal inconsistency, and a vagueness, which makes them useless." The aspiration of Beard and of the committee as a whole was to win for their relativist theses formal ratification by the profession as a whole, and Bulletin 54 was to be the monument of their triumph. The Randall-Haines essay had celebrated the victory in advance. With what they described as the recent general acceptance of relativism, "American historiography had," they said, "come of age." As a relativist monument, Bulletin 54 seemed in the event to be an illustration of one of the tongue-in-cheek "laws" the English historian C. Northcote Parkinson announced in the 1950s. Exquisite monumental expression, he declared, was attained only by institutions in steep decline, or even total collapse. St. Peter's was erected long after the great days of the papacy, the House of Commons was completed only after parliament had begun to decline, the Palais des Nations was formally opened only after the League had practically ceased to exist. And so it was with Bulletin 54.[49]

As the discussions of relativism among historians generated by Bulletin 54 were petering out, "critical" or "analytical" philosophy of history was in the process of becoming a respectable subdivision of academic philosophy. Unlike the older "speculative" or "substantive" philosophy of history, the new subdiscipline was concerned not with overall interpretive schemes, but with the immanent logic of historical inquiry. Philosophers centered their attention not on the objectivity question, but rather on the

---

[48]Brinton review of Bulletin 54, *Journal of Modern History* 18 (1946): 341; Handlin review, *New England Quarterly* 19 (1946): 538; Handlin, "Memorandum on *Theory and Practice in Historical Study*," 10 June 1947, Curti Papers, 38–4.

[49]Holt, "An Evaluation of the Report on Theory and Practice in Historical Study," *Pacific Historical Review* 18 (1949): 236; Randall and Haines, "Controlling Assumptions," 51; Parkinson, *Parkinson's Law, or the Pursuit of Progress* (London, 1959), 83–94.

nature of historical explanation. The catalyst of this concern was a 1942 article by Carl G. Hempel in which he argued that Karl Popper's "covering law" model of scientific explanation was equally applicable to history. In the words of one of the leading members of the new subdiscipline, "it could be said without exaggeration that until about 1965 the critical philosophy of history *was* the controversy over the covering-law model."[50]

Popper had held that to offer a causal explanation of an event in the empirical sciences was "to deduce a statement which describes it, using as premises of the deduction one or more *universal laws*, together with certain singular statements, the *initial conditions*." (Explanation and prediction were thus mirror images of each other: explanation was "retrodiction.") "Historical explanation, too," Hempel said, "aims at showing that the event in question was not 'a matter of chance,' but was to be expected in view of certain antecedent or simultaneous conditions."

It is highly instructive, in examining the adequacy of a suggested explanation, to attempt a reconstruction of the universal hypotheses on which it rests. . . . Consider, for example, the statement that the Dust Bowl farmers migrate to California 'because' continual drought and sandstorms render their existence increasingly precarious, and because California seems to them to offer so much better living conditions. This explanation rests on some such universal hypothesis as that populations will tend to migrate to regions which offer better living conditions. But it would obviously be difficult accurately to state this hypothesis in the form of a general law which is reasonably well confirmed by all the relevant evidence available. . . . Analagous remarks apply to all historical explanations in terms of class struggle, . . . tendency to conspicuous consumption, etc.: All of them rest on the assumption of universal hypotheses which connect certain characteristics of individual or group life with others; but in many cases, the content of the hypotheses which are tacitly assumed in a given explanation can be reconstructed only quite approximately.[51]

Hempel acknowledged that given these difficulties one could perhaps expect from historians no more than "explanation sketches," and in his own later writings, as well as those of philosophers sympathetic to his viewpoint, the model was elaborated and qualified with the introduction of "normic laws," "truisms" as grounds for historical explanation, stochastic laws, and "laws" of less than universal applicability. But despite

---

[50]Hempel, "The Function of General Laws in History," *Journal of Philosophy* 39 (1942), reprinted in Patrick Gardiner, ed., *Theories of History* (Glencoe, Ill., 1959), 344–56; Louis O. Mink, "The Divergence of History and Sociology in Recent Philosophy of History," in Patrick Suppes et al., eds., *Logic, Methodology and Philosophy of Science, IV* (Amsterdam, 1973), 730.
[51]Popper, *The Logic of Scientific Discovery* (1934; English trans., New York, 1959), 59; Hempel, 349–50.

Objectivity reconstructed

all the modifications made to bring the model more into line with historical practice, the application of the Hempelian formula to history retained
a prescriptive flavor. When historians "subsumed [phenomena] under
some general idea which is not amenable to any empirical test," Hempel
wrote, "it amounts to a pseudo-explanation which may have emotive
appeal and evoke pictorial associations, but which does not further our
theoretical understanding of the phenomena under consideration." The
prescriptive tone was continued in the writings of Hempelians like May
Brodbeck, who wrote of historians' "obscurantist appeals to 'judgment'
and 'intelligibility'."[52]

Historians saw the Hempelian model of historical explanation as a
condescending and dismissive critique of existing historical practice. This
was as true for the handful, like Lee Benson, who endorsed it, as for the
overwhelming majority who rejected it as irrelevant to historical practice.
In fact, most of the philosophers who addressed themselves to the question had little interest in existing historical practice, either in criticizing it
or in reforming it. Their concern was with the nature of logical inference.
Historical explanation was of interest as the limiting case of a general
model of scientific explanation. Hempel himself, like many of those involved in the defense or elaboration of his model (Brodbeck, Nagel,
Michael Scriven), was a philosopher of science. Other philosophers who
involved themselves in the controversy (Patrick Gardiner, Morton
White, Arthur Danto), sometimes had a particular interest in history, but
were principally concerned with the extent to which the rational reconstruction of historical explanation might elucidate more general philosophical propositions.

Historians often misunderstood, and sometimes willfully misrepresented, the nature of the philosophers' exercise, which was the rational
reconstruction of one dimension of historical discourse. The feisty J. H.
Hexter wrote that Morton White's and Arthur Danto's "fiddling around"
with history produced "sophistical flimflam." He quoted White's observation, with respect to the analysis of the structure of historical explanation, that "The vast differences that human beings exhibit do not prevent
us from X-raying them in an effort to discern the skeletal structure that
each of them possesses." Hexter went on to characterize White's position
as being that "All we know about the structure of the human body, all the
truth accessible to us about it, is what the roentgenologist finds by X-raying the skeleton; all the rest has to do with its color, texture, and beauty,
and is mere fleshing out." In quoting White, Hexter omitted the imme-

---

[52]Hempel, 353; Brodbeck, "Explanation, Prediction, and 'Imperfect' Knowledge," *Minnesota Studies in the Philosophy of Science, Vol. III* (Minneapolis, 1962), reprinted in
Brodbeck, ed., *Readings in the Philosophy of the Social Sciences* (London, 1968), 389.

diately following two sentences, thus reversing his meaning. "Naturally," White wrote in the passage which Hexter omitted, "if upon discovering this structure a roentgenologist were to come to the absurd conclusion that men are nothing but skeletons, we should regard him as mad. And in the same way, if a logician of narrative, upon discovering its structure, were to conclude that narratives are nothing but logical conjunctions of certain kinds of statements, we should regard him as mad too."[53]

Some of those philosophers who defended the applicability of the covering law model to history were at the same time strong defenders of the objectivity of historical knowledge. But support of the covering law model by no means entailed an objectivist position in historiography. Popper, the original creator of the model, made clear his repudiation of objectivity as a plausible goal for history, and took what was, though not labeled as such, a very "relativist" stance. Few historical interpretations, he said, were really testable; they were "more or less interesting points of view"; there was "necessarily a plurality of interpretations which are fundamentally on the same level of both suggestiveness and arbitrariness"; historians should "be clear about the necessity of adopting a point of view . . . state this point of view plainly, and always . . . remain conscious that it is one among many." In a passage that might have been written by Becker or Beard, he said that "each generation has its own troubles and problems, and therefore its own interests and its own point of view."

It follows that each generation has a right to look upon and re-interpret history in its own way. . . . After all, we study history because we are interested in it, and perhaps because we wish to learn something about our own problems. But history can serve neither of these two purposes if, under the influence of an inapplicable idea of objectivity, we hesitate to present historical problems from our point of view. And we should not think that our point of view, if consciously and critically applied to the problem, will be inferior to that of a writer who naively believes . . . that he has reached a level of objectivity permitting him to present "the events of the past as they actually did happen."

Popper, in all other respects a determined antirelativist, was probably driven to this position by both the rigor of his standards for objective knowledge and his zeal to unmask Marxist claims to be presenting the scientific truth about history.[54]

---

[53]Hexter, "The One That Got Away," *New York Review of Books* 8 (9 February 1967): 24, 26–27; White, *Foundations of Historical Knowledge* (New York, 1965), 220–21. See White's response and Hexter's rejoinder, ibid., 23 March 1967, 28–31.

[54]*The Poverty of Historicism* (1957; rev. ed., New York, 1964), 151–52; *The Open Society and Its Enemies* (2 vols., 1945; rev. ed., London, 1962), 267–68.

The postwar philosophical climate was, in a general way, hostile to cognitive relativism, and to the pragmatism and the continental idealism with which many of Becker and Beard's philosophical critics associated their historical relativism. But with the passage of time fewer and fewer of the analytical philosophers of history defended the traditional norms of historical objectivity. The majority, whatever their views on the applicability of covering law theory to history, concluded that in selecting elements either of a description or of an explanation, historians had no choice but to make decisions based largely on their own values and intentions.

Shortly after the war, Morton White, as part of his analysis of Progressive thought, wrote a searching critique of Beard's relativism, and a defense of historical objectivity. Historians, he said, could overcome the vexatious problem of selection by making their selection "representative," in a way analagous to the randomizing procedures of sociologists. Maurice Mandelbaum, who called himself an "unmitigated objectivist," and who was the philosopher who more than any other continued to devote himself to the refutation of historical relativism, claimed White, along with Arthur Danto, as allies. But within a few years White announced that he had modified his earlier "objectivistic" approach, and Mandelbaum was criticizing the implicit relativism of White's characterization of how historians evaluate each other's work:

We feel [White wrote] that the author has written a narrative which, in the light of our acquaintance with the facts, and our estimate of their importance, is on the whole good. . . . One approves of the history because the author seems to look at the evidence with one's eyes and one's heart . . . and to feel about him that he is a kindred spirit, one who would see the same figure as we would in a Rorschach inkblot, or who would first see the duck-rabbit of Jastrow and Wittgenstein as a duck, just as we did every time we looked at it. . . . They have converging interests without articulating them, so two mutually resonant historians may have a similar value-orientation but not bother to make explicit that shared orientation when they praise each other's work.

Similarly Danto proved an unreliable ally for Mandelbaum. In his most comprehensive treatment of the question Danto argued the old "noble dream" of a completely verisimilitudinous account was not even a proper ideal at which historians should aim.

In the nature of the case historians are obliged to aim, not at a reproduction but at a kind of organization of the past. . . . This . . . I shall try to exhibit as logically dependent upon topical interests which motivate historians, so that, if I am right, historical relativism will finally be vindicated. It will be vindicated in the sense that it is, in a general way, correct, and that we cannot conceive of history without organizational schemes, nor of historically organizing schemes apart from specific human interests.[55]

The Canadian philosopher William H. Dray was a particular favorite of those who followed the debate on explanation because, in the words of one leading historian, he brought "philosophical support and respectability to historians' visceral reaction against . . . 'the covering law theory.'" Dray preferred a "rational action" model of explanation, one with close affinities to R. G. Collingwood's conception of historical explanation as "rethinking." Dray was influenced in this decision by considerations which appealed to many contemporary historians. Dray believed the rational model of explanation to be particularly congenial to a libertarian metaphysical position and "logically compatible with indeterminism regarding human actions." Moreover, history for Dray was irretrievably one of the "humanities," and he said that his chief complaint against accepting covering law doctrine in history was "not the difficulty of operating it, in either fully deductive or mutilated form. It is rather that it sets up a kind of *conceptual barrier* to a humanistically oriented historiography."[56]

Covering law theorists were widely criticized by historians for dealing with abstract examples, rather than drawing their conclusions from the writing of professional historians, and Dray was praised by historians for grounding himself in practice. But his conclusions, he observed, were "not, perhaps, what they had in mind in urging that theorizing about history take care to concern itself with actual historical practice," because after surveying the relevant literature he concluded that historians "will never know 'objectively' what caused the Civil War." For Dray, as for White and Danto, the sticking point was selection. Historians' choice of

---

[55]White's critique of Beard and his "objectivistic" approach are in his *Social Thought in America: The Revolt Against Formalism* (New York, 1949), and "Toward an Analytic Philosophy of History," in Marvin Farber, ed., *Philosophical Thought in France and the United States* (Albany, 1950), 705–26. Mandelbaum's claim that White and Danto shared his rejection of relativism is in his "Concerning Recent Trends in the Theory of Historiography," *Journal of the History of Ideas* 16 (1955): 508–9. White repudiates his earlier position in "The Logic of Historical Narration," in Sidney Hook, ed., *Philosophy and History: A Symposium* (New York, 1963), 23, 28–29. (White's *Foundations of Historical Knowledge* [New York, 1965] went even farther in a "relativist" direction.) Mandelbaum's characterization of White's later views is in his comment on White's paper, Hook, ed., *Philosophy and History*, 52. For Danto, see his *Analytical Philosophy of History* (Cambridge, 1968), 111.

[56]Leonard Krieger, "Comments on Historical Explanation," in Hook, ed., *Philosophy and History*, 136; Dray, "The Historical Explanation of Actions Reconsidered," ibid., 131–33.

causes to discuss, Dray concluded, did not just happen to be based on value judgments; the conclusions were logically dependent on them. No value-free ground of selection was possible.[57]

Those philosophers who defended the objectivity of history often set up standards for the legitimate scope of history which were quite restrictive. John Passmore believed that historians had to severely limit the scope of their work if they were to attain objectivity. "Historians," Passmore said, "write books . . . with what seem to me to be preposterous titles—titles like *The History of England*. . . . The fact of the matter is that there is no such subject as *The History of England*." Mandelbaum thought that the extension of historical inquiry beyond narrowly and precisely defined parameters "necessarily lead[s] to the theory of historical relativism." In a period when history was broadening to encompass many new areas, few historians were prepared to restrict the discipline's range to satisfy philosophers' objectivist scruples.[58]

It is difficult to say how closely postwar historians followed the controversies among philosophers of history. AHA executive secretary Boyd Shafer characterized the debates among Hempel, Dray, et al. as resembling "the arguments of the later scholastics." In the opinion of his successor, Paul L. Ward, historians had paid "strikingly little attention to them." In Leonard Krieger's view, historians found the philosophers' discussions "either opaque or irrelevant." Bernard Bailyn was surely speaking for many of his colleagues when he said that however interesting these issues were to philosophers, neither he nor any historian he knew found them at all helpful to their professional work. Jürgen Herbst, who in the 1960s surveyed theoretical offerings in two hundred history departments, found concern with philosophy of history "peripheral": "Those historians who seek to plead for greater self-awareness in the historical profession convey a hard-to-define but very noticeable sense of being propagators of a minority and perhaps even declining cause."[59]

Historians directed more scorn toward Hempel's covering law model than they did toward any of the other writings of philosophers who

---

[57]"Some Causal Accounts of the American Civil War," *Daedalus* 91 (1962): 587.

[58]Passmore, "The Objectivity of History," *Philosophy* 33 (1958), reprinted in William H. Dray, ed., *Philosophical Analysis and History* (New York, 1964): 84–85; Mandelbaum, "Recent Trends," 515.

[59]Shafer, "The Study of History in the United States: Some Affirmations, Some Doubts," *Bulletin of the American Association of University Professors* 50 (1964): 235; Ward, *Elements of Historical Thinking* (Washington, D.C., 1971), 31; Krieger, review of White, *Foundations of Historical Knowledge*, *AHR* 73 (1968): 1092; Bailyn, "The Problems of the Working Historian: A Comment," in Hook, ed., *Philosophy and History*, 93–94; Herbst, "Theoretical Work in History in American University Curricula," *History and Theory* 7 (1968): 348.

interested themselves in history. It seemed to many historians a philosophical stalking horse for a takeover of history by the social sciences. For historians, as for Dray, its scientism violated their sense of history as one of the humanities. And, in the cold war climate where "determinism" of any kind was vaguely associated with Marxism, it could be regarded as ideologically obnoxious as well. But the work of Hempel and those in his camp was seen as only the most egregious example of what Krieger termed "academic imperialism by the mother country of all the sciences."[60]

The principal issue for mid-twentieth-century historians, as it had been for the founders of the profession in the late nineteenth century, was autonomy. Earlier, historians had sought to win autonomy for the historical profession from speculative philosophy of history, with its overarching interpretive schemes. Now historians sought to maintain that autonomy in the face of what seemed to them epistemological supervision by analytic philosophers of history. Naturally the greatest resentment was directed toward those philosophers who were most critical of existing practice, or, more precisely, existing conceptualization of practice. But from the standpoint of full professional autonomy, it was as offensive to be patted on the head by a philosopher for doing things right as it was to be scolded for doing them wrong.

Historians, in discussing the work of philosophers of history, repeatedly stressed the theme of autonomy. Paul L. Ward gave high praise to G. R. Elton's 1967 *The Practice of History*, despite his disagreements with many of Elton's prescriptions, because the English scholar had avoided contemporary theoretical discussions, and made a "welcome contribution to the case for the autonomy of history." C. Vann Woodward insisted that history was "sui generis." John Higham thought that an unintended consequence of the philosophers' disputes was to strengthen historians' conviction of the "special character of historical knowledge." "History as a type of investigation and study," Lloyd Sorenson wrote, "is much older than modern science and had attained to distinctive methods and procedures when science was still trying to account for the horn on the unicorn." Leonard Krieger, in articles and reviews spoke again and again of "the sovereign rights of the historian," and of the historian's "autonomous province." If the historian surrendered that autonomy, Krieger warned, "he loses his soul."[61]

[60]Krieger, "Comments on Historical Explanation," 137.
[61]Ward, review of Elton, *History and Theory* 8 (1969): 119; Woodward, "Report on Current Research: American History," *Saturday Review of Literature* 36 (4 April 1953): 16;

It may be doubted whether in any circumstances historians would have closely followed the philosophers' discussions of historical epistemology, presented, as they often were, in the arcane symbol system of modern logic. But the professional insistence of the autonomy of historians' standards from philosophers' strictures made it almost a professional duty to tune out the philosopher's arguments. (Some made an exception for R. G. Collingwood, whose *The Idea of History* was more acceptable to the profession precisely because Collingwood, in addition to being as much historian as philosopher, repeatedly echoed the cry of "the autonomy of history.") Whatever the nuances of postwar historians' substantive differences on issues of epistemology they were as one on the relevant tribunal which should adjudicate them. Judgments on such questions, insofar as they were necessary at all, would be made "autonomously," within the profession.

IV

After the wrangling over Bulletin 54 in the 1940s died down, it is only in a philosopher's "rational reconstruction" that one can speak of a full-scale debate on objectivity within the historical profession. At most one can describe a desultory conversation, with few of the participants presenting fully worked out positions, and none of them offering much that was original. It was the critics of interwar relativism who were most deeply committed on the issue, and who expressed themselves with the greatest force.

Attacks on Becker's and Beard's relativism were often ancillary to attacks on the Progressive tradition in scholarship which they represented. This was most clearly the case with Robert E. Brown, whose explanation of Becker's and Beard's substantive mistakes in terms of their misconceived epistemology was discussed in Chapter 11. His attacks on Beard in his treatment of the Constitution were so personal and vituperative that the book was rejected by the AHA's Beveridge Prize Committee largely on those grounds. A year later Brown's *Middle-Class Democracy and Revolution in Massachusetts* was awarded an honorable mention on condition that what Edmund S. Morgan called "pointless and offensive" characterizations of Becker and Beard be eliminated. When Brown gave two lectures on relativism at a 1955 conference, his remarks were so

Higham et al., *History*, 143; Sorenson, "Historical Currents in America," *American Quarterly* 7 (1955): 244; Krieger, review of White, in *AHR* 73 (1968): 1094; review of H.- I. Marrou, *De la Connaissance Historique*, and W. H. Dray, *Law and Explanation in History*, *AHR* 64 (1959): 333; "The Horizons of History," *AHR* 63 (1957): 73.

extreme that, according to one participant, they "turned even those who were originally neutral to a fierce defense of Beard, and to a lesser extent of Becker."[62]

The grasslands historian James C. Malin also combined attacks on interwar relativism with denunciation of the New Deal "collectivism" with which he associated it. Because he saw himself living in a "censored world" in which "the only way I could have the freedom to print what I wanted to say was to print privately," Malin personally financed the publication of a number of attacks on relativism in the forties and fifties. He found a few supporters among those who shared his sense of political and professional isolation. William B. Hesseltine, who abandoned his earlier socialist allegiance after the war, hailed one of Malin's volumes for combating

efforts . . . to call on historical data to support social planning and to bolster the drive for the totalitarian welfare state. Aided and abetted by historians, by the American Historical Association, and by the Social Science Research Council, the collectivists, calling themselves "liberals," have maintained that historical data is subjective . . . and that history should serve the "presentist" functional end of advancing a reformed social order. . . . Professor Malin's faith in historical scholarship is an inspiration in these days of the anti-intellectualism of presentist social science "frames of reference."

But most younger historians took a dim view of Malin's polemics, and his books received a cool reception in professional journals. John Higham explained to Merle Curti why his highly critical review of Malin's *On the Nature of History* was not as severe as it might have been: "A man who has given his life to patient scholarship and who with senile foolishness has embarked in his later years on an embittered crusade for which he is not intellectually equipped deserves a gentle treatment which he himself is incapable of giving to others." David W. Noble, describing Malin's behavior at a conference, said that he "was so obviously off balance or more bluntly crazy that we didn't take him seriously enough to get mad at him."[63]

[62]Reports of Beveridge Committee deliberations for 1953 and 1954 in AHA Papers, Boxes 431, 429; on Brown's lectures, David Lowenthal to Merle Curti, 27 August 1955, Curti Papers, 24–21. Slightly after the period now under review Brown published, privately, a full-scale attack on Becker's relativism, which charged Becker with having skated on "the thin ice of Communism." (Brown, *Carl Becker on History and The American Revolution* [East Lansing, Mich., 1970], 170.)

[63]Malin on publishing his own works, in letter to Fred Shannon, 4 April 1947, Shannon Papers, Box 1; Hesseltine on Malin in ms. review of *On the Nature of History*, Hesseltine Papers, M66–132/8; Higham to Curti, 4 October 1955, Curti Papers, 19–20; Noble to Curti, undated, ibid., 28–7.

Attacks on interwar relativism and defense of disinterested objectivity as a professional norm were not restricted to the historiographical right. Edward Pessen offered a ringing affirmative to his title question "Can the Historian Be Objective?" As an example of new historical truths established through objective inquiry, not by wishy-washy "fair-mindedness" or "impartiality," and certainly not the result of new frames of reference, he listed "Herbert Aptheker's story of near incessant rebellion against slavery" as one of the new findings which demonstrated "the difference between the invalid and the valid or objective."[64]

A number of articles offered refutations of this or that thesis of Becker and Beard. Perez Zagorin observed that many people mistakenly confuse knowledge with certainty; then he charged Becker with denying the possibility of historical knowledge on the basis of this error—a denial Becker had never made. Like a number of other critics of relativism, Zagorin used the imagery of disease. Becker was representative of "that prolonged malady of skepticism which yet afflicts us." Harry J. Marks sought to refute Beard's contention that historians' principles of selection were "relative," by concentrating on Beard's acknowledgment that one can know many "individual truths" about the past. His argument reflected the endurance of the cumulativist vision of the founding fathers of the profession.

Once it has been granted . . . that a part of the objective truth, albeit a small fraction, can be stated about a part of the past . . . there is nothing inherent in [Beard's] logic to prevent new studies from evolving additional objective truths about this given segment of the past. And further studies add further truths, and so on, accumulating more and more truths. . . . It is . . . possible to accumulate larger and larger proportions of the unattainable "whole truths" about this given sector of the past until one would have collected so overwhelming a bulk of truths that each new increment . . . could not seriously alter the fundamental features of the picture. It is thus possible within the Beardian limitations to secure an objectively truthful account approaching a limit ("the whole truth") closely enough, eventually, so that "the whole truth" would not be substantially different.[65]

The most often cited "refutation" of interwar relativism was Chester MacArthur Destler's "Some Observations on Contemporary Historical Theory," published in the *American Historical Review* in 1950. Much of Destler's argument aimed at exposing the poisoned roots of relativism. It

[64]*Bulletin of the Association of American Colleges* 51 (1955): 325.
[65]Zagorin, "Professor Becker's Two Histories: A Skeptical Fallacy," *AHR* 62 (1956): 4; Marks, "Grounds Under Our Feet: Beard's Relativism," *Journal of the History of Ideas* 14 (1953): 630.

derived, he said, largely from Croce, who "helped lay the intellectual foundations of Italian Fascism." (Destler sought to prove that Becker had stolen all his ideas from Croce and had then clumsily attempted to cover his tracks: "ideological plagiarism of a complete type . . . protected by outright prevarication.") John Dewey was another "subjectivist" influence denounced at length. For Destler, only historical work deformed by presentism had to be rewritten by successive generations of historians.

The rewriting of history will become necessary . . . only where investigation and interpretation have rested predominantly or exclusively upon "leading principles and hypotheses" derived from the author's own day. Even then, basic revision is called for only when new data is discovered or old evidence is more ably appraised. Edward Gibbon's masterpiece is still the classic work for the centuries between the time of Marcus Aurelius and the capture of Constantinople by the Turks, corrected and brought up to date historically by the able editorship of J. B. Bury.

Defending himself against criticism for publishing Destler's article, AHA managing editor Guy Stanton Ford said "I have no illusions about Destler as a philosopher but I thought he might break enough china to get a rejoinder from some of the owners of the shop." But by the early 1950s most of the old proprietors were not very zealous about protecting their merchandise, which even they, along with many of their customers, regarded as rather shopworn.[66]

In response to Destler's *AHR* article Merle Curti, with a few others, wrote a letter to *The Review* asserting that Destler had misrepresented Becker and Beard's position, but they did not elaborate this point, concentrating on the defense of John Dewey, who was still alive. In his presidential address to the Mississippi Valley Historical Association in 1952, Curti defended relativists against the charge that they had exaggerated the "democratic theme" in American history, but the emphasis was on the legitimacy of the theme. All historians' work, he said, had been "influenced by dominant or competing movements of thought in their time or by the position they held in society" and this was no more true of avowed relativists or presentists than of their critics. But he saw the issue

[66]Destler, *AHR* 55 (1950); quotations from 504, 517–18. The quotation in parentheses is from Destler to Boyd Shafer, 17 March 1959, AHA Papers, Box 502, seeking publication of an article detailing his charges against Becker, which were only hinted at in the earlier *AHR* article. Ford's remark was in his 21 September 1950 letter to John Herman Randall, Jr., AHA Papers, Box 358. Destler's article was later published as "The Crocean Origins of Becker's Historical Relativism" in *History and Theory* 9 (1970): 334–42; it was rebutted by Hayden V. White in "Croce and Becker: A Note on the Evidence of Influence," ibid. 10 (1971): 222–27.

declining in importance, and did not again address himself to it in a serious way. The decline of the controversy seemed to him to demonstrate the truth of Dewey's contention that "problems are often not solved . . . they merely give way to others."[67]

Erstwhile followers of Becker's and Beard's doctrines were increasingly reluctant to defend their teachings. Leo Gershoy endorsed the judgment that Becker was "an exciting but poor epistemologist." Louis Gottschalk, both in his textbook on historical method and in his AHA presidential address, put a good deal of distance between himself and his mentor. Often the topic of Becker's and Beard's relativism was discreetly avoided. Guy Stanton Ford in an eight-page obituary of Becker made no reference to his relativism. The posthumous Festschrift for Beard, which Howard K. Beale edited, contained only the most brief and casual mention of his relativism.[68]

Among that minority of postwar historians who concerned themselves at all with the challenge the relativists had posed to the norm of objectivity, most were neither concerned to refute relativism nor to defend it. Of the numerous works which touched on the question, only Cushing Strout's *Pragmatic Revolt in American History* was centrally concerned with the relativist critique, and Strout's was the only treatment which offered a systematic evaluation of Becker's and Beard's epistemology. Like a number of other commentators, Strout gave the two men high marks for having had the courage to incur "the puzzled hostility of those scholars for whom conventional assumptions and habits were still adequate." But he criticized their "exaggerated pragmatism," and their tendency "to reduce the historical imagination to a mere weapon in present struggles"; they "woke historians from their dogmatic slumbers at the

---

[67]Letter by Curti, Bert J. Loewenberg, John Herman Randall, Jr., and Harold Taylor, *AHR* 56 (1951): 450–52; "The Democratic Theme in American Historical Literature," *MVHR* 39 (1952): 26; "John Dewey's Theory of History," ms. in Curti Papers, 15–4. Curti's students privately reassured him that they shared his dismay at Destler's attack on relativism. John Higham called it "a tissue of exaggerations. . . . Why do you suppose that Destler is infected with such animus? . . . Can the article be seen perhaps as a defensive reaction, as a return to tradition in the face of present world challenges?" (Letter of 11 May 1950, Curti Papers, 19–19.) David W. Noble assured Curti that if he criticized Becker and Beard it was in a friendly fashion, the better to defend them against "fashionable, irrational criticism" like that of Destler. (Undated [1955] letter, ibid., 28–7.)

[68]Gershoy review of Burleigh Taylor Wilkins, *Carl Becker*, *AHR* 67 (1962): 453; Gottschalk, *Understanding History* (New York, 1954); "A Professor of History in a Quandry," 59 (1954): 273–86; Ford, *American Philosophical Society Yearbook, 1945*, 338–46; *Charles A. Beard: An Appraisal* (Lexington, Ky., 1954). Gershoy did, by invitation, respond to a critique of Becker's thought by Perez Zagorin: see his "Zagorin's Interpretation of Becker: Some Observations," *AHR* 62 (1956): 12–17.

price of a skepticism which, instead of being constructively provisional, threatened to become destructively final."[69]

Other historiographical works published in the fifties and sixties either summarized relativist themes without evaluative comment, or made passing critical remarks, as when John Higham censured Becker and Beard for "slurring" the clear distinction between judgments of fact and judgments of value. All of these works were concerned to historicize relativism. They sought to understand it as a reflection of a moment in American cultural history, tied to a Progressive vision now discredited, or as a stage in the dialectical development of American historical thought, which had now attained greater sophistication. To historicize a doctrine is always, to some greater or lesser extent, to subtly undermine it, to suggest that it is *vieux jeu*. Becker, Beard, and their allies had understood this well, and had stressed the time-bound origins of received objectivist doctrine, and its association with nationalist and conservative ideologies held in low regard at the time when they wrote. Now the tables were turned, and their relativism was made to appear a somewhat quaint artifact of a bygone period; the companion of either a naive faith in progress, or an overreaction to disappointment in the failure of that progress to materialize.[70]

Paradoxically, a paradox that Becker and Beard would have relished, it was most often on pragmatic grounds that the relativists' pragmatic theory of truth was rejected. Dozens of commentators deplored the effect of relativism on historians' morale. Roy F. Nichols complained that the writings of the relativists had "tended to create confusion in some minds" and "lessened self-confidence." Others were concerned with perpetuating the posture of objectivity as a defensive shield. Edward Kirkland, who was active on the American Association of University Professors' academic freedom committee, thought that in the era of McCarthyism, on "utilitarian" grounds, "an emphasis upon the frame of reference theory weakened our defenses against the Philistine and the barbarian." Stanley Pargellis of the Newberry Library was continually trying to get corpora-

---

[69](Ithaca, N.Y., 1958), 2, 158–59, 161.
[70]Higham et al., *History*, 133–34. Higham devoted only a few paragraphs to Becker's and Beard's epistemological thought in a work whose avowed central focus was shifting substantive interpretations. Hofstadter, in his discussion of Beard in *The Progressive Historians*, avoided evaluating his relativism. Robert A. Skotheim (*American Intellectual Histories and Historians* [Princeton, 1966]) dealt only in passing (and nonevaluatively) with relativism. David W. Noble, in *Historians Against History: The Frontier Thesis and the National Covenant in American Historical Writing Since 1830* (Minneapolis, 1965), discussed Becker and Beard at length but gave the merest mention to their relativism.

tions to make their records available to historians, promising businessmen that only objective (i.e., not unsympathetic) scholars would have
access to them. "I have gone on record as defending the objectivity of the
historical profession," he wrote to Paul W. Gates, "and . . . I need
ammunition." Ray Billington, representing historians on the Social Science Research Council, argued that relativistic thought in history weakened his hand in arguing for funds against the claims of the "harder"
social sciences. Vann Woodward, with a concern reminiscent of Voltaire's fear of talking atheism in front of the servants, worried about the
consequences for the profession of relativist doctrines, "loosely construed" by the laity: "Becker and Beard could be pictured as the Martin
Luther and Philip Melanchthon of the American faith. They preached a
sort of secular Reformation of relativism, a new Protestantism that gives
licence to the layman to consult the sacred text for himself and seek out its
meaning without mediation of the priesthood."[71]

No professional consensus was reached on the objectivity question in
the postwar years, though in what one later historian called "The Era of
No Hard Feelings" there was a strong tendency toward middle-of-the
road convergence. As we have seen, various elements in the culture pushed historians toward an objectivist and spectatorial posture, while other
tendencies emphasized the need for moral commitment and engagement.
Probably a desire to distinguish between "autonomous" historians' discourse and the antiseptic language of hyperempiricist social scientists led
some humanistic historians to be more evaluative and judgmental than
their principles allowed. In the postwar decades almost fifty American
universities initiated doctoral programs in history, which meant that for
the first time a substantial section of the profession was engaged in directing doctoral dissertations. To the extent that much of one's professional
life was spent supervising the production of what were usually pedestrian
monographs, which at best could be designated "a contribution," there
was strong internal psychological pressure to place a higher valuation on
the genre.

Certainly there was no agreement on the level of ideological commitment regarded as consistent with good professional practice. Richard
Hofstadter laid out the opposing arguments in a fashion which reflected
his own ambivalence, and that of many of his generation, but in language

[71]Nichols, "Postwar Reorientation," 78–79; Kirkland to Merle Curti, 24 January 1942,
   Curti Papers, 22–18; Pargellis to Paul W. Gates, 6 June 1944, Gates Papers; Billington,
   draft article intended for SSRC *Items* (never printed), attached to 9 April 1953 letter to
   Gates, Gates Papers; Woodward, *American Attitudes Toward History* (inaugural lecture
   as Harmsworth Professor of American History) (Oxford, 1955), 20.

which made his own inclinations clear, and in this, too, he was probably reflecting a generational sensibility:

Historians . . . are caught between their desire to count in the world and their desire to understand it. On one side their passion for understanding points back to the old interest in detachment, in neutrality, in critical history and the scientific ideal. But the terribly urgency of our political problems points in another direction, plays upon their pragmatic impulse. . . . In the end most historians will be persuaded less by the arguments than by the dictates of their temperaments. In the American temperament there is a powerful bias toward accepting the pragmatic demand upon history. . . . The urgency of our national problems seems to demand, more than ever, that the historian have something to say that will help us. . . . Against this, the professional case for detachment seems at first overwhelmingly strong. Most of us think we have other and better criteria of a historical work than its usefulness as a source of battle cries or slogans. . . .

Yet . . . the case for the historian *engagé*—and I mean here the case for him *as a historian*, not as a public force—also has its strengths. . . . Present-mindedness, though it has been responsible for major errors, has often brought with it a major access of new insight—bearing error and distortion not in arbitrary solitude but in a kind of fertile if illicit union with intellectual discovery. . . . The great fear that animates the most feverishly committed historians is that our continual rediscovery of the complexity of social interests . . . may give us not only a keener sense of the structural complexity of our society in the past, but also a sense of the moral complexity of social action that will lead us toward political immobility. . . . History does seem inconsistent with the coarser rallying cries of politics. Hence I suppose we may expect that the very idea of complexity will itself come under fire once again, and that it will become important for a whole generation to argue that most things . . . are not complex but really quite simple. This demand I do not think the study of history can gratify. . . . There may be comfort in it still. . . . History may remain the most humanizing among the arts.[72]

There were a few realms in which value-consensus was so nearly universal that it took on the aura of objective truth, and in which historians felt free to editorialize without compromising objectivity: "internationalism" and acceptance of "the responsibilities of world power" in the realm of foreign policy; racial egalitarianism on issues touching black-white relations. But these were the exceptions. If it was less frequently urged that historians approach their work totally purged of values, it was often demanded that these be kept under tight rein. H. Stuart Hughes thought values were useful for the historian if "mastered," "transcended," "controlled." He applied this criterion in criticizing Fritz Stern, a refugee from Nazi Germany, for making obvious his detestation of three intellec-

---

[72]*Progressive Historians*, 463–66.

tual precursors of Nazism: "I wish Mr. Stern had refrained from such questionable devices as throwing in an 'alas' at the triumph of Hitler. I wish there had been some trace of ambiguity in the historian's mind, the lingering, regretful sympathy for an enemy which, since Ranke, has characterized the best of cultural history in the German tradition."[73]

Except for always permissible paeans to the liberal tradition, the overt acknowledgment that one's history was written from a determinate overarching perspective was restricted to a handful of avowedly Christian historians, all of whom made clear that it was in their faith that they found the resolution of vexing problems of historical objectivity. For Kenneth Scott Latourette a Christian interpretation was something of a Beardian "act of faith," an answer to the problem of finding an ordering scheme with which to resolve the problem of selection. Rather more assertively, George V. Taylor argued that unlike secular historians of the French Revolution, each of whom, from Carlyle to Lefebvre, had "developed an interpretation consistent with his own views, his nationality, his party affiliation, his social status, and the experience of the generation in which he shared," the Christian historian had a timelessly valid perspective. His interpretation of the revolution was informed by his conviction that "undertakings originating in pride or cupidity ultimately destroy themselves. Otherwise Hell triumphs and the Gospel makes no sense." Arthur S. Link thought secular notions of objectivity "a snare and delusion." Secular historians could "live scrupulously, morally, righteously by the law of historical method" but that method "leaves us in vast darkness. It tells us that there are facts but does not tell us what they mean. . . . We cannot take an honest view of human history unless we acknowledge God's work through human kind in history." Such frank avowals were exceedingly rare, and were certainly unknown to most of those who read Taylor on the French Revolution or Link on Woodrow Wilson. When George Rawick's dissertation committee at the University of Wisconsin insisted that he make his Marxist perspective explicit, he had good grounds for thinking it "a bit of a violation of academic freedom to make a Marxist state clearly his frame of reference when *no one* else is asked to do so." (He reluctantly acceded.)[74]

Most historians gave little thought to "the objectivity question" in the

---

[73]"Is Contemporary History Real History?" *American Scholar* 32 (1963): 520; review of *The Politics of Cultural Despair*, *Political Science Quarterly* 77 (1962): 266.

[74]Latourette, "The Christian Understanding of History," *AHR* 54 (1949): 261; Taylor, "Prospectus for a Christian Consideration of the French Revolution," *Historical Magazine of the Protestant Episcopal Church* 25 (1956): 365, 375; Link, "The Historian's Vocation," *Theology Today* 19 (1962): 77–78, 87; Rawick to Merle Curti, 5 February 1957, Curti Papers, 34–24.

postwar years, a native predisposition reinforced by the warnings against philosophical indulgence which they received from the leaders of the profession. There was perhaps a bit more hesitation about using the term "objectivity"; a disposition among many to substitute softer terms like "fairness," "judiciousness," or "balance." "Definitive" also experienced a slight decline as a word of praise, except in the case of monographs on subjects so narrow that it was unlikely anyone would ever look at them again. Probably among the majority of historians who continued to praise works for their objectivity there were some who used the word in an altered sense: referring to rigorous testing of hypotheses, rather than "approaching a subject without preconceptions" or "letting the facts speak for themselves." But the latter locutions continued to be so freely employed that it is likely that those who used "objectivity" in the newer sense were a minority.

The most plausible characterization of the prevailing tacit epistemology of professional historians in the postwar years was made by Bruce Kuklick. He argued that historians, without being aware of the fact, or even acknowledging it as a model, had adapted "ideal observer" theory from moral philosophy. Taking over an idea common to "moral sense" philosophers of the eighteenth century, for whom "right" was what God approved, later thinkers substituted a hypothetical omniscient and dispassionate "ideal observer." One could approximate correct moral judgments by emulating the ideal observer. The ideal observer of moral philosophy, Kuklick noted, "has the characteristics attributable to the ideal historian": "There will be one correct evaluation in every situation calling for evaluation. . . . It will be necessary, at least theoretically, for everyone finally to agree on the truth-value of any evaluation. . . . Evaluations— similarly to the assertions of science—may thus be declared 'objective.'"

One central . . . problem is to reconcile the evaluative overtones of much historical narrative with the idea that what is "objective" is "value-free." In actual historical practice, however, the model settles precisely this conflict. The ideal observer theory eschews the notion that evaluations are "non-cognitive" and insists that they are empirical in exactly the same way as are the judgments of science. . . . Their evaluations naturally issue from a proper comprehension of the facts. . . .

Interpretative disputes in history are bitter and unamenable to settlement . . . but on a further explication of the model, their existence becomes easily explicable. Making an evaluation consists in part in *attempting* to put ourselves into the position of an ideal observer. Because this is ultimately impossible, however, there may be disagreement about the evaluatively significant reactions of an ideal observer. . . . If two people come to different conclusions concerning an evaluation, one of them, at least, in trying to put himself in the place of an ideal observer, *must* have failed. One of them, that is, has simply mistaken his reaction to a set of conditions basically reflecting his own biases for a reaction to a much more purified set of conditions. . . . The closer one thought oneself to be approaching the status of ideal observer, the more positive would be one's belief that others making opposing evaluations were, by definition, wrong. . . . Every interpretative dispute . . . indicates that someone has in effect confused his own biases with the impartiality of an ideal observer.[75]

Among those historians who attempted to deal with the relativist challenge, the most common attitude was what has been termed, in another connection, "restriction by partial incorporation," though in this case "rejection by partial incorporation" might be more accurate. Becker and Beard were frequently acknowledged to have performed an important service in freeing historians from the belief that "the facts spoke for themselves." Strout wrote that Becker had mounted such a devastating assault on received icons like "cold, hard facts" and "objective detachment," that "it is hard to believe that anyone with an intellectual conscience can ever revive them again in their old meaning without wincing, even though he may rightly feel that Becker's own theory is far from adequate as a philosophy of history." For most historians it was regarded as useful to be reminded how social circumstances had shaped historical scholarship in the past. Historians then proceeded to revive Hume's riddle of induction: it was illegitimate to infer present social influence on historical interpretation from the demonstration that it had been ubiquitous in the past. "Rejection through partial incorporation" could take various forms. One was voiced by Ralph H. Gabriel. The profession, he said, "has now rejected Charles A. Beard's doctrine of relativity. . . . Their awareness of the problem, plus their critical methods, make possible a practicable objectivity." In a much quoted phrase, Oscar Handlin announced that the historical profession had "learned to live with relativism." What was proposed seems to have been "living with" relativism as one lives with eczema: it's not fatal, simply an annoying chronic itch that's best ignored; it only gets worse if you scratch it.[76]

It was a strategy which worked well enough for the postwar years, when, as we have seen, a multitude of factors furthered the reconstruction of the norm of objectivity, and the repudiation of the relativist

[75]"The Mind of the Historian," *History and Theory* 8 (1969): 316, 319, 327, 329–30.
[76]The term "restriction through partial incorporation" was coined by the political scientist Harold D. Lasswell with reference to strategies of coping with revolutionary ideologies. David Riesman employed it in discussing the defusing or trivialization of Freudian propositions in consequence of the piecemeal and watered-down fashion in which they are

critique. It would not prove so serviceable in the drastically changed circumstances of the years that were to follow.

encountered. (Lasswell, *World Politics and Personal Insecurity* [New York, 1935], 5; Riesman, "The Themes of Heroism and Weakness in the Structure of Freud's Thought," in his *Individualism Reconsidered* [Glencoe, Ill., 1954], 365–87.) Strout, *Pragmatic Revolt*, 30. Gabriel's remark from his "History and the American Past," in Robert E. Spiller and Eric Larrabee, eds., *American Perspectives* (New York, 1961), 16; Handlin, quoted in Richard D. Challener and Maurice Lee, "History and the Social Sciences: The Problem of Communications," *AHR* 61 (1956): 331–32.

PART IV

Objectivity in crisis

13

◁══▷

The collapse of comity

The mood of affirmation and consensus which dominated American society from the early 1940s to the early 1960s had been, on the whole, congenial to an objectivist posture. Scholars celebrated the end of seriously divisive conflicts in the era of the "end of ideology." With agreement not only on ends, but to a considerable extent on means as well, residual problems were largely technical, objectively soluble through expertise. Historians' objectivism was usually qualified and tolerant. For various reasons, including the strictures of the interwar relativists, there had been, in these years, somewhat diminished confidence that historians' interpretations would converge on a single Truth, but every reason to believe that the boundaries of disagreement would continually narrow. For practical purposes, so long as historical accounts remained within these limits a certain amount of perspectival relativism could be tolerated without abandoning a larger commitment to objectivity. This was a philosophically makeshift, but psychologically and sociologically appealing, stance: why should one jeopardize professional comity by loudly insisting that one's own version was the objective truth and that one's colleague's version, which differed only in emphasis and nuance, was biased or partisan?

During the decade of the sixties the ideological consensus which provided the foundation for this posture collapsed, and it was not to be reconstructed in subsequent decades. The political culture lurched sharply left, then right; consensus was replaced first by polarization, then by fragmentation; affirmation, by negativity, confusion, apathy, and uncertainty. The consequences of all this turmoil for the idea of historical objectivity were various, and often contradictory.

The sixties were years of distrust, both of the leading institutions in society and of those who were their spokesmen. Brazen mendacity by the federal government increased in the course of the decade, and produced a concomitant increase in skepticism about "official truth," and for some, about truth of any kind—not least the academic. Not all official lying was delegated to those with impeccable scholarly credentials like Professors Schlesinger, Bundy, Rostow, or Kissinger, but enough of it was to destroy the presumption that in judging veracity the pronouncements of highly regarded academics should be automatically accepted, or even get the benefit of the doubt.

When journalists came under attack by Vice-President Spiro Agnew and Chicago Mayor Richard Daley for not reporting "objectively," what was most often at issue was their failure to accept official versions of the actions and fortunes of American troops in Vietnam; of the police in front of the Conrad Hilton. Tom Wicker of the *New York Times* saw many of the demands for journalistic objectivity as "serv[ing] the interests of those official sources with which the fetish of objectivity is primarily concerned." His colleague David Halberstam seconded his observations on what he called "the basic rule of journalistic theology."

Objectivity was prized and if objectivity in no way conformed to reality, then all the worse for reality. . . . In truth, despite all the fine talk of objectivity, the only thing that mildly approached objectivity was the form in which the reporter wrote the news, a technical style which required the journalist to appear to be much dumber and more innocent than in fact he was. So he wrote in a bland, uncritical way which gave greater credence to the utterances of public officials, no matter how mindless these utterances.

Still another former *Times* correspondent, J. Anthony Lukas, reported feeling while working for the *Times* that "what my editors were telling me was that objectivity meant that I should write within *their* definition of, within their unquestioned assumptions about, reality." Meanwhile, academic students of the media wrote of objectivity as an empty and formalistic "strategic ritual." For analysts of press coverage of the Vietnam War, "objectivity" was simply not a category of thought, as they devoted themselves to the exploration and explication of the mechanisms by which presentations were slanted this way and that.[1]

Responses to the climate of mendacity and mistrust varied. For many it

---

[1]Wicker, "The Tradition of Objectivity in the American Press—What's Wrong with It," *Proceedings of the Massachusetts Historical Society* 83 (1971): 84; Halberstam, quoted in Michael Parenti, *Inventing Reality: The Politics of the Mass Media* (New York, 1986), 52–53; Lukas, comment in "Ragtime Revisited: A Seminar with E. L. Doctorow and Joseph Papaleo," *Nieman Reports* 31 (Summer/Autumn 1977): 48–49.

produced cynicism about the very idea of truth and objectivity. If everyone was lying, if there was no one who could be trusted, why not simply believe whatever one found congenial and convenient? For others, and in general this was true of the most militant and activist critics of the government, the urgent task was to substitute their Truth for the lies and distortions of the state and its allies. Noam Chomsky's book-length essay "Objectivity and Liberal Scholarship" was dedicated to demonstrating liberals' deplorable failure to be objective. In this and subsequent writings he never wavered in his confidence that his own analyses met the highest standards of objectivity.[2]

With the heating up of the political atmosphere there were strong opposite pulls on scholars: toward leaping into the arena, "exposing lies," "speaking truth to power"; or toward leaving the stadium altogether, turning one's back on increasingly raucous and ill-tempered debate. Calls for a "relevant" scholarship—mostly from students, occasionally from younger faculty—were met by an academic backlash which made a virtue of irrelevance. In the classroom, in various forms of campus turmoil, and in miscellaneous ructions in professional associations, all the terms and concepts associated with "the objectivity question" were repeatedly at the top of the agenda.

Above all, historical objectivity became problematic because historians could not agree on what philosophers call the "explanandum"—that which is to be explained. At the extremes it was the "America" of the *Love It or Leave It* bumper sticker versus "Amerika" spray-painted by student militants on a campus wall. Historical writing which could explain the triumphs of the former was not much good at explaining the iniquities of the latter, and vice versa. Most historians, to be sure, were not found at the extremes, but the center had lost its vitality. The broad agreement on fundamentals which had endured, even during periods of strain and dissidence like the years between the wars, broke apart. And there appeared for the first time something hitherto unknown in the American historical profession: substantial and systematically "oppositional" historiographical tendencies.

I

The new, left-oriented historians who became visible within the profession during the 1960s came to be capitalized, reified, and often tacitly

---

[2]Chomsky's essay in his *American Power and the New Mandarins* (New York, 1969), 23–158.

homogenized as "New Left historians." This was a largely empty and misleading designation, lumping together individuals of the most diverse orientation, and often, innocently or maliciously, associating them with the most extreme wing of the student movement. In a comprehensive review of the work of a range of "New Left" historians stretching from Stephan Thernstrom to Eugene Genovese, Irwin Unger informed the readers of the *American Historical Review* that the group was united by their "conviction of America's total depravity." In fact, although there were some dissident historians who had ties to the student and youth insurgency which was labeled "New Left," at least as many either had no connection with the movement, or viewed it with a jaundiced eye. In any case, the rapid fragmentation and disintegration of the student movement made clear what a heterogeneous phenomenon it was, and the uselessness of the phrase "New Left" for describing any definable ideological tendency.[3]

To be sure, the new, left historiography and the student New Left had some important common roots. Both arose around 1960 in a climate characterized by the decline of McCarthyism, frustration with the mindlessness of politics in the Eisenhower years, admiration for the emerging civil rights movement in the South, the first stirrings of opposition to the nuclear arms race, and the turmoil in the Communist movement occasioned by Khrushchev's Twentieth Party Congress speech and the Soviet suppression of the Hungarian Revolution. It was a time when H. Stuart Hughes ran as a "peace candidate" for the U.S. Senate; when the future high priest of neoconservatism, Norman Podhoretz, published Staughton Lynd's revisionist account of cold war origins in *Commentary* and considered himself Lynd's ally in working to create a "new radicalism" freed of illusions about the USSR.[4]

There was an important generational difference between those (uncapitalized) new, left historians who received their doctorates in the late 1950s or early 1960s, and those who came along thereafter. Members of the former group often had firsthand experience in the "old" left, several having been what might be called "red romper toddlers," with youthful involvement, sometimes starting in their teens, in the Communist Party or its periphery. At age thirteen James Weinstein had been a delegate to the last meeting of the American Youth Congress in 1941, and spent several years in a factory doing political work for the CP, as had David Montgomery, among others. Staughton Lynd recalled "arguing as a ripe

---

[3]"The 'New Left' and American History: Some Recent Trends in United States Historiography," *AHR* 72 (1967): 1246.
[4]Podhoretz, *Breaking Ranks* (New York, 1979), 189.

Marxist of 14 against the 'Browder line' which . . . [advocated] dissolving the CP [and] declaring the class struggle at an end." Howard Zinn joined the party in his late teens and remained an active member for almost ten years. Eugene Genovese was expelled from the party while an undergraduate "for having zigged when I was supposed to zag." Herbert Gutman reported that he had "flirted briefly but intensely with the Communist movement"—which may have been an understatement. Aileen Kraditor described herself in 1969 as "a graduate of the Old Stalinist Left [whose] heart is with the young people, especially the saner hippie-anarchistic types."[5]

Others in this first cohort had youthful ties to the social democratic wing of the Old Left: Gabriel Kolko and Jesse Lemisch had been members of the barely socialist Student League for Industrial Democracy. A number of historians who went to Harvard, like Stephan Thernstrom and N. Gordon Levin, were influenced by the social democratic Marxism of Barrington Moore. Some—George Rawick and Richard N. Hunt, along with the present writer and a few other future historians—had been, during the mid-1950s, in the "Shachtmanite" Young Socialist League, then in the process of evolving from dissident Trotskyism to the left wing of social democracy. And there were those in this first cohort who are best described as "left liberals," young historians like Barton Bernstein and Christopher Lasch, critical of American liberals' accommodation to the cold war and to McCarthyism, but without, at this stage, anything that could be called a socialist commitment.

There is no hard-and-fast line to be drawn between this cohort of left historians and those who came along a few years later, but there were, overall, some distinctions worth noting. The sensibility of the former group had been shaped in the fifties and they were, for the most part, culturally very "straight," whereas those who came along later, attending college or graduate school during the tumultuous late sixties, were more

[5]Weinstein to Paul Buhle, 8 February 1968 and 20 March 1969, Radical America Papers, 1–16; Lynd, "Prospects for the New Left," *Liberation* 15 (January 1971): 18; for Zinn, see August Meier and Elliott Rudwick, *Black History and the Historical Profession: 1915–1980* (Urbana, Ill., 1986), 165; Genovese, quoted in Arnold Beichman, "Study in Academic Freedom," *New York Times Magazine*, 19 December 1965, 14; Gutman, interview in Henry Abelove et al., eds., *Visions of History* (New York, 1984), 188; Kraditor to Paul Buhle, 9 July 1969, Radical America Papers, 2–3. In 1955 a witness before the House Committee on Un-American Activities reported that when he had attended a Communist summer camp in the late 1940s, Gutman, a counselor, had attempted to recruit him into CP activity and had confided in 1950 that he was a party member. (Testimony of Stanley Wechkin, U.S. Congress, House, Committee on Un-American Activities, *Investigation of Communist Activities, New York Area—Part 5 [Summer Camps]*, 84th Congress, 1st sess. [1955], 1327–44.)

likely to display a countercultural sensibility, and were more likely than those in the previous group to have an activist orientation. Prominent in the second wave were a number of "red diaper babies" like Eric Foner and Robert Starobin—children of that substantial group who had entered the Communist Party milieu during its heyday, between 1936 and 1948. Unlike those in the former cohort, who entered a sellers' market, and had usually attained tenure before the academic depression set in during the seventies, many of this second group eventually left the profession.

The only previous occasion when a new historiographical tendency had burst so suddenly upon the scene was just before World War I, when the much less radical New and Progressive historians appeared. The same schools, Columbia and Wisconsin, were the nurseries of both developments; the overwhelming majority of the first two generations of radical historians received their degrees from those two institutions. Columbia's role was probably mainly due to its location in the capital of American left politics. No members of its history department seem to have played an important role in inspiring or supporting a left consciousness. As a primarily commuter institution, Columbia provided a poor framework of community.

It was quite otherwise with Wisconsin, which throughout the 1950s had been something of a "Progressive" holdout against more conservative historiographical currents. Its faculty contained a number of historians who in various ways served as models to graduate students, a significant portion of whom were New York Jews of leftist background, for whom Wisconsin served an "Americanizing" function. George Rawick, a student at Wisconsin in the mid-1950s, recalled in a letter to Merle Curti that Curti had served as an inspiration to him in becoming an *American* radical, "not just someone in the 'internal emigration' which has been the home of so many New York radicals." Paul Breines, a graduate student at Madison a few years later, thought that "leftist Jews who identified with [William Appleman] Williams were trying to submerge their Jewishness in his very American socialism or even his socialist Americanism."[6]

In the light of all this it is not surprising that Madison was the site of the first, and in many ways the most important, organized vehicle for the new historiographical left—the graduate student journal *Studies on the Left*, which began publication in 1959. Young leftist historians, like Stephen Ambrose, the future biographer of Eisenhower, expressed a desire

[6]Rawick to Curti, 24 November 1961, Curti Papers, 34–24; Breines, "With George Mosse in the 1960s," in Seymour Drescher et al., eds., *Political Symbolism in Modern Europe: Essays in Honor of George L. Mosse* (New Brunswick, N.J., 1982), 295.

to publish in the journal, even though it would probably hurt his academic career in the South. To appear in *Studies*, he wrote one of its editors, would be "visible proof I'm helping the cause, whatever that is." And the journal was received enthusiastically by more senior scholars, not themselves on the left, who were discontented with what John Higham had called the "cult of consensus." Higham himself contributed an appreciative review of William A. Williams's work to *Studies*. In *Commentary*, Andrew Hacker, who had voted for Nixon in 1960, hailed its appearance as "a revolt against . . . prevailing orthodoxies[:] conservative professor-scholars [who] have been mere celebraters, the liberals [who] have hidden behind methodological barricades."[7]

Insofar as the young leftist historians regarded themselves as Marxists, they were the inheritors of an ambiguous legacy. The classic Marxist texts provided an overall model of society and of historical change—the centrality of modes of production, and of class struggle—but little in the way of concrete exemplars of their application. There had been some important Marxist historical studies of European history, particularly of various aspects of the transition from feudalism to capitalism. But there had been very little significant work on the United States—and the great majority of new, left historians were Americanists. This was not necessarily a disadvantage. In France, for example, Marxist scholarship on the French Revolution had degenerated into what François Furet mocked as *le catéchisme révolutionnaire*. No such procrustean bed governed the work of the new generation of American leftists. Their work, though frequently employing Marxist categories, was notable for its heterodoxy. Descriptions of "open door imperialism" had little in common with traditional Leninist theory; the concept of corporate liberalism had no precedent in classic texts; studies of the working-class movement were on the whole "culturalist" rather than "economistic"; the work of Genovese and his associates on the slave South stressed the errors and inadequacies of treatments by Marx and Engels.

There were some important aspects of the Marxist historiographical legacy which were not merely unuseful, but in fact served as an antimodel for the new generation. In the era of the Second International, Marxist historical theory and practice had been mechanistically determinist. Then, under Stalinist influence, it veered off into a voluntarism that was put at the disposal of current Soviet requirements. In the United States, historians associated with the Communist Party were sometimes dogmat-

[7]Ambrose to James Weinstein, 12 November 1963, *Studies on the Left* Papers, 1–4; Hacker, "The Rebelling Young Scholars," *Commentary* 30 (1960): 406.

ic and sectarian. More often their work had hardly any Marxist theoretical content at all, and shaded off into celebratory accounts of struggle and
resistance—"the people" versus "the interests." (The failure of historians
associated with the Communist Party to make their theoretical orientation explicit was one of the principal complaints of the young historians
who had recently broken from the party's embrace, and was a practice
they were determined to abandon.) Although, especially before the late
1950s, all Western Communist historians subordinated themselves to
their parties' demands, American Communist historians, like the CPUSA
as a whole, were the most servile of any in the West. Following the
Hungarian Revolution in 1956 a number of leading British historians,
notably Christopher Hill and E. P. Thompson, left the Communist Party. But even those who stayed, like Eric Hobsbawm and V. G. Kiernan,
joined in publicly condemning their party's refusal to disassociate itself
from the Soviet intervention in Hungary. In the United States, the leading Communist historian, Herbert Aptheker, produced the party's official defense of Soviet tanks assaulting Hungarian workers.[8]

In their innovative use of the Marxian legacy, and in their break with
some of the more discreditable aspects of that legacy, the young leftist
historians were certainly "new." But there was very little that was new or
unorthodox about the epistemological posture of the radical historians; it
was, as Marxism had traditionally been, overwhelmingly objectivist.
Marx and Engels, particularly the latter, and even more their subsequent
interpreters, emphasized the objective and scientific character of Marxism. Trotsky was at one with his enemy Stalin when he declared history
to be "a science no less objective than physiology." Aptheker denounced
"bourgeois academicians" for denying the existence of "real objectivity."
This was to remain the orthodox view. Some years later, when a writer
close to the American CP had favorable things to say about Kuhn's
Structure of Scientific Revolutions he was rebuked in the official party
organ *Political Affairs*:

The reactionary aspect of Kuhnianism stems from his rejection of the objective
content of the truth of scientific knowledge. For if physical science itself can be
shown to be nothing more than a succession of subjective models, then . . . social
science also would have no objective content. . . . Those who say capitalist
oppression is a reality are just as right (or wrong) as those who deny it. . . .

---

[8]Letter from British historians in *New Statesman and Nation* n.s. 52 (1 December 1956):
701; Aptheker, *The Truth About Hungary* (New York, 1957).

[Kuhn] is encouraging an ideological trend which has a paralyzing effect upon millions.[9]

In the main, young radical historians were firmly committed to the realist, objectivist, and antirelativist tradition of the left. William A. Williams, something of a godfather to *Studies on the Left*, wrote Curti of his disagreement with Beard's and Becker's relativist theses. He insisted that with sufficient effort historians could wrench themselves free of background and values to "see things as they really were." Staughton Lynd, writing to one of the editors of *Studies*, underlined his commitment to "objective truth," his rejection of the idea that "there is one truth for radicals and another truth for other people." Jesse Lemisch wrote of the radical historian's obligation to "pursue truth, adhere to the most rigorous standards of evidence and proof, and try to make history a science." When his contract at the University of Chicago was not renewed, he invited readers of the student newspaper to "ponder the irony in the judging of a scholar who believes very firmly in the pursuit of truth by men of more relativistic bent."[10]

Leftist historians were convinced that what they were offering was not just objectively true, but that it was *the* truth. An editorial in the inaugural issue of *Studies on the Left* argued that the objective, unvarnished truth was radical, that no act was more radical than disclosing it.

Arnold Hauser has observed that the French bourgeoisie of the nineteenth century rejected naturalism in art from its "perfectly correct feeling that every art that describes life without bias and without restraint is in itself a revolutionary art." In 1912, Woodrow Wilson shrewdly expressed a similar feeling current within the American bourgeoisie. "The radicalism of our time . . . ," he observed, "does not consist in the things that are proposed, but in the things that are disclosed." The relentless disclosure of the nature and causes of social institutions and developments is, in our own time, also radical.

[9]Trotsky, "What Is Historical Objectivity?" (1933), quoted in Baruch Knei-Paz, *The Social and Political Thought of Leon Trotsky* (Oxford, 1978), 497; Aptheker, review of William Z. Foster, *Outline Political History of the Americas, Masses & Mainstream* 4 (March 1951): 88; John Pappademos and Beatrice Lumpkin, "The Scientific Outlook Under Attack," *Political Affairs* 53 (November 1974): 31, 34.
[10]Williams to Curti, undated, Curti Papers, 45–11; Williams review of J. H. Plumb, *The Death of the Past, Nation* 210 (9 March 1970): 280; Lynd to Eleanor Hakim, 13 March 1961, *Studies on the Left* Papers, 6–8; Lemisch, "Radical Scholarship as Scientific Method and Anti-Authoritarianism, Not 'Relevance,'" *New University Conference Papers* 2 (1970) (unpaginated pamphlet); "A Word on the Lemisch Case," *Chicago Maroon*, 19 May 1967. (The printed text of the first quotation from Lemisch reads "peruse" rather than "pursue" truth, but I have assumed that this is a typographical error.)

The theme of "the radicalism of disclosure" recurred in the writing of the new generation of leftists. "The naked truth really is revolutionary in its implications," wrote Lynd. Gabriel Kolko spoke of this kind of radicalism, "a primary commitment to truth . . . and myth destruction," as "simply too embarrassing for perpetual toleration." The Latin Americanist John Womack wrote that

the most radical thing there is, is the truth about something. In a world of many kinds of lies, coerced, compulsive, and deliberate . . . it's not only a communist but a revolutionary act just to tell the truth. And the most important truth about Latin American history, so far as I know, is the history of classes there, which means the struggles between them. And so I teach the most important thing I can think of in my field.[11]

But without intending to, the new radical historians, by the very fact of their sudden emergence, challenging fundamental assumptions of existing mainstream historiography on a variety of fronts, inevitably raised the issue of historical objectivity. If the previous framework for interpreting American history was objectively true, the radicals' perspective could not be; or, more threateningly, vice versa.

Virtually all the themes which emerged in professional indictments of the first generation of left historians for violating the canons of objectivity are to be found in Irwin Unger's *AHR* survey, written in 1965 though not published until 1967. There was the psychologizing of dissidence. Young leftists' "assault on the New Deal" was oedipal, "an adolescent blow for independence . . . in rejecting it they are rejecting their fathers and their fathers' faith." They had a contempt for "pure history" ("for its own sake"); their concerns were governed "not by the natural dialogue of the discipline but by the concerns of the outside cultural and political world." They failed to maintain a cool and detached rhetorical style: they were "often bad tempered" and "sometimes allow the tone and rhetoric of the picket line and the handbill to invade their professional work." Leftists' criticism of twentieth-century reform was ideologically predetermined, rather than being "the inevitable conclusion imposed by the facts." They suffered from "exaggerated present-mindedness" and partisanship, the enemies of objective historical truth. Above all, unlike most members of the previous generation of historians, they failed to maintain the "political neutrality" that was so important for scholarship.[12]

[11]"The Radicalism of Disclosure," *Studies on the Left* 1 (Fall 1959): 3–4; Lynd to Eleanor Hakim, 13 March 1961, *Studies on the Left* Papers, 6–8; Kolko, "Government and University in America," in Conor Cruise O'Brien and William Dean Vanech, eds., *Power and Consciousness* (New York, 1969), 138; Womack interview in *Visions of History*, 259.
[12]Unger, "New Left," 1253, 1262–63, 1252, 1263.

While on a philosophical level the young leftist historians were conventionally objectivist, and while they seemed to have no more spontaneous desire to raise epistemological questions than most other members of the profession, they had recognized from the outset the issues that would be raised by their work, and in the first issue of *Studies* launched a preemptive strike.

In academic circles, the term "objectivity" is generally used to indicate the dispassion, the non-partisanship with which the "true scholar" approaches his work. It is also frequently used to indicate the prevalent, or "majority" view. . . . Many, perhaps most students . . . have made the subtle and all-important equation between quality on the one hand, and acceptability or market value on the other, and are well on their way to a bright academic future. The objectivity here assumed is reducible to the weight of authority, the viewpoint of those who are in a position to enforce standards, the value judgments of the not so metaphorical market-place of ideas. Similarly, the use of the term to indicate scholarly dispassion is, at bottom, a way of justifying acceptance . . . of the status quo. When a man is digging up facts to support traditional and accepted interpretations . . . he may, without too much difficulty, prevent himself from becoming impassioned. . . . On the other hand when a scholar arrives at a radical or unconventional interpretation, he may very well become excited by what he is doing. For the act of contradiction involves emotions more tumultuous than those aroused by the state of acceptance. Scholarly dispassion is the true medium of the scholar satisfied with (or browbeaten by) things as they are.

"Partisanship or commitment," it was argued, "no more eliminates the possibility of objectivity than 'neutrality' or the supposed lack of theory or of ideology guarantees it." Indeed, the *Studies* editors said, if the leftist was "a scholar as well as a malcontent, an honest researcher as well as a radical,"

his very partisanship, bias, call it what you will—gives him a kind of objectivity. Because he stands opposed to established institutions and conventional conceptions, the radical scholar possesses an unconcern for their safety or preservation which enables him to carry inquiry along paths where the so-called "objective" conservative or liberal scholar would not care to tread.[13]

There was some variation in how far this argument was pushed. Most leftist historians agreed with Barrington Moore's observation that "in any society the dominant groups are the ones with the most to hide about the way society works," and that to the extent that radicals took a jaundiced

[13] "Radicalism of Disclosure," 2; David Eakins, "Objectivity and Commitment," *Studies on the Left* 1 (Fall 1959): 53; "Radicalism of Disclosure," 3.

view of dominant ideology they were more likely to penetrate to the truth, to resemble Mannheim's "free floating intelligentsia." Another theme in Mannheim's strategy for avoiding relativism was adopted by Howard Zinn, when he argued that "the closest we can come to that elusive 'objectivity' is to report accurately *all* of the subjectivities in a situation." Accounts from the slaveowner's point of view should be complemented with a picture from a slave's-eye view, and in practice, since historiography was slanted toward the former, the historian would be restoring balance by emphasizing the latter. Others went farther than Zinn in hinting that there was something objectively truer about the viewpoint of the oppressed, but while, or because, this was the official American Communist view, none of the younger leftist historians explicitly adopted this position. All agreed that acknowledged identification with those on the bottom of society was at worst no more distorting, or inconsistent with objectivity, than unacknowledged identification with those on top.[14]

The long-standing association of "balance" with a nonpolitical objectivity was challenged as a meretricious centrist device to seize the epistemological high ground. The act of balancing, David Eakins argued in *Studies*, was intensely political, involving constant adjustment to remain equidistant from shifting criteria of what were extreme and impermissible positions.

The most serious criticism of this whole effort is that it is wholly independent of evidence—hence of objectivity. The decision to maintain balance or neutrality, in this sense, is an *a priori* decision that has nothing whatever to do with facts or the weighing of facts. The balancer is as committed as any ideologue, but without a real frame of reference of his own other than the prevailing mood of the moment.

Somewhat surprisingly, since there was no shortage of targets, leftists rarely attacked "partisanship" or "present-mindedness" in the work of mainstream scholarship. In part this was a consequence of their concern with empirical rather than *Weltanschauunglich* issues. More important was that they were too involved in producing their own work, which, in the new climate, they hoped would in due course displace that of the

---

[14]Moore, *Social Origins of Dictatorship and Democracy: Lord and Peasant in the Making of the Modern World* (Boston, 1966), 522; Zinn, *The Politics of History* (Boston, 1970), 41. Reviewing Zinn's book, Aptheker maintained that "a 'slave-oriented' historiography of slavery does not merely 'fill out the picture' of that institution; it *is* the picture. That is, if one wants to know what the institution of slavery was he must go to the slave, to those who endured it; there is the *objective* picture of that institution." (*Political Affairs* 49 [October 1970]: 57.)

previous generation by the weight of its evidence and the cogency of its argument.[15]

The early and mid-1960s was a period of optimism and decreasing marginalization for the growing American left. In the United States in the twentieth century, liberal ascendancy has traditionally provided the climate in which left dissidence flourishes, from Progressivism, through the New Deal, to the Kennedy-Johnson years. In this period the most salient enemies of liberals and centrists were on the right: die-hard segregationists, the John Birch Society, the Goldwater movement. Lyndon Johnson, partially in response to a socialist-inspired catalyst, Michael Harrington's *The Other America*, declared "war on poverty," and won an overwhelming electoral victory running on the most left-leaning liberal platform of modern times. On foreign policy questions, large numbers of liberals joined with the growing left movement in opposition to the Kennedy-sponsored Bay of Pigs invasion and Johnson's intervention in the Dominican Republic.

In this climate, and in an academic bull market, leftist historians had good grounds to see bright prospects for their eventual acceptance within the profession. Though their work was often sharply criticized, it was also honored. Walter LaFeber's first book, for example, won the AHA's Beveridge Prize in 1962. And leading radical historians had positions at universities of the first rank: Barton Bernstein at Stanford, Gabriel Kolko at Pennsylvania, LaFeber at Cornell, Jesse Lemisch at Chicago, Staughton Lynd at Yale. Lynd urged radicals to "enter the mainstream of scholarly discussion . . . and whenever possible publish in conventional scholarly journals." His own experience, he said, was that "good work, however iconoclastic, can get published." Compared to most periods in the past it was an era of good feeling, both within the left, and between left and center. In this atmosphere, leftist historians, though by no means unaware of the difficulties in their path, seemed confident that they were starting on a steady march to historiographical triumph: "truth is great, and shall prevail."[16]

Although the national controversy over the Vietnam War was the principal catalyst of the unprecedented tumult and acrimony which racked the historical profession in the late 1960s, the war itself was seldom a cause of major divisiveness. Like most academics, the great majority of historians deplored it. But antiwar protest in the late 1960s raised questions which not only produced acrimonious debates between leftist and

[15]Eakins, "Objectivity and Commitment," 52.
[16]Lynd to Eleanor Hakim, 13 March 1961, *Studies on the Left* Papers, 6–8.

liberal historians, but polarized the left itself, producing battle scars
which even twenty years later had not entirely faded. At issue were the
relationship between the demands of citizenship and scholarship; the
"neutrality" of not just this or that work of scholarship, but of the institutions of scholarship themselves; and, related to both of these, the attitude
to adopt toward often disorderly and occasionally violent attacks on these
institutions, and challenges to their hierarchical organization.

It would be an exaggeration to speak of the polarization of left historians into two distinct and mutually hostile camps. The groups which
emerged were both heterogeneous; both shared fundamental values
which distinguished them from the liberal center; and a number of radical
historians were not clearly affiliated with either. But, with all this said, it
is convenient to speak of one group, younger on the whole, including
many graduate students, rather more countercultural and with a more
activist orientation, in which the leading figures were Staughton Lynd,
Howard Zinn, and Jesse Lemisch; a second group, including more members with a Communist background, somewhat better established, and
with a more traditionalist scholarly orientation, which included Eugene
Genovese, Christopher Lasch, and James Weinstein.

The leaders of the first group, along with a great part of their following, had devoted much of their time in the sixties to active political
engagement. Both Lynd and Zinn had extended involvement in the civil
rights struggle in the South, where both had taught at black colleges; both
traveled to Hanoi in connection with their antiwar work; both, along
with Lemisch, had personally participated in disruptive campus protest.
Almost all the members of this camp were enthusiastic supporters of "the
Movement," and were usually at best ambivalent about the university and
the historical profession. Jeffrey Kaplow wrote one of the editors of
Studies on the Left that his view of "Ivory tower universities" was such
that "the mere thought of making a career in one of them sometimes
prompts suicidal tendencies"; James Gilbert wrote a friend that he had
"an open mind" on the question of destroying the university. In the case
of younger militants, ambivalence could give way to "schizophrenia," as
in this account by Mark Naison of taking his Ph.D. orals during the 1968
Columbia strike, an account which also contains some interesting observations on faculty response to the events.

Fayerweather Hall [was] occupied at the precise moment my exams began. . . .
My orals board, composed of Richard Hofstadter and some equally uptight, but
less renowned professors, began their questioning amidst the sounds of breaking
furniture, shouts of rage and pride, fragments of falling plaster and chants of
"shut it down." . . . The behavior of the faculty members was curious. They were

not, as I expected, unusually hostile to me, but absolutely tickled pink at the prospect of keeping the institutional ritual alive amidst the surrounding chaos. They regarded themselves as the carriers of the light of civilization among the depredations of the strange new barbarians who had somehow exploded into their lives. Every time plaster fell on their heads they felt a strange thrill; they alone stood between America and Totalitarianism. . . .

I sensed, during the whole awful comedy, that they were more interested in their own performance than in mine. There was no question that I would pass; the issue was: could they retain the composure to ask good questions. They did. I gave the expected-unexpected answers. . . . I played the game by all the rules. Man, they knew that I was for everything happening in that bldg, from the breaking of the furniture to the slugging of professors, but I would express my values in measured tones, over a glass of sherry, and make a final chivalric gesture. I would escort them out of the building. And so the final act featured mark naison, in a suit & tie . . . leading rh, dwight miner, equally attired, out of the window of an occupied bldg in front of 2000 people, raising my fist dramatically when friends asked whether I passed, & feeling at once overjoyed at having the whole fucking mess over with, and guilty at deserting my brothers inside. . . . SCHIZOPHRENIA! You better believe it.[17]

Much of student protest activity was directed at the university simply because it was there, ready to hand. But it was also true that the university was connected in countless ways to the hated "military-industrial complex," from the calculation of class rank which determined which young men would be drafted for the war to Pentagon-sponsored secret research. Young leftists beginning to make careers in the university feared its corrupting influence—the moral consequences of a full-time choice for the academy over political activism. Lynd wrote:

Whatever our social origins, the university is a marvelously effective instrument for making us middle-class men. First it sets us in competition with one another. . . . We become emotionally engaged in the upward scramble, and whatever our rhetoric, in fact let the university become the emotional center of our lives. . . . It is a very peculiar sort of radicalism which permits one only to be arrested in summertime, or obliges one to hurry home from Hanoi to be on time for a seminar. But that is the kind of radical one has to be so long as one's first commitment is to university life. . . . We ourselves must have a foot solidly off the campus . . . alternate years of full-time intellectual work with years of full-time work for the Movement. . . . Nothing in the Communist Manifesto, or for that matter the New Testament, assures us that at age thirty-five or forty we should expect to achieve economic security for the rest of our lives. Disgorge the bait of tenure, and the problem of making a living can solve itself year-by-year.

[17]Kaplow to Eleanor Hakim, undated, *Studies on the Left* Papers, 5–6; Gilbert to Paul Buhle, 24 October 1968, *Radical America* Papers, 1–16; Naison to Paul Buhle, undated (Spring 1968), *Radical America* Papers, 2–14.

Rejection of the idea of a full-time academic career was connected to the
New Left theme of "wholeness." "In resistance to a dehumanizing social
system," Arthur Waskow wrote, "radical historians . . . are questioning
the whole bureaucratic-'rational' assumption of the split in roles between
citizen and scholar."[18]

Opposition to bureaucratic rationality and to hierarchy inevitably also
influenced some young leftists' attitude to the community of historians.
The introduction to a special issue of *Radical America* devoted to left
historiography spoke of its editors' ambivalence on that score. On the
one hand, they had had, at Wisconsin, cordial and intellectually rewarding experiences with members of the faculty, and they endorsed the
profession's rigorous standards of proof.

On the negative side, the profession seems to us a bad combination of a gentlemen's clubhouse and a bureaucracy. . . . Even today faculty members at the most
prestigious universities, who largely set the tone for the profession as a whole,
enjoy an income level and social status that sets them well apart from the lower
classes in society. . . . It is . . . a bureaucracy in which younger men progress by
producing tangible evidence of their merit (publications). In this constant struggle
to advance, the history profession itself becomes the source of all values for those
who depend on its approbation for their employment. It is an unhealthy
atmosphere.

Jesse Lemisch, in addition to joining the denunciation of hierarchy and
competitiveness per se, argued that professional hierarchy impeded the
growth of knowledge; that "what we know of scientific revolutions and
of the sociology of knowledge clearly indicates that meritocracy wars
with truth."

The system which gives greater power to those with allegedly better ideas is
inevitably a system for impeding innovation in ideas. . . . Those with power will
define ideas which resemble their own as "excellent" and will encourage those
ideas; it is not so much a matter of weeding out nonsense as of defining as
nonsense what is to be weeded out. . . . While holding . . . to the *most rigorous of
standards* the radical scholar should oppose the joining together of power and
alleged merit, the institutionalization of standards. . . . Because he has a stake in
rigor and in truth, the radical scholar will oppose authority, deference, hierarchy:
in the classroom, in the university, in the professional association. Combining the

[18]Lynd, "Intellectuals, the University, and the Movement," speech delivered to founding
meeting of New University Conference (Spring 1968), published as pamphlet (Boston,
n.d.); Waskow, "Radicals, Conservatives, and History: 1969," *AHA Newsletter* 8 (February 1970): 27–28. Lynd later acknowledged that "while I was very much discontented at
Yale, maybe I wasn't discontented enough to have turned my back on it and looked in
new directions unless they pushed me out." (1977 interview in *Visions of History*, 151.)

anti-authoritarianism of the New Left with the anti-authoritarianism of scientific method, the radical defers to no authority but that of evidence and proof.[19]

There was a strong moralistic tone to much of the substantive and programmatic writing of members of this camp, joined to an emphasis on history which would be immediately useful. The activist scholar, Howard Zinn wrote, would "decid[e] from a particular ethical base what is the action-need of the moment, and . . . concentrate on that aspect of the truth-complex which fulfills that need."

> If we start from the ethical assumption that it is fundamentally wrong to hold in bondage . . . another human being, and that the freeing of such persons requires penetrating the moral sensibilities of a nation, then it is justifiable to focus on those aspects of the complexity which support this goal. . . . You are not telling the whole truth . . . but you are emphasizing that portion of the truth which supports a morally desirable action.

He urged an historiography which would "recapture those few moments in the past which show the possibility of a better way of life than that which has dominated the earth thus far." Most members of this group heartily endorsed student cries for relevance in the classroom. Lynd rejected the argument that it was the proper task of radical scholars to analyze systems of oppression with greater precision and sophistication. "Is this not quibbling while Rome burns?" he asked. "Can it satisfactorily define the scholar's task to be able to say 'I told you so' amid the ruins? Should we be content with measuring the dimensions of our prison instead of chipping, however inadequately, against the bars?"[20]

No doubt many factors, including the temperamental, inclined the activist faction to this historiographical orientation. But in Lynd's case, and in that of at least some sizable number of those associated with him, it

[19]*Radical America* 4 (November 1970): 1–2; Lemisch, "Radical Scholarship as Scientific Method and Anti-Authoritarianism, Not 'Relevance,'" *New University Conference Papers* 2 (1970) (unpaginated pamphlet). Lemisch's remark on scientific revolutions probably derived from one of the many common misreadings of the work of Thomas Kuhn.
[20]Zinn, "Abolitionists, Freedom-Riders, and the Tactics of Agitation," in Martin Duberman, ed., *The Antislavery Vanguard: New Essays on the Abolitionists* (Princeton, 1965), 430–31; *Politics of History*, 47; Lynd, "Historical Past and Existential Present," in Theodore Roszak, ed., *The Dissenting Academy* (New York, 1968), 107. Zinn also urged historical study for left self-criticism: to "show how good social movements can go wrong, how leaders can betray their followers, how rebels can become bureaucrats, how ideals can become frozen and reified." (*Politics of History*, 51.) And Lemisch engaged in a running battle with Lynd and others of his comrades in defense of "irrelevant" scholarship. (See his "Who Will Write a Left History of Art While We Are All Putting Our Balls on the Line?"—appended as rejoinder to Lynd's "Intellectuals . . . and the Movement" (note 18, above).

was rooted in a political and strategic evaluation of the contemporary scene. Impressed by the surge of leftist energy, and exhilarated by the temporary victories of students from Columbia to Nanterre, many believed that on what might be the eve of the American October, analytical scholarship was beside the point. There was a hint of Third World romanticism in this perspective, as when Lynd termed oral history of working-class communities "guerrilla history." In any event, his apocalyptic perspective was clear. "It seems to me," he wrote a friend, "that American society is 'objectively overripe' and that the thing to do is to change it. . . . In the last analysis revolution will happen if there are revolutionaries who *want* enough to make it. . . . I think that America will pass from New Leftism to more-or-less underground resistance against an American fascism without an intervening stage of electoral politics."[21]

As the historiographical posture of the group around Staughton Lynd was rooted in a political and strategic evaluation, so was that of the group whose central figures were Genovese, Lasch, and Weinstein, and the evaluations were diametrically opposed. Indeed, the second was deliberately formulated in opposition to that of the first. Genovese spoke of a struggle that "might take a century to mature," and foresaw a period of "political retreat but intellectual advance." He mocked "fantasies of revolutionary apocalypse—of a grand denouement that features the overthrow of the American state by an invincible army of acid-heads and suburbanites." Lasch attacked Lynd's argument that repression served the left. The position was "ill-informed and irresponsible," stemming both from a misreading of history and the New Left delusion that a minority of committed activists could make a revolution in the United States.[22]

Members of this group saw in the most militant wing of the student movement what E. P. Thompson in a retrospective evaluation called "the revolting bourgeoisie doing its own revolting thing . . . the expressive and irrationalist, self-exalting gestures of style that do not belong to a serious and deeply rooted, rational revolutionary tradition." Though the tone in which campus activists were criticized might vary, all agreed that targeting the university as the enemy was a totally misconceived and suicidal

[21]Lynd, "Guerrilla History in Gary," *Liberation* 14 (October 1969): 17; Lynd to "Norm" [Fruchter?], undated but probably 1966, *Studies on the Left* Papers, 6–8.
[22]Report of Genovese's remarks at 1965 Socialist Scholars Conference, *Studies on the Left* 5 (Fall 1965): 5; Genovese to Paul Buhle, 24 September 1970, *Radical America* Papers, 1–14; Lasch, "The Revival of Political Controversy in the Sixties," in *The Agony of the American Left* (New York, 1969), 203–4.

strategy. None in this camp maintained that the existing university was in fact a neutral institution; all were critical of its bureaucratic and hierarchical structure. Campaigns directed against the university's subservience to militarism were regarded as right and proper. Lasch confessed that like other members of his generation, he found himself "uncomfortable in academic life and often at odds with the profession and the university." But the university as such had to be defended, not attacked—primarily, though not exclusively, on prudential grounds. Given a long-term strategy, and the conditions of American life, it was, Genovese argued, the only viable home for effective work by the great majority of left intellectuals. "This fact," he said, "must shape our attitude toward the university as an institution, and it must be understood to impose certain limits and restrictions (compromises, if you will) on those who seek its protection." On a realistic assessment of the balance of political forces, "politicization" of universities would tilt them to the right. Works of scholarship were not "neutral"; Genovese described his own work as consistently "political in intent." "I have never written a line," he said, "that has not been . . . a political intervention." But unless the university, as an "arena of ideological contention," remained formally neutral, socialists could find no base there.[23]

But the argument for the defense of the university—more precisely, the ideal of the university—was not just prudential. Weinstein wrote one of the younger leftist historians that having to live for a long time in the existing social order entailed "building on whatever is good in this society . . . preserv[ing] the better of our institutions—those that embody something of the ideal of freedom and self-development. . . . The ideal of truth, which is at least rhetorically . . . a central part of university self-image, is an ideal to be carried over into socialism and transcending capitalism." Both Lasch and Genovese endorsed the strategic doctrine of the Italian Communist Antonio Gramsci, who had argued that in the West socialist transformation would be accomplished not by a swift "war of movement," as in Russia, but through a protracted "war of position," in which the cultural front was by no means the least important. The task of socialist intellectuals was, in Genovese's paraphrase of Gramsci, "fashioning a world view appropriate to the movement and society they wish

[23]Thompson, 1976 interview in *Visions of History*, 10; Lasch, foreword to 1973 edition of Richard Hofstadter's *American Political Tradition* (New York, 1973), xxiii-xiv; Genovese, "On Being a Socialist and a Historian," in his *In Red and Black: Marxian Explorations in Southern and Afro-American History* (New York, 1972); Genovese, "A Reply to Criticism," *Radical History Review* 3 (September 1976): 106-7.

to see born." Often this would involve drawing on older values, embodied in the traditions of humanistic scholarship, which the present ruling
class was in the process of discarding.[24]

A corollary of the long-term Gramscian strategy was that demands for
scholarship which was immediately relevant were rejected out of hand. If
activist criteria of relevance were frequently narrow and anti-intellectual,
Genovese leaned so far in the other direction that he virtually embraced a
cult of irrelevance. "All good (true, valid, competent) history," he wrote,
whether on Dante's religious views or the shipbuilding industry in Bor-
deaux, served the socialist cause; "all poor (false, invalid, incompetent)
history serves the interest of our enemies." Few, even among his closest
associates, went quite as far as Genovese along these lines, but the
grounds of his rejection of demands for "useful" history had considerable
resonance for those who had shared his experience with the Communist
Party. "The demand for ideological history, for 'class truth,' for 'partisanship in science,'" he wrote, "has ended in the service of a new elite, a
new oppressor."[25]

Battles between the two camps of left historians were fought in various
arenas, and produced a number of casualties. *Studies on the Left* ceased
publication after a struggle between "scholars" and "activists" proved
irreconcilable; the same conflict first polarized and then destroyed the
annual Socialist Scholars Conference and other ventures in left ecumenism. "La lutte finale" came at the December 1969 meeting of the American Historical Association. A radical caucus drawn from the activist wing
of the left launched a campaign to pass a resolution against the war, to run
Lynd for president of the AHA against the official candidate, Robert R.
Palmer, and in various ways to restructure the association. Jesse Lemisch,
writing to his comrades before the meeting, noted the great discrepancy
between the "pathetic" disorganization of the insurgents and the fear that
they inspired in "the establishment." He proposed that they might take
advantage of this.

"There is a specter haunting the professors." Maybe they watch too much televi-
sion. Often, just as the lone ranger was about to be destroyed by Indians, the
U.S. cavalry would show up, or so it seemed, but it was actually Tonto, the
friendly Indian, setting off cartridges in a frying pan. Maybe we should do some
of this, i.e., come on very tough, frighten them into thinking that there are
literally millions of us.

[24]Weinstein to Paul Buhle, 15 November 1967 and 6 June 1968, *Radical America* Papers, 3–
16; Genovese, "Socialist and Historian," 12.
[25]"Socialist and Historian," 4, 9–10.

Establishment anxiety was real enough, and there was a concerted mail campaign to get "counterrevolutionaries" to attend the business meeting. The AHA Council produced its own proposals for structural reform. Richard Hofstadter, commenting on the council's constitutional amendments expressed his pleasure at "the way in which the sober purpose of keeping control in the hands of the sane majority of the establishment's members is accounted for in fine populist rhetoric." Just as real was the "pathetic" ineptitude of the insurgents. Following New Left norms of openness, Xeroxed copies of correspondence among the rebels on how to proceed, including Lemisch's "Tonto strategy," were put on the reserve shelves of the library at the State Historical Society of Wisconsin for the edification of would-be recruits. The correspondence was promptly recopied and sent to AHA headquarters by members of the Wisconsin history faculty.[26]

At the 1969 business meeting the insurgents were defeated on every front. Palmer easily outpolled Lynd for the presidency; the constitutional amendments aiming at maintaining elite control passed just as easily; the antiwar resolution sponsored by the radical caucus was decisively rejected. Both wings of the left seemed to inhabit a realm of fantasy or, at a minimum, to be intoxicated with their own rhetoric. Lynd's fantasies were grandiose. Even after the AHA had, by constitutional change, armored itself against transient majorities at its business meetings, Lynd wrote of the radicals being in a position to "take power" in the association. Genovese's fantasies were paranoid. He predicted that if the antiwar resolution passed, there would be a purge of the AHA, since all members who dissented would be forced to leave the organization. (This phenomenon was not observed at universities like Harvard where the faculty had passed an antiwar resolution, or in other academic associations which had done likewise, nor, for that matter, in the AHA, when, a few years later, it quietly followed suit.) Genovese, in language so extreme that he alienated many of his closest supporters, labeled the Lynd group "totalitarians," and in an at-the-top-of-his-lungs conclusion to a speech at the business meeting, urged the association to "put them down, put them down hard, and put them down once and for all."[27]

In all of this "the objectivity question" was often the vehicle through

---

[26]Lemisch to Arthur Waskow, 13 September 1969, Lynd/Radical Caucus/AHA Papers, Box 2; Hofstadter circular letter, 1 December 1969, and copy of Hofstadter to AHA executive secretary Paul Ward, 25 August 1969, both in Cochran Papers, Boxes 5 and 7, respectively.

[27]Lynd, "Prospects for the New Left," 26; Genovese's remarks quoted in the *Washington Post*, 29 December 1969.

which quite different agendas were pursued. Terms with positive valence ("disinterested," "evenhanded") were claimed for one's own camp; those with negative connotations ("present-minded," "partisan") were ascribed to one's enemies. To be sure, alignments were frequently confusing, and pronouncements were sometimes Delphic. Reviewers of Howard Zinn's *Politics of History* could not decide whether he was embracing or seeking to escape from relativism; Genovese repeatedly attacked ideological scholarship (bad) and simultaneously urged that universities be arenas of ideological contention (good). Even with a scorecard it was often difficult to tell the players and their positions.

But in the main, strategic conceptions, and concomitant choices of allies and opponents, dictated postures. For those in the Lynd camp, the allies were militants in the street, the principal enemy was mainstream historical scholarship. Jesse Lemisch, in a speech which concluded by invoking Ranke, attempted to seize the objectivist high ground for the left, and demonstrate, through a detailed examination of the work of the consensus historians, that it was they who were systematically present-minded.

The politics which mainstream historians have admired are unreal and unprincipled; their history has aimed further to insulate those politics from reality. But the Left will continue to present the real alternatives. . . . Fire us, expel us, jail us, we will not go away. We exist, and people like us have existed throughout history, and we will simply not allow you the luxury of continuing to call yourselves politically neutral while you exclude all of this from your history. You cannot lecture us on civility while you legitimize barbarity. You cannot fire us for activism without having your own activism exposed. You cannot call apologetics "excellence" without expecting the most rigorous and aggressive of scholarly replies. We were at the Democratic Convention, and at the steps of the Pentagon. . . . And we are in the libraries, writing history, trying to cure it of your partisan and self-congratulatory fictions, trying to come a little closer to finding out how things actually were.[28]

Genovese and Lasch, as part of a strategy aimed at "convinc[ing] liberals and conservatives that the culture they value cannot be preserved without a fundamental reform of American society," and winning a place for leftist academic work in the university, directed their principal fire at the Lynd camp for "sneer[ing] at objectivity," for hostility to the values of scholarship. Genovese excoriated Lynd for his "distrust of the intel-

[28]Lemisch, *On Active Service in War and Peace: Politics and Ideology in the American Historical Profession* (Toronto, 1975), 117. The original paper, delivered at the 1969 meeting of the AHA, was entitled "Present-Mindedness Revisited: Anti-Radicalism as a Goal of American Historical Writing."

ligentsia," his "antirationalism," his "subjectivity," above all for his "ahistorical" belief in absolute moral standards. Lasch heaped scorn on Howard Zinn's ethical and presentist criteria for choosing which truths to emphasize. With Genovese, he urged the academic world to repudiate "the cynical conclusion that all scholarship is subjective and 'ideological.'"[29]

If the sleeping objectivity question was awakened by the emergence of an historiographical left it was not primarily because the left mounted any philosophical assault on norms of objectivity, which by and large it accepted. In part what raised the question anew was the strident tone of the new debates, and the tumultuous climate in which they took place. Historically, the posture of objectivity had always been closely associated with values of civility, moderation, and order. Formally, Lemisch's fiery oration at the 1969 AHA meeting was a Rankean attack on present-mindedness. But few traditionalists who venerated the father of modern historical scholarship, and believed in writing history "wie es eigentlich gewesen," could take much pleasure at Lemisch's invocation of Ranke's words, at the conclusion of a savage attack on the previous generation of historians, and to the accompaniment of raised fists and cries of "Right on!" A referee for the *Journal of American History*, to which Lemisch had submitted his AHA talk, wrote to the *Journal*'s editor: "I don't know how you can tell him that he simply cannot do this, and that he certainly cannot do it in the pages of the *Journal*. He probably believes that he can, which says something about how far he and his ilk are estranged from civilization."[30]

Beyond all this, the emergence of the historiographical left was but one dimension of a process of ideological polarization, disorientation, and fragmentation taking place throughout the academic world. At the beginning of the decade of the sixties one could find no better representatives of the liberal academic center than Walter Johnson, chairman of the University of Chicago History Department, and Oscar Handlin, Harvard's premier Americanist. By the end of the decade Johnson was drafting the radical caucus's resolution denouncing American imperialism and the murder of the Black Panthers; Handlin was signing advertisements for Richard Nixon. Disorientation was at least as common as polariza-

[29]Lasch and Genovese, "The Education and the University We Need Now," *New York Review of Books* 13 (9 October 1969): 23–24; Genovese, "Socialist and Historian," 9–10; Genovese, "Staughton Lynd as Historian and Ideologue" (originally published in 1968), in *Essays in Red and Black*, 366, 359, 357; Lasch, foreword to 1973 edition of *American Political Tradition*, xx–xxi; Lasch and Genovese, 26.

[30]Anonymous referee's report, quoted in Thomas Schofield's introduction to Lemisch, *On Active Service*, 5.

tion. Wayne Cole wrote a colleague that he had long considered himself "well to the 'left' . . . now it seems strange to be viewed as . . . conservative in the Department and profession." A vaguely liberal "consensus of the competent" had been the bedrock of postwar historians' confidence in objectivity; increasingly, that rock was reduced to rubble.[31]

II

Manifestly Genovese's assessment of the short-term prospects for the left was correct, and Lynd's egregiously wrong: nothing remotely resembling the revolutionary crisis Lynd anticipated appeared. If left-wing scholars were to make a contribution to socialist transformation, at best a far-distant prospect, it would be in the stacks, and not in the streets. But, a generation later, the across-the-board program and process of ideological contestation which Genovese and his associates had proposed had not materialized either. Lynd had not been entirely mistaken in emphasizing the co-optive power of the profession, though characteristically he had focused on the risk of moral corruption of the individual scholar, rather than the ways in which the organization and values of the profession worked to restrict and defuse conflict and confrontation. Ever increasing specialization, and the concentration of leftists in a handful of specialties, localized conflict; a deeply entrenched empiricist orientation worked to direct attention toward data rather than theory; the high value placed on moving toward scholarly convergence inclined members of the profession to incorporate bits and pieces of heterodox analyses, rather than confront them head-on. All of this, of course, took place within a larger context which saw the center of gravity of American political culture steadily move ever farther to the right.

This is not to say that left historiography was without impact, or that ideological conflicts did not take place. Marxist scholarship, both European and American, became more acceptable within the profession, though frequently somewhat grudgingly, as work was praised "despite" its Marxist orientation, or for not allowing that point of view to be "too obtrusive." Increasingly, major departments decided that the addition of Marxist historians to their permanent ranks would be a desirable complement to other orientations, and a bridge to a growing body of scholarship. But that body of scholarship as a whole was something less than the sum of its parts. Certainly it did not, in the aggregate, constitute anything

[31]Johnson draft resolution (for presentation to the 1970 meeting of the OAH) enclosed with Johnson to Lynd, 18 March 1970, Lynd/Radical Caucus/AHA Papers, Box 3; Cole to Norman Graebner, 9 August 1971, Graebner Papers.

like the historical component of that "alternative world view" which Genovese had hoped for. Most notably, there was no overall synthetic work which embodied the new perspective, as the Beards' *Rise of American Civilization* had between the wars; as, on a smaller scale, interpretive essays by Hartz, Boorstin, and Potter had in the era of consensus.[32]

It was probably not a coincidence that the left historical scholarship which had the greatest influence on the profession was work which could as easily be used for conservative as for radical purposes. Books by Gabriel Kolko (*The Triumph of Conservatism*) and James Weinstein (*The Corporate Ideal and the Liberal State*), but also work by William A. Williams and his students, advanced the idea of "corporate liberalism." Extending the consensus historians' onslaught on the Progressive vision of "the people versus the interests," twentieth-century liberalism, from Theodore Roosevelt to Franklin Roosevelt and beyond, was reinterpreted as a strategy of stabilizing capitalism through a collaborative effort of big business, government, and organized labor. It was a strategy by which class collaboration was substituted for class conflict; in which all parties shared an interest in smoothing out business cycles through regulation, expanding overseas markets, and cooperating to increase the size of the economic pie while keeping the distribution of shares, and power, unaltered.

Work by Kolko and Weinstein meshed with "corporatist" theories being developed by nonleftists like Alfred Chandler, Samuel Hays, and Robert Wiebe, and Europeanists like Charles Maier—all of whom viewed the development with more equanimity. While there was dissent from some liberal historians whose icons were being attacked, by and large work in this tradition received a favorable reception. Some young leftists in the early 1970s, and Herbert Gutman in the early 1980s, criticized work on "corporate liberalism" for its pessimism: reading back into the past, they said, the mood of a later period of discouragement about possibilities of transformative action from below. There was, in any case, no denying that when pushed to its conclusion, work in this tradition, despite its quasi-left provenance, was redolent of some of those consensus themes which many on the left had found most offensive. According to one recent critic, "there is about their description of the modern world an unmistakable aura of inevitability." It was

a subtle version of the same normative view of protest, dissent, and alternative visions that characterizes consensus history. Agrarian radicals, fundamentalists,

---

[32]One possible exception to this generalization is William A. Williams's *Contours of American History*, which was certainly influential, but too idiosyncratic and allusive to constitute a framework for synthesis.

militant minorities, and others who have opposed the centralizing tendencies of modern society may not be the "paranoid" sociopaths that consensus historians at times described. But they are, in the organizational view, essentially irrelevant, clinging to a vision of society doomed to obsolescence by the relentless march of history.[33]

The great majority of young radical historians entered one or another subdivision of social history. Even before the left influx, that area of historical scholarship was *the* growth industry within the profession. As a percentage of all dissertations in history, studies in social history quadrupled between 1958 and 1978, overtaking intellectual history, previously the hot field for young scholars. While a great deal of new social-historical scholarship, beginning in the late 1950s, was informed by Parsonian sociology and by "modernization theory," social history remained, as it had always been, a field relatively hospitable to young radicals. As someone once remarked, thoroughgoingly conservative social historians were about as numerous as Republican folk singers. While the entry into social history of a great many young radicals pushed it somewhat farther to the left, for various reasons it never became the center of a left bid for intellectual hegemony within the profession, as some on the left had hoped and as many on the right feared.[34]

The inspiration for a good deal of the new social history came from E. P. Thompson's 1964 *The Making of the English Working Class.* Surely no work in European history ever so profoundly and so rapidly influenced so many American historians. Thompson, of course, had a special appeal to those on the left. He was the prime—indeed, perhaps the sole— exemplar of Lynd's model radical historian who continued to produce scholarly work of high quality while keeping one foot outside the academy, and devoting much of his time to political activity. *The Making of the English Working Class* was avowedly partisan, suffused with moral passion. It was dedicated to creating a Marxist historiography which abandoned the "construction engineer's metaphor" of base and super-

[33]Disparagement of "corporate liberalism" in "New Radical Historians in the Sixties: A Survey," *Radical America* 4 (November 1970): 104–6, and Gutman interview (1982) in *Visions of History*, 204; long quotation from Alan Brinkley in his "Writing the History of Contemporary America," *Daedalus* 113 (Summer 1984): 133–34.

[34]Calculations by Robert Darnton, "Intellectual and Cultural History," in Michael Kammen, ed., *The Past Before Us: Contemporary Historical Writing in the United States* (Ithaca, N.Y., 1980), 334. Any such generalization depends on definitions, and whether one lumps or splits subcategories. Mine is a lumping definition, referring to studies of the everyday experience of popular classes, whether in cities, factories, or the home; regardless of the race or gender of those studied: it thus includes much (though not all) of what are sometimes separately designated as urban, labor, family, black, and women's history.

structure; which broke with "economistic" determinism, and focused rather on "lived experience" and the agency of those at the bottom of society. Thompson attacked the practice and motives of mainstream academics who denied the centrality of class and class struggle. But he was equally critical of the way the concept had frequently been employed by Marxists. He reconceptualized class in a fashion which one of his American admirers called "a quenching shower of spring rain across a parched landscape of arid, static definitions."

Sociologists who have stopped the time-machine and, with a good deal of conceptual huffing and puffing, have gone down to the engine-room to look, tell us that nowhere at all have they been able to locate and classify a class. They can only find a multitude of people with different occupations, incomes, status-hierarchies, and the rest. Of course, they are right, since class is not this or that part of the machine, but *the way the machine works* once it is set in motion—not this interest and that interest, but the *friction* of interests—the movement itself, the heat, the thundering noise. Class is a social and cultural formation . . . which cannot be defined abstractly, or in isolation, but only in terms of relationship with other classes. . . . When we speak of *a* class we are thinking of a very loosely defined body of people who share the same congeries of interests, social experiences, traditions and value-systems, who have a *disposition* to *behave* as a class, to define themselves in their actions and in their consciousness in relation to other groups of people in class ways. But class itself is not a thing, it is a happening.[35]

In its focus on spontaneous forms of protest, and the ways in which subordinate classes forged their own oppositional postures, *The Making of the English Working Class* opened important new areas for exploration, and inspired important work. But whereas some who acknowledged their indebtedness to Thompson, like Genovese, retained Thompson's emphasis on class, others who expressed similar indebtedness, like Herbert Gutman, were relatively silent on the question. From a professional historical, or Marxist, point of view there were some serious weaknesses in *The Making*, some of which Thompson later acknowledged, and which were much less evident in his later work. There was a tendency to inflate the significance and exaggerate the element of spontaneity in sometimes ephemeral protest. The focus on the standpoint of the oppressed sometimes gave short shrift to the significance of structures of domination. Overall—and this tendency increased as Thompson was drawn more and more deeply into polemics with Marxist structuralists—there

[35] Alan Dawley, "E. P. Thompson and the Peculiarities of the Americans," *Radical History Review* 19 (1978–79): 39; Thompson, "The Peculiarities of the English," *Socialist Register*, 1965, 357.

was an empiricism which sometimes almost shaded off into the position that "the facts spoke for themselves."

Many of those who sought to follow Thompson's example in writing history "from the bottom up" had much less discipline and sophistication than the master, and the weaknesses in Thompson's work were often exaggerated in that of epigones. On the one hand, there were inspirational accounts which contained overdrawn portrayals of lower-class militancy. On the other hand, there were studies which, in their absorption with the minutiae of everyday underclass existence, sometimes degenerated into sentimental antiquarianism or, at any rate, social history as G. M. Trevelyan had defined it: history "with the politics left out." This latter tendency was furthered by some leading social historians not of the left, for one of whom the field would have "arrived" when "the history of menarche is widely recognized as equal in importance to the history of monarchy."[36]

As so often in the case of influential writings, the timing of their arrival is crucial. Thompson's work appeared on the American scene at a time when there was widespread enthusiasm for a deinstitutionalized understanding of politics joined to a variety of radical-democratic and libertarian currents. As that tide receded, the political thrust of Thompsonian social history was often lost; it had, wrote Geoff Eley and Keith Nield, "lost the discipline of its organizing insights and was left marooned on a sea of increasingly diffuse cultural analysis." *A fortiori*, this was seen by disgruntled leftists as characteristic of social history as a whole. Tony Judt, in a particularly ill-tempered attack on what he saw as dominant tendencies in the field in the seventies, wrote of its political marginalization, the encouragement which practitioners received to concentrate on the "avowedly insignificant."

Meanwhile the political history of the ruling class has survived unscathed the threat to its hegemony of interpretation in those things that matter, rather in the way that an international corporation will grant a degree of workers' control on the shop-floor, smiling the while, in the knowledge that this is not where the true power lies.

Eugene Genovese had urged the depoliticization of the universities so that a politicized scholarship would be free to flourish—a hope he now

---

[36]Peter N. Stearns, "Coming of Age," *Journal of Social History* 10 (1976): 250. The phrase "history from the bottom up," popularized by Jesse Lemisch in the 1960s, and probably independently coined, dated back to at least 1923, when Frederick Jackson Turner used it in a letter. (Turner to Carl William Blegen, 16 March 1923, Turner Papers, Box 32.)

found disappointed. Writing with Elizabeth Fox-Genovese he insisted on the continuing centrality of the politics and economics of class relations. The Genoveses deplored "massive attempts by social historians to deflect attention to the bedrooms, bathrooms, and kitchens of each one's favorite victims." The shift, they said, "owes much to the reigning preference for private satisfaction over public purpose."

> As admirable as much of the recent social history has been and as valuable as much of the description of the life of the lower classes may eventually prove, the subject as a whole is steadily sinking into a neoantiquarian swamp presided over by liberal ideologues, the burden of whose political argument—notwithstanding the usual pretense of not having a political argument—rests on an evasion of class confrontation. It should therefore come as no surprise that so many leading lights are ex-Marxists, ex-new Leftists, and ex-Communists who have fallen silent on political matters as well as on the class content of historical process but who desperately cling to the subject matter of the lower classes to shore up eroding credentials.

Responding in 1980 to the criticisms of Judt, and implicitly to that of Eley and Nield and the Genoveses, Edward Shorter told them that their concerns were out of date—no longer fashionable. "Listen, Tony. . . . What you don't realize is that in most university towns nowadays people aren't all that *interested* in the Worker's Struggle. They're concerned with women now, with lifestyles, and why everyone's so unhappy."[37]

Changes in the political climate also had a powerful effect on un-depoliticized social historians who continued to wrestle with that hardy perennial "Why Is There No Socialism in the United States?" For generations this question had occupied both those historians who were asking, "Why (Thank God) Is There No Socialism in the United States?" and those asking, "Why (Goddamit) Is There No Socialism in the United States?" From the sixties onward there were more historians asking the latter question, but the answers offered did little to advance the search for an answer beyond explanations offered by Louis Hartz in the fifties. New scholarship in European history, notably William Sewell's work on early French socialism, tended to sustain Hartz's argument that the absence of an organic, corporatist, feudal past in the United States deprived Ameri-

---

[37]Eley and Nield, "Why Does Social History Ignore Politics?" *Social History* 5 (1980): 267; Judt, "A Clown in Regal Purple: Social History and the Historians," *History Workshop* 7 (1979): 87; Genovese and Fox-Genovese, *Fruits of Merchant Capital* (Oxford, 1983), x; "The Political Crisis of Social History: A Marxian Perspective," *Journal of Social History* 10 (1976): 213–15; Shorter, "'Clowns in Regal Purple'—A Response," *Theory and Society* 9 (1980): 673.

can workers of a collective memory sustaining an anticapitalist world view. To be sure, scholars found traces of such an outlook in eighteenth- and nineteenth-century artisans, whose anticapitalist rhetoric centered on the charge that the new productive system was transforming their labor into a commodity. But all of this simply underscored the fact that, in the United States as in Europe, the most militant working-class activity was associated with the transition to rather than from capitalism.

While labor historians succeeded in demonstrating that American working-class history was considerably more turbulent than had appeared to be the case in previous representations, the history of radical labor militancy was, at least in the long run, and usually in the short as well, a history of defeat—certainly of failure to sustain a successful socialist movement. Werner Sombart's 1906 *Warum gibt es in den Vereinigten Staaten keinen Sozialismus?* directed itself to the striking contrast between the growth of mass socialist parties in Europe and the absence of such formations in the United States. It was American exceptionalism that subsequent generations of scholars had sought to explain. By the late 1980s, American leftist scholars had experienced two decades of disappointment and disillusionment at the fate of the left abroad. In 1968 there was the failure of both the Prague Spring and "les événements de mai" in Paris; there was the degeneration of Third World socialisms into bureaucracy and repression; the collapse of "Eurocommunism"; the dismal record of the Mitterand government in France. The list could be extended almost indefinitely. Where was the socialist "success" abroad with which American socialist "failure" had been contrasted?

American leftists had often turned to the European past for visions of the American future. Perhaps it was the other way round. Perhaps Gertrude Stein had been right when she said that the United States was not the youngest nation, but the oldest, since it was the first to enter the twentieth century. Younger leftist social historians, like Sean Wilentz and Eric Foner, urged an abandonment of the thesis of "American exceptionalism," an abandonment which implied a break with the most fundamental Marxist assumptions. Rather than continuing to wrestle with Sombart's question, Foner said, one might more fruitfully ask, "why has there been no socialist transformation in any advanced capitalist society?"

Perhaps because mass politics, mass culture, and mass consumption came to America before it did to Europe, American socialists were the first to face the dilemma of how to define socialist politics in a capitalist democracy. Perhaps, in the dissipation of class ideologies, Europe is now catching up with a historical process already experienced in the United States. . . . Only time will tell whether the United States has been behind Europe in the development of socialism, or ahead of it, in socialism's decline.[38]

If social history had traditionally been relatively hospitable to radicals, there had been no field more establishmentarian than diplomatic history. But it was in that realm that left dissidence had its greatest impact, largely because historiographical controversies were fueled by the great debate on American foreign policy in the sixties and early seventies—a debate which cut much deeper than such debates in the past. In 1940–41, when isolationists and interventionists confronted each other, the issue was what we should *do*. Both of the contending parties had agreed on two propositions: that it would be a great misfortune if American young men were sent off to fight in a European war; that it would be a great misfortune if Hitler established permanent dominion over Europe. The debate was not a confrontation of opposing values, but had to do with which of two shared values should have precedence; which misfortune one had to accept to avoid the other.

The foreign policy debate which began in the sixties—enormously exacerbated and dramatized by the Vietnam War, but not, particularly among historians, initiated by that conflict—was not just about what we should do, but about who we *were*. Was the United States, as most historians had said, a traditionally isolationist nation, dedicated to minding its own business; a nation which, despite an aberrant spasm at the turn of the century, had been overwhelmingly anti-imperialist; a nation which had only slowly, reluctantly, and in self-defense, come to accept "the responsibilities of world power?" Or had the traditional version gotten it all wrong? Were we, in fact, something very, very different?

Generational experience was central to the conflict which emerged in the interpretation of American foreign policy. For diplomatic historians whose shaping experience was either the "battle against isolationism" in 1940 and 1941 or, as the received version had it, America's grudging recognition of a renewed totalitarian menace after 1945, the great truth about the history of American foreign relations was its tradition of noninvolvement in the affairs of the outside world; the American people's reluctance to recognize the need to defend their vital interests abroad. For a good many of those who came of age after the mid-1950s the dominant

[38]Foner, "Why Is There No Socialism in the United States?" *History Workshop Journal* 17 (1984): 74–76. Cf. Wilentz, "Against Exceptionalism: Class Consciousness and the American Labor Movement, 1790–1920," *International Labor and Working Class History* 26 (Fall 1984): 1–24, with critical comments by Nick Salvatore and Michael Hanagan immediately following.

experience, and one whose historical roots seemed worth exploring, was American globalism and interventionism: a worldwide network of military bases, the increasingly routine American practice of attempting to overthrow or subvert regimes considered "unfriendly."

The single most important figure in the reconceptualization of the history of American foreign policy was in fact a member of the "Munich generation"—William Appleman Williams of the University of Wisconsin, an Annapolis graduate who, abandoning a career as a professional naval officer after his service in World War II, turned to the study of history. In *The Tragedy of American Diplomacy* (1959), and in subsequent works, Williams, and others who came to be designated members of the "Wisconsin school," sought to show that turn-of-the-century American imperialism, rather than being a brief departure from traditional national policy, was in fact continuous with early-nineteenth-century frontier expansion and early-twentieth-century U.S. domination of Latin America, which had grown by the middle of the century to a drive for global hegemony. Williams's characterization of American "open door imperialism" was, by his own account, influenced by contemporary English scholarship on "the imperialism of free trade." But in a larger sense his central theme of overseas expansion as the psychic heritage of the frontier mentality, and as a strategy consistently preferred over redistributive domestic policies for solving the problem of underconsumption, harked back to hints dropped by Frederick Jackson Turner, and the theory of imperialism advanced by John A. Hobson at the turn of the century. The recurring ambiguity in Williams's treatment of American expansionism—was it the inevitable consequence of the structure of American capitalism or a "cruel convenience" which could be reversed by a political act of will—reflected the tension between Turner's pessimistic streak and Hobson's reforming zeal.

From the early sixties onward, historians identified with the Wisconsin school followed, elaborated, and modified the approaches laid down by Williams. Though their work varied considerably in the relative weight given to economic, ideological, and political influences on policy, their investigations converged in seeing American devotion to overseas expansion as the red, white, and blue thread running through the past century of the country's history. Before the 1960s the community of American diplomatic historians had traditionally closely identified with the goals of policymakers, with a concomitant agreement in principle on the grounds for judging policy. This consensus did not survive that decade. When, in the early 1970s, Norman Graebner distributed a questionnaire to several hundred of his colleagues, which asked them to evaluate the "success" of

American foreign policy in the nineteenth and twentieth centuries, the responses made him realize that the question was no longer answerable in the old way. Many of Graebner's respondents wrote him that they couldn't answer the question. From their perspective, policies which were "successful" in accomplishing the stated or unstated aims of those who promoted them were politically and morally disastrous.[39]

Given the larger implications of their theses, it is not surprising that the work of Williams and those associated with him on nineteenth- and early-twentieth-century American expansion evoked a hostile response from a large section of the community of diplomatic historians. But controversies over events in the relatively distant past were mild compared to the ill-tempered and vituperative debate which broke out in the sixties over the origins of the cold war, a debate which frequently filled the pages of general-circulation periodicals. The explicit issues in debate were important enough, but what made the controversy so highly charged were the implicit questions it raised, which had to do with nothing less than the United States' moral standing in the world.

In American thinking about international relations no theorem was more influential than that which asserted there was a close moral affinity between a nation's foreign and domestic policies—benevolent democratic regimes which were pacific and defensive, brutal despotisms which were aggressive and expansionist. This proposition had been a staple of American thinking about diplomacy since the nineteenth century. The assertion that the domestic terror and messianic ideologies of "totalitarian" regimes found their inevitable counterpart in those regimes' limitless drive for conquest was simply an updating and systematization of what had long been the conventional wisdom.

It was the equivalence between aggression and depravity, between a defensive posture and virtue, which had led Andrew McLaughlin to interpret the thesis that Germany had not been responsible for World War I as tantamount to saying that his son had died fighting "on the wrong side." No one in the twenties had been saying precisely that. But by the sixties an increasing number of Americans, especially in the universities, were saying something very similar with respect to the ongoing Vietnam War. In 1965 the defense of Eugene Genovese's academic freedom at Rutgers became the leading issue in the New Jersey gubernatorial race, after he had said, at an early teach-in, "I do not fear or regret the impending Viet Cong victory in Vietnam. I welcome it." Within the next few

---

[39]Graebner, "The State of Diplomatic History," Society for Historians of American Foreign Relations *Newsletter* 4 (March 1973): 5.

years such remarks became commonplace, as a substantial number of Americans regretfully concluded not just that the war was ill-advised, but that we were on the wrong side.[40]

What "cold war revisionism" did was to extend questions being raised about American policy in Vietnam to the larger issue of the genesis of the global conflict between the West and the Communist world. Until the 1960s the all-but-unquestioned historical truth about the origins of the cold war held that it was, in Arthur Schlesinger, Jr.'s words, "the brave and essential response of free men to communist aggression." The core of the revisionists' position was that at the end of World War II, Soviet policy was dominated by a concern with security and reconstruction rather than expansion and global subversion; that visceral anti-Sovietism decisively colored the perceptions of American officials; that a variety of American actions—particularly the failure to accept the inevitability of a Soviet sphere of influence in Eastern Europe—had unnecessarily escalated international tensions and prevented the establishment of a postwar modus vivendi. To one degree or another most revisionists saw a commitment to postwar American hegemony via open door imperialism as an underlying theme of U.S. policy.[41]

If revisionists agreed on this much, they agreed on little else. There were crosscutting divisions between "liberal" and "radical," "hard" and "soft," revisionists. There were those who in their analyses stressed American economic motives and the extension of the open door, those who stressed American messianic ideology, and those who tried to synthesize the two. Perhaps the most important division was between those who focused on contingent events and the role of personalities, and those who emphasized the alleged structural determinants of American policy. Some revisionists maintained that the decision to drop the atomic bomb on Hiroshima was dictated by anti-Soviet motives, but many others rejected this view. There were those who saw a sharp break in American policy with Truman's accession to the presidency, while others saw a fundamental continuity between Roosevelt and his successor.

The sixties provided a congenial climate for a revised view of the origins of the cold war. If fewer and fewer at this time accepted that American "vital interests" were at stake in Southeast Asia, was it not reasonable to ask if the same was true of Eastern Europe in the 1940s? If more and

---

[40]Genovese, quoted in Kirkpatrick Sale, *SDS* (New York, 1973), 184.
[41]Schlesinger, "Origins of the Cold War," *Foreign Affairs* 46 (1967): 23. The phrase was Schlesinger's characterization of the "orthodox" view: by 1967 he was prepared to acknowledge that the cold war was not a "pure" case of Russian aggression and American response. (Ibid., 52.)

more Americans in the sixties could concede that China had a legitimate interest in the regimes on her borders, might not this also have been the case with the USSR earlier on? If ill-considered American global interventionism had landed us in this bloodiest manifestation of the cold war, was it not at least worth considering whether the same hubris had been responsible for the larger conflict of which it was a part? Manifestly by the sixties the United States was overseeing an empire. Could scholars comfortably argue that it had been acquired, as had been said of the British Empire, "in a fit of absence of mind"?

Such "presentist" questions were reinforced by revelations from newly opened archives and newly published memoirs, together with the evolution of mainstream scholarship, all of which on the whole tended to sustain most of the core revisionist assumptions. That Russia's postwar posture had been defensive, and that acceptance of a Soviet sphere of influence in Eastern Europe had offered the only possible basis of accommodation, were accepted by all but the most hawkish scholars. Herbert Feis, a staunch antirevisionist, admitted privately that "the intense quest for exports by the capitalist countries was inadvisable and always an impending source of conflict." He deplored "the fanaticism with which from the time of Secretary Hull, Will Clayton, and Dean Acheson the American Government has made itself the exponent of trade expansion." Particular interpretations which had been central to the orthodox version had to be abandoned. Stalin, whose alleged promotion of armed insurgency in Greece had been the justification for the Truman Doctrine, had, it was now acknowledged, opposed that initiative. The invitation to the Soviets to participate in the Marshall Plan had been presented as evidence of continuing American goodwill. Contemporary documents made it clear that the invitation was purely for show—that it had been carefully framed to insure Soviet rejection. George Kennan's *Memoirs*, intended to demonstrate his cool realism, revealed rather an anguished moralist in the grip of a visceral anti-Sovietism.[42]

For those committed to the defense of postwar American foreign policy, while treating the Vietnam War as an aberration, fending off the revisionist challenge was more than an academic exercise. Given the broad and deep-seated commitment to the equation between aggressive behavior and depravity, the confirmation of primary Soviet responsibility for the conflict was a fundamental patriotic duty if American virtue was to be defended. (Additionally, one could not satisfactorily justify hundreds of billions of dollars in continuing defense budgets on the basis of a

---

[42]Feis to Arthur Schlesinger, Jr., 7 May 1971, Feis Papers, Box 32.

thesis of avoidable misunderstanding, let alone one which attributed greater bellicosity to America.) There was a personal element as well. To accept the revisionist theses was not just to challenge older historians' interpretations, but, in the case of many of them, to besmirch the crusade to which they had devoted much of their youth. As early as 1966, Schlesinger sounded the alarm: it was necessary to "blow the whistle before the current outburst of revisionism regarding the origins of the cold war goes much further."[43]

Those dedicated to discrediting revisionist theses employed a variety of strategies. One was red-baiting. "The fact that in some aspects the revisionist thesis parallels the official Soviet argument," wrote Schlesinger, "must not, of course, prevent consideration of the case on its merits, nor raise questions about the motives of the writers, all of whom, so far as I know [*sic*], are independent-minded scholars."

> For Brutus is an honourable man;
> So are they all, all honourable men.

(Privately, Schlesinger had described William A. Williams to the executive secretary of the AHA as "a pro-Communist scholar.") John Lewis Gaddis asserted that the revisionists applied "the classical Leninist model of imperialism" to postwar American foreign policy, something which none of them had done. Herbert Feis protested to the editor of the *New York Times Book Review* that whereas the text of a letter he had submitted to the *Review* stated that revisionist historians' work closely followed the interpretation of Communist writers, the letter as published substituted "Marxian" for "Communist." "I meant Communist, not merely Marxian . . . most of the writings and analyses of the historians of the New Left seemed to me just poor imitations of Communist official doctrine. . . . Have you by any chance members of the New Left on your staff who are protecting their pals?"[44]

The very term "New Left" as applied to revisionist historians was a far from innocent appellation, and it continued to be employed by antirevisionists like Gaddis well into the 1980s, long after its inappropriateness had become evident. By aggregating a carefully selected list of writers—

[43]Schlesinger, letter to the editor, *New York Review of Books* 7 (20 October 1966): 37. Subsequently he characterized this remark as "somewhat intemperate." ("Origins of the Cold War," 23.)

[44]Schlesinger, "Origins of the Cold War," 24; Schlesinger to Boyd Shafer, 1 July 1954, AHA Papers, Box 367; Gaddis, "The Emerging Post-Revisionist Synthesis on the Origins of the Cold War," *Diplomatic History* 7 (1983): 172–73; Feis to John Leonard, 15 April 1971, Feis Papers, Box 32.

including the most vulnerable, and omitting the most circumspect—all cold war revisionists could be tarred with the New Left brush, and made collectively responsible for whatever errors or exaggerations were contained in the work of anyone so designated. And, of course, there were errors and exaggerations in revisionist work, along with other defects. Gar Alperowitz, in arguing that anti-Soviet motives were central in the decision to bomb Hiroshima, was pushing to the limit Richard Hofstadter's maxim that "if a new or heterodox idea is worth anything at all it is worth a forceful overstatement." Gabriel Kolko consistently overestimated calculation and continuity in American policy. The tone of all of his writings was dogmatic and arrogant, and he could reasonably be charged with giving Soviet versions of events a benefit of the doubt which they did not deserve. Others were corrigible on other scores.

The chef d'oeuvre of antirevisionism, the shrillest blast of the whistle which Schlesinger had sought, was Robert Maddox's *The New Left and the Origins of the Cold War*, which before its publication collected a formidable array of sponsors, including Feis, Schlesinger, and Oscar Handlin. Deliberately ignoring the theoretical framework offered by revisionists, and formally abstaining from any evaluation of their theses, the book examined "representative" examples of the use of evidence in seven well-known revisionist accounts. Maddox's conclusion was that "without exception" the books he subjected to scrutiny were farragoes of falsification and fabrication; that even "granting a generous allowance for mere carelessness," the authors' "pervasive misusages of the source materials" could only be explained as willful and deliberate; that their works had no claim to scholarly standing.[45]

Maddox's conclusion, if accepted by the community of diplomatic historians, would have been fatal for cold war revisionism within the profession. Schlesinger and Handlin expressed satisfaction that Maddox

---

[45]*The New Left and the Origins of the Cold War* (Princeton, 1973), 10–11. The authors treated were Gar Alperowitz, Diane Shaver Clemens, D. F. Fleming, Lloyd C. Gardner, David Horowitz, Gabriel Kolko, and William A. Williams. One of Maddox's "New Leftists" (Fleming) was an old Wilsonian who celebrated his eightieth birthday in the year Maddox's book was published; another (Horowitz) was a radical journalist without academic credentials, who subsequently became a Reaganite. (Neither Fleming nor Horowitz had any credibility within the historical community.) Of the five remaining authors treated, only Alperowitz, Gardner, and Kolko were central figures in the revisionist venture—and it was well known that Alperowitz's principal conclusions had been rejected by most revisionists. Maddox's attack on Williams's *Tragedy of American Diplomacy* was directed to the one out of seven chapters in that sweeping interpretive essay which dealt with the origins of the cold war. (Williams's empirical research all dealt with the nineteenth century.) In the case of Clemens, whose *Yalta* Maddox put under the microscope, his critique was limited to five pages in her concluding chapter.

had proven his case. The book was hailed in right-wing journals for "uncovering an academic Watergate" and disclosing the "intellectual sorcery" of the revisionists. But academic reviewers were on the whole unimpressed, which led Handlin to expatiate on "the ultimate betrayal of the profession," "preach[ing] the academic coverup." While almost all professional historians commented unfavorably on what Norman Graebner called Maddox's "unnecessary spirit of vindictiveness," their more important conclusion was that even in his own hyperempiricist terms, Maddox had not made his case. Where real errors had been disclosed they were adjudged for the most part inconsequential. More often, the items in Maddox's catalogue of horrors seemed to the reviewers matters of interpretation on which honest scholars might differ.[46]

After a brief flurry of attention, Maddox and his bombshell-turned-firecracker disappeared from view. While sharp criticism continued to be directed at revisionist works, they were not to be thus blown out of the water. Other lines of attack were employed. Historians of the older generation sometimes invoked the authority of their gray hairs. Lawrence S. Kaplan asked how any of the revisionists could "truly understand the origins of the Cold War unless they were of an age to experience World War II and its immediate aftermath." H. Stuart Hughes found revisionist accounts by younger historians who did not experience the events firsthand "out of focus"—they lacked the "feel and taste" of the 1940s. Schlesinger thought that those with "no vivid memories of Stalinism" might fail to appreciate the perceptions, and language, of his own generation. Younger historians, he wrote, erred in failing to realize that when in the 1940s those like himself voiced their opposition to Communism they were not responding to a polycentric phenomenon: "Communism had a clear and specific meaning . . . it didn't mean Titoism, or Trotskyism, or Maoism . . . but purely and simply Stalinism." (This explanation was received skeptically by those who recalled that in 1945, Schlesinger had described a nineteenth-century journalist who had supported the Paris Commune as "one of the first American Communist fellow travelers.")[47]

[46]The two phrases from the right appeared, respectively, as the title of Claire Z. Carey's review in *The Intercollegiate Review* 9 (Winter 1973–74): 51, and in Jack Chatfield's review, *National Review* 25 (1973): 904–5; Handlin's remarks in "The Failure of the Historians," *Freedom at Issue* 32 (September-October 1975): 5; Graebner review of Maddox, *Pacific Historical Review* 43 (1974): 138–39. The review which particularly outraged Handlin was that by Warren F. Kimball, "The Cold War Warmed Over," *AHR* 79 (1974): 1119–36.

[47]Kaplan, "Response" to Gaddis, "Post-Revisionist Synthesis," 194; Hughes, "The Second Year of the Cold War," *Commentary* 48 (August 1969): 27; Schlesinger, "Origins of the Cold War," 22–23; Schlesinger, "Communication" to *AHR* 78 (1973): 190–91; Schlesinger, *The Age of Jackson* (Boston, 1946), 409, 508.

Though Schlesinger's memory may have been inexact, the larger point he was making directs attention both to the principal source of "orthodox" dismay at cold war revisionism, and to the grounds on which the controversy might be, if not resolved, at least moderated. As so often, the dispute over the origins of the cold war had been moralistic, a matter of apportioning guilt, blame, or responsibility. With some exceptions, moralism among the contenders was more characteristic of the orthodox than of the revisionists. A recurring theme in antirevisionist arguments was that it was astigmatic, if not vaguely obscene, to ignore the evils of the Stalinist regime, to evaluate the foreign policy of the Soviet Union without consideration of its domestic horrors. H. Stuart Hughes attacked revisionists for their "reluctance to plumb the full monstrousness in Stalin's character"; Oscar Handlin, for attempting to "establish a moral parity in the post-war world between the United States and the Soviet Union." Schlesinger said that the great omission of the revisionists was "the fact that the Soviet Union was *not* a traditional national state." The key was agreement on the "big truth" of Stalinist depravity. If that were acknowledged all around, one could continue to wrangle over particulars, but at least a measure of historiographical détente might be achieved.[48]

The problem faced by defenders of the orthodox version of the cold war was not unlike that which had confronted southerners in the late nineteenth century with respect to the historiography of slavery, the Civil War, and Reconstruction. Given the centrality of the cold war in American society since the 1940s, it is only a slight exaggeration to say that cold war revisionism threatened the myth which defined and justified the postwar American polity, as northern scholarship in the previous century had threatened white southerners' self-image and confidence in their own righteousness. In that case, as we have seen, the key was consensual agreement on black inferiority. Once that was granted, one could acknowledge that slavery had been often cruel and had become anachronistic; even that secession was a mistake; that the Ku Klux Klan might have been guilty of excesses. But, on the premise of black inferiority, actions taken to preserve white supremacy were understandable, and, even if mistaken, to be judged charitably. As acknowledgment of black inferiority was the key to a history acceptable to white southerners a hundred years earlier, acknowledgment of Soviet depravity (and thus the moral superiority of Western society) was for defenders of American

---

[48]Hughes, "The Cold War and Detente," *New York Review of Books* 26 (19 February 1976): 4; Handlin, introduction to Robert J. Maddox, "Cold War Revisionism: Abusing History," *Freedom at Issue* 15 (September-October 1972): 2; Schlesinger, "Origins of the Cold War," 46.

policy. If this was granted, substantial concessions could be made on particular interpretations, because nothing done to combat the "evil empire," no matter how ill-advised or excessive, could narrow the great moral gulf which separated the two superpowers.

This was the key to the partial cooling out of the controversy, on the basis of "postrevisionism," the label attached to interpretations of the origins of the cold war which incorporated many of the revisionist findings, but did so within a context which emphasized Soviet depravity and American virtue. Its first and fullest expression was John Lewis Gaddis's *United States and the Origins of the Cold War*, which unlike Maddox's book won widespread academic approbation, and garnered three professional prizes. Gaddis's narrative of the actual conduct of wartime and postwar Soviet-American diplomacy frequently had more in common with revisionist than with orthodox accounts. He saw the Soviet posture as defensive rather than expansionist. He acknowledged that during the war Roosevelt had indicated to the Russians that "they could count on a free hand in Eastern Europe"—a position abruptly reversed after 1945. On the key points in contention, he granted that Soviet but not American "vital interests" were at stake. The reviewer for the *American Historical Review* suggested that had Gaddis's arguments been presented six or seven years earlier, they would have led the work to be labeled "an example of New Left history."[49]

But Gaddis did not limit himself to a diplomatic recital, the level on which his work could lead to unacceptably "revisionist" conclusions. Throughout the book he treated American leaders as heavily constrained by calculation of the difficulties of going against public opinion, and the possibility of electoral costs if a more accommodating policy were pursued. "Surely," he wrote, it would be "uncharitable, if not unjust, to condemn officials for rejecting courses of action which, to them, seemed intolerable." In a conclusion which William H. McNeill generously described as "rather glib," Gaddis explained why, whatever the course of diplomacy, whatever the rights and wrongs of the substantive issues in dispute, the onset of the cold war was primarily the responsibility of the Soviet Union, precisely because of the vices of its political system, the virtues of ours.

> If one must assign responsibility for the Cold War, the most meaningful way to proceed is to ask which side had the greater opportunity to accommodate itself, at least in part, to the other's position. . . . Revisionists have argued that American

---

[49]*The United States and the Origins of the Cold War, 1941–1947* (New York, 1972), 134, 354–55; Kimball, 1123.

policy-makers possessed greater freedom of action, but their view ignores the constraints imposed by domestic politics. Little is known even today about how Stalin defined his options, but it does seem safe to say that the very nature of the Soviet system afforded him a larger selection of alternatives than were open to leaders of the United States. The Russian dictator was immune from pressures of Congress, public opinion, or the press. This is not to say that Stalin wanted a Cold War. . . . But his absolute powers did give him more chances to surmount the internal restraints on his policy than were available to his democratic counterparts in the West.[50]

Other postrevisionist works varied in their assessment of blame or responsibility, but all emphasized Soviet depravity. For Vojtech Mastny the matter was straightforward: "the evils of the Soviet system were the ultimate cause of the Cold War." In a very different fashion, Daniel Yergin's *Shattered Peace* was inclined to assign greater responsibility to the United States, focusing on the visceral and rigid anti-Sovietism of the American diplomatic establishment. But it won broad approval, because, as Charles Maier noted, Yergin "temper[ed] his basically revisionist critique with evocations of Stalin's domestic repression."[51]

The extent of convergence should not be exaggerated: the moderation of controversy, to the extent that it occurred, was as much the result of temporary exhaustion as of anything else. The greatest limitation of the analogy with the nineteenth-century debate was that in the earlier case there was a powerful will to achieve reconciliation, which, while not completely absent, was much less powerful in the grumpy and sullen mood of the 1970s and 1980s. For most revisionists, Gaddis's postrevisionism was simply "orthodoxy restated." Yergin's narrative account, because of its avoidance of questions of structural determination, was "a toothless revisionism." The most intransigent traditionalists found Gaddis wishy-washy, and Yergin beyond the pale.[52]

And with the passage of time, there were shifts in the grounds of contention. "Orthodoxy" was attacked from a new (in fact a very old) direction. The conventional wisdom on the cold war had originally been formulated in response to Republican charges that Democratic administrations had been, perhaps treasonably, too accommodating to the

[50]*Origins of the Cold War*, 357, 360–61; McNeill, review of Gaddis, *Pacific Historical Review* 43 (1974): 287.
[51]Mastny, *Russia's Road to the Cold War: Diplomacy, Warfare, and the Politics of Communism, 1941–1945* (New York, 1978), 312; Maier, "Marking Time: The Historiography of International Relations," in Kammen, *Past Before Us*, 370–71.
[52]Barton J. Bernstein, "Cold War Orthodoxy Restated," *Reviews in American History* 1 (1973): 460 (review of Gaddis); Carolyn Eisenberg, "Reflections on a Toothless Revisionism," *Diplomatic History* 2 (1978): 295 (review of Yergin).

USSR, rather than that they had been too intransigent. Now these charges, minus the imputation of treason, were revived. Oscar Handlin endorsed the explanation of the cold war advanced by Aleksander Solzhenitsyn—"a novelist with integrity enough to value the truth." The cold war began at Yalta

as the cowardly pens of Roosevelt and Churchill, anxious to celebrate their victory with a litany of concessions, signed away Estonia, Latvia, Lithuania, Moldavia, Mongolia, condemned to death or to concentration camps millions of Soviet citizens, created an ineffectual United Nations Assembly, and finally abandoned Yugoslavia, Albania, Poland, Bulgaria, Rumania, Czechoslovakia, Hungary, and East Germany.

By the mid-1980s Gaddis was hailing the "striking new interpretation," in fact an amalgam of the old orthodoxy and even older Republican charges against Roosevelt and Truman, that "the primary cause of the Cold War was Stalin's own ill-defined ambition. . . . A secondary cause was the West's failure to act soon enough to stop him." Theodore Draper, who had been one of the most vocal antirevisionists, was warning against the resurgence, among neoconservatives, of the McCarthyite version of the "Yalta surrender."[53]

In a symposium on postrevisionism at the 1983 meeting of the Organization of American Historians, Lloyd Gardner said that debate was probably pointless since "we will not convince one another." Bruce Kuniholm thought that given the wide differences in assumptions and judgments, any agreement reached "will always be as much a matter of fashion as of 'truth.'" In part these remarks indicated acceptance of a perspectival relativism: a number of review articles on the cold war controversy used the Kuhnian language of "incommensurable paradigms." In part they signaled recognition that America was putting the Vietnam experience behind it.[54]

In his 1968 presidential address to the American Historical Association, John K. Fairbank had called the Vietnam War "an object lesson in historical nonthinking." Greater historical sophistication, he said, could have averted a situation in which probably the greatest menace to mankind was "the American tendency to overrespond to heathen evils abroad, either by attacking them or by condemning them to outer dark-

---

[53]Handlin, *Truth in History* (Cambridge, Mass., 1979), 160–61, citing Solzhenitsyn, "The Big Losers in the Third World War," *New York Times*, 22 June 1975, sec. 4; Gaddis, "Post-Revisionist Synthesis," 176; Draper, "Neoconservative History," *New York Review of Books* 32 (16 January 1986): 5–15.
[54]Gardner and Kuniholm, responses to Gaddis, "Emerging Post-Revisionist Synthesis," 191 and 201–2, respectively.

ness." After a generation of revisionist and postrevisionist scholarship, much of it devoted precisely to exploring and analyzing the roots of the phenomenon which Fairbank deplored, the fashion in American foreign policy was once again messianic rhetoric and global interventionism. In the 1960s Robert Freeman Smith and Ronald Radosh had been members of the Wisconsin school, and severe critics of American intervention in Latin America. In the age of Reagan they were denouncing the menace of leftist regimes in the hemisphere. A survey of diplomatic historians in the early 1980s reported that those who had moved to the right during the last ten years were three times as numerous as those who had moved to the left. It remained to be seen exactly how "fashionable" American diplomatic historiography would become.[55]

III

It is not always easy to clearly identify a dominant interpretive orientation within the historical profession in any given period, but usually something more or less adequate can be patched together. The designation "conservative evolutionist" probably applies to the great majority of American historians from the 1880s through the first decade of the twentieth century. "Progressive" historiography had strong support from the teens through the forties, and "consensus" interpretations thereafter, and while in neither case did these orientations drive all competitors from the field, no great violence is done to the record by employing these labels as roughly descriptive of the leading schools in these successive periods. Certainly it is true that in each period most historians found one or another of these schema both coherent and satisfying.

A striking feature of the American historical profession in the last twenty years has been its inability to move toward any overarching inter-

[55]Fairbank, "Assignment for the '70's," *AHR* 74 (1969): 873, 879; survey cited in Jeffrey Kimball, "The Influence of Ideology on Interpretive Disagreement: A Report on a Survey of Diplomatic, Military and Peace Historians on the Causes of 20th Century U.S. Wars," *History Teacher* 17 (1984): 364. The case of Radosh is particularly interesting. He is best known for *The Rosenberg File* (New York, 1983), co-authored by Joyce Milton. In it, Radosh concluded that the case against Julius Rosenberg was solid, and that leftist protests of "frame-up" were without foundation. In the controversy which followed the book's publication, Radosh was feted and fawned upon by the right and center, while receiving rough treatment from various sections of the left. Throughout, Radosh's greatest supporter on the left was the historian James Weinstein, since become editor and publisher of the socialist newspaper *In These Times*. Weinstein's consistent defense of the book cost him considerable personal abuse, canceled subscriptions, and the like. By 1986, Radosh, in the course of rebutting an article favorable to the Sandinista regime, noted that it appeared in "the ostensibly democratic socialist *In These Times*." (Radosh, "Nicaraguan Myths," *Partisan Review* 53 [1986]: 68.)

pretation which could organize American, or for that matter, non-American, history. Perhaps even more significantly, rather than there being vigorous competition between schools, each confidently pressing the claims of its own scheme, potential contenders seem to be in the process of breaking down, with many of their erstwhile promoters experiencing declining confidence in either their coherence or capacity to satisfy.

Schools of historical interpretation are never politically neutral. Overall views of the past are tied in countless ways to visions of the present and future. Which is to say that they are, in a broad sense, "ideological." In Chapter 3, I suggested that, broadly conceived, an ideology can be said to include (1) beliefs about the way things are, (2) beliefs about the way things ought to be, and (3) an ensemble of propositions about the relationship between the first two. Increasingly throughout the 1970s, and dramatically by the 1980s, not only was there no ideological consensus within the American intellectual community, but many of those previously committed to particular ideological perspectives were experiencing deep crises of confidence in their adequacy. The discontent and disarray were both academic and political. Scholarly experience suggested their inability to explain the past; political discouragement and disillusionment led to doubts about their adequacy as orientations in the present. There was confusion about what was, both now and in the past; uncertainty about what ought to be, beyond the vaguest generalizations; and, for the most part, not the foggiest notion of how "is" and "ought" could converge. The only proposition that seemed likely to command a plurality was the meta-ideological conviction that is and ought, however pictured, were diverging.

While a deeply pessimistic *Weltanschauung* is by no means inconsistent with historical scholarship of the highest order—the case of Henry Adams is the most obvious American example—it is difficult to imagine a national historical profession, conscious of its social responsibilities, organizing scholarly work around such a view. And almost equally hard to imagine it forming the tacit consensual basis on which historical scholarship is judged "objective."

The left presence within the historical profession from the 1960s onward was substantial compared to previous periods, but its strength is often exaggerated. In no important historical specialty were leftists a majority; in no major history department were they more than a small minority. The ranks of the historiographical left were depleted by the departure from the profession of most of those who had been associated with the Lynd faction of radical historians. Some, like Lynd himself, who became a lawyer, found other employment. No doubt for many younger leftists whose first taste of academic life was in the exhilarating late sixties, the campus climate in the decades that followed was too bland for their taste, and they drifted away. A handful of left historians emigrated abroad; a few emigrated to the right. And, of course, from the early seventies the continuing job crisis excluded many who would have found permanent positions in the sixties.

What left historians did achieve was a certain legitimacy. As the election of Louis Gottschalk to the presidency of the AHA at a relatively young age had been a deliberate symbol of the acceptance of Jews within the profession, so the selection in 1978 of Eugene Genovese, at an even younger age, as president of the Organization of American Historians signaled the legitimacy of the left. The naming of John Womack, who called himself a (small "c") communist, as chairman of the Harvard History Department was perhaps an even more significant symbol of left "arrival." When left historical scholarship first appeared in the mid-sixties, it often received rather grudging tolerance, as when Robert R. Palmer reluctantly advised the editor of the *AHR* to let a young radical's work appear in the *Review*: "Otherwise it might seem that the *AHR*, as an organ of the establishment . . . seem to be trying to silence him or brush aside ideas emanating from the Left." But within the next decades leftists became a recognized constituency, not unlike other constituencies based on region or historical specialty, and as such fully entitled to representation on professional committees, on programs at professional meetings, and in professional journals.[56]

But the very acceptance of radical historians as legitimate participants in a pluralistic professional discourse carried with it the likelihood that particular aspects of their work would be assimilated in a way which defused its bite—a process we have observed earlier in this chapter, and which, in another connection, I have referred to as "restriction through partial incorporation." And what was true of left scholarship was equally true of left scholars. Unlike that of blacks and women, whose identity is harder to shed, leftists' political identification could gradually attenuate until it was little more than a sentimental memory. It was awareness of these dangers that led E. P. Thompson, while stressing the importance of radical historians' participating fully in mainstream academic life, to warn that they should never allow themselves "to become wholly dependent upon established institutions." They had to occupy

some territory that is, without qualification, their own: their own journals, their own theoretical and practical centers—places where no one works for grades or

[56]Palmer to Henry Winkler, 7 January 1966, AHA Papers, Box 846.

for tenure but for the transformation of society; places where criticism and self-criticism are fierce, but also mutual help and the exchange of theoretical and practical knowledge; places that prefigure in some ways the society of the future.[57]

Various ventures of this kind were launched in the seventies. One was Eugene Genovese's *Marxist Perspectives*, a somewhat slick quarterly, intended to serve as both a forum for Marxist scholarship and a vehicle through which Marxists could engage those "on the other shore." Perhaps in part because of the ambiguity of its purpose, the journal never seemed to find its focus, and if it prefigured the society of the future, that future is bleak: following dissension among its editors, it ceased publication after two years. Meanwhile, a much younger group, some of whom as graduate students had been members of the Lynd caucus, began publishing the *Radical History Review*. This was a more raucous and countercultural journal, which evolved from a crudely reproduced bulletin into a major outlet for left scholarship—still going strong after a dozen years. (To the extent that the *Radical History Review* prefigures the society of the future, its citizens will have a lot of fun.) But in the very years that historical studies written from a left perspective multiplied, and won professional respect, the political morale of leftists was repeatedly battered by successive defeats abroad, and the all but total collapse of left and working-class movements at home. And at the same time, the theoretical core of left perspectives—Marxism—was starting to be perceived by many of its former followers as disintegrating.

Until the 1960s there had been so little serious Marxist historical scholarship that, as with the old aphorism about Christianity, it could be said the problem with Marxism was not that it had failed, but that it hadn't been tried. Hostility to Marxist currents within the Anglo-American academic community was so pervasive, and so often both ill-informed and manifestly politically motivated, that anyone even mildly skeptical of the conventional wisdom was likely to suspect that there must be a good deal of value in anything so widely anathematized. And, of course, there was, as attested by the work of great power and originality which began to be produced by highly talented Marxist historians in the English-speaking world. That work gave credence to their claims for Marxism as the overarching theoretical orientation which, suitably modified and "modernized," could offer a comprehensive understanding of the past. But as "Marxist" scholarship flourished, the modifications and modernizations multiplied to the point that the coherence and distinctiveness

[57]March 1976 interview with Thompson, *Visions*, 22–23.

of what remained became very doubtful. With the increasing emphasis on culture and consciousness, how far back did one have to reach to find materialist determination "in the last instance?" Did not newer Marxist stress on the relative autonomy of state and bureaucracy stretch to the breaking point their links to the mode of production? Marx's theory of exploitation through the extraction of surplus value might be sublime moral philosophy, but how useful was it as a tool of economic analysis? How many epicycles could one introduce into the Marxist taxonomy of class identity before it collapsed of Ptolemaic overload? As these questions were being raised with greater and greater urgency, there was a deep crisis in the interpretation of what had always been the center of the Marxist model, the French Revolution. Work by scholars in England, France, and the United States effectively challenged so many axiomatic propositions about this paradigm of "bourgeois revolution" that the subject became an embarrassment to Marxists throughout the western world.

Most American leftist historians were "Thompsonians," lining up with the author of *The Making of the English Working Class* in his continuing debate with supporters of French structuralist Marxism; endorsing his effort to develop a distinctively Marxist historiography which allowed for contingency, stressed human agency, was expressed in an "empirical idiom." But Thompson's effort to define a coherent and distinctive Marxist tradition which steered a course between dogmatism and eclecticism met with very limited success, as he himself admitted.

Some, without abandoning a left commitment, went further. Perhaps the most important American journal of critical Marxist thought was *Telos*, an interdisciplinary venture whose leading figures included several historians. In the late seventies one of its editors noted that for the last few years almost everyone associated with the journal had been "independently developing a fairly elaborate critique of Marxism."

Since everything in Marxism has turned out to be either wrong or trivial, maybe we should dump such a theoretical albatross. . . . Very few of us still believe in the falling rate of profit, the inherent revolutionary character of the proletariat, . . . materialism understood in any of the ordinary senses, . . . or the ridiculous claims of "scientificity" for Marxism. . . . We must stop blaming Kautsky, Engels, Lenin, or Stalin for "Marxism" in the effort to pump formaldehyde into a theoretical cadaver. . . . Looking back over the last eight years, it can be said that our historical function has been primarily to provide Marxism with a decent burial.[58]

In the late seventies and early eighties the *Radical History Review* published interviews with eight of America's leading leftist historians. All

[58]Paul Piccone, "Internal Polemics," *Telos* 31 (Spring 1977): 178–79.

of the eight referred in one way or another to the importance of Marxism, its influence on their thought, the distinctive contributions Marxism had to offer, and the questions it raised. But none identified him- or herself as a Marxist; none suggested that Marxism constituted a sufficient method or world view. And none suggested any alternative candidate. Natalie Davis spoke of her devotion to demonstrating "that things don't have to be the way they are now." David Montgomery thought it important to show that "the working class has always formulated alternatives to bourgeois society in this country." Herbert Gutman saw his work as "transform[ing] historical givens into historical contingencies." John Womack was concerned to combat the widespread belief that "Niggers and Indians don't hurt like white people. . . . Poor people don't hurt like rich people." "Teaching about pain," he said, "is the most important thing history can do." The volume in which the interviews were collected was entitled *Visions of History*. The interviews, said the editors, "reveal the basic unity of purpose that all radical historians share": a determination, following Marx, "not only to interpret the world, but to change it." No group of historians in recent years had done more to advance the interpretation of the world; their determination to fulfill the second half of the injunction may have remained intact, but the "vision" of how it was to be accomplished—either through structural determination or any foreseeable human agency—was not to be found.[59]

Historically, "conservatism" is as much a child of the French Revolution as are ideologies of the left. The values of conservatism—order, tradition, legitimacy—were defined against the revolution, and in practice the center of conservatism is often "counterrevolution." Since revolution is rare, what passes for conservatism is often anachronistic, as when McCarthyites, in the 1950s, directed their fire against domestic Communists whose trivial influence had long since dissipated. So it was with "neoconservatism," which often degenerated into neo-McCarthyism, in the late 1970s and 1980s. Academic neoconservatives' principal targets were the leftist turmoil on and off the campuses in the sixties, and its aftermath, the temporary victory of the McGovern forces in the Democratic Party in 1972. By the time that neoconservatism became an organized force in the late 1970s, when peace had returned to the campus, and the right had become ascendant, it was doing battle with ghosts and chimeras. As Daniel Bell, who increasingly distanced himself from his former neoconservative associates, observed, ideologues of the right

---

[59]Davis, Montgomery, Gutman, Womack and the editors quoted in *Visions*, 114, 180, 203, 260–61, and xi respectively. There *were* American historians who continued to call themselves Marxists, particularly among students of the American South.

could not afford to acknowledge the change. Through "a parochialism which has stopped time . . . one never loses an enemy but reincarnates him in different guises in order to maintain one's original momentum."[60]

In the late sixties a beleaguered counterrevolutionary posture was common among academics distressed by turmoil on and off the campus. But neoconservative scholars continued to maintain that posture long after it had become more than a little ridiculous. In 1986, Secretary of Education William J. Bennett warned that "nowadays [*sic*] . . . campus radicals . . . see the university as a kind of fortress at war with society, an arsenal whose principal task is to raise revolutionary consciousness, frustrate the government, discredit authority and promote a radical transformation of society." The Harvard historian Richard Pipes described attitudes within the historical profession in ways which most found unrecognizable. "The majority of practicing historians," he wrote in 1979, view the Bolshevik Revolution as "a progressive event . . . pav[ing] the way for the triumph of freedom and equality." Gertrude Himmelfarb saw the dominant tendencies in the historical profession in 1983 as radical, dedicated to "a trashing of the past . . . a degradation of history and also, therefore, a degradation of the present, which has always been presumed to be our heritage from the past."[61]

Neoconservative scholars traduced their adversaries in a style reminiscent of the most intemperate young radicals of the sixties. The targets were not infrequently historians, even when the marksmen were not. Allan Bloom of the University of Chicago accused Sir Moses Finley of being a Marxist ideologue, Edmund Morgan of having cravenly prostituted his scholarship to "keep in the good graces of the wave of the future." The most extreme example of neoconservative misrepresentation came from the medievalist Norman Cantor, who denounced Lawrence Stone as a long-time Marxist, "peddl[ing] . . . a more subtle and poisonous Marxism than traditional Leninism." Under Stone's influence Princeton University had become "a central school for indoctrination of the young in Marxist ideology." This was rather too much for Himmelfarb, who, repeating the argument of 1950s liberal anti-Communists who disliked McCarthy for discrediting the cause, chastised Cantor for using the term "Marxist" so loosely, and thus "distract[ing] attention

[60]Bell, "Our Country—1984," *Partisan Review* 51/52 (1984/1985): 630–31.
[61]Bennett, speech prepared for delivery to American Jewish Committee, *New York Times*, 15 May 1986, B12; Pipes, "The Revolution: Conventional Attitudes," *New York Times Book Review*, 30 December 1979, 7; Himmelfarb, contribution to symposium *Our Country and Our Culture: A Conference of the Committee for the Free World* (New York, 1983), 52–53.

from . . . historians to whom it does properly apply and who are influential enough to warrant serious concern." And it was counterproductive for the cause in the case of J. H. Hexter, who remarked that some years ago, in response to the "McGovernizing" of his party and insolent students, he "began a slow quiet crawl to the right—and there I find Norman Cantor. Guess I'll start crawling back."[62]

In fact, while the rightward drift in the political culture was reflected in various academic disciplines, history was relatively untouched by conservative currents. It had long been a commonplace that America, "born liberal," lacked a conservative tradition in the European sense: organicist, legitimist, antiliberal. The few representatives of this tradition in the American historical profession never had much influence before the 1960s, and had no more thereafter. While right-of-center academic journals proliferated in other disciplines, the only explicitly conservative historical venture was *Continuity*, which began publication in 1980. Its masthead included the traditional conservative Thomas Molnar, the anti-Progressive Forrest McDonald, the antirevisionist Robert Maddox, and Aileen Kraditor, who at some point in the seventies moved across the spectrum from left to right. The journal's inaugural statement announced that *Continuity* would publish scholarship committed to "the quest for truth for its own sake; the superiority of our free society, with all its faults, to any practicable alternative; legitimate authority; and the presumptive value of tradition as the accumulated wisdom of the past." It would criticize "historiographical idols" which contributed to "the current erosion of scholarly discourse within the academy and to the fashionable vilification of our country among intellectuals throughout our society." Five years after *Continuity* began publication, its circulation was 300, less than one-tenth that of the *Radical History Review*. It was a curiosity, without influence or even visibility. A sense of "continuity" was precisely what was missing from American society from the sixties onward, which could lead a moderately conservative historian like David Donald of Harvard to despair of his vocation.

What undergraduates want from their history teachers is an understanding of how the American past relates to the present and the future. But if I teach what I believe to be the truth, I can only share with them my sense of the irrelevance of

---

[62]Cantor, letter to *New Criterion* 4 (December 1985): 86–87; Himmelfarb and Hexter letters, ibid., 4 (March 1986), 85 and 86. Cantor's original article, which initiated the exchange, was "The Real Crisis in the Humanities Today," ibid., 3 (June 1985): 28–38. For Bloom on Finley, see his review of Finley's *Ancient Slavery and Modern Ideology*, *New York Times Book Review*, 11 January 1981, 8, 19; on Morgan, his "University Standards and the Decline of Humane Learning," in John W. Chapman, ed., *The Western University on Trial* (Berkeley, 1983), 160–61.

history and of the bleakness of the new era we are entering. . . . Perhaps my most useful function would be to disenthrall them from the spell of history, to help them see the irrelevance of the past.

In both American and European history some individual works exhibited a strong conservative tilt, but even these were not very numerous. If the left had tried and failed to create an overarching historiographical framework congenial to its views, the right did not even attempt such a task.[63]

The most serious breakdown of interpretive framework, and ideological faith as well, was not at the extremes of left and right, but in the broad liberal center which had united the vast majority of American historians around a faith in orderly progress. Formally, professional historians disparaged the teleological "Whig interpretation of history," in which historical actors were graded according to whether they advanced or retarded the growth of liberalism and democracy. But in a larger sense a liberal, Whiggish orientation had continued to guide the pens of most American historians and gave larger meaning to their monographic labors. By the 1970s and 1980s both Americanists and Europeanists found this framework no longer satisfactory. Bernard Bailyn wrote that the old structure, "which explained the present in terms of an inferior but improving past" had been completely eroded, and there was no substitute in sight to take its place. William H. McNeill, reviewing American scholarship on European history in the 1970s, offered the image of "a powerful fountain whose jet ascended high into the air, only to break up into unstable, inchoate shapes, dispersing in every direction before commencing a glorious descent."

The cascade of a descending fountain is entrancing to the beholder—far more spectacular, in fact, than the narrowly focused, ascending jet. But the fountain can persist only if an ascending jet sustains descending multiplicity. . . . The jet has been turned off. European history has lost the necessary focus on some kind of fundamental meaning such as once was provided by the liberal vision of the human condition. . . . Without such an organizing vision of the whole, how long can we expect the variety and technical virtuosity of the decade of the 1970s to be sustained?[64]

For those who were liberals in the narrower sense, supporters of the liberal wing of the Democratic Party, American politics after 1968 was a scene of unmitigated disaster. The liberal electoral base steadily eroded,

---

[63]"Statement of Policy," *Continuity* 1 (Fall 1980): [ii]; Donald, "Our Irrelevant History," *New York Times*, 8 September 1977, reprinted in *AHA Newsletter* 15 (December 1977): 3–4.
[64]Bailyn, "The Challenge of Modern Historiography," *AHR* 87 (1982): 3; McNeill, "Modern European History," in Kammen, ed., *Past Before Us*, 109.

liberal social programs were eviscerated, and a successful effort was mounted to deliberately redistribute income from the poorest to the richest segments of society. With no end in sight to the rightward march of politics, erstwhile liberal figures rushed to climb on the neoconservative bandwagon. If the 1964 election had been a referendum on the welfare state, racial equality, and the avoidance of nuclear confrontation, it was the last such referendum won by liberals; every subsequent augury pointed in the opposite direction—signaling a reversal of the long-term course of American political developments in the twentieth century.

But discouragement and disillusionment were also common among those who were liberals in the broader, "Hartzian" sense, the sense in which almost all Americans are liberals. The fundamental values and assumptions of the American liberal tradition in this broader sense all came to be at risk. The most sophisticated theorists of liberal democracy explained that voting was irrational, and that it was well that most of the potential electorate appeared to share this view, because widespread participation in the democratic process could destabilize the system. "Justice," according to the most advanced thinkers, was not a transcendent social ideal, but "allocative efficiency." In the view of a growing group of social theorists—left, right, and center—the liberal malaise was not transient, but epochal, the tragedy of its triumph, which only revealed itself gradually, over centuries. Michael Walzer of the Institute for Advanced Study was impressed by the observation of the neoconservative Irving Kristol that bourgeois society had lived for years off "the accumulated capital of traditional religion and traditional moral philosophy," capital it did not effectively renew. For all of its achievements, Walzer said, liberalism "has been parasitic not only on older values but also and more importantly on older institutions and communities."

And these latter it has progressively undermined. For liberalism is above all a doctrine of liberation. It sets individuals loose from religious and ethnic communities, from guilds, parishes, neighborhoods. It abolishes all sorts of controls and agencies of control: ecclesiastical courts, cultural censorship, sumptuary laws, restraints on mobility, group pressure, family bonds. It creates free men and women, tied together only by their contracts—and ruled, when contracts fail, by a distant and powerful state. It generates a radical individualism and then a radical competition among self-seeking individuals. What made liberalism endurable for all these years was the fact that the individualism it generated was always imperfect, tempered by older restraints and loyalties, by stable patterns of local, ethnic, religious, or class relationships. An untempered liberalism would be unendurable. That is the crisis the neo-conservatives evoke: the triumph of liberalism over its historical restraints.[65]

[65]Walzer, "Nervous Liberals," *New York Review of Books* 26 (11 October 1979): 5–6.

The acceleration in the pace of recent history was paralleled by an acceleration in the succession of historiographical sensibilities. The fifties was the "era of no hard feelings" among historians—the decade of consensus, and "the end of ideology." Hard on its heels came the violent acrimony and polarization of sensibilities in the hyperideological sixties. Polarized consciousness overlapped with, but ultimately gave way to, the confused fragmentation which accompanied the ideological *Gotterdämmerung* of the seventies and eighties, when even the pragmatic, liberal welfare-capitalist ideology of the end-of-ideologists threatened to collapse.

In the postwar period a chastened objectivism had been the natural concomitant of a convergent mood—of substantive consensus, optimism, and goodwill. The historiographical consequences of the following periods of polarization and fragmentation were by no means as clear. On the one hand, those most committed to ideological postures were the most likely to insist on the objectivity of their findings—that it was they who saw clearly; their antagonists who saw darkly, through ideologically tinted glass. On the other hand, the need to restore comity within a polarized profession could lead to a resigned perspectivalism, and abandonment of hope for convergence on unitary truth. Robert Berkhofer saw American historians irreconcilably split into rival camps, "social scientific" and "radical," with "no hope of a congenial fusion."

The logical underpinnings of each paradigm are mutually exclusive in ultimate source of theory, in method and criteria of verification, and in moral and political positions. The two histories are not like two ships passing in the night upon the same sea of history; rather, they are like two ships sailing upon two quite different oceans. . . . In consequence, their chances of communicating seem only slightly less remote than their chances of colliding.[66]

Both Bailyn and McNeill had seen fragmentation rather than polarization as the most noteworthy characteristic of the 1970s and 1980s, but they responded very differently to the phenomenon. Bailyn's response was transcendence through value-freedom. He believed it "possible to approach that ultimate stage in historical interpretation where partisanship is left behind"; to produce an historical account which was "neither whig nor tory, idealist nor materialist, liberal nor conservative." McNeill's response to the crisis of faith was a call for historians to dedicate themselves to the care and repair of public myth; for them to be, recognizing the "elastic" character of truth, "truth-seeking mythogra-

---

[66]Berkhofer, "The Two New Histories: Competing Paradigms for Interpreting the American Past," *OAH Newsletter* 11 (May 1983): 11–12.

phers," shaping "shared truths that provide a sanction for common effort."[67]

Despite their differing prescriptions, both Bailyn and McNeill had responded to historiographical fragmentation and confusion by seeking a unifying version of the past, one that could appeal to all sections of the community, national in Bailyn's case, global in McNeill's. But as they wrote, important elements within the American historical community were moving in the opposite direction, deliberately employing particularistic criteria to fashion accounts serviceable to particularistic constituencies. It is to this development that we now turn.

[67]Bailyn, "The Central Themes of the American Revolution: An Interpretation," in Stephen G. Kurtz and James H. Hutson, eds., *Essays on the American Revolution* (Chapel Hill, N.C., and New York, 1973), 15, 23; McNeill, "The Care and Repair of Public Myth" (1982), and "Mythistory, *or* Truth, Myth, History, and Historians" (his 1985 AHA presidential address), both reprinted in McNeill, *Mythistory and Other Essays* (Chicago, 1986), 7, 22.

14

◁ ━━━━━━━━━━━━━━━━━━━━━━━━━━━━━━ ▷

Every group its own historian

Over the last hundred years no component of the synthesis of ideas which went to make up the norm of historical objectivity had been more central and enduring than "universalism." Truth was one, the same for all peoples. It was, in principle, accessible to all and addressed to all. Particularist commitments—national, regional, ethnic, religious, ideological— were seen as the enemies of objective truth. They had to be transcended if unitary truth was to be approached. Ranke's commanding reputation rested in large part on the perception that he had risen above narrow nationalism and parochialism. American historians had taken from Francis Bacon not only their notions of the inductive method, but also his warnings against the "Idols of the Cave": particularistic commitments which blocked access to universal truth. Historians were attracted to those schools of social science which believed that empathic identification and *Verstehen* were legitimate methods of comprehension, but insisted, along with the social scientists, that these devices were available to all investigators, and were not the special prerogative of insiders. The close connection which historians saw between detachment and objectivity made them sympathetic to Mannheim's celebration of the vantage point of free-floating and socially detached observers, whose liberation from particularist loyalties allowed them to approach closer to objectivity.

American historians, as compared with historians of other nationalities, had always been especially attached to universalist norms, and were proud that these norms had strengthened as the profession developed—a particularly urgent task in a country with strong regional loyalties, and a multiethnic population. The process of professionalization had seen the gradual victory of national over particularist interpretations, and increasingly universalistic patterns of recruitment to the profession.

With the sharp decline in the number of historians who could lay claim to "forefathers in 1776" (or for that matter, 1876), insider claims, such as those voiced by Carl Bridenbaugh in 1962, became rarer, and were regarded as not just tasteless but fundamentally wrongheaded. There was an additional consideration. In every other country the great majority of professional historians wrote the history of their own national community, and frequently disparaged the capacity of outsiders to penetrate its *Geist* or *génie*. American historians, by contrast, were substantially more cosmopolitan in their subject matter. Within the profession as a whole, and in every major department of history, historians of the United States were a minority, most practitioners studying societies with which they had no organic connection. To acknowledge insider privilege would be to devalue either one's own work, or, at a minimum, that of most of one's colleagues.

The entry of large numbers of Jews into the upper reaches of the profession in the 1950s and early 1960s was widely seen as the fulfillment of universalist norms. It was otherwise with the arrival of blacks and women from the late sixties onward. For their rise to prominence within the profession coincided with a new, assertive, particularist consciousness which both directly and indirectly challenged universalist norms. They defined themselves not as "historians who happened to be Negroes," with a consensually acceptable integrationist standpoint, but as *black* historians, committed to one or another form of cultural nationalism; not "historians who happened to be women," seeking proportional representation in textbooks for members of their sex, but *feminist* historians with an overriding loyalty to their sisters, and agendas which called for a thoroughgoing transformation of historical consciousness. Jews, upon entering the profession, had insisted that they were "just like everyone else, except more so," committed to a sensibility which was not just integrationist but usually assimilationist as well. In a different cultural climate the new black and female entrants stressed the distinctiveness of their vision, and often were highly critical of central values of the profession.[1] Assertive particularism had implications not just for academic universalism in the abstract, but for values as basic to academic life as a commitment to "telling the whole truth." No one, it seems safe to say, tells the truth all the time. Other values intervene. We tell white lies to safeguard the feelings of those we care about. Often there are conflicts of

---

[1] With a few noteworthy exceptions the Jews who rose to prominence within the profession did not venture into Jewish history; they certainly never attempted to define a "Jewish perspective"; it is probably not coincidental that the leading figures in developing the "consensus" interpretation of American history were all of Jewish background.

loyalties. When writing letters of recommendation, loyalty to clients conflicts with loyalty to colleagues. And, as a rule, we do not tell "the whole truth" to an enemy if we have good reason to believe that the enemy will use the information imparted to hurt or destroy us. In their academic writing scholars strive to present "the whole truth and nothing but the truth" for a variety of reasons, not least among them fear of the embarrassment which follows being caught doing otherwise—a fear which various institutionalized mechanisms are devised to reinforce. But beyond such prudential considerations, the obligation of complete scholarly frankness has a principled foundation. It implies commitment to solidarity in a common venture; a loyalty, superior to any other loyalties, to allies in the collective scholarly search for increased knowledge and understanding. If those ties of solidarity are weakened; if they are seen as subordinate to other loyalties; in the limiting case, if other members of the scholarly community are seen as enemies rather than as allies, the principled basis for academic openness and objectivity is in serious jeopardy.

Newer particularistic sensibilities also challenged universalist assumptions about cognitive style and modes of discourse. Turn-of-the-century racists had asserted that blacks were naturally subjective, whites objective. The popular belief that women were naturally intuitive while men were analytic has a long history. These were propositions which Negroes and women in the academy had scornfully repudiated as racist or sexist slanders. Enlightened egalitarians had consistently maintained that the approved academic cognitive style, including all the elements which went to make up objectivity, was uncorrelated with color or gender. In the seventies and eighties a substantial number of black and feminist scholars denied that blacks were, in Kenneth Stampp's words, "innately . . . only white men with black skins"; that women differed from men only in their reproductive systems. Serious claims were made for distinctive discursive and cognitive styles among blacks and women—differences which might possibly, in some distant future, be synthesized with those of white males, but ought on no account to be assimilated to them.

From the sixties onward black and feminist historians anticipated theses advanced by Michel Foucault about the relation between power and knowledge: the "disciplining" of subordinate groups through being made the object of "disciplines"; arguments by Edward Said about the occidental construction of "the Orient"; concern by ethnographers about the legitimacy of their franchise to describe and define non-Western cultures. (These discussions will be briefly treated in Chapter 15.) Other challenges to universalism came from "Public History," which sought to

legitimize historical work designed for the purposes of particularist constituencies. In the historiographical as in the political realm, *e pluribus
unum* was falling on evil days.

I

During the twenty years following the publication of his *From Slavery to
Freedom* in 1947, Negro history, so far as the profession was concerned,
was represented above all by John Hope Franklin. This was something of
a paradox, since Franklin always denied that he was a "Negro historian."
His career was a demonstration that without sacrificing dignity, or pandering to whites, it was possible for a Negro to reach the heights of
professional honor and respect, and to have warm relations of collegiality
with leading white historians. In 1956, after teaching for twenty years at
black universities, he became the first black historian to receive a regular
faculty appointment at a white institution (Brooklyn College). Franklin
was always deeply committed to the universalist and objectivist norms of
the profession, to faith in America, and to optimism about the attainment
of racial justice through integration. In both his life and his work, Franklin was the model Negro historian for white liberals in the 1950s. He
became something of an antimodel for a new generation of black historians in the sixties and seventies.

   Much of Franklin's scholarly work had nothing to do with blacks,
which was the basis of his consistent claim that he was not a "Negro
historian" but a "historian of the South" who happened to be a Negro.
Franklin not only rejected the label "Negro historian" for himself, but
deplored the fact that "Negro history" had been established as a separate
area of inquiry early in the century. He expressed sympathy for those of
his predecessors who had insulated themselves against racist attacks from
white scholars by carving out the field, but argued that by so doing they
had perpetuated their ghettoization, and held back the integration of
blacks into the mainstream of the profession.

   In denying that blacks had privileged "insider" access to the black
experience, Franklin was in some measure protecting himself. To grant
that skin color conferred epistemological privilege would be to denigrate
the value of his own studies of white southerners. But it was his universalist ethos and rejection of particularist claims which dictated his choice
of subject matter, not the other way round. His criticism of the profession, like his criticism of the American polity, was always directed to the
gap between principles which he wholeheartedly accepted, and performance which he frequently found wanting.

Historians, operating under Ranke's mandate to write history as it actually happened . . . could not bring themselves to write about runaway slaves as normal, freedom-loving human beings. . . . In refusing to face the facts of history and in refusing to use the same canons of scholarship to judge all peoples, such historians forfeited their own claims of being scientific just as surely as the founding fathers had forfeited their claims that they were shaping political institutions in the interests of all the people.

Despite humiliations and rebuffs, of which he himself had had his full share, Franklin said that the Negro historian must resist "the temptation to pollute his scholarship with polemics, diatribes, arguments. . . . If he yields to this attractive temptation, he can by one act destroy his effectiveness and disqualify himself as a true and worthy scholar." The positive role for the Negro scholar was "to combat the forces that isolate him and his people and, like the true patriot that he is, to contribute to the solution of the problems that all Americans face in common."[2]

The postwar decades had seen slow but steady progress in desegregation, the decline of the most blatant forms of racism and discrimination, and the possibility, for men like Franklin, to achieve levels of success within white society unimaginable before World War II. By the early sixties optimism about the prospects for successful racial integration, the consistent theme of Franklin's work, was as high in the historical profession as in the rest of American society, and Franklin was the symbol of that integrationist optimism. And then, like so much else in those years, it all fell apart.

Black anger and impatience were hardly unknown before the sixties, but in the face which blacks turned to whites these were often disguised. Franklin wrote of having frequently repressed his true feelings—finding catharsis, in the wake of racial slights, by writing angry pieces which he then consigned to his desk drawer. In the mid-sixties white Americans were confronted with the full fury of a new generation of blacks who wore no such masks. Bloodied southern civil rights workers came to be disillusioned with the fruits of their "nonviolent" efforts, and with the prospects of cooperation with whites. Blacks in northern ghettos exploded in paroxysms of violence. Most of the new militants repudiated an "Americanism" rooted in older integrationist tactics, called for "black power," termed themselves "black nationalists."[3]

[2]"George Washington Williams and the Beginnings of Afro-American Historiography," *Critical Inquiry* 4 (1978): 658–59; "The Dilemma of the American Negro Scholar," in Herbert Hill, ed., *Soon, One Morning: New Writing by American Negroes, 1940–1962* (New York, 1969), 73, 76.
[3]For Franklin's "blowing off steam" in unpublished writings, see "Dilemma," 74–75.

"Black nationalism" is an ambiguous term. In the past it had sometimes meant "Back to Africa"; sometimes the establishment of an "autonomous black belt" in the South. In the sixties very few so-called black nationalists envisioned an independent black polity. The demand for "black power" was primarily tactical, an effort to build a power base to challenge structures of oppression, rather than pursue piecemeal integration. For some left-nationalists, black revolutionaries would be the vanguard of a broader transformation of American society, perhaps in alliance with Third World forces as well as with whites. But above all, black nationalism was cultural. It was an insistence on the distinctiveness of the American black experience, that blacks constituted "a nation within a nation." At a minimum, as with all proto-nationalisms, "black power" meant that blacks rather than whites should have the power to define and interpret black history.

The best publicized instance of blacks' resentment at white appropriation of their past came with the publication in 1967 of novelist William Styron's *Confessions of Nat Turner*. It was open to question whether the memory of Nat Turner and his 1831 slave revolt figured as largely in black folk memory as militants maintained. But as the leader of what was by far the largest black insurgency in the history of the United States, Turner certainly was a central symbol for the militants themselves, the outstanding example of that heroic, revolutionary consciousness which they sought to create in the present, and celebrate in the past. Styron's depiction of Turner, though sympathetic, was of an anguished soul, psychically maimed, and ambivalent to the point of paralysis. Not the sort of shining example the new black consciousness demanded, or that, in other circumstances, any patriotic history could tolerate in a national hero. The English Americanist Marcus Cunliffe, discussing the black outcry against the book, doubted whether, even 170 years after his death, "Americans would be indifferent to a description of George Washington in the act of masturbating." Though there were many debates over how much imaginative freedom the historical novelist should be allowed, the principal issue was who owned the black past. "You've Taken My Nat and Gone" was black historian Vincent Harding's charge against Styron, an indictment echoed in one way or another by most of Styron's black critics. The extravagant praise of Styron's work by white historians from Eugene Genovese and Martin Duberman to Vann Woodward and Arthur Schlesinger was an added provocation; further evidence of white determination to control blacks' history.[4]

[4] Cunliffe, "Black Culture and White America," *Encounter* 34 (January 1970): 30; Harding, in John Henrik Clarke, ed., *William Styron's Nat Turner: Ten Black Writers Respond* (Boston, 1968), 23–33.

The Styron controversy prefigured increasingly common assertions that it was blacks who should be the ones to write black history. This position was by no means new. It was Franklin's universalist stance, not that of the sixties militants, which was exceptional among twentieth-century black historians. Leaders of the Association for the Study of Negro Life and History, which began publishing the *Journal of Negro History* in 1916, had maintained the position for reasons which combined territoriality and conviction. Carter G. Woodson, founder of the association, was convinced that "if the story of the Negro is ever told it must be done by scientifically trained Negroes." "Men of other races," he wrote, "cannot function efficiently because they do not think black." There had been divisions of opinion as to how exclusive a sway blacks should exercise, but dependence on white philanthropic support, and contemporary norms of deference, had worked to moderate the claims of even those who sought monopoly. In any case, in earlier decades, so few white historians concerned themselves with the history of blacks as subjects that black historians had in fact enjoyed a near monopoly in the field. By the sixties the circumstances were very different. Whites were not only writing about blacks, but teaching courses, frequently to overflow crowds, on black history, and habits of black deference had given way to often belligerent assertiveness. A new generation of black historians aggressively challenged the claims of any whites to speak authoritatively on *their* past.[5]

Kenneth Stampp was told by militants that, as a white man, he had no right to write *The Peculiar Institution.* Herbert Gutman, presenting a paper to the Association for the Study of Negro Life and History, was shouted down. A white colleague who was present (and who had the same experience), reported that Gutman was "shattered." Gutman pleaded to no avail that he was "extremely supportive of the black liberation movement—if people would just forget that I am white and hear what I am saying . . . [it] would lend support to the . . . movement." Among the most dramatic incidents of this sort was the treatment accorded Robert Starobin, a young leftist supporter of the Black Panthers, who delivered a paper on slavery at a Wayne State University conference in 1969, an incident which devastated Starobin at the time, and was rendered the more poignant by his suicide the following year. The black historian Vincent Harding, who was in the audience, ostentatiously walked out during Starobin's talk. One of the two black commentators was Sterling Stuckey, who mocked Starobin's interpretation of slave letters by reading

---

[5] Woodson and Wesley, quoted in August Meier and Elliott Rudwick, *Black History and the Historical Profession: 1915–1960* (Urbana, Ill., 1986), 289.

them aloud in black rather than white accents. The other was Julius
Lester, who attacked Starobin for his presumption in attempting to write
about blacks. Both left immediately after Lester's comments, and before
Starobin's rebuttal, "to catch a plane." After Starobin's suicide Lester
wrote:

> It was one of those situations that are unavoidable when blacks and whites come
> together in post–Black Power America, a situation in which people are not indi-
> viduals, but historical entities, playing out a drama whose beginnings are now so
> submerged that we will never find them. And, in these days, any white man who
> devotes himself to teaching and writing about black history must have the forti-
> tude and strength of a bull elephant, because blacks will let him know that his
> presence is unwanted and undesirable. Whether this attitude is just or unjust is
> scarcely a question. In absolute terms it is obviously unjust. Historically, it is the
> present reality, and that day at Wayne State University my heart ached for Bob,
> though I didn't know him, but I knew what I had to do to him. He had to be
> attacked and I did so. . . . I bowed to the demands of history that day and will
> loathe myself forever for having done so. History makes its demands, but one
> does not have to accede to them. . . . All too often we let ourselves be History's
> willing victims, and, that day History demanded that I treat another human being
> as a category and I, not without hurting inside, acceded.[6]

The new separatist consciousness was hostile not just to histories of
blacks by whites, but also to integrationist accounts produced by
"Negroes" like Franklin, who were often privately referred to scornfully
as "oreos"—black on the outside, but white at the core. "The Negro
history movement has had its day," Stuckey wrote. "Its premises were
exploded at Watts and Detroit when the armies of occupation moved in
to put down the desperate rebellions. As faith in America waned among
the black masses . . . young black intellectuals and artists had no interest
whatever in focusing on the 'progress' of their people, on their patriotism." Harding wrote that Franklin, and other Negro historians of his
generation, had "internalized America and its 'promise,'" and put their
faith in "'well-meaning' whites." "Negro History" had to give way to
"Black History":

> While Negro History almost never questioned the basic goodness and greatness
> of American society, while it assumed its innate potential for improvement (pro-

---

[6]Stampp and Gutman anecdotes in Meier and Rudwick, ibid., 292–93; for Starobin, see
Linda Rennie Forcey, "Personality in Politics: The Commitment of a Suicide" (Ph.D.
dissertation, State University of New York at Binghamton, 1978), 159–66; Lester, "Suicide of a Revolutionary," *Liberation* 15/16 (Spring 1971): 64. Between the Wayne State
meeting and Starobin's suicide, he and Lester established reasonably cordial relations by
correspondence.

vided it was ready to read additional volumes on Negro History), Black History has peeped a different card. . . . Black History allows us no hope in white saviors. It insists that we grow up—black. Our fathers in Negro History still generally lived in an age of belief in white deliverers. Our maturity and our fulfillment demand unbelief.[7]

The consciousness which substituted "black" for "Negro" history merged with the broader movement for programs in "Black Studies" in colleges and universities, many of which became bastions of militantly separatist black nationalism. While administrators rejected on principle demands by blacks for autonomous control of Black Studies programs, that all faculty in the programs be black, and that white students be excluded from some or all of the courses offered, these were occasionally granted in practice. At some institutions coherent interdisciplinary programs were established. But jerry-built structures, hastily conceded out of faculty and administrators' guilt and fear, were rather more common, at a time when, as Cunliffe observed, "white facial muscles ache with nervous smiling, black ones with intimidating scowls." In all, perhaps as many as five hundred colleges and universities had established Black Studies programs by the early 1970s. By the 1980s only about half of them survived, usually with few students, as well as depleted and demoralized faculties who produced little published scholarship, and sometimes still in operation only because academic administrators found it marginally less embarrassing to keep them in operation than to close them down.[8]

The decline of Black Studies as the institutionalization of separatist black consciousness was almost as rapid as its rise, in which it followed the fortunes of the nationalist movements in the ghetto which had brought it into being. But separatist black consciousness, in various, somewhat transmuted forms, was considerably more enduring, particularly in history. And those who practiced the new black history were by no means only, or even mainly, black.

In the late 1960s most white historians whose work touched in one way or another on the black experience were ambivalent about the new Black

[7]Stuckey, "Twilight of Our Past: Reflections on the Origins of Black History," in John A. Williams and Charles F. Harris, eds., *Amistad 2* (New York, 1971), 287–88; Harding, "Beyond Chaos: Black History and the Search for the New Land," in Williams and Harris, eds., *Amistad 1* (New York, 1970), 275, 278–79, 285–86.
[8]Cunliffe, "Black Culture," 22. The observation about scholarly productivity refers to those whose primary affiliation—and loyalty—was to Black Studies, rather than to those with a strong disciplinary base, who for one reason or another *also* participated in the programs. Most productive black historians had some connection or other with Black Studies programs.

Studies programs. But they were not at all ambivalent about demands for the exclusion of whites from scholarly inquiry in this area, which they rejected out of hand. Lawrence Levine, who was beginning to study black folklore, experienced a sense of déjà vu. What was being put forward was a "new historical obscurantism" which exactly paralleled what he took to be Carl Bridenbaugh's suggestion, some years earlier, that it was incongruous for Levine, as a Jew of recent immigrant background, to study William Jennings Bryan. "This was a period," Eugene Genovese later recalled, "in which any white working in black history had to take a lot of crap."

We all felt it, but my attitude was I'm not going to take the crap. After awhile I didn't get very much because I quickly developed a reputation for being quite savage. One of these guys would get up and run off at the mouth about who are you to write about black people and I'd look him straight in the eye and say, "you're an idiot," and proceed from there. I didn't enjoy it but the point was I didn't know how else to handle this. Either you do that or you retreat.[9]

Few of the younger white historians of black history—Genovese is the only important exception—explicitly labeled their perspective "nationalist." But in practice all in one way or another, though paradoxically, the "nationalist" Genovese less than others, abandoned the traditional universalist, "ideal observer" posture which had been so central to the ethos of objectivity. The received universalist orthodoxy contrasted "insiders," with potentially distorting particularist commitments, and "outsiders," with less commitment, more detachment, and thus more likelihood of viewing matters objectively. The newer white historians who dealt with black issues insisted that their commitment to the black cause was every bit as deep as that of blacks, which it seemed to be. Though integrationists of the older generation, like Woodward and Stampp, had certainly written out of deep moral commitment to racial equality, younger scholars' commitment had been much more activist. Nearly all of the newer generation of historians had been heavily involved in sit-ins, demonstrations, and other forms of protest.[10]

"Of history and its consequences," Conor Cruise O'Brien has written, it may be said:

"Those who can, gloat; those who can't, brood." Englishmen are born gloaters; Irishmen born brooders. . . . A reformed gloater—an English liberal say, or a

---

[9]Levine, "The Historian and the Culture Gap," in L. P. Curtis, Jr., ed., *The Historian's Workshop* (New York, 1970), 325–26; Genovese, quoted in Forcey, 166.
[10]Meier and Rudwick, *Black History*, chaps. 2 and 3, passim.

Swede—feels, I think, a sense of guilt about South Africa; this is because he still identifies himself, probably without being entirely conscious of the fact, with the master race. The brooder, making the opposite identification, feels no sense of guilt, only a sense of outrage.

O'Brien's remarks are suggestive in considering the difference in the dimensions of black history addressed by gentile and Jewish scholars in the sixties and seventies. While there are some exceptions to the rule, those who have written the most influential studies of white attitudes and behavior toward blacks were almost all gentiles—David Brion Davis, George Frederickson, Winthrop Jordan, Morgan Kousser, James McPherson; those who wrote of blacks as subjects, were overwhelmingly Jewish—Ira Berlin, Herbert Gutman, Lawrence Levine, Leon Litwack, George Rawick. Whatever the reason for the disproportionate number of Jews who wrote about blacks from the black point of view, what is important for our purposes is the profound identification of all members of this latter group of historians, Jewish and gentile, with blacks. Though white, they prided themselves on "thinking black"; of being the reverse of "oreos"—vanilla wafers with chocolate filling. George Rawick, commenting on black historian John Blassingame's *Slave Community*, spoke of a new group of historians, mostly black, but including whites like Gutman and himself. Whatever his criticisms of Blassingame's book, he wanted to emphasize that it was "a work that is 'ours' rather than 'theirs.'" And the claim was sometimes accepted across the color line. The black historian Nell Painter, arguing that black and white historians had quite different sensibilities, acknowledged that "not all whites hold what I'm calling 'white' views; Lawrence Levine and Herbert Gutman, for instance, are able to think about history in what I'd call 'black' ways." It was this group of historians, who whatever their race, "thought black," who were representative of the new style and focus in black history.[11]

The principal theme of the earliest black (or rather "Negro") history in

---

[11]O'Brien, *To Katanga and Back* (London, 1962), 31; Rawick, "Some Notes on a Social Analysis of Slavery: A Critique and Assessment of *The Slave Community*," in Al-Tony Gilmore, *Revisiting Blassingame's "The Slave Community": The Scholars Respond* (Westport, Conn., 1978), 17–18; Painter, "Who Decides What Is History?" *Nation* 234 (6 March 1982): 277. The generalization about the difference in focus between gentiles and Jews applies with greatest force to those who came of scholarly age in the sixties and seventies, though one could observe it in the previous generation: Woodward and Stampp writing the history of racism and oppression from the white side, Herbert Aptheker and Philip Foner emphasizing black agency. By the 1980s the injunction to "think black" had become so powerful that the distinction began to break down. The examples of Aptheker and Foner suggest a partial explanation for the difference: Jews were considerably more likely to have a background in left politics—to be presocialized into identification with the oppressed.

the twentieth century was what has been termed "contributionism." For the most part integrationist in thrust, and written by blacks, it emphasized the achievements of noteworthy members of the race. For blacks it would be a spur to effort and enhance self-esteem. Insofar as it was read by whites, contributionist history suggested that blacks could be valuable members of the national community. Contributionism, at least as traditionally conceived, rapidly reached a point of diminishing returns. For perfectly explicable reasons there had not been that many black high achievers in most of the more important realms of American life. As one tried to expand the list one moved with embarrassing rapidity down to "contributions" that wouldn't get a footnote if made by someone white.

After 1945 a new theme became dominant. Also integrationist in orientation, but this time written mostly by and for whites, postwar historiography emphasized white oppression of blacks, and the toll it had taken, particularly under slavery, but also in its aftermath. Its avowed or tacit intention was to promote a sense of responsibility and guilt in its white audience, though the detailed exposure of patterns of racism and domination was not at all uncongenial to most blacks. But there was a political and rhetorical problem in work of this kind, which Dwight Macdonald once noted in socialist discourse. If capitalism was as inhuman and destructive as socialists maintained, its victims must have been psychologically maimed and brutalized. On the other hand, if workers were as noble and stalwart as they were in socialist depictions, could the system within which they had developed really be all that oppressive? This conundrum was inherent in all areas of black history, but particularly in treatments of slavery which emphasized its harshness and brutality.

In the older historiography of Ulrich Phillips, slavery had been a benign institution. Blacks were childlike by genetic inheritance. Kenneth Stampp's 1956 *The Peculiar Institution* challenged both Phillips's defense of slavery and his racist portrayal of blacks. Stampp pictured the institution as brutal and oppressive, and emphasized slave resistance rather than docility. He acknowledged that there were some slaves who lost their manhood, but for the most part their appearance of subservience was a disguise assumed to deceive the owners. Hailing Stampp's work, Woodward wrote that it exposed slavery for the atrocity that it was, and "left in shreds" the legend of "the gay, carefree black clown." Macdonald's conundrum remained latent in Stampp's work, but was to appear in all its starkness in Stanley Elkins's *Slavery* published three years later.[12]

---

[12]Woodward review of *The Peculiar Institution*, New York *Herald Tribune Book Review*, 21 October 1956, 6.

For Elkins, the "gay, carefree black clown" was no legend, but the predictable result of a closed and total system of oppression, similar in operation to Nazi concentration camps, and with parallel infantilizing consequences for their inmates. He was in accord with Stampp in rejecting Phillips's benign view of the plantation, but accepted Phillips's description of "Sambo" as the typical slave, with the difference that where Phillips had seen Samboism as a racial trait, Elkins's explanation was environmental, and could hardly be described as racist since it allegedly paralleled the process that Elkins's fellow Jews had undergone behind Hitler's barbed wire. "Absolute power for [the slaveowner] meant absolute dependency for the slave—the dependency not of the developing child but of the perpetual child."[13]

Elkins's book was the most extreme example of what in retrospect came to be termed the "damage," "victimization," or "deficit" model of black history, which in the course of the sixties and seventies was overwhelmingly repudiated by scholars. Sambo-bashing was the principal agenda of the field, and Elkins became the *bête blanche* of black history. As usual, those who came out on top saw the outcome as a victory for "the facts." Carl Degler thought it clear that "the flood of new evidence, whether traditional or novel, destroyed Sambo." The principal lesson to be derived from the fate of Elkins's work, he said, was that "historical evidence is crucial." Ideology might propose, but documentation disposed. And, again, as usual, losers saw it differently. Elkins's view was that by the late 1960s "the entire 'damage' argument, as applied to any aspect of Negro life in America, had become ideologically untenable." On the question of what was decisive in the controversy—*not* the relative merits of the respective approaches—Elkins had much the stronger case. The older model was abandoned because members of the newer generation of historians refused to accept that twentieth-century blacks were "damaged" as human beings, that they were (merely) "victims," that there was anything "deficient" about their culture.[14]

The question of damage became a highly charged contemporary issue in the bitter controversy surrounding Assistant Secretary of Labor Daniel Moynihan's 1965 report "The Negro Family: The Case for National Action." Moynihan's aim was to shift federal attention from legal equal-

---

[13]*Slavery* (Chicago, 1959), 130.
[14]Degler, "Why Historians Change Their Minds," *Pacific Historical Review* 45 (1976): 176, 179; Elkins, "The Two Arguments on Slavery," Appendix VI of *Slavery* (3d. ed., Chicago, 1976), 271. My remarks on the relative weight of ideology and evidence in responses to Elkins's work apply only to the question of "Sambo"; the balance seems to me quite different with respect to the evaluation of other theses advanced in *Slavery*.

ity to what, following the black psychologist Kenneth Clark, he called the "tangle of pathology" in northern ghettos, which would prevent those caught in its coils from taking advantage of formal equality of opportunity. He described communities in which "the fabric of conventional social relationships has all but disintegrated." Though the situation was the consequence of white racism and oppression, it was by now "capable of perpetuating itself without assistance from the white world." At the center of the tangle Moynihan located broken and matriarchal families. He saw family breakdown as primarily a consequence of black unemployment ("at disaster levels for 35 years"), and furthered by a welfare system which penalized families in which adult males were present. Accordingly his proposed remedies centered on jobs, job training, and changes in welfare allocation. But the roots of the problem went deeper. Slavery and post-Emancipation oppression in the South had systematically undermined the self-confidence of black males. In the most hyperbolic passage in a document not generally given to understatement, he cited Elkins in support of the proposition that "it was by destroying the Negro family under slavery that white America broke the will of the Negro people."[15]

The report produced a storm of protest from blacks and from white liberals and radicals. It was widely denounced as a racist slander of the black community. Critics denied that ghetto life was "a tangle of pathology"; if there was pathology, it was not to be found in the black family, which was a healthy adaptive response to white oppression. Any pathologies in the ghetto were not a legacy of slavery but the direct consequences of racism and discrimination in the here and now. The psychologist William Ryan, who in the turmoil surrounding the report coined the phrase which made him famous—"blaming the victim"—not only described the report's focus as "a subtle form of racism," but saw the invocation of history as a smokescreen:

We are told the Negro's condition is due to his "pathology," his values, the way he lives, the kind of family life he leads. The major qualification—the bow to egalitarianism—is that these conditions are said to grow out of the Negro's history of being enslaved and oppressed—*generations ago.* . . . Liberal America is pleading guilty to the savagery and oppression against the Negro that happened 100 years ago, in order to escape trial for the crimes of today.

Finally, the report was seen as not just wrong, but harmful. The novelist Ralph Ellison charged that "sociologists [are] propagating an image of the

[15]Lee Rainwater and William L. Yancey, *The Moynihan Report and the Politics of Controversy* (Cambridge, Mass., 1967), 43, 93, 66, 62, 76.

Negro condition which is apt to destroy our human conception of ourselves just at the moment when we are becoming politically free."

From one perspective, slavery was horrible and brutalizing. . . . And the Negro
writer is tempted to agree. "Yes! God damn it, wasn't that a horrible thing!" And
he sometimes agrees to the next step, which holds that slaves had very little
humanity because slavery destroyed it for them and their descendants. That's
what the Stanley M. Elkins "Sambo" argument implies. But . . . there is from *my*
perspective something further to say. I have to *affirm* my forefathers. . . . I am
forced to look at these people . . . and conclude that there is another reality
behind the appearance of reality which they would force upon us as truth. Any
people who could endure all of that brutalization and keep together, who could
undergo such dismemberment and resuscitate itself, and endure until it could take
the initiative in achieving its own freedom is obviously more than the sum of its
brutalization. Seen in this perspective, theirs has been one of the great human
experiences and one of the great triumphs of the human spirit in modern times.[16]

The Moynihan Report did not succeed in reorienting federal policy
toward blacks, but the report, and the controversy surrounding it, contributed a sense of urgency to reorienting black history. The Elkins thesis
no longer was of "merely historical interest," but was perceived as central
to contemporary debates on social policy; part of the larger outlook
which led Nathan Glazer, who had been closely associated with both
Elkins and Moynihan, to assert that the black American "has no values
and culture to guard and protect." It was the Moynihan controversy
which led Herbert Gutman to set aside his studies in labor history, and
begin work on what became *The Black Family in Slavery and Freedom*.
Lawrence Levine explicitly aimed his *Black Culture and Black Consciousness* at Glazer's disparagement of black culture and values. The mid-1960s
were both the high point of "black and white together, we shall overcome," and the time after which there was no longer any place for whites
in the movement. White historians could at least participate vicariously
by defending the historical reputation of the constituency with which
they so deeply identified.[17]

[16]Ryan, "Savage Discovery: The Moynihan Report" (1965), reprinted in Rainwater and
Yancey, 464; "'A Very Stern Discipline': An Interview with Ralph Ellison," *Harper's* 234
(March 1967): 76, 83–84.
[17]Nathan Glazer and Daniel Patrick Moynihan, *Beyond the Melting Pot: The Negroes,
Puerto Ricans, Jews, Italians, and Irish of New York City* (Cambridge, Mass., 1963), 53;
Gutman, *The Black Family in Slavery and Freedom* (New York, 1974), xvii; Levine,
Black Culture and Black Consciousness (New York, 1977), 443. Glazer, besides collaborating with Moynihan, had contributed the introduction to the first paperback edition
of Elkins's *Slavery*—the form in which it first reached a large audience. For Gutman's
continued hostile engagement with Moynihan, fourteen years after his report had appeared (and disappeared), see "The Moynihan Report: Black History Seduced and Abandoned," *Nation* 229 (1979): 232–36.

The new black history treated blacks as healthy subjects rather than maimed objects; emphasized collective strength rather than individual weakness; made black culture and the black community its central focus. The new school was strongly influenced by E. P. Thompson's stress on lower-class self-activity, and some of its major themes were inspired by the pioneering studies of black religion, folklore, and music which young black scholars produced in the sixties. The new work rested heavily on previously little-used black sources, particularly the more than forty volumes of slave narratives published on Rawick's initiative. But at least as significant as these positive influences was the negative and reactive agenda of black history. As consensus history was, above all, "counter-Progressive" history, the new black history was one long assault on the theses and general outlook of Elkins, Moynihan, and Glazer.

No force is as energizing and unifying as a shared enemy, which no doubt accounts for much of the power and excitement of the new black history published during the 1970s. The field attracted an extraordinarily talented and energetic group of historians, who explored difficult new terrain with innovative and imaginative approaches, and with a level of conceptual sophistication rarely equaled in American scholarship. Never before had any group of historical specialists constituted such an interactive and cooperative community, regularly sharing data and reading each other's work in manuscript. Much of the new work was not only technically accomplished, but written with a literary grace and evocative power unusual among professional historians. Members of the new school effectively refuted the exaggerations and distortions of those who had seen only damage in the black past. Inevitably, in the process, they introduced exaggerations and distortions of their own.

There was an all but universal commitment to accentuating the positive in the black experience, bracketing or minimizing the negative, particularly anything which suggested damage or pathology. Individual historians differed a good deal in how heavily their work was constrained by this commitment, but to one degree or another, all shared it. Differences were not a function of skin color. Gutman and Rawick, along with the black historian Leslie Owens, were among those who wrote almost exclusively about black strength. Black historians like John Blassingame and Thomas Holt joined with Genovese in greater willingness to acknowledge damage.

Black culture, and the institutions of the black community, were almost always treated as an unambiguously positive heritage. Lawrence Levine's tribute to the poetic beauty, richness of imagery, and emotional intensity in slaves' religious music was offered as evidence of a strong communal consciousness, a refutation of the theses of damage and deficit. His treatment of spirituals ignored what W. E. B. Du Bois had noted three-quarters of a century earlier: that above all they were "Songs of Sorrow," with "eloquent omissions and silences. Mother and child are sung, but seldom father." Rawick was one of many who argued that slave folklore, particularly trickster tales, represented "the social insights of a people and express a most sophisticated view of human life"; Brer Rabbit "manages to assert himself and his humanity and overcome . . . victimization." This was certainly an important dimension of the stories, but there was another side, rarely mentioned, which Elkins noted:

Many of Brer Rabbit's tricks are responses to the requirements of self-defense and survival. But many others seem gratuitous. . . . He steals or cheats the other animals out of more of their food than he needs . . . a lady who resists his wooing he kills, skins, and smokes over hickory chips. He assembles his neighbors to help him build a spring house, and when this act of community is accomplished he has them all drowned. . . . Rabbit callously sacrifices his own wife and children to save himself. There may be much "complexity and ambiguity" in the tales . . . and "levels of meaning," but one thing about them is clear and simple enough: their "hero" is at best one nasty little hustler.

"In that world of lying, stealing, duplicity, and murder," Elkins concluded, "there is no friendship, no affection, and no mutual trust; 'family' counts for nothing, and of 'community' there is not a shred."[18]

Gutman's magnum opus, justly praised for its moving evocation of black fortitude, was from first to last an attorney's brief in the case of *The Black Family v. Daniel Patrick Moynihan*, and in lawyerly fashion Gutman gave not a point away to the adversary. Every aspect of the black family was portrayed as strong and adaptive. He minimized or denied what was weak, maladaptive, or suggestive of "victimization." Again, the more nuanced views of Du Bois received no consideration. Though Gutman used quotations from Du Bois as epigraphs to chapters, he never mentioned, let alone confronted, the evidence and conclusions of Du Bois (in his 1908 *The Negro Family*), which flatly contradicted Gutman's wholly affirmative picture of black family stability, and pictured serious weakness along with strength. Perhaps Gutman was right and Du Bois wrong, but Gutman's failure even to consider Du Bois's contemporary

---

[18]Levine, *Black Culture and Black Consciousness* (Oxford, 1977), 30, 443; Du Bois, *The Souls of Black Folk* (Chicago, 1903), 259; Rawick, *From Sundown to Sunup: The Making of a Black Community* (Westport, Conn., 1972), 97, 100; Elkins, *Slavery* (3d. ed.), 282–83. Elkins's remarks on Brer Rabbit were directed not at Rawick's discussion but at an early treatment by Levine.

testimony suggested a posture so adversarial that contrary views were dismissed in advance.

Within the generally celebratory new black historiography, two inter-related themes stood out. One was "resistance." Previously historians had disparaged Herbert Aptheker's 1943 *American Negro Slave Revolts* for, in Rawick's words, "portraying black slaves as virtually always on the barricades," and no one had denounced Aptheker for exaggerating rebelliousness more vehemently than Genovese. Both Rawick and Gen-ovese changed their evaluations. Genovese wrote that "specifics apart, he had been much closer to the truth than I on the way in which slave revolts . . . have to be understood." The relative scarcity of armed rebellion in North America as compared to other areas was explained more with reference to demography (the black-white ratio in the population) and topography (the absence of places of refuge) than in terms of any docility in the American slave. Blacks, both under slavery and thereafter, were depicted as constituting a community of resistance—and resistance was redefined. There was greater emphasis on running away, damaging prop-erty, spitting in the soup and pissing in the coffee. "Whereas Western scholarship has frequently confused resistance with bloodshed," Leslie Owens wrote, "Africans have often perceived it as an inner stance coiled to preserve identity." In a way which had many parallels to Jewish histo-rians' discussions of the behavior of Jews during World War II, resistance came to be equated with endurance and survival. Responding to criticism that in *The Slave Community* he had slighted resistance, John Blassingame made the analogy explicit: "The most apt characterization of the slave's behavior is that Lucy Dawidowicz used . . . [in] *The War Against the Jews*: 'They learned not only to invent, but to circumvent; not only to obey, but to evade; not only to submit, but to outwit. Their tradition of defiance was devious rather than direct, employing nerve instead of force.'"[19]

The even more pervasive theme of the autonomy of the black commu-nity and black culture vis-à-vis white America, even under slavery, was directed against claims of blacks' "dependency." It was also directed against Stampp's tacitly integrationist assertion that "innately Negroes *are*, after all, only white men with black skins, nothing more, nothing less," which was now read as both condescending and mistaken. Ameri-

---

[19]Rawick, *Sundown to Sunup*, 74–75; Rawick, "Social Analysis of Slavery," 19; Genovese, "Introduction to the New Edition" of his *In Red and Black* (Knoxville, 1984), xlv; Owens, "The African in the Garden," in Darlene Clark Hine, ed., *The State of Afro-American History* (Baton Rouge, 1986), 35; Blassingame, "Redefining *The Slave Commu-nity*: A Response to the Critics," in Gilmore, 136.

can blacks' African heritage was frequently invoked. In earlier days, Negro historians had systematically minimized the African legacy. Acknowledgment of any such "savage" survivals would be an obstacle to integration. Now they maximized it, and, almost as rapidly as "black" had replaced "Negro," the preferred term became "Afro-American." Gutman, in arguing for the autonomous development of the black family, stressed its African roots. The Christianity of slaves could hardly be treated as wholly "autonomous," but Genovese, in his discussion of slave religion, argued that the absence of a conception of original sin in African thought made the slave's theology distinctive.

Men and women in bondage were clearly not autonomous in the ordinary sense of the term. What was insisted upon was their inner autonomy; their capacity to mold their own norms, and institutions like the family, rather than having their consciousness shaped by the masters. Elkins's case for infantilization required that the plantation be a "closed" system, like a concentration camp. The argument for the autonomy of the slave community and culture mandated that historians pry open the system to allow social space for autonomous development. One way in which this was commonly done was the privileging of life after hours. This approach was explicit in the title of George Rawick's *From Sundown to Sunup: The Making of the Black Community*. Even Blassingame, who thought the theme of autonomy had been exaggerated, wrote of life in the quarters as the "primary" shaping experience. What went on during the working day was a far less important "secondary environment." At its extreme, work in this vein suggested Teflon slaves, all but immune to the system which oppressed them. There were many grounds on which Genovese's *Roll, Jordan, Roll* and *Time on the Cross* by Robert Fogel and Stanley Engerman were criticized. But for many younger historians what was most objectionable about the two works was that both argued against a fully autonomous slave culture, for some black internalization of white values. Genovese did this with his Hegelian portrayal of a master-slave dialectic, and paternalistic hegemony; Fogel and Engerman, much more crudely, with their picture of slaves thoroughly embracing a bourgeois work ethic. Neither work was consistent with the view that pictured "free slaves," who in the words of one of the younger scholars, "by passing their unique set of cultural themes from generation to generation . . . were able to resist most of white teaching, set themselves apart from white society, and mold their own cultural norms and group identity."[20]

[20]Blassingame, *The Slave Community* (New York, 1972), 41; Thomas L. Webber, *Deep Like the Rivers: Education in the Slave Quarter Community, 1831–1865* (New York, 1978), 261–62.

By the mid-1980s the frameworks which had been adumbrated in the 1960s, though still dominant, were starting to creak a bit at the joints. As Hofstadter had written of the Progressive Historians and the principle of conflict, the new historians of the black experience had pushed the mood of affirmation and the themes of resistance and autonomy so far that to go any farther could only result in caricature. Some members of the next cohort were objecting to the unrelievedly positive portrayal of black history; the unwritten rule against any but the most dismissive attention to "damage"; what one young historian called the myth of "the utopian slave community."[21]

It is a truism that all historical writing, at least on highly charged subjects, is the product of a particular moment in time, which shapes historians' decisions about what needs to be explained; which often leads them to conclude that their social responsibilities require that they write history of a certain sort. But some moments are more momentary than others. The black historiography of the seventies stands as a monument to the fruitful energies which presentist concerns can mobilize—and as an illustration of their sometimes untoward consequences.

Working in civil rights organizations during the 1950s, George Rawick had been struck by how few blacks joined in; by the generally low level of black activism. Independently of Elkins he concluded that slavery had created a dependent personality type among blacks which had endured until the present. When he read Elkins's work he embraced it. Within a few years, however, as a result of working with a new generation of black militants he reversed himself. It was, he said, no longer possible to write black history which stressed victimization. "Unless we find the real historical roots of Black Power we are faced with a situation unparalleled in world history: a massive revolutionary movement which comes from nowhere and is born fully grown." By the 1980s not much was left of the "massive revolutionary movement" which for Rawick, as for many others, had cried out for historical explanation.[22]

After two decades in which by every measure ghetto pathology had deepened, black leaders were talking very differently in the 1980s than they had in the 1960s. When the Moynihan Report appeared, the National Association for the Advancement of Colored People had taken the lead in attacking its emphasis on black family breakdown. In 1983 the execu-

---

[21]Peter Kolchin, "Reevaluating the Antebellum Slave Community: A Comparative Perspective," *JAH* 70 (1983): 581. Cf. Laurence Shore, "The Poverty of Tragedy in Historical Writing on Southern Slavery," *South Atlantic Quarterly* 85 (1986): 147–64.
[22]Rawick, *Sundown to Sunup*, 74, n. 2; Rawick, "The Historical Roots of Black Liberation," *Radical America* 2 (July 1968): 1.

tive director of the NAACP put the "precipitous slide of the black family" at the top of the group's agenda. Eleanor Holmes Norton, former chairman of the Equal Employment Opportunity Commission, wrote of the crisis of the black ghetto family as the center of the "self-perpetuating . . . predatory ghetto subculture . . . originating in the historic atrocity of slavery." Whatever opportunity there had been to check family decline, Norton said, had been lost in the anti-Moynihan backlash, "driving the issue from the public agenda and delaying for a generation the search for workable solutions." The black sociologist William J. Wilson agreed, adding that "a new emphasis on the positive aspects of the black experience tended to crowd out older concerns."

Arguments extolling the strengths and virtues of black families replaced those that underlined the deterioration of black families. In fact, aspects of ghetto behavior described as pathological in the studies of the mid-1960s were reinterpreted or redefined as functional . . . because . . . blacks were displaying the ability to survive. . . . Ghetto families were described as resilient and as adapting creatively to an oppressive racist society.

Both Norton and Wilson were speaking much more of sociologists than of historians, and in any case it is unlikely that a different scholarly focus would have done much to redirect social policy in the seventies and eighties. But the troubling thought remained that insofar as the new black historiography of the seventies had discernable social impact, it was to divert attention from the urgent needs of the constituency which those who produced it were dedicated to serving.[23]

Most members of the generation of young white historians who wrote the history of blacks in the seventies had left-wing backgrounds or involvement in the civil rights movement. Insofar as they were disproportionately Jews, they were products of the years when Jews were, in O'Brien's terms, brooders rather than gloaters. Certainly no one can confidently predict what new interpretations of the black experience will be forthcoming from a generation formed in the climate of the eighties. The continued momentum of the great body of scholarship which germinated in the sixties will surely continue to be influential. But much has changed in the succeeding twenty years. Concern with blacks is no longer fashionable with white liberals, now more concerned with issues of the

[23]Benjamin Hooks of the NAACP, quoted in Daniel Patrick Moynihan, *Family and Nation* (San Diego, 1986), 55; Norton, "Restoring the Traditional Black Family," *New York Times Magazine*, 2 June 1985, 79, 93; Wilson, "The Black Underclass," *Wilson Quarterly* 8 (Spring 1984): 89; Wilson, "The Urban Underclass," in Leslie W. Dunbar, ed., *Minority Report* (New York, 1984), 77–78.

environment, and the politics of sexuality and reproduction. It is by no means impossible to imagine that in an era of ever increasing conservatism and privatization of consciousness, and with the growing respectability of a frequently crypto-racist sociobiology, the thrust of seventies scholarship will be reversed: that a professional consensus will form around some version of "damage," but one whose policy orientation is malign neglect.[24]

If the future direction of white historical writing on blacks is unknowable, generalizations about the present relationship of black historians to the overwhelmingly white historical profession are very difficult to formulate. Though many whites had, with some success, striven to "think black," and while many younger black historians had been successfully integrated into the profession, and internalized all of its norms, there remained a good deal of de facto segregation of consciousness. Some black historians, like Vincent Harding, had always maintained a certain distance from the profession. From his earliest writings, Harding had scoffed at "white" notions of detachment and objectivity. His 1981 magnum opus, *There Is a River: The Black Struggle for Freedom in America*, combined religious messianism and revolutionary black nationalism in an account which portrayed slaves as constantly on the verge of insurrection. White academic reviewers did not quite know what to make of the book, which wasn't scholarly history as they understood it. The black historian Nell Painter, who unlike Harding was an "integrated professional," noted this fact with some asperity, and said that black historians, on the contrary, were quite comfortable with Harding's approach. She saw no likelihood of a convergence of sensibilities in the near future.[25]

It would be difficult to find two more highly placed black historians than John Blassingame and Nathan Huggins, holders of the chairs in Afro-American history at Yale and Harvard, respectively. Unlike Harding, both Blassingame and Huggins had in the late sixties underlined their allegiance to traditional professional values. Both had spoken out against substituting myth for history, and for the maintenance of balance and objectivity in black scholarship. Ten or fifteen years later, when each wrote a major synthetic account of the black experience (in Blassingame's case in collaboration with Mary F. Berry), mainstream white historians were as much at a loss as they were in confronting Harding's work.

---

[24]From the late 1960s onward *Commentary*, the semiofficial house organ of neoconservatism, has carried more sustained criticism of the new black history, and more defenses of the "damage" thesis (and of Moynihan) than any other journal. Awareness of this may be one reason why those with opposing views have clung to them so tenaciously.
[25]Painter, "Who Decides What Is History?" 276–78.

Blassingame's *Long Memory*, a synthesis of three hundred years of black history, was a catalogue of white oppression and unavailing black protest, acknowledging neither nuance nor even change over time. Huggins's *Black Odyssey* was, he said, like Harding's book, conceived not in the ordinary academic mode, but as "epic": "the strokes are broad, antithesis muted or denied." Both books, he said, were written by blacks for blacks, in a distinctively black mood and idiom. Most white academic critics responded to Blassingame's and Huggins's works with the same nervous bewilderment with which they had greeted Harding's *There Is a River*: they "weren't history." Some younger black historians agreed; others vigorously dissented. The issue of the existence, and legitimacy, of a distinct, unassimilable "black perspective" on history was clearly going to be unresolved for some time to come.[26]

II

Women's history was at least as great a particularist threat to professional norms of universalism as black history, and there were striking parallels in the ways in which the two developed. Both had their origins in the rise of new forms of militancy and collective consciousness outside the academy, and, once launched, grew with extraordinary rapidity into major historical fields. Those involved in both ventures were torn between professional obligations and a commitment to serving the psychic and political needs of their external constituencies and movements. In both cases arguments for at least semiautonomous cultures, with distinctive values and institutions, were forcefully advanced. With women, as with blacks, these constructs proved more ambiguous in their political consequences than their authors had originally believed.

Unlike blacks, women had been members of the organized historical profession from the beginning. But in many respects they were almost as marginalized as blacks. Among other things, most leading woman historians had been employed at institutions for "their own kind." In a variety

[26]Huggins, "Integrating Afro-American History into American History," in Hine, *Afro-American History*, 164. One interesting feature of the book which Blassingame wrote with Berry is that while in his previous work he had acknowledged the scholarly assistance of both black and white historians, all of the dozen historians thanked in the preface of *Long Memory* were black. Other black historians moved in the opposite direction. Armstead Robinson, as a graduate student, had been a moving spirit behind the establishment of a separate Black Studies program at Yale in 1968. In the early 1980s he declined to be interviewed for Meier and Rudwick's *Black History* on the Franklinian grounds that he was not a specialist in black history, but a Civil War and Reconstruction historian. (Meier and Rudwick, *Black History*, 300.)

of ways women were kept at arm's length, but the imperatives of chivalry demanded that they be given recognition. From early on, women were accorded token representation on committees of the major historical associations (which didn't matter much). But, with the rarest exceptions, they were excluded from membership in major departments (which mattered a great deal). At the beginning of the sixties there were no women at all among the total of 160 full professors in the ten highest ranking graduate departments of history; 4 women among the 128 associate and assistant professors in those departments. At the end of that decade of unprecedented growth there were a total of 274 full professors in the ten departments, of whom 2 were women; of the by then 317 associate and assistant professors in the top departments, 5 were women.[27]

"Affirmative action" of various kinds, which many denounced as an unbearable affront to universalist and meritocratic norms, was undertaken to countervail a legacy of gender discrimination that was undeniable. The ends of affirmative action programs were universalist rather than particularist, intended to further integration rather than separatism. In the professional associations (which still didn't matter that much, and where concessions could be made without substantial cost), women went from tokenism to substantial overrepresentation. In 1985 a majority of the members of the executive board of the Organization of American Historians were women. In the elections for the leading positions in the American Historical Association in 1984, women won all six of the contests in which men were slated opposite women; in 1985 they won seven of nine such contests, including those for president and vice-president. By the mid-1980s, as a result of preferential treatment, women's representation on the programs of professional meetings was a good deal more than proportional. Encouraged by this fact, but distressed at the continued presence on the AHA program of a number of sessions in which all the participants were male, the chairperson of the AHA's Committee on Women in the Profession, advanced a suggestion which went beyond integrationism, and repudiated not just separatism, but pluralism as well. She suggested that it might be time for the AHA Council to "avoid approving sessions that are racially or gender segregated."[28]

[27]Calculations based on tables in summary of the report of the AHA's Ad Hoc Committee on the Status of Women in the Profession, *AHA Newsletter* 9 (September 1971): 20. Stated differently, at the beginning of the decade women held 1.397 percent of the most highly prized positions in the profession; at its end, 1.385 percent.

[28]The seven out of twelve members of the 1985 OAH executive board who were women included two of the past three presidents of the organization, whose principal permanent official was also a woman (Executive Secretary Joan Hoff-Wilson). For AHA election results, see *AHA Perspectives* 23 (January 1985): 3, and 24 (January 1986): 3. For repre-

Affirmative action in the 1970s scored victories in hiring as well, but met greater resistance, particularly at the most important institutions. Affirmative action programs had been designed with the dizzying growth of the sixties in mind. As one feminist journal put it, "Women Get a Ticket to Ride After the Gravy Train Has Left the Station." Overall, women's representation among the ranks of academically employed historians increased substantially, though disproportionately in temporary and part-time positions, and at lower-ranked institutions. By the end of the seventies, after a decade of effectively resisting pressure for affirmative action, the top ten departments had 5 (out of 294) women full professors, with a slight increase in women's representation in lower ranks. A tabulation of Ph.D.'s in American history from major universities showed women's share of new degrees rising dramatically, from 10 percent in 1970 to 30 percent in 1980. But this was an artifact of young men choosing not to enter academic life. The human reality behind the percentages was 30 women and 283 men in 1970; 29 women and 68 men in 1980.[29]

Women historians were by no means all historians of women, nor were they necessarily feminists. Most women historians of the older generation were neither, and in fact often opposed both feminism and the establishment of women's history as a separate field. In its late-twentieth-century embodiment, feminism was less a doctrine of equal rights—though it was that also—than of the liberation of consciousness; more an ideology of difference than of sameness. For feminists, while the particular forms which the oppression of women had assumed varied over time, and under different social systems, it was ubiquitous, from the boardroom to the

sentation of women on OAH and AHA programs, see "Assessing the Past, Looking to the Future: A Report by the OAH Committee on the Status of Women," special insert in *OAH Newsletter* 14 (May 1986): 4; Alice Kessler-Harris, "Annual Report of the Committee on Women Historians," *AHA Perspectives* 24 (February 1986): 9 (also the source of the suggestion on ending "segregated" sessions).

[29]Figures for women in top departments in 1979–80 from Joan W. Scott, "Politics and Professionalism: Women Historians in the 1980s," *Women's Studies Quarterly* 9 (Fall 1981): 25. Calculations of women's share of history doctorates in 1970 and 1980 based on figures in "Assessing the Past," 3. (For technical reasons, Harvard was not included among the four dozen institutions surveyed, but this omission could hardly have significantly skewed the overall picture.) The forty-eight history departments which turned out the largest number of Ph.D.'s in 1984–85 averaged 13 Americanists in their ranks. A majority had either one woman or none in this contingent; women's representation was usually less in the more highly ranked departments. (Ibid., 2.) Pressure to hire blacks was on the whole resisted less: there weren't that many available candidates; at most, they threatened a "takeover" of one small field, given that almost all specialized in black history; except in the South, black male historians were probably perceived as less of a threat to the folkways of the white male academic culture than were white women.

bedroom. Academic feminism thus insisted that gender was as central a category of analysis as race or class, and that any scholarly work which failed to give it due weight was fatally flawed. In history the feminist perspective was much more than a matter of including those who had been "hidden from history," but rather a transforming vision with revolutionary implications for the understanding of all human activities. Of particular relevance for our purposes, feminists consistently and repeatedly denounced the universalistic and "value-free" pretensions of traditional scholarship as masks for maintaining the domination of a male-centered world view. Their posture was avowedly perspectival, committed, and skeptical of objectivist claims. Moreover, for many feminists the ideology of "difference" extended to fundamental questions of cognitive style and epistemological values.

Since time immemorial the complaint of male historians about women colleagues had echoed that of Professor Henry Higgins in *My Fair Lady*: "Why can't a woman be more like a man?"—rigorous and objective, rather than intuitive and subjective. An especially favored female colleague would receive, with mixed emotions, the ultimate accolade: "She thinks like a man." That men and women had different cognitive styles was not simply locker room lore. A substantial body of psychological research suggested that, as a result of nature, nurture, or some combination of the two, boys were considerably more likely to think analytically, and display the kind of aggressive intellectual style associated with high-level intellectual productivity. Girls, wrote the psychologist Eleanor Maccoby, summarizing several studies, "tend to be more influenced by the opinions of others . . . are more conforming to what they perceive to be the social demands of the situation they are in."

It is probably these conformist tendencies that help them to excel at spelling and punctuation—the kinds of performance for which there is only one socially prescribed right answer. But for higher-level intellectual productivity, it is independence of mind that is required—the ability to turn one's back on others . . . while working alone on a problem—and it is just this which girls . . . appear to find so difficult to do.

There were, of course, women with a "male" cognitive style, but, Maccoby said, they paid a price for this in personal anxiety—which, in turn, interfered with intellectual productivity. Parents of girls thus faced a dilemma: did they want to encourage intellectuality at the price of "femininity"? Academic women had for the most part either ignored such findings, denounced them as wrongheaded, or argued that whatever disadvantages women suffered from in this realm could be overcome by an effort of will. On the whole, like Maccoby, they accepted "male cognitive style" as normative; they simply denied that it was necessarily "male."[30]

A later generation of feminists had a changed perspective. Embracing rather than rejecting "difference," feminist psychologists, philosophers, and historians of science explored, and transvalued, men's and women's thoughtways. Feminists employing D. J. Winnicott's object-relations theory argued that fundamental differences in the process by which male and females separated themselves from their mothers led to fundamentally different postures toward the external world, including, for scholars, the objects of study. In the words of the philosopher Sandra Harding:

A rational person, for women, values highly her abilities to empathize and "connect" with particular others and wants to learn more complex and satisfying ways to take the role of the particular other in relationships. . . . For men, in contrast, a rational person values highly his ability to separate himself from others and to make decisions independent of what others think—to develop "autonomy". . . . No wonder women's relational rationality appears to men immature, subhuman, and threatening. No wonder men's objectifying rationality appears to women alien, inhuman, and frightening.

Feminist historians of science traced modern conceptions of objectivity and rationality to the seventeenth-century scientific revolution, when scientists, breaking with previous conceptions of the relations between knower and known, framed inquiry in adversarial terms of domination and power: "squeezing the truth out of Dame Nature's anus." Evelyn Keller, in her study of the Nobel laureate Barbara McClintock emphasized the "holism" which characterized McClintock's work, which contrasted to prevailing reductionist approaches. It was unclear how much impact all of this had on women historians, but it certainly had its attractions, since the themes stressed in the literature on women's cognitive style—empathy, seeing globally and contextually—were precisely those often privileged in discussions of historical consciousness. And there were indications of a new willingness on the part of women historians to stress their gender in describing their modes of inquiry. Natalie Zemon Davis wrote of her "maternal" attitude to the past, "wanting to bring people to life again as a mother would want to bear children."[31]

[30]Maccoby, "Feminine Intellect and the Demands of Science," *Impact of Science on Society* 1 (1970): 17, 19, 24, 26–27.
[31]Harding, "Is Gender a Variable in Conceptions of Rationality? A Survey of Issues," *Dialectica* 36 (1982): 235–36; for "Dame Nature," see Ian Hacking, "Liberating the Laboratory," *New Republic* 193 (15–22 July 1985): 48; interview with Davis in *Visions of History* (New York, 1983), 113.

In principle, feminist perspectives in history were as relevant to such male activities as war and diplomacy as they were to realms in which women dominated. In practice, though there were repeated programmatic statements pressing this point, little such work was done. Feminist perspectives were not restricted to those women historians who wrote the history of women. But while among historians of women a deep feminist commitment was all but universal, among women in other areas it was usually neither as profound nor as widespread. One consequence of this was that the impact of feminist perspectives on history was more restricted in scope than it might otherwise have been, or might be in the future. The other side of this coin was that it was in women's history, which in practice was the feminist history of women, that the full force of the new antiuniversalist sensibility made itself felt. By the late 1970s the assertion that women's history could only be legitimately written from a feminist standpoint was no longer being argued; it was a settled question, beyond argument.

The very staking out of a distinct territory designated "women's history" constituted an antiuniversalist manifesto. So too was the rejection by most women historians of the integrationist strategy of "mainstreaming" women's history into general history courses and texts, scorned as a recipe to "add women and stir." Interdisciplinary programs in Women's Studies were neither as well-funded nor as administratively autonomous as Black Studies had been. When Black Studies programs had been established (before the gravy train left the station), the very word "black" was loaded with ideological significance. The designation "Women's Studies," rather than "Feminist Studies" was a bit disingenuous, probably representing, one feminist historian said, "an implicit recognition that expediency favors maintenance of a token of traditional academic 'objectivity.'" Whatever their connection with Women's Studies programs, historians of women were on history department budgets, and the nuances of their ambivalent relations to the male-dominated historical profession varied a good deal from case to case. But the frequency with which they chose to publish major work in interdiscplinary feminist journals, the patterns of their acknowledgments of scholarly assistance, and other informal indications, strongly suggested that for most, the feminist community was at least as salient a reference group as was the profession. Albeit with variations in nuance and emphasis, all feminist historians shared the belief that "sisterhood," a bond of solidarity and mutual support, was both historical reality and contemporary moral imperative.[32]

[32]Marilyn J. Boxer, "For and About Women: The Theory and Practice of Women's Studies in the United States," in Nannerl O. Keohane et al., eds., *Feminist Theory: A Critique of*

The major themes in black history were all present in women's history: overcoming historical neglect; stressing the contributions of the group; an emphasis on oppression, with its troublesome complement, victimization and damage; a search for foreparents in protest and resistance; finally, a celebration of an at least semiautonomous separate cultural realm, with distinctive values and institutions. In the case of black history a tradition had developed over many decades, and one can see a pattern of changing emphases. Women's history grew so rapidly that often-contradictory themes arose more or less simultaneously.[33]

Though many aspects of the black experience had been neglected by historians, by the time the new black history arrived on the scene the significance of the black presence in the United States was not in question. Women, half of the population, had hardly a walk-on role. Given the continuing focus in historical scholarship on male-dominated realms, it was perhaps unreasonable to expect equal time. But surely something was seriously amiss when twenty-four out of twenty-five leading American history texts published in the sixties and seventies devoted considerably less than 1 percent of their pages to women. "Contributionism" in black history peaked at a time when the consensual orientation was integrationist. Negro historians experienced no inner conflict in documenting black contributions to white society. By the time historians of women arrived on the scene, and sought to "make the invisible woman visible," a feminist sensibility had developed which resisted accepting male-centered definitions of importance and excellence: they were often deeply ambiva-

---

Ideology (Chicago, 1982), 240. No generalization about the way in which feminist historians balanced the competing claims of professionalism and sisterhood can be more than impressionistic. Certainly formal avowals cannot be taken at face value, since working inside the profession to advance the cause of women mandated one posture, while continued participation in the discourse of women's history dictated another. Though I have stressed the particularist claims of sisterhood, there were many historians of women— particularly those who also thought of themselves as social historians, or historians of the family—for whom loyalty to the profession was of equal or greater importance. Because there were so few men in women's history one rarely heard claims for an exclusive franchise, but the work of men sometimes received a cool reception. One woman historian speculated about the extent to which "the rather inordinate interest of male scholars in the history of women's sexuality serves to provide them with titillating reading material and reinforce phallocentric views of women's nature." (Hilda Smith, "Female Bonds and the Family: Recent Directions in Women's History," in Paula A. Treichler et al., eds., *For Alma Mater: Theory and Practice in Feminist Scholarship* [Urbana, Ill., 1985], 284.)

[33] No field of historical inquiry had ever grown as rapidly. A survey of the incidence of articles about women in the major journals of five academic disciplines showed an overall increase from 2 percent of all articles in 1966 to 7 percent in 1980. During the same period articles in historical journals about women went from half of 1 percent to just under 12 percent. (Ellen Carol DuBois et al., *Feminist Scholarship* (Urbana, Ill., 1985), 164–69.)

lent about writing a "compensatory" story of women's contributions
which tacitly accepted a male framework.[34]

There were other problems with a contributionist, or compensatory
orientation. Pressed too far, it tacitly minimized the extent to which
women had been excluded from full participation in society. Much contributionist work was also the history of resistance; celebration of those
"women worthies" who had led campaigns for suffrage, women's trade-
union struggles, and the like. But this theme too presented difficulties,
since many late-twentieth-century feminists were convinced that those
who in earlier days had led political and economic struggles on behalf of
women had been victims of "false consciousness": they had been naive in
their belief that women's cause could be pursued in alliance with men,
and they had failed to realize that the prime locus of their oppression was
in the patriarchal family. One result was that like some discussions of
nineteenth-century black leadership by black nationalist historians, historical treatments of past women leaders were sometimes condescending
toward those whose concerns were not what the historians thought they
ought to have been.

Before the new black history made its appearance in the sixties, a
previous generation had not only documented the pervasiveness of racism
and discrimination, but exposed the prejudices which informed earlier
scholarly work. By the sixties almost all white historians readily acknowledged the depth of past and present oppression of blacks, and were
at least formally committed to racial equality. This was neither difficult
nor threatening to white male academics, particularly outside the South.
The forms of discrimination had been public and palpable, and in any
case, whatever prejudices whites had toward blacks, they usually didn't
have more than casual contact with them. They had little opportunity to
practice discrimination or interest in doing so. Men's association with
women was daily and often intimate. The forms of oppression were for
the most part subtle and generally unacknowledged—sometimes, at least
on a conscious level, even by its victims. For men to confront the manifold dimensions of their own discriminatory attitudes and behaviors was
as difficult and threatening a demand as could be conceived. Some,

---

[34]Calculations based on figures in Dolores Barracano Schmidt and Earl Robert Schmidt,
"The Invisible Woman: The Historian as Professional Magician," in Berenice A. Carroll,
ed., *Liberating Women's History* (Urbana, Ill., 1976), 45–48. I have not independently
verified the figures on pages devoted to women. Since the article was written for polemical
purposes, I suspect that borderline cases did not get the benefit of the doubt, and in any
case, this is a crude measure. But even if one doubled the pages which Schmidt and
Schmidt say were devoted to women, eighteen of the twenty-five texts would still score
under 1 percent.

mostly of a younger generation, made a concerted effort; most did it halfheartedly, or not at all. And most male historians' commitment to gender equality was ambivalent at best. As of 1969, when William O'Neill published his *Everyone Was Brave: A History of Feminism in America*, it was inconceivable that an historian would write of blacks as O'Neill did of women, in his preface: "I have avoided the question of whether or not women ought to have full parity with men. . . . Since we do not know what genuine equality would mean in practice, its desirability cannot fairly be assessed."[35]

Documenting the range of ways in which women had been oppressed, and even forcing acknowledgment of women's existence on the profession, was a necessary item on the women's history agenda of the seventies. But the very fact of having to undertake such a rudimentary task was demeaning. When, as it inevitably did, the effort revealed the depth of male-centeredness, complacency, and even misogyny in the existing historical literature, the result was often further alienation of feminists from the profession. The documentation of oppression, particularly in domestic life, was an emotionally charged activity in other ways. A white historian of slavery might have a more difficult time than a black historian in achieving psychic identification with a slave, but even the black historian was more than a century removed in time, and light years in social circumstances, from the institutions of chattel slavery. Black scholars had to make almost as great an imaginative leap as whites. A woman historian of oppression within the patriarchal family had usually been raised in one. More often than not her own domestic arrangements carried daily reminders of the price traditional arrangements exacted. The focus on modes of male domination which had changed relatively little over time made its historical study a very "undetached" exercise. Insofar as many women historians had only recently come to the perception of their collaboration in their own victimization, the subject had an even greater charge. It was this sort of thing which accounted for the tone of much writing in women's history—for example, the common employment of the evocative "phallocentric" in place of the scientistic "androcentric" as a general term for a male-oriented outlook.

The move from a focus on women's oppression to women's culture was on the whole a response to the same considerations which operated in black history. In Gerda Lerner's words, an emphasis on oppression "makes it appear either that women were largely passive or that, at the most, they reacted to male pressures or to the restraints of patriarchal

---

[35]*Everyone Was Brave* (Chicago, 1969), viii.

society." As in the black case, an antireductionist argument could turn into a tacit reductionism of another kind. To treat women "only" as victims of oppression was not just a very partial view, but "once again places them in a male-defined conceptual framework: oppressed, victimized by standards and values established by men." Which was fair enough, but it was hardly less reductionist to argue, as Lerner and other feminist historians did, that the "true" history of women was the story of "their ongoing functioning in that male-defined world *on their own terms.*" One reason for shifting the focus from victimization to women's autonomous activity was stated frankly by Carroll Smith-Rosenberg, who said that she had gradually realized that emphasizing male oppression of women had turned her into an "historian of men," when she wanted to be an historian of women.[36]

There were various ways in which feminist historians effected the transition from an historiography which stressed women's subordination and victimization to one which emphasized their agency and autonomy. Probably the most important, and certainly the most imaginative, was the reconceptualization of the history of middle-class women in nineteenth-century America. The "cult of true womanhood," which arose early in the century, had defined women as pure and submissive. It was the ideological justification for their restriction to a largely domestic "women's sphere." But, feminist historians argued, women had not experienced this ghettoization as victims. Rather, within that sphere, they had created a "rich and empowering culture of women." The "women's sphere," it was maintained, was the seedbed of organized political feminism. To alter the metaphor, friendship and support networks became "crucibles in which collective acts of rebellion were formed."[37]

But the theme of resistance, at least political resistance, was less central to the new work than insistence on the autonomy of the woman's world, that women's values were distinctive and not to be assimilated to those of men. The most original, provocative, and sophisticated work in this area was by Smith-Rosenberg, who argued for the existence of a nineteenth-century female world "in which men made only a shadowy appearance"; a world filled with female rituals "so secret that men had little knowledge of them, so pervasive that they patterned women's lives from birth to

[36]Lerner, "Placing Women in History" (1975), in *The Majority Finds Its Past* (New York, 1979), 147–48; Smith-Rosenberg, in "Politics and Culture in Women's History: A Symposium," *Feminist Studies* 6 (1980): 61.
[37]DuBois, *Feminist Scholarship*, 56; Rayna Rapp et al., "Examining Family History," in Judith L. Newton et al., eds., *Sex and Class in Women's History* (London, 1983), 244.

death." Smith-Rosenberg was explicit about the "explosive" political implications of her work:

If we assert that nineteenth-century women in particular, and perhaps all women, constitute an autonomous female culture, we assert that women's separate sphere and experiences are the product, not of men's ghettoization of women, but of women's distinctive psychosexual and biological nature. We then unambiguously proclaim women's absolute Otherness.

A number of historians of women argued that it was precisely the decay of a separate women's world which accounted for the decline of feminism in the early twentieth century, and that a revival of separatism had energized the women's movement in the sixties and seventies.[38]

The concentration on autonomous women's culture was not accepted by all feminist historians. Those with a continuing left commitment, entailing solidarity with male comrades, were more likely than others to question both its historiographical and contemporary-strategic implications. Socialist-feminists also shared in the general uneasiness on the left concerning the new social history's concentration on the private realm. Elizabeth Fox-Genovese acknowledged that work which treated women as "the Other" had, "at its most rich and complex . . . taught us much." But she saw it as "capitulat[ion] to official history's insistence upon the universal claims of female biology." It did not, she said, necessarily challenge mainstream history, "or rather, it poses a challenge so extreme as to make interchange next to impossible." But it was work which emphasized women's autonomy and a distinctive women's culture which dominated the field. When that orientation was joined to the consensual insistence on bringing an explicitly feminist orientation to bear on problems past and present, the generally separatist implications of most feminist history were clear enough.[39]

The logical conclusion of militant black separatism was political nationalism, involving emigration, or at least total withdrawal from white society. More realistically, a kind of moral and cultural emigration was called for. Such a prospect was in truth not at all disturbing to most whites, for whom the black presence was troubling, and black absence welcomed. The logical conclusion of separatist feminism was lesbianism. Smith-Rosenberg, and she was by no means alone in this, made explicit

[38]Smith-Rosenberg, "Hearing Women's Words: A Feminist Reconstruction of History," in her *Disorderly Conduct: Visions of Gender in Victorian America* (New York, 1985), 28, 41.
[39]Fox-Genovese, "Placing Women's History in History," *New Left Review* 133 (1982): 14.

the homoerotic dimension of the bonds of sisterhood which she celebrated. She somewhat tentatively endorsed the view that heterosexuality
was "an artificial construct imposed upon humanity." The Stanford historian Estelle Freedman embraced not just a separatist historiographical
orientation, and a separatist strategy for the present, but said that the
history of separatism "helps explain why the politics of lesbian feminism
have been so important in the revival of the women's movement."

Lesbian feminism, by affirming the primacy of women's relationships with each
other and by providing an alternative feminist culture, forced many nonlesbians
to reevaluate their relationships with men, male institutions, and male values. In
the process, feminists have put to rest the myth of female dependence on men and
rediscovered the significance of woman bonding. I find it personally gratifying
that the lesbian feminist concept of the woman-identified woman has historical
roots in the female friendships, networks, and institutions of the nineteenth
century. The historical sisterhood . . . can teach us a great deal about putting
women first, whether as friends, lovers, or political allies.

While only a minority of feminist historians were or became lesbians, a
much larger number were inclined to agree that heterosexuality was to
some substantial extent a male-imposed construct. A common response
was a kind of political or cultural lesbianism. Lesbians were honored as
serious feminists, much as Jews accorded special respect to those who
demonstrated the depth of their Zionism by emigrating to Israel. Even if
women did not physically separate themselves from men—and many, in
various ways, did—a kind of moral separatism was fairly widespread. All
of this was a good deal more threatening to academic life, and the domestic life of male academics, than black separatism had been.[40]

Many of the central issues in women's history came together dramatically in the mid-1980s in the case of *Equal Employment Opportunity
Commission v. Sears, Roebuck, & Co.* The EEOC, in seeking to prove
that Sears had discriminated against women with respect to jobs in commission sales, presented evidence concerning the company's procedures
for selecting such personnel, and alleged inadequacies in its affirmative
action program. But the centerpiece of its case was the undisputed statistical underrepresentation of women among those members of the total
Sears sales force who held the better-paying commission positions. The
heart of Sears' defense was that one could only infer discrimination from
this statistical pattern on the assumption that women were equally inter-

---

[40]Smith-Rosenberg, "Hearing Women's Words," 32; Freedman, "Separatism as Strategy:
Female Institution Building and American Feminism, 1870–1930," *Feminist Studies* 5
(1979): 524–25.

ested in commission sales positions, which, Sears claimed, they were not. Many women, Sears maintained, "fear or dislike . . . the competitive, 'dog-eat-dog' atmosphere of most commission sales divisions"; feared nonacceptance by customers in selling such traditionally "male" items as hardware and automotive supplies; and disliked the high-pressure sales techniques associated with commission selling. Overall, Sears said, "the crux of the issue" was "the reasonableness of the EEOC's a priori assumptions of male/female sameness with respect to preferences, interests, and qualifications."[41]

Opinions and testimony to this effect offered by Sears managers were, if not tainted, at least suspect. One member of the legal team representing Sears, having been formerly married to an historian of women, was aware that much recent scholarship in women's history tended to support Sears' contentions that women's values and interests could not be assumed to be the same as men's, and in the end it was his ex-wife, Rosalind Rosenberg of Barnard, who became Sears' expert witness. In her previous academic work Rosenberg had been skeptical of arguments for a distinctive "women's culture," but in her testimony she was able to draw on a body of recent historical literature which differentiated women's values and interests from those of men.

The EEOC's statistician, she told the court, "assumes that given equal opportunity women will make the same choices that a man would make. . . . That assumption is based on a traditionally male model of how people behave in the universe, that . . . the most important thing is economic maximation." Women, rather more than men, she said, "have goals and values other than realizing maximum economic gain . . . values shaped in earlier eras." Women were "more interested than men in the cooperative, social aspects of the work situation." Many women shared the view that for them work should be subordinated to family obligations, and chose jobs that complemented those obligations over jobs that offered increased earnings. "The overwhelming weight of modern scholarship in women's history," Rosenberg said, "supports the view that disparities in the sexual composition of an employer's workforce . . . are consistent with an absence of discrimination on the part of the employer."

I myself might prefer a world in which as many women as men placed career ahead of family, in which as many women as men were ready, willing, and able to sell furnaces . . . but that is not our world today. I have tried to show that nothing

[41]"Post-Trial Brief of Sears, Roebuck and Co.," 9, 11–12; "Trial Brief of Sears, Roebuck and Co.," 21; in *EEOC v. Sears*, Civil Action No. 79–C–4373, U.S. District Court for the Northern District of Illinois, Eastern Division, 9, 11–13, quoted in Ruth Milkman, "Women's History and the Sears Case," *Feminist Studies* 12 (1986): 383–84.

about our history, and nothing in the best recent scholarship about women in our history, would lead one to expect otherwise.[42]

On the narrow point at issue Rosenberg had no difficulty making an effective case. A much more difficult task faced Alice Kessler-Harris, chosen by the EEOC to rebut Rosenberg. And her job was not made easier by the fact that Rosenberg had been able to cite Kessler-Harris's *Out to Work: A History of Wage-Earning Women in the United States* on behalf of Sears' argument that women's own attitudes were an important factor limiting their full and equal participation in the work force. Married women's failure to take jobs during the Great Depression, Kessler-Harris had written, was a result of "ideological constraints that continued to operate even in this period of crisis." Until quite recently, she had said in her book, "the ideology of the home still successfully contained most women's aspirations." Elsewhere Kessler-Harris had expressed the view that women "harbor values, attitudes, and behavior patterns potentially subversive to capitalism," an assertion that Rosenberg, in surrebuttal, found "at odds with her testimony . . . that women are as likely as men to want Sears' most highly competitive jobs, those in commission sales."[43]

Embarrassed at having her own work used against her, Kessler-Harris tried to talk around the narrowly posed question, and to advance broader arguments, but the format defeated her. She found herself offering testimony in which, as she later acknowledged, "subtlety and nuance were omitted . . . complexities and exceptions vanished from sight." It was, in fact, a bit worse than that. The rules of the game were such that Rosenberg had only been required to show that women's values and attitudes played some role in their choice of jobs; Kessler-Harris was required to assert that they played no role. In an impossible situation Kessler-Harris advanced impossible arguments. "Where opportunity has existed," she told the court, "women have never [*sic*] failed to take the jobs offered. . . . Failure to find women in so-called non-traditional jobs can thus only [*sic*] be interpreted as a consequence of employer's unexamined attitudes or preferences, which phenomenon is the essence of discrimination."[44]

[42]Trial Transcript, 10357–58 (11 March 1985); "Offer of Proof Concerning the Testimony of Dr. Rosalind Rosenberg," pars. 1–2, 19; "Written Rebuttal Testimony of Dr. Rosalind Rosenberg" (June 1985), pars. 1, 16; all quoted in Milkman, "Sears Case," 385–88.
[43]*Out to Work* (Oxford, 1982), 259, 296, 311; Kessler-Harris, "American Women and the American Character: A Feminist Perspective," in John Hague, ed., *American Character and Culture* (Westport, Conn., 1979), 228; Rosenberg, letter to *Chronicle of Higher Education* 32 (2 July 1986): 22.
[44]Kessler-Harris, "Equal Employment Opportunity Commission v. Sears, Roebuck and Company: A Personal Account," *Radical History Review* 35 (1986): 74; "Written Testimony of Alice Kessler-Harris" (June 1985), pars. 6, 13, quoted in Milkman, "Sears Case," 376.

The outcome was hardly in doubt, not because of the relative skill of the historical witnesses, and not even for reasons having much to do with whether Sears did in fact discriminate, but because the EEOC had so structured its argument that an historian much less adept than Rosenberg could have knocked it over. No historian could have done much more than Kessler-Harris to defend that argument against assault. The judge's verdict (there was no jury) was delivered in January 1986. He found the EEOC's statistical argument fatally flawed, primarily because of its assumption that there were no differences in women's interests and values which could account for their underrepresentation among commission sales personnel. The judge described Rosenberg as "a highly credible witness . . . offer[ing] reasonable, well-supported opinions." His verdict cited the view of Rosenberg and another Sears witness that "women tend to see themselves as less competitive." Neither, he said, contended "that all women have these tendencies or preferences, and the court has not drawn any such inference from their testimony. They have merely attempted to describe the overall tendencies of many women." The testimony of Kessler-Harris, he said, "focus[ed] on small groups of unusual women and their demonstrated abilities in various historical contexts, not on the majority of women or their interests."

For example, Dr. Kessler-Harris testified about the experience of women during both World Wars, who took jobs such as welders, shipfitters, and crane operators, as well as similar experiences of other women in unusual circumstances throughout history. It is *not* an issue in this case that *some* women are both capable and interested in holding commission sales jobs in traditional male product areas, such as automotive, plumbing, furnaces and fencing. This is obviously true. The real question is what percentage of women versus men . . . at Sears stores during 1973 to 1980, were capable and interested.[45]

Various conclusions were drawn from the trial. To Jonathan Wiener the case demonstrated what left-feminists had argued all along, that "arguments about distinctive female values play into the hands of conservatives." For Kathryn Kish Sklar the case illustrated the dilemma of contemporary feminism: "When we admit difference, it goes overwhelmingly against women. On the other hand, to deny difference may also prove futile. I lament the way this case has shown that admitting difference is a negative thing." Another feminist thought that at a minimum the lesson of the Sears case was that

We ignore the political dimensions of the equality-versus-difference debate at our peril, especially in a period of conservative resurgence like the present. . . .

[45]628 F. Supp. 1264 (N.D. Ill. 1986), 1308, 1314.

Feminist scholars must be aware of the real danger that arguments about "difference" or "women's culture" will be put to uses other than those for which they
were originally developed.[46]

For some the case was a scholarly morality play, showing, in Thomas
Haskell's words, that "justice is better served by truth than zealotry."
Carl Degler thought the controversy surrounding the case would harm
women's history by "mak[ing] it seem simply a polemical subject and not
. . . a real field of scholarly inquiry." Rosenberg, in this view, emerged as
the spokesperson for the disinterested historical truth, in all its sometimes
painful complexity. But neither of the two opposing expert witnesses was
"disinterested." Neither had taken a "tell the truth though the heavens
fall" posture. Both decided to testify based on their respective evaluations
of the political consequences of the verdict. And their decisions to testify
were also based on a priori beliefs about Sears' guilt or innocence which
in neither instance seemed very well grounded.[47]

For Kessler-Harris, "the success of Sears' lawyers would undermine
two decades of affirmative action efforts and exercise a chilling effect on
women's history as a whole. . . . The potential consequences were terrify-
ing." It does not seem an exaggeration to say that for Kessler-Harris,
Sears was guilty until proven innocent, inherently complicit in the discrimination endemic to the capitalist system. Sears was, in her words, "at
best, a potentially discriminatory employer." "Why not," she asked,
"give women, rather than employers, the benefit of the doubt?" She
invoked an avowedly instrumentalist criterion in choosing what explanation of disparity to adopt. After the trial, tacitly retreating from the
position she had taken on the witness stand, she said that the real question
was

not whether discrimination is the *only* explanation, but whether it is . . . the best,
most appropriate explanation for statistical disparities? . . . The point is that, in a
case that is about discrimination, to argue that discrimination was not the likely
explanation is to lend one's expertise to the argument that other explanations are
more plausible.[48]

[46]Wiener, "Women's History on Trial," *Nation* 241 (1985): 180; Sklar, quoted in Carol
Sternhell, "Life in the Mainstream: What Happens When Feminists Turn Up on Both
Sides of the Courtroom," *Ms.* 15 (July 1986): 89; Milkman, "Sears Case," 394.
[47]Haskell, letter to *The Nation* 241 (1985): 410; Degler quoted in Sternhell, "Mainstream,"
88.
[48]Kessler-Harris, "Personal Account," 75, 59, 71; Kessler-Harris, quoted in Sternhell, 51;
"Personal Account," 63. Kessler-Harris's criterion of the "best" or "most appropriate"
explanation was exactly that which R. G. Collingwood explicated as the sensible principle
of selecting relevant causes in practical life: the cause that we can do something about. (See
An Essay on Metaphysics [1940; reprinted Chicago, 1971], 302–12.)

Rosenberg's critique of the inferences drawn by the EEOC statistician would have been equally cogent whether or not Sears had discriminated, but she repeatedly insisted that her decision to testify for Sears was based on her certainty that Sears had not discriminated. Her grounds for this belief were no less a prioristic than Kessler-Harris's opposing conviction. One was the absence of complainants. "I said in the beginning, 'If there's ever a complainant in this case, I'm not going to testify, which strikes me in retrospect as a little bit crazy . . . but for me, symbolically, the absence of complainants was critical." The absence of complainants at the trial was, however, purely a function of the EEOC's self-defeating strategy of sole reliance on statistical evidence. Her confidence in Sears' innocence was, she said, furthered by the fact that they were represented by the law firm of Chuck Morgan, whom she had respected for many years as a civil rights lawyer. (Which seems equivalent to inferring the innocence of Loeb and Leopold from the fact that they were defended by Clarence Darrow.) The overall thrust of Rosenberg's testimony tended to undermine the plausibility of her belief that Sears had not discriminated. As she pointed out, there were very substantial historical and cultural influences which probably led many women to conclude, against their self-interest, that commission selling was inappropriate for women. Was it less probable that many of the thousands of male Sears middle managers shared these views, which were in their self-interest, and that these historically determined cultural stereotypes influenced their selection decisions? And, like Kessler-Harris, Rosenberg based her decision to testify on a calculation about what would aid the cause of women. In her view a victory for the EEOC would have discouraged other companies from enacting good-faith affirmative action programs.[49]

The problems of feminist historians in the courtroom were not theirs alone. When committed scholars enter the legal arena, they uphold the highest academic standards when circumstances allow; when circumstances don't, they fudge. Until the Sears case the best known example of historians' involvement in the legal process was in *Brown v. Board of Education*. The Supreme Court asked the attorneys for both sides to address the question of the "intentions of the framers"; whether those who proposed and ratified the Fourteenth Amendment had intended to outlaw school segregation. Henry Steele Commager, when approached by the NAACP, told them to drop the point, since the unhelpful answer to the Court's question was "no." John Hope Franklin, Vann Woodward, and Alfred Kelly were among those who helped the NAACP

[49]Rosenberg, quoted in Milkman, "Sears Case," 392–93.

respond. The principal contribution of the historians involved was to devise ways of evading a direct answer to the question. Kelly recalled:

The problem we faced was not the historian's discovery of the truth, the whole truth and nothing but the truth. . . . It is not that we were engaged in formulating lies; there was nothing as crude and naive as that. But we were using facts, emphasizing facts, bearing down on facts, sliding off facts, quietly ignoring facts, and above all, interpreting facts in a way to do what Marshall said we had to do— "get by those boys down there."

In *Brown v. Board of Education*, unlike in *EEOC v. Sears*, obfuscation was precisely what the Court desired, it having already determined, on other grounds, to decide for the plaintiff, even if the historical evidence went the other way. By the highest standards of academic rectitude, Franklin et al. were no doubt in scholarly honor bound to submit an *amicus curiae* brief which cut through the NAACP's evasions. They should have informed the Court that if it wished to interpret the Fourteenth Amendment according to the framers' intentions, segregation must remain.[50]

What most disturbed feminist historians was what they regarded as the apostasy of one of their number. Rosenberg had not been the first historian of women approached by Sears. When Kathryn Kish Sklar was asked to testify, she told Sears that "they were wasting their time. There was no way . . . that I was going to testify against the EEOC in this case. I didn't feel I could testify against the individual rights of women to equal employment opportunity." Carl Degler also turned down Sears, a decision he originally described as based on his reluctance to "us[e] historical evidence as a justification for limiting opportunities," but which he later characterized as stemming "partly from simple laziness, partly from cowardice, partly because I didn't care to compromise my feminist bona fides."[51]

Hostility to Rosenberg was no doubt exacerbated by the fact that the case took place in the wake of the defeat of the Equal Rights Amendment, and in a general climate of feminist retreat. Ellen DuBois termed Rosen-

[50]Kelly, "When the Supreme Court Ordered Desegregation," *U.S. News and World Report*, 5 February 1962, 88. (Kelly's reference is to then NAACP legal director, later Supreme Court justice, Thurgood Marshall.) See also Richard Kluger, *Simple Justice* (New York, 1977), chap. 24. In *Brown*, of course, the historians were not testifying, but preparing in-house memoranda for the lawyers. Therefore, they did not publicly assume individual responsibility for the use to which their labors were put. They were not cross-examined on the cogency or relevance of their arguments.

[51]Sklar, quoted in Sternhell, "Mainstream," 86–87; Degler's first explanation quoted in Wiener, "Women's History on Trial," 179; second explanation in Sternhell, "Mainstream," 88.

berg's testimony "an attack on working women and sexual equality." Women historians, she said, "have an obligation to remain honest to our feminist origins by, at the very least, ensuring that our scholarship is not used for an anti-feminist purpose." Renate Bridenthal reported that most people were appalled that Rosenberg "put her skills in the service of a company when we mostly identify with the position of women workers and the Women's Movement."

Some people think she was misguided, that she made a mistake. Others think it was more than that, that she was stupid or evil. Personally, I can't believe anyone could be so stupid. I'm more inclined to believe she was defending a class interest as she understood it.

Sandi Cooper wrote that Rosenberg had acted immorally in "us[ing] the labors of other scholars . . . to demonstrate the validity of second-class status for women." Kessler-Harris said that "the issue is purely this":

You would not lie in your testimony, but you also would not say or write something as a historian solely to hurt a group of people. . . . [Rosenberg] was prepared to testify that other women—working class women, poor women, non-white women—had not wanted well-paying jobs, and would not willingly make the kinds of compromises she herself had made in order to succeed at them. What was to be gained by such testimony?[52]

At a meeting of over 150 feminist scholars at Columbia University's Women and Society Seminar in December 1985, where the case was discussed, Rosenberg had not a single defender. Later that month the Coordinating Committee of Women in the Historical Profession passed a resolution which avoided mentioning Rosenberg by name, but which expressed the belief that "we have a responsibility not to allow our scholarship to be used against the interests of women struggling for equity in our society." A few women historians deplored the acrimony of the controversy. Some privately criticized Kessler-Harris's testimony; and there were no doubt those who expressed their ambivalence through

---

[52]DuBois, quoted in Wiener, "Women's History on Trial," 179, and in Karen J. Winkler, "Two Scholars' Conflict in Sears Sex-Bias Case Sets Off War in Women's History," *Chronicle of Higher Education* 31 (5 February 1986): 8; Bridenthal, quoted in Sternhell, "Mainstream," 48–49; Sandi Cooper's reference to Rosenberg's testimony as "an immoral act" appeared in a circular letter, cited in Sternhell, ibid., 88; Cooper's quoted remarks in her "Women's History on Trial," *Conference Group on Women's History Newsletter* 16 (October 1985): 6; Kessler-Harris's first two sentences quoted in Samuel G. Freedman, "Of History and Politics: Bitter Feminist Debate," *New York Times*, 6 June 1986, B1, B4; second two sentences from her "Personal Account," 59.

silence. The only historians to publicly support Rosenberg were two males, Degler and Haskell.[53]

Feminist historians were members of both the community of feminists and the community of historians, with all of the potential for conflicting loyalties that such dual citizenship entails. Of all the illusions in which we seek refuge, none is more pathetic than that which holds out the prospect of satisfactorily resolving irreconcilable claims. In such circumstances, we cannot steer between, but rather ricochet off, the rocks on either side of the channel, inevitably getting a bit bruised in the process. In the Sears case Rosenberg's feminist credentials and Kessler-Harris's scholarly credibility were each bruised, though not, one hopes, irreparably. So long as dual citizenship continues, and there is no reason to believe that it will not, conflicts of this kind will recur.

III

As a result of their commitment to provide a usable past for their respective constituencies, black and feminist historians in the academy had introduced into historiography strong particularist currents which contradicted the universalist ethos of scholarship. But though their external commitments were often deeply felt, their work, cast in an academic idiom, and appearing in academic media, rarely reached a lay audience. Virtually all of them were firmly embedded in a culture of academic professionalism. Their avowedly perspectival and particularist sensibilities implicitly challenged universalist norms, but their institutional location, and socialization into institutional values, constrained how far they could push that challenge. In a separate development, a movement arose within the historical profession which not only directly assaulted universalist assumptions, but sought to institutionalize particularism,

---

[53]Report on Columbia Seminar and CCWHP resolution in Milkman, "Sears Case," 391–92; for Degler and Haskell, see above, note 47. The issues in *EEOC v. Sears* resembled those in the Moynihan Report controversy. Rosenberg was arguing that active, current discrimination, and the absence of formal opportunity, was not an adequate explanation of women's disadvantaged state—that historically conditioned cultural factors needed to be taken into account. This was approximately the point Moynihan had been making with respect to ghetto blacks, and which brought down on his head the wrath of historians of blacks, as Rosenberg's testimony made her anathema to historians of women. There were the same charges that history was being used to divert attention from contemporary discrimination: "History should never have been in that courtroom," Kessler-Harris said. There was even identical rhetoric: Kessler-Harris called Rosenberg's testimony "a classic example of blaming the victim." (Kessler-Harris, quoted in Sternhell, "Mainstream," 91; Kessler-Harris, "Personal Account," 70.)

calling into question not only standard notions of objectivity, but traditional conceptions of "historical professionalism" as well.

We have seen how, at the turn of the century, the professionalization of history and the establishment of norms of objectivity were intimately linked, each process reinforcing the other. A national historical profession would transcend provincialism and particularism. Amateurs who adjusted their findings to the tastes and values of their audience would be displaced by professionals loyal only to objective truth; in an academic environment historians would be insulated from outside pressures. Thus objectivity as individual moral aspiration would be reinforced by powerful social and institutional buttresses.

At the center of the ideal of professionalism, and with obvious relevance to the way in which professionalism furthered objectivity, was "professional autonomy." The ideal-typical professional was an individual practitioner to whom clients deferred. The professional's livelihood was held to depend not upon satisfying any particular client, but rather was a consequence of upholding universalistic professional standards which the laity as a whole would honor. At the core of traditional definitions of professionalism was the proposition that while a client could engage the services of a professional, it was the professional, and not the client, who determined how the services were rendered: what pill to prescribe, what motion to file.

Not all professions had their origins in independent practice, and in the course of the twentieth century even members of "free professions," like doctors and lawyers, were increasingly becoming salaried employees. But as the de facto autonomy of other professionals declined, that of academics rose. They, too, were employees of large bureaucratic organizations, but the university as employer had less and less control over academics' work. How much one taught might be decided by employers, but hardly ever what took place in the classroom. In the case of scholarly writing, university administrations might establish quantitative guidelines for tenure or promotion, but judgments of content were delegated to members of the discipline involved. While scholars' increasing autonomy from institutional pressure could hardly guarantee objectivity, that autonomy was generally seen as one of its principal social preconditions.

By no means all of those in traditional academic disciplines were to be found on campuses. A substantial proportion of all natural scientists were employed by government or industry. In the social sciences, psychologists might work for the penal system or attempt to manipulate the consciousness of an industry's work force; sociologists were employed in marketing or in welfare administration; economists plied their trade at various levels of government and business. Even when members of these disciplines retained regular academic affiliations, they were often engaged in consulting or part-time work for government and industry. From the beginning these external connections had raised difficult questions of objectivity—and of professional ethics. History was in this regard among the least worldly of disciplines. Almost all professional historians were employed within the academy. When Mary O. Furner wrote a book on the tension between "advocacy and objectivity" among professionalizing social scientists at the turn of the century, she excluded historians from her study on the grounds that unlike other social scientists their professional practice was confined to the campus. Black and feminist historians in the academy often experienced the pull of external loyalties which competed with scholarly norms of detachment and objectivity. But the strength of the pull was reduced by the very fact that it was external—at some distance from the universalist standards and values of their immediate environment.[54]

After the onset of the academic job crisis of the seventies increasing numbers of historians found off-campus employment in what came to be called "public history," an omnibus designation covering a range of activities whose only common feature was that they were conducted outside university precincts. Each of the modes of public history, though each in different ways, raised the objectivity question. In the aggregate, the public history phenomenon produced calls for a reexamination, redefinition, and reevaluation of the very idea of historical professionalism.

One wing of public history was indeed "public," though "popular" is probably a more accurate term. Hundreds of young historians, who in a better job market would have secured teaching positions, went to work for local historical societies and museums, infusing new energy into what had previously been a somnolent realm. Others were employed in oral history projects, historical film-making, and other activities aimed at gathering and presenting historical materials in nontraditional ways. There was often a populist aura to work of this kind: "history of, by, and for the people." A number of historians in this field saw themselves less as authoritative experts than as "facilitators," helping every group to be its own historian. Sometimes, wrote one young member of the movement, who explicitly invoked Becker's authority, "this merely means helping to bring to the front the information, understanding, and consciousness that is already there."

[54]Furner, *Advocacy and Objectivity: A Crisis in the Professionalization of American Social Science, 1865–1905* (Lexington, Ky., 1975), xii-xiii.

More often it means a much more painstaking process of confronting old interpretations, removing layer upon layer of ideology and obfuscation. . . . [Public
history] promises us a society in which a broad public participates in the construction of its own history. . . . It seems to answer the question of whose public?
whose history? with a democratic declaration of a faith in members of the public
at large to become their own historians and to advance their knowledge of
themselves.[55]

But much of what went under the name of "public history" was in fact
"private history," historical work in the service of government agencies,
businesses, or other organizations with very particularist agendas inconsistent with universalist norms of disinterested objectivity. Some so-
called applied history was concerned with policy analysis—producing
reports, exclusively for in-house circulation, which advised on the lessons
of the past for current policymaking. Other historians were employed in
straightforward advocacy. When working in the area of historic preservation they mustered evidence to demonstrate, on behalf of a client, that a
given building was or was not deserving of landmark status. They argued
the historic rights of this or that Indian tribe to disputed lands. In water-
rights cases they sought to establish that at some point in the past a river
was or was not navigable. Much work of this kind involved historians
serving as expert witnesses, as in *EEOC v. Sears*, though sometimes it
meant backroom work for a legal team, as in *Brown v. Board of Education*. A great many public historians found employment in producing
professionally certified official histories for both government agencies
and private corporations.

The challenge to traditional notions of historical detachment and objectivity was least bothersome in that public history which was truly "public," but even in that realm local funding tilted presentations toward
particularist celebration. Work in oral history was often marked by uncritical overidentification with informants and the privileging of their
perspective. And without effective mechanisms for critical review, exaggeration and bias frequently proceeded unchecked. In the public history
that was really private, the case was much clearer. In principle, historical
policy analysis aimed at "let the chips fall where they may" objective
truth, though none of the chips were to be subjected to public scrutiny.
In practice, historians doing such work were seriously constrained by
having to conduct inquiries whose terms and assumptions were set by
others, and by the necessity of framing conclusions not overly threaten-

[55]Ronald J. Grele, "Whose Public? Whose History? What Is the Goal of a Public Historian?" *The Public Historian* 3 (Winter 1981): 46–48.

ing to the interests of their readers, who were also their immediate superiors. Those engaged in advocacy history necessarily highlighted those aspects of the historical record which supported the case they were making, and did their best to sweep under the rug or trivialize discrepant findings. In the face of ambiguous evidence they were under constant pressure to make their assertions confident and unequivocal. Official historians, though they might strive to protect their reputations or consciences by including mildly critical remarks, were for practical purposes engaged in public relations. One public historian told a seminar that while it would be unethical to destroy an embarrassing file in corporate archives, the proper course was to segregate it under lock and key so that its existence would not become known. Another leader in the field acknowledged that those undertaking "client-oriented research" should prepare themselves to face pressure to "bend the findings to the whims or the project design that the client has in mind."[56]

"The objectivity question" was a sore point with public historians, and their programmatic writings returned to it again and again, almost always with a defensive tone. The "Editor's Preface" to the first issue of the movement's journal, *The Public Historian*, observed that "some academics may raise objections to the notion of the historian as an agent for an organization" but asserted that "keeping a code of ethical behavior is not impossible." Public historians could and would "adhere to the highest ideals of objectivity and dispassionate analysis required by the academy." In the same issue, Robert Kelley, describing the program in public history at the University of California at Santa Barbara, said that at its center was a seminar in which students wrestled with the problem of how staff historians could "keep their integrity, when under pressure to produce desired results." Aspiring public historians had to confront "the ethical complexities of being a 'house historian' who nonetheless is going to call the shots as the evidence dictates."[57]

There were various efforts to draft codes of ethics for public historians, but the resulting texts demonstrated the difficulty in balancing professional responsibility to clients and scholarly norms. The Code of the National Council on Public History combined injunctions to protect clients' secrets unless required to divulge them by court order; to avoid

---

[56]Darlene Roth, "The Mechanics of a History Business," *The Public Historian* 1 (Spring 1979): 36; Lawrence B. de Graaf, "Summary: An Academic Perspective," ibid., 2 (Spring 1980): 69.

[57]G. Wesley Johnson, "Editor's Preface," *The Public Historian* 1 (Fall 1978): 9; Kelley, "Public History: Its Origins, Nature, and Prospects," ibid., 24, 28.

muckraking by presenting findings to the public "in a responsible manner"; to "serve as advocates of economic or political interests only when such a position is consistent with objective historical truth." A declaration that "historians are dedicated to the truth" was immediately followed by a gloss which observed that "flagrant [*sic*] manifestations of prejudice, distortions of data, or the use of deliberately misleading interpretations are anathema." It is little wonder that one member of the Society for History in the Federal Government, commenting on that organization's draft code of ethics, expressed concern that it would "fall into the hands of our academic brethren, confirming their darkest suspicions about our branch of the craft."[58]

Some of those engaged in advocacy history argued that while the way in which public history arrived at objective truth differed substantially from procedures followed by academic scholars, the end result was equivalent. "Are Expert Witnesses Whores?" asked J. Morgan Kousser, who had frequently served in that capacity in voting rights cases. There was, he argued, a fundamental difference between the world of academic scholars, who, in principle, were disinterested, pursuing truth "linearly," and how things worked in the courtroom.

In the adversary tradition . . . truth is assumed to emerge, if at all, as part of a dialectical process. The lawyer's ideal world is, in this respect, rather like Adam Smith's: when every lawyer seeks simultaneously to maximize the chances of his or her own client, assuming that each abides by some fundamental rules of fairness, an Invisible Hand guides the process toward the maximum production of truth.

The adversary process, he concluded, "provide[s] a safeguard at least equal to those in academia." Ronald C. Tobey extended Kousser's argument beyond the legal realm to public history in general. Academic scholarly ethics, which assumed the disinterestedness and integrity of the historian, were, he said, both in principle and in practice inadequate in the public sphere. "Partiality in presentation and consequent distortion" were intrinsic to advocacy history. But he was confident that nevertheless public history could produce objective results, on the basis of his tenuous presumption that "parties whose interest is opposed to that of the spon-

[58]National Council on Public History, "Ethical Guidelines for the Historian," *The Public Historian* 8 (Winter 1986): 64; anonymous comment quoted in Martin Reuss, "Federal Historians: Ethics and Responsibility in the Bureaucracy," ibid., 16.

sors of the research will come forward and critique the scholarship or its implications."[59]

Another common theme in public historians' discussions of objectivity is hinted at in Kousser's reference to safeguards "at least equal to those in academia." The *tu quoque* argument recurred time and again. Peter Stearns, one of the most active promoters of public history, wrote that "a conventional discipline that regularly produces myopically patriotic school texts can hardly claim that its present clients induce no distortion in results." Revisionist diplomatic historians, and feminist historians, were, he said, just as "instrumentalist" as those in public history. Otis L. Graham, Jr., of the University of North Carolina, another leader in the movement, said that "only in degree and in type, but not in kind, does the academic historian experience a different set of corrupting pressures than the friends of Clio who work outside."

Within just the last year or so I have been involved in tenure reviews or professional advancement decisions concerning individuals in labor history and women's history. These are flourishing subfields, where professionalism is strong. In each case it is hard to imagine a historian employed by a town, a bank, a neighborhood, or a federal agency encountering more pressure from involved interests who wished to keep the bad news suppressed and the good news up front, to close out the discussion or constrain it.[60]

And for some public historians the defense of their field took the form of what might be called "opportunistic relativism," the assertion that the very idea of objectivity was outmoded and obsolete. One wrote that the

---

[59]Kousser, "Are Expert Witnesses Whores? Reflections on Objectivity in Scholarship and Expert Witnessing," *The Public Historian* 6 (Winter 1984): 15–16; Tobey, "The Public Historian as Advocate: Is Special Attention to Professional Ethics Necessary?" ibid., 8 (Winter 1986): 22, 28–29. To avoid any possible misunderstanding, I should say that for myself I have no difficulty in giving Kousser the answer he desires in response to his flamboyantly worded title question: "no," or at least, "rarely." A whore turns tricks for those whom she despises, usually mechanically and contemptuously. Historians serving as expert witnesses have been, for the most part, "nice girls," who only go to bed with—or on behalf of—those whom they love, and perform with genuine passion. My guess is that Kousser's own expert-witnessing, which has mostly concerned southern legislators' intention to discriminate in electoral districting, involved no tension between academic and advocacy standards. But I think it unlikely that this experience is generalizable. I call Tobey's presumption "tenuous" because it assumes equality of resources, and access to archival materials, among potential critics—a state of affairs which may, sometimes, exist in legal proceedings, but which could hardly be expected to be the rule in the case of, for example, official histories of business and government agencies.
[60]Stearns, "Applied History: Policy Roles and Standards for Historians," in Daniel Callahan et al., eds., *Applying the Humanities* (New York, 1985), 238; Graham, "Intellectual Standards in the Humanities," ibid., 268.

"Rankean" conception of scholarship as totally honest and candid was "very influential in its time," but that experience had shown it to be unrealistic. Another told the readers of *The Public Historian* that "the unblemished scholar-historian who speaks freely, objectively, truthfully, and purely to an audience entirely of his own choosing was dismissed long ago as a fantasy." Those who still clung to this fantasy "would have us tell the truth, no matter what: no matter good taste . . . no matter the predisposition . . . of audience." Good historians, by contrast, knew that "revealing history in any form is always an opportunity for thoughtful and *responsible* presentation, not simply an opportunity to 'tell the truth'—spill the beans . . . and damn the consequences."[61]

Public historians' defensiveness on the objectivity question was generated at least as much by professional status-anxiety as by epistemological scruples. Academic historians, whatever their private thoughts about the status of public history, and its compatibility with traditional norms of the profession, were generally reluctant to criticize its practices. Most of the public historical community was made up of their own students, who in a depressed job market had either to become public historians or leave the profession altogether. To cavil at their compromises with traditional academic norms no doubt seemed like adding insult to injury. Public historians nevertheless perceived, probably correctly, that academics looked down on them. David F. Trask, chief historian of the State Department, complained that historians in the federal government were "treated patronizingly in the profession and even relegated to second-class status within it" because they were seen as "cynical servants of power who delivered biased history to order." "The prevailing attitude in academe," wrote another public historian, "is that public history is an alternative career option for less talented graduate students."[62]

Until the 1970s the question of whether history was properly described as a "profession" or a "learned discipline" was little more than a terminological quibble. It had little practical import, since unlike the situation in other fields, there were hardly any professional historians who were not employed by colleges or universities. Studies of the history of history usually casually conflated the process of disciplinary organization with

[61]Barbara Benson Kohn, "Corporate History and the Corporate History Department: Manufacturers Hanover Trust Company," *The Public Historian* 3 (Summer 1981): 35; Darlene R. Roth, letter to the editor, ibid., 5 (Winter 1983): 6–7.
[62]Trask, "Public History in the Washington Area," *The Public Historian* 1 (Fall 1978): 39; David Brumberg, "The Case for Reunion: Academic Historians, Public Historical Agencies, and the New York Historians-in-Residence Program," ibid., 4 (Spring 1982): 88.

"professionalization," which in turn was all but universally regarded as a positive development.

All of this was to change. There was, in the first place, throughout the culture, a transvaluation of "professionalism." The respect accorded lawyers plummeted in the wake of Watergate. Declining faith in the authority of physicians was reflected in the growing number of malpractice suits. Left-wing cultural critics like Ivan Illich and Christopher Lasch joined with free-market deregulationists like Milton Friedman in denouncing the baneful consequences of submission to professional expertise and professional monopoly. Whereas an earlier generation of sociologists had treated the advance of professionalization as an unambiguously good thing, many younger sociological analysts of professionalism, like Magali Sarfatti Larson and Randall Collins, treated it with a skepticism that shaded off into cynicism, and they were joined in this by academic historians like Burton Bledstein and David F. Noble. Even an academic historian as conservative and circumspect as Thomas Haskell found the new cynicism "salutary."

> Laymen have been retreating before the expanding claims of organized professional experts for over a century, and now the time has come to set limits to professional power. The retreat of the laymen must be halted before it turns into a rout, and cynicism about the motives of professional people may be a useful weapon against professionalism run wild.[63]

At the same time, as historians began a more systematic investigation of the growth of organized knowledge, several of those engaged in this venture began to insist that previous writers on the subject had illegitimately conflated client-oriented professions and research-oriented academic disciplines. Charles Rosenberg wrote that in studying the institutionalization of knowledge "perhaps the most useful distinction to be made is that between the professions and the learned disciplines." Laurence Veysey seconded Rosenberg's view, pointing out that the brochure in which Johns Hopkins University announced its first graduate programs spoke of them as offering "advanced (not professional) study." Commenting on the growing tendency to separate the history of disciplines from the history of professions, a development which on the whole he approved, Haskell speculated whether "the undoubtedly strong appeal of this distinction derives from the desire of today's academicians to

---

[63]Haskell, "Professionalization as Cultural Reform," *Humanities in Society* 1 (1978): 103.

purify their line of descent and disassociate themselves from some of the more affluent offspring of the university movement in an age of substantial public disenchantment with professional experts of all kinds."[64]

The arrival of public historians on the scene gave substance to the question of whether history was "a profession" or "a learned discipline," and complicated the search for a consensually satisfactory answer. For many public historians the "professional" label was precisely what they were offering to prospective employers. *The Public Historian* announced in its first issue that the journal was "dedicated to the proposition that historians are professional people, who possess certain marketable skills which can be practiced in the governmental, business, education, or general research areas." Deprived of academic status, public historians clung all the more tenaciously to their status as professionals. Feeling scorned by academic historians, they asserted their professionalism all the more stridently. The various codes of ethics for public historians were promulgated at least in part as symbols of professional status—their Hippocratic oath.[65]

At the same time, the populist stream within public history was hostile to "elitist" professionalism, and this stream was fed by the wellsprings of antiprofessional sentiment in the 1970s and 1980s. But whether public historians regarded "professional" as an honorific or a pejorative term, they were brought together by their shared hostility to the monopolistic claims of academic history. The conventional wisdom had always celebrated J. Franklin Jameson's success in "professionalizing" history by pushing amateurs out and establishing the domination of university-based scholars. For public historians the profession's hero was transformed into villain. The editor of *The Public Historian* wrote of Jameson's having encapsulated history within "the proverbial ivory tower." "The triumph of the professional was complete, and so was his isolation." Another public historian denounced what he saw as the sexism implicit in Jameson's disparaging local historical societies' collections as comprising "the poke bonnets and spinning wheels of all garrets." Jameson's remarks, he said, "indicate the extent to which the local history world was identified with the . . . 'feminine' context of the home as

---

[64]Rosenberg, "Toward an Ecology of Knowledge: On Discipline, Context, and History," in Alexandra Oleson and John Voss, eds., *The Organization of Knowledge in Modern America, 1860–1920* (Baltimore, 1979), 443; Veysey, "The Plural Organized Worlds of the Humanities," ibid., 61–62; Haskell, "Are Professors Professional?" *Journal of Social History* 14 (1981): 491.

[65]"Editor's Preface," *The Public Historian* 1 (Fall 1978): 8.

opposed to the 'masculine' arena of world events on which professional historians focused."[66]

Public history is so new a phenomenon that it is difficult to assess its future role in the culture of American historiography. Professional courtesy has mandated a formally positive response to public history by the professorate, and by the two major national professional organizations, the American Historical Association and the Organization of American Historians. But this surface unanimity can conceal as much as it reveals. In the absence of any more-satisfactory indicators, it is at least suggestive to look at the markedly different responses to the public history phenomenon by the executive secretaries of those two bodies, which at least hint at the range of responses which public history has evoked.

The AHA is the senior of the two organizations, and by far the more traditional. Though it includes thousands of Americanists, most of its membership is made up of historians studying other parts of the globe. When asked questions about the future of "the profession" by an interviewer from *The Public Historian*, AHA executive secretary Samuel R. Gammon repeatedly and pointedly responded with references to "our learned society." He spoke of the necessity of a "sense of elitism" to sustain morale in any organization. Asked about the attitude of the overwhelmingly academic AHA Council to the inclusion of public historians in the organization, Gammon replied, benevolently albeit a trifle condescendingly, that he was aware of no opposition to "bringing in all historians of whatever variety, persuasion, or subspecialty, including . . . those outside of the profession who are sympathetic to the profession— history buffs."[67]

By the mid-1980s the membership of the Organization of American Historians had almost caught up to the hitherto much larger AHA, and its ranks included a far greater proportion of the nation's academic Americanists. Shortly before being chosen executive secretary of the OAH, Joan Hoff-Wilson discoursed on the past and future of history in the United States, with special reference to its domination by academics, a phenomenon she considered disastrous. She hailed Herbert Baxter Adams for having tried to keep a balance between "amateur or independent historians" and "professional or academic historians," and she deplored the victory of his successors in "wrenching" the AHA from "the less scholarly, less exclusive historians." Hoff-Wilson attacked the version of history's past promulgated by "the curators of Jameson's legacy." She

[66]"Editor's Preface," ibid., 5; Brumberg, "Case for Reunion," 74;
[67]Philip L. Cantelon, "The American Historical Association and Public History: An Interview with Samuel R. Gammon," *The Public Historian* 6 (Winter 1984), 49, 50, 56–57.

thought it ironic that the AHA had established a Jameson Fellowship and Jameson Prize "at the very moment when his much lauded 'administrative genius' for turning the association over to the academics is being questioned." She offered a prescription which was startling coming from one on the brink of being named chief executive officer of what remained an overwhelmingly academic organization. If organized historical activity was to flourish in the coming decades, Hoff-Wilson said, "the independent [i.e., nonacademic] scholar must, as at the turn of the previous century, either share equally or dominate both the leadership and rank-and-file."[68]

The founding fathers of the American historical discipline had grounded objectivity in a program of universalism versus particularism, nationalism versus localism, and professionalized versus amateur history. By the 1980s all of the elements of this program had become problematic.

[68]Hoff-Wilson, "Is the Historical Professional an 'Endangered Species'?" ibid., 2 (Winter 1980): 6, 7–8, 9, 16.

15

The center does not hold

When the American historical profession was born in the last third of the
nineteenth century, various features of the surrounding culture converged to mandate an austere objectivity as the appropriate posture for
practitioners of the emerging discipline. In the last third of the twentieth
century the wind was blowing from a quite different direction, assaulting
the old ideal of objectivity with unprecedented force. A century earlier
the forces mandating a posture of objectivity had won a sweeping victory.
In the late twentieth century antiobjectivist influences met fierce resistance, producing a level of often angry dispute over "the objectivity
question" which, together with developments discussed in the immediately preceding chapters, destroyed the broad professional consensus
which had marked the immediate postwar decades.

There were, starting in the 1960s, two quite separate assaults on the
idea of objectivity. The first, the Dionysian, was boisterous, flamboyant,
and, at least so far as the academic world was concerned, ephemeral. The
"counterculture" of drugs and mysticism, with its celebration of a radical
subjectivity, hostile to all academic and scientific pretensions to objectivity, was from first to last almost exclusively a student phenomenon—
hardly more enduring than goldfish-swallowing. Those who embraced its
precepts disappeared from the academy as a matter of principle, following
the injunction to "tune in, turn on, and drop out." A tiny handful of
junior faculty members became apostles of the new dispensation: Yale
law professor Charles Reich, Harvard psychologist Timothy Leary. It
was Theodore Roszak, a Princeton-trained medievalist no less, who
coined the term "counterculture" and happily proclaimed that its followers had "turned from objective consciousness as if from a place inhabited by plague." But except for a slight relaxation of faculty dress codes

and speech habits, few scholars, and historians least of all, were influenced by the counterculture except to be repelled by it.[1]

Much more substantial, widespread, and enduring was the Apollonian assault on received norms of objectivity. From the 1960s onward the objectivist assumptions and foundations of many academic disciplines came to be undermined by currents of thought emanating from culturally very "straight" scholars. In one field after another distinctions between fact and value and between theory and observation were called into question. For many, postures of disinterestedness and neutrality increasingly appeared as outmoded and illusory. It ceased to be axiomatic that the scholar's or scientist's task was to represent accurately what was "out there." Most crucially, and across the board, the notion of a determinate and unitary truth about the physical or social world, approachable if not ultimately reachable, came to be seen by a growing number of scholars as a chimera. And with skepticism about that telos, the meaning of "progress" in science and scholarship became problematic. The objectivity question, in one form or another, moved to the top of disciplinary agendas.

Overall, one could speak of a "second crisis of historicism." The first, largely German, crisis, at the turn of the century, had been moral. Within an academic community whose members were overwhelmingly conventionally religious, the historicizing and relativizing of ethical and religious standards caused widespread personal anxiety. The second, late-twentieth-century, crisis of historicism was cognitive: the anxiety of highly professionalized academics occasioned by the historicizing and relativizing of knowledge. Practitioners of individual disciplines, and the academic community as a whole, had learned to live without moral absolutes, or to bracket moral questions. But for those with a now much more professionalized consciousness, belief in the objective status of their disciplinary labors could play as central a role in psychic equilibrium as a timeless morality did in the case of their predecessors.

There is no satisfactory term with which to describe the multiple but loosely convergent assaults on received notions of objectivity which swept across the academic world from the 1960s onward. The most common designation is "postmodern." We are alleged to be living in a "postmodern condition" (Jean-François Lyotard), which encompasses "postmodern politics" (Sheldon Wolin), "postmodern science" (Stephen Toulmin), and a forest of other "posts." "Postmodern" has been em-

[1]*The Making of a Counter Culture: Reflections on the Technocratic Society and Its Youthful Opposition* (New York, 1969), 215.

ployed so promiscuously and with such varied and contradictory meanings that it has been emptied of content. As with "postindustrial,"
"poststructuralist," and the like, the locution is symbolic of a circumstance of chaos, confusion, and crisis, in which everyone has a strong
suspicion that conventional norms are no longer viable, but no one has a
clear sense of what is in the making.

It is hard to say how many historians attended to the currents here
surveyed; certainly awareness varied a great deal. The work of Thomas
Kuhn was inescapable in practically every realm, that of Clifford Geertz
hardly less so. Intellectual historians were more concerned with the new
"textualism" in literary studies than were quantitative social historians;
historians of professions more attentive to Michel Foucault than were
diplomatic historians. But the whole was a good deal more than the sum
of its parts, if only because of the intense mutual interaction between the
new dissident tendencies, which spread over the entire academic landscape. A fresh breeze for some, acid rain for others. However the new
tendencies were evaluated, they constituted a central element of the context in which historians thought about objectivity in recent decades.

I

For historians—as for those in every other discipline, as for the man in
the street—the natural sciences had always been the bedrock upon which
the idea of objectivity was founded. Mid-twentieth-century historians
were less inclined than their late-nineteenth-century predecessors to appropriate the label "scientific" for their own labors, and it was only a
small minority within the profession who deliberately modeled their procedures after those of the natural sciences. But the example of the scientist
was no less a bench mark against which historians' progress toward objectivity was measured. Though "objectivity" had various facets and dimensions, science was the supreme exemplar of all of them.

Few historians or other nonscientists, or for that matter practicing
scientists themselves, had an explicit theoretical model of the nature of
science, but what the French call the *vulgate anonyme* was the more
powerful for not being systematically articulated. Science was dedicated
to "the truth" about the natural world: bringing its descriptions into
correspondence with "what was out there." There were two views of the
temporal relation of fact and theory, though both agreed on the authority
of fact over theory, and agreed also that fact and theory were clearly
distinguishable. In the older inductivist view, scientists, with an open
mind, unclouded by preconceptions, first observed the facts, then

devised theories based on these facts, and confirmed by them. In the Popperian view, theory came first. There was room for the bold hypothesis, the inspired guess, the dazzling flash of insight. But having produced hypotheses, scientists immediately subjected them to the most rigorous empirical test—correspondence with the facts—and indeed devoted their best efforts to disproving their speculations. Theories were only worthwhile insofar as they were not falsified by the facts, at which point they were ruthlessly abandoned. Science advanced by the overthrow of inferior theories when new facts were discovered which falsified them. They were then replaced by new theories which were more accurate, more comprehensive, "closer to the truth."

Science was both cumulative and progressive. Unlike other realms, in which particularist loyalties might produce partisan results, science was universalistic. Whereas findings in other fields might reflect the preferences of the investigator, science was value-neutral. Other disciplines suffered from the intrusion of ideological currents, but science proceeded in serene isolation from such distorting influences. Scholars in other fields might occasionally succumb to dogmatism, stubbornly clinging to cherished beliefs in the face of evidence, but the modern scientist was the sworn enemy of dogma of any kind. The ideal-typical scientist was Promethean and iconoclastic. All of these propositions were both descriptive and normative. Insofar as they had sometimes been violated, the result had been "bad science"—a setback to the collective venture of selflessly moving toward depicting nature "wie es eigentlich gewesen." Though few historians explicitly framed their understanding of historical objectivity in terms of this model, its assumptions permeated objectivist arguments in the historical community.

There had been, as we have seen, some questions raised about received notions of science between the wars, but these were mainly directed at inductivist fictions, abandoned by postwar philosophers of science. "Relativity" and "complementarity" may have shaken some historians' sense of a determinate, Newtonian universe, but these were esoteric doctrines, usually ill-understood, and their area of application—the subatomic and the extraterrestrial—hardly impinged on that broad middle realm where the historian operated. Historical relativists had characteristically contrasted the historian's problematic access to reality with the immediacy enjoyed by the scientist. Whereas the historian saw as through a glass darkly, the scientist confronted things face-to-face. Doubts about historical objectivity continued to be expressed in terms of the inherent inability of history, because it dealt with willful, rational actors, to be fully "scientific." Mannheim, following Marx, had granted science an exemp-

Objectivity in crisis

tion from the sociology of knowledge. Postwar historians who had kept up with these things (i.e., had read Karl Popper) understood that science might never, as was once thought, achieve absolute closure; that no scientific theory could ever finally and definitively be pronounced "true." But there was no doubt that "progress toward the truth"—toward objective correspondence with the reality of the natural world—was the essence of the scientific venture.

None of the elements in the received notions of science or of scientific objectivity survived unscathed from the close criticism to which they were subjected from the 1960s onward. Conducted by historians, philosophers, and sociologists of science, the questioning of the old vulgate proceeded with astonishing rapidity, and with ramifications in every field of knowledge.

It is a commonplace that Thomas Kuhn's 1962 *The Structure of Scientific Revolutions* was the vehicle which introduced the general academic world to what may be called, to be in fashion, "postpositivist" or "postempiricist" conceptions of science. Arthur Danto has pointed out how ironic it was that Kuhn's book first appeared as a volume in the *Encyclopedia of Unified Science*, a monument to positivism and empiricism.

His theory of scientific revolution subverted the enterprise that sponsored it, and opened the way to discussing science as a human and historical matter instead of a logical *Aufbau* of some immaculate formal language. . . . Instead of history being connected to the wider body of science by a logical *Anschluss*, the natural sciences themselves became matters for the kinds of interpretation the earlier theorists had identified as the methodological prerogative of the human sciences: ways of reading the world. To be sure, there now really was a unity of science, in the sense that all of science was brought under history rather than, as before, history having been brought under science construed on the model of physics.[2]

Kuhn's book was clearly and powerfully written, filled with persuasive examples, devoid of the arcane vocabulary and symbols which had made philosophy of science a closed book to most laymen. Kuhn's ideas were quickly taken up by scholars in fields far removed from the natural sciences. It would be hard to nominate another twentieth-century American academic work which has been as widely influential; among historical books it would appear to be without serious rival. Without disparaging Kuhn's originality, one should bear in mind that in many ways his book represented a bringing together of ideas which were being developed by a

---

[2]*Narration and Knowledge* (New York, 1985), xi-xii. I have rearranged the order of Danto's remarks.

number of scholars at the time. Indeed, in the Guggenheim application which Kuhn submitted to support the writing of *Scientific Revolutions*, he wrote that while the ideas he was bringing together were "original in this context," what he proposed was "primarily a work of synthesis."[3]

At the very core of the received view of science was the authority of fact over theory—and the certainty that there were independent observations which either confirmed or falsified theories. In a series of works in the 1950s and 1960s, most notably his 1958 *Patterns of Discovery*, Norwood Russell Hanson argued persuasively that "there is more to seeing than meets the eye": that facts were thoroughgoingly "theory laden," dependent on acceptance of the very theory which they were meant to test. Whereas previously philosophers had spoken of scientists seeing the same thing but interpreting it differently, Hanson sought to show that the two processes were inseparable. To the extent that scientific observation could be shown to be thus constrained, the idea of theories being straightforwardly confirmed or falsified by observations or facts fell apart.

While Hanson, and others, focused on what they saw as the myth of a "neutral observation language," Michael Polanyi called into question the notion that dogma was antithetical to science. Polanyi, who was, as we have seen, a strong defender of the autonomy of the Republic of Science against external control, argued, in Burkean fashion, that there was "reason in tradition," and that what he explicitly termed "suppression of evidence" might be necessary in order to preserve a viable tradition. "There must be at all times a predominantly accepted scientific view of the nature of things. . . . A strong presumption that any evidence which contradicts this view is invalid must prevail. Such evidence has to be disregarded, even if it cannot be accounted for, in the hope that it will turn out to be false or irrelevant." Stubbornly, "irrationally" clinging to received theory in the face of discrepant evidence—regarded as pathological in other fields, and unthinkable in the sciences—was, Polanyi suggested, a necessary element in the conduct of science.[4]

The Structure of Scientific Revolutions incorporated these and other ideas, extended them, and produced a synthesis which offered a powerful alternative to the received version of the internal dynamics of science. Despite the efforts of many social scientists to treat the work as an instruction manual to make their own disciplines more "scientific" and "objective," this was far from Kuhn's intention: Indeed, he sought to

---

[3]Kuhn's Guggenheim application quoted in Daniel Goldman Cedarbaum, "Paradigms," *Studies in History and Philosophy of Science* 14 (1983): 177–78.
[4]"The Potential Theory of Adsorption: Authority in Science Has Its Uses and Its Dangers," *Science* 141 (1963): 1012.

explain what made the mature natural sciences fundamentally different from other realms; what made their characteristic fruits objective in a way which other scholarly products were not; what made scientific knowledge progress in ways in which, to use his examples, art, political theory, or philosophy do not. In the process, "scientific objectivity" and "scientific progress" were redefined in ways which challenged the conventional understandings of these terms.

What for Kuhn distinguished a mature science was that it operated within a "paradigm"—an ambiguous term which included exemplary scientific achievements or model experiments, metatheoretical and ontological assumptions (amounting to a disciplinary *Weltanschauung*), methodology, instrumentation, and research agenda—the whole enforced by formal and informal institutional arrangements which insured its hegemony. The very rigidity and restriction of vision a paradigm imposed made possible the focused effort and precision of match between observation and theory characteristic of mature sciences. After a scientific field had come to be organized under a governing paradigm, its development, according to Kuhn, took place in two quite different ways. Kuhn's account of both of these modes of advance differed markedly from the received version.

The vast majority of scientific activity he described as "normal science," puzzle solving within the framework of the paradigm, conducted by scientists who were indoctrinated into it with a rigidity exceeded only by orthodox theology. For scientists operating within a paradigm, the paradigm was not a self-consciously held and contingent theory about the way things might be hypothetically considered. It was a quite unselfconscious and unquestioned conviction about the way things are. Paradigms were not just constitutive of science; they were, in an important sense "constitutive of nature as well." In the ordinary course of things, paradigmatic assumptions were unfalsifiable. After Newton's second law of motion, or Dalton's chemical law of fixed proportion, became paradigmatic, no observation or experimental results could refute them. It was precisely the tenacity with which fundamental assumptions were held, the "attempt to force nature into the preformed and relatively inflexible box that the paradigm supplies" which accounted for the consensual objectivity of normal scientific findings, because the paradigm defined both what were relevant soluble problems and what, within the assumptions of the paradigm, constituted universally satisfactory solutions. Normal science was likewise guaranteed to "progress"—in part because progress was defined as the articulation of the paradigm itself through a variety of mopping-up operations; in part because the pursuit of questions to which the paradigm did not promise a solution was discouraged; most importantly, because agreement on fundamentals freed practitioners from distractions, and allowed them to devote their full efforts to producing an increasingly close fit between ever more refined findings and theories consistent with the paradigm's overarching assumptions.[5]

This was a view of "normal science" which many scientists endorsed as congruent with their own experience, and one which served as a model for many subsequent historical investigations. But in its suggestion that dogma was the precondition, not the antithesis, of scientific advance, and in its corollary—the "normal" scientist as tradition-bound puzzle-solver, rather than bold adventurer—it fundamentally contradicted the orthodox Promethean image. And by its suggestion that "objectivity" and "progress," as traditionally understood, were meaningful only within an unfalsifiable frame of reference, it threatened the larger world view based on absolutist understandings of those terms.

Though Kuhn's normal science was inconsistent with the image of the scientist as conquistador, his depiction of the "scientific revolution," in which a community abandoned one paradigm for another, posed a much more direct challenge to the standard view of objectivity. In the older view, a scientific revolution was simply theoretical modification writ large. An influential theory, when contradicted by the facts, was on that account abandoned and replaced by a more accurate and more comprehensive theory which did everything the old theory had done, and more besides. There might be a few stubborn holdouts, who were, by that token, being "unscientific," but the empirical and logical demonstration that the new theory meshed more closely with observation, and "approached closer to the truth" won over the community in question.

Kuhn challenged this version at every point. Paradigms were not abandoned when "falsified" by evidence. "If any and every failure to fit were ground for theory rejection, all theories ought to be rejected at all times." For Kuhn, as we have seen, paradigms were immune to straightforward falsification. Paradigms did, to be sure, accumulate "anomalies"—phenomena they could not, as yet, explain. But this was not in itself a source of weakness. Indeed, it was precisely the lack of good fit between data and theory that set the puzzle-solving agenda of normal science. Some anomalies always persisted, and scientists worked around them, directing their attention to less recalcitrant problems. As anomalies continued to

[5]*The Structure of Scientific Revolutions* (2d. ed., enlarged, Chicago, 1970), 166, 109–110, 78, 24, 162–66.

resist explanation, when for one reason or another research came to center on areas in which anomalies accumulated, and when the accumulation of irresolvable anomalies came to be seen as more than merely as yet unsolved puzzles, a sense of crisis ensued. In these circumstances, determined not simply by the existence of numerous anomalies, which were a constant fact of scientific life, but by the collective unease of the scientific community, the time was ripe for an alternative paradigm which would vie for community allegiance. If the new paradigm-candidate was successful, and future work came to be organized in the new way, and with the new assumptions which it mandated, a "scientific revolution" had taken place.

Kuhn used various metaphors to describe the process. "Revolution" itself, "a choice between incompatible modes of community life," was a metaphor drawn from politics. He likened paradigm change to a gestalt switch, an instantaneous total reconfiguration. And he used the language of religious conversion, reporting how scientists spoke of "scales falling from the eyes." Consistent with his rejection of a "Whig interpretation" of the history of science, Kuhn did not scorn "counterrevolutionaries," those who had resisted the new order. Their conviction that ultimately "nature can be shoved into the box the paradigm provides" might sometimes have become stubborn or pigheaded, but it was that very conviction that made normal scientific advance possible.[6]

Whether the metaphor was drawn from politics, the psychology of perception, or religion, a scientific revolution was not to be understood as a matter of "rational" demonstration of the superiority of the new view (as "rationality" was traditionally defined), or as the triumph of a manifestly "truer" outlook accomplished simply by the deployment of evidence and logic. A new paradigm might deal more satisfactorily with some anomalies which had proved recalcitrant under the old, but the older paradigm usually explained many things which the new one could not. Overall, adoption of a new paradigm could be expected to involve substantial loss, as well as gain, of explanatory power. Indeed, in its early stages this would inevitably be the case, since a schema which had been elaborated and articulated over many years yielded to one which was undeveloped. In any case, it was by no means easy to make judgments of comparative explanatory power because the very criteria of what counted as an explanation might be at issue. Shortly before Newton arrived on the scene up-to-date scientists had banished Aristotelian and scholastic explanations which spoke of the "essences" of material bodies. Saying that an

[6]Ibid., 94, 122, 151–52.

object fell because its "nature" directed it toward the center of the universe was denounced as occult nonsense, or at best an empty tautology. It was in this spirit that Molière mocked the physician who explained opium's function as a soporific by reference to its "dormitive" qualities. To its opponents, acceptance of Newton's view of gravity as innate attraction would "return science to the Dark Ages." It was not explanation at all, but "mere prediction."[7]

With a new paradigm, not only what counted as an explanation but what counted as facts could change, along with the meaning of key terms like "force" and "mass." Paradigms were thus often at least partially "incommensurable." There was no neutral observation language, no set of terms not themselves saturated in a paradigm, by which rival claims could be measured against each other. Repeatedly, and always in qualified language which revealed his uneasiness with the seemingly idealist implications of the phrase, Kuhn wrote of scientists operating under different paradigms as "living in different worlds."

The very ease and rapidity with which astronomers saw new things when looking at old objects with old instruments may make us wish to say that, after Copernicus, astronomers lived in a different world.

Lavoisier . . . saw oxygen where Priestley had seen . . . dephlogisticated air and where others had seen nothing at all. . . . At the very least, as a result of discovering oxygen, Lavoisier saw nature differently. And in the absence of some recourse to that hypothetical fixed nature that he "saw differently," the principle of economy will urge us to say that after discovering oxygen Lavoisier worked in a different world.

In a sense that I am unable to explicate further, the proponents of competing paradigms practice their trades in different worlds. . . . That is not to say that they can see anything they please. Both are looking at the world, and what they look at has not changed. But in some areas they see different things, and they see them in different relations one to the other. That is why a law that cannot even be demonstrated to one group of scientists may occasionally seem intuitively obvious to another.[8]

---

[7]Ibid., 104–5, 163.
[8]Ibid., 117, 118, 150. Cf. 111, 112 for other examples of the diffidence with which Kuhn employed the expression. Kuhn's use of the technical term "incommensurable" has occasioned a certain amount of confusion, which might have been avoided had he initially made its meaning clear. A number of quite reputable dictionaries, reflecting sloppy common usage, equate it with "incomparable"—clearly not Kuhn's meaning, since he frequently wrote of scientists comparing theories and paradigms. The word, first employed in ancient mathematics, means having "no common measure" or, metaphorically, "no common language." As Kuhn wrote some years later, "The claim that two theories are incommensurable is . . . the claim that there is no language, neutral or otherwise, into

The first sentence of *The Structure of Scientific Revolutions* had advanced the suggestion that "History, if viewed as a repository for more than anecdote or chronology, could produce a decisive transformation in the image of science by which we are now possessed." For many of his readers Kuhn's own writings, together with the writings of others who wrote in the same spirit, did precisely that. That body of work was conducted in no debunking spirit. There was no more devoted celebrant of the scientific venture than Kuhn. But to those for whom science was meaningful only insofar as it was teleological, approaching closer and closer to "the objective truth," Kuhn's picture was unacceptably "relativist," a characterization he neither accepted nor unequivocally repudiated.

We are all deeply accustomed to seeing science as the one enterprise that draws constantly nearer to some goal set by nature in advance. But need there be any such goal? Can we not account for both science's existence and its success in terms of evolution from the community's state of knowledge at any given time? Does it really help to imagine that there is some one full, objective, true account of nature and that the proper measure of scientific achievement is the extent to which it brings us closer to that ultimate goal?

Later scientific theories are better than earlier ones for solving puzzles in the often quite different environments in which they are applied. That is not a relativist's position, and it displays the sense in which I am a convinced believer in scientific progress. Compared with the notion of progress most prevalent among both philosophers of science and laymen, however, this position lacks an essential element. A scientific theory is usually felt to be better than its predecessors . . . because it is somehow a better representation of what nature is really like. One often hears that successive theories grow ever closer to, or approximate more and more closely to, the truth. Apparently generalizations like that refer not to the puzzle-solutions and the concrete predictions derived from a theory but rather to its ontology, to the match, that is, between the entities with which the theory populates nature and what is "really there." . . . There is, I think, no theory-independent way to reconstruct phrases like "really there"; the notion of a match between the ontology of a theory and its "real" counterpart in nature now seems to me illusive in principle. Besides, as a historian, I am impressed with the implausibility of the view. . . . Though the temptation to describe that position as relativistic is understandable, the description seems to me wrong. Conversely, if

which both theories, conceived as sets of sentences, can be translated without residue or loss. No more in its metaphorical than its literal form does incommensurability imply incomparability." ("Commensurability, Comparability, Communicability," *Proceedings of the 1982 Biennial Meeting of the Philosophy of Science Association* [2 vols., East Lansing, Mich., 1983], 671.

the position be relativism, I cannot see that the relativist loses anything needed to account for the nature and development of the sciences.[9]

Though Kuhn's historicism, and the general turn to a historical view of scientific development, produced a revolution in the generally accepted view of science, in one crucial respect that revolution was limited and traditionalist. At no point did Kuhn ever abandon the orthodox "internalist" posture which, as we have seen, dominated historiography of science in the postwar years.[10]

The autonomy of science from external agendas had always been a key element in the received notion of scientific objectivity, as it was for most disciplines' claim to objectivity. And nowhere was this more true than in history, where skepticism about the discipline's freedom from such concerns had been a central element in doubts about historical objectivity. In *Scientific Revolutions*, and in his subsequent theoretical writings, Kuhn was more aggressively internalist than in his earlier substantive historical studies; more insistent that science be considered as an autonomous realm, insulated from external social and intellectual currents. In addition to whatever other factors inclined Kuhn to an internalist orientation, his epistemology virtually demanded such a posture, if scientific objectivity, albeit somewhat redefined, was to be preserved.

In Karl Popper's depiction of science there was a sharp distinction between hypothesis formation and hypothesis testing, contexts of discovery and of justification. For Popper, since hypotheses were immediately subjected to potentially falsifying tests, it was of no consequence if they came from outside science; once they entered science, there was a binding algorithm of choice and decision. For Kuhn, who acknowledged no such algorithm, and offered no criterion of scientific acceptability other than the unforced consensus of scientists, it was of the greatest importance that their judgment be seen as based on "purely scientific" values if the authority of that consensus was to be respected, as he clearly wished it to be. He explicitly stipulated that when external values came to play a large role in scientific judgment, scientific progress became problematic, or might even come to an end. If he occasionally made passing mention of external factors, he characteristically did so in order to trivialize them. They might

[9]*Scientific Revolutions*, 171, 206–7. For a slightly different formulation of Kuhn's response to the charge of "relativism," see "Reflections," 264–65.
[10]Kuhn's fullest statements on "internalism" are in his "History of Science," *International Encyclopedia of the Social Sciences* (New York, 1968), reprinted in Kuhn, *The Essential Tension: Selected Studies in Scientific Tradition and Change* (Chicago, 1977), 105–26, and "History of Science," in Peter D. Asquith and Henry E. Kyburg, Jr., eds., *Current Research in Philosophy of Science* (East Lansing, Mich., 1979), 121–28.

influence the timing of the recognition of anomalies, but "technical breakdown would still remain the core of the crisis." Though individual scientists might have their vision shaped by extrascientific factors, the lesson drawn from this was that attention should be directed away from individuals and toward the group.[11]

It is important here to remember that Kuhn's view of theory choice subjected him to a barrage of criticism for having grounded scientific truth in "mob rule"; for advocating an "irrationalist" position. The main line of his defense was that scientists, applying purely scientific values, could not possibly be described as "a mob"; that it was oxymoronic to describe autonomous scientific judgment as "irrational." One cannot know whether in the absence of a rhetorical context in which he was on the strategic defensive, Kuhn would have clung so tenaciously to an internalist view. But some powerful motive is needed to explain what could lead Kuhn, who was himself, before he turned to history, one of the thousands of physicists mobilized for the defense effort, to describe practitioners of mature sciences as working on problems "no longer presented by the external society but by an internal challenge to increase the scope and precision of the fit between existing theory and nature."[12]

Kuhn's reliance on the collective judgment of the scientific community was based on the shared values which that community brought to theory appraisal. He suggested that these included accuracy, consistency, breadth, simplicity, and fruitfulness. When scientists disagreed, it was because it was often not clear how these values should be applied, and even less clear how they should be assigned relative weights, when, as often happened, one theory scored higher on one criterion, another on another. He acknowledged that not even all the values in this core list were always operative, and that the list was not exhaustive. On the basis of his own previous historical studies, as well as those of others, it could be shown that external cultural and ideological factors had substantially influenced which values dominated a particular community at a given time, their interpretation, and their relative weighting. Of equal importance, extrascientific considerations could be shown to have been important in how scientists perceived facts with which theories were to be aligned. Despite Kuhn's personal commitment to an internalist posture,

[11] For Kuhn's view of the dire consequence of the intrusion of externalities, see "Reflections," 262–63; and "Objectivity, Value Judgment, and Theory Choice," in *Essential Tension*, 333; for his trivialization of them, see *Scientific Revolutions*, 69, 152–53.

[12] "The History of Science," *Essential Tension*, 119. Though Kuhn later produced a "strictly historical" study of twentieth-century physics, from the mid-1960s onward he interacted increasingly with philosophers and not historians—with all the marginalization of context which that implies.

his attack on the view that theory choice was algorithmic opened the door to the serious consideration of "externalities" which could be shown to have been important if not decisive in determining scientific truth at different times and places.

Just as Kuhn's work was taking hold, "externalist" studies in the history of science began to multiply. Work in Renaissance and early modern science collapsed older notions of a sharp distinction between science on the one hand, and magic, religion, superstition on the other. More to the point, it made clear that Giordano Bruno's heliocentrism was inexplicable without reference to his hermeticism; that the early history of chemistry was incomprehensible unless one understood the alchemic and scriptural concerns of the Paracelsians; and that all of these "extrascientific" elements, and others besides, lay at the foundations of Newton's work.

It was no different when one moved to more recent times. Histories which showed the impact of science on social thought, like Hofstadter's *Social Darwinism*, posed no threat to standard notions of the autonomy of science. But dozens of studies of the development of evolutionary theory showed that the lines of influence were often reversed, and that one might, with equal cogency, speak of "Manchesterian biology." It was argued that central elements of the Darwinian model, such as "progress toward perfection," derived from nineteenth-century ideology rather than the fossil record. Other scholars described the influence on evolutionary thought of Malthusian propositions about struggle for survival, and other ideas drawn from contemporary political economy. The historical *Ideologiekritik* of nineteenth-century evolutionism became a weapon in late-twentieth-century scientific debate. The paleontologist Stephen Jay Gould, coauthor of the theory that evolution proceeded episodically rather than uniformly, saw gradualism as "the standard argument among nineteenth-century liberals trying to preserve the social order against increasing threats (and practices) of revolution." "Darwin," Gould said, "did not 'see' gradualism in the rocks."[13]

The most broadly influential body of externalist work in the history of science was undoubtedly that of the French philosopher and historian Michel Foucault, several of whose books appeared in English translation during the decade of the seventies. Much of his work concerned medicine and psychiatry, but it extended to all realms of thought. One of Foucault's central concepts was the "episteme"—not, as in Kuhn's "paradigm," the organizing assumption of an autonomous scientific communi-

---

[13]Darwin, *On the Origin of Species by Natural Selection* (London, 1859), 489; Gould, "Evolution: Explosion, Not Ascent," *New York Times*, 22 January 1978, E5.

ty, but "the totality of relations that can be discovered, for a given period, between the sciences when one analyses them at the level of discursive regularities." His recurring emphasis on rupture and discontinuity in discourse historicized and relativized any stable truth-claims. Foucault's later work became increasingly concerned with the relation between social purpose, social institutions, and the establishment of knowledge: the nexus between scientific disciplines and the "disciplining" of those subject to them, indeed, constituted by them. Scientific truth was not "the reward of free spirits . . . nor the privilege of those who have succeeded in liberating themselves." It was

a thing of this world . . . produced only by virtue of multiple forms of constraint. And it induces regular effects of power. . . . "Truth" is linked in a circular relation with systems of power which produce and sustain it, and to effects of power which it induces and which extend it. A "regime" of truth.[14]

Finally, the received view of the scrupulous and dispassionate scientist received a further blow from historical investigations which showed that Sir Isaac Newton had fudged his record of observations in the *Principia* to lend support to his theories, and that Mendel had done something similar in his genetic reports. The phenomenon could not be dismissed as "pre-professional." The American Nobel laureate Robert Millikan had done precisely the same thing in the twentieth century. (This raised the awkward question of whether greater rectitude would have retarded scientific progress by making the scientific community more reluctant to accept originally only loosely supported theories which were later vindicated.) There was a great uproar over the revelation that the English psychologist Sir Cyril Burt had fabricated influential findings out of whole cloth. James Watson's somewhat sordid account of the background to the discovery of *The Double Helix* was the most widely read contribution to the revised public picture of the scientist. "Watson has told the truth about the motivation and behavior of scientists," wrote one scientific reviewer, "and he has not helped their public image."

The myth of the objective, unselfish scientist, consumed even unto death with the fire of curiosity, a slave to the desire to know has somehow survived the cynicism of the times. Sinclair Lewis' Martin Arrowsmith is the archetype, and for those who don't read much there are always Edward G. Robinson and Paul Muni giving up their lives and reputations to save us from syphilis and rabies. The truth

---

[14] *The Archaeology of Knowledge* (1969; English trans., New York, 1972), 191; "Truth and Power," in his *Power/Knowledge: Selected Interviews and Other Writings, 1972–1977* (New York, 1980), 131–33.

is rather different and "Honest Jim" has told it. . . . Science is a form of competitive and aggressive activity, a contest of man against man that provides knowledge as a side product. That side product is its only advantage over football.[15]

When the American historical profession was founded, unquestioned assumptions about the nature of science, and scientific objectivity, had played a central role in rendering unproblematic the profession's constituent beliefs. One hundred years later the radical questioning of these assumptions was to play just as central a role in rendering those beliefs deeply problematic. As the scientizing of history had provided the discipline with a stable objectivist foundation, the historicizing of science destabilized that foundation. In the early 1970s Arnold Thackray, soon to be named editor of *Isis*, the leading American journal in history of science, said that those in his specialty were, within the overall discipline, those least likely to find acceptable or attractive the program of writing history "wie es eigentlich gewesen." Modern history and philosophy of science were, he said, congenial to relativists, antithetical to traditionalists. By the beginning of the 1980s he defined the central contested questions in the history of science as: "Can logical or historical distinctions between science and magic be sustained? Is science culture free in any but a trivial sense? Is progress or truth a useful concept around which to organize historical work? . . . Is science essentially an ideology or form of oppression?" It was a far cry from "scientific history" as understood by the founders.[16]

II

In the postwar years historians had shunned philosophy at least in part because the dominant analytic tradition was perceived as either disparaging history because it was incapable of arriving at scientific certitude, or manipulating it in a scientistic direction. Beginning in the sixties Ameri-

---

[15]Richard S. Westfall, "Newton and the Fudge Factor," *Science* 179 (1973): 751–58; Curt Stern and Eva R. Sherwood, *The Origin of Genetics: A Mendel Source Book* (San Francisco, 1966); Gerald Holton, "Subelectrons, Presuppositions, and the Millikan-Ehrenhaft Dispute," *Historical Studies in the Physical Sciences* 9 (1978): 166–224; L. S. Hearnshaw, *Cyril Burt, Psychologist* (London, 1979); Richard C. Lewontin, "'Honest Jim' Watson's Big Thriller about DNA," *Chicago Sun-Times*, 25 February 1968, reprinted in Gunther S. Stent, ed., *The Double Helix: Text, Commentary, Reviews, Original Papers* (New York, 1980), 186.

[16]"Science: Has Its Present Past a Future?" in Roger H. Stuewer, ed., *Historical and Philosophical Perspectives of Science* (Minneapolis, 1970), 120–21; "History of Science," in Paul T. Durbin, ed., *A Guide to the Culture of Science, Technology, and Medicine* (New York, 1980), 21.

can academic philosophy moved in a quite different, much more radical, and, for many, a much more threatening direction. It called into question the central philosopher's quest since Descartes, which had united members of warring schools for three hundred years: establishing an Archimedean point upon which knowledge could be grounded. "Reading the *Meditations* as a journey of the soul," wrote the American philosopher Richard Bernstein, "helps us to appreciate that Descartes' search for a foundation or Archimedean point is more than a device to solve metaphysical and epistemological problems."

It is the quest for some fixed point, some stable rock upon which we can secure our lives against the vicissitudes that constantly threaten us. The specter that hovers in the background of this journey is not just radical epistemological skepticism but the dread of madness and chaos where nothing is fixed, where we can neither touch bottom nor support ourselves on the surface. With a chilling clarity Descartes leads us with an apparent and ineluctable necessity to a grand and seductive Either/Or. *Either* there is some support for our being, a fixed foundation for our knowledge, *or* we cannot escape the forces of darkness that envelope us with madness, with intellectual and moral chaos. . . .

At the heart of the objectivist's vision, and what makes sense of his or her passion, is the belief that there are or must be some fixed, permanent constraints to which we can appeal and which are secure and stable. At its most profound level the relativist's message is that there are no such basic constraints except those that we invent or temporally (and temporarily) accept. . . . The primary reason why the *agon* between objectivists and relativists has become so intense today is the growing apprehension that there may be nothing—not God, reason, philosophy, science, or poetry—that answers to and satisfies our longing for ultimate constraints, for a stable and reliable rock upon which we can secure our thought and action.[17]

The contemporary American philosophers who have called for the abandonment of the quest for objective certitude have drawn their inspiration from a variety of continental, English, and American sources. Though united in their desire to break free from "Cartesian anxiety," and their rejection of received notions of objectivity, they have disagreed on precisely what is to be put in its place, and, depending on how they define the term, whether to characterize their own position as "relativistic."

Nelson Goodman of Harvard cheerfully accepted "radical relativism" as a description of his position, so long as it was clear that this was not taken to imply that any version could be accepted as true, or that there was no such thing as falsehood. He denied that among conflicting ver-

---

[17]*Beyond Objectivism and Relativism: Science, Hermeneutics, and Praxis* (Philadelphia, 1983), 18–19.

sions of the world one was necessarily "right" and others "wrong." Many versions of the world could be right at the same time even when these right versions could not be mutually reconciled. We "cannot test a version by comparing it with a world undescribed, undepicted, unperceived . . . all we learn about the world is contained in right versions of it." "A version is taken to be true when it offends no unyielding beliefs and none of its own precepts. Among beliefs unyielding at a given time may be long-lived reflections of laws of logic, short-lived reflections of recent observations, and other convictions and prejudices ingrained with varying degrees of firmness."

How . . . are we to accommodate conflicting truths without sacrificing the difference between truth and falsity. Perhaps by treating these versions as true in different worlds. Versions not applying in the same world no longer conflict; contradiction is avoided by segregation. A true version is true in some worlds, a false version in none. Thus the multiple worlds of conflicting true versions are actual worlds, not the merely possible worlds or nonworlds of false versions. So if there is any actual world, there are many. For there are conflicting true versions and they cannot be true in the same world. . . . When we consider conflicting true versions and their several worlds, paradox enters. This sometimes leads to utter resignation, sometimes to an irresponsible relativism that takes all statements as equally true. Neither attitude is very productive. More serviceable is a policy common in daily life and impressively endorsed by modern science: namely, judicious vacillation. After all, we shift point of view and frame of reference for motion frequently from sun to earth to train to plane, and so on. The physicist flits back and forth between a world of waves and a world of particles as suits his purpose. We usually think and work within one world-version at a time . . . but we shift from one to another often. When we undertake to relate different versions, we introduce multiple worlds. When that becomes awkward, we drop the world for the time being and consider only the versions. We are monists, pluralists, or nihilists not quite as the wind blows but as befits the context.[18]

Goodman's colleague Hilary Putnam, also one of the most influential academic philosophers of the sixties and seventies, repudiated the "relativist" label because, unlike Goodman, Putnam did take it to imply that "every conceptual system is . . . just as good as every other." Putnam broke with the "metaphysical realism" with which he was long associated. "On this perspective," wrote Putnam, "the world consists of some fixed totality of mind-independent objects. There is exactly one true and complete description of 'the way the world is.' Truth involves some sort of correspondence relation between words . . . and external things and

[18]Goodman, *Ways of Worldmaking* (Indianapolis, 1978), 94, 3–4, 17; "Notes on the Well-Made World," *Partisan Review* 51 (1984): 277–78.

sets of things." Against this "externalist" or "God's eye point of view," Putnam proposed "realism for us," which he called "internalist" because it holds that

what objects does the world consist of? is a question that it only makes sense to ask *within* a theory or description. Many "internalist" philosophers, though not all, hold further that there is more than one "true" theory or description of the world. "Truth," in an internalist view, is some sort of (idealized) rational acceptability—some sort of ideal coherence of our beliefs with each other and with our experiences *as those experiences are themselves represented in our belief system*—and not correspondence with mind-independent or discourse-independent "states of affairs." There is no God's Eye point of view that we can know or usefully imagine; there are only the various points of view of actual persons reflecting various interests and purposes that their descriptions and theories subserve.[19]

The most prominent antifoundationalist in recent years has been Richard Rorty: the most widely discussed in philosophical journals; the most widely read by nonphilosophers; the most repeatedly insistent on the need for philosophy to abandon "the neurotic Cartesian quest for certainty." "Relativism," said Rorty, was a straw man.

"Relativism" is the view that every belief on a certain topic, or perhaps about *any* topic, is as good as every other. No one holds this view. Except for the occasional cooperative freshman, one cannot find anybody who says that two incompatible opinions on important topics are equally good. The philosophers who get *called* "relativists" are those who say that the grounds for choosing between such opinions are less algorithmic than had been thought.[20]

For Rorty a contingent "solidarity," participation in an ongoing "conversation," was all that was available to us. "The Enlightenment's search for objectivity has often gone sour. . . . Setting aside the desire for objectivity altogether . . . we should think of human progress as making it possible for human beings to do more interesting things and be more interesting people, not as heading towards a place which has somehow been prepared for humanity in advance. Our self-image would employ images of making rather than finding." He described

a fundamental choice which confronts the reflective mind: that between accepting the contingent character of starting-points, and attempting to evade this contingency. To accept the contingency of starting-points is to accept our inheritance from, and our conversation with, our fellow-humans as our only source of guid-

---

[19]Putnam, *Reason, Truth and History* (Cambridge, Mass., 1981), 54, 49–50.
[20]"Pragmatism, Relativism, and Irrationalism," in his *Consequences of Pragmatism* (Minneapolis, 1982), 166.

ance. To attempt to evade this contingency is to hope to become a properly-programmed machine. This was the hope which Plato thought might be fulfilled . . . when we passed beyond hypotheses. Christians have hoped it might be attained by becoming attuned to the voice of God in the heart, and Cartesians that it might be fulfilled by emptying the mind and seeking the indubitable. Since Kant, philosophers have hoped that it might be fulfilled by finding the a priori structure of any possible inquiry, or language, or form of social life. If we give up this hope, we shall lose what Nietzsche called "metaphysical comfort," but we may gain a renewed sense of community. Our identification with our community—our society, our political tradition, our intellectual heritage—is heightened when we see this community as *ours* rather than *nature's*, *shaped* rather than *found*, one among many which men have made. In the end . . . what matters is our loyalty to other human beings clinging together against the dark, not our hope of getting things right. James, in arguing against realists and idealists that "the trail of the human serpent is over all," was reminding us that our glory is in our participation in fallible and transitory human projects, not in our obedience to permanent nonhuman constraints.

Rorty called upon philosophy to abdicate its role as monitor of the legitimacy of truth claims. As moral philosophers had advanced the idea of "situation ethics," Rorty wanted "situation epistemology"; the end of a do-all correspondence standard of objectivity, and its replacement by standards relative to the changing purposes of changing disciplinary communities in changing circumstances. These criteria might be, on some level would always be, pragmatic.[21]

Literary studies had not, traditionally, been a realm which had wholeheartedly adopted the most rigorous academic norms of objectivity and scientificity, in large measure because it was a field which came relatively late to full professionalization. Many of the twentieth century's most highly regarded literary critics never had university connections. It was only after World War II that criticism became an academic pursuit. Within the university, literary studies, when not philological, or historical and biographical, had often been characterized by an impressionistic estheticism.

It was the proclaimed mission of the "New Criticism," which became dominant in the years after World War II, to change this. Despite the involvement of many of its leading spokesmen in the Southern Agrarians' protest against science and technology, the New Critics avowed that they would make the study of literature scientific. "Criticism," wrote John Crowe Ransom, "must become more scientific, or precise and systemat-

---

[21]"Solidarity or Objectivity," in John Rajchman and Cornel West, eds., *Post-Analytic Philosophy* (New York, 1985), 16, 10; "Pragmatism, Relativism, and Irrationalism," 166.

Objectivity in crisis

ic, and this means that it must be developed by the collective and sustained effort of learned persons—which means that its proper seat is in the universities." Allen Tate called for a focus on the "specific objectivity" of the text. Cleanth Brooks attacked "critical relativism" which ignored universal criteria of formalist evaluation. The critic, discarding externalities and prejudices, would penetrate to the determinate meaning of a text through the close analysis of the interaction of its words without the intervention of an authorial will. In their classic article "The Intentional Fallacy," William K. Wimsatt and Monroe C. Beardsley argued, in a fashion which paralleled claims for the objectivity of science, that by making the text an autonomous "public" artifact, independent of its author's will or its context, objectivity of interpretation could be achieved.[22]

Competing tendencies, far from questioning the norms of objectivity and scientificity, merely argued that the New Critical orientation did not deliver what it promised; that in practice it failed to produce convergent and authoritative interpretations. E. D. Hirsch pressed for accepting the author's meaning as the normative ideal of interpretation on the grounds that only in this way could subjectivity be avoided. He urged "a ruthlessly critical process of validation." "Conflicting interpretations can be subjected to scrutiny in the light of the relevant evidence, and objective conclusions can be reached. . . . Devising . . . hypotheses [in literary interpretation] is not in principle different from devising experiments which can sponsor decisions between hypotheses in the natural sciences." The so-called Chicago neo-Aristotelians believed that through the extension and refinement of classical categories a "poetic science" could be created with uniform procedures and standards of judgment. Northrop Frye, in his 1957 *Anatomy of Criticism*, offered a sort of proto-structuralism, laying down objective laws of literary form which could free interpretation from "value judgments." "The critic should see literature as, like a science, a unified, coherent, and autonomous created form . . . not determined by any external historical process. This total body of literature can be studied through its larger structural principles . . . [:] conventions, genres, and recurring image-groups, or archetypes." Structuralism, when it first arrived on American shores, was welcomed as an antidote to a "criticism plagued by an excess of possibilities." By adopting a struc-

[22]Ransom, "Criticism, Inc.," in *The World's Body* (New York, 1938), 329; Tate, "Miss Emily and the Bibliographer" (1940), in his *Collected Essays* (Denver, 1959), 57; Brooks, "Criticism, History, and Critical Relativism," *The Well Wrought Urn: Studies in the Structure of Poetry* (New York, 1947), 212; Wimsatt and Beardsley, *Sewanee Review* 54 (1946).

turalist orientation, criticism, like other disciplines, could make demonstrable, objective "progress." Roland Barthes, referring to his own structuralist period, spoke of his "rêve euphorique de scientificité."[23]

As the 1960s gave way to the 1970s, and structuralism to "poststructuralism," what had been the solution became the problem. The focus on language, the ultimate foundation of all varieties of structuralism, came to appear less as a key than as a lock which sealed the door of the "prison-house of language," a prison to which author, text, context, and reader were sentenced for all eternity. There was increasing acceptance of the idea that the relationship between signifier and signified was arbitrary, and that the two could never quite coincide, an idea which undermined assumptions of the determinacy of meaning. On the increasingly shared assumption that language was prior to meaning, language was seen as not only decisively shaping, but also subverting, the intention of an author. The very concept of an individual and autonomous "author" was questioned. When Barthes abandoned the quest for an objective, structuralist science of literature, he repudiated its implicit claim that there could be a metalanguage of criticism, through which one looked disinterestedly at the language of a text. By the time of his *S/Z* (1970) he saw the "text" as without any determinate meaning or boundaries, irreducibly plural, an endless play of signifiers.

Whereas previously the aim of criticism had been to penetrate to the determinate and coherent meaning of texts, the deconstruction of Jacques Derrida and his American followers proclaimed the omnipresence of inherent contradictions, indeterminacies, and discontinuities. In the words of one commentator:

By scrutinizing the words on the page harder than new criticism ever had, deconstruction discovered not their translucent and free-standing autonomy but, in a radical defamiliarization, their dark, even opaque, character as writing, black marks on white paper; not the organic unity that binds together irony, paradox, and ambiguity in a privileged, indeed redeemed and redeeming, language, but unrecuperable rhetorical discontinuity.

Deconstructive practice, itself admittedly "contaminated" by its own language, aimed at unraveling antitheses and pregnant absences in texts,

[23]Hirsch, *Validity in Interpretation* (New Haven, 1967); Richard McKeon, quoted in Walter Sutton, *Modern American Criticism* (Englewood Cliffs, N.J., 1963), 160; Frye, "The Critical Path: An Essay on the Social Context of Literary Criticism," in Morton W. Bloomfield, ed., *In Search of Literary Theory* (Ithaca, N.Y., 1972), 160; Robert Scholes, *Structuralism in Literature: An Introduction* (New Haven, 1974), 167; Barthes, quoted in Philip Thody, *Roland Barthes: A Conservative Estimate* (London, 1977), 107.

showing how they contradicted their own first principles. Whereas the New Critics had urged the close reading of a text isolated from its distracting context, Derrida's most quoted remark—"il n'y a pas d'hors-texte"—proclaimed not the irrelevance of that which was outside the text, but rather the "textuality" of all of life and history.[24]

Among the most influential American literary theorists who denied the determinacy of meaning was Stanley Fish. For Fish, meaning inhered not in the author's intentions, nor in the text itself, but in the reader's act of interpretation. Whereas earlier he had agreed with his predecessors on "the need to control interpretation lest it overwhelm and obscure texts, facts, authors, and intentions," he came to argue that "interpretation is the source of texts, facts, authors, and intentions." Rather than "restoring" or "recovering" texts, he was "in the business of making texts and of teaching others to make them." The superiority of his approach, he said, was that it was liberating. "It relieves me of the obligation to be right (a standard that simply drops out) and demands only that I be interesting (a standard that can be met without any reference at all to an illusory objectivity)." Fish later retreated a bit from this position. There were standards of right and wrong, but only within transient interpretive communities. It was the continuing succession of different orientations within these communities which explained why, though "a Shakespeare sonnet is only 14 lines long, we haven't been able to get it right after four hundred years." His description of these interpretive communities bore a striking resemblance to Kuhn's communities of "normal scientists," with the abandonment of the goal of pursuing timeless truth which that position entailed.

Interpretations rest on . . . assumptions—about what is possible, necessary, telling, essential, and so on—so deeply held that they are not thought of as assumptions at all; and because they are not thought of as assumptions, the activities they make possible and the facts they entail seem not to be matters of opinion or debate, but a part of the world. . . . Rational debate—about whether or not a work is ironic or about anything else—is always possible; not, however, because it is anchored in a reality outside it, but because it occurs in a history, a history in the course of which realities and anchors have been established, although it is always possible, and indeed inevitable, that they will have to be established again.[25]

[24]Howard Felperin, *Beyond Deconstruction: The Use and Abuses of Literary Theory* (Oxford, 1985), 110.
[25]*Is There a Text in This Class?* (Cambridge, Mass., 1980), 16, 180, 174, 367; "Short People Got No Reason to Live: Reading Irony," *Daedalus* 112 (1983): 190.

Literary scholars, pursuing the capacity of language to shape that which it represented, moved far beyond their traditional domain of a growing but relatively fixed literary canon. Edward Said, in *Orientalism*, analyzed at length the "discursive consistency" with which Western scholars had constituted the East. He (ambiguously) disavowed the notion that there was "such a thing as a real or true Orient" which he was counterposing to the construction of the Orientalists. Despite his argument that Islam had been fundamentally misrepresented in the West, Said thought that "the real issue is whether indeed there can be a true representation of anything, or whether any and all representations, because they *are* representations, are embedded first in the language and then in the culture, institutions, and political ambience of the representer."

If the latter alternative is the correct one (as I believe it is), then we must be prepared to accept the fact that a representation is *eo ipso* implicated, intertwined, embedded, interwoven with a great many other things besides the "truth," which is itself a representation. What this must lead us to methodologically is to view representations (or misrepresentations—the distinction is at best a matter of degree) as inhabiting a common field of play defined for them, not by some inherent common subject matter alone, but by some common history, tradition, universe of discourse. Within this field, which no single scholar can create but which each scholar receives and in which he then finds a place for himself, the individual researcher makes his contribution. Such contributions, even for the exceptional genius, are strategies of redisposing material within the field; even the scholar who unearths a once-lost manuscript produces the "found" text in a context already prepared for it, for that is the real meaning of *finding* a new text. Thus each individual contribution first causes changes within the field and then promotes a new stability, in the way that on a surface covered with twenty compasses the introduction of a twenty-first will cause all the others to quiver, then to settle into a new accommodating configuration.[26]

Meanwhile other literary scholars extended their area of investigation to the discursive practices, rhetorical devices, and narrative strategies in which knowledge was constituted in a variety of realms. To mention but a single instance of a growing genre, one English professor analyzed the ways in which the style manual of the American Psychological Association shaped discourse within that field in an increasingly procrustean behaviorist framework. (The manual grew from seven pages in 1929 to 32 pages in 1944 to 61 pages in 1952, and over 200 by 1974, by which time psychologists were constrained to act not just like behaviorists, but like

[26]*Orientalism* (New York, 1978), 322, 272–73.

laboratory rats in a maze.) Though literary scholars increasingly stirred up trouble in other domains, their central effect was reflexive: to "deconstruct" the traditional assumption of their own field. By the 1980s, practitioners who could agree on nothing else, and by that time there were few who *could* agree on anything else, were unanimous in proclaiming the "crisis" in literary studies. Though that crisis had many dimensions, its core was the collapse of consensus on the viability of the search for stable and determinate meanings.[27]

III

The social science disciplines, albeit very unevenly, were also caught up in the epistemological revolution which began in the 1960s. Although the highly charged political atmosphere of the period sometimes raised the stakes of controversies about objectivity in the social sciences, it was for the most part "strictly academic" considerations which initiated debates, and contributed the categories in which heterodox views were advanced.

Up to the 1960s philosophy of the social sciences had been, in the main, an extension of the dominant positivist and empiricist philosophy of the natural sciences. Those who dominated discussions in the former realm—Carl Hempel, Rudolph Carnap, Ernest Nagel—wrote a good deal on the philosophy of social science as well. The received view of social science epistemology was almost isomorphic with that of the natural sciences. Occasional dissenters, like Peter Winch, whose 1958 *The Idea of a Social Science* was popular among American historians anxious to escape the grip of scientization, accepted the conventional view of *Naturwissenschaft*, and argued that the social sciences were *geisteswissenschaftlich*, and thus ought not to be assimilated to natural science models.

As the postpositivist/postempiricist current in philosophy of science developed, its theses were quickly reflected in discussions of social science epistemology. Social scientists began to speak of the ultimate unfalsifiability, and "incommensurability," of their theories and descriptions. As more and more work was done in the history of the social sciences the relativistic implications of any historicization of belief made themselves felt, and *Ideologiekritiken* of disciplinary assumptions followed. The notion of the natural science as value free, based on the belief in a clear distinction between facts and values, had been taken over by the

[27]Charles Bazerman, "Codifying the Social Scientific Style: The APA Publication Manual as a Behaviorist Rhetoric," paper delivered at 1984 University of Iowa symposium on "The Rhetoric of the Human Sciences."

grand tradition in social science. As that distinction came to be questioned even in the natural sciences, it was *a fortiori* at risk in the social sciences. A growing body of analysts argued that there could be no "neutral observation language" in the social sciences, and that description as well as the choice of explanations were inherently value-laden. In *The Political Sciences*, Hugh Stretton offered the example of cannibalism.

One aspect of cannibal raiding classifies it as sin; I recognize it as being like my own sins. Another aspect of cannibal raiding identifies it as war . . . ; I know which civilized wars it thus resembles. Another aspect classifies it as food-gathering; I see myself picking lemons from my tree or buying a can of beans in the local supermarket. Another aspect—based on some less obvious causal propositions— identifies it as a release of social tensions; I see myself kicking the cat, driving aggressively. . . . Another aspect classifies it as a mechanism for establishing individuals' qualifications for manhood or social promotion; I see myself learning to shave, cramming for my B.A. examinations, trying to make the serious bits of this book more original and the original bits more serious. It took an abstract and subtle social science to make these last identifications, and they all have different manipulative implications. One makes the abolition of cannibalism look easy, another hard, another nearly impossible. Some imply that it could be simply abolished, others that its functions would need to be replaced. One suggests abolition by moral abjuration or religious conversion, another by police prohibition, another by economic development, another by social reconstruction.[28]

In a separate development, but one furthered by the perceived inapplicability of natural science models to the social world, some social scientists came to look increasingly to the humanities, to hermeneutics, and to recent literary theory as approaches which might be more useful to their work than the procedures of the sciences. Paul Ricoeur offered the model of "meaningful action considered as a text." The interpretive approach Ricoeur recommended was not one which would ultimately reveal a transparent and unified reality. It was a "hermeneutics of suspicion," for which the symbol had unfathomable depth and opacity. The political theorist Charles Taylor envisioned a hermeneutical social science which would be "unformalizable," and would have no "brute data" and no "verification procedure"; in which some important claims would be "nonarbitrable by further evidence" and in which "each side can only make appeal to deeper insight on the part of the other": "a scandalous result according to the authoritative conception of science in our tradition."

[28] *The Political Sciences: General Principles of Selection in Social Science and History* (New York, 1969): 149–50.

There are . . . good grounds . . . for opting for hermeneutical sciences of man. But we cannot hide from ourselves how greatly this option breaks with certain commonly held notions about our scientific tradition. We cannot measure such sciences against the requirements of a science of verification; we cannot judge them by their predictive capacity. We have to accept that they are founded on intuitions which all do not share, and what is worse, that these intuitions are closely bound up with our fundamental options. These sciences cannot be *"wertfrei"*; they are moral sciences in a more radical sense than the eighteenth century understood. Finally, their successful prosecution requires a high degree of self-knowledge, a freedom from illusion, in the sense of error which is rooted and expressed in one's way of life; for our incapacity to understand is rooted in our own self-definitions, hence in what we are. To say this is not to say anything new: Aristotle makes a similar point in Book I of the *Ethics*.   But it is still radically shocking and unassimilable to the mainstream of modern science.[29]

The impact of these currents varied greatly among individual disciplines in the social sciences. Economics, despite a few dissidents, remained firmly committed to the positivist program of generating objective laws of economic behavior, based on its reification of *homo oeconomicus*. In political science, there was much talk of having passed into a "postbehavioral" era, but no consensus emerged as to what had replaced it. The increasing acceptance of the "bargaining" model, and other borrowings from economics, was the most prominent tendency. On the whole only political theorists, somewhat marginal to the mainstream of the discipline, paid much attention to postpositivist currents, aside from those who tried to use Kuhn's model as a recipe for making political science a "real" science by agreeing on a paradigm. (Most economists believed that they had already reached that stage of disciplinary nirvana.) Within sociology, though a positivist orientation remained dominant, several important currents either explicitly or implicitly discussed the social world in "textual" and "constructivist" ways; treated reality as something "made" rather than "found." Though antiobjectivist currents passed through all these disciplines, and produced a certain amount of acrimonious controversy and fragmentation, in none did they produce general epistemological crisis.

Of all the social science disciplines, it was in anthropology that the "objectivity question" assumed the greatest centrality in recent decades,

[29]"Interpretation and the Sciences of Man," *Revue of Metaphysics* 25 (1971), reprinted in Paul Rabinow and William M. Sullivan, *Interpretive Social Science: A Reader* (Berkeley, 1979), quotations from pp. 65–71. Ricoeur, "The Model of the Text: Meaningful Action Considered as a Text," which originally appeared in *Social Research* 38 (1971), is reprinted in the same collection.

and where it was most divisive. In the postwar years anthropology had stressed the unity rather than the variety of cultures. The discourse of the discipline was often belligerently scientistic, and its principal subject matter was determinate behaviors and structures. In what became popular anthropological jargon, the dominant approach was "etic," centering on what was particular, concrete, measurable, and describable in a denotative metalanguage, as opposed to "emic" orientations, attempting holistic understanding "from the native's point of view." (The terms were derived—obviously with considerable extension—from "phonetic" and "phonemic.") Anthropology, in the "etic" mode, addressed its subject matter from an Archimedean point. "We have," said a semiofficial spokesman, "taken our stand beyond—above—existing cultures." By the late sixties strong countercurrents to the postwar orientation began to appear.[30]

Of the two forms of relativism, moral and cognitive, with which that discipline had wrestled since its inception, the issues raised by the former never regained their former salience. Ethnographic fieldwork continued to demand of its practitioners at least a bracketing of overt expressions of moral disapprobation. The original program of cultural relativism had as one of its aims winning tolerance for customs that diverged from stable and puritanical American norms. As one moved from the sixties to the seventies and eighties it was hard to conceive of practices so deviant or kinky that they could not be found just off Main Street.

From the late 1960s onward it was cognitive relativism which came to trouble the profession, in large part because, for complex reasons, ethnographic attention came increasingly to focus on systems of belief, meaning, and symbol. There was nothing in such a focus which was inherently hostile to a posture of scientific objectivity. Claude Lévi-Strauss described his structural analysis of myth as preparing the way for a "scientific anthropology" which "should be able to set up experiments for the purpose of verifying its hypotheses and deducing, on the basis of certain guiding principles, hitherto unknown properties of the real world." But the structuralist program for uncovering the universal grammar of culture had few American followers, and the American anthropologists who dealt with myth, magic, and primitive belief systems not only were little influenced by structuralism, but also moved away

[30]Eric R. Wolf, *Anthropology* (in the series Humanistic Scholarship in America) (Englewood Cliffs, N.J., 1964), 59, 94, 96. For the evolution of terminology, see Paul Jorion, "Emic and Etic: Two Anthropological Ways of Spilling Ink," *Cambridge Anthropology* 8 (1983): 41–68.

from the empiricism and positivism which had characterized the discipline in the postwar years.[31]

The spectre of thoroughgoing cognitive relativism hovered over the continuing debate among English and American scholars concerning the "rationality" of Azande witchcraft—whether there was a metacultural criterion by which Azande beliefs could be pronounced "true" or "false"; whether a clear distinction could be made between magic and science. Following Durkheim, Robin Horton continued to insist that a crucial distinction could be made, having to do principally with the "closed" as opposed to "open" nature of the alternative thoughtways. By the early 1980s Horton, though by no means prepared to collapse the distinction, admitted that the differences were considerably more fuzzy and nuanced than he had once thought. His critics, in Horton's summary, had insisted that

the tradition-bound thinker is *more* critical and reflective, and *less* conservative, than I make him, and that the modern, scientifically-trained thinker is *less* critical and reflective, and *more* conservative, than I make him. So far as the world-view associated with a society is concerned, they insist that the typical traditionalistic world-view is far more open to change and external influence than I allow, and that the typical modern world-view is rather less open to change than I would like to think.

"By and large," Horton granted, "they have proved their point."[32]

Whereas Horton's experience with primitive belief systems led him, though with diminishing certitude, to stress the contrast between traditional and scientific thought, Mary Douglas's investigations of implicit and inarticulate areas of tribal consciousness took a reflexive turn. "If they use appeals to the *a priori* in nature as weapons of coercion or as fences around communal property," she wrote, "it is probable that we do likewise." The contrast between Horton and Douglas is clearest in their response to Durkheim's separation of the traditional and the modern with respect to rationality and the social determination of knowledge. Where Horton stressed the distinction, Douglas deconstructed it. For her it was precisely the sort of *aporia* which Derrida et Cie. found in the texts they examined. In her view Durkheim, by failing to push his thought to his logical conclusion, missed the opportunity to rank with Marx and Freud, and integrate his unpursued insight with theirs. Durkheim's failure, in Douglas's view, stemmed from two unwarranted assumptions. One was

<hr/>

[31]Lévi-Strauss, *The Naked Man: Introduction to a Science of Mythology, 4* (New York, 1981), 153.
[32]Horton, "Tradition and Modernity Revisited," in Martin Hollis and Steven Lukes, eds., *Rationality and Relativism* (Cambridge, Mass., 1982), 210–11.

his conviction that primitives are utterly unlike modern westerners, an assumption which would have been corrected had he spent as much as a week in the field. The other was his unquestioned belief in "objective scientific truth, itself the product of our own kind of society."

Durkheim used the sacred-profane dichotomy to develop a completely sociological theory of knowledge. The theory comes to a halt in his thinking when it reaches objective scientific truth. It peters out when it seems about to conflict with the most widely held beliefs of his own day. . . . It is timely to inquire again about the philosopher's bogey of relativism. Bracket aside Durkheim's wish to protect from defilement the values of his own community as a distracting illustration of the value of his theory—then follow his thought through to the bitter end: we seem to have a thoroughly relativised theory of knowledge. The boundaries which philosophers rally instinctively to protect from the threat of relativism would seem to hedge something very sacred. . . . Anyone who would follow Durkheim must give up the comfort of stable anchorage for his cognitive efforts. His only security lies in the evolution of the cognitive scheme, unashamedly and openly culture-bound, and accepting all the challenges of that culture. It is part of our culture to recognise at last our cognitive precariousness. . . . It is part of our culture to be forced to take aboard the idea that other cultures are rational in the same way as ours. Their organisation of experience is different, their objectives different, their successes and weak points different too. The refusal to privilege one bit of reality as more absolutely real, one kind of truth more true, one intellectual process more valid, allows the original comparative project dear to Durkheim to go forward at last.[33]

The foremost American representative of the new anthropological sensibility has been Clifford Geertz. Prodigiously prolific, he is the author of several highly acclaimed ethnographies, as well as dozens of critical and reflective essays, all written in a lively, highly personal, and aphoristic style which appears to irritate as many as it delights. More influential than any other single figure within the discipline, he is also the anthropologist best known and most cited outside of it. (The editors of the proceedings of a recent conference of American intellectual historians described Geertz as "virtually the patron saint" of the meeting.) As director of the Social Science School of the Institute for Advanced Study, which every year brings together a new collection of emerging or established leaders of social science disciplines, he has occupied an unparalleled strategic location.[34]

---

[33]*Implicit Meanings: Essays in Anthropology* (London, 1978), xv-xviii.
[34]John Higham and Paul K. Conkin, eds., *New Directions in American Intellectual History* (Baltimore, 1979), xvi. Kuhn, Higham and Conkin reported, ran Geertz a close second. It is worth noting that many of the historians who have spent a year at the institute, particularly those dealing with recent centuries, have come to its social science rather than its historical school.

Objectivity in crisis

Though his early work was concerned with comparative problems of economic development in new nations, Geertz soon came to personify the echt-emic anthropologist: holistic, concerned with "the native's point of view," taking a semiotic view of culture, a textual view of reality, and a hermeneuticist view of the task of the social sciences. "Believing with Max Weber, that man is an animal suspended in webs of significance he himself has spun, I take culture to be those webs, and the analysis of it to be therefore not an experimental science in search of law but an interpretive one in search of meaning." Geertz has never sought to codify his approach, and his epistemological observations have been cast in his characteristic allusive, and, in consequence, frequently elusive, style. Insofar as one can speak of him as having a "position" on these issues it has largely been defined by him in negative terms.[35]

"Cultural analysis is (or should be)," he writes, "guessing at meaning, assessing the guesses, and drawing explanatory conclusions from the better guesses, not discovering the Continent of Meaning and mapping out its bodiless landscape." He was an early (1964) critic of the pejorative use of the term "ideology," and on numerous occasions made it clear that he thought all ways of thinking were "ideological" in nontrivial senses. The approach with which he identified had, he said, no room for "the strict separation of theory and data, the 'brute fact' idea . . . , the claim to moral neutrality and the Olympian view, the 'God's truth' idea." Though not a direct participant in the debate on "scientific rationality," he declined an invitation to appear as an expert witness for those seeking to oust "creationism" from the schools on the grounds that he would hurt their cause, since his testimony would depict the boundary between science and religion as much fuzzier than it was held to be by the anticreationists.[36]

Following his usual practice, Geertz, in his fullest statement on "objectivity" and "relativism," expressed himself negatively. His position, in both the cognitive and moral domains, was "Anti-Anti-Relativism." He mocked the embattled defenders of objectivity who were "afraid reality is going to go away unless we believe very hard in it."

We are being offered a choice of worries. What the relativists, so-called, want us to worry about is provincialism—the danger that our perceptions will be dulled,

[35]"Thick Description: Toward an Interpretive Theory of Culture," in his *Interpretation of Cultures* (New York, 1973), 5.
[36]Ibid., 20; "Blurred Genres: The Refiguration of Social Thought," *American Scholar* 49 (1980), reprinted in his *Local Knowledge: Further Essays in Interpretive Anthropology* (New York, 1983), 34; remarks on creationism delivered orally at 1984 University of Iowa symposium on "The Rhetoric of the Human Sciences."

our intellects constricted, and our sympathies narrowed by the overlearned and overvalued acceptances of our own society. What the anti-relativists, self-declared, want us to worry about, and worry about and worry about, as though our very souls depended upon it, is a kind of spiritual entropy, a heat death of the mind, in which everything is as significant, thus as insignificant, as everything else: anything goes, to each his own, you pays your money and you takes your choice, I know what I like, not in the south, *tout comprendre, c'est tout pardonner*. . . .

I myself find provincialism altogether the more real concern so far as what actually goes on in the world. . . . The image of vast numbers of anthropology readers running around in so cosmopolitan a frame of mind as to have no views as to what is and isn't true, or good, or beautiful, seems to me largely a fantasy. There may be some genuine nihilists out there, along Rodeo Drive or around Times Square, but I doubt very many have become such as a result of an excessive sensitivity to the claims of other cultures; and at least most of the people I meet, read, and read about, and indeed, I myself, are all-too-committed to something or other, usually parochial. "'Tis the eye of childhood that fears a painted devil": anti-relativism has largely concocted the anxiety it lives from.[37]

Anthropologists a generation younger than Geertz, some of them his students, extended the critique of positivism and objectivism by focusing on the nature of the ethnographic encounter, and its representation. Whereas Geertz has been skeptical of cross-cultural generalizations, members of this group doubted the legitimacy of Geertzian synthetic, often synechdocal, claims for intracultural characterization. The 1967 publication of Malinowski's diary, with its repeated reference to "cheeky niggers," was one catalyst for this concern, as was, more generally, heightened sensitivity to tacit racism at home and abroad. With the shift of ethnographic focus to systems of meaning rather than of behavior there was increasing skepticism about the adequacy of anthropologists' fairly rudimentary, rapidly attained "working knowledge" of indigenous language as a basis for sweeping "emic" characterizations. Much of the classic ethnographic literature had been produced in a colonial context, to which, looking back from the postcolonial 1960s and 1970s, its authors seemed willfully blind. Michel Foucault's various meditations on the relation between knowledge and power, as well as Said's explicit location of this relation in the encounter of the West with "the Other," stimulated many younger anthropologists to greater self-consciousness about the nature of their elders', and their own, relations with "natives." Geertz's "thick description," one young anthropologist wrote, was "thick with extravagant assumptions," notably that "social relationships constitute an observer-independent reality" which could be accurately described. He was charged by another critic with "fail[ure] to acknowledge reflectively the influence of the data-generating encounter."[38]

Work in the history of anthropology, whose principal audience was anthropologists rather than historians, was particularly important in raising epistemic questions. George Stocking, influenced by Kuhn's treatment of the social constitution of scientific truth, analyzed the strategies by which the emerging anthropological profession established its products' claim to scientific validity. James Clifford, a younger historian of anthropology, brought to bear the full battery of modern literary theory in a number of studies of ethnographic representation. He directed attention to the process by which dialogic discourse becomes monologic and authoritative text, using, inter alia, the example of Geertz's classic account of the Balinese cockfight.

"The Balinese" function as author of Geertz's textualized cockfight. . . . It is tempting to compare the ethnographer with . . . the traditional critic, who sees the task at hand as locating the unruly meanings of a text in a single, coherent intention. . . . The ethnographer transforms the research situation's ambiguities and diversities of meaning into an integrated portrait. But it is important to notice what has dropped out of sight. The research process is separated from the texts it generates and from the fictive world they are made to call up. . . . The dialogical, situational aspects of ethnographic interpretations tend to be banished from the final representative text. . . . Geertz's abrupt disappearance into his rapport—the quasi-invisibility of participant-observation—is paradigmatic. . . . We are seldom made aware of the fact that an essential part of the cockfight's construction as a text is dialogical, talking face-to-face with particular Balinese rather than reading culture "over the[ir] shoulders."[39]

In the last decade younger anthropologists have moved beyond programmatic statements and critiques of existing practice. They have been producing a growing body of substantive ethnographic work which is frequently dialogic in form, and almost always stresses the "negotiated" and "constructed" nature of the reality it describes. It is thoroughly "postmodern" in the explicit authorial presence and insistence on the "textual" nature of what is produced. If, as in Clifford's account of Geertz's procedures, the author's disappearance in favor of "the culture

---

[38]Paul J. Magnarella, review of Geertz et al., *Meaning and Order in Moroccan Society*, *American Anthropologist* 82 (1980): 676–77; Vincent Crapanzano, review of the same work, *Economic Development and Cultural Change* 29 (1981): 859.

[39]Clifford, "On Ethnographic Authority," *Representations* 1 (1983): 131–33; Geertz, "Deep Play: Notes on the Balinese Cockfight," *Daedalus* 101 (1972), reprinted in his *Interpretation of Culture*, 412–53.

speaking for itself" is an inauthentic device for the attainment of problematic authority, at least some members of the following generation have opted for an anthropology which ties "an Other that is created as a relation to Self, and a Self that emerges in its encounter with the Other."[40]

There was one academic realm in which those who argued about "objectivity" and "determinacy" were playing for more than academic stakes. From *Brown v. Board of Education* through the *Roe v. Wade* abortion decision and beyond, the American judiciary came to be in fact what it had always been in principle: a coequal branch of government, whose "legislation" was often more consequential than anything produced by Congress. In an era of unprecedented judicial activism, the question "Quo Warranto?" loomed with ever greater urgency. Legislative decisions are justified by the legislators' notions of their constituents' best interests, but judges' decisions, particularly when they go against majority views, have to claim to be based on something more objective than personal preference. As one legal scholar recently put it, "'I like it' is not a very good argument, but 'the Constitution says so,' stated with appropriate emphasis and in a sincere tone, can be persuasive." But by the 1960s and 1970s there were hardly any members of the legal community prepared to argue that constitutional adjudication was clear-cut—that, in Justice Roberts's classic phrase, the Court's only duty was "to lay the article of the Constitution which is invoked beside the statute which is challenged and to decide whether the latter squared with the former."[41]

The Critical Legal Studies movement which emerged in the 1970s was clearly the intellectual descendent of interwar Legal Realism, but the progeny were in every way more radical than their ancestors. Where the Realists had regretfully noted that existing deductive jurisprudence was indeterminate, followers of CLS renounced the very notion of a coherent and predictable jurisprudence. Sanford Levinson of the Stanford Law School wrote that

it would obviously be nice to believe that *my* Constitution is the true one and therefore that my opponents' versions are fraudulent, but that is precisely the belief that becomes steadily harder to maintain. They are simply *different* Constitutions. There are as many plausible readings of the United States Constitution as there are versions of *Hamlet*, even though each interpreter, like each director,

[40] Kevin Dwyer, *Moroccan Dialogues: Anthropology in Question* (Baltimore, 1982), 272. Recent work of this sort is surveyed and summarized in George E. Marcus and Michael M. J. Fischer, *Anthropology as Cultural Critique: An Experimental Moment in the Human Sciences* (Chicago, 1986).
[41] Mark Tushnet, "Legal Scholarship: Its Cause and Cure," *Yale Law Journal* 90 (1981): 1210; *United States v. Butler*, 297 U.S. 1, 62 (1936).

might genuinely believe that he or she has stumbled onto the one best answer to the conundrums of the texts. That we cannot walk out of offending productions of our national epic poem, the Constitution, may often be anguishing, but that may be our true constitutional fate.

While most Realists had seen problems of "subjectivity" as isolable difficulties in carrying out a program grounded in "the rule of law," critical scholars in the 1970s and 1980s saw the problems from a Wittgensteinian view of the relativism inherent in "the concept of rules."[42]

The Critical Legal Studies movement was unique among the antiobjectivist tendencies surveyed in this chapter in being a movement of the left, "neo-" or "post-" Marxist. Its critique of what it saw as the incoherencies and contradictions of liberal jurisprudence went considerably farther than that of the Realists, who had never questioned the capitalist order, and tended, like the Progressive Historians, to reduce outcomes to self-conscious and self-interested decisions of actors within the political and legal system.

History was a key weapon in the CLS armory. Morton Horwitz of Harvard, whose 1977 *The Transformation of American Law* won the Bancroft Prize for history, saw the fundamentally unhistorical orientation of legal scholarship as a defense of the rationalizing enterprise which sought to "suppress the real contradictions in the world, to make the existing world seem to be necessary . . . part of the nature of things." Legal scholars' hostility to history, Horwitz said, was based on recognition of its subversive potential, its capacity to show that "the rationalizing principles of the mainstream scholars are historically contingent." Robert Gordon, another CLS legal historian, argued that

our accustomed ways of thinking about law and history are as culturally and historically contingent as "society" and "law" themselves. Though we can never completely escape from the limitations of our environment, we can [undertake] a self-conscious effort to relativize our own consciousness . . . relativize our understanding of the past's relation to the present . . . see that our conventional views of that relation are mediated by familiar narrative story-lines, that are so deeply entrenched in our consciousness that we are often unaware of their rule over our conception of reality. These story-lines, like other mentalities have a history filled with ideological purposes, and there always exist—and so we always may draw upon—competing stories that impress the same historical experience with radically divergent meanings.[43]

---

[42]"Law as Literature," *Texas Law Review* 60 (1982): 391–92. Levinson is not formally a member of the Conference on Critical Legal Studies, but his writings parallel many of the themes in the work of those formally affiliated with CLS.

[43]Horwitz, "The Historical Contingency of the Role of History," *Yale Law Journal* 90 (1981): 1057; Gordon, "Critical Legal Histories," *Stanford Law Review* 36 (1984): 101–2.

In addition to the project of relativizing and delegitimizing legal consciousness through historical analysis, CLS scholars analyzed legal texts with a technique they called "trashing," a combination of deconstruction and *Ideologiekritik*. The method, according to one practitioner, was to "take specific arguments very *seriously* in their own terms; discover they are actually *foolish* ([tragi-]*comic*); and then look for some (external observer's) *order* (*not* the germ of truth) in the internally contradictory incoherent chaos we've exposed."[44]

Numerically CLS supporters constituted a small fraction of the community of legal scholars, though like the Realists before them, they were a particularly strong presence at some of the nation's most important law schools, notably Harvard and Stanford, and they played a role disproportionate to their numbers in setting the terms of debate within the field. Leading mainstream scholars, like the very unradical G. Edward White of the University of Virginia, were prepared to concede that the CLS critique had effectively demolished the central tenets of postwar legal thinking: the ideas "that process leads to justice . . . that advocacy leads to truth . . . that expertise leads to wisdom." One of the most noteworthy aspects of recent controversies in jurisprudence is that many of the opponents of Critical Legal Studies are almost as likely as its supporters to seek guidance from the work of Kuhn, Rorty, Geertz, and Fish. Discourse in legal scholarship became increasingly "textual," distributed along a continuum between "strong textualists" who emphasized the malleability of texts, and "weak textualists" who emphasized boundaries to the possibilities of interpretation. In the writings of mainstream legal theorists like Ronald Dworkin and Owen Fiss, traditional claims to cognitive objectivity were abandoned, legal interpretation was seen as hermeneutic (analogous to the interpretation of literature), and their hopes for avoiding radical indeterminacy rested in the authority of professional communities of interpreters to decree some readings "off the wall."[45]

Recent criticisms of received views of truth and objectivity in psychoanalysis were of particular interest to historians, because in many ways they recapitulated the interwar critique of historical objectivity by Beard and Becker, in both their less and their more cogent moments. And, more than in any other field, recent epistemological debates in psychoanalysis have explicitly referred back to earlier discussions of the objectivity question in historiography.

As H. Stuart Hughes, among many other postwar scholars, pointed

[44]Mark G. Kelman, "Trashing," *Stanford Law Review* 36 (1984): 293.
[45]White, "The Inevitability of CLS," *Stanford Law Review* 36 (1984): 663–65, 670; Dworkin, "Law as Interpretation," in Mitchell, *Politics of Interpretation*, 249–70; Fiss, "Objectivity and Interpretation," *Stanford Law Review* 34 (1982): 739–63.

out, the analyst's "professional and moral goal is the same as that of the historian: to liberate man from the burden of the past by helping him to understand that past." Though Hughes sensed a close affinity between psychoanalysis and history, in part because both were attacked by "literal-minded devotees of science," the goal of both was "objective truth." For the philosopher of history Hans Meyerhof the two modes of inquiry were alike in aiming "to eliminate the personal equation . . . make the findings . . . as 'objective' as possible. . . . In both fields we can and do . . . distinguish between science and fiction."[46]

That psychoanalysis was devoted to unearthing objective truth, producing an account which "corresponded" to buried psychic reality, was an unquestioned axiom within the field. From his earliest to his last writings, Freud consistently maintained that the knowledge unearthed in a successful analysis met the most stringent criteria of a correspondence theory of truth, and that only such knowledge could be beneficial to the patient. In 1937, in the evening of his life, Freud was even willing to express serious doubts about the range and permanency of psychoanalysis' therapeutic efficacy. But in the same year he reaffirmed his lifelong belief that the analyst's final reconstruction of the repressed psychic life of the analysand was the objective historical truth about repressed psychic reality. In arriving at this goal the analyst faced fewer difficulties than the historian or archaeologist, because "all of the essentials are preserved; even things that seem completely forgotten are present somehow and somewhere." Though the analyst's reconstructions were informed by certain general theoretical assumptions, the approved procedure was thoroughly empiricist and might even be termed inductive. The patient's "free associations" were taken in by the analyst, who maintained a posture of "evenly-hovering attention." Tentative interpretations, and larger reconstructions based on these interpretations, were tested, modified, and ultimately verified in the ongoing explorations. A well-conducted analysis produced its cure through the patient's justified conviction of the historical truth of the analyst's reconstruction.[47]

---

[46]Hughes, "History and Psychoanalysis: The Explanation of Motive" (1961), in his *History as Art and as Science* (New York, 1964), 46–47; Meyerhof, "On Psychoanalysis as History," *Psychoanalysis and the Psychoanalytic Review* 49 (Summer 1962): 11.

[47]"Constructions in Analysis," in James Strachey, ed., *The Standard Edition of the Complete Psychological Works of Sigmund Freud*, vol. 23 (London, 1964), 260. For Freud's pessimistic assessment of psychoanalysis as therapy, see "Analysis Terminable and Interminable," ibid., 211–53. Freud was scornful of Hans Vaihinger's talk of "practical fictions" in *The Philosophy of "As If"*: its demand was "one that only a philosopher could put forward. A man whose thinking is not influenced by the artifices of philosophy will never be able to accept it." (*The Future of an Illusion* [1927], in *Standard Edition*, 21:29.)

Until the 1960s the dominant self-image of the psychoanalytic profession, particularly in the United States—was positivist and scientific. Within the last two decades this orientation has come to be challenged, accompanied by a lively historical and biographical debate whether the "essential" Freud was a biologist of the mind (Frank Sulloway) or a humanist lost in translation (Bruno Bettelheim). Whatever individual writers' views on the past of the movement, there has arisen a strong disposition to reconceive the ongoing psychoanalytic venture as hermeneutic rather than scientistic, a development which was, to use the language of psychoanalysis, "overdetermined." Within the medical-psychiatric community, which increasingly became a subspecialty of pharmacology, psychoanalysis was no longer "where the action was," and it experienced a continuing crisis of recruitment. Meanwhile, among the laity, it priced itself out of reach. Philosophers, following Popper, though sometimes with much greater sophistication, continued to attack the scientific status of psychoanalysis because of the alleged "unfalsifiability" of both its theoretical propositions and clinical diagnoses. Analysts never succeeded in producing—indeed, shrank from attempting—statistical demonstration of its superiority to alternative therapies. At the same time, Freudian approaches were gaining ever greater currency in disciplines like literary criticism and cultural anthropology, in which a "hermeneutic turn" was congenial. The development of a hermeneutic conceptualization of the discipline, which had the not overlooked consequence of immunizing it from meeting difficult philosophical and scientific criteria, was cheered on by sympathetic philosophers, notably Jürgen Habermas and Paul Ricoeur.

Nothing in the adoption of a hermeneuticist posture per se involved forswearing criteria of veridicality. Practitioners of the "human sciences," though they employed a different mode of explanation, had traditionally been as insistent as those working within the natural sciences in defending the objectivity of their labors. By the late twentieth century received notions of objectivity were as much at risk in the latter realm as in the former, and skepticism about the nature of the "truths" uncovered by psychoanalysis might well have arisen without the hermeneutic turn. Psychoanalysts who abandoned mimetic notions of reconstruction cited Kuhn and Feyerabend as well as Barthes and Fish, and rounded out their arguments with reference to the other usual suspects: Foucault, Geertz, Goodman, and the rest. But the direction taken by analysts who distanced themselves from the positivist model of archaeological reconstruction was decisively shaped by their alliance with the humanities, and an emphasis on language, literature, and "narrativity."

The work of two of the most influential analysts who led in this development, Donald Spence and Roy Schafer, illustrates the very different paths which led to the new view, and the way in which convergent conceptualizations could reflect what appear to be quite disparate sensibilities. Both men rejected Freud's positivist, archaeological model, and the notion that there are knowable, discrete bits of reality "out there" (or "in there") out of which the analytic life history is reconstructed. For both, facts were irretrievably theory-laden. Both rejected a criterion of correspondence for judging the adequacy of analytic interpretation. For both, the new life history which emerges from analysis is made, not found. Both, albeit understandably somewhat gingerly, spoke of the "fictive" nature of analytic constructions. Both took an explicitly relativistic stance, but where Spence's was a relativism of limitations, Schafer's was a relativism of possibilities.

Spence's starting point was distress at the opacity of language. He repeatedly emphasized its potentiality for concealment rather than its capacity to reveal. The titles of his early papers suggest his rattling at the bars of the prison house of language, his attempt to penetrate the linguistic barrier between the analyst and "reality": "Computer Measurement of Process and Content in Psychoanalysis"; "Tracing a Thought Stream by Computer." In his later work, cybernetic dreams had faded, but he continued to decry the absence of unmediated and transparent media of communication. In his major work, *Narrative Truth and Historical Truth*, there were complaints that "language is both too rich and too poor to represent experience adequately," "there is no one-to-one correspondence between text and reality." Archaeological reconstruction could not function when one had, at most, "contaminated" descriptions of pillars and paving stones, not the objects themselves. Moreover, the analyst was self-deceived in believing that the combination of the patient's free association and the analyst's evenly hovering attention could produce anything but chaos. One party or the other was necessarily, if unwittingly, imposing narrative order. The resulting construction was not empirically verifiable, and constructions arrived at in this fashion could not cumulate for the advancement of theory. Since historical truth was unavailable in analysis, one settled, *faute de mieux*, for narrative truth, which would cohere even if it would not correspond.[48]

Like Spence, Schafer's starting point was the language of psychoanalysis, but whereas Spence had seen language as barrier, Schafer

[48]Papers in, respectively, *Transactions of the New York Academy of Sciences* 31 (1969) and *Psychoanalysis and Contemporary Science* 2 (1973); quotations from *Narrative Truth* (New York, 1982), 49, 51.

stressed its potential for reconceptualizing Freudian metapsychology and reforming psychoanalytic practice. In his early work he called for a replacement of the scientistic language of energy, force, and drive, which implied that individuals were objects, and the substitution of "action language" which emphasized human agency and responsibility. As Schafer turned to the study of narrative he saw the traditional Freudian "drive narrative," rooted in nineteenth-century physiology and neuroanatomy, as being far from the only sort of story that could be told.

The drive narrative tells the partly moralistic and partly Darwinian-scientific tale that at heart we are all animals, and it sets definite guidelines for all the tales we tell about ourselves and others. By following these guidelines, we fulfill two very important functions, albeit often painfully and irrationally. We simultaneously derogate ourselves (which we do for all kinds of reasons), and we disclaim responsibility for our actions. Because these functions are being served, many people find it difficult to accept the proposition that drive is a narrative structure, that is, an optional way of telling the story of human lives.[49]

For Schafer it was the task of the analyst and analysand to collaborate in constructing a coherent and useful *version* of the latter's psychic life history, one among many possible versions, since there was "no single knowable reality as a final test of truth." Psychoanalysis, for Schafer, offered "a narrative method for constructing a second reality," which, following Nelson Goodman, he called "a kind of worldmaking."

Although this second reality sometimes overlaps the ordinary, conscious . . . reality of everyday life, it need not do so, and in crucial respects it does not do so. In many ways, the second reality of psychoanalysis is more akin to the reality constructed in poetry, story, visual arts. . . . It both supplements and competes with . . . conventionalized reality. Both kinds of reality are constructions. Each construction has its uses.

The analyst should say to the patient: "This second reality is as real as any other. In many ways it is more coherent and inclusive and more open to your activity than the reality you now vouch for and try to make do with. On this basis it also makes the possibility of change clearer and more or less realizable, and so it may open for you a way out of your present difficulties." In constructing a life history on these pragmatic grounds one entered the world of "fictions" ("an approach to reality . . . an organized set of beliefs and a corresponding way of defining facts"), but this very awareness of what one was doing, allowed one to avoid "myth"

[49]*The Analytic Attitude* (New York, 1983), 225–26.

("ultimate, unchangeable assertions about reality pure and simple . . . claim[ing] direct access to one and only one clearly ascertainable world").[50]

The resemblance between elements of postpositivist psychoanalytic thought and that of interwar historical relativists is striking. Spence's turn to a relativist orientation in the wake of his disappointed earlier scientism parallels Beard's odyssey. His distinction between the allegedly unmediated access to reality of the natural scientist and the analyst seeing through a glass darkly recapitulates an invalid distinction common to both Beard and Becker. Schafer's emphasis on the pragmatic purposes for which "everyman" constructs a usable history closely follows Becker's argument. Comparison between relativism in history and in psychoanalysis was pursued more systematically by other psychoanalysts who reexamined Freudian epistemology and practice. Richard Geha, who went farther than any other analyst in adopting a "subjectivist idealist" position, was inclined to invoke Croce and Collingwood. Edwin Wallace, though disavowing a "naive Rankean notion of the facts," took an objectivist stance, and generally endorsed the antirelativist strictures of Lovejoy and Mandelbaum.[51]

Above all, the resemblance lay in seeking to overthrow the reign of a solely correspondence theory of truth, which had been the bedrock of traditional epistemology in both fields, and pressing the claims of its competitors, "coherence" and "pragmatic" theories. In the traditional view it was assumed that latent coherence and pragmatically beneficial consequences would naturally follow from an account which "corresponded." Spence, Schafer, and their allies within psychoanalysis, like the historical relativists, argued that no possible single account could exactly correspond, and that many possible competing accounts could do so "more or less." In their view, while correspondence did not necessarily entail coherence or utility, coherence and utility required a good deal of correspondence, since no account not substantially anchored in reality could ever, in practice, be judged coherent, practical, or in any other sense "true." In their dethroning of correspondence as the all-powerful and sufficient criterion of truth, the dissident analysts were pursuing the same agenda as their colleagues in other disciplines. Their positive program paralleled that enunciated by Becker in "Everyman His Own Histo-

[50]Ibid., 255–56, 235, 276, 283.
[51]Richard E. Geha, "On Psychoanalytic History and the 'Real' Story of Fictitious Lives," *International Forum for Psychoanalysis* 1 (1984): 221–92; Edwin R. Wallace IV, *Historiography and Causation in Psychoanalysis: An Essay on Psychoanalytic and Historical Epistemology* (Hillsdale, N.J., 1985).

rian." The pasts men created were "as a whole perhaps neither true nor false, but only the most convenient form of error." Each generation "must inevitably play on the dead whatever tricks it finds necessary for its own peace of mind."[52]

IV

The fortunes of nontraditional approaches and epistemologies varied a good deal from discipline to discipline. Nowhere did they fail to meet fierce resistance. Just as dissidence was variously motivated, and took different forms, yet was, broadly speaking, convergent, so it was with the responses of its opponents.

Many of the objections raised were purely intellectual, centering on inconsistencies and exaggerations in the new currents. The ambiguities in Kuhn's use of the term "paradigm" was one of the most notorious instances, as was what many historians of science found to be an overdrawn contrast in his work between "normal" and "revolutionary" science. Many philosophers thought that Rorty let his enthusiasm run away with his judgment in defining a pragmatic tradition that stretched from Dewey to Heidegger. In literary studies, critics like Wayne Booth combined respectful attention to Stanley Fish's theses with detailed arguments designed to show that while texts might not be univocal, there was such a thing as irony which could be located in a text, and not just in the mind of the reader. Edward Said seemed to be trying to have it both ways by denying the existence of a "real" Orient, and savaging Orientalists for misrepresenting it. And there were those in anthropology, legal studies, and the psychoanalytic community who produced sharp, reasoned critiques of this or that aspect of the dissidents' work.

Many had professional reasons for questioning the new approaches. In literary studies there was a good deal of discussion of the difficulty, if not impossibility, of teaching literature in a language clotted with the jargon of deconstructionism. Anthropologists who were appreciative of the often penetrating insights of Geertzian ethnography thought it an approach too idiosyncratic, too dependent on personal qualities of the ethnographer, to be widely recommended as general practice. The insistence,

---

[52]Becker, *Everyman His Own Historian* (New York, 1935), 245, 253. Schafer, echoing a point made repeatedly by Beard and Becker, made it clear that he did not believe that any view was as good as any other: "we can identify wrong, false, or inadequate answers to the questions we put to reality, even though we allow that there are many right, true, or adequate answers to them rather than just one such answer." (Schafer, "Misconceiving Historiography and Psychoanalysis as Art," *International Forum for Psychoanalysis* 1 [1984]: 368.)

common to most of the dissidents, on the irretrievably ideological nature of standpoints, seemed to threaten the possibility of professional discourse which transcended ideologies. Across the board there was understandable professional distress and resentment at the arrogant claims sometimes made by zealots that the new dispensations rendered existing traditions of inquiry obsolete, together with the technical skills with which they were practiced.

But the crisis occasioned by the wave of dissidence went far beyond debate over particular theses, methodologies, or research agendas. There was an almost religious repugnance for the new orientations, since they threatened what in individual disciplines, and in academic life as a whole, was sacred. "The only person who holds nothing sacred," Mary Douglas writes, "is the one who has not internalised the norms of any community." For (many) professors of English it was the "canonical" status of a body of literary work which was sacred; for (practically all) legal scholars it was the Constitution. Those who questioned that status were guilty not just of error, but of sacrilege, and were demonstrating their unfitness to continue as members of the community. Thus, for University of Chicago law professor (later judge) Richard Posner, the Critical Legal Studies scholars were "unassimilable and irritating foreign substances in the body of the law school."[53]

The attacks, coming as they did, all at once, in a wide variety of fields, and, as we have seen, with considerable interaction and mutual reinforcement, seemed to challenge not just this or that set of disciplinary assumptions, but the very foundations of science and scholarship as a whole. Though dissidence had different particular targets in different fields, fundamental assumptions common to all areas of knowledge were at risk: the determinacy of meaning; distinctions between fact and value, and between knower and known; traditional canons of what it meant to be "rational"; perhaps above all—a proposition too banal to articulate and too sacred to question—that the meaning, and the justification, of scientific and scholarly work was "progress toward the truth."

For many members of the academy, these were not historically contingent aspects of contemporary civilization but the essence of civilization itself. The literary scholar E. D. Hirsch found English studies beset by "anti-rationalism, faddism, and extreme relativism," but the problem transcended his own field.

Scholars are right to feel indignant toward those learned writers who deliberately exploit the institutions of scholarship—even down to its punctilious conventions

---

[53]Douglas, *Implicit Meanings*, xv; Posner, "The Present Situation in Legal Scholarship," *Yale Law Journal* 90 (1981): 1128.

of footnotes and quotations—to deny the whole point of the institutions of scholarship, to deny, that is, the possibility of knowledge. It is ethically inconsistent to batten on institutions whose very foundations one attacks. It is logically inconsistent to write scholarly books which argue that there is no point in writing scholarly books.

The multisided onslaught produced among a great many scholars a beleaguered sense of defending the life of the mind against enemies who had infiltrated the fortress and were attacking from within.[54]

The assaults on traditional epistemology had either coincided with, or followed closely upon, a wave of political assassinations, ghetto rioting, a general unraveling of the culture, and, most immediately relevant to academics, campus turmoil. One common response was to accuse epistemological dissidents of giving aid and comfort to "anti-intellectual" leftist student insurgency, and the more bizarre manifestations of the counter-culture. For the philosopher of science Imre Lakatos, Kuhn's position, albeit unintentionally, "would vindicate . . . the basic political credo of contemporary religious maniacs ('student revolutionaries')." Robert Nisbet predicted that Hugh Stretton, whose *Political Sciences* he thought quite cogent, would become a hero in "the more literate quarters of . . . epistemological nihilism. . . . Though he will certainly enjoy brief heroic status . . . he will yet become like certain refugees from Berkeley who, having sown the wind, avoided the whirlwind by retreating behind institute doors or else snuggling under eastern ivy." To anthropologist Marvin Harris, Geertzian ethnography had made common cause with the religious fanatics of Jonestown:

Many of those who might normally be expected to defend a rational and scientific view . . . of social life and human history in general have abandoned the barricades or actually joined the cultists. What now passes for wisdom among my own colleagues is that science is a Western disease . . . that all descriptions of social life are fabrications; and that empirical research is nothing but a bourgeois dirty trick.[55]

All of this shaded off into charges of "irrationalism" and "nihilism." The former epithet was most often employed against postpositivist philosophers and historians of science, with Kuhn the most visible and most frequent target. Kuhn, according to Dudley Shapere, was maintaining that "the decisions of a scientific group to adopt a new paradigm cannot

---

[54]*The Aims of Interpretation* (Chicago, 1976), 13.
[55]Lakatos, "Falsification and the Methodology of Scientific Research Programmes," in Imre Lakatos and Alan Musgrave, *Criticism and the Growth of Knowledge* (Cambridge, 1970), 93; Nisbet, "Subjective Sí! Objective No!" *New York Times Book Review*, 5 April 1970, 36; Harris, "No End of Messiahs," *New York Times*, 26 November 1978, E21.

be based on good reasons of any kind." Israel Scheffler attributed to
Kuhn the view that "adoption of a new scientific theory is an intuitive or
mystical affair," while according to Imre Lakatos, "in Kuhn's view scientific revolution is irrational, a matter for mob psychology." Judith Buber
Agassi saw critics of objectivity in sociology as "influenced by anarchistic
irrationalism, by Che Guevara's emotionalism, and by Mao's primitive
collectivism." The accusation of nihilism was commonly directed at
deconstructionists. René Wellek charged that their "extreme skepticism
and even nihilism would . . . 'deconstruct,' as they say, all literary study,
interrupt tradition, dismantle an edifice built by the efforts of generations
of scholars and students." But it was even more frequently directed at
those in the Critical Legal Studies movement. For Owen Fiss of Yale,
theirs was "the deepest and darkest of all nihilisms . . . it threatens our
social existence and . . . public life as we know it in America . . . it
demeans our lives."[56]

Despite recurrent attempts to conflate political and epistemological
dissidence, academic "postmodernism," with the single exception of the
explicitly leftist CLS, defied political categorization. Most of the central
figures in the various movements—Kuhn, Rorty, Fish, Geertz—were
either moderate liberals or moderate conservatives. In particular disciplinary heterodoxies there was sometimes a leftward-leaning element: a
few Marxist deconstructionists, some Marxoid externalist historians of
science, post-Geertzian anthropologists who were unhappy with the *maî-
tre's* neglect of issues of power. But the new movement of thought was on
the whole quite apolitical. Indeed, some of the sharpest attacks on new
academic currents came from the left.

Marxists, in proportion to their orthodoxy, were unhappy with what
they saw as the "idealist" implications of Kuhn's position. Most on the
left took a dim view of Rorty. "When [he] actually participates in the
ongoing conversation," wrote political theorist William Connolly, "he
constantly wards off dangerous or disturbing possibilities within it."

Rorty's language tranquilizes and comforts his fellow Americans, first, by
celebrating the technocratic values, self-conceptions, and economic arrangements
operative in (though not exhaustive of) American institutions and, second, by

---

[56]Shapere, "Meaning and Scientific Change," in Robert G. Colodny, ed., *Mind and Cos-
mos: Selected Essays in Contemporary Science and Philosophy* (Pittsburgh, 1966), 67;
Scheffler, *Science and Subjectivity* (Indianapolis, 1967), 18; Lakatos, "Falsification," 178;
Agassi, "Objectivity in the Social Sciences," in R. J. Seeger and R. S. Cohen, eds.,
Philosophical Foundations of Science (Dordrecht, 1974), 306; Wellek, "Destroying Liter-
ary Studies," *New Criterion* 2 (December 1983): 8; Fiss, "Objectivity," 763 (order of
Fiss's remarks slightly rearranged).

implying that once these endorsements have been offered there is not much more to be said. Rorty's prose inhibits discursive mobilization of political energies; it closes the conversation before it manages to disturb the sense that all is well with America. . . . Rorty drops out of the conversation just when it should become more intense and demanding.[57]

The most celebrated American attack on postmodernism in literary studies, Gerald Graff's *Literature Against Itself*, was, Graff said, written from an "old Left" standpoint, and grew out of Graff's distaste for the way academics had "come to reduce political alignments to matters of style and epistemology." And no one was more savage with deconstructionism than the Marxist literary theorist Terry Eagleton, for whom it was "the last uncolonized enclave in which the intellectual can play, savouring the sumptuousness of the signifier in heady disregard of whatever might be going on in the Elysée palace or the Renault factories."[58]

Marvin Harris's animus against Geertz, and "emic" ethnography in general, reflected his belief that it was an approach which "fulfills the conservative bias inherent in institutionalized social science."

No amount of knowledge of . . . rules and codes can "account for" phenomena such as poverty; underdevelopment; imperialism; . . . ethnic and class conflict; exploitation, taxation, private property; pollution and degradation of the environment; the military-industrial complex; political repression; . . . unemployment; or war. These phenomena, like everything else that is important to human beings . . . cannot be scientifically understood as manifestations of codes or rules.

Even the opponents of the neo-Marxist Critical Legal Studies movement were by no means all conservatives. Left-activist lawyers, seeking to extend traditional notions of "rights," did not warm to CLS arguments that constitutional rights were "a hallucination . . . shared, imaginary attributes . . . that don't in fact exist." Owen Fiss, a liberal and egalitarian opponent of the Burger Court, denounced CLS "nihilism" because it undermined "confidence in the existence of the values that underlie the litigation of the 1960's."[59]

It is no criticism of the defenders of traditional epistemologies, whether of the left or of the right, to note that they offered very few new argu-

[57]Connolly, "Mirror of America," *Raritan* 3 (1983): 129, 131.
[58]Graff, "Teaching the Humanities," *Partisan Review* 51/52 (1984–85): 852; Eagleton, *Literary Theory: An Introduction* (Minneapolis, 1983), 141, 144–45.
[59]Harris, *Cultural Materialism: The Struggle for a Science of Culture* (New York, 1980), 284–85; Duncan Kennedy and Peter Gabel, "Roll Over Beethoven," *Stanford Law Review* 36 (1984): 34; Fiss, "The Supreme Court, 1978 Term—Foreword: The Forms of Justice," *Harvard Law Review* 93 (1979): 16–17.

ments for the determinacy of meaning and of reference, the distinction between fact and value, truth as correspondence, the possibility of disinterested inquiry, cumulative progress toward the truth, and the other elements of the objectivist program. Their view was that "if it ain't broke, don't fix it." There was, to be sure, sometimes a more assertive tone to objectivist arguments, which probably owed something to the new climate of criticism, but the arguments themselves were extensions of earlier traditions, and were not devised as responses to the new critiques. This was true as well of the only substantially original objectivist thesis, which was in law. There some (mostly right-wing) scholars claimed to be able to ground a "value-free" jurisprudence in "allocative efficiency," based on the algebra of neoclassical economics. But while the "Law and Economics" movement was a direct challenge, both epistemologically and ideologically, to Critical Legal Studies, it developed independently, not in response to CLS.

If there was a single rallying cry of those who condemned the new tendencies in all the disciplines in which epistemological dissidence threatened, it was "Back to Popper!" In literature, Gerald Graff praised Popper for "show[ing] us a way out of the paralysis of post-Kantian thought," by emphasizing the "'resisting reality' that the current way of talking about fictions fails to respect," while E. D. Hirsch thought that Popper had shown the flaw in "dogmatic relativism" by exposing "The Myth of the Framework . . . the central bulwark of irrationalism." In anthropology Robin Horton sought to defend the distinction between primitive and Western thought on the basis of an "amended and developed" version of Popper's work. Improbably, even in psychoanalysis, Popper's outstanding example of a pseudoscience, one extended defense of the traditional scientism of psychoanalysis against the hermeneutic turn based itself on Popper, whose philosophy could be used to sustain the old view, "if what Popper has explicitly stated about psychoanalysis is ignored."[60]

Especially in the study of science, there was a new, nervous realization of the relativist potential of histories which were either externalist or thoroughgoingly historicist. An article in *Science* asked, half seriously, "Should the History of Science Be Rated X?"—dangerous to the morals and morale of practitioners. In the work of those of his colleagues who

---

[60]Graff, *Literature Against Itself: Literary Ideas in Modern Society* (Chicago, 1979), 204; Hirsch, *Aims*, 148; Horton, "Tradition and Modernity Revisited," 201; James G. Blight, "Must Psychoanalysis Retreat to Hermeneutics: Psychoanalytic Theory in the Light of Popper's Evolutionary Epistemology," *Psychoanalysis and Contemporary Thought* 4 (1981): 149.

pushed externalism to its limits, historian of science Robert J. Richards could hear "the ticking message of the intellectual anarchist." Charles C. Gillispie warned those attending a meeting of the American Association for the Advancement of Science to keep a close eye on historians of science, "lest the field fall prey to those who would use history against science." Mary Hesse worried that "even if the autonomy of internal intellectual factors could be sustained, the tendency of internal history would still be towards relativizing canons of rationality." The threat of relativism was even greater when one acknowledged "external," "nonrational" factors. "Throwing more light on a picture," she warned, "may distort what has already been seen." Lakatos, to preserve the autonomy of science, and protect it from relativism, would limit its history to "rational reconstruction." He suggested that one could "relate the internal history *in the text*, and indicate *in the footnotes* how actual history 'misbehaved' in the light of its rational reconstruction."[61]

One of the most interesting cases of retreat from the relativistic implications of historicism was that of E. H. Gombrich, whose work in the 1950s and early 1960s had stressed that "there is no innocent eye," that the "reality" we see is controlled by conventions, which are in turn imposed by culture. Gombrich's work was a major influence on philosophers like Nelson Goodman, and literary theorists like Murray Krieger, among many others. Kuhn described Gombrich's work as tending in many of the same directions as his own, and being "a source of great encouragement to me." Analogies between the "conventionalism" of Gombrich and Kuhn were frequently made. Krieger called Gombrich's work "an early version of the deconstructive move," licensing a view of all signs as conventional, none any longer "natural." From the mid-1960s onward, as his work was used for purposes of which he came to disapprove, or came to be seen as part of a relativist movement which he deplored, Gombrich progressively drew back from his earlier positions. Like so many others, he often cited Popper. His later work was, in his words, "intended to establish the study of the visual image as a scientific enterprise," the displacement of "subjectivity and convention" by "proven facts." Western naturalistic art since the Renaissance was not just

[61]Stephen G. Brush, "Should the History of Science Be Rated X?" *Science* 183 (1974): 1164–72; Richards, *Darwin and the Emergence of Evolutionary Theories of Mind and Behavior* (Chicago, 1987), 13; Gillispie (paraphrased), in William J. Broad, "History of Science Losing Its Science," *Science* 207 (1980); Hesse, "Reason and Evaluation in the History of Science," in Mikuláš Teich and Robert Young, eds., *Changing Perspectives in the History of Science* (Cambridge, 1973), 129–30, 143; Lakatos, "History of Science and Its Rational Reconstruction," in Y. Elkana, ed., *The Interaction Between Science and Philosophy* (Atlantic Highlands, N.J., 1974), 216.

another code, but progressive movement toward "true" or "correct" representation.[62]

No doubt there were, as Geertz had said, "genuine nihilists out there, along Rodeo Drive or around Times Square." One could indeed find Rorty's "occasional cooperative freshman" who struck a posture so "relativistic" that he or she could find no grounds for choosing between incompatible views. But the dissident academics whose views have here been surveyed were not nihilists, and not (that sort of) relativists. Their rejection of older notions of objectivity and truth, the traditional foundations of knowledge, and hitherto standard ways of adjudicating truth claims, made all the more urgent their need to find a new place to stand.

In one way or another, virtually all followed Kuhn in regarding truth as ultimately social, and locating epistemic authority in their respective disciplinary communities. Popperians might gag at this. W. W. Bartley III referred to "the absurd autistic idea that intellectual issues are settled in university departments." But most "postmodern" scholars, in the natural and social sciences, as well as the humanities, were convinced that no more satisfactory foundation was to be had.[63]

It was not, after all, a new idea. Indeed, it was the epistemological rationale for the professionalizing program of scholars and scientists at the end of the nineteenth century, the establishment of authoritative "communities of the competent." Charles S. Peirce, a central figure in the movement, had defined truth as "the opinion which is fated to be ultimately agreed to by all who investigate." As Thomas Haskell has pointed-ed out, a strict interpretation of Peirce's criterion was pessimistically fatalist: truth cannot be known until the end of time. But a slightly loosened reading is dramatically different. "Recognizing the fallibility of all truth claims, act in accordance with the current best opinion of the existing community of inquirers."[64]

A key assumption which rendered Peirce's social definition of truth satisfactory was his faith that inquiry would inevitably produce con-

---

[62]Kuhn, "Comments on the Relations of Science and Art" (1966), reprinted in *The Essential Tension*, 340–41; Krieger, "The Ambiguities of Representation and Illusion: An E. H. Gombrich Retrospective," *Critical Inquiry* 11 (1984): 184; Gombrich, "Representation and Misrepresentation," ibid., 197. See also Krieger's "Optics and Aesthetic Perception: A Rebuttal," ibid., 11 (1985): 502–8.

[63]"A Popperian Harvest," in Paul Levinson, ed., *In Pursuit of Truth: Essays on the Philosophy of Karl Popper on the Occasion of His 80th Birthday* (Atlantic Highlands, N.J., 1982), 270.

[64]"Professionalism *versus* Capitalism: R. H. Tawney, Emile Durkheim, and C. S. Peirce on the Disinterestedness of Professional Communities," in Haskell, ed., *The Authority of Experts* (Bloomington, Ind., 1984), 207.

vergent results, that "the processes of investigation, if only pushed far enough, will give one certain solution to each question to which they apply it." Investigators

may at first obtain different results, but, as each perfects his method and his processes, the results are found to move steadily together toward a destined centre. . . . Different minds may set out with the most antagonistic views, but the progress of investigation carries them by a force outside of themselves to one and the same conclusion. This activity of thought by which we are carried, not where we wish, but to a fore-ordained goal, is like the operation of destiny. No modification of the point of view taken, no selection of other facts for study, no natural bent of mind even, can enable a man to escape the predestinate opinion.[65]

The foremost late-twentieth-century exponent of a Peircean conception of truth was Richard Rorty, not coincidentally, since Rorty defined himself squarely within the pragmatist tradition. He urged, as we have seen, the substitution of "solidarity" for "objectivity." On the macrocosmic and political level, Rorty's "solidarity" was diachronic: solidarity with the "conversation of the West," "the conversation that is us."

We . . . want to imagine conversations between ourselves . . . and the mighty dead. We want this . . . because we would like to be able to see the history of our race as a long conversational interchange. We want to be able to see it that way in order to assure ourselves that there has been rational progress in the course of recorded history—that we differ from our ancestors on grounds which our ancestors could be led to accept. . . . We need to imagine Aristotle studying Galileo or Quine and changing his mind, Aquinas reading Newton or Hume and changing his, etc. We need to think that . . . the mighty mistaken dead look down from heaven at our recent successes, and are happy to find that their mistakes have been corrected. This means that we are interested not only in . . . the Aristotle who walked the streets of Athens . . . but in . . . an ideally reasonable and educable Aristotle. . . . An ideal Gulag guard can eventually be brought to regard himself as having betrayed his loyalty to his fellow-Russians. . . . Each of these imaginary people, by the time he has been brought to accept such a new description of what he meant or did, has become "one of us." He is our contemporary, or our fellow-citizen, or a fellow-member of the same disciplinary matrix.

On the everyday and academic level, solidarity was synchronic: inquiry and truth claims could only be grounded in contemporary disciplinary practice. In a private letter Rorty wrote of his suspicion that "civilization reposes on a lot of people who take the normal practices of the[ir] disci-

---

[65]"How To Make Our Ideas Clear" (1878), in Charles Hartshorne and Paul Weiss, eds., *Collected Papers of Charles Sanders Peirce* (Cambridge, Mass., 1931–60), 5: 407.

pline with full 'realistic' seriousness . . . the practitioners of . . . inquiry reserving their irony for after-hours."[66]

Peirce's confidence in a solidarity which eventuated in convergent discourse was a plausible act of faith at a time when organized and institutionalized inquiry was just getting under way. Its extension to the social and political realm seemed equally plausible in the era of liberal ascendancy. Rorty thought the best argument for shifting from objectivity to solidarity was that the former—"the traditional Western metaphysico-epistemological way of firming up our habits"—"simply isn't working anymore." But when Rorty wrote, was "solidarity" working any better—diachronically in an age of radical discontinuity, synchronically in a period of polarization and fragmentation?[67]

By the mid-1980s, ideological appeals to the "conversation that is us" seemed to many simply bourgeois mystification. This, in fact, had been the view of the philosopher's father, the independent Marxist journalist James Rorty. He thought Americans would do well to rid themselves of "the democratic dogma expressed in the phrase 'We, the people.' We have never had in this country any such identity of interest as is implied in that first person plural."[68]

If a jaundiced view of the ersatz foundationalism provided by invoking the Western liberal "conversation that is us" came from the left, as analagous skepticism came from dissidents in the Soviet bloc, there was nothing ideological about the perception that "communities of the competent" were not, in fact, steadily marching toward convergent truth. Hard as one might try, it was impossible to locate that emerging Peircean scholarly consensus which was to sustain objectivity in place of old-style foundationalism. In virtually every disciplinary realm, very much including the historical, one found either factional polarization, or fragmented chaos which made factionalism seem, by comparison, like a kind of order.

---

[66]"The Historiography of Philosophy: Four Genres," in Rorty et al., eds., *Philosophy in History* (Cambridge, 1984), 51–52; Rorty to Sanford Levinson, 28 April 1981, quoted in Levinson's "Law as Literature," 401.
[67]Rorty, "Solidarity or Objectivity," 15.
[68]James Rorty, *Where Life Is Better* (New York, 1936), 169, quoted in William Stott, *Documentary Expression and Thirties America* (London, 1973), 239.

16

There was no king in Israel

Taken together, the developments recounted in the last three chapters constituted a sweeping challenge to the objectivist program of the founding fathers of the historical profession. Ideological disarray replaced the consensus on which ideas of objectivity had always depended so heavily. The resurgence of particularist tendencies further undercut the objectivist vision of a convergent past. Various "postmodern" intellectual currents worked together to chip away at the philosophical foundations of the objectivist posture.

But if the challenge was powerful, resistance was hardly less so. The forces of inertia, combined with sometimes willful obliviousness to the implications of new developments, were very strong. And for many historians, who were all too aware of the threatening consequences of new currents, the chosen response was a circling of the wagons, traditionalist backlash, and reasserting more forcefully than ever the validity of received thoughtways.

History's epistemological crisis was played out against a background of depression which was both material and moral. For members of all academic disciplines, and for historians more than most, the lush years of the sixties were followed by years of famine which seemed likely to last out the century. At the same time there was a widespread sense that the historical profession was coming apart at the seams: that it had become, in William Bouwsma's words, "little more than a congeries of groups, some quite small . . . which can speak only imperfectly to each other." And on no issue was mutual incomprehension greater, the fragmentation of discourse more total, than on "the objectivity question."[1]

[1]Bouwsma, "Specialization, Departmentalization and the Humanities," American Council of Learned Societies *Newsletter* 36 (Summer-Fall 1985): 2.

I

There were various causes of the great academic depression which began in the 1970s, but at its heart was a crisis of overproduction. Exhilarated by prospects of seemingly endless expansion, doctoral programs had turned out new would-be college teachers at an ever increasing rate: the number of new history Ph.D.'s who emerged annually tripled in the course of a decade, peaking at over twelve hundred a year in the early seventies. It was simply assumed that there would be jobs for all. By the late sixties the handwriting was on the wall, but it was a few years before academics could bring themselves to read it. The baby boom had ended: by the mid-eighties the college-age population would be shrinking, the shrinkage would not turn around until the mid-nineties, and the pool of potential undergraduates would not return to previous levels before the twenty-first century. Caution and contraction were to replace the ebullient expansionism of the sixties.

The job crunch was at its worst in the early seventies, as large numbers of those who had opted for a career in history during the days of the sellers' market found themselves too far into the pipeline to back out, and trudged ahead even though there was now only twilight at the end of the tunnel. At the 1970 meeting of the American Historical Association there were 2,481 applicants for 188 listed positions, and competition was so fierce that security measures had to be introduced to keep those seeking jobs from destroying invitations to interviews addressed to their competitors. An AHA committee drafted a statement which it asked graduate departments to distribute to applicants, warning them that "employment opportunities for Ph.D.s in history . . . are likely to be few in the next two decades"; advising them to re-examine their "commitments, capabilities, and aspiration" before embarking on graduate study. Supply and demand moved closer together as graduate enrollments in history fell: by the early eighties only half as many history Ph.D.'s were coming out each year as a decade earlier. But nothing like the former equilibrium had been reached: in the mid-sixties fewer than 10 percent of history Ph.D.'s were still looking for a job when they received the degree; by the late seventies and early eighties, more than one-third were still looking at graduation time. And the jobs that were available were often not all that attractive, many being temporary or part-time positions, as cautious or budget-conscious administrators were reluctant to make long-term commitments. The prospects for young scholars replacing retirees diminished as legislation raised the mandatory retirement age from sixty-five to seventy, and then—albeit with a brief suspension of the application of the law to universities—removed that limit as well. The mean age of faculties steadily rose; departments which had previously included in their ranks a substantial contingent of assistant professors—traditionally the vehicle for the introduction of new ideas and approaches—became "tenured in," with few junior members, or even none at all.[2]

For those who had secure jobs, standards of living declined. As with the turnaround in the job market, the pinch was felt all the more because the downturn came in the immediate wake of a period of economic advance. During the sixties the salaries of academics had risen substantially—considerably more rapidly than in other sectors of the labor market. In the seventies the professorate was particularly hard hit by inflation: from 1970–71 to 1984–85 the salaries of academics, in constant dollars, fell by 15 percent, putting them approximately back where they were at the beginning of the sixties. Over the same period the real income of professional and managerial personnel in both government and the private sector increased by about 20 percent. In an era of belt-tightening, university administrations reduced allocations for travel, photocopying, library purchases, and the like, while changes in the tax laws eliminated previous deductions and began to tax some previously sheltered perquisites—all of which reduced scholars' disposable income still further. Professors' social status, as measured by survey researchers, remained about the same relative to other occupations, but their standing in American society experienced an absolute decline as part of the general crisis of confidence in traditional elites. Within the university, faculty members reported that both their autonomy and their participation in institutional decision making was eroding. One study in the mid-eighties called the shift in power away from faculty and toward administration "probably the most important change in higher education that has occurred in recent years"; another spoke of a widespread movement "from faculty hegemony to student consumerism . . . from education community to economic industry."[3]

[2]J. Anthony Lukas, "Historians' Conference: The Radical Need for Jobs," *New York Times Magazine*, 12 March 1972, 47; AHA Committee on Ph.D. Programs in History, "Statement to prospective graduate students on professional opportunities: the 'Job Crisis'" (Washington, D.C., 1972); AHA *Perspectives* 24 (March 1986): 7; Howard R. Bowen and Jack H. Schuster, *American Professors: A National Resource Imperiled* (New York, 1986), 184. In 1983–84 Bowen and Schuster compared reports from leading graduate departments in thirty-two disciplines on changes in enrollment figures for advanced graduate students. History reported a greater decline than any other field. (Ibid., 293.)
[3]Bowen and Schuster, *American Professors*, 84–89, 127; Ann E. Austin and Zelda F. Gamson, *Academic Workplace: New Demands, Heightened Tensions* (Washington, D.C., 1984), 3, 18; Shirley M. Clark, Carol M. Boyer, and Mary Corcoran, "Faculty and Institutional Vitality in Higher Education," in Clark and Darrell R. Lewis, eds., *Faculty*

The academic depression did not hit all disciplines with equal force. Generally the decline was greatest in fields which offered no opportunity for extra-academic employment, or which in other ways had less practical payoff. There had always been differences in the salary scales of faculty in professional schools and those in the arts and sciences. In response to market considerations these differences widened, and within the arts and sciences previously minor differences widened as well. One senior historian told an interviewer that he and his colleagues would rather not know how much an assistant professor of economics was being paid: "we're . . . afraid of the humiliation." At many institutions departmental budgets were closely tied to enrollments—a disaster for historians, whose classes came to be more and more depopulated. At some colleges this was the result of a move toward reducing or eliminating required history courses; everywhere it was a consequence of students voting with their feet against the liberal arts generally. In the course of the seventies the percentage of undergraduates majoring in history fell by almost two-thirds. As of the mid-1980s the American Historical Association reported a continuing decline in undergraduate history enrollments, with no end in sight.[4]

Not all historians were so unlucky as to have their salaries dependent upon enrollment, but few could fail to be discouraged by the flight from history—at least professional history—which proceeded outside as well as inside the academy. History's role in the schools continued to decline. Whereas around 1960 most public high school students studied one year of world history and one of American history, by 1985 most took only one year of American history; at the elementary school level, many states eliminated their eighth-grade American history course to "avoid repetition." All of this, of course, was simply the continuation of a trend which dated from early in the century. And, as had long been true, historians were at a loss as to how the trend could be reversed. Likewise, professional historians continued to lament their failure to win the attention of a popular audience, and there were the by now somewhat ritualistic exhortations about the need for historians to address themselves to the laity.

Vitality and Institutional Vitality (New York, 1985), 23. A 1979 survey asked respondents whether it would be a good thing or a bad thing to have a member of one of several listed groups as President of the United States. By margins of two to one or better, those who replied thought it would be good for the country to have a business executive, a woman, a black, or a Jew as president. A majority of those with an opinion thought it would be bad for the country to have a college professor in the Oval Office. Professors could perhaps take some consolation from the fact that labor leaders, atheists, and priests were rejected by even wider margins. (Bowen and Schuster, *American Professors*, 133.)
[4]Bowen and Schuster, *American Professors*, 156; AHA *Perspectives* 22 (November 1984): 3; Kathleen Neils Conzen and Irene D. Neu, "The State of the Job Crisis in the Historical Profession," *OAH Newsletter* 12 (February 1984): 12.

For some years the AHA sought to develop a popular magazine of history, with editorial fare which would be "diverse, exciting, and irresistibly appealing"; in 1986 the plan was abandoned for lack of resources. Within the profession one looked in vain for successors to the generation of Handlin, Hofstadter, and Woodward, who had had at least some success in reaching out to the educated nonprofessional. With the exception of a few problematic ventures in "public history," professional historians' audience was more than ever confined to each other, plus a dwindling student constituency.[5]

Sooner or later the academic depression would pass, or at least ameliorate. But historians faced another and deeper crisis, which seemed likely to be more enduring. Though, as always, a few cranky commentators grumbled about a "decline of standards," there was no general dissatisfaction with the quality of individual historical works, which, most agreed, need not fear comparison with the scholarship of earlier periods. It was the status of the venture as a whole which dismayed historians. By the 1980s more and more practitioners were reluctantly concluding that even by the most generous definition, history no longer constituted a coherent discipline; not just that the whole was less than the sum of its parts, but that there was no whole—only parts.

II

No aspect of academic life is as taken for granted as the division of inquiry into separate disciplines—institutionally embodied as learned societies at the national or international level, as departments on individual campuses. Though scholars, as a result of quaint anachronistic terminology, are all technically "doctors of philosophy," in practice they receive certification to practice individual disciplines, and secure employment through disciplinary networks. At the campus level it is the discipline which competes for curricular space, for students, and for a larger share of institutional resources.

Most modern academic disciplines emerged through secession—as physics, chemistry, biology and the rest emerged from undifferentiated "natural philosophy," or as political science, economics, sociology, and history broke with the omnibus American Social Science Association in the late nineteenth century. In the majority of cases the establishment of an autonomous discipline was grounded in claims to exclusive sov-

[5]Diane Ravitch, "Decline and Fall of Teaching History," *New York Times Magazine*, 17 November 1985, 50, 101; "AHA Considering Popular History Magazine," *AHA Newsletter* 19 (September 1981): 4.

ereignty over a distinctive subject matter, though territorial claims were commonly joined to assertions that a discipline also shared a particular approach, theoretical assumptions, or concern with a particular set of problems. Since no master cartographer ever laid out a map of academic disciplines, and the way in which knowledge came to be divided was usually the result of contingent circumstances and political struggles, the problem of establishing general criteria of what constituted a bona fide discipline had rarely arisen. In practice, disciplinary organization was simply accepted as given, resting above all on the confidence of members of each discipline that theirs was a coherent and well-defined area of scholarship; on tacit acceptance of each group's claims by those in every other group. It was precisely this confidence which fell apart in the seventies and eighties—not, to be sure, in history alone, but in history more than in any other discipline. In no other field was there such a widespread sense of disarray; in no other discipline did so many leading figures express dismay and discouragement at the current state of their realm. And the frequency with which such expressions appeared seemed to increase with each passing year.

Theodore Hamerow recalled the remark of J. Franklin Jameson in 1923 that up to that time professional historians had been "tun[ing] the instruments of the Muses"; that now it was time to "let the concert begin." But, Hamerow wrote in 1986, "there has been no concert nor is there likely to be one."

The first generation or two of professional historians was sustained by a belief that the growing mass of primary materials and monographic studies would ultimately help scholarship arrive at . . . broader insight into the past. . . . The historians of today have largely abandoned this faith. The course of scholarship has made it appear visionary. They are intimidated by the complexity of the past, by the bewildering variety of what mankind has experienced on earth. They despair of being able to bring order out of chaos.

John Higham, discussing relations between Americanists and European-ists in the United States, had a sense of "a house in which inhabitants are leaning out of many open windows gaily chattering with the neighbors while the doors between the rooms stay closed." Thomas Bender described the historical discipline as fragmented into a large number of autarkic boxes, with each field "studied in its own terms, each with its own scholarly network and discourse."[6]

[6]Hamerow, "The Professionalization of Historical Learning," *Reviews in American History* 14 (1986): 327; Higham, "Paleface and Redskin in American Historiography: A Comment," *Journal of Interdisciplinary History* 16 (1985): 111–12; Bender, "Wholes and Parts: The Need for Synthesis in American History," *JAH* 73 (1986): 127–28.

Even within subdisciplinary communities there was a sense of disorganization and an absence of consensual agendas. Karl F. Morrison, surveying the medieval field, saw one of its most striking features as "the contrast between the ideal of . . . coherence and the reality of fragmentation." Robert R. Palmer, summing up the current state of work in French history, noted the multiplication of microscopic studies which, while "extremely interesting to those who can understand them," seemed to contribute to no larger whole. In the history of international relations, Charles Maier saw "little sense of collective enterprise." Intellectual history, said Robert Darnton, was in no sense a coherent enterprise. "It has no governing *problématique*. Its practitioners share no sense of common subjects, methods, and conceptual strategies." Describing the state of early modern history, Bernard Bailyn saw inquiries "ramifying in a hundred directions at once [with] no coordination among them."

Paths cross and identities merge, and historiography grows ever broader—and, one would have thought, deeper and more meaningful. But depth of understanding is a function, at the least, of coherence, and the one thing above all else that this outpouring of historical writing lacks is coherence. . . . The absence of effective organizing principles in modern historiography—its shapelessness, its lack of general coherence—is not simply the result of the immense increase in writing. It stems . . . from deeper roots. Many of the most energetic historians have forsaken the general goals of history for technical problem-solving. . . . Perhaps that is the way historical understanding must grow. But, whether or not that is so, large areas of history, including some of the most intensively cultivated, have become shapeless, and scholarship is heavily concentrated on unconnected technical problems.[7]

The collapse of professional historical study as an even minimally cohesive venture was the result of a number of gradual developments—a confluence of evolutionary changes which had accelerated in recent decades and which, both singly and in combination, at some point "went critical." It was an illustration of old aphorisms: that quantitative change eventually becomes qualitative change; that while the camel can keep lurching along as one adds straw after straw, the final straw will break its back. At the autopsy, even in the unlikely event that one could manage to

[7]Morrison, "Fragmentation and Unity in 'American Medievalism,'" in Michael Kammen, ed., *The Past Before Us: Contemporary Historical Writing in the United States* (Ithaca, N.Y., 1980), 50; Palmer, "A Century of French History in America," *French Historical Studies* 14 (1985): 173–74; Maier, "Marking Time: The Historiography of International Relations," in Kammen, *Past*, 355; Darnton, "Intellectual and Cultural History," in Kammen, ibid., 337; Bailyn, "The Challenge of Modern Historiography," *AHR* 87 (1982): 2–7.

pick out *the* final straw, its contribution to the beast's demise would have been no greater than that of those added earlier.

The increase in the sheer size of the historical profession necessarily had fragmenting consequences. As a community grows beyond a certain point it ceases to *be* a community. It breaks down into subcommunities, which themselves, in time, may subdivide, so that an effective community can be re-created. By the 1980s the time was long past when the profession as a whole constituted a community in any meaningful sense. As attendance at annual meetings of the American Historical Association moved well into four figures, the gatherings ceased to be, even vestigially, the occasion for the exchange of ideas—a function which was in any case excluded by the way in which substantive sessions were organized. The formal presentation of papers, never less than several hundred in recent years, was an opportunity for young job seekers to display their wares; for the untenured to add something to their *vitae*; for more-established historians to offer prepublication advertisements for forthcoming works. Annual meetings had always served as job markets; now this function crowded out all others. In the course of the seventies, membership in the AHA fell by more than a third, while new organizations founded on the basis of specialist interests multiplied; serious intellectual interaction was reserved for the meetings of specialist groups or for ad hoc gatherings. (By the early 1980s there were seventy-five specialist historical organizations affiliated with the AHA; many more, including some of the most important, with no formal affiliation.) Philip Curtin, in his presidential address to the association, saw declining identification with the historical discipline as a whole, and increasing identification with specialist associations, as "the expression, not the cause, of intellectual splintering that has been going on for decades." Editors of the *American Historical Review* repeatedly bemoaned the absence of submissions of general interest: a futile plaint, since there no longer were any topics of general interest. The most significant new work appeared in specialist journals.[8]

[8]Curtin, "Depth, Span, and Relevance," *AHR* 89 (1984): 2–3. The way in which substantive sessions were organized at meetings of the AHA was the best evidence that the ostensible purpose of the gathering was not taken seriously. Typically there would be three tenuously connected papers, edited with a cleaver so as to be (almost) deliverable in the allotted time. The shredded remnants were read aloud as rapidly as the speakers' lips and tongues could move, while pretending not to notice the chairperson pointing at the clock. There followed one or two "prepared" comments cobbled together at the last moment because the paper had only just arrived. Then, if time allowed, there would be a couple of usually rambling and off-the-point remarks from the floor. The conclusion was often a plea to the audience (friends and family of the speakers, those on search committees sampling the merchandise, and a collection of incurable innocents in search of enlightenment) to exit the room as rapidly as possible because the hotel staff had to arrange it for a luncheon now overdue. If there is exaggeration in this description, it is slight; if there are exceptions, they are rare.

The collapse of community was frequently replicated at the departmental level as well. As departments of forty and fifty or more members became common, they inevitably became bureaucratized, and either subdivided into formal or informal subdepartments, or became mere administrative holding companies. In some of the larger departments members barely knew each other by sight, much less had any idea of what most of their colleagues were up to. With the increase in the size of departments, the number of specialized course offerings doubled and sometimes trebled between the late forties and the late seventies. Whereas well into the postwar period it was common for an individual faculty member to offer a general survey course on American or European history, by the 1980s such courses—if they were offered at all—were typically subdivided into segments, each in the hands of specialists. All of this inevitably meant an increasingly narrow (and often almost random) curriculum, particularly for graduate students. In no other discipline did holders of a Ph.D. have less in the way of common experience.[9]

But the most important way in which sheer expansion conduced toward narrow specialization and fragmentation, both in student training and in scholarly production, was the exponential growth in the quantity of scholarly historical works which filled library shelves. This was a problem for all scholars and scientists, who whatever their discipline are expected to keep up with the literature in their field. But historians, if they are to deal with more than the narrowest subjects in the narrowest possible fashion, rely more on the surrounding literature than any other group of practitioners. Much historical work is based on original investigations in archival material; indeed, historians make something of a fetish of the primary source, particularly if unpublished. But, committed as they are to both contextualism and synthesis, they are much more dependent than others on the work of colleagues. No other discipline is as insistent that both graduate education in a field and the writing of a work of history require mastery of all of the relevant secondary literature.

As recently as a generation ago this requirement was not unrealistic, since even in quite broadly defined fields, or on subjects of major interest, the monographic literature was manageable in size. By the 1980s the kind of mastery to which historians had once aspired, and which professional norms still demanded, escaped even full-time bibliographers. "Only a besotted Faust," said Bernard Bailyn, would attempt to keep up with even a major fraction of the work being done in early modern history. Inevitably, the training of graduate students became narrower and narrower, while in their search for dissertation topics which had not "been

9For figures on the multiplication of course offerings, see Darnton, "Intellectual and Cultural History," in Kammen, *Past*, 350–52.

done," more and more turned to subjects of less and less significance. Whereas in earlier times the most ambitious mature scholars had undertaken works of synthesis which integrated the labors of others, now the proliferation of monographic works made such attempts seem quixotic.[10]

Among all members of the academic community it has long been accepted as axiomatic that increased knowledge leads to increased understanding. But what does "understanding" mean? In the sciences, though there is some reluctance to acknowledge the fact, the bottom-line criterion of understanding is frequently technical and pragmatic. The community of physicists demonstrates an impressive level of understanding of nuclear physics when it can make a bomb that goes off; cardiologists validate their understanding when the heart transplant is not rejected. Even when the criteria are not technological, in almost all of the natural sciences, and many of the social sciences as well, understanding is measured by predictive power—indeed, equated with it: "knowledge is power." Historians have never claimed the capacity to predict: their aspiration, insofar as it transcends compiling an accurate chronicle, is holistic comprehension—a rather different sort of understanding.

There is a sense in which one can speak of "historical knowledge"—verified, accurate statements about the past—as something accumulating on library shelves. But "historical understanding" is in the mind of a human being or it is nowhere. Even within restricted realms, historical knowledge (of the sort libraries build annexes to house) increased past the capacity of human minds to contain, let alone assimilate, it. What, then, of understanding? Up to a point it had been sound doctrine that increased knowledge led to increased understanding. Past that point it was arguable

---

[10]Bailyn, "Challenge," 2. In the case of graduate education, my own experience twenty-five years ago contrasted with that of students today illustrates the point nicely. Those of us at Columbia who in the early sixties prepared for oral examinations in modern European history since the Renaissance were expected, whatever our capacity to read works in foreign languages, to familiarize ourselves with the entire English-language corpus of professional historical scholarship in that vast field, which was then assumed to constitute a foundation shared by all modern Europeanists. The task was certainly time-consuming, but it was by no means impossible. There were perhaps five or six books on nineteenth-century France, two or three on eighteenth-century Germany, comparable numbers treating other times, places, and topics. Then, starting in the sixties, came the flood: by the seventies there were approximately as many American academic works on modern European history published each year as there were on the total "backlist" in 1960. The old assumption that a hardworking student should have a comprehensive grasp of the literature of a major field became hopelessly out-of-date. For a sense of the orders of magnitude involved, cf. the AHA's comprehensive *Guide to Historical Literature* (New York, 1961), and William H. McNeill's quantitative survey of books on modern European history published in the decade 1968–78, in his "Modern European History," in Kammen, *Past*, 95–112.

that knowing more could mean understanding less. Orthodox historical method continued to decree that any reputable generalization had to be consonant with all the discoverable evidence. As findings accumulated which pointed in quite opposite directions, it became virtually impossible to make a generalization which was not falsified in advance by some substantial body of data. In retrospect one could see the extent to which in the past it was precisely lacunae in historical knowledge which had provided imaginative space for the construction of those interpretive patterns which had been the foundation of "historical understanding."

Expansion of the size of the profession, and of the quantity of historical literature, was paralleled by the expansion of history's scope. One should perhaps not make too much of the fact that Herbert Baxter Adams chose "Professor of Institutional History" as the title of his chair at Johns Hopkins in the 1880s, but it surely was the case that when professional history was organized it was primarily dedicated to the study of institutions—mostly though not exclusively political—in northwestern Europe and the United States. It was a finite domain, and in principle a coherent one.

The expansion of history's realm was gradual, dating at least from the emergence of the New Historians in the first years of this century. But for many years programmatic statements about the need to broaden history's scope were little heeded; well into the post-World War II period the overwhelming majority of professional historical work was quite traditional. As late as 1958 fewer than 20 percent of completed dissertations in history dealt with social, cultural, or intellectual issues. This share more than doubled over the next twenty years. Over the same period dissertations in the old political-diplomatic-constitutional core went from almost half to less than a third: still, to be sure, a plurality, but a center, if indeed it was that, which no longer exercised sufficient gravitational pull to keep the other elements within the discipline in orbit. In the mid-1950s there were fewer than a dozen professional historians specializing in Africa; by the end of the 1970s there were six hundred.[11]

From the sixties onward, historians prided themselves on the extent to which their studies had been "broadened" and "enriched"—moving away from a focus on a very limited range of activities, undertaken by a restricted group of persons, in a few areas of the world, to encompassing everything that everybody had done everywhere. Realms of the human past which had hitherto been left to other disciplines—the history of

[11]Figures from Darnton, "Intellectual and Cultural History," in Kammen, ibid., 353, and Philip D. Curtin, "African History," also in Kammen, ibid., 114–15.

education, law, art, philosophy, literature—increasingly became the subject of investigation by professional historians. The expansion of history's
scope was like a film of the history of science run backward, with astronomy, geology, botany, and physiology moving in reverse to gather under
the old umbrella of natural philosophy.

The expansion of historians' interests produced work of great interest
and originality, but the discipline gradually came to recognize that the
price of lateral expansion was a loss of definition for the venture as a
whole. How could one describe what it was that historians did when no
one could imagine anything which they didn't do? Those who had pushed the program of expanding history's domain had always argued that the
ultimate result would be a broader and deeper synthesis: an updated
version of the founding fathers' vision of the gradual additions of bricks
to a cumulative edifice. But whereas the materials which the founders had
fabricated were usually all of a type, historians by the seventies and
eighties were bringing to the building site Carrara marble and vinyl tile,
Thermopane and leaded glass, tapestries and plywood paneling. No one
could possibly put all of this stuff together without creating an architec-
tural monstrosity; perhaps tacit recognition of this was one of the factors
inhibiting attempts at synthesis. For the profession, the ultimate consequence of the diffusion of concerns was the loss of any sense of participating in a common venture. Vann Woodward noted that history had once
been described as "a habitation of many mansions"; by the 1980s it
seemed to him more like "scattered suburbs, trailer camps and a
deteriorating central city."[12]

The expansion of history into new realms inevitably involved historians crossing disciplinary boundaries, and members of other disciplines
proved no more respectful of historians' territorial claims than historians
were of theirs. As with other developments that challenged the autonomy
and integrity of history, the increasing permeability of its borders was not
a new development, but rather an acceleration of previously gradual processes. At the same time it was part of a crisis of disciplinary identity
which was taking place in all quarters of the academy.

In the natural sciences old disciplinary allegiances had been breaking
down for many years, as evidenced by the emergence of such hybrid
fields as geophysics, biochemistry, and no doubt, before long, astro-
botany. In the sciences the development of transdisciplinary or su-
pradisciplinary fields had countervailed the tendency toward compart-

---

[12]Woodward, "A Short History of American History," *New York Times Book Review*, 8
August 1982, 14.

mentalization of inquiry. Rather than scientists becoming ever narrower and more specialized, the Nobel laureate Sir Peter Medawar argued a generation ago, "the opposite is the case."

One of the distinguishing marks of modern science is the disappearance of sectarian loyalties. Newly graduated biologists have wider sympathies today than they had in my day, just as ours were wider than our predecessors'. At the turn of the century an embryologist could still peer down a microscope into a little world of his own. Today he cannot hope to make head or tail of development unless he draws evidence from bacteriology, protozoology, and microbiology generally; he must know the gist of modern theories of protein synthesis and be pretty well up in genetics.

In the biological and physical sciences even formal disciplinary organization was periodically being reshuffled, replacing loyalty to traditional fields with a problem orientation in which institutional form followed what was functional for inquiry. A typical example was this announcement by a major university in 1984:

As of July 1, the departments of biochemistry and molecular biology and the department of molecular genetics and cell biology replaced the departments of microbiology, biochemistry, and biophysics and theoretical biology. . . . Faculty chose in which of the two departments they would maintain their primary appointment. . . . [The] chairman of the reorganization committee, said the streamlining reflects the current principal areas of biological research. . . . [The] associate dean of biological sciences, said the reorganization "will more accurately reflect the current and developing interests of the faculty."[13]

No such far-reaching formal reorganization seemed likely in the case of the social sciences and humanities, but there was nevertheless widespread recognition of what Clifford Geertz called a blurring of genres: "a phenomenon general enough and distinctive enough to suggest that what we are seeing is not just another drawing of the cultural map—the moving of a few disputed borders, the marking of some more picturesque mountain lakes—but an alteration of the principles of mapping." In the opinion of sociologist Donald Levine, the boundaries of disciplines had been "irreparably sundered."

---

[13]Medawar, *The Art of the Soluble* (London, 1967), 115; "Biological Sciences Reorganization Reflects Current Areas of Study," *University of Chicago Magazine* 76 (Summer 1984): 3–4. The remarkable flexibility which the natural sciences have shown in reordering their components is probably in part a consequence of large-scale funding of mission- or problem-oriented research, which supported new ventures and exerted a powerful push toward whatever reorganization was necessary to direct the appropriate mix of talents to the problem at hand.

Each of the disciplines has established beachheads or won converts among the practitioners of other disciplines. At present there are probably few major concepts, methods, or problems that belong exclusively to a single social science discipline; those that do will probably not long remain so. Anthropologists interpret dreams to find motives; psychoanalysts scrutinize documents to find the causes of war; . . . economists do field work to study behavior patterns in primitive societies. . . . Who, now, is prepared to grant anthropology sole jurisdiction over the study of culture, economics over exchange, political science over power, or psychology over motivation?[14]

As historians ventured onto what had been the turf of others, often employing unfamiliar concepts, methods, and vocabulary, traditionalists frequently complained that whatever the merits of the new work it "simply wasn't history"; that the scholars who produced it, whatever their formal affiliations, weren't functioning as historians. Historians for whom theirs was unambiguously a "humanistic" study had long railed against the emergence of a social scientific sensibility among their colleagues. Such complaints continued, as in Jacques Barzun's fulminations against "psycho-history" and "quanto-history." But now the intrusion of new approaches from humanistic fields was seen as equally objectionable, and equally threatening to the integrity of the profession. William Bouwsma, reviewing a collection of work by younger intellectual historians, expressed dismay that rather than closing the gap between intellectual history and the rest of the discipline, "the 'new perspectives' displayed here seem largely designed to widen the gap by claiming for it novel responsibilities that do not appear to have much to do with historical study. . . . Their . . . work seems less and less shaped by the historical consciousness and an historian's questions."[15]

Meanwhile, members of other disciplines were producing historical studies of considerable breadth and power which had a good deal of influence on historians: Theda Skocpol and Charles Tilly from sociology, Walter Dean Burnham and Barrington Moore from political science, Sidney Mintz and Eric Wolf from anthropology, not to mention the economists who had largely taken over economic history, and those who dealt with the history of other realms which had traditionally been treated under other disciplinary rubrics but which now fell within the ambit of a

---

[14]Geertz, "Blurred Genres: The Refiguration of Social Thought," in his *Local Knowledge* (New York, 1983), 20; Levine's remarks from an unpublished draft manuscript, quoted by permission of the author.

[15]Barzun, *Clio and the Doctors: Psycho-History, Quanto-History, and History* (Chicago, 1974); Bouwsma, review of Dominick LaCapra and Steven L. Kaplan, eds., *Modern European Intellectual History, History and Theory* 23 (1984): 232–33.

"totalizing" historical discipline. While historians naturally differed in their evaluation of particular historical works by nonhistorians, all but a few crusty elders agreed that on the whole the historical discipline was stimulated and enriched by such contributions. And no historian could fail to be cheered by the foothold which historical consciousness gained in traditionally ahistorical social science disciplines. But as the University of Chicago economists never tire of reminding their colleagues, "there's no such thing as a free lunch": the price of enrichment was an increase in centrifugal tendencies within history. Historians who were attracted to sociological models and modes of inquiry were at odds with those of an anthropological turn of mind; those for whom economistic approaches seemed most fruitful were scornful of those who adopted a psychoanalytic orientation—and vice versa.[16]

As modes of thought from other disciplines entered into history they brought with them their characteristic forms of expression, which further disrupted the unity of the historical enterprise. History had always prided itself on employing everyday language; its freedom from jargon. As a rule, disciplinary jargon is integrative in its consequences: those who share it have an "in group" sense of solidarity (and superiority) vis-à-vis the baffled laity. But *sub*disciplinary jargon, incomprehensible to fellow members of the discipline not within the charmed circle, can be seriously disintegrative. As subcommunities of historians came to express themselves in the language of statistics, depth psychology, structuralist Marxism, and semiotics, the result was not just that they communicated less effectively with the laity—they weren't doing all that well in plain English anyway—but that they had increasing difficulty in speaking to each other.

[16]Paradoxically, it was anthropology—the social science discipline which in its holistic orientation most resembled history—which did more to promote fragmentation within history than any other intruder from across the border. Anthropology's holism was traditionally focused on a local (usually tribal) society as an integrated system with its unique folkways and cultural values, and this orientation heavily influenced what was perhaps the hottest historical field in the seventies and eighties: community studies. The vogue of community studies was paradoxical, for, as Michael Zuckerman noted, "Once we studied American history as if it were national when it was much more nearly local. Now we rush to recover the localities when the nation is manifestly the salient scale of our lives." ("Myth and Method: The Current Crisis in American Historical Writing," *History Teacher* 17 [1984]: 234.) Anthropologically influenced localist holism was one of the major fragmenting influences at work within history in recent years. In principle, monographs on communities were often conceived as "case studies" of broader phenomena and processes. In practice, as one survey noted, the studies disclosed "a particularism . . . which makes it hazardous to advance almost any generalization." (Richard Beeman, "The New Social History and the Search for 'Community' in Colonial America," *American Quarterly* 29 [1977]: 426.)

Besides contributing to a breakdown of communication within the discipline, subdisciplinary jargon also occasioned intramural resentment, for reasons which Ortega y Gasset had pointed to in a 1925 essay on the hostile response to modern art:

When a man dislikes a work of art, but understands it, he feels superior to it; and there is no reason for indignation. But when his dislike is due to his failure to understand, he feels vaguely humiliated and this rankling sense of inferiority must be counter-balanced by indignant self-assertion.

For Ortega, who loathed democracy and equality, it was the inaccessibility of the work of cultural modernists which was its greatest merit: it "compel[s] the people to recognize itself for what it is: . . . inert matter of the historical process, a secondary factor in the cosmos of spiritual life." At the same time the new art "helps the elite to recognize themselves and one another in the drab mass of society and to learn their mission which consists in being few and holding their own against the enemy." Just as one cannot ascribe to Stravinsky and Pirandello the agenda of elitism and condescension which Ortega saw as the function of their work, so it would be unjust to make those ascriptions in the case of those who expressed their historical findings in language inaccessible to the majority of their fellow historians. But this fact did not prevent many historians from feeling both put upon and put down; experiencing arguments couched in terms they could not comprehend as a subtle or not so subtle form of condescension.[17]

Historians who wanted to know the basis for Robert Fogel and Stanley Engerman's conclusion that slaves were only moderately exploited were told that the answer was

$$E_x = \frac{B}{\displaystyle\sum_{t=0}^{n} \frac{\lambda_t(\alpha_1 P_{ct} Q_t L_t^{-1})}{(1+i)^t}} \cdot$$

The dust jacket of a recent work in intellectual history carried the prediction by Mark Poster that "no historian who reads and comprehends this book will ever write in the same way again." This promise (or threat) was limited by the qualifying "and comprehends": while the author of the book helpfully provided a glossary of such terms as "distransitivity," "actantial/actant," and "psychologeme," there were no entries for terms

[17] José Ortega y Gasset, *The Dehumanization of Art and Other Essays on Art, Culture, and Literature* (Princeton, 1948), 6–7.

which presumably all but the hopelessly illiterate commanded, like "chrononym," "dromomatics," and "intradiegetic." These examples are admittedly extreme and atypical—though they are drawn from two of the liveliest areas of contemporary historical scholarship. Technical and arcane terminology helps communities of specialists communicate easily and with precision, and it is pointless to cavil at it. But the increasing use of such language within history not only furthered the decline in the profession's sense of wholeness but produced a fair amount of resentment as well.[18]

Newer modes of discourse also made it more difficult for historians to evaluate each other's work. When *Time on the Cross* appeared in 1974, many traditional historians felt themselves, in Vann Woodward's words, "coerced by references to 'vast research effort involving thousands of man and computer hours' and inconceivable mountains of statistical data." Historians, Winthrop Jordan said, "tend[ed] to simply roll over and say, 'Gee Whiz.'" The most effective and systematic criticism of *Time on the Cross* was produced by Fogel and Engerman's fellow "cliometricians"— more often trained in economics than in history. The most telling critiques of psychoanalytically oriented history came from those fully socialized into that mode of thought; it was all but impossible to have a serious critical encounter with much recent work in European intellectual history without being fluent in Derridese. The point should not be overstated: historians could and did offer cogent, even devastating, criticisms of work whose conceptual foundations they barely understood. It was certainly not the case that all common standards of evaluation disappeared, but they became much less consensual than they had been. Historians, nervously and guiltily, were increasingly inclined to delegate judgments of merit to members of the relevant subcommunities.[19]

Centrifugal forces of various sorts had killed the founders' vision of a unified and cohesive historical discipline, and there seemed no prospect

---

[18]Fogel and Engerman, *Time on the Cross: Evidence and Methods—A Supplement* (Boston, 1974), 124; Sande Cohen, *Historical Culture: On the Recoding of an Academic Discipline* (Berkeley, 1986).

[19]Woodward, "The Jolly Institution," *New York Review of Books* 21 (2 May 1974): 3; Jordan, quoted in Robert W. Merry, "History by Computer: Can It Tell The Story," *National Observer*, 9 November 1974, 7. Consensual, and especially *authoritative*, evaluation was made even more difficult by the increasingly common practice by some major journals of assigning books for review to young and unknown scholars. In 1980 the editor of the *Journal of American History* announced with satisfaction that nearly 60 percent of recent reviews were by first-time reviewers. (Lewis Perry, "Editor's Report, 1979–80," *JAH* 67 [1980]: 487.) Probably most young reviewers did a more conscientious job than old-timers for whom the task had become routinized, but their judgments inevitably lacked the authority wielded by established figures.

of resurrection. At least for the foreseeable future there appeared no hope that historians' work would converge to produce the sort of integrated syntheses which had long been the discipline's aspiration. The historical profession of the 1980s would have been quite unrecognizable to those who had established it in the 1880s, and no doubt many of the first generation of historians would have been dismayed at the collapse, or even abandonment, of so many of their hopes and expectations. But it is a commonplace that one could say the same thing of what the Founding Fathers of the American republic would make of the United States today. Neither in the case of the nation nor the discipline did transformation beyond recognition imply instability or imminent demise; rather, it simply meant that all things change, and in some periods more rapidly than others. Like any analogy, that between nations and disciplines can be pushed too far, but it is nevertheless suggestive.

Though we know that in the overall history of mankind the organization of the world into nation-states is a relatively recent development, the concept of nationality and of national loyalty have been around for long enough to seem part of the natural and eternal order of things. Certainly they have proved enduring in the face of all challengers, from Marx's claim that "the workingmen have no country" to a world economy dominated by multinational corporations. In our own century, separatist and secessionist movements have almost never succeeded in sundering the nation; nations have retained their identity even when incorporated into supranational institutions; national loyalty has proven at least as powerful as competing cross-national allegiances, whether religious or ideological. Whatever the cogency of antinational arguments, whatever the abstract merits of alternative forms of political organization, nations—for better or for worse—seem here to stay.

As the world political order is founded on nations, the constituent units of the world of scholarship are disciplines. While it is well to remind ourselves that they were created by man in (relatively recent) historic time, and formed no part of God's six-day agenda, they seem almost as "given" and enduring as the nation. At least in the humanities and social sciences they are as capable of inspiring fierce loyalty, not to say chauvinism. Even in a world dominated by the nation-state there is a handful of true cosmopolitans, of both the aristocratic right and the revolutionary left. And in the world of scholarship there are a few "supradisciplinarians": old-style intellectuals with what might be called a "predisciplinary" consciousness; "postdisciplinarians" whose primary allegiance is to newly formed communities of shared academic interests which include members of several disciplines. But they are a small minor-

ity, and against the entrenched power of the disciplines, they seem
destined to remain so. Separate disciplines may be, as many have argued,
an anachronism, but if so, they are anachronisms which are going to be
around for some time.[20]

As disciplines grew to resemble empires more than nations, many formally reorganized themselves as confederations of subdisciplines. One
could no longer simply join the American Anthropological Association:
it was necessary to combine a "basic" membership ($35) with member-
ship in one of sixteen "units" ranging in price from the archaeology
section (also $35) down to the biological anthropology section (a bargain
at $10). The American Psychological Association published twenty sepa-
rate "primary journals" in specialized fields, and had forty-four separate
divisions, each with its own elected officers and executive committee,
ranging from consumer psychology to psychology and the arts. The
Modern Language Association held the record for the number of separate
divisions: seventy-six, including six divisions of French literature by
period, plus one for "French literature outside Europe"; separate divisions for "sixteenth- and seventeenth-century Spanish poetry and prose"
and "sixteenth- and seventeenth-century Spanish drama." Again, each
had a full set of officers and an executive committee; each had corporate
responsibility for a portion of the annual program; the MLA as a whole
was governed by a congress of ambassadors from the divisions.

The historical profession has always resisted formalizing its de facto
segmentation: while there have always been informal arrangements to
assure representation of all constituencies among the leading officers of
the AHA, the mystique of participation in a common, holistic venture
has inhibited historians from following the model of the disciplinary
associations just mentioned. History has also been constrained from

[20]Within the historical profession the attenuation of disciplinary loyalty appeared first and
was most marked among historians of non-Western portions of the globe, who were
frequently heavily involved in area studies programs, and sometimes felt at least as much
kinship with those from other disciplines with a shared focus on a cultural area as with
fellow historians who knew nothing of their area—and perhaps cared less. But a number
of those who worked on American or European topics were also, depending on their
specializations, often more intellectually engaged with colleagues in other disciplines of
shared substantive interests or shared sensibility than with fellow historians. As more
interdisciplinary journals and associations were established, there came to be alternate foci
of attention and activity. The phenomenon of the joint appointment also worked to
attenuate purely disciplinary loyalty. At the University of Chicago—almost certainly not
a typical example—as of 1987 fully half of the members of the History Department also
held appointments in other units of the university, and others were heavily involved in
area studies programs without appointive powers. Yet for all this, the overwhelming
majority would unhesitatingly and unequivocally identify themselves as historians, with
other commitments relegated to a subordinate position.

adopting such a model not because it is less fragmented than others, but because it is more fragmented. Laurence Veysey reflected on the consequences of what he termed the "truly awesome subdivision" within the profession.

The discipline of history . . . has become far more minutely specialized than such neighboring fields as sociology or economics . . . [and historians] have . . . much less to say to each other . . . even if this may mean they also less often bother to argue with each other. Historians are subdivided quadruply, by nation or region of the globe, by time period, by thematic category . . . and by cognitive predilection, sometimes, but not always tied to a political outlook. . . . All that unites historians is a concern for the evolution over time of whatever it is they study. . . . This is something . . . to be sure. . . . But it is far less compelling as an attribute in most contexts than the diversity of outlooks and interests that splinter historians into minute subgroups, each with its own hierarchy of respected authorities.

For the historical profession formally to institutionalize fragmentation would be formally to acknowledge its permanence, which it was not prepared to do. Even were it prepared to do so, the crosscutting fissures Veysey noted made impossible any such (relatively) neat separations as those between the MLA's Shakespeare division and its Chaucer division, between cultural and physical anthropology.[21]

The bad news was that the American historical profession was fragmented beyond any hope of unification. The good news was that the fragments were doing very well indeed. New fields were explored in innovative ways; historical works of considerable originality and even brilliance appeared every year. Among subcommunities of historians there were higher levels of fruitful interaction and higher critical standards than at any time in the past. Those American historians who studied other regions of the globe were increasingly integrated into historical communities abroad; it became much more common for the works of American historians to be translated into the language of those communities, and receive respectful treatment. At the level of everyday practice, things had never been better.

One thing the American historical community could not do was sustain a disciplinewide discussion on the meaning of the historical venture as a whole. On "the objectivity question"—as on other questions once of common concern, on which historians, even when they had disagreed, had communicated with each other—discourse across the discipline had effectively collapsed.

[21]Veysey, "The United States," in Georg G. Iggers and Harold T. Parker, eds., *International Handbook of Historical Studies* (Westport, Conn., 1979), 158.

III

The level of concern with epistemological issues within the American historical profession had never been high—compared either with other American academic disciplines or with historical communities abroad. But from the mid-1930s through the mid-1960s programs of the American Historical Association, and the pages of the *American Historical Review*, had periodically devoted at least some minimal attention to philosophical questions. From that time forward, when there was widespread recognition of a cognitive crisis in the academic world at large, and when the annual meetings and official journals of other disciplines in the humanities and social sciences were increasingly given over to epistemological introspection, the attention devoted to such questions within the American historical community as a whole sank to a new low. The *AHR* all but eliminated historiological questions from its pages; at the 1986 meeting of the AHA not one of the 123 sessions was devoted to any epistemological issue. Perhaps this was simply a continuing reflection of what Michael Kammen described in the 1980s as the "utter indifference" of the overwhelming majority of American historians to issues of epistemology or philosophy of history. Alternatively, it could be seen as tacit recognition that the issues involved were too hot to handle—in any case, dangerously divisive in an already sufficiently fragmented community. With the founding of *History and Theory* in the sixties, concern with the cognitive foundations of the historical venture was formally ghettoized as an esoteric concern, like business history or the history of South Dakota. Henceforth, in J. H. Hexter's words, this "specialized journal undert[ook] custody of historical navel-watching in the United States."[22]

By the seventies and eighties American professional historians' attitudes on the objectivity question were so heterogeneous that it was impossible to identify anything resembling a dominant sensibility. As always, for the great majority of historians, postures were implicit rather than explicit, which makes any taxonomy of positions both arbitrary and slippery. But for heuristic purposes one can describe several rough groupings or tendencies.

The matter-of-fact, antitheoretical and antiphilosophical objectivist empiricism which had always been the dominant stance of American

[22]Kammen, "Historical Knowledge and Understanding," paper delivered at a 1986 symposium at the University of Chicago, 27; Hexter, "Carl Becker and Historical Relativism" in his *On Historians* (Cambridge, Mass., 1979), 34. As of 1986 only one member of *History and Theory*'s ten-person editorial board was an American historian; most were philosophers.

historians continued to be enormously powerful. For those in this group it remained taken for granted that truth was "out there"; something found, rather than made; unitary, not perspectival. Though interpretation was necessary, it was at bottom the facts that mattered. While those sharing this orientation might have qualified or modified this or that element in the program of the founding fathers of the profession, they remained attached to its fundamental tenets. Works of history were praised for approaching "objectivity"; the most highly esteemed might win the coveted appellation "definitive."

On relinquishing the editorship of the *American Historical Review* in 1985, Otto Pflanze warned historians that while models and theories had their uses, they had a dangerous "seductive power," which could divert historians from their prime obligation to come as close as humanly possible to reporting on the past "wie es eigentlich gewesen." J. H. Hexter, in a series of books and articles widely admired by historians, proclaimed his "willful ignorance" of recent philosophy (he was particularly proud of never having read Wittgenstein), and held that issues of historical credibility were resolvable through "common sense." The goal of history was to "come close to an account of things past that approaches maximum verisimilitude." He insisted that historians, following tested, professionally approved procedures, in fact regularly succeeded in "giving an account of the past as it actually was." Hexter's books on historical epistemology, David Donald said, "raise thinking about the nature of the historical enterprise to a new level of intelligence and sophistication."[23]

All of this was "business as usual." Writing at the end of the seventies, Laurence Veysey maintained that for all of historians' greater sophistication in method and argumentation,

> it remains true that the very highest amount of prestige is still awarded to an historian who uncovers (no matter how he does it) some incontestable yet previously unknown fact of undeniably major importance. Discovery is what still counts the very most. . . . On this most fundamental level, standards of historical excellence have not changed all that much in the last hundred years.

This was surely an exaggeration. Historians who had done no more than uncover important new facts were respected, but the profession had often bestowed its highest honors on those whose contributions were primarily

---

[23]Pflanze, "Report of the Editor . . . A Parting Word," *AHA Annual Meeting, 1985* (Washington, D.C., 1985), 114; Hexter, *The History Primer* (New York, 1971), 20, 270; *Doing History* (Bloomington, Ind., 1971), 18, 70; Donald, review of *Doing History* and *The History Primer*, *Commentary* 54 (November 1972): 99. Philosophers—and philosophically inclined historians—were less impressed. See, e.g., review of *The History Primer* by Bruce Kuklick, *History and Theory* 11 (1972): 352–59.

interpretive. Yet it remained true that the veneration of the incontrovertible fact had been the single most enduring theme in the ethos of the profession, and that traditional objectivism and empiricism were gaining added strength from currents within the profession which in other respects were dissident.[24]

Zealous quantifiers like J. Morgan Kousser insisted that "history is better than ever" precisely because it was becoming scientific, value-free, and objective; it would be tragic if on the brink of triumph history, "regress[ed] into a prescientific . . . stage." "Thompsonian" social history in the United States was on the whole even more empiricist than that of the master, and Thompson himself endorsed Hexter's "reality rule"—the historian should tell "the most likely story that can be sustained by the relevant existing evidence." Insofar as American leftist historians followed English debates in which Thompson savaged structuralist-Marxists while they in turn attacked his empiricism, most lined up solidly behind Thompson. Overall, as Henry May observed, the capacity of historians to incisively criticize each other's works had outrun the capacity of historians to produce works that could withstand such criticism. A prudent response, particularly for younger scholars in a dismal market, was to limit themselves to the recounting of the verifiable, avoiding risky interpretive flights. At the same time, the unprecedented ideological heterogeneity of recent scholarship meant that the only grounds for anything resembling an evaluative consensus on an historical work was whether it had its facts straight.[25]

While the old positivist/empiricist/objectivist sensibility remained powerful, there was at the same time a strong current of skepticism toward traditional notions of objectivity within the profession, the roots of which were to be found in the developments recounted in Chapters 13, 14, and 15. Earlier postures of detachment gave way to more explicit avowals of commitment, as when Daniel Boorstin, in the early eighties, co-authored a work subtitled *A Conservative Textbook for Conservative Times*. In the face of ideological polarization and fragmentation, many found that insistence on unitary truth meant paying too high a price in acrimony at the departmental as well as the national-professional level, and tacitly abandoned it in the interest of comity. Nonspecialists could not unravel the complex statistical arguments advanced by the authors

---

[24]Veysey, "The United States," 168–69.
[25]Kousser, "Ironies of Abolition," *Times Literary Supplement*, 1 February 1985, 123–24; Kousser, "Must Historians Regress? An Answer to Lee Benson," *Historical Methods* 19 (1986): 62, 78; Thompson, *The Poverty of Theory and Other Essays* (New York, 1978), 195, n. 37; May, paraphrased in Veysey, "The United States," 168–69.

and critics of *Time on the Cross*, but it was possible for all historians to follow and appreciate the numerous ideological critiques of that allegedly value-neutral work. It became increasingly common for historians to combine empirical criticism of colleagues' work with systematic attention to their hidden ideological agendas, not just in treatments of relatively recent events, but on topics ranging from slavery in antiquity to medieval and Renaissance Venice. At both scholarly meetings and in scholarly journals the device of the review-symposium became institutionalized, typically bringing together critics chosen as representatives of differing ideological standpoints.[26]

If black and feminist historians, whose standpoint was often un-abashedly perspectival, were to be accepted as legitimate members of the profession, insistence on a "God's eye view" was impossible to maintain. But perspectivalism which challenged the traditional objectivist posture was also implicit in historical accounts "from the bottom up," or "from the native's point of view." Here, too, it was not just that the sensibilities of new groups of historians were inconsistent with old verities, but that other historians faced a choice between either relaxing traditional objectivist criteria or reading important constituencies out of the discipline.

The influence of antiobjectivist currents of thought coming from other disciplines is difficult to evaluate exactly, and all but impossible to trace in the case of any given individual. But in the aggregate they clearly made many historians aware of how problematic received views of objectivity had become in contemporary thought—an awareness signaled by the increasing frequency with which "objective" and "objectivity" were put in quotation marks by historians. The original objectivist posture elaborated by historians in the late nineteenth century had combined various elements into an interlocking whole. As particular items in that complex came to be seen as questionable—the aim of "reconstruction," the primacy of fact over theory, the distinction between fact and value or between fact and interpretation, the historian as neutral judge—many historians had increasing difficulty in knowing what objectivity meant, and were often inclined to dismiss it as an outdated construct, while by no means necessarily disavowing all of its constituent elements.

In general, new currents in philosophy and literature were felt most strongly by intellectual and cultural historians. Paul Conkin was not unrepresentative of intellectual historians in the eighties when he mocked the "naive realism" which believed that "a 'real' past is now firmly in

---

[26]Boorstin and Brooks Mather Kelly, *A History of the United States: A Conservative Textbook for Conservative Times* (Lexington, Mass., 1981).

place, waiting to be known insofar as we can find any means of knowing it." He could conceive of no "minimal bedrock" of established fact on which historical inferences could firmly rest. Historical facts, Conkin said, were "only what everyone agrees upon at any time. . . . No facts demonstrably correspond to a historical reality." But newer thoughtways also affected many working in social history, which was becoming increasingly concerned with Geertzian questions of meaning and symbolic representation, rather than material or narrowly behavioral dimensions of existence. While some historians who employed Freudian categories in their work had as positivist a view of psychoanalysis as the founder, others, like Peter Loewenberg, argued that for the historian as for the analyst, subjectivity ("countertransference") was not an intrusion to be guarded against but should become "an accepted element in historical writing."[27]

As "social scientific" history arose in the 1950s it had borrowed not only concepts and methods, but also the then regnant positivism and empiricism of social science disciplines, which in this respect mirrored contemporary philosophy of the natural sciences. There continued to be those, like Kousser, who clung to the original conception of the venture. But from the late sixties onward historians who considered themselves social scientists rather than humanists were often among those who most forcefully distanced themselves from some of the key elements in the older positivist and empiricist position. Michael Kammen, discussing the way in which explicit value judgments were "very much in vogue" in the seventies, noted that it was precisely the historians closest to the social sciences who were "most commonly given to moralizing in their work," and who had adopted an "explicitly ideological approach." Erik Monkkonen, an aggressive quantifier, while insisting that there was "one reality, one truth" said that along with most of his colleagues he was "rela-

---

[27]Conkin, review of Oscar Handlin, *Truth in History*, *History and Theory* 19 (1980): 228, 230; Loewenberg, "Historical Method, the Subjectivity of the Researcher, and Psychohistory," *Psychohistory Review* 14 (Fall 1985): 30–31. In practice, historians employed subjectivity at their risk. Throughout his account of Black Mountain College, Martin Duberman included his personal meditations on the material he uncovered. Discussing the shabby treatment accorded a homosexual faculty member, he mused in print as to whether he was exaggerating the college's offense as "a function of my own indignation as a homosexual, a potential victim." Reviewers were critical of what they regarded as an intrusive authorial presence. Laurence Veysey, while finding merit in some parts of the work, thought it a device by which Duberman dramatized himself, and he "vot[ed] against any general shift into the subjective mode in scholarly writing." Paul Conkin thought the book "embarrassing, pretentious, the very epitome of bad taste." (Duberman, *Black Mountain: An Exploration in Community* [New York, 1972], 227; review by Veysey, *Harvard Educational Review* 43 [1973]: 262–63; review by Conkin, *JAH* 60 [1973]: 512.)

tivistic with regard to the nature of facts," which were simply "theoretical postulates." In the late sixties Robert Berkhofer, another leading figure among social scientifically oriented historians, cited Kuhn in support of his view that historians neither "reconstructed" nor "recaptured" the past, but rather picked out those bits of data which they could organize within the framework of a (transient) theory, producing "a highly selective account of a postulated past reality." By the mid-1980s he was bemused by "historical fundamentalists" who continued to insist on the primacy of facts over interpretation; like Rip Van Winkle, they had been napping for twenty years.[28]

Perhaps the most striking feature of the way in which historians signaled their abandonment of traditional objectivist axioms was the casual, matter-of-fact fashion in which they did so; the sometimes condescending attitude they adopted toward those who clung to what they regarded as outworn shibboleths. Joan W. Scott expressed astonishment that a critic of *Women, Work, and Family*, which she had coauthored with Louise Tilly, could imagine that "somehow Tilly and I believe we are writing 'value neutral,' objective history." Walter LaFeber, writing to a friend who had collated diplomatic historians' opinions about their work, was amazed at the number of those who spoke of their "objectivity." Reading the paper, he said, "was a good education for me, because I tend to forget that there are still that number of people in our profession who believe that." Eugen Weber concluded a massive textbook by telling its readers that "all the historian may hope to do is to record a passing point of view as honestly and as thoughtfully as he knows how: not to . . . cut a slice out of the pie of Truth, but to suggest plausible interpretations to his time and indicate to others who come later how his own age mirrored itself in its past."[29]

In the thirties, forties, and fifties, doubts about historical objectivity had a clear reference point: the theses advanced by Becker and Beard. There were no identifiable leaders of the mood of diffuse skepticism about objectivity which many historians shared from the sixties onward, and by no stretch of the imagination could one describe the phenomenon

[28]Kammen, "Clio and the Changing Fashions: Some Patterns in Current American Historiography," *American Scholar* 44 (1975): 490; Monkkonen, "The Challenge of Quantitative History," *Historical Methods* 17 (1984): 87; Berkhofer, *A Behavioral Approach to Historical Analysis* (New York, 1969), 22–26; Berkhofer, review of Robert Fogel and G. R. Elton, *Which Road to the Past? AHR* 90 (1985): 105.
[29]Scott, "Reply to the Hilden Critique," *International Labor and Working Class History* 16 (Fall 1979): 17; LaFeber to Norman Graebner, 11 February 1973, Graebner Papers; Weber, *A Modern History of Europe* (New York, 1971), 1125.

as a "movement," or even "school of thought." The noncrusading non-members of this nonschool had no need of leadership. But those who viewed the new mood with alarm required a symbolic embodiment of extreme "nihilistic relativism" within the profession, and Hayden White was made to order for the role.

The point of departure for this most radical representative of the episte-mological avant-garde was an "old-fashioned" insistence that history was preeminently a branch of literature. Other historians who had either proclaimed themselves or been labeled "relativists" had centered their analysis on historians' differing ideological commitments. For White, who called himself "a genuine pluralist . . . who is even prepared to bear the label of radical relativist in matters having to do with *historical knowl-edge*," it was the historian's poetic consciousness which was decisive. The most important thing to know about an historian was whether he or she prefigured the historical field according to the literary trope of metaphor, metonymy, synecdoche, or irony. While "tropological strategy" was fun-damental, each trope had elective affinities with one of four modes of emplotment (romance, comedy, tragedy, satire), four modes of explana-tion (formist, organicist, mechanist, contextualist), and four ideologies (anarchism, conservatism, radicalism, liberalism).[30]

Though trained conventionally as a medievalist, White was almost from the very beginning of his career a very "unprofessional" historian who had little regard for traditional values of the discipline—above all for the idea that the past should be studied "for its own sake." For him, anyone who pursued historical study as an end in itself was "either an antiquarian, fleeing from the problems of the present into a purely per-sonal past, or a kind of cultural necrophile . . . who finds in the dead and dying a value he can never find in the living." His consciousness is per-haps best described as "pre-professional." From his earliest to his latest writings he made invidious comparisons between what he saw as the current debased state of historiography, and earlier centuries when it was truly a "moral science," whose task was "less to remind men of their obligation to the past than to force upon them an awareness of how the past could be used to effect an ethically responsible transition from pres-ent to future."[31]

In Europe, and even more in the United States, one of the earliest tasks

[30]White, "Historical Pluralism," *Critical Inquiry* 12 (1986): 486. White's italicization of "historical knowledge" in his relativist avowal was presumably intended to exclude, for example, moral relativism.
[31]White, "The Burden of History," *History and Theory* 5 (1966): 125, 132.

professionalizing historians set for themselves was the emancipation of "history proper" from nefarious speculative philosophy of history. For White the two realms were "distinguishable only in emphasis, not in their respective contents": "every philosophy of history contains within it the elements of a proper history, just as every proper history contains within it the elements of a full-blown philosophy of history." In his 1973 *chef d'oeuvre, Metahistory: The Historical Imagination in Nineteenth-Century Europe*, White applied the same formalist literary analysis to philosophers of history (Hegel, Marx, Nietzsche, Croce) as he did to historians (Michelet, Ranke, Tocqueville, Burckhardt). Burckhardt, said White, had more in common with Flaubert and Baudelaire than with Ranke.[32]

If the distinction between history and philosophy of history had been basic to historians, the most sacred boundary of all was that between history and fiction, and nothing outraged historians more than White's blurring of that dividing line. White did not deny that the historian dealt with events which were, in principle, observable, and which had a specific location in time and space, while imaginative writers were not so restricted. But for him the differences between a work of history and a novel were both less interesting and less significant than the similarities. They resembled each other not just in form, but in aim as well. According to White the image of reality which the novelist constructed corresponded to a domain of human experience no less "real" than that to which the historian referred, and the historian faced the same problem in creating coherence as did the novelist. The idea that there were two kinds of truth "which the Western prejudice for empiricism as the sole access to reality has foisted upon us" disguised the fact that historians and novelists alike had to meet criteria of both correspondence and coherence in their accounts. The conventional distinction between the two realms underestimated the constraints on the writer of fiction and overestimated those on the historian. Historical stories, like all others, were made rather than found.

We may seek to give our lives a meaning of some specific kind by telling now one and now another kind of story about them. But this is a work of construction rather than of discovery. . . . Neither the reality nor the meaning of history is "out there" in the form of a story awaiting only a historian to discern its outline and identify the plot that comprises its meaning.

---

[32] *Metahistory* (Baltimore, 1973), 427–28; "The Fictions of Factual Representation" (1976), in his *Tropics of Discourse: Essays in Cultural Criticism* (Baltimore, 1978), 124.

White denied that there was any single correct view of any event or process, but rather many correct views, "each requiring its own style of representation."[33]

White's relativism was not that of Rorty's "cooperative freshman," for whom any view was as good as any other, but an only moderately careless reading of White's work could lead to that conclusion. His view that history was "essentially" like literature, could, like any essentialism, easily be conflated with the reductionist proposition that it was "nothing but" literature, and that differences between the two were trivial. White's apparent indifference to empirical criteria in evaluating histories was also a function of his view, heterodox within the profession, that "a specifically *historical* inquiry is born less of the necessity to establish *that* certain events occurred than of the desire to determine what certain events might *mean* for a given group, society, or culture's conception of its present tasks and future prospects." Thus, in reading White's observation, at the conclusion of *Metahistory*, that "when it is a matter of choosing among . . . alternative visions of history, the only grounds for preferring one over another are *moral* or *aesthetic* ones," it was important to note that he wrote of "visions" rather than "versions."[34]

Throughout his work, White's trivializing of questions of evidence was in the service of his arguments for the "made" rather than "found" nature of historical accounts, his belief in the legitimacy of pluralism, and above all his existentialist quasi obsession with the historian's liberty of choice. It is not too much to call him historiography's philosopher of freedom.

One must face the fact that, when it comes to the historical record, there are no grounds to be found in the record itself for preferring one way of construing its meaning rather than another.

[33]White, "Fictions," 121–22; "Historical Pluralism," 487. Norman Hampson, a highly regarded English historian of the French Revolution, had made an argument similar to White's with respect to the difficulty of drawing a line between history and fiction, but appearing as it did in a somewhat obscure English journal, it probably passed completely unnoticed within the American historical profession. ("History and Fiction: Where Does the Difference Lie?" Manchester Literary and Philosophical Society: *Memoirs and Proceedings* 106 [1963–64]: 64–73.)

[34]White, "Historical Pluralism," 487; *Metahistory*, 433. To cite only one example of numerous misreadings of White, noteworthy precisely because it came from a sophisticated and meticulous scholar, there was Georg Iggers's review of *Metahistory*. Iggers framed a quotation from White as follows: "The fact that all history is perspectivistic and reflects the ideological commitments of the historian does not permit us to conclude categorically that the criteria by which the historian arrives at his conclusion are entirely 'aesthetic or moral rather than epistemological in character.'" What White in fact wrote on the page Iggers cited was: "the best grounds for choosing one perspective on history rather than another are ultimately aesthetic or moral rather than epistemological." (*Reviews in European History* 2 [1976]: 180; *Metahistory*, xii.)

We can tell equally plausible, alternative, and even contradictory stories . . . without violating rules of evidence or critical standards. . . . One can imagine not only one or two but any number of alternative stories of . . . any . . . culturally significant event, all equally plausible and equally authoritative by virtue of their conformity to generally accepted rules of historical construction.

Though arguing that belief in an immanent order in history is no more plausible or implausible than the view that it is inherently meaningless, he was hostile to systems of thought which rendered the world comprehensible because "to the extent to which they succeed in doing so, these ideologies deprive history of the kind of meaninglessness which alone can goad the moral sense of living human beings to make their lives different for themselves and their children . . . to endow their lives with a meaning for which they alone are fully responsible."[35]

Though the extent to which White advocated an unrestrained or "absolute" relativism was exaggerated, he was given to formulations which seemed to imply that "transtropal" or "transideological" academic discourse was all but impossible. Kuhn had made it clear that when he described competing paradigms as "incommensurable" he was using the word in a technical sense: he was not saying that they were "incomparable," or that communication breakdown between those operating within different paradigms was more than partial. White went a good deal farther. The work of each master historian he treated constituted an "effectively closed system of thought, incommensurable with all the others appearing in contention with it." Many historians would give at least qualified assent to White's suggestion that

it is fruitless . . . to try to arbitrate among contending conceptions of the nature of the historical process on cognitive grounds which purport to be value-neutral in essence, as both Marxist and non-Marxist social theorists attempt to do. The best reasons for being a Marxist are moral ones, just as the best reasons for being a Liberal, Conservative, or Anarchist are moral ones.

[35]"The Politics of Historical Interpretation: Discipline and De-Sublimation," in W. J. T. Mitchell, ed., *The Politics of Interpretation* (Chicago, 1983), 136–37; "Historical Pluralism," 488; "Politics of Historical Interpretation," 134. For reasons which are not entirely clear, White maintained that "for those who deny the adequacy of narrative historiography to the representation of real events, the issue of pluralism does not arise. For contemporary non- or anti-narrative historians, historical accounts are either true or false, intelligible or unintelligible." ("Historical Pluralism," 493.) This is manifestly false, as evidenced by the numerous historians who present their analytic schemes as one among many legitimate ways of conceptualizing the past. One may speculate that despite White's strictures concerning the fatuity of the "history as art" versus "history as science" dichotomy, and his explicit recognition that scientific knowledge is no less "constructed" than historical knowledge, he, like so many others, was still fighting old battles which pitted humanists against social scientists.

But the immediately following sentence, while containing a grain of truth, made a much stronger claim. "The Marxist view of history is neither confirmable nor disconfirmable by appeal to 'historical evidence,' for what is at issue between a Marxist and a non-Marxist view of history is the question of precisely what counts as evidence, and what does not." Arguably this was a plausible description of the nineteenth-century confrontation between Marxist and non-Marxist views of history. But as a description of late-twentieth-century encounters between Marxist and non-Marxist historians it was wide of the mark. Insofar as it had a timeless and prescriptive dimension, as White's use of the present tense suggests, it denied the possibility of fruitful professional discourse except within communities of believers. And this, of course, was one of the major and legitimate concerns of those who worried about the impact of relativism within the historical discipline.[36]

Though White was the central symbolic figure of what came to be designated as the new "rhetorical relativism," he was by no means the only historian for whom a literary or linguistic orientation led to fundamental questioning of traditional objectivist epistemology. Some thought White's dissidence went a bit too far; others thought it didn't go far enough; there were those, like Dominick LaCapra, who thought that both were true. Like White, LaCapra took a dim view of the current state of the discipline, and sought to revive pre-professional conceptions of the venture: "a Renaissance ideal of historiography . . . in which scholarly research is intimately linked to 'rhetorical' and ethicopolitical discourse." Like White, he sought the unification of history and criticism, and regarded the attempt to establish the autonomy of history as part of the problem, not part of the solution. LaCapra deplored historians' exclusively "documentary" or "objectivist" model of knowledge. In a sentence which could have been written by White, he complained that "Mr. Gradgrind has been the modern historian's alter ego."[37]

But LaCapra denied that the alternative was a "'presentist' quest for liberation from the 'burden' of history through unrestrained fictionalizing and mythologizing." White, LaCapra said, had done more than anyone else in the United States to "wake historians from their dogmatic slumbers." But, he said, White "simply reverses the positivistic mythology of a mimetic consciousness and substitutes for it an idealistic mythology which converts the former meaningful plenum of the 'record' into dead matter or even a void." The subjective relativism in White's work

---

[36]*Metahistory*, 432, 284.
[37]LaCapra, *History and Criticism* (Ithaca, N.Y., 1985), 9, 17, 20.

was a product of a mistaken conception of the historian as a "free shaping agent with respect to an inert, neutral documentary record." It obscured the way in which the documentary record itself was "always already" textually processed before the historian came to it. Extreme documentary objectivism and relativistic subjectivism were "mutually supportive parts of the same larger complex."

> The objectivist historian places the past in the "logocentric" position of what Jacques Derrida calls the "transcendental signified." It is simply there in its sheer reality, and the task of the historian is to use sources as documents to reconstruct past reality as objectively as he or she can. The objectivist falsely sees the attempt to question precritical and unreflective certainty about the nature of history as tantamount to denying that people bleed when they are cut—and that they do not bleed signification. The relativist simply turns objectivist "logocentrism" upside-down. The historian places himself or herself in the position of "transcendental signifier" that "produces" or "makes" the meaning of the past.[38]

Against what he saw as false alternatives, and drawing on the work of various continental theorists, LaCapra advocated an encounter between the historian and the texts which he variously described as "dialogic," "transferential," or "worklike." Active dialogue with the past would involve strenuous contestation with texts, help to decide "what deserves to be preserved, rehabilitated, or critically transformed in tradition," and at the same time question the historian's posture of omniscient narrator. In transferential relationships with the past "the processes at work in the object of study acquire their displaced analogues in the historian's account." As contrasted with objectivist or "documentary" approaches, which had their role, but which risked denying the historian's own historicity, a worklike approach was "critical and transformative . . . deconstruct[ing] and reconstruct[ing] the given . . . bringing into the world something that did not exist before in that significant variation, alteration, or transformation." He was suspicious of attempts to find (or invent) unity and order in the past, "and by implication in one's own life and times," and of the search for "closure, undivided origin, coherent structure, determinate meaning." Opposing the efforts of E. D. Hirsch in

[38]"Rethinking Intellectual History and Reading Texts" (1980), in his *Rethinking Intellectual History: Texts, Contexts, Language* (Ithaca, N.Y., 1983), 63; "A Poetics of Historiography: Hayden White's *Tropics of Discourse*" (1978), ibid., 72; *History and Criticism*, 34–35; "Poetics of Historiography," 79–80; *History and Criticism*, 137–38. While both White and LaCapra drew heavily on contemporary literary theory, in White's case the decisive influence was structuralist; the considerably younger LaCapra was of a poststructuralist generation, and he was much more favorably disposed than White to such figures as Derrida and Foucault.

literary history and Quentin Skinner in the history of political thought to seek closure in authorial intention, LaCapra defined the point of inquiry as not ending an argument but making it "as informed, vital, and undogmatically open to counterargument as possible." A "good" interpretation, while resolving those documentary questions capable of verification, should seek not closure but rather an opening to new avenues of criticism and self-reflection.[39]

Historians like White and LaCapra had, in principle, opened an entirely new dimension of "the objectivity question" by introducing into American historiography a reprocessing of influential contemporary continental thought. In practice, their work had little positive resonance within the historical profession, and practically none outside the subdiscipline of European intellectual history. Even within that realm, most who responded affirmatively to their work were either those professionally concerned with the study of contemporary figures like Foucault or Derrida, or professionally marginal historians whose primary allegiance was to interdisciplinary communities with a membership made up largely of literary theorists, cultural critics, and philosophers. The work of White, LaCapra, and those historians closely associated with them, characteristically appeared in *Modern Language Notes*, *Representations*, *New Literary History*, *Critical Inquiry*, or the published proceedings of interdisciplinary symposia; scarcely at all in mainstream historical journals. Among modern-European intellectual historians a typical response was that of Michael Ermath, who expressed concern that the new intellectual history, in its borrowing from extrahistorical sources, might be "cutting itself off from recognizably historical thinking . . . wind[ing] up as metahistory, parahistory, or some form of cultural-linguistic criticism. . . . It could turn into 'semiohistory,' then semihistory, and eventually nonhistory."[40]

If intellectual historians of Europe gave at best a very mixed reception to the work of White and LaCapra, and the continental currents of thought they embodied, historians of American thought either failed to respond at all or greeted the new currents with hostile skepticism. A 1979 collection of essays entitled *New Directions in American Intellectual History* avoided consulting any European signposts: there was not a single reference to the approaches of Bakhtin, Barthes, Derrida, Gramsci, Goldmann, or Lukacs; Lévi-Strauss was mentioned only to be put down; the handful of references to Foucault were mostly disparaging. There was

[39]"Rethinking," 61, 17; *History and Criticism*, 11; "Rethinking," 30, 68, 38.
[40]Ermath, "Mindful Matters: The Empire's New Codes and the Plight of Modern European Intellectual History," *Journal of Modern History* 57 (1985): 521–22.

Objectivity in crisis

a nativist tone to Cushing Strout's discussion of Hayden White. After detailing the various foreign influences on White, Strout wrote that

seen . . . as a muse of myths and tropes, Clio is transformed . . . to a dark lady who speaks with a charming if somewhat artificial French accent. . . . Appropriately it was French thinkers who originally made everything a matter of language, according to the principle of *Pygmalion*'s Professor Higgins that "the French don't care what you do actually, so long as you pronounce it properly."

In more muted form the same nativism could be seen in David Hollinger's description of how Europeanists, unlike Americanists, were being tempted by "the imperial possibilities presented by twentieth-century views of language."

Perhaps we shall soon witness a linguistic imperialism comparable to other imperialisms of the recent academic past. . . . Among the potential volunteers for these new International Brigades . . . are scholars who think of themselves as "intellectual historians." . . . Whatever the destiny of the new empire of language now gaining ground in departments of philosophy, anthropology, and comparative literature, the study of American intellectual history will best prosper if it [is] . . . resistant in true "Republican" fashion to the ambition of private developers and imperialists.[41]

Counterbalancing the "rhetorical relativists," in fact weighing a good deal more heavily on the scales, was a tendency which might be alternatively designated "neo-objectivist" or "hyperobjectivist," with an absolutist commitment to the old creed. Though those in this camp were naturally among the strongest critics of White and others associated with him, hyperobjectivism did not arise in response to hyperrelativism. The two developments appeared more or less simultaneously; if anything, neo-objectivism arrived on the scene a bit before rhetorical relativism.

Neo-objectivism was a reactive or "backlash" movement, though not all those in this group concentrated on the same targets. Most often, the catalyst for neo-objectivism was "the sixties"—a term of art which encompassed student insurgency and faculty members who had cravenly or opportunistically condoned it; Black Studies, Women's Studies, and affirmative action programs; "ideological" scholarship (of the left), and any scholarship not pursued "for its own sake." For many hyperobjectivists bitter memories of the sixties, and often-exaggerated estimates of its resi-

[41]John Higham and Paul Conkin, eds., *New Directions in American Intellectual History* (Baltimore, 1979); Strout, *The Veracious Imagination: Essays on American History, Literature, and Biography* (Middletown, Conn., 1981), 10, 12–13; Hollinger, "American Intellectual History: Issues for the 1980s," *Reviews in American History* 10 (1982): 315–16.

due, were lumped together with various relativistic, "postmodern" currents into an undifferentiated and monstrous Other which had to be combated if liberal rationalism was to survive.

In history, as in other domains surveyed in Chapter 15, the implausibility of conflating sixties leftism and hyperrelativism did little to inhibit those who insisted on the linkage. Militantly leftist historians had little taste for White, and the feeling was reciprocated. An editorial in the *Radical History Review* insisted that leftists would be in the forefront of those rejecting White's suggestion that history should be considered a rhetorical construction. White declared his repugnance for revolution of any kind: "whether directed by leaders who profess a science of society and history or by celebrators of political 'spontaneity.'" But the conflation was an article of faith. In a symposium on *Metahistory* one historian wrote of the "dangerous and destructive" implications of the book: the kind of "intellectual liberation" which White offered not only "destroy[s]" any criterion of truth" but also "personal responsibility and ultimately freedom itself." The book, he said, represented a "fleeting moment in our intellectual history":

when revolution and antiestablishmentarianism became linked with both Nietzschean-existentialist and neo-Marxist notions of anarchistic individualism; when science and knowledge itself could be seen by some to be in the service of a stultifying conformity or even a bourgeois tyranny; it was in that fleeting moment, sometime in the 1960s, that the conception of *Metahistory* was formed, and it is that moment which it represents.

Another historian, reviewing *Metahistory*, thought White's work could most plausibly be seen as "an apology for the 'engaged' historical writing which has become fashionable in recent years."[42]

The impact of "the sixties" on historiographical consciousness is perhaps best illustrated in the case of Oscar Handlin. Though often irascible, his overall posture in the postwar decades had been tolerant. It was Handlin who had announced that the historical profession had "learned to live with relativism." The book which made him famous—his 1952 Pulitzer Prize-winning *The Uprooted*—was, as David Rothman wrote in a retrospective evaluation, "frankly and unembarrassedly engaged[,] . . . personal, value-laden," making no claims to "pure objectivity." In other books published in the same decade he had made a point of the presentist

[42]*Radical History Review* 31 (1984): 2; White, "Politics of Historical Interpretation," 125; Eugene Golob, "The Irony of Nihilism," *History and Theory*, Beiheft 19 ("*Metahistory*: Six Critiques") (1980): 64–65; Stanley Pierson in *Comparative Literature* 30 (1978): 180–81.

concerns which informed his work. In one he had described himself as "a historian who searched the record of the past for clues to the problems of the present"; in another he had written of himself "seeking, by looking backward, some meaning for the present . . . aid[ing] all those who seek such meaning to shape their vision of the future."[43]

In the late sixties, student turmoil at Harvard and elsewhere, and particularly what he perceived as the cowardly response of faculty and administrators, opened Handlin's eyes to a broader collapse of standards in the academy—"the tolerance of plagiarists, loafers, incompetents, drunkards." The historical discipline, in its de facto acceptance of affirmative action programs on behalf of blacks and women, its politicization, and its tacit acceptance of shoddy and tendentious scholarship, had abandoned those standards of universalism, detachment, and intellectual rigor which had once been the pride of the community of scholars he had joined decades earlier. Moral decay in the university and the historical profession was part of a larger crisis of moral relativism in American society, which had passed over into cognitive relativism. "An affluent and indulgent society . . . mistook flaccid permissiveness for tolerance. Everything went because nothing was worth defending, and the legitimate right to err became the disastrous obliteration of the difference between error and truth."[44]

In these circumstances the profession could no longer afford to "live with relativism." Chief among the ills from which the historical discipline suffered was the abandonment of faith that truth was "absolute," and knowable "if earnestly pursued." Historical truth, defined by Handlin as "correspondence of a representation with its object," was to be found "in the small pieces which together form the record." Handlin had been renowned for the boldness of his interpretations, and his sensitivity to the uses of social science theory in historiography. In the 1970s he saw the discipline of history mortally threatened by the blurring of the line between fact and interpretation, and "rejection of allegiance to the fact"—a change he traced back to the influence of Soviet historical practice on American historians. Contempt for the sovereignty of the fact had become epidemic within the profession.

[43]Rothman, "*The Uprooted*: Thirty Years Later," *Reviews in American History* 10 (1982): 318, 311; Handlin, *Race and Nationality in American Life* (Boston, 1957), xii; Handlin, *Adventure in Freedom: Three Hundred Years of Jewish Life in America* (New York, 1954), viii-ix.

[44]Handlin, "The Vulnerability of the American University," *Encounter* 35 (July 1970): 28, 25; "History: A Discipline in Crisis?" *American Scholar* 40 (1971): 446–64; *Truth in History* (Cambridge, Mass., 1979), 410.

Lofty discussion of paradigms evades the discomfort of factual criticism, which thereupon becomes a pursuit unworthy of scholars. . . . Yet the first and, sometimes, the sufficient test of the worth of a book is accuracy of detail. . . . It is difficult enough, and achievement enough, to get the record straight. To have put the evidence in order, that is, to have brought it as close as possible to correspondence with the occurrence in the past, should be sufficient reward for the historian. Properly speaking, that is the task most appropriate to this scholarly discipline.

Once among the most *engagé* of historians, Handlin, after the experience of the sixties, and in the light of its pernicious legacy, insisted that historians could only be true to their vocation by pursuing truth as an end in itself, without instrumental purpose. He concluded his valedictory with a plea that in an era hostile to the enterprise of truth, historians ponder the example of clerks in the Dark Ages, who in a similar time had "retir[ed] from an alien world to a hidden monastic refuge [where] now and again one of them at least was able to maintain a true record."[45]

The aggregated Other could take different forms in the minds of historians with differing agendas. In a brief for history as social science, written in the immediate aftermath of the campus turmoil of the late sixties, David Landes and Charles Tilly described two camps. One, which included all social scientific historians, was firmly rooted in the Western rational tradition: it pursued the ideal of objective historical truth for its own sake; avoided ideological bias and the use of history for purposes of indoctrination. The "other" camp was made up of a diverse collection of those who repudiated the ideal of discovering "what really was" in favor of private visions (the historian as literary artist) or political purpose (the historian as activist); those who would privilege a particular ethnic perspective; and those who purported to find latent political agendas in "ivory tower" scholarship. Pursued far enough, all these tendencies wound up in extreme subjectivism or nihilism. Their attack "focus[ed] with special sharpness on quantitative work, precisely because it embodies better than any other kind of history the . . . aspirations of the historian as scientist."[46]

Gertrude Himmelfarb saw a different aggregation. Radicals' politicization of history, combined with "increased use of quantification, models and other social science techniques," had led not to greater confidence in history's objectivity, but to "an increased sense of relativism and subjec-

[45]*Truth in History*, 405, 409, 116, 140–41, 414–15.
[46]Landes and Tilly, eds., *History as Social Science* (Englewood Cliffs, N.J., 1971), 5–6, 13–16.

tivism." Marxist-oriented scholarship, together with various other new currents in historiography, were threatening objectivity and "denigrating the rule of reason."

It is not only political history that the new historian denies or belittles. It is reason itself: the reason embodied in the polity . . . the reason inherent in the historical enterprise, in the search for an objective truth that always eludes the individual historian but that always (or so it was once thought) informs and inspires his work. This rationality is now consciously denied or unconsciously undermined by every manner of new history: . . . by anthropological history exploring such nonrational, indeed primitive, aspects of society as kinship . . . ; by psychoanalytic history dwelling on the irrational, unconscious aspects of individual and collective behavior; . . . by *engagé* (and *enragé*) history that is as much a work of advocacy as of analysis; . . . by the new history of every description asking questions of the past that the past did not ask of itself, for which the evidence is sparse and unreliable and to which the answers are necessarily speculative, subjective, and dubious.[47]

Responding to Himmelfarb, Lawrence Stone criticized her for her "misguided onslaught on the new social history" which stirred up divisions among scholars whose common faith in the reasoned search for truth was under attack.

Today, we need to stand shoulder to shoulder against the growing army of enemies of rationality. By that I mean the followers of the fashionable cult of absolute relativism, emerging from philosophy, linguistics, semiotics, and deconstructionism. These are truly "denigrating the power of reason," since they tend to deny the possibility of accurate communication by the use of language, the force of logical deduction, and the very existence of truth and falsehood.

The same theme of the need to bury old methodological differences in the face of new threats was sounded in Robert Fogel and G. R. Elton's *Which Road to the Past?* The formerly antagonistic spokesmen for "traditional" and social scientific history reported how, since 1968, they had been led to "a more ecumenical view" of history. The book constituted a mutual nonaggression pact between two hitherto warring positivistic schools in order to combat the common enemy of postpositivism, and in particular to make war on the relativistic tendency to "subordinate facts to theory."[48]

[47]Himmelfarb, "The New History," *News York Times Book Review*, 17 August 1980, 3; "Denigrating the Rule of Reason: The 'New History' Goes Bottom-up," *Harper's* 268 (April 1984): 88.

[48]Stone, letter to *Harper's* 268 (June 1984): 4–5; Fogel and Elton, *Which Road to the Past? Two Views of History* (New Haven, 1983), 123, 126.

The most spirited defense of a hyperobjectivist position came from Peter Gay, probably the leading European intellectual historian of his generation—certainly the most prolific and wide-ranging. Like so many others, he had been angered by the campus events of the late sixties, "when academic discourse in the United States, and elsewhere, was poisoned by the strident calls for relevance." Teachers, he said, could avoid losing their students only at the cost of abandoning their "old ideal of objectivity," and thus losing their self-respect. Gay insisted that Ranke's wish to relate the past as it actually happened was "neither a fatuous fantasy nor a concealed ideology"; rather it was "a difficult but perfectly realistic expectation." For Gay the historian's "ordering" of material was merely formal. "The order itself is something the historian does not make; he finds it." Even the division of history into periods was "not a construction but a discovery. The order, the period, are there." Not only did the tree in the forest fall, whether or not any historians were there to record the event, it "fell in only one way." He apologized for having entitled his magnum opus *The Enlightenment: An Interpretation.* "I suppose," he said, " '*the* Interpretation' would have sounded immodest; but it would have been what I meant."[49]

There is a paradox in trying to evaluate the relative weight of hyperobjectivist and hyperrelativist tendencies in the historical profession. In political campaigns we heavily discount candidates' public estimates of their own support; listen with a jaundiced ear to their accounts of the ground swell of sentiment they command. In matters intellectual, the opposite is often the case, since moral merit attaches to defying the Zeitgeist. Thus H. Stuart Hughes, who deplored what he described as a "regression toward positivism" feared that it was the wave of the future. He contrasted the postwar decades, when history was alive with new ideas and interpretations, and scholars took risks, to a present marked by "a return to the earlier obsession with archival research," and a future in which "*Sitzfleisch* alone will be prized, and thought will be at a discount." Conversely, neo-objectivists repeatedly described themselves as a beleaguered minority countering a pervasive "fashionable" relativism. Gay wrote of a relativist and subjectivist position having, by the mid-1970s, "secured an almost monopolistic dominance among historians." The founding fathers of the historical profession had used military metaphors when speaking of their conquest of objectivity: the armies of new Ph.D.'s marching out to establish its claims in the hinterland. A

[49]Gay, "Against the Gravediggers," *Studies on Voltaire and the Eighteenth Century* 152 (1976): 837–38; Gay, *Style in History* (New York, 1974), 199, 217, 211.

century later those most committed to the program of the founding fathers depicted themselves as doomed defenders of Masada or the Alamo.
Gordon Wood, writing on behalf of what he called "the old fashioned
methodology" of nineteenth-century positivism, acknowledged how
"philosophically naive . . . even philosophically absurd" it appeared in a
"relativist-minded age," but would have historians cling to it, "as we wait
for modernism to engulf us."[50]

Hyperobjectivism of the Handlin variety was a minority position within the profession, though a larger minority than allegedly "fashionable"
hyperrelativism. But when joined to historians' traditional empiricism,
hyperobjectivism could be very powerful indeed. Just how powerful was
demonstrated in the "David Abraham Case," the best-publicized historical controversy of the 1980s. The brouhaha was not simply about epistemology; indeed, there was nothing simple about the entire affair. All
participants agreed that it raised serious questions of scholarly ethics, and
of ideological zealotry; there was much difference of opinion about
whose ethics and whose zealotry violated traditional academic norms.
The affair certainly shed a good deal of light on the breadth of differences
within the profession on the nature and purpose of the historical
venture.[51]

In 1981, Princeton University Press published Abraham's *The Collapse
of the Weimar Republic: Political Economy and Crisis*—a revised version
of his 1977 University of Chicago doctoral dissertation. Both in the
United States and abroad almost all reviews were favorable, and most
were enthusiastic. Previous historical writing about industry and politics
in late Weimar had for the most part been directed to the question of
business complicity in the rise of Hitler; demonstrating the presence (or
absence) of the "smoking gun" which would link industrialists to the
Nazi movement. Reviewers, whether or not they looked favorably on
Abraham's structuralist-Marxist approach, praised him for breaking out
of what had become a sterile debate. His theoretical concern was with

---

[50]Hughes, "Contemporary Historiography: Progress, Paradigms, and the Regression Toward Positivism," in Gabriel Almond et al., eds., *Progress and Its Discontents* (Berkeley,
1982), 245, 247–48; Gay, *Art and Act: On Causes in History—Manet, Gropius, Mondrian*
(New York, 1976), ix-x; Wood, "Writing History: An Exchange," *New York Review of
Books* 29 (16 December 1982): 59; Wood, review of Handlin's *Truth in History, Journal of
Modern History* 53 (1981): 89.
[51]At this point a warning to the reader is in order. David Abraham was my student, and is
my good friend. I do not believe that the account which follows is biased or tendentious in
any of the usual senses of those words, but the reader should know at the outset that I am
not at all "neutral" about David Abraham, his persecution, or his persecutors.

conditions of stability in capitalist democracies, and his study of Weimar was an attempt to demonstrate how previously viable compromises between various sectors of industry, agriculture, and labor became unworkable under the impact of political and economic crisis, leaving elites with no alternative to an authoritarian solution. The victory of Nazism was portrayed as the unintended consequence of systemic breakdown.

Not all reviewers were favorable. In an East German journal Abraham was indicted for using "Bonapartism theory . . . [as] an instrument for the whitewashing of the big bourgeoisie and its responsibility for barbarism and war." And the Yale historian Henry Turner, who was in the last stages of work on his *German Big Business and the Rise of Hitler*, the fullest statement of the "no smoking gun" position, attacked Abraham's model as schematic, unilluminating, and unoriginal in the *Political Science Quarterly*. Despite the overwhelmingly positive response his book received in more than thirty reviews, not all was sunshine in Abraham's life. The Princeton History Department had voted to recommend Abraham for tenure, but the university's administration rejected the recommendation. Though he had to look for another job, his prospects seemed bright. As of the spring of 1983, with favorable reviews rolling in, and with his work being hailed by Weimar scholars as a seminal contribution, his future seemed assured. He was on his way to becoming a major figure in the profession. In a way he did, though not as anticipated.[52]

By his own account, Turner was outraged by the favorable reception Abraham's work was receiving—particularly the enthusiasm with which it was greeted at a Harvard colloquium on Weimar in March 1983. While in his *Political Science Quarterly* review Turner had concentrated on the substance of Abraham's argument ("warmed over" dogmatic Marxism fueled by a desire to discredit capitalism), Turner now took a different tack. He wrote circular letters to numerous historians in Germany and the United States attacking Abraham's scholarship; he urged Princeton University Press to remove the book from circulation; finally, he sent a letter to the *American Historical Review* to inform its readers that the book's scholarship was not just deficient but fraudulent. Abraham's book cited "a letter of October 6, 1931, as evidence about reactions to a meeting that took place five days later," and "a letter written on November 26, 1932, attributed to a man who died five months earlier." The book, Turner said, included references to "a nonexistent book," "a nonexistent

---

[52]W. Ruge, review in *Zeitschrift für Geschichtswissenschaft* 30 (1982): 290; Turner review in *Political Science Quarterly* 97 (1982–83): 739–41.

journal article," and the "outright invention" of "nonexistent archival documents."[53]

Abraham, after returning to Germany to recheck archival material, replied in the October 1983 issue of the *AHR* in which Turner's letter appeared. He apologized for citing a letter of October 6 rather than one of October 12 immediately following it in the file; for mistakenly assuming that a "Dr. Scholz" referred to in the archives was the deceased Dr. Ernst Scholz; and for defective citations to the book and article in question, which were not only quite existent, but not all that difficult to identify on the basis of the information he had provided. To the most serious charge of all—wholesale fabrication of archival material—Abraham replied that he had indeed made incorrect inferences about the authorship of a report and its recipient, but that while the errors were regrettable, there was nothing "nonexistent" about the documents. He concluded by observing that there were substantive interpretive differences between Turner and himself which could not be resolved "by appeal to some purely neutral technical principles of disinterested scholarship." Further, that "if there is a *Methodenstreit* lurking here between what one might call positivists and conceptualists," it should be pursued at that level, rather than by seizing on technical mistakes "to discredit a detailed and comprehensive argument without confronting it."[54]

No one took a poll, but there was a general feeling that Abraham had done reasonably well in the exchange, that the public recounting of his errors was sufficient punishment, that his apology was acceptable, and that Turner's characterization of Abraham's errors was uncalled-for and offensive. At this point another actor took his place on center stage: Gerald Feldman of Berkeley, who was "moved to take a stand by comments made to me that Abraham has satisfactorily responded to Turner." Feldman had served as one of the referees of Abraham's manuscript for Princeton University Press and had recommended that it be accepted,

---

[53]*AHR* 88 (1983): 1143. For Turner's being "furious" at the praise which Abraham received at the Harvard colloquium, and on this moving him to circularize historians, see Colin Campbell, "History and Ethics: A Dispute," *New York Times*, 23 December 1984, 19. Copies of Turner's letter to Miriam Brokaw of Princeton University Press, 28 May 1983, and of Turner's circular letters, in my possession.

[54]*AHR* 88 (1983): 1148–49. There was a third participant in the *AHR* exchange, T. W. Mason, author of the original review of Abraham's book which had appeared in the journal. Mason noted other errors by Abraham in reporting and characterizing some individuals' views (errors addressed by Abraham in his reply) but remained convinced that the book was a largely successful effort to "raise the argument to a higher plane of structural analysis . . . at which the motivations and the choices of individuals are secondary in the sense that they are heavily determined by economic and institutional pressures" (p. 1144).

despite "severe reservations about the argument and method," particularly its Marxist concepts and terminology. At the time of the Princeton tenure decision Feldman, whose views were solicited, had recommended against promotion. Privately, Feldman had indicated his complete agreement with Turner's criticisms. After the response to the *AHR* exchange he "went public," or rather semipublic, in widely distributed circular letters attacking Abraham, to which Feldman appended copies of a draft manuscript by his student Ulrich Nocken describing errors in Abraham's book beyond those cited by Turner. Clearly there were additional errors, but what was one to make of them? How were they to be explained and what was their significance in evaluating both the book and its author?[55]

For Feldman and Turner, what was involved was not, properly speaking, error at all, but fraud: a brazen attempt by a dishonest pseudoscholar to hoodwink the academic community through deception and fabrication. They sometimes vacillated on the question of motive, implying that at least in some instances criminal negligence rather than straightforward criminality might have been involved, but throughout they kept returning to the assertion that Abraham had worked with malicious intent. "This is not petty larceny," Turner told an interviewer; "it is the Brink's robbery of German history." Abraham had, Feldman said, "invented" documents, "knowingly lied," and engaged in "a systematic effort to cover up the truth." Feldman held that the "errors" in the book were neither random nor inconsequential; rather they were deliberate, and indispensable to its thesis; if corrected, "they would completely reverse much of its argument." Misstatements were so pervasive, said Feldman, that the book constituted "a veritable menace to scholars." Turner claimed that if the errors were corrected "there is nothing left." Feldman joined Turner in demanding that the book be withdrawn from circulation. Since the book was "not correctible," Feldman said that it would be "unpardonable" for the Princeton University Press to proceed with a projected revised edition, and he threatened reprisals if it went ahead.[56]

---

[55]Feldman, "Dear Colleagues" circular letters of 28 November 1983 and 26 February 1984, both in my possession. Feldman's charges and Abraham's reply, with rejoinders by each, were eventually published in *Central European History* 17 (June-September 1984): 159–290. The cover date is misleading: the issue in fact appeared in the summer of 1985, a year and a half after the beginning of the widespread informal distribution of the charges. See also Nocken, "Weimarer Geschichte(n)," *Vierteljahrschrift für Sozial- und Wirtschaftsgeschichte* 71 (1984): 505–27, a somewhat toned-down version of the two drafts of the Nocken manuscript distributed earlier, and Abraham, "Business Wars: On Contributions to Weimar Scholarship," ibid., 72 (1985): 329–52.

[56]Feldman, letter to the editor of *The Nation* 240 (1985): 322; Turner, quoted in Karen J. Winkler, "Brouhaha over Historian's Use of Sources Renews Scholars' Interest in Ethics Codes," *Chronicle of Higher Education* 29 (6 February 1985): 9; Feldman circular letters,

Abraham offered a rather different version. There were, he said, numerous errors in his book, more than he had thought at the time of his exchange with Turner, though not nearly so many as was being alleged. He offered a "mundane" explanation.

Much of the research . . . was done during a year-and-a-half stay in Germany while I was a graduate student. While doing that research, I committed the embarrassing and elementary error of hasty and niggardly note taking. The consequence was that my transcriptions sometimes yielded quotations that were elided or not precise. My then practice of sometimes translating and transcribing on the spot served me ill, particularly given my technical competence in German at the time. Worst, over the next several years, going back to my notes, I sometimes mistook summaries of documents for quotations. Such research practices, of course, cannot be defended.

The errors were particularly serious—he in fact termed them "inexcusable"—because historians often use a book not to evaluate its argument but for particular quotations or citations and "there are simply too many errors in my work." Rather than deny his errors, Abraham said, he had not only acknowledged them, but gone on to solicit evidence of error from Turner, and other scholars in the United States and Germany, and revisit all the archival collections, so that they might be corrected in a revised edition. He denied categorically that he had "invented" anything, or that there was anything either deliberate or patterned about the errors. They were the result of carelessness, not deviousness: some helped his argument, some hurt it, most were matters of illustrative detail that neither helped nor hurt. At the very end of his detailed published reply to Feldman's charges he presented, in parallel columns, both the original and the corrected versions of the passages in his book which had been most heavily attacked for "fabrication," "tendentious misquotation," and the like. The device demonstrated that deplorable as the errors were, his argument was sustained at least as well by the corrected as by the original versions. It was a rhetorical tour de force insofar as it showed that there were no rational grounds for him to have deliberately falsified. At the same time, nothing could more infuriate empiricists than this demonstra-

cited in preceding note; Feldman to Miriam Brokaw of Princeton University Press, 20 May 1983 and 24 February 1984, also in my possession. In another letter Feldman warned the Press that if the book were not withdrawn from circulation, "you should know that the request will be repeated by me in very choice company and . . . a further decision to continue marketing the book will be made a matter of public record in what I write." (Quoted in Jonathan Wiener, "Footnotes to History," *Nation* 240 [1985]: 181.)

tion of the relative autonomy of the argument from details of the evidence.[57]

Feldman distributed his circular letters just as Abraham entered the job market, and since "this profession needs to be protected against people like David Abraham," he made a particular target of institutions where Abraham was under consideration. Feldman was "pleased to say I was directly or indirectly involved in stopping four places from hiring Abraham"—the University of Texas at Austin, the University of Tel Aviv, the University of California at Santa Cruz, and Catholic University. The position at Tel Aviv would have involved, in addition to a teaching appointment, responsibility for a research library. This, said Feldman, would have been "like putting Dracula in charge of a blood bank." At Santa Cruz more than two-thirds of the history department wrote to the *AHR* protesting Feldman's "effort to intimidate colleagues" via a campaign of letters and telephone calls, including threats "to go to the Board of Regents, if necessary" to block Abraham's appointment. At Catholic University, where both the department and the dean's committee on tenure and promotion recommended Abraham's appointment, Feldman learned of the prospect only at the last moment, and succeeded in convincing the dean to reject the recommendation. All the members of the Catholic University search committee wrote to the AHA's professional division asking for the establishment of guidelines "to assure fairness to any candidates who might, in the future, be the object of similar campaigns to deny them employment."[58]

There was an unsuccessful attempt, supported though not, Feldman said, initiated by him, to get the University of Chicago to rescind Abraham's Ph.D. This led the university's president, Hanna Holborn Gray, to join with Stanley Katz, Carl Schorske, and others in a protest to the AHA against Feldman's activities. Feldman had greater success in another realm: whether or not his intervention was decisive is impossible to

---

[57]Abraham, "A Reply to Gerald Feldman," *Central European History* 17 (1984): 183–84, 237–39. At most, as Abraham recognized, the device could refute charges of rationally calculated falsification: "Conspiratorial theories are notoriously impossible to refute, since they can be 'immunized' by the addition of ad hoc hypotheses of 'incompetent dishonesty,' 'supererogatory manipulation,' etc. Ultimately they can only be rejected on grounds of implausibility." (Ibid., 198, n. 44.)

[58]Feldman on protecting the profession, in his circular letter of 27 March 1984, quoted in Abraham, "Reply," 197. Feldman is quoted on his interventions in Winkler, "Brouhaha," 9. Feldman on "Dracula" is quoted in Campbell, "History and Ethics," 19. The letters from Santa Cruz and Catholic University faculty are quoted in Abraham, "Reply," 179–80, n. 5.

tell, but Princeton University Press canceled plans for a revised edition of Abraham's book. Both Feldman and Turner were gratified by the decision of the AHA Council in December 1984 to cancel the inquiry into their activities which had been begun by its professional division, and Feldman cited the council's action as evidence of the propriety of his interventions. The discipline's system of criticizing colleagues, the council said, "works as it should." Above all, Feldman and Turner could take satisfaction in having succeeded in their avowed aim of driving Abraham out of the historical profession. As of 1988 Abraham, then in his early forties, was enrolled in law school.[59]

The dominant themes in the campaign waged by Turner and Feldman were outrage and incredulity. They were outraged that a book containing numerous demonstrated factual errors could be so widely acclaimed; incredulous that few leaders in the profession joined their crusade, and that many even had the temerity to defend Abraham. In the case of Turner the nexus between anti-Marxism and hyperempiricism was manifest. Several years before the Abraham imbroglio he had dismissed Marxist historiography of Germany as unworthy of serious consideration since "almost without exception" it rested on fraudulent scholarship and "egregious misrepresentation of factual information." In his 1985 *German Big Business and the Rise of Hitler* he insisted that "only through gross distortion can big business be accorded . . . even [a] major role in the downfall of the Republic." Those guilty of such distortions were moved by the antibusiness bias endemic to the historical profession; neo-Marxist interpretations were being used "in an effort to discredit and undermine societies with capitalist economies and to legitimize repressive anti-capitalist regimes." He was not unhappy to be labeled "a vulgar factologist." It was through close empirical investigation, rather than "grandiose theories," that the truth about business and politics in Weimar could be known. Feldman, though impatient with Marxist theorizing, was less global in his condemnation of it than Turner, but equally insistent that what mattered most in history was "the facts." He concluded an address at the 1984 meeting of the AHA by quoting from Fogel and Elton on the primacy of evidence over interpretation. Enthusiastically reviewing Turner's long-awaited book in the *American Historical Review*,

[59]The initiative at the University of Chicago and ensuing protest are reported in Wiener, "Footnotes," 181. The AHA Council's decision and Turner and Feldman's satisfaction with it, are reported in Colin Campbell, "Academic Fraud Inquiry Is Dropped," *New York Times*, 3 January 1985, C22. For Feldman's invocation of the AHA Council's action, see his "A Response to Abraham's 'Reply,'" *Central European History* 17 (1984): 247, n. 2. A second, revised edition of Abraham's book was eventually published by Holmes & Meier (New York and London) in late 1986.

he adopted the posture, fashionable among neo-objectivists, of being defiantly "unfashionable":

One can only welcome Turner's explicit and implicit rejection of a pervasive historiographical high fashion and trendiness that encourages airy "interpretations," unverifiable constructs, irrelevant concepts and outright violations of common sense as high intellectual adventure.[60]

Outrage and incredulity were also the characteristic responses of Abraham's defenders. For them what was outrageous was the indefatigable zeal with which Abraham was being pursued, and the irregular procedures employed in that pursuit—procedures which, until it was too late, made it impossible for Abraham's replies to catch up with the accusations. The irregularity of denunciation-by-circular carried out by senior figures, combined with (mostly Feldman) putting his weighty thumb on the scales to prevent a junior historian from finding employment, seemed a classic case of abuse of power. Feldman's procedure, said Stanley Katz, "was calculated not to inform but to intimidate." There was incredulity, mixed with outrage, at Turner's and Feldman's repeated insistence that Abraham had been not just careless but deliberately deceptive. Lawrence Stone found nothing at all unlikely in Abraham's account of the "mundane" source of his errors.

When you work in the archives you're far from home, you're bored, you're in a hurry, you're scribbling like crazy. You're bound to make mistakes. I don't believe any scholar in the Western world has impeccable footnotes. Archival research is a special case of the general messiness of life.

---

[60]Turner, ed., *Reappraisals of Fascism* (New York, 1975), x-xi; Turner, *German Big Business*, 340, 350–51, 356, 357, 359; Feldman, "German Economic History," *Central European History* 19 (1986): 185; Feldman review of Turner, *AHR* 90 (1985): 718. In his review Feldman said the book was "characterized by a careful analysis of . . . sources and a painstaking evaluation of the evidence they provide undertaken by a scholar more interested in getting at the truth they contain than in verifying any preconceived idea or abstract theory" (p. 717). Numerous other reviewers disagreed. Geoffrey G. Field described Turner as "a man with a mission"—to refute the calumnies which leftists had heaped on German business. (*New York Times Book Review*, 27 January 1985, 28.) F. L. Carsten found in the book signs of "special pleading" and failure to even present, let alone deal with, readily available material which contradicted his arguments. (German Historical Institute [London], *Bulletin* 22 [Summer 1986]: 20–23.) In Germany, H.-A. Winkler found Turner's exculpatory verdict contradicted by his own evidence, while Klaus Wernecke charged that documents cited by Turner "say the opposite" of what Turner reported, and that Turner offered "falsified" versions of articles in a probusiness journal, while suppressing other relevant material, in order to misrepresent industrialists' attitude to the Nazis. (Winkler, "Schuldlos am Dritten Reich?" *Die Zeit*, 21 March 1986, 17; Wernecke, "In den Quellen steht zuweilen das Gegenteil," *Frankfurter Rundschau*, 17 May 1986, ZB4.)

There was incredulity also at what Carl Schorske termed a sad confusion between "facticity" and historical truth. "When all the errors are corrected, the argument will stand exactly; the historical configuration will not change; the interpretive logic of the book will be upheld." Charles S. Maier, though critical of aspects of Abraham's argument, and deploring its errors, thought it "unwarranted to seek to discredit the book on the basis of these errors." Abraham's stimulating and challenging thesis was, Maier wrote, not ultimately dependent on the sorts of errors his account contained. Thomas Bender thought the attack on Abraham revealed a "gnawing defensiveness" in the profession about the status of history. The incident, he wrote, "in ways I cannot grasp—must be very threatening to make men of considerable intelligence and standing defend publicly the absolute certitude of historical fact, a position both philosophically untenable and historiographically naive."[61]

It is difficult to generalize about the response of the profession as a whole to the Abraham affair. Some who had earlier been supporters of Abraham backed off when it turned out that there were more errors in the book than those originally cited by Turner. Others, who had originally been impressed by the charges against Abraham, changed their minds when his full reply appeared in the summer of 1985, too late to do him much good. There was widespread skepticism about the Turner-Feldman vocabulary of "invention" and "fabrication," but at the same time a suspicion within that vast majority of the profession who had not examined the evidence that "where there's smoke there's fire." Some on the historiographical left reflexively leaped to Abraham's support on grounds of ideological solidarity. But there was a larger traditional empiricist group with a predisposition to believe that those with explicit theoretical commitments, and in particular Marxists, were more likely than other historians to play fast and loose with evidence. This in turn was connected with the neo-objectivist conflation of leftism and hyperrelativism, and insofar as Abraham was perceived as part of this undifferentiated and threatening Other, his cause suffered.[62]

[61]Katz and Stone, quoted in Wiener, "Footnotes," 181–82, 180; Schorske on "facticity," quoted in Campbell, "History and Ethics," 19; other remarks from Schorske quoted in Wiener, "Footnotes," 183; Maier, "The Vulnerabilities of Interwar Germany," *Journal of Modern History* 56 (1984): 91; Bender, "'Facts' and History," *Radical History Review* 32 (1985): 81–82.

[62]The ideological dimension of the dispute was more salient in Germany than in the United States. In Germany the issue of whether Weimar's collapse (and the rise of Nazism) was the result of structural characteristics of German society or of contingent political events was always highly charged, and was becoming more so as a resurgent conservative historiography tried to provide Germany with a "positive past." To the extent that American historians of Germany were caught up in this dispute, it may have moved them this way or that on the Abraham case.

Professional historians might sympathize with Abraham, but found it awkward and embarrassing to defend one who had confessed to numerous "inexcusable" errors, let alone hire him. Most were upset by the episode and simply wished it would go away. Certainly this was the attitude of the AHA Council, which had another motive as well. "A lot of people felt the reputation of the profession was on the line," said then AHA president, William McNeill. The long *New York Times* story on the Abraham affair appeared on the eve of the council's decision to cancel the investigation into Turner and Feldman's conduct. On its front page the *Times* reported that historians were asking "whether undiscovered errors and serious misquotations may not flaw countless modern works of history," and inside reported the chairman of the University of Texas search committee's opinion that if other works of scholarship were subjected to the same kind of scrutiny, they would exhibit errors like Abraham's. This was a theme reiterated in numerous discussions of the case. Lawrence Stone, for example, reported being told that when a second edition of Sir Lewis Namier's landmark *Structure of Politics at the Accession of George III* was being planned, the publishers found "endless, countless, minor errors." In explaining the council's action, AHA officials told the *Times* that the council had been "angered" by suggestions that many works of professional history had errors comparable to Abraham's.[63]

The trope of synecdoche, in which the part is presented as a microcosm of the whole, is one that the historian is well advised to employ with great caution. It would be overreaching by a long stretch to take the outcome of the Abraham case as emblematic of the dominant historiographical sensibility of the 1980s. It might, as a result of contingent circumstances, have turned out differently, and there were at least as many participants who voiced their hostility to hyperempiricism and neo-objectivism as there were historians who actively or tacitly embraced them, not to speak of those whose responses were governed by other considerations. But it remains true that the "bottom line"—Turner and Feldman triumphant, and Abraham out of the profession—was a striking demonstration of the continued power of the empiricist-objectivist alliance.[64]

There were attempts of various kinds to cope with history's many-

[63]Campbell, "History and Ethics," 1, 19; Stone, quoted in Wiener, 180; McNeill, quoted in Winkler, 9; Campbell, "AHA Council Declines to Take Up Abraham Case," C22.

[64]Observers both within history and in such adjacent disciplines as anthropology, sociology, and political science agreed that the case would have had a very different outcome in those other fields. While errors would have been censured, not so much would have been made of them, and greater weight would have been put on Abraham's conceptual contribution. Depending on one's point of view, this difference, and its consequences, was the historical discipline's pride or its shame.

sided crisis. One of the most talked-about developments within the profession in the late 1970s and early 1980s was what Lawrence Stone claimed was a "revival of narrative," which dovetailed with J. H. Hexter's call for much greater attention to "the rhetoric of history"—and in particular of historical narrative.[65]

The idea of a revival of narrative had several obvious attractions to historians. As disciplinary identities became blurred, historians could define the distinctive essence of their craft, their autonomous realm, as "telling stories." In the face of multiplying centrifugal forces within the historical discipline a narrative focus could be integrative. Immediately after deploring the profession's fragmentation, Bernard Bailyn called the writing of "essential narratives . . . the great challenge of modern historical scholarship." A number of historians—Vann Woodward was particularly eloquent on this issue—saw a revival of narrative as a strategy by which historians could win back the lost popular audience. For various sections of the historical community a narrative focus had special appeal. To those who had always disliked social scientific and quantitative history, or who, like Stone, were questioning their earlier far-reaching claims on its behalf, narrative offered an alternative road. For some still battling against the Hempelian "deducto-nomological" model of historical explanation a revival of narrative was connected to the assertion that there was at least equal explanatory power in "following a story."[66]

For several reasons the revival of narrative proved an evanescent phenomenon, and an idea which stirred up as much opposition as enthusiasm. Stone's examples of the new wave of narrative histories seemed to many commentators not narratives at all by any reasonable definition, and Stone himself later confessed that perhaps "narrative" wasn't quite the word he'd been looking for. Many objected to the inherent political conservatism of narrative histories, in which structures were implicitly accepted as a given background against which individual actors shaped events, treating those structures as unproblematic. Narratives were thus conservative in a sense which transcended the left-right continuum: in the USSR accounts of Stalinism which focused on the deeds of the dictator, rather than structural determinants, were "conservative" in their tacit exculpation of the system. In the United States in the 1980s the ideological valence of narrativity seemed clear to leftists. Joan W. Scott described the call for a return to narrative as the rallying cry of conservative histo-

[65]Stone, "The Revival of Narrative: Reflections on a New Old History," *Past and Present* 85 (November 1979); Hexter, "The Rhetoric of History," *International Encyclopedia of the Social Sciences* (New York, 1968), reprinted in his *Doing History*.
[66]Bailyn, "Challenge," 7; Woodward, "Short History."

rians; Erik Monkkonen perceived it as offering "an interesting parallel with Reaganism and the New Right: a demand for a return to simpler times and simpler tales, for a world no longer mired in complexity and opacity." For others the issue was methodological. Allan Bogue saw the narrativist crusade as connected to the "stubbornness, inertia . . . [and] vested interests" of beleaguered historical traditionalists, and Morgan Kousser denounced the "revivalism of narrative" as an attempt to turn back the historiographical clock. Whatever else it might offer, the prospect of a revival of narrative seemed to drive historians farther apart, not bring them together.⁶⁷

From Samuel Eliot Morison and Allan Nevins to Peter Gay, Oscar Handlin, and Jack Hexter, those who had stressed the importance of literary quality in history, and were inclined to privilege narrative form, had often also been those who had most strongly insisted on the objectivity of history. Could a revival of narrative contribute to firming up objectivist defenses? From the 1960s onward no one had done more to stress the significance of narrative and "the rhetoric of history" than Hexter. "Rhetoric," he wrote, had been "ordinarily deemed icing on the cake of history, but . . . it is mixed right into the batter. It affects not merely the outward appearance of history . . . but its inward character, its essential function—its capacity to convey knowledge of the past as it actually was." For Hexter, the function of historical narrative was mimetic: to reproduce a story lived in the past, whose structure and appropriate mode of representation were latent in the events themselves. The historian first discovered in the historical record the meaning of past reality, then accurately and artfully represented what he or she had found.⁶⁸

But in attempting to combine a focus on narrative construction with a

---

⁶⁷Stone, "A Life of Learning," *ACLS Newsletter* 36 (Winter-Spring 1985): 18–19; Scott, "Comment," in symposium "Agendas for Radical History," *Radical History Review* 36 (1986): 43; Monkkonen, letter to *New York Times Book Review*, 5 September 1982, 21; Bogue, "Systematic Revisionism and a Generation of Ferment in American History," *Journal of Contemporary History* 21 (1986): 144–45; Kousser, "The Revivalism of Narrative," *Social Science History* 8 (1984). There were other objections as well. On the other side of the Atlantic, Sir Moses Finley was not persuaded that the public "craves narrative accounts" and would seek them out in preference to analytic presentations, citing the fact that "Kitto's *The Greeks* is by far the best-selling work on the subject since the Second World War, and my little book, *The Ancient Greeks*, has also had a much wider circulation than any narrative account, both in ten or a dozen languages." ("'Progress' in Historiography," *Daedalus* 106 [Summer 1977]: 129.) The German social historian Jürgen Kocka's objection to a return to a narrative mode was that insofar as the arguments of narratives were implicit rather than explicit they could not be confronted and discussed in a way which advanced historical knowledge. (Kocka's observation made to me in private conversation.)
⁶⁸Hexter, "Rhetoric," in *Doing History*, 68.

strong commitment to historical objectivity, Hexter impaled himself on the horns of a dilemma, underlining the dangers which a narrative or rhetorical focus posed for objectivist epistemology. Hexter, in the summary of the philosopher Louis O. Mink, was committed to four propositions: (1) the aim of historical writing is the representation of the past "wie es eigentlich gewesen"; (2) the historical knowledge which historians communicate involves not just isolated facts, but structures of interrelationship; (3) narrative form both exhibits these structures and is needed to communicate much of historical knowledge; (4) proper narrative is meticulously crafted by the historian. The dilemma, said Mink, was that "given (2) and (3), (1) and (4) cannot both be true."

> Historical actuality has . . . its own complex structure . . . ; narrative has another . . . of an entirely different order. It could be no more than a lucky accident if the structure of narrative ever successfully represented the structure of historical actuality; but even worse, no one could possibly know whether it did, since to do so would require *comparing* the two and thus would require knowing the structure of historical actuality in itself independently of *any* representation of it. But this is impossible.
>
> The dilemma could be avoided by giving up—*really* giving up—either (1) or (4); then the remaining three propositions would be consistent. . . . The price for giving up (1) is relativism (a *bête noire* for Hexter). . . . On the other hand, the price of giving up (4) is a crushing dullness (also a *bête noire* for Hexter), since the only historiographical form *directly* supported by evidence is bare chronology. . . . [Hexter's] positive contribution to the theory of historiography is the attempt to elaborate criteria for the achievement and communication of historical knowledge which would be both true and illuminating. . . . This is achieved by holding together incompatible criteria by main strength. To sustain this precarious alliance a sort of mental oscillation is required: to forget temporarily how much imagination goes into the construction of a narrative when one is thinking about the *otherness* of historical actuality, and to forget temporarily the distance which separates one from that actuality when one is thinking about the coherence and force of the story one tells or is trying to tell. Hexter might reply that there is very little point in historians' worrying over how it is possible to do something which in fact [Hexter claims] they do all the time as a matter of course. . . . But in a *theory* of historiography one cannot evade a problem by calling it only theoretical.[69]

Historians as well as philosophers came to realize that for those committed to the defense of historical objectivity, a literary or narrativist orientation was dangerous. In his objectivist manifesto, *Truth in History*,

[69]Mink, "The Theory of Practice: Hexter's Historiography," in Barbara C. Malament, ed., *After the Reformation: Essays in Honor of J. H. Hexter* (Philadelphia, 1980), 19–20.

Oscar Handlin had complained that historians had "locked themselves apart from the changes that have transformed the English language since the time of Joyce, Eliot, and Pound." More than one reviewer of the book found this an astonishing observation for Handlin to make, since he was recommending precisely the kind of modernist outlook which had undermined faith in objectivity. Gordon Wood, reviewing a narrative history of the American Revolution, warned that the account was so selective that the author "plays into the hands of all those who like Hayden White argue that historical narrative is just another form of fiction." On the objectivity question, as on questions of ideology and methodology, narrativity offered no basis for the convergence of historical consciousness.[70]

Finally, there were a handful of historians who had no doubt that the discipline's traditional ideas of objectivity were "in crisis," and whose writings attempted to mediate, or at least mitigate, the crisis. Unlike hyperobjectivists they did not angrily dismiss the newer ways of thinking; unlike hyperrelativists they did not embrace them; unlike most of those in the middle they attempted a serious encounter with "postmodern" currents. Two of the profession's most highly regarded and least parochial American intellectual historians, David Hollinger and Thomas Haskell, were at least tacitly engaged in an effort to find a new, and possibly consensual, grounding for the historical venture.

Of the two, Hollinger was more committed both to damage control and to accentuating the positive. Like others who took it for granted that old postures were no longer tenable, he used ironic quotation marks when he wrote of historians "discovering" the "objective truth," and praised Kuhn for "breaking down . . . the old monolithic concept of objectivity." He understood better than most commentators that Kuhn and Rorty were not radicals who aimed at debunking science and scholarship, but rather were men of essentially conservative temperament, who wanted to ground existing practices on a new foundation. He applauded their fundamental historicism, and sought to enlist them in intellectual historians' old battles: against Hempelians and positivistically inclined social scientific historians; in support of narrative modes of presentation and explanation; in defense of at least a qualified autonomy of history from philosophers' prescriptions. Among the things Hollinger found most attractive in Kuhn was that his "sociological sense of what makes an idea true exercises an important control on 'perspectivism,' and prevents

---

[70]Handlin, *Truth in History*, 9; Wood, "Star-Spangled History," *New York Review of Books* 29 (12 August 1982): 8.

it from turning into the more complete relativism of 'every man his own historian.'" Like Kuhn and Rorty themselves, he wanted to neutralize the most radical implications of their thought; like them, Hollinger found something approaching a functional equivalent for objectivity in disciplinary consensus. He indulged in a bit of what the literary theorists call "creative misreading" in claiming Kuhn's authority for the view that history was a "proto-science." But in a larger sense, he was correct in seeing in Kuhn, and Rorty as well, a willingness to grant a sort of "primal validity" to historical scholarship, based on trust in the truth-seeking motives of historians, and in the community of critical inquiry which they constituted. In a general way, Hollinger's efforts resembled those of the postwar historians who had dealt with the interwar relativist critique by a strategy of "restriction through partial incorporation." But by the last decades of the twentieth century, in a very different cultural and political climate, in which traditional thoughtways faced a broader and more systematic challenge, accommodation could be reached only on the basis of more far-reaching concessions to the critics of the objectivist posture.[71]

Thomas Haskell was somewhat less inclined to play the role of centrist statesman. He admired the work not just of Kuhn and Rorty, but also that of more controversial figures like Stanley Fish and the textualist legal scholars of the Critical Legal Studies movement. Haskell had long been concerned with the establishment of "authoritative" academic knowledge and how its claims were grounded. His *Emergence of Professional Social Science* had focused on the Peircean faith in communities of the compe-

---

[71]Hollinger, "Perry Miller and Philosophical History" (1968), in his *In the American Province: Studies in the History and Historiography of Ideas* (Bloomington, Ind., 1985), 164–65; review of Kuhn's *Essential Tension, AHR* 83 (1978): 1232; "T. S. Kuhn's Theory of Science and Its Implications for History" (1973), *In the American Province*, 124, 119; cf. "The Voice of Intellectual History in the Conversation of Mankind: A Note on Richard Rorty" (1982), ibid. I use the phrase "creative misreading" to describe the following: In "T. S. Kuhn's Theory of Science," 119, Hollinger wrote, "Fortunately Kuhn's sense of validity has a corollary for knowledge-producing communities that fall short of the tightly organized, clearly successful research consensus of the developed sciences. These 'proto-sciences,' as Kuhn calls disciplines like history and most of the social sciences, both generate and test—however imperfectly—'testable propositions.'" Hollinger documents this assertion with a footnote reference to a passage in which Kuhn wrote: "there are many fields—I shall call them proto-sciences—in which practice does generate testable conclusions. . . . I think, for example, of fields like chemistry and electricity before the mid-eighteenth century, of the study of heredity and phylogeny before the mid-nineteenth, or of many of the social sciences today." The "many" (not "most") social sciences to which Kuhn referred probably included such fields as experimental psychology, micro-economics, and perhaps some areas of sociology; there was, in any case, no hint that history was included. ("Reflections on My Critics," in Imre Lakatos and Alan Musgrave, eds., *Criticism and the Growth of Knowledge* [Cambridge, 1970], 244.)

tent, which had underwritten the establishment of disciplines in the late nineteenth century. With engaging frankness he confessed that though he believed in the theory of evolution "with nearly the same degree of confidence that I feel about the existence of the table I am writing on," that belief rested not on reason but purely on his deference to the authority of scientists. Were it not for that deference, he would find creationist accounts no more inherently implausible than those of evolutionists. Though Haskell was in no danger of becoming a creationist, he conceded that the old grounding was not what it had once been; that recent onslaughts had "left in tatters" the old Peircean confidence in academic authority. He thought that "no straightforward answer" could be given to the question whether, in the late twentieth century, professional communities of inquiry had any special access to the truth. Like Hollinger, he sought to defend a moderate relativism against a Nietzschean "epistemological left," which was at least as troubling to him as the older, objectivist, "epistemological right." Much more than Hollinger, Haskell was disturbed by moral relativism, which he saw as intimately associated with cognitive relativism. He worried that the thoroughgoing contextualism of Kuhn's work could, in other hands, lead to "bland neutrality in the face of evil." In both the moral and cognitive realms he was concerned to find "anchors." Revulsion at the horrors of Nazi Germany was "one of the principal anchors of the twentieth-century mind," and however tempting it was to accommodate to relativism, "we know that we cannot permit that anchor to break loose." In the cognitive realm, for all his acknowledgment of the weakened authority of disciplinary communities, he expressed a deeply felt need to cling to them. "We know they won't hold under the severest strain, but in high wind and shoal water, even a light anchor is vastly superior to none at all."[72]

[72]Haskell, "Introduction" to Haskell, ed., *The Authority of Experts: Studies in History and Theory* (Bloomington, Ind., 1984), x-xi; "Response" to Bouwsma, "Specialization," American Council of Learned Societies, *Newsletter* 36 (Summer-Fall 1985): 15, 12; "Deterministic Implications of Intellectual History," in Higham and Conkin, eds., *New Directions*, 138–39, 145; "Introduction," xxxvii. Haskell has amplified and extended his reflections on these issues in "The Curious Persistence of Rights Talk in the 'Age of Interpretation'" (*JAH* 74 [1987]: 984–1012), which appeared when this book was at the page proof stage. It is an eloquent and moving statement of Haskell's anguish at the "fashionable" tide of radical historicism which "throbs and swells in hopes of filling the entire cosmos." Though his principal concern in the article is with moral relativism, he devotes much of his attention to cognitive relativists. From their "laid-back, happy-go-lucky tone" one would never know that "the doctrine had teeth, much less fangs"; that they would lead us over the brink into an intellectual and moral abyss. He contrasts the active role which Becker and Beard played in the earlier crisis of historicism with the apparent obliviousness of all but a few contemporary historians to what he describes as a continuation of the same debate. Haskell leaves "open" the question whether "the absence

Both Hollinger and Haskell were attempting to stake out an epistemological "vital center"—a middle-of-the-road grounding for the historical
venture. This was a not unworthy endeavor; one which they conducted
with great subtlety, modesty, and circumspection; one which, in other
circumstances, might have attracted considerable attention and support.
But as of the 1980s, hardly anybody was listening. Sensibilities were too
diverse to be gathered together under any ecumenical tent. As a broad
community of discourse, as a community of scholars united by common
aims, common standards, and common purposes, the discipline of history had ceased to exist. Convergence on anything, let alone a subject as
highly charged as "the objectivity question," was out of the question. The
profession was as described in the last verse of the Book of Judges.

In those days there was no king in Israel; every man did that which was right in
his own eyes.

How long "those days" will continue is anyone's guess. With the triumph of professionalized, scientific history at the turn of the century,
historians were confident that problems of historical knowledge had been
definitively resolved. Surveying the development of historical theory
through the 1930s, Bulletin 54 of the Social Science Research Council
announced that with the victory of relativism, American historiography
had "come of age." In the early 1960s historians congratulated themselves
on having successfully transcended relativism, and having established a
mature and permanent equilibrium in a "practical" objectivity. The reader
will understand my unwillingness to join the ranks of these failed proph-
ets by predicting the indefinite continuation of present chaos (or some
other outcome). In any case, as I have attempted to show, the evolution
of historians' attitudes on the objectivity question has always been closely
tied to changing social, political, cultural, and professional contexts. It
would take a bolder spirit than mine to predict all of these futures, their
interactions, and their consequences.

In the introduction, I called this book an inquiry into what professional historians have thought they were doing, or ought to be doing, when
they wrote history. The book's aim, I said, was to provoke my fellow
historians to greater self-consciousness about the nature of our activity,

of historians from the current field of battle testifies to the imperturbable good sense of a
discipline that has both feet firmly planted in empirical inquiry, or to the dullness of a
discipline smugly unaware of its own theoretical commitments and so busy sifting through
its own overspecialized and underconceptualized scholarly productions that its members
no longer have time to be intellectuals." (Pp. 991, 990, 985.)

to stimulate alternative ways of thinking about works of history and the claims made on their behalf. At moments I think I may have succeeded; much of the time not. "In the domain of expression," Jean-Paul Sartre once told an interviewer, "success is necessarily failure." He wrote of how "it is *impossible* to succeed, since at the outset you set yourself the goal of failure (to capture movement in immobile objects, for instance)."

The moment comes when you just can't take the work any further. . . . At this point, my friend Giacometti explains, you can throw your piece of sculpture in the rubbish bin or exhibit it in a gallery. So there it is. You never quite grasp what you set out to achieve. And then suddenly it's a statue or a book. The opposite of what you wanted. If its faults are inscribed methodically in the negative which you present to the public, they at least point to what it might have been. And the spectator becomes the real sculptor, fashioning his model in thin air, or reading the book between the lines.[73]

[73]Sartre, *Between Existentialism and Marxism* (1974; English trans., New York, 1976), 19–20.

Appendix

◁═══▷

Manuscript collections cited

Adams, George B. Papers. Historical Manuscripts Collection, Yale University Library, New Haven, Conn.

Adler, Selig. Papers. University Archives, State University of New York, Buffalo, N.Y.

American Historical Association (including *American Historical Review*) Papers. Manuscripts Division, Library of Congress, Washington, D.C.

Americans for Democratic Action Papers. State Historical Society of Wisconsin, Madison.

Ames, Herman V. Papers. University Archives, University of Pennsylvania, Philadelphia.

Andrews, Charles M. Papers. Historical Manuscripts Collection, Yale University Library, New Haven, Conn.

Bailey, Thomas A. Papers. University Archives, Stanford University, Palo Alto, Calif.

Barnes, Harry Elmer. Papers. Archive of Contemporary History, University of Wyoming Library, Laramie.

Barzun, Jacques. Papers. University Archives, Columbia University, New York.

Becker, Carl L. Papers. Department of Manuscripts and University Archives, Cornell University, Ithaca, N.Y.

Bemis, Samuel Flagg. Papers. Historical Manuscripts Collection, Yale University Library, New Haven, Conn.

Buck, Solon J. Papers. Manuscripts Division, Library of Congress, Washington, D.C.

Burr, George L. Papers. Department of Manuscripts and University Archives, Cornell University, Ithaca, N.Y.

Carman, Harry J. Papers. University Archives, Columbia University, New York.

Cheyney, Edward P. Papers. University Archives, University of Pennsylvania, Philadelphia.

Cochran, Thomas C. Papers. University Archives, University of Pennsylvania, Philadelphia.

Crane, Verner W. Papers. Michigan Historical Collections, Bentley Historical Library, University of Michigan, Ann Arbor.

Cross, Arthur Lyon. Papers. Michigan Historical Collections, Bentley Historical Library, University of Michigan, Ann Arbor.

Curti, Merle E. Papers. State Historical Society of Wisconsin, Madison.

Dodd, William E. Papers. Manuscripts Division, Library of Congress, Washington, D.C.

Farrand, Max. Papers. Huntington Library, San Marino, Calif.

Feis, Herbert. Papers. Manuscripts Division, Library of Congress, Washington, D.C.

Fish, Carl Russell. Papers. State Historical Society of Wisconsin, Madison.

Ford, Guy S. Reminiscences. Columbia Oral History Collections, Butler Library, Columbia University, New York.

Gabriel, Ralph H. Papers. Historical Manuscripts Collection, Yale University Library, New Haven, Conn.

Gates, Paul W. Papers. Department of Manuscripts and University Archives, Cornell University, Ithaca, N.Y.

Gottschalk, Louis. Papers. Department of Special Collections, Joseph Regenstein Library, University of Chicago, Chicago.

Graebner, Norman A. Papers. University Archives, University of Illinois, Urbana.

Griswold, A. Whitney. Presidential Papers. Historical Manuscripts Collection, Yale University Library, New Haven, Conn.

Hayes, Carlton J. H. Papers. University Archives, Columbia University, New York.

Hesseltine, William B. Papers. State Historical Society of Wisconsin, Madison.

Hicks, John D. Papers. Bancroft Library, University of California, Berkeley.

Holt, W. Stull. Papers. University Archives, University of Washington, Seattle.

Hutchinson, William T. Diary. Department of Special Collections, Joseph Regenstein Library, University of Chicago, Chicago.

Illinois, University of. History Department Papers. University Archives, University of Illinois, Urbana.

Jameson, J. Franklin. Papers. Manuscripts Division, Library of Congress, Washington, D.C.

Knaplund, Paul. Papers. State Historical Society of Wisconsin, Madison.

Lee, Dwight E. Papers. University Archives, Clark University, Worcester, Mass.

Lerner, Max. Papers. Department of Manuscripts and University Archives, Yale University Library, New Haven, Conn.

Lippmann, Walter. Papers. Department of Manuscripts and University Archives, Yale University Library, New Haven, Conn.

Lynd/Radical Caucus/AHA Papers. State Historical Society of Wisconsin, Madison.

McLaughlin, Andrew C. Papers. Michigan Historical Collections, Bentley Historical Library, University of Michigan, Ann Arbor.

Merriman, Roger B. Papers. Massachusetts Historical Society, Boston.

Mississippi Valley Historical Association (including *Mississippi Valley Historical Review*) Papers. Nebraska State Historical Society, Lincoln.

Morgenstern, George. Papers. Archive of Contemporary History, University of Wyoming Library, Laramie.

Nevins, Allan. Papers. University Archives, Columbia University, New York.

Notestein, Wallace K. Papers. Department of Manuscripts and University Archives, Yale University Library, New Haven, Conn.

Pratt, Julius. Papers. Buffalo and Erie County Historical Society, Buffalo, N.Y.

Radical America Papers. State Historical Society of Wisconsin, Madison.

Randall, James G. Papers. Manuscripts Division, Library of Congress, Washington, D.C.

Schlesinger, Arthur M. Oral History Memoir. Columbia Oral History Collections, Butler Library, Columbia University, New York.

Schlesinger, Arthur M. Papers. University Archives, Harvard University, Cambridge, Mass. (Some of Schlesinger's papers are held separately in Harvard's Houghton Library, and where reference is made to these, the fact is indicated in the notes.)

Schmitt, Bernadotte. Papers. Manuscripts Division, Library of Congress, Washington, D.C.

Sellers, James L. Papers. Nebraska State Historical Society, Lincoln.

Shannon, Fred A. Papers. University Archives, University of Illinois, Urbana.

Shotwell, James T. Reminiscences. Columbia Oral History Collections, Butler Library, Columbia University, New York.

Studies on the Left Papers. State Historical Society of Wisconsin, Madison.

Turner, Frederick Jackson. Papers. Huntington Library, San Marino, Calif.

Van Tyne, Claude H. Papers. Michigan Historical Collections, Bentley Historical Library, University of Michigan, Ann Arbor.

Wish, Harvey. Papers. University Archives, Case Western Reserve University, Cleveland, Ohio.

Index

Abbott, Wilbur C., 241
abolitionism, 77, 338, 351n
Abraham, David, 612–21
academic freedom, 64–68, 198–200, 242n, 245n, 323, 325–32, 405, 408, 447, 511
Acton, Lord, 40, 73
ad hominen, argumentum, 219–21
ad verecundiam, argumentum, 221–22
Adams, Brooks, 33, 38n, 64
Adams, Charles Kendall, 70
Adams, George B., 29, 30, 91, 114, 126n
Adams, Henry, 30, 33, 59, 81, 458
Adams, Herbert Baxter, 33, 48, 69n, 78, 87–88, 520, 583
Adams, James Truslow, 193
Adler, Cyrus, 69n
Agassi, Judith Buber, 566
Agassiz, Louis, 35–36, 74–75
Allardyce, Gilbert, 311
Allen, Frederick Lewis, 193, 341
Allen, James S., 225
Alperowitz, Gar, 451
Alvord, Clarence W., 94n, 131–32, 140, 182, 203n
Ambrose, Stephen, 420–21
American Association of University Professors, 67–68, 326
American Heritage, 194
American Historical Association, 21, 26, 48, 49, 58, 200n, 362, 365, 400, 492, 520, 574, 580
and Abraham case, 618, 621
and academic freedom 200n, 329–30
and history in schools, 70, 71, 186, 189–91, 368–71

internal politics of, 183–84, 321, 363, 434–35
meetings of, 58, 77, 113, 580, 593
officers of, 49, 115–16, 365, 591
and popular history magazine, 194–97, 577
and World War I, 121, 127
and World War II, 302
American Historical Review, 15, 48, 54, 58, 59, 121–22, 200, 203–4, 331, 580, 593
American Revolution, 82–84, 198, 336–37
American Studies, 381
Anderson, Frank Maloy, 119n, 127, 212
Andrews, Charles M., 46, 82, 83, 101, 173n, 178, 193, 266
Anglo-Saxonism, 80–84
anthropology, 143–44, 227, 284, 285, 471, 548–55, 563, 568, 587n, 591
see also cultural relativism
anti-Catholicism, 46, 174n, 203n, 366n, 388
antirelativism, 164–66, 260–63, 265–66, 274, 295–301, 347, 390–92, 552, 564–70
anti-Semitism, 15, 69n, 172–74, 203n, 338–41, 365–66, 376n
Aptheker, Herbert, 225, 245n, 327, 402, 422, 426n, 479n, 486
Arnold, Thurman, 148, 150, 161, 252, 253
Association for the Study of Negro Life and History, 225, 475
Ausubel, Herman, 374
Aydelotte, William O., 322n, 385

633